COMPUTER SCIENCE

An Overview

FIFTH EDITION

COMPUTER SCIENCE

An Overview

J. GLENN BROOKSHEAR
Marquette University

An imprint of Addison Wesley Longman, Inc.

Reading, Massachusetts ▪ Harlow, England ▪ Menlo Park, California ▪ Berkeley, California
Don Mills, Ontario ▪ Sydney ▪ Bonn ▪ Amsterdam ▪ Tokyo ▪ Mexico City

Sponsoring Editor Susan Hartman
Production Supervisor Kathleen A. Manley
Production Services Sandra Rigney
Text Design Sandra Rigney
Cover Design Diana Coe
Artist Ben Turner Graphics
Composition Compset
Prepress Buyer Caroline Fell
Marketing Manager Tom Ziolkowski
Senior Manufacturing Coordinator Judith Y. Sullivan

Library of Congress Cataloging-in-Publication Data

Brookshear, J. Glenn.
Computer science : an overview / J. Glenn Brookshear.
p. cm.
Includes bibliographical references and index.
ISBN 0-8053-4632-5
1. Computer science. I. Title.
QA76.B743 1997
004--dc20 96-22969
CIP

Access the latest information about Addison-Wesley titles from our World Wide Web page: `http://www.aw.com/cseng/`

3 4 5 6 7 8 9 10—MA—00999897

To my parents
Garland and Reba Brookshear

Preface

I wrote this book to provide a comprehensive overview of computer science, one that presents a thought-provoking introduction to the key issues and concepts throughout the field. I have done this with two audiences in mind.

Computer Science Majors

The first audience consists of computer science majors in the early stages of their academic careers. Students at this stage tend to equate computer science with programming because that is essentially all they have seen. Yet computer science is much more than programming. In turn, beginning computer science students need exposure to the breadth of the subject in which they are planning to major. Providing this exposure is the purpose of this book. It gives students an overview of computer science—a foundation from which they can understand the relevance and interrelationships of future courses. Without such a perspective, students easily become immersed in the details of specialized courses and never understand the true scope and dynamics of the field. In short, this book is an ideal text for computer science curricula endorsing the breadth-first approach as popularized by the report of the ACM/IEEE-CS Joint Curriculum Task Force.

Students of Other Disciplines

I also designed this book with majors of other fields in mind. Too often these students are channeled into courses that merely teach specific skills in a specialized, rather than a generic, environment. The subject matter of these courses is often time-sensitive, limited in portability, or not developed to a depth to be useful outside the classroom. Any benefits from such courses dissipate quickly after the semester is over. In contrast, I feel that a computer science course for nonmajors should present an overall picture of the science. This, in fact, is the model used in the natural sciences and is the model on which this book is designed. After taking a course based on this text, students will have obtained an understanding of computer science that will continue to pay dividends well into the future. Indeed, they will have been educated rather than trained.

Fifth Edition

As represented by the book's new design, this fifth edition reflects the most extensive renovation of the text to date. Although it maintains the same chapter-by-chapter structure as previous editions, many topics have been added, some minor topics have been deleted, and much of the remaining material has been rewritten to provide an up-to-date and relevant picture of the science of computing. The following are some general comments that should help you become acquainted with this new edition.

Many themes run throughout the text, including the role of abstraction, the recognition of alternative solutions, and the dynamics of the subject under study. The goal is for students to see computer science as a broad, evolving science rather than a textbook subject to be categorized, memorized, and forgotten. The text's approach to problem solving is exemplary.

I believe that students do not become true problem solvers by following a particular problem-solving methodology. They become problem solvers over a period of time during which they are required to apply and refine their problem-solving skills in a thought-provoking environment. Thus, as in previous editions, this fifth edition repeatedly challenges its readers to look beyond the status quo and to sharpen their creative skills. Rather than avoiding topics considered deep or complex, I have searched for clear explanations; I have encouraged thought by alluding to relationships between different topics; and I have added many new problems at the end of both sections and chapters.

Another theme of this edition regards ethical, social, and legal issues. I do not believe that a student's awareness is aroused by presenting these topics in an isolated chapter. An appreciation of such issues is developed and altered as one's knowledge of the science and the ramifications of its application grows. Thus you will find topics relating to social, ethical, and legal issues appearing throughout this fifth edition rather than being grouped into a chapter of their own. Examples include vandalism in the context of networks, professionalism and rights of ownership in the context of software engineering, and security in the context of operating systems, networks, and database systems. Moreover, to stimulate thought and discussion, I have added *Questions of Ethics* at the end of each chapter. You will find this theme explicitly introduced in the introductory chapter.

As for specific changes, topics that have been added include an introduction to digital circuitry, an increased emphasis on the concept of a process, an introduction to the client/server model, an extended discussion of the Internet in general and the TCP/IP protocol suite in particular, a more thorough coverage of language translation, the Java® programming language, and an increased emphasis on the object-oriented paradigm including its influence in software engineering and database design. Examples of topics that have undergone major updates or revisions include operating system architecture and programming language concepts. In turn, such topics as the network database model and serializable schedules have been dropped.

Pedagogical Features

This text is the product of many years of teaching. As a result, it is rich in pedagogical aids. Paramount is the abundance of problems to enhance the student's participation. Each section within a chapter closes with *Questions/Exercises* to challenge students to think independently. This feature reviews the material just discussed, extends the previous discussion, or hints at related topics to be covered later. These questions are answered in Appendix F.

Each chapter after the introduction closes with three sets of problems. The first of these is a set of *Chapter Review Problems* that are designed to serve as "homework" problems in that they cover the material from the entire chapter and are not answered in the text. Following these problems is a set of *Questions of Ethics* that are designed for thought and discussion. Many of them can be used to launch research assignments culminating in short written or oral reports. Following these questions is a set of *Additional Activities* that are designed for readers with prior computing experience. These problems tend to ask the reader to relate prior knowledge to the material in the text, sometimes through programming assignments and sometimes through experimentation. Many of these problems are excellent sources for term projects.

Each chapter also ends with a list called *Additional Reading* that contains references to other materials relating to the subject of the chapter. The Web site, described later in this preface, is also a good place to look for related materials.

Another pedagogical aid is the use of optional sections. These sections are marked in the table of contents. The fact that a section is declared optional does not mean that its material is more difficult or should be skipped. It merely means that the material in later (nonoptional) sections does not rely on these sections. The purpose of identifying these sections is to allow students to reach later portions of the text more quickly than would otherwise be possible. For example, many instructors may wish to skip or postpone much of the material on machine architecture, operating systems, and networks in order to spend more time on algorithm development and representation as discussed in Chapters 4 and 5. The use of optional sections allows such modifications yet leaves the material available to more inquisitive students or courses with different goals.

Laboratory Materials

Supplementary laboratory manuals that are coordinated with the text are available from the Addison-Wesley Web site free to adopters. These manuals, one for the language Pascal, one for C, and another for C++, are for courses with an introductory-level programming component and are designed for a closed laboratory that meets once a week for approximately two hours. Each manual contains material for at least 16 laboratory sessions (many are optional) that teach the rudiments of the particular language and provide experiments that reinforce material in the parent text.

Each laboratory session consists of explanatory material, activities for the students that are presented in a true experiment format that encourages investigation, and post-laboratory problems that ask students to apply their knowledge outside the closed laboratory environment.

Web Site

This text is supported by a World Wide Web site at `http://www.aw.com/cseng/authors/brookshear/compsci/compsci.html`. At this site you will find laboratory manuals, supporting software, and general information relating to the text. It also contains links to other resources that may be of interest. This site will provide a dynamic environment in which supplementary materials and related information will be offered and updated in a timely manner.

Acknowledgments

I first thank those of you who have supported this book by reading and using it in previous editions. I am honored.

With each new edition, the list of those who have contributed to the book grows. Today this list includes J. M. Adams, C. M. Allen, D. C. S. Allison, B. Auernheimer, P. Bankston, M. Barnard, K. Bowyer, P. W. Brashear, C. M. Brown, B. Calloni, M. Clancy, R. T. Close, D. H. Cooley, F. Deek, B. Dredge, M. J. Duncan, N. E. Gibbs, J. D. Harris, D. Hascom, P. Henderson, L. Hunt, L. A. Jehn, K. Korb, G. Krenz, J. Liu, T. J. Long, C. May, S. J. Merrill, J. C. Moyer, M. Murphy, J. P. Myers, Jr., D. S. Noonan, G. Rice, N. Rickert, J. B. Rogers, G. Saito, W. Savitch, J. C. Schlimmer, J. C. Simms, M. C. Slattery, J. Slimick, J. A. Slomka, D. Smith, J. Solderitsch, R. Steigerwald, L. Steinberg, W. J. Taffe, J. Talburt, P. Tromovitch, and M. Ziegler. To these individuals I give my sincere thanks. I also thank Sandra Rigney, my production editor, for guiding me through this fifth edition. A special thank you goes to Phil Bender, Mary Boelk, and Jody Jung for writing the laboratory manuals.

And, I thank my wife Earlene and daughter Cheryl for putting up with an author living in the house.

J. G. B.

Contents

Introduction 1

0.1 The Study of Algorithms 2
0.2 The Development of Algorithmic Machines 6
0.3 The Evolution of Computer Science 9
0.4 The Role of Abstraction 10
0.5 Ethical/Social/Legal Repercussions 11

Questions of Ethics 11 *Additional Reading 12*

PART ONE
MACHINE ARCHITECTURE 13

CHAPTER ONE
Data Storage 15

1.1 Storage of Bits 16
1.2 Main Memory 22
1.3 Mass Storage 25
1.4 Coding Information for Storage 29
***1.5** The Binary System 35
***1.6** Storing Integers 38
***1.7** Storing Fractions 44
***1.8** Communications Errors 48

Chapter Review Problems 52 *Questions of Ethics 56*
Additional Activities 56 *Additional Reading 57*

*Sections marked by an asterisk are optional in that they provide additional depth of coverage that is not required for an understanding of future chapters.

CHAPTER TWO
Data Manipulation 58

2.1 The Central Processing Unit 59
2.2 The Stored-Program Concept 62
2.3 Program Execution 66
2.4 Other Architectures 71
***2.5** Arithmetic/Logic Instructions 75
***2.6** Computer–Peripheral Communication 79

Chapter Review Problems 84 *Questions of Ethics 88*
Additional Activities 88 *Additional Reading 88*

PART TWO
SOFTWARE 89

CHAPTER THREE
Operating Systems and Networks 91

3.1 The Evolution of Operating Systems 92
3.2 Operating System Architecture 96
3.3 Coordinating the Machine's Activities 102
***3.4** Handling Competition Among Processes 106
3.5 Networks 110
***3.6** Network Protocols 117

Chapter Review Problems 126 *Questions of Ethics 128*
Additional Activities 129 *Additional Reading 129*

CHAPTER FOUR
Algorithms 130

4.1 The Concept of an Algorithm 131
4.2 Algorithm Representation 133
4.3 Algorithm Discovery 140
4.4 Iterative Structures 146
4.5 Recursive Structures 155
4.6 Efficiency and Correctness 171

Chapter Review Problems 177 *Questions of Ethics 181*
Additional Activities 181 *Additional Reading 182*

CHAPTER FIVE

Programming Languages 183

5.1 Historical Perspective 184
5.2 Traditional Programming Concepts 193
5.3 Program Units 203
***5.4** Language Implementation 210
***5.5** Parallel Computing 219
***5.6** Declarative Programming 222

Chapter Review Problems 227 *Questions of Ethics 230*
Additional Activities 231 *Additional Reading 231*

CHAPTER SIX

Software Engineering 232

6.1 The Software Engineering Discipline 233
6.2 The Software Life Cycle 234
6.3 Modularity 239
6.4 Development Tools and Techniques 244
6.5 Documentation 250
6.6 Software Ownership and Liability 252

Chapter Review Problems 253 *Questions of Ethics 256*
Additional Activities 257 *Additional Reading 257*

PART THREE

DATA ORGANIZATION 259

CHAPTER SEVEN

Data Structures 261

7.1 Arrays 262
7.2 Lists 265
7.3 Stacks 271
7.4 Queues 275
7.5 Trees 280
7.6 Customized Data Types 288
7.7 Object-Oriented Programming 292

Chapter Review Problems 296 *Questions of Ethics 300*
Additional Activities 300 *Additional Reading 301*

CHAPTER EIGHT

File Structures **302**

8.1 Sequential Files 303
8.2 Text Files 308
8.3 Indexed Files 311
8.4 Hashed Files 315
8.5 The Role of the Operating System 321

Chapter Review Problems 323 *Questions of Ethics 325*
Additional Activities 326 *Additional Reading 326*

CHAPTER NINE

Database Structures **327**

9.1 General Issues 328
9.2 The Layered Approach to Database Implementation 331
9.3 The Relational Model 333
***9.4** Object-Oriented Databases 345
***9.5** Maintaining Database Integrity 346

Chapter Review Problems 350 *Questions of Ethics 353*
Additional Activities 353 *Additional Reading 354*

PART FOUR

THE POTENTIAL OF ALGORITHMIC MACHINES **355**

CHAPTER TEN

Artificial Intelligence **357**

10.1 Some Philosophical Issues 358
10.2 Image Analysis 361
10.3 Reasoning 363
10.4 Control System Activities 367
10.5 Using Heuristics 372
10.6 Artificial Neural Networks 377
10.7 Applications of Artificial Intelligence 383

Chapter Review Problems 391 *Questions of Ethics 394*
Additional Activities 394 *Additional Reading 395*

CHAPTER ELEVEN

Theory of Computation **396**

11.1 A Bare Bones Programming Language 397
11.2 Turing Machines 402
11.3 Computable Functions 407
11.4 A Noncomputable Function 411
11.5 Complexity and Its Measure 415
11.6 Problem Classification 422

Chapter Review Problems 427 *Questions of Ethics 429*
Additional Activities 429 *Additional Reading 430*

APPENDICES **431**

A ASCII 433
B Circuits to Manipulate Two's Complement Representations 434
C A Simple Machine Language 437
D Program Examples 439
E The Equivalence of Iterative and Recursive Structures 446
F Answers to Questions/Exercises 448

Index 475

COMPUTER SCIENCE

An Overview

Introduction

0.1 The Study of Algorithms
0.2 The Development of Algorithmic Machines
0.3 The Evolution of Computer Science
0.4 The Role of Abstraction
0.5 Ethical/Social/Legal Repercussions

Computer science is the discipline that seeks to build a scientific foundation for a variety of topics, including computer design, computer programming, information processing, algorithmic solutions of problems, and the algorithmic process itself. In turn, it provides the underpinnings for today's computer applications as well as the foundations for tomorrow's applications. It follows that we cannot become knowledgeable in computer science by studying only a few topics as isolated subjects or by merely learning how to use the computing tools of today. Rather, to understand the science of computing, we must grasp the scope and dynamics of a wide range of topics.

This book is designed to provide such a background. It presents computer science through an integrated introduction to the subjects that constitute a typical university computer science curriculum. The book can therefore serve as a foundation for beginning computer science students or as a source for other students seeking an introduction to the science behind today's computer-oriented society.

0.1 The Study of Algorithms

We begin with the most fundamental concept of computer science—that of an algorithm. Informally, an **algorithm** is a set of steps that defines how a task is performed.[1] For example, there are algorithms for constructing model airplanes (expressed in the form of instruction sheets), for operating washing machines (usually displayed on the inside of the washer's lid), for playing music (expressed in the form of sheet music), and for performing magic tricks (Fig. 0.1).

[1]More precisely, an algorithm is an ordered set of unambiguous, executable steps that defines a terminating activity. These details are discussed in Chapter 4.

Figure 0.1 An algorithm for a magic trick

Effect: The performer places some cards from a normal deck of playing cards face down on a table and mixes them thoroughly while spreading them out on the table. Then, as the audience requests either red or black cards, the performer turns over cards of the requested color.

Secret and Patter:

Step 1. From a normal deck of cards, select ten red cards and ten black cards. Deal these cards face up in two piles on the table according to color.

Step 2. Announce that you have selected some red cards and some black cards.

Step 3. Pick up the red cards. Under the pretense of aligning them into a small deck, hold them face down in your left hand and, with the thumb and first finger of your right hand, pull back on each end of the deck so that each card is given a slightly backward curve. Then place the deck of red cards face down on the table as you say, "Here are the red cards in this stack."

Step 4. Pick up the black cards. In a manner similar to that in step 3, give these cards a slight forward curve. Then return these cards to the table in a face-down deck as you say, "And here are the black cards in this stack."

Step 5. Immediately after returning the black cards to the table, use both hands to mix the red and black cards (still face down) as you spread them out on the tabletop. Explain that you are thoroughly mixing the cards.

Step 6. As long as there are face-down cards on the table, repeatedly execute the following steps:

6.1. Ask the audience to request either a red card or a black card.

6.2. If the color requested is red and there is a face-down card with a concave appearance, turn over such a card while saying, "Here is a red card."

6.3. If the color requested is black and there is a face-down card with a convex appearance, turn over such a card while saying, "Here is a black card."

6.4. Otherwise, state that there are no more cards of the requested color and turn over the remaining cards to prove your claim.

In the domain of computing machinery, algorithms are represented as **programs** within computers. Programs are collectively called **software** in contrast to the machinery itself, which is known as **hardware.** Before a machine can perform a task, an algorithm for performing that task must be discovered and represented as a program. As a result, the study of algorithms plays a central role in computer science.

The study of algorithms began as a subject in mathematics. The search for algorithms was a significant activity of mathematicians long before the development of today's computers. The major goal of that search was to find a single set of directions that described how any problem of a particular type could be solved. One of the best known consequences of this early search for algorithms (and one of the more elementary examples of it) is the long division algorithm for finding the quotient of two multiple-digit numbers. Another example is the Euclidean algorithm (discovered by the ancient Greek mathematician Euclid) for finding the greatest common divisor of two positive integers (Fig. 0.2).

Once an algorithm for performing a task has been found, the performance of that task no longer requires an understanding of the principles on which the algorithm is based. Instead, the performance of the task is reduced to the process of merely following directions. (One can follow the long division algorithm to find a quotient or the Euclidean algorithm to find a greatest common divisor without understanding why the algorithm works.) In a sense, the intelligence required to perform the task is encoded in the algorithm.

It is through this ability to capture and convey intelligence by means of algorithms that we are able to build machines that display intelligent behavior. Consequently, the level of intelligence displayed by machines is limited by the intelligence that can be conveyed through algorithms. Only if we find an algorithm that directs the performance of a task can we construct a machine to perform that task. In turn, if no algorithm exists for performing a task, then the performance of that task lies beyond the capabilities of machines.

Figure 0.2 The Euclidean algorithm for finding the greatest common divisor of two positive integers

Description: This algorithm assumes that its input consists of two positive integers and proceeds to compute the greatest common divisor of these two values.

Procedure:

Step 1. Assign M and N the value of the larger and smaller of the two input values, respectively.

Step 2. Divide M by N, and call the remainder R.

Step 3. If R is not 0, then assign M the value of N, assign N the value of R, and return to step 2; otherwise, the greatest common divisor is the value currently assigned to N.

A major undertaking throughout the computing field, then, is the development of algorithms, and consequently a significant part of computer science is concerned with issues relating to that task. In turn, we can gain an understanding of the breadth of computer science by considering some of these issues. One such issue deals with the question of how algorithms are discovered in the first place—a question that is closely related to that of problem solving in general. To discover an algorithm for solving a problem is essentially to discover a solution for the problem. It follows that studies in this branch of computer science draw heavily from such areas as the psychology of human problem solving and theories of education. We consider some of these ideas in Chapters 4 and 6.

Once an algorithm for solving a problem has been discovered, the next step is to represent the algorithm so it can be communicated to a machine or to other humans. This means that we must transform the conceptual algorithm into a clear set of instructions and represent these instructions in an unambiguous manner. Studies emerging from these concerns draw from our knowledge of language and grammar and have led to an abundance of algorithm representation schemes (known as programming languages) based on a variety of approaches to the programming process (known as programming paradigms). We consider some of these schemes in Chapter 5.

In many instances, such as in business environments, the development of programs does not require the discovery of radically new algorithms. Rather, the major obstacle in these cases is to identify what automated systems are needed and how these new systems will interact with existing ones. (Will the new employee benefits system blend with the existing personnel records system?) In such cases, the task of program development is seen as a small part of the overall business management process. Combining this insight with the realization that the algorithmic structure of large automated systems must be engineered in much the same way as the machines themselves has led to the branch of computer science known as software engineering. Today, research in this field is providing automated organization and planning systems that allow nonprogrammers to develop the systems they need without technical assistance. We study software engineering in Chapter 6.

Still another important branch of computer science deals with the design and construction of machines. We consider these topics later in this introduction as well as in Chapters 1 and 2. Although our study of computer architecture incorporates some discussions of technological issues, our goal is not to master the details of how today's architecture is implemented in electronic circuitry. That would lead us too far into the subject of electrical engineering. Moreover, just as yesterday's gear-driven calculators gave way to electronic devices, today's electronics may soon be replaced by other technologies, a prime candidate being optics. Our goal is to understand enough of today's technology so that we can appreciate its ramifications in today's machines as well as its influence on the development of computer science.

Ideally, we would like the architecture of computers to be a consequence solely of our knowledge of algorithmic processes and not be limited by the capabilities of technology. That is, rather than allowing the dictates of technology to determine machine design and thus the way we represent algorithms, we would like our knowledge of algorithms to be the driving force behind modern machine architecture. As technology advances, this dream is becoming more of a reality. Today, it is possible to construct machines that allow algorithms to be represented as multiple sequences of instructions that are executed simultaneously (Chapter 2) or as patterns of connections between numerous processing units, in much the same way that our minds represent information as links between neurons (Chapters 2 and 10).

Another context in which we study computer architecture relates to data storage and retrieval. Here the internal features of a machine are often reflected in the machine's external characteristics. We consider these features and ways of avoiding their undesirable effects in Chapters 1, 7, 8, and 9.

Closely related to the design of computing machinery is the design of a machine's interface with the outside world. How, for example, will algorithms be inserted into a machine, and how will the machine be told which algorithm to execute? Resolving such problems in an environment in which the machine is expected to provide a variety of services requires the solution to many problems involving coordination of activities and resource allocation. We investigate some of these solutions in our discussion of operating systems in Chapter 3.

As machines have been asked to perform more and more intelligent tasks, computer science has turned to the study of human intelligence for leadership. The hope is that by understanding how our own minds reason and perceive, we will be able to design algorithms that mimic these processes and thus transfer these capabilities to machines. The result is the area of computer science known as artificial intelligence, which leans heavily on research in such areas as psychology, biology, and linguistics. We discuss some of these topics in artificial intelligence in Chapter 10.

The search for algorithms to direct increasingly complex tasks also leads to questions regarding the ultimate limitations of algorithmic processes. If no algorithm exists for performing a task, then that task cannot be performed by a machine. We say that a task that can be described by an algorithm is algorithmic. In short, then, machines are only capable of performing algorithmic tasks.

The realization that there are nonalgorithmic tasks surfaced as a subject in mathematics in the early 1900s with the publication of Kurt Gödel's incompleteness theorem. This theorem essentially states that in any mathematical theory encompassing our traditional arithmetic system, there are statements that can be neither proved nor disproved. In short, any complete study of our arithmetic system lies beyond the capabilities of algorithmic activities.

The desire to study the limitations of algorithmic methods that followed Gödel's discovery led mathematicians to design abstract machines for executing algorithms (this was before technology was able to provide actual machines for investigation) and to study the theoretical powers of such hypothetical machines. Today, this study of algorithms and machines forms the theoretical backbone of computer science. We discuss some of these topics in this area in Chapter 11.

0.2 The Development of Algorithmic Machines

The abstract machines hypothesized by mathematicians in the early 1900s form an important part of the family tree for today's computers. Other branches of that tree extend much further back in time. Indeed, the quest for machines that perform algorithmic tasks (which we will call algorithmic machines) has had a long history.

One of the first computing devices was the abacus. Its history has been traced as far back as the ancient Greek and Roman civilizations, and it is still used today. The machine is quite simple, consisting of beads strung on rods that are in turn mounted in a rectangular frame. As the beads are moved back and forth on the rods, their positions represent stored values. It is in the positions of the beads that this "computer" represents and stores data. Data input is accomplished by a human who positions the beads; data output consists of observing the bead positions. For control of an algorithm's execution, the machine relies on the human operator. Thus the abacus alone is merely a data storage system; it must be combined with a human to create a complete algorithmic machine.

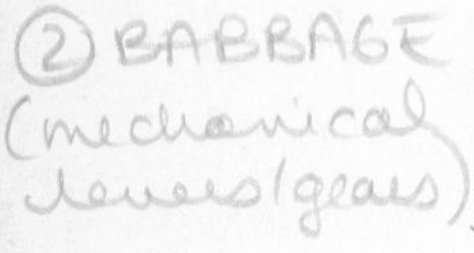

In more recent years the design of computing machines was based on the technology of gears. Among the inventors were Blaise Pascal (1623–1662) of France, Gottfried Wilhelm Leibniz (1646–1716) of Germany, and Charles Babbage (1792–1871) of England. These machines represented data through gear positioning, with data being input mechanically to establish gear positions (Fig. 0.3). Output

Figure 0.3 A prototype of Babbage's difference engine (Courtesy of International Business Machines Corporation. Unauthorized use not permitted.)

from Pascal's and Leibniz's machines was achieved by observing the final gear positions in much the same way that we read the numbers on a car's odometer. Babbage, on the other hand, envisioned a machine that would print output values on paper so that the possibility of transcription errors would be eliminated.

As for the ability to follow an algorithm, we can see a progression of flexibility in the machines. Pascal's machine was built to follow only the addition algorithm. Consequently, the appropriate sequence of steps was embedded into the structure of the machine itself. In a similar manner, Leibniz's machine had its algorithms firmly embedded in its architecture, although it offered a variety of arithmetic operations from which the operator could select. Babbage's machine, in contrast, was designed so that the sequence of steps the machine was to perform could be communicated to the machine in the form of holes in paper cards.

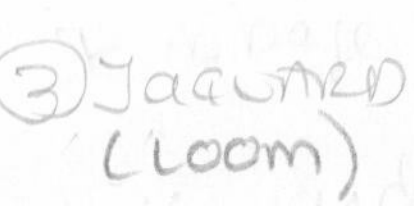

This idea of communicating an algorithm via holes in paper was not originated by Babbage. In 1801 Joseph Jacquard had applied a similar technique to control weaving looms in France (Fig. 0.4). In particular, he developed a loom in which the steps to be performed during the weaving process were determined by patterns of holes in paper cards. In this manner the algorithm followed by the machine could be easily changed to produce different woven designs.

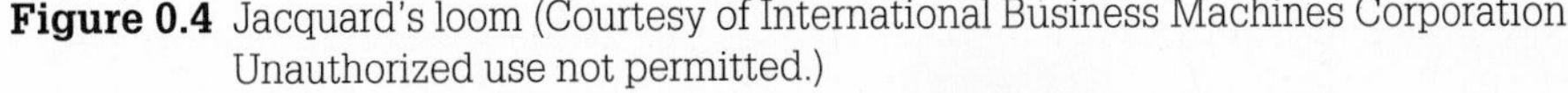

Figure 0.4 Jacquard's loom (Courtesy of International Business Machines Corporation. Unauthorized use not permitted.)

Later, Herman Hollerith (1860–1929) applied the ideal of representing information as holes in paper cards to speed up the tabulation process in the 1890 U.S. census. It was, in fact, this work by Hollerith that led to the creation of IBM.

The technology of the time lacked the precision required to popularize the complex gear-driven calculators of Pascal, Leibniz, and Babbage. Not until electronics began to supplement mechanical devices could technology support the theoretical developments taking place in the embryonic science of computing. Examples of this advance include the electromechanical machine of George Stibitz, completed in 1940 at Bell Laboratories, and the Mark I, completed in 1944 at Harvard University by Howard Aiken and a group of IBM engineers (Fig. 0.5). These machines made heavy use of electronically controlled mechanical relays. In this sense they were obsolete almost as soon as they were built, because other researchers were applying the technology of vacuum tubes to construct totally electronic digital computers. The first of these machines was apparently the Atanasoff–Berry machine, constructed during the period from 1937 to 1941 at Iowa State College (now Iowa State University) by John Atanasoff and his assistant, Clifford Berry. Another was a machine called COLOSSUS, built in England to decode German messages during the latter part of World War II. Other, more flexible machines such as the ENIAC (electronic numerical integrator and calculator) developed by John Mauchly and J. Presper Eckert at the Moore School of Electrical Engineering, University of Pennsylvania, soon followed.

From that point on, the history of algorithmic machines is one of advancing technology, the most notable steps being the invention of transistors and the

Figure 0.5 The Mark I computer

subsequent development of integrated circuits. Today, desktop-size machines known as personal computers (PCs) as well as their smaller, portable cousins known as laptops have more computing power than the room-size machines of the 1940s.

0.3 The Evolution of Computer Science

Such conditions as limited data storage capabilities and detailed, time-consuming programming procedures restricted the complexity of the algorithms to which early machines were applied. However, as these limitations began to disappear, machines were applied to increasingly larger and more complex tasks. As attempts to express the composition of these tasks in algorithmic form began to tax the abilities of the human mind, more and more research efforts were directed toward the study of algorithms and the programming process.

It was in this context that the theoretical work of mathematicians began to pay dividends. Indeed, as a consequence of Gödel's incompleteness theorem, mathematicians had already been investigating those questions regarding algorithmic processes that advancing technology began to raise. With that, the stage was set for the emergence of a new discipline known as computer science.

Today, this new discipline has established itself as the science of algorithms. As we have seen, the scope of this science is broad, drawing from such diverse subjects as mathematics, engineering, psychology, biology, business administration, linguistics, and others. In the following chapters we discuss many of the topics of this science. In each case our goal is to introduce the central ideas in the subject, the current topics of research, and some of the techniques being applied to advance knowledge in the area. For example, our discussion of programming is not geared toward developing programming skills but concentrates on the principles behind the programming tools of today, how these tools have evolved, and the problems current research is trying to overcome.

As we progress through this study of topics, it is easy to lose track of the overall picture. We therefore collect our thoughts by identifying some questions that define the science of computing and provide the focus for its study.

- Which problems can be solved by algorithmic processes?
- How can the discovery of algorithms be made easier?
- How can the techniques of representing and communicating algorithms be improved?
- How can our knowledge of algorithms and technology be applied to provide better algorithmic machines?
- How can the characteristics of different algorithms be analyzed and compared?

Note that the theme common to all of these questions is the study of algorithms (Fig. 0.6).

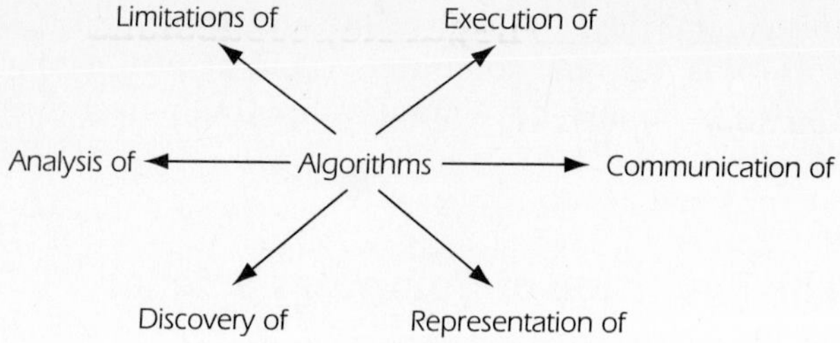

Figure 0.6 The central role of algorithms in computer science

0.4 The Role of Abstraction

Today's computer systems are extremely complex when viewed in all their detail, and such a mountain of intricacy can quickly overwhelm the human mind. It is common therefore to view such systems at various levels of detail. At each level we envision the system in terms of components whose internal characteristics we ignore. This allows us to concentrate on how those components interact with other components at that level and how they are used to construct higher-level components.

The distinction between the external properties of a component and the internal details of the component's construction is known as **abstraction.** Abstraction is an important simplification technique with which our society has created a lifestyle that would otherwise be impossible. For example, few of us understand how the various conveniences of daily life are actually implemented. We eat food and wear clothes that we ourselves cannot produce. We use electrical devices without understanding the underlying technology. We use the services of others without knowing the details of their activities. With each new advancement a small part of society chooses to specialize in its implementation, while the rest of society learns to use the results as **abstract tools,** that is, as tools whose interior implementation we need not understand. In this manner, society's warehouse of abstract tools expands and society's ability to advance further increases.

Abstraction is a recurring theme throughout computer science. It is by means of abstraction that today's large, complex hardware and software systems are designed, constructed, and managed, and it is by means of abstraction that the science is able to advance. In fact, our study itself will progress through a hierarchy of abstractions, beginning in Chapters 1 and 2 with issues relating to how individual steps of an algorithm are executed within a machine and progressing up to the topics in Chapter 11 that involve properties of entire classes of algorithms.

0.5 Ethical/Social/Legal Repercussions

Computer science, as well as other sciences and technologies, is blurring many distinctions on which our society has based decisions in the past and is even challenging many of society's principles. What is the difference between the presence of intelligent behavior and the presence of intelligence itself? When does life begin and when does it end? What is the difference between a plant and an animal? Such questions are forcing the individual to reassess his or her beliefs and often to reconstruct the very foundation of those beliefs.

Computer science is generating such questions in a variety of contexts. In law, questions arise regarding the degree to which software can be owned and the rights and liabilities that accompany that ownership. In ethics, individuals are faced with numerous options that challenge the traditional principles on which their behavior is based. In government, questions arise regarding the extent to which computer technology and its applications should be controlled.

Resolving these dilemmas in a rational manner requires a basic knowledge in the relevant science or technology. For a society to make rational decisions regarding the storage and disposal of nuclear waste, its members must comprehend the effects of radiation, understand what is required to protect against its dangers, and grasp a realistic image of the time span over which the radiation risk will persist. Likewise, to determine whether governments or companies should be allowed to develop large, integrated databases containing information about its citizens or customers, members of that society must have a basic understanding of the capabilities, limitations, and ramifications of database technology. The chapters in this text provide such fundamental knowledge in the field of computer science.

Scientific expertise does not necessarily provide clear and decisive solutions to many of the social questions generated by that science, however. There is often no single correct answer, and many solutions are compromises between opposing views. Thus life in today's society requires more than scientific and technical knowledge. It requires the ability to listen, to recognize other points of view, to carry on a rational debate, and to expand one's own opinions as new insights are gained. To assist in the development of these skills, each chapter of this text ends with a segment called Questions of Ethics. In a sense, these questions represent subject matter that is just as important as the technical material discussed within the chapters.

QUESTIONS OF ETHICS

The following questions are provided to help you understand some of the ethical/social/legal issues associated with the field of computing as well as investigate your own beliefs and their foundations. The goal is not merely to answer these questions. You should also consider why you answered as you did and whether your justifications are consistent from one question to the next.

1. The premise that our society is different from what it would have been without the computer revolution is generally accepted. Is our society

better than it would have been without the revolution? Is our society worse? Would your answer differ if your position within society were different?

2. Is it acceptable to participate in today's technical society without making an effort to understand the basics of that technology? For instance, do members of a democracy, whose votes often determine how technology will be supported and used, have an obligation to try to understand that technology? Does your answer depend on what technology is being considered? For example, is your answer the same when considering nuclear technology as when considering computer technology?
3. By using cash in financial transactions, individuals have traditionally had the option to manage their financial affairs without service charges. However, as more and more of our economy is becoming automated, financial institutions are implementing service charges for access to these automated systems. Is there a point at which these charges unfairly restrict an individual's access to the economy? For example, suppose an employer pays employees only by check, and all financial institutions place a service charge on check cashing and depositing. Are the employees unfairly treated? What if an employer insists on paying only via direct deposit?
4. When interactive television or an equivalent phenomenon becomes a household reality, to what extent should a company be allowed to retrieve information from children (perhaps via an interactive game format) regarding the household? For example, should a company be allowed to obtain a child's report on his or her parents buying patterns? What about information about the child?
5. To what extent should a government regulate computer technology and its applications? Consider, for example, the issues mentioned in Questions 3 and 4. What justifies governmental regulation?
6. To what extent will our decisions regarding technology in general, and computer technology in particular, affect our grandchildren?
7. As technology advances, our educational system is constantly challenged to reconsider the level of abstraction at which topics are presented. Many questions take the form of whether a skill is still necessary or whether students should be allowed to rely on an abstract tool. Students of trigonometry are no longer taught how to find the values of trigonometric functions using tables. Instead, they use calculators as abstract tools to find these values. Some argue that long division should also give way to abstraction. What other subjects are involved with similar controversies? Will the use of video technology someday remove the need to read? Do automated spell checkers eliminate the need for spelling skills?

ADDITIONAL READING

Dejoie, D., G. Fowler, and D. Paradice. *Ethical Issues in Information Systems.* Boston: Boyd & Fraser, 1991.

Forester, T., and P. Morrison. *Computer Ethics: Cautionary Tales and Ethical Dilemmas.* Cambridge, Mass.: MIT Press, 1990.

Goldstine, J. J. *The Computer from Pascal to von Neumann.* Princeton, N.J.: Princeton University Press, 1972.

Johnson, D. G. *Computer Ethics,* 2nd ed. Englewood Cliffs, N.J.: Prentice-Hall, 1994.

Johnson, D. G. *Ethical Issues in Engineering.* Englewood Cliffs, N.J.: Prentice-Hall, 1991.

Mollenhoff, C. R. *Atanasoff: Forgotten Father of the Computer.* Ames: Iowa State University Press, 1988.

Randell, B. *The Origins of Digital Computers.* New York: Springer-Verlag, 1973.

Shurkin, J. *Engines of the Mind.* New York: W. W. Norton, 1984.

PART ONE

MACHINE ARCHITECTURE

A major process in the development of a science is the construction of theories that are confirmed or rejected by experimentation. In some cases these theories lie dormant for extended periods, waiting for technology to develop to the point that they can be tested. (Many theories about our solar system are only now being tested, whereas others will remain untestable for years to come.) In other cases the capabilities of current technology influence the concerns of the science. (The reality of space travel has generated research on the effects of weightlessness as well as on ways to build better spacecraft.)

The development of computer science possesses both of these characteristics. We have already seen that the science grew from theories that originated well before technology could produce the machines envisioned by early researchers. Even today, our advancing knowledge of algorithmic processes is leading to new machine designs that challenge the limits of technology. In contrast, other subjects in the science are rooted in the application of today's technology. In sum, computer science is a blend of theoretical research and advancing technology, each influencing the other in a mutually beneficial relationship.

It follows that to appreciate the role of various subjects within computer science, one should understand the basics of today's technology and how it influences the design and implementation of today's computers. Providing this foundation is the purpose of the following two chapters. In Chapter 1 we discuss techniques by which information is represented and stored inside computers. In Chapter 2 we discuss ways in which today's machines manipulate data.

CHAPTER ONE

Data Storage

1.1 Storage of Bits
Gates and Flip-Flops
Other Storage Techniques
Hexadecimal Notation

1.2 Main Memory
Main Memory Organization
Organization Within a Cell

1.3 Mass Storage
Disk Storage
Compact Disks
Tape Storage
Logical Versus Physical Records

1.4 Coding Information for Storage
Representing Symbols
Representing Numeric Values
Representing Other Types of Data

***1.5 The Binary System**
Binary Addition
Fractions in Binary

***1.6 Storing Integers**
Excess Notation
Two's Complement Notation

***1.7 Storing Fractions**
Floating-Point Notation
Round-Off Errors

***1.8 Communication Errors**
Parity Bits
Error-Correcting Codes
Issues of Application

In this chapter we consider issues associated with date representation and storage within a computer. At times we will address issues of technology, since these matters are often reflected in the external characteristics of today's machines. However, most of our discussion will deal with topics that will be germane to computer design well after today's technologies have been replaced with those of tomorrow.

*Sections marked by an asterisk are optional in that they provide additional depth of coverage that is not required for an understanding of future chapters.

1.1 Storage of Bits

Today's computers represent information as patterns of bits. A **bit** (binary digit) is one of the digits 0 and 1, which, for now, we will consider merely as symbols with no numeric meaning. Indeed, we will see that the meaning of a bit varies from one application to another. Storing a bit within a machine requires a device that can be in one of two states, such as a switch (on or off), a relay (open or closed), or a flag pole (raised or lowered). One state is used to represent 0, the other to represent 1. Our immediate goal is to consider ways in which bits are stored within today's machines.

Gates and Flip-Flops

We begin by introducing the operations AND, OR, and XOR (exclusive or) as summarized in Fig. 1.1. These operations are similar to the arithmetic operations TIMES and PLUS in that they combine a pair of values, the operation's input, to produce a third value, the operation's output. Note, however, that the only digits manipulated by the AND, OR, and XOR operations are 0 and 1; these operations are thought of as manipulating the values true and false—1 for true, 0 for false. Operations that manipulate true/false values are called **Boolean operations**, in honor of the mathematician George Boole.

The Boolean operation AND is designed to reflect the truth or falseness of an expression formed by combining two smaller expressions with the conjunction *and*. These expressions have the generic form

P AND *Q*

where *P* represents one expression and *Q* represents another, for example,

Kermit is a frog AND Miss Piggy is an actress.

The inputs to the AND operation represent the truth or falseness of the compound expression's components; the output represents the truth or falseness of the compound expression itself. Since an expression of the form P AND Q is true only when both of its components are true, we conclude that 1 AND 1 should be 1, whereas all other cases should produce an output of 0, in agreement with Fig. 1.1.

In a similar manner, the OR operation is based on compound expressions of the form

P OR *Q*

where, again, *P* represents an expression and *Q* represents another. Such expressions are true when at least one of their components is true, which agrees with the OR operation depicted in Fig. 1.1.

There is not a single conjunction in the English language that captures the meaning of the XOR operation. XOR produces an output of 1 when one of its inputs is 1 and the other is 0. For example, a statement of the form *P* XOR *Q* means "either *P* or *Q* but not both."

0	0	1	1
AND 0	AND 1	AND 0	AND 1
0	0	0	1
0	0	1	1
OR 0	OR 1	OR 0	OR 1
0	1	1	1
0	0	1	1
XOR 0	XOR 1	XOR 0	XOR 1
0	1	1	0

Figure 1.1 The AND, OR, and XOR operations

The operation NOT is another Boolean operation. It differs from AND, OR, and XOR in that it has only one input. Its output is the opposite of that input; if the input of the operation NOT is true, the output is false, and vice versa. Thus, if the input of the NOT operation is the truth of falseness of the statement

Fozzie is a bear

then the output would represent the truth or falseness of the statement

Fozzie is not a bear.

A device that produces the output of a Boolean operation when given the operation's input values is called a **gate.** Gates can be constructed from a variety of technologies such as gears, relays, and optic devices. Today's computers usually implement gates as small electronic circuits in which the digits 0 and 1 are represented as voltage levels. We need not concern ourselves with such details, however. For our purposes, it suffices to represent gates in their symbolic form, as shown in Fig. 1.2. Note that the AND, OR, XOR, and NOT gates are represented by distinctively shaped diagrams, with the input values entering on one side and the output exiting on the other.

Gates such as these provide the building blocks from which computers are constructed. One important step in this direction is depicted in the circuit in Fig. 1.3. This is a particular example from a collection of circuits known as flip-flops. A **flip-flop** is a circuit that has one of two output values; its output remains fixed until a temporary pulse from another circuit causes it to shift to the other value. In other words, the output will flip or flop between two values under control of external stimuli. As long as both inputs in the circuit in Fig. 1.3 remain 0, the output (whether 0 or 1) will not change. However, temporarily placing a 1 on the upper input will force the output to be 1, whereas temporarily placing a 1 on the lower input will force the output to be 0.

Let us consider this claim in more detail. Without knowing the current output of the circuit in Fig. 1.3, suppose that the upper input is changed to 1 while the lower input remains 0 (Fig. 1.4a). This will cause the output of the OR gate to

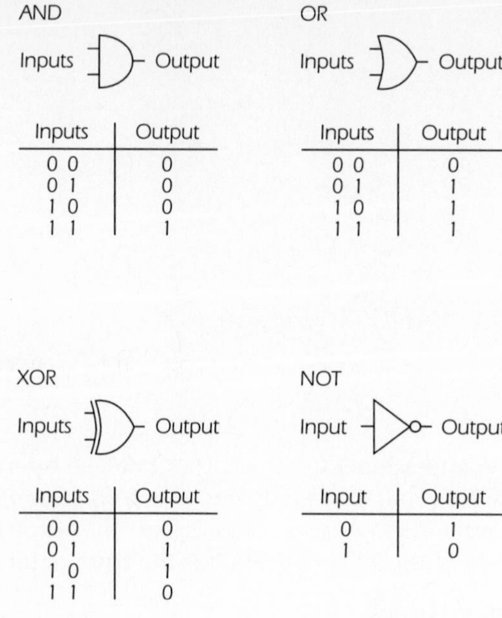

AND

Inputs	Output
0 0	0
0 1	0
1 0	0
1 1	1

OR

Inputs	Output
0 0	0
0 1	1
1 0	1
1 1	1

XOR

Inputs	Output
0 0	0
0 1	1
1 0	1
1 1	0

NOT

Input	Output
0	1
1	0

Figure 1.2 The pictorial representation of AND, OR, XOR, and NOT gates as well as their input and output values

Figure 1.3 A simple flip-flop circuit

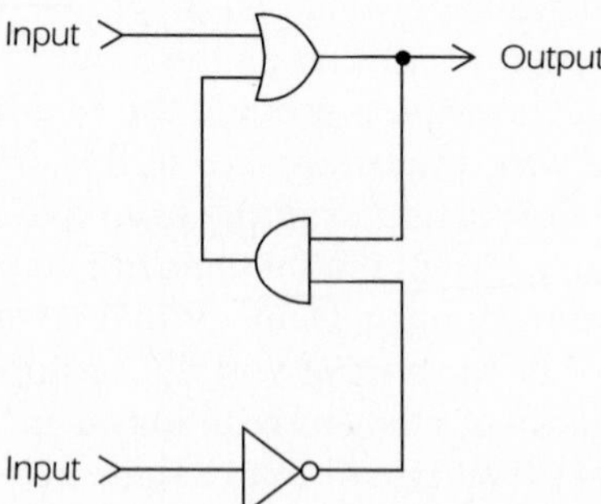

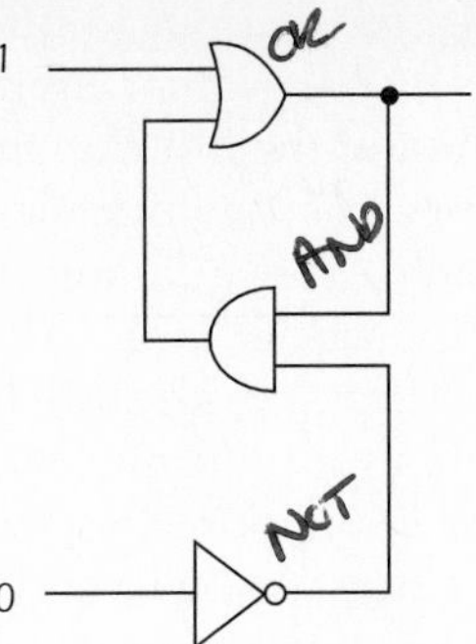

(a) 1 is placed on the upper input.

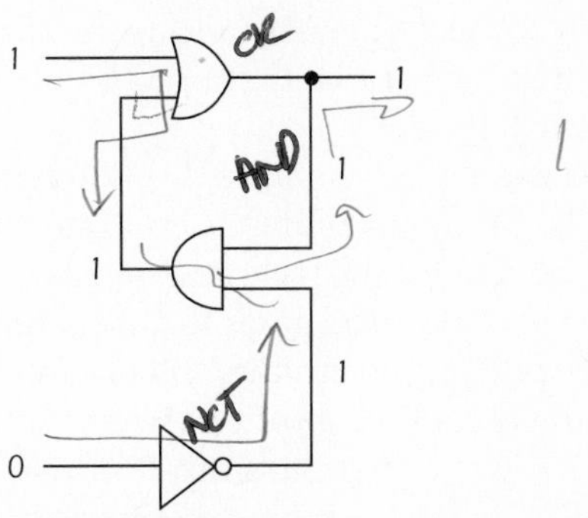

(b) This causes the output of the OR gate to be 1 and, in turn, the output of the AND gate to be 1.

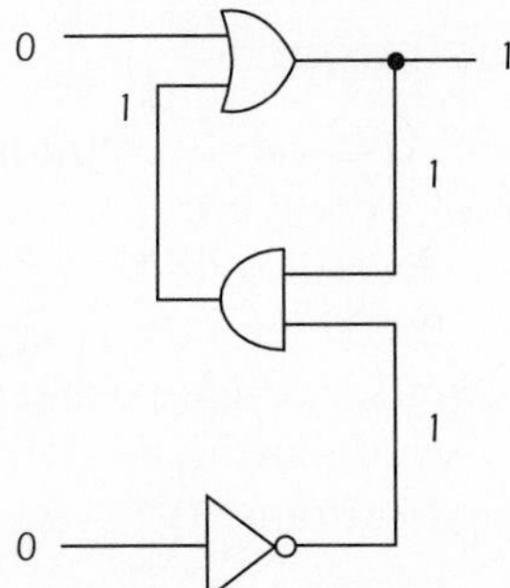

(c) The 1 from the AND gate keeps the OR gate from changing after the upper input returns to 0.

Figure 1.4 Setting the flip-flop's output to 1

be 1, regardless of the other input to this gate. In turn, both inputs to the AND gate will now be 1, since the other input to this gate is already 1 (obtained by passing the lower input of the flip-flop through the NOT gate). The output of the AND gate will then become 1, which means that the second input to the OR gate will now be 1 (Fig. 1.4b). This guarantees that the output of the OR gate will remain 1, even when the upper input to the flip-flop is changed back to 0 (Fig. 1.4c). In summary, the flip-flop's output has become 1, and this output value will remain after the upper input returns to 0.

In a similar manner, temporarily placing the value 1 on the lower input will force the flip-flop's output to be 0, and this output will persist after the input value returns to 0.

The significance of a flip-flop from our perspective is that it is ideal for the storage of a bit within a computer. The value stored in a flip-flop can be observed and changed easily by other electronic circuits. Moreover, flip-flops can be made so small that millions of them can be placed on a single wafer (called a **chip**) no larger than a dime.

Gates and circuits such as flip-flops provide our first example of the use of abstract tools. We can use gates as building blocks when designing computer circuitry without concern for the technical details of each gate's internal construction. Moreover, once we have used gates to design flip-flops or other circuits, we can use these larger components as building blocks for more complex systems. To demonstrate, Fig. 1.5 shows another flip-flop circuit with the same external properties as the one in Fig. 1.3. When designing a flip-flop, one considers the pros and cons of these two options. But, when designing a larger circuit in which a flip-flop is used, one puts the internal details of the flip-flop aside and concentrates on how the flip-flop, as a complete unit, interacts with the other components in the larger system.

Other Storage Techniques

In the 1960s machines commonly contained many small donut-shaped rings of magnetic material, or **cores,** threaded on wires. By passing electric current through the wires, each core could be magnetized or remagnetized in one of two directions. Later, the direction of the magnetic field could be detected by observing its effect on an electric current passing through the center of the core. Thus a core provided a means of storing a bit. Such systems are obsolete today due to their size and power requirements.

Figure 1.5 Another way of constructing a flip-flop

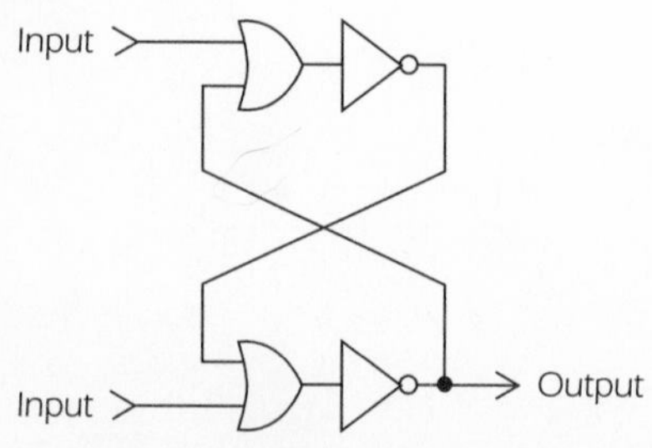

Magnetic technology is still used for bit storage within machines, however. Later in this chapter we will see that today's machines record bits on magnetic material in much the same way that music is recorded on magnetic tape. We will also learn how laser technology is used to record bit patterns.

Differences in the properties of electronic flip-flops and magnetic (or laser) storage devices represent pros and cons in their application. In favor of the flip-flop is the fact that it is entirely electronic and can therefore be manipulated more quickly than today's magnetic or laser devices, which, we will see, require physical motion for their operation. For this reason, devices such as flip-flops are used for the storage of bits in a computer's internal circuitry. However, an electronic flip-flop loses the information intrusted to it when its power source is turned off. In contrast, a magnetic or laser storage device maintains its data and so is commonly used for the construction of storage systems in which longevity is important.

Hexadecimal Notation

When considering the internal activities of a computer, we must deal with strings of bits, some of which can be quite long. Unfortunately, the human mind has difficulty handling such detail. Merely transcribing the pattern 101101010011 is tedious and error-prone. To simplify the representation of bit patterns, therefore, we usually use a shorthand notation called **hexadecimal notation.** This notation takes advantage of the fact that bit patterns within a machine tend to have lengths in multiples of four. In particular, hexadecimal notation uses a single symbol to represent four bits, meaning that a string of twelve bits can be represented by only three symbols.

Figure 1.6 presents the hexadecimal coding system. The left column in this figure displays all possible bit patterns of length four; the right column shows

Figure 1.6 The hexadecimal table

Bit pattern	Hexadecimal representation
0000	0
0001	1
0010	2
0011	3
0100	4
0101	5
0110	6
0111	7
1000	8
1001	9
1010	A
1011	B
1100	C
1101	D
1110	E
1111	F

the symbol used in hexadecimal notation to represent the pattern to its left. Using this system, the bit pattern 10110101 is represented as B5. This is obtained by dividing the bit pattern into substrings of length four and then representing each substring by its hexadecimal equivalent—1011 is represented by B and 0101 is represented by 5. In this manner the 16-bit pattern 1010010011001000 can be reduced to the more palatable form A4C8.

We will use hexadecimal notation extensively in the next chapter. There you will come to appreciate its efficiency.

Questions/Exercises

1. What input bit patterns will cause the following circuit to produce an output of 1?

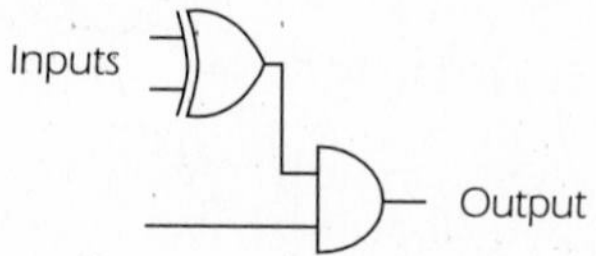

2. In the text we claimed that placing a 1 on the lower input of the flip-flop in Fig. 1.3 (while holding the upper input at 0) will force the flip-flop's output to be 0. Describe the sequence of events that occurs within the flip-flop in this case.
3. Assuming that both inputs to the flip-flop in Fig. 1.5 are 0, describe the sequence of events that occurs when the upper input is temporarily set to 1.
4. Use hexadecimal notation to represent the following bit patterns:
   a. 0110101011110010 b. 111010000101010100010111
   c. 01001000
5. What bit patterns are represented by the following hexadecimal patterns?
   a. 5FD97 b. 610A c. ABCD d. 0100

1.2 Main Memory

For the purpose of storing data, a computer contains a large collection of circuits, each capable of storing a bit. This bit reservoir is known as the machine's **main memory.**

Main Memory Organization

The storage circuits in a machine's main memory are arranged in manageable units called **cells** (or words), with a typical cell size being eight bits. In fact, bit collections of size eight have become so popular that the term **byte** is now widely used in reference to bit collections of that size.

Small computers used in such household devices as microwave ovens may have main memory sizes measured in hundreds or fewer of cells, whereas large computers used to store and manipulate extensive amounts of data can have billions of cells in their main memories. The size of a machine's main memory is often measured in terms of 1,048,576-cell units. (The value 1,048,576 is a power of two, namely 2^{20}, so it is more natural as a unit of measure within a computer than an even 1,000,000.). The term *mega* is used to indicate this unit of measure. The abbreviation MB is often used for the term *megabyte*. Thus a memory of 4MB contains 4,192,304 (4 × 1,048,576) cells, each of which is one byte in size. Other units of measuring memory size are kilobyte (abbreviated as KB), which is equal to 1024 bytes (2^{10} bytes, and gigabyte (abbreviated as GB), which is equal to 1024MG, or 2^{30} bytes.

To identify individual cells in a machine's main memory, each cell is assigned a unique name, called its **address.** The system is analogous to, and uses the same terminology as, the technique of identifying houses in a city by addresses. In the case of memory cells, however, the addresses used are entirely numeric. To be more precise, one envisions all the cells being placed in a single row and numbered in this order starting with the value zero. The cells in a machine with a 4MB memory would be therefore addressed as 0, 1, 2, . . . , 4192303. Note that such as addressing system not only gives us a way of uniquely identifying each cell but also associates an order to the cells (Fig. 1.7), giving us phrases such as "the next cell" or "the previous cell."

To complete the main memory of a machine, the circuitry that actually holds the bits is combined with the circuitry required to allow other circuits to store and retrieve data from the memory cells. In this way, other circuits can get data from the memory by electronically asking for the contents of a certain address (called a read operation), or they can record information in the memory by requesting that a certain bit pattern be placed in the cell at a particular address (called a write operation).

Figure 1.7 Memory cells arranged by address

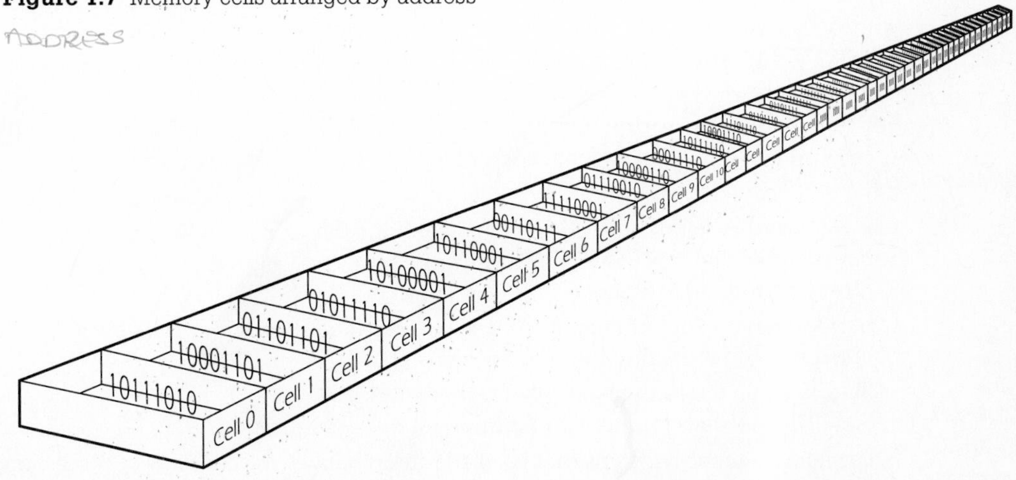

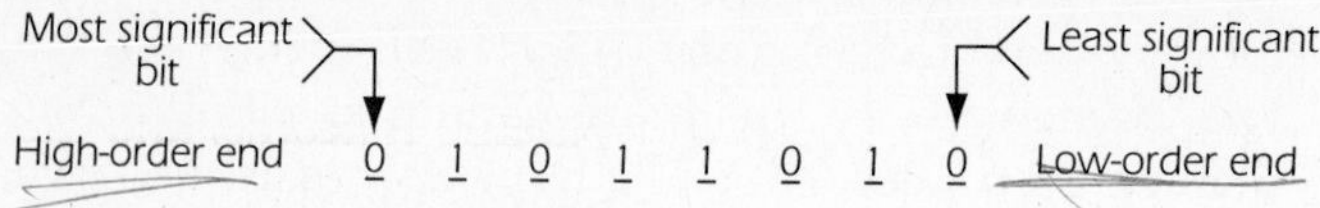

Figure 1.8 The organization of a byte-size memory cell

An important consequence of organizing a machine's main memory as small, addressable cells is that each cell can be referenced, accessed, and modified individually. A memory cell with a low address is just as accessible as one with a high address. In turn, data stored in a machine's main memory can be processed in any order desired, and thus a machine's main memory is often referred to as **random access memory (RAM)**. This random access of small data units is in stark contrast to the mass storage systems that we will discuss in the next section, in which long strings of bits must be manipulated as a block.

Organization Within a Cell

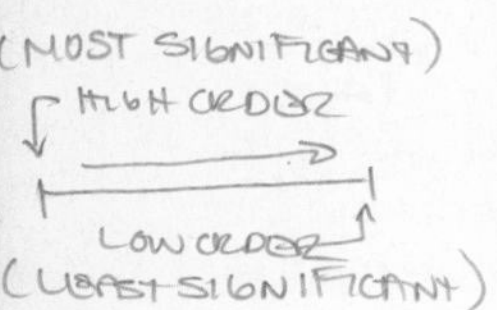

We envision the bits within a memory cell as being arranged in a row. We call one end of this row the **high-order** end and the other the **low-order** end. Although there is no left or right within a machine, we imagine the bits arranged in a row from left to right with the high-order end on the left. The bit at this end is often called either the high-order bit or the **most significant** bit; similarly, the bit at the other end is referred to as the low-order bit or the **least significant** bit. Thus we may represent the contents of a byte-size cell as shown in Fig. 1.8.

An important consequence of the ordering of both the cells in main memory and the bits within each cell is that the entire collection of bits within a machine's main memory is essentially ordered in one long row. Pieces of this long row can therefore be used to store bit patterns that may be longer than the length of a single cell. In particular, if the memory is divided into byte-size cells, one can still store a string of 16 bits merely by using two consecutive memory cells.

Questions/Exercises

1. If the memory cell whose address is 5 contains the value 8, what is the difference between writing the value 5 into cell number 6 and moving the contents of cell number 5 into cell number 6?
2. Suppose you want to interchange the values stored in memory cells 2 and 3. What is wrong with the following sequence of steps:

   Step 1. Move the contents of cell number 2 to cell number 3.
   Step 2. Move the contents of cell number 3 to cell number 2.

   Design a sequence of steps that correctly interchanges the contents of these cells.
3. How many bits would be in the memory of a computer with 4KB memory?

1.3 Mass Storage

Limitations of technology, economic concerns, and the necessity of maintaining backup copies of sensitive data dictate that the main memory of a computer rarely fills the needs of all the machine's applications. Thus most machines are provided with **mass storage** systems (also called **secondary memory**) in addition to their main memory. Data is traditionally stored on these systems in large units called **files**. Among the disadvantages of mass storage systems is that they typically require mechanical motion and so are slow in storing or retrieving data compared to the machine's main memory which performs all activities electronically. Among the advantages of mass storage is that, in many cases, it is cheaper than main memory and the medium on which it records data can be removed from the machinery and stored elsewhere for backup purposes.

You will hear the terms *on-line* and *off-line* in relation to devices that can be either attached to or detached from a machine. **On-line** means that the device or information is connected and readily available to the machine without human intervention. In contrast, **off-line** means that human intervention is required before the device or information can be accessed by the machine, perhaps because the device must be turned on or the medium holding the information must be inserted into some mechanism.

Disk Storage

The most common form of mass storage in use today is disk storage, in which a thin spinning disk with magnetic coating is used to hold the data. Read/write heads are placed above and/or below the disk so that as the disk spins, each head traverses a circle, called a **track**, around the disk's upper or lower surface. Since each track can contain more information than we would normally want to manipulate at any one time, tracks are divided into arcs called **sectors** on which information is recorded as a continuous string of bits (Fig. 1.9).

By repositioning the read/write heads, sectors on different concentric tracks can be accessed. In turn, a disk storage system consists of many individual sectors, each of which can be accessed as an independent string of bits. The number of tracks per surface and the number of sectors per track vary greatly from one disk system to another. However, sector sizes tend to be either 512 bytes or 1024 bytes.

Figure 1.9 A disk storage system

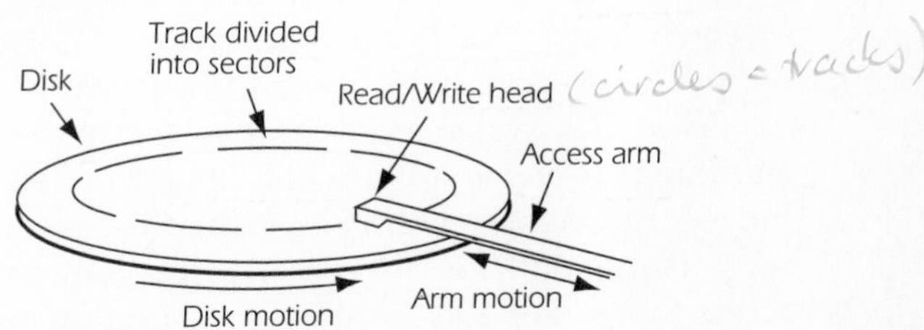

The location of tracks and sectors is not a permanent part of a disk's physical structure. Instead, they are marked magnetically through a process called **formatting** (or initializing) the disk. This process is usually done by the disk's manufacturer, resulting in what are known as formatted disks. Fortunately, most computer systems can reformat disks when a format is not compatible. Reformatting a disk destroys all the information that was previously recorded on the disk.

The capacity of a disk storage system depends on the number of disks used and the density in which the tracks and sectors can be placed. Lower-capacity systems consist of a single plastic disk known as a diskette or, since the disk is flexible, by the less prestigious title of floppy disk. Such diskettes are available in diameters of 5¼ and 3½ inches. (The 3½-inch varieties, being housed in rigid plastic cases, do not constitute as flexible a package as their larger cousins that are housed in paper sleeves.) Although diskette capacities tend to be limited to a few megabytes, they are easily inserted and removed from their corresponding read/write unit and are easily stored. As a consequence, diskettes provide a good medium for off-line storage of information.

High-capacity disk systems, capable of holding several gigabytes, consist of perhaps five to ten rigid disks mounted on a common spindle, one on top of the other, with enough space for the read/write heads to slip between the platters. The fact that the disks used in these systems are rigid leads them to be known as hard-disk systems, in contrast to their floppy counterparts. To allow for faster rotation speeds, the read/write heads in these systems do not touch the disk but instead "float" just above the surface. The spacing is so close that any particle of dust could jam between the head and disk surface, destroying both (a phenomenon known as a *head crash*) Thus hard-disk systems are housed in cases sealed at the factory.

Several measurements are used to evaluate a disk system's performance. One, **seek time**, measures the time required to move the read/write heads from one track to another. Other measurements include **rotation delay** or **latency time** (half the time required for the disk to make a complete rotation, which is the average amount of time required for the desired data to rotate around to the read/write head once the head has been positioned over the desired track), **access time** (the sum of seek time and rotation delay), and **transfer rate** (the rate at which data can be transferred to or from the disk).

Hard-disk systems generally have significantly better characteristics than floppy systems. Since the read/write heads do not touch the disk surface in a hard-disk system, one finds rotation speeds on the order of 3000 to 4000 revolutions per minute, whereas disks in floppy-disk systems rotate in the 300 revolutions-per-minute range. Consequently, transfer rates for hard-disk systems, usually measured in megabytes per second, are much greater than those associated with floppy-disk systems, which tend to be measured in kilobytes per second.

Since disk systems require physical motion for their operation, both hard and floppy systems suffer when compared to speeds within electronic circuitry. Indeed, delay times within an electronic circuit are measured in units of nanoseconds (billionths of a second) or less, whereas seek times, latency times, and access times of disk systems are measured in milliseconds (thousandths of a second). Thus the time required to retrieve information from a disk system can seem like an eternity to an electronic circuit awaiting a result.

Compact Disks

The technology of mass storage is continually evolving. Today, optical systems that challenge the popularity of magnetic devices are on the market. Most prominent is the compact disk (CD), which is compatible with those in the music industry except that computer CD players tend to spin the CD faster to obtain higher data transfer rates.

These disks, approximately 5 inches in diameter, consist of reflective material covered with a clear protective coating. Information is recorded on them by creating variations in their reflective surfaces. This information can then be retrieved by monitoring these irregularities with a laser beam as the disk spins. In contrast to magnetic disk storage in which information is recorded on separate, concentric tracks, information on a CD is stored on one continuous track that spirals around the CD like a groove in an old-fashioned record. The fact that positions on a CD are identified by track numbers is a convenient, yet inaccurate, carryover of magnetic disk terminology, rather than a reference to the existence of physically separate tracks on the CD.

Today, the most common use of compact disk storage devices is in the context of read-only devices called CD-ROM (compact disk read-only memory). These disks are purchased with information already recorded on them. Due to their enormous storage capacities (at least 600MB), such disks are capable of storing multimedia presentations in which audio and video data are combined to present information in a more interesting and more informative manner than would be possible by means of traditional text. Today's market provides CD-ROMs containing musical scores combined with audio recordings of the works, a brief bibliography of the composers, and perhaps a discussion of the significance of the works. Other CD-ROMs contain complete encyclopedias that include video presentations of historical events. Moreover, CD-ROMs are rapidly becoming the medium of choice for the distribution of large software systems.

CD systems in which stored data can be altered are also available. For example, systems using magneto-optical drives record information by essentially melting the CD's reflective surface with a laser beam and then rearranging it by magnetic fields before it cools again.

Tape Storage

An older form of mass storage device uses magnetic tape (Fig. 1.10). Here information is recorded on the magnetic coating of a thin plastic tape that is in turn wound on a reel for storage. To access the data, this tape is mounted in a device called a tape drive that typically can read, write, and rewind the tape under control of the computer. Tape drives range in size from small cartridge units, called streaming tape units, that use tape similar in appearance to that in stereo systems to older, large reel-to-reel units. Although the capacity of these devices depends on the format used, some can hold several gigabytes.

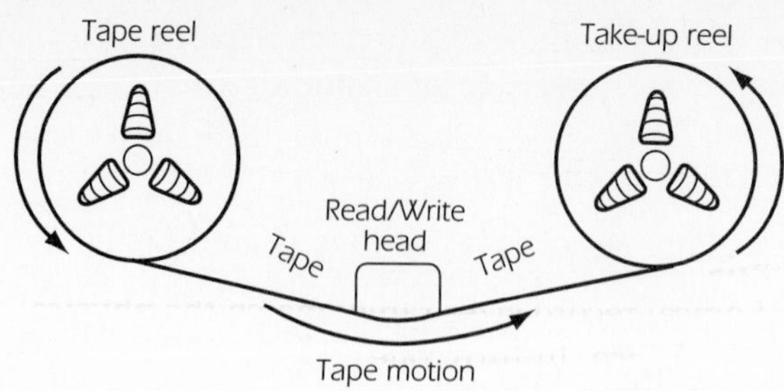

Figure 1.10 A tape storage mechanism

Modern streaming tape systems divide a tape into segments, each of which is magnetically marked by a formatting process similar to that of disk storage devices. Each of these segments contains several tracks that run parallel to one another lengthwise on the tape. These tracks can be accessed independently, meaning that the tape ultimately consists of numerous individual strings of bits in a manner similar to the sectors on a disk.

A major disadvantage of streaming tape systems is that moving between different positions on a tape can be very time-consuming owing to the significant amount of tape that must be moved between the reels. Thus tape systems have much longer data access times than disk systems in which different sectors can be accessed by short movements of the read/write head. In turn, tape systems are not popular for on-line data storage but are used mainly in off-line, backup storage applications. Indeed, streaming tape units have become the de facto standard for backup storage on small computer systems.

Logical Versus Physical Records

Whereas data in a machine's main memory can be referenced by individual byte size cells, the physical properties of mass storage devices dictate that data stored on these systems be manipulated in multiple byte units. For example, each sector on a magnetic disk must be handled as one long string of bits. A block of data conforming to the physical characteristics of a storage device is called a **physical record**.

Figure 1.11 Logical records versus physical records on a disk

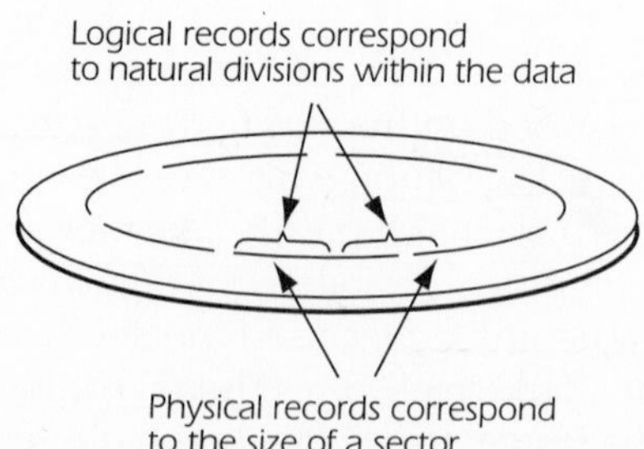

In contrast to the division of data into physical records whose sizes are determined by the characteristics of the storage device, the file being stored usually has natural divisions. For example, a file containing information regarding a company's employees is conveniently divided into a block of information for each employee. Such naturally occurring blocks of data are called **logical records**.

Logical record sizes rarely match the physical record size dictated by a mass storage device. In turn, one may find several logical records residing within a single physical record or perhaps a logical record split between two or more physical records (Fig. 1.11). The result is that a certain amount of unscrambling is associated with retrieving data from mass storage systems.

Questions/Exercises

1. What advantage does a hard-disk system gain from the fact that its disks spin faster than those in a floppy-disk system?
2. When only one side of a disk is used for storing data, it is called single-sided. When both surfaces are used, we say it is double-sided. Drives for double-sided disk are provided with two read/write heads (one for each side) that are mechanically linked so that they move as a single unit and always traverse tracks directly opposite each other on the two surfaces. When recording data on a double-sided disk, should we fill a complete side before starting the other or alternate between the surfaces by filling each opposing track pair before moving to the next pair?
3. Why should the data in a reservation system that is constantly being updated be stored on a disk instead of on tape?
4. Suppose that logical records of 450 bytes each are to be stored on a disk whose sectors consist of 512 bytes each. Give an argument to the effect that only one logical record should be stored per physical record even though this means that 62 bytes of each sector will be wasted.

1.4 Coding Information for Storage

We now take a closer look at the techniques used for representing information in terms of bit patterns.

Representing Symbols

One procedure for representing data within a machine is to design a code in which different symbols (such as the letters of the alphabet or punctuation marks) are assigned unique bit patterns and to store the information as coded sentences in main memory or on mass storage media. In the early years of computers many such codes were designed and used in connection with different pieces of equipment, producing a corresponding proliferation of communication problems.

To alleviate this situation, the American National Standards Institute (ANSI) adopted the **American Standard Code for Information Interchange (ASCII**, pronounced "as'–kee"), which has become extremely popular. This code uses bit patterns of length seven to represent the upper- and lowercase letters of the English alphabet, punctuation symbols, the digits 0 through 9, and certain control information such as line feeds, carriage returns, and tabs. Today, ASCII is often extended to an eight-bit-per-symbol format by adding a 0 at the most significant end of each of the seven-bit patterns. This technique not only produces a code in which each pattern fits conveniently into a typical byte-size memory cell but also provides 128 additional bit patterns (those obtained by assigning the extra bit the value 1) that can represent symbols excluded in the original ASCII. Unfortunately, because vendors tend to use their own interpretations for these extra patterns, data in which these patterns appear are often not easily transported from one vendor's application to another.

Appendix A shows a portion of ASCII in an eight-bit-per-symbol format, and Fig. 1.12 demonstrates that, in this system, the bit pattern

01001000 01100101 01101100 01101100 01101111 00101110

represents "Hello."

Although ACSII is the most common code used today, other more extensive codes, capable of representing documents in a variety of languages, are gaining in popularity. One of these, **Unicode**, was developed through the cooperation of several of the leading manufacturers of hardware and software. This code uses a unique pattern of 16 bits to represent each symbol. As a result, Unicode consists of 65,536 different bit patterns—enough to allow the most common Chinese and Japanese symbols to be represented. A code that will probably compete with Unicode is being developed by the **International Standards Organization (ISO)**, of which ANSI is a member. Using patterns of 32 bits to represent symbols, this code has the potential of representing more than 17 million symbols. Which of these codes will ultimately win the vote of popularity remains to be seen.

Representing Numeric Values

Although the method of storing information as coded characters is quite useful, it is inefficient when the information being recorded is purely numeric. To see why, suppose we want to store the number 25. If we insist on storing it as coded symbols in ASCII using one byte per symbol, we need a total of 16 bits. More-

Figure 1.12 The message "Hello." in ASCII

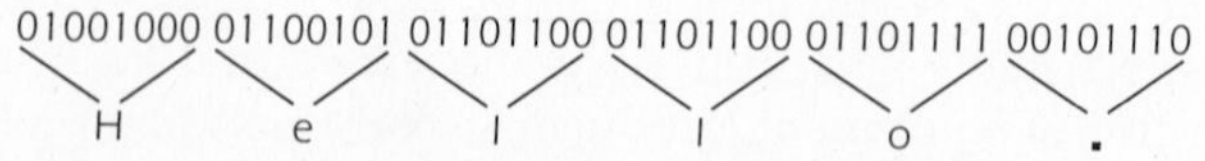

over, the largest number we can store using 16 bits is 99. A more efficient approach is to store the value in its base two, or binary, representation.

Binary notation is a way of representing numeric values using only the digits 0 and 1 rather than the digits 0, 1, 2, 3, 4, 5, 6, 7, 8, and 9 as in the traditional decimal, or base ten, system. Recall that in the base ten system each position in a representation is associated with a quantity. In the representation 375, the 5 is in the position associated with the quantity one, the 7 is in the position associated with ten, and the 3 is in the position associated with the quantity one hundred (Fig. 1.13). Each quantity is ten times that of the quantity to its right. The value represented by the entire expression is obtained by multiplying the value of each digit by the quantity associated with that digit's position and then adding those products. To illustrate, the pattern 375 represents (3 × hundred) + (7 × ten) + 5 × one).

The position of each digit in binary notation is also associated with a quantity except that the quantity associated with each position is twice the quantity associated with the position to its right. More precisely, the rightmost digit in a binary representation is associated with the quantity one (2^0), the next position to the left is associated with two (2^1), the next is associated with four (2^2), the next with eight (2^3), and so on. For example, in the binary representation 1011, the rightmost 1 is in the position associated with the quantity one, the 1 next to it is in the position associated with two, the 0 is in the position associated with four, and the leftmost 1 is in the position associated with eight (Fig. 1.13b).

To extract the value represented by a binary representation, we follow the same procedure as in base ten—we multiply the value of each digit by the quantity associated with its position and add the results. For example, the value represented by 100101 is 37, as shown in Fig. 1.14. Note that since binary notation uses only the digits 0 and 1, this multiply-and-add process reduces merely to adding the quantities associated with the positions occupied by 1s. Thus the

Figure 1.13 The decimal and binary systems

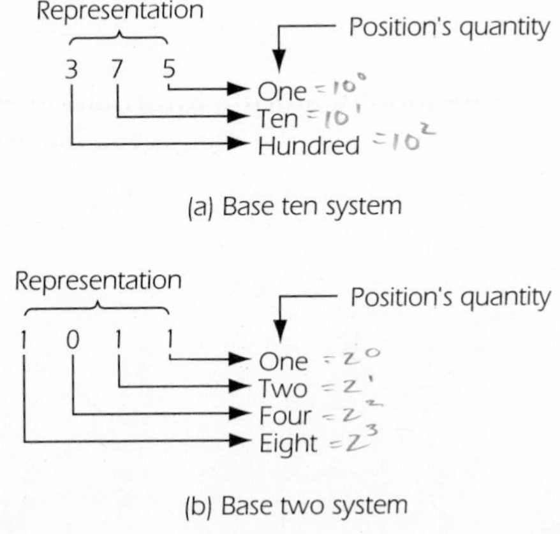

binary pattern 1011 represents the value eleven, because the 1s are found in the positions associated with the quantities one, two, and eight.

Note that the sequence of binary representations obtained by counting from zero to eight is the following:

0
1
10
11
100
101
110
111
1000

There are numerous approaches to generating this sequence, and although not elegant in theoretical content, they do provide a quick way of obtaining the binary representation for small values. One approach is to imagine a car's odometer whose display wheels contain only the digits 0 and 1. The odometer starts at 0 and rotates to a 1 as the car is driven. Then, as that 1 rotates back to a 0, it causes a 1 to appear to its left, producing the pattern 10. The 0 on the right then rotates to a 1, producing 11. Now the rightmost 1 rotates back to 0, causing the 1 to its left to rotate to a 0 as well. This in turn causes another 1 to appear in the third column, producing the pattern 100.

For finding binary representations of large values, you may prefer the more systematic approach described by the algorithm in Fig. 1.15. Let us apply this algorithm to the value thirteen (Fig. 1.16). We first divide thirteen by two, obtaining a quotient of six and a remainder of one. Since the quotient was not zero, step 2 tells us to divide the quotient (six) by two, obtaining a new quotient of three and a remainder of zero. The newest quotient is still not zero, so we divide it by two, obtaining a quotient of one and a remainder of one. Once again we divide the newest quotient (one) by two, this time obtaining a quotient of zero and a remainder of one. Since we have now acquired a quotient of zero, we move on to step 3, where we learn that the binary representation of the original value (thirteen) is 1101.

Figure 1.14 Decoding the binary representation 100101

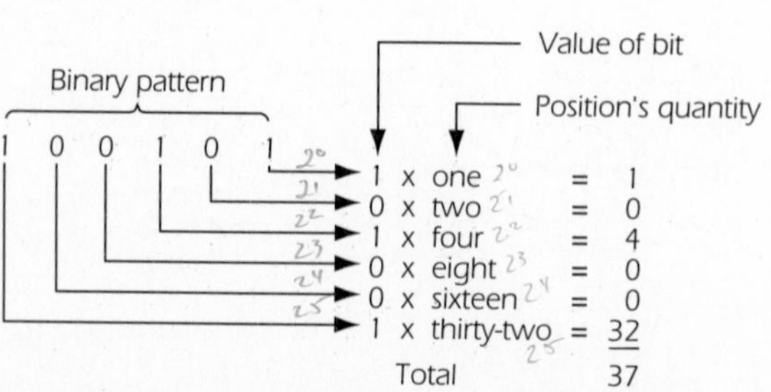

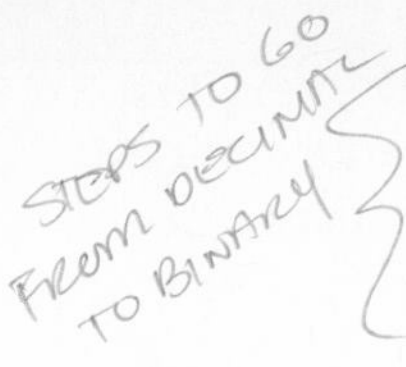

Step 1. Divide the value by two and record the remainder.

Step 2. As long as the quotient obtained is not zero, continue to divide the newest quotient by two and record the remainder.

Step 3. Now that a quotient of zero has been obtained, the binary representation of the original value consists of the remainders listed from right to left in the order they were recorded.

Figure 1.15 An algorithm for finding the binary representation of a positive integer

Recall our original problem of storing numeric data. Using binary notation, in one byte we can store any integer between 0 and 255 (00000000 to 11111111), and given two bytes, we can store the integers from 0 to 65535. This is a drastic improvement over the ability to store only the integers from 0 to 99 when coding characters using one ASCII pattern per byte.

For this and other reasons, it is common to store numeric information in a form of binary notation rather than in coded symbols. We say "a form of binary notation" because, the straightforward binary system just described is only the basis for several numeric storage techniques used within machines. Some of these variations of the binary system are discussed later in this chapter. For now, we merely note that a system called two's complement notation is common for storing whole numbers because it provides a convenient method for representing negative numbers as well as positive. For representing numbers with fractional parts such as 4½ or ¾, another technique, called floating-point notation, is used. Thus a particular value (such as 25) may be represented by several different bit patterns (coded characters, two's complement notation, or in floating-point notation as 25⁄1); conversely, a particular bit pattern may be given several interpretations.

At this point, we should mention a significant problem with numeric storage systems that we deal with in more depth later. Regardless of the pattern size that a machine might allocate for the storage of numeric values, there will still be val-

Figure 1.16 Applying the algorithm in Fig. 1.15 to obtain the binary representation of thirteen.

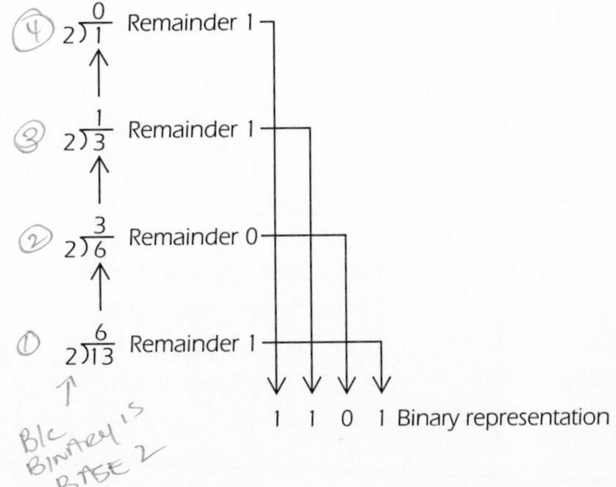

ues too large or fractions too small to be stored in the space allotted. The result is the constant potential for errors such as overflow (values too large) and round-off (fractions too small) that must be dealt with, or an unsuspecting computer user can soon be faced with a multitude of erroneous data.

Representing Other Types of Data

Today's computer applications involve more than just character and numeric data. They include pictures, audio, and video. In comparison to character and numeric storage systems, the techniques for representing data of these additional forms are in their infancy and consequently are not as standardized across the data processing community.

One popular way of storing pictures is to consider the picture as a collection of dots, each of which is called a **pixel,** short for "picture element." In its simplest form, an entire picture can be represented as a long string of bits representing the rows of pixels in the picture, where each bit is either 1 or 0 depending on whether the corresponding pixel is black or white. Color pictures are only slightly more complicated, since each pixel can be represented by a combination of bits indicating the color of that pixel.

Representations of this form are collectively called **bit maps,** meaning that the bit pattern is little more than a map of the picture being represented. Popular bit map systems include TIFF (Tag Image Format File) and GIF (Graphic Interchange Format). Photographs are often represented in a bit map form known as JPEG (Joint Photographic Experts Group). The major disadvantage of these systems is that a picture cannot be rescaled to any arbitrary size. It can be printed using one printer pixel to represent an original pixel or perhaps using a two-by-two block of printer pixels to represent a single original pixel. The later would produce a bigger display than the former, but sizes between these two would be awkward.

To overcome this scaling problem, a picture can be stored as a set of directions explaining how the picture is to be drawn rather than as a pixel-by-pixel representation. For example, a line in the picture could be represented as the instruction to draw a straight line between two particular points. Such a description leaves the details of how that line is drawn to the device that ultimately produces the picture rather than insisting that the device reproduce a particular pixel pattern. It also provides a description that is compatible with any size coordinate system that might be specified when the output is requested.

The various fonts available on today's printers and monitors are usually represented in this manner to provide flexibility in character size, resulting in **scalable fonts.** For example, TrueType® (developed by Microsoft and Apple Computer) is a system for describing how symbols in text are to be drawn. Likewise, PostScript® (developed by Adobe Systems) provides a means of describing characters as well as more general pictorial data.

Still other methods of representing data include MPEG (Motion Picture Experts Group), is for video and audio, and DXF (Drawing Interchange Format), for computer-aided design (CAD) systems in which images must be rotated and rescaled on a monitor screen.

Questions/Exercises

1. Here is a message coded in ASCII using eight bits per symbol. What does it say?

   01000011 01101111 01101101 01110000 01110101 01110100
   01100101 01110010 00100000 01010011 01100011 01101001
   01100101 01101110 01100011 01100101

2. In the ASCII code, what is the relationship between the codes for an uppercase letter and the same letter in lowercase?
3. Code these sentences in ASCII:
   a. Where are you?
   b. "How?" Cheryl asked.
   c. 2 + 3 = 5.
4. Describe a device from everyday life that can be in either of two states, such as a flag on a flagpole that is either up or down. Assign the symbol 1 to one of the states and 0 to the other, and show how the ASCII representation for the letter *b* would appear when stored with such bits.
5. Convert each of the following binary representations to its equivalent decimal form:
   a. 0101 b. 1001 c. 1011 d. 0110
   e. 10000 f. 10010
6. Convert each of the following decimal representations to its equivalent binary form:
   a. 6 b. 13 c. 11 d. 18 e. 27 f. 4
7. What is the largest numeric value that could be represented with three bytes if each digit were coded using one ASCII pattern per byte? What if binary notation were used?
8. An alternative to hexadecimal notation for representing bit patterns is **dotted decimal notation** in which each byte in the pattern is represented by its base ten equivalent. In turn, these byte representations are separated by periods. For example, 12.5 represents the pattern 0000110000000101 (the byte 00001100 is represented by 12, and 00000101 is represented by 5), and the pattern 100010000001000000000111 is represented by 136.16.7. Represent each of the following bit patterns in dotted decimal notation.
   a. 0000111100001111 b. 001100110000000010000000 c. 0000101010100000

1.5 The Binary System

Before pursuing the numeric storage techniques used in today's machines, we need a few more details about the binary representation system.

Binary Addition

To add two values represented in binary notation, we begin, just as we did with base ten in elementary school, by memorizing the addition facts (Fig. 1.17). These facts are used to add two strings of decimal digits. That is, add the digits

```
   0      1      0      1
 + 0    + 0    + 1    + 1
 ---    ---    ---    ---
   0      1      1     10
```

Figure 1.17 The binary addition facts

in the right-hand column, write the least significant digit of this sum under the column, carry the more significant digit of the sum (if there is one) to the next column to the left, and proceed by adding that column. To solve the problem

```
  00111010
+ 00011011
----------
```

we begin by adding the rightmost 0 and 1; we obtain 1, which we write below the column. Now we add the 1 and 1 from the next column, obtaining 10. We write the 0 from this 10 under the column and carry the 1 to the top of the next column. At this point, our solution looks like this:

```
         1
  00111010
+ 00011011
----------
        01
```

We add the 1, 0, and 0 in the next column, obtain 1, and write the 1 under this column. The 1 and 1 from the next column total 10; we write the 0 under the column and carry the 1 to the next column. Now our solution looks like this:

```
       1
  00111010
+ 00011011
----------
      0101
```

The 1, 1, and 1 in the next column total 11; we write the low-order 1 under the column and carry the other 1 to the top of the next column. We add that 1 to the 1 and 0 already in that column to obtain 10. Again, we record the low-order 0 and carry the 1 to the next column. We now have

```
     1
  00111010
+ 00011011
----------
    010101
```

Now we add the 1, 0, and 0 from the next to the last column, obtaining 1, which we record below the column with nothing to carry. Finally, we add the last column, which yields 0, and record this under the column. Our final solution is this:

```
  00111010
+ 00011011
----------
  01010101
```

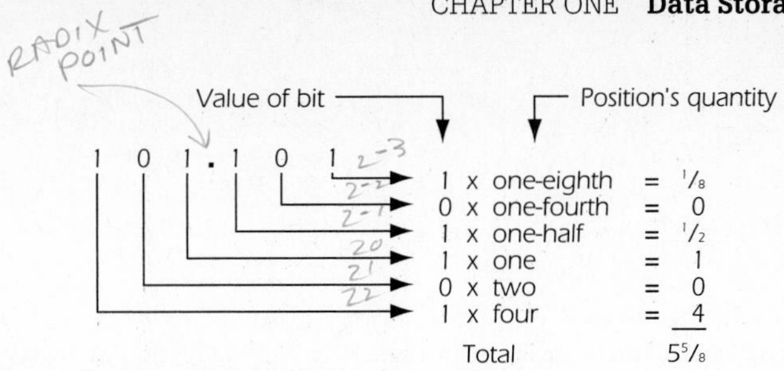

Figure 1.18 Decoding the binary representation 101.101

Fractions in Binary

To extend binary notation to accommodate fractional values, we use a **radix point** in the same role as the decimal point in decimal notation. That is, the digits to the left of the point represent the integer part of the value and are interpreted as in the binary system discussed previously. The digits to its right represent the fractional part of the value and are interpreted in a manner similar to the other bits, except their positions are assigned fractional quantities. That is, the first position to the right of the radix is assigned the quantity ½, the next position the quantity ¼, the next ⅛, and so on. Note that this is merely a continuation of the rule stated previously: Each position is assigned a quantity twice the size of the one to its right. With these quantities assigned to the bit positions, decoding a binary representation containing a radix point requires the same procedure as used without a radix point. In particular, we multiply each bit value by the quantity assigned to that bit's position in the representation. To illustrate, the binary representation 101.101 decodes to 5⅝, as shown in Fig. 1.18.

For addition, the techniques applied in the base ten system are also applicable in binary. That is, to add two binary representations having radix points, we merely align the radix points and apply the same addition process as before. For example, 10.011 added to 100.11 produces 111.001, as shown here:

```
   10.011
 + 100.11
 --------
  111.001
```

Questions/Exercises

1. Convert each of the following binary representations to its equivalent decimal form:

   a. 101010   b. 100001   c. 10111   d. 0110   e. 11111

2. Convert each of the following decimal representations to its equivalent binary form:

   a. 32   b. 64   c. 96   d. 15   e. 27

3. Convert each of the following binary representations to its equivalent base ten form:

a. 11.01   b. 101.111   c. 10.1   d. 110.011   e. 0.101

4. Express the following values in binary notation:

a. $4\frac{1}{2}$ b. $2\frac{3}{4}$ c. $1\frac{1}{8}$ d. $\frac{5}{16}$ e. $5\frac{5}{8}$

5. Perform the following additions in binary notation:

a.	b.	c.	d.
11011	1010.001	11111	111.11
+ 1100	+ 1.101	+ 1	+ .01

1.6 Storing Integers

When searching for an efficient technique for representing whole numbers as bit patterns, we might try the binary notation presented in Section 1.4, except that we often need to store negative values as well as positive ones. We therefore need a notational system that encompasses both positive and negative integers. Mathematicians have long been interested in numeric notational systems, and many of their ideas have turned out to be very compatible with the design of electronic circuitry and so are used extensively in computing equipment. In this section we consider two of these notational systems, excess notation and two's complement notation.

Excess Notation

One method of representing integer values is **excess notation.** Each of the values in an excess notation system is represented by a bit pattern of the same length. To establish an excess system, we first select the pattern length to be used, then write down all the different bit patterns of that length in the order they would appear if we were counting in binary. Next, we observe that the first pattern with a 1 as its most significant bit appears approximately halfway through the list. We pick this pattern to represent zero; the patterns following this are used to represent 1, 2, 3, . . . ; and the patterns preceding it are used for –1, –2, –3, ... The resulting code, when using patterns of length four, is shown in Fig. 1.19. There we see that the value 5 is represented by the pattern 1101 and –5 is represented by 0011.

Note that in an excess notation system it is easy to distinguish the patterns that represent negative values from those that do not. Those that represent negative values have a 0 as their most significant bit, and those that do not represent negative values have a 1 as their most significant bit. The most significant bit is often called the **sign bit.** In excess notation a sign bit equal to 0 indicates a negative value, and a sign bit equal to 1 indicates a positive or zero value.

The system represented in Fig. 1.19 is known as excess eight notation. To understand why, first interpret each of the patterns in the code using the traditional binary system and then compare these results to the values represented

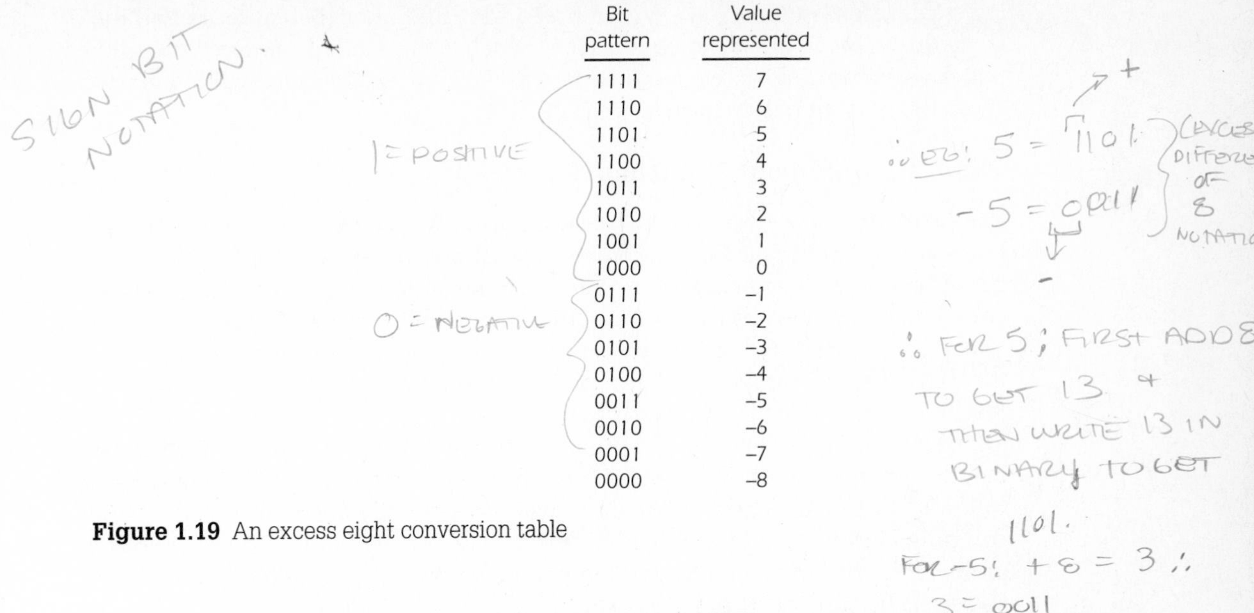

Bit pattern	Value represented
1111	7
1110	6
1101	5
1100	4
1011	3
1010	2
1001	1
1000	0
0111	–1
0110	–2
0101	–3
0100	–4
0011	–5
0010	–6
0001	–7
0000	–8

Figure 1.19 An excess eight conversion table

in the excess code. In each case, you will find that the binary interpretation exceeds the excess code interpretation by the value 8. For example, the pattern 1100 normally represents the value 12, but in our excess system it represents 4; 0000 normally represents 0, but in the excess system it represents –8. In a similar manner, an excess system based on patterns of length five would be called excess 16 notation, because the pattern 10000, for instance, would be used to represent 0 rather than representing its usual value of 16. Likewise, you may want to confirm that the three-bit excess system would be known as excess four notation (Fig. 1.20).

Based on these observations, we obtain a quick method of coding values when using excess notation. To code a value using excess eight notation, we need to add 8 to the value, write the result in base two, and then add leading 0s (if required) to obtain a pattern of four bits. For example, to code the value 5 us-

Figure 1.20 An excess notation system using bit patterns of length three

Bit pattern	Value represented
111	3
110	2
101	1
100	0
011	–1
010	–2
001	–3
000	–4

ing excess eight notation, we would first add 8, giving us the value 13, and then write this value in binary to obtain 1101, which is the desired pattern. To find the pattern representing –5, we would add 8 to obtain the value 3, which in binary is 11, so the four-bit pattern we desire is 0011.

Two's Complement Notation

The most popular system for representing integers within today's computers is **two's complement notation.** Like excess notation, this system uses a fixed number of bits to represent each of the values in the system. Figure 1.21 shows two's complement systems based on bit patterns of length three and four. Such a system is constructed by starting with a string of 0s of the appropriate length and then counting in binary until the pattern consisting of a 0 followed by 1s is reached. These patterns represent the values 0, 1, 2, 3, ... The patterns representing negative values are obtained by starting with a string of 1s of the appropriate length and then counting backward in binary until the pattern consisting of a 1 followed by 0s is reached. These patterns represent the values –1, –2, –3, ... (If counting backward in binary is difficult for you, merely start at the very bottom of the table with the pattern consisting of a 1 followed by 0s, and count up to the pattern consisting of all 1s.)

Note that in a two's complement system, the negative values are represented by the patterns whose sign bits are 1; in turn, a 0 sign bit indicates that the value represented is either zero or positive. You should also note the convenient relationship between the patterns representing positive and negative values of the same magnitude. These patterns are identical when read from right to left, up to

Figure 1.21 Two's complement notation systems

Using patterns of length three		Using patterns of length four	
Bit pattern	Value represented	Bit pattern	Value represented
011	3	0111	7
010	2	0110	6
001	1	0101	5
000	0	0100	4
111	–1	0011	3
110	–2	0010	2
101	–3	0001	1
100	–4	0000	0
		1111	–1
		1110	–2
		1101	–3
		1100	–4
		1011	–5
		1010	–6
		1001	–7
		1000	–8

and including the first 1. From there on the patterns are complements of one another. (The **complement** of a pattern is the pattern obtained by changing all the 0s to 1s and all the 1s to 0s; 0110 and 1001 are complements.) For example, in the four-bit system in Fig. 1.21 the patterns representing 2 and –2 both end with 10, but the pattern representing 2 begins with 00, whereas the representing –2 begins with 11. This observation leads to an algorithm for converting back and forth between bit patterns representing positive and negative values of the same magnitude. We merely copy the original pattern from right to left until a 1 has been copied, then we complement the remaining bits (change all the remaining 1s to 0s and 0s to 1s) as they are copied (Fig. 1.22).

Understanding these basic properties of two's complement systems also leads to an algorithm for decoding two's complement representations. If the pattern to be decoded has a sign bit of 0, we need merely read the value as though the pattern were a binary representation. For example, 0110 represents the value 6, because 110 is binary for 6. If the pattern to be decoded has a sign bit of 1, we know the value represented is negative and all that remains is to find the magnitude of the value. We do this by copying the original pattern from right to left until a 1 has been copied, then complementing the remaining bits as they are copied, and finally decoding the pattern obtained as though it were a binary representation.

For example, to decode the pattern 1010, we first recognize that since the sign bit is 1, the value represented is negative. Hence, we convert the pattern to 0110, recognize that this represents 6, and conclude that the original pattern represents –6.

Addition in Two's Complement Notation To add values represented in two's complement notation, we apply the same algorithm that we used for binary addition, except that all bit patterns, including the answer, are the same length. This means that when adding in a two's complement system, any extra bit generated on the left of the answer by a final carry must be truncated. Thus

Figure 1.22 Coding the value –6 in two's complement notation using four bits

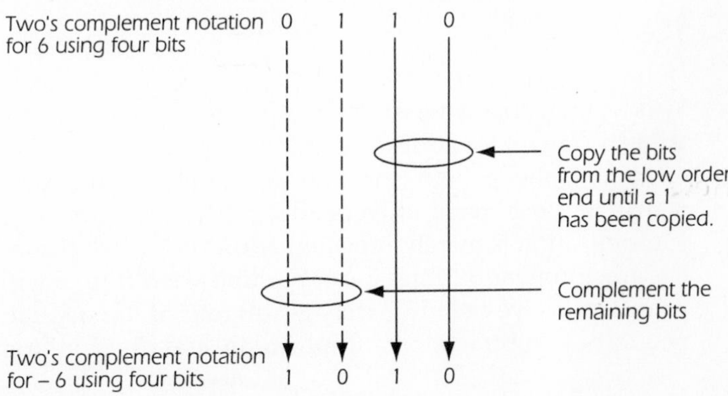

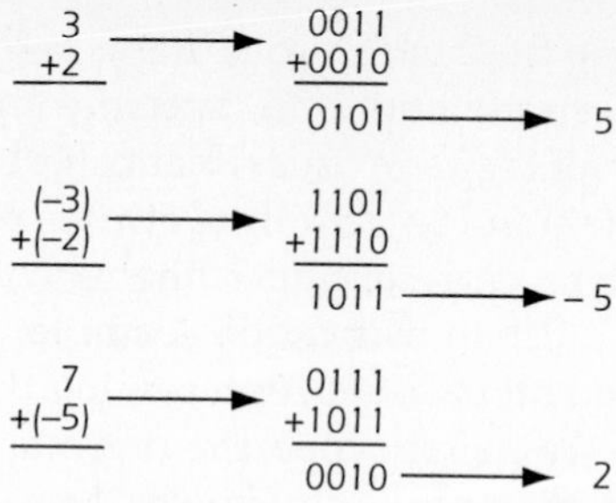

Figure 1.23 Addition problems converted to two's complement notation

"adding" 0101 and 0010 produces 0111, and "adding" 0111 and 1011 results in 0010 (0111 + 1011 = 10010, which is truncated to 0010).

With this understanding, consider the three addition problems in Fig. 1.23. In each case we have translated the problem into two's complement notation (using four bits), performed the addition process previously described, and decoded the result back into our usual decimal notation.

Observe that if we were to use the traditional techniques taught in elementary school, the third problem would require an entirely different process (subtraction) than the previous problems. On the other hand, by translating the problems into two's complement notation, we can compute the correct answer in all cases by applying the same computational algorithm. This, then, is the advantage of two's complement notation: Addition of any combination of signed numbers can be accomplished using the same algorithm.

In contrast to elementary schoolchildren, who must first learn to add and later to subtract, a machine using two's complement notation needs to know only how to add and negate. For example, the subtraction problem 7 – 5 is the same as the addition problem 7 + (–5). Consequently, if a machine were asked to subtract 5 (stored as 0101) from 7 (stored as 0111), it would first change the 5 to –5 (represented as 1011) and then perform the addition process of 0111 + 1011 to obtain 0010, which represents 2, as follows:

$$\begin{array}{r} 7 \\ \underline{-5} \end{array} \rightarrow \begin{array}{r} 0111 \\ \underline{-0101} \end{array} \rightarrow \begin{array}{r} 0111 \\ \underline{+1011} \\ 0010 \end{array} \rightarrow 2$$

We see, then, that when two's complement notation is used to represent numeric values, a circuit for addition combined with a circuit for negating a value is sufficient for solving both addition and subtraction problems. (Such circuits are shown and explained in Appendix B.) The benefits do not stop there, however. Multiplication is merely repeated addition, and division is repeated subtraction (6/2 is the number of times 2 can be subtracted from 6 without getting a negative result). Thus we can ultimately get all four of the standard arithmetic operations of addition, subtraction, multiplication, and division from these two circuits.

The Problem of Overflow One problem we have avoided in the preceding examples is that in any of the numeric systems we have introduced, there is a limit to the size of the values that can be represented. When using two's complement with patterns of four bits, the value 9 has no pattern associated with it so we could not hope to obtain the correct answer to the problem 5 + 4. In fact, the result would appear as –7. A similar problem arises if patterns of five bits are used and we try to represent the value 17. Such an error is called **overflow.** When using two's complement notation, this might occur when adding two positive values or when adding two negative values. In either case, the condition can be detected by checking the sign bit of the answer. That is, an overflow is indicated if the addition of two positive values results in the pattern for a negative value or if the sum of two negative values appears to be positive.

The point is that computers can make mistakes. So, the person using the machine must be aware of the dangers involved. Of course, because most machines manipulate longer bit patterns than we have used here, larger values can be computed without causing an overflow. Many machines use patterns of 32 bits for storing values in two's complement notation, allowing for positive values as large as 2,147,483,647 to accumulate before overflow occurs. If still larger values are needed, the technique called **double precision** is often used. This means that the length of the patterns used is increased from that which the machine normally uses. Another approach to the problem is to change the units of measure. For instance, finding a solution in terms of miles instead of inches results in smaller numbers being used and may still provide the accuracy required.

Questions/Exercises

1. Convert each of the following excess eight representations to its equivalent decimal form without referring to the table in the text:

   a. 1110 b. 0111 c. 1000
   d. 0010 e. 0000 f. 1001

2. Convert each of the following decimal representations to its equivalent excess eight form without referring to the table in the text:

   a. 5 b. –5 c. 3 d. 0 e. 7 f. –8

3. Can the value 9 be represented in excess eight notation? What about representing 6 in excess four notation? Explain your answer.

4. Convert each of the following two's complement representations to its equivalent decimal form:

   a. 00011 b. 01111 c. 11100
   d. 11010 e. 00000 f. 10000

5. Convert each of the following decimal representations to its equivalent two's complement form using patterns of eight bits:

   a. 6 b. –6 c. –17 d. 13 e. –1 f. 0

6. Suppose the following bit patterns represent values stored in two's complement notation. Find the two's complement representation of the negative of each value:

a. 00000001 b. 01010101 c. 11111100

d. 11111110 e. 00000000 f. 01111111

7. Suppose a machine stores numbers in two's complement notation. What are the largest and smallest numbers that could be stored if the machine uses bit patterns of the following lengths?

a. four b. six c. eight

8. In the following problems, each bit pattern represents a value stored in two's complement notation. Find the answer to each problem in two's complement notation by performing the addition process described in the text. Then check your work by translating the problem and your answer into decimal notation.

a.	b.	c.	d.	e.
0101	0011	0101	1110	1010
+ 0010	+ 0001	+ 1010	+ 0011	+ 1110

9. Solve each of the following problems in two's complement notation, but this time watch for overflow and indicate which answers are incorrect because of this phenomenon.

a.	b.	c.	d.	e.
0101	0101	1010	1010	0111
+ 0011	+ 0110	+ 1010	+ 0111	+ 0001

10. Translate each of the following problems from decimal notation into two's complement notation using bit patterns of length four, then convert each problem to an equivalent addition problem (as a machine might do), and finally perform the addition. Check your answers by converting them back to decimal notation.

a.	b.	c.	d.	e.
6	3	4	2	1
+ 1	− 2	− 6	+ 4	− 5

11. Can overflow ever occur when adding values in two's complement notation when one value is positive and the other is negative? Explain your answer.

1.7 Storing Fractions

In contrast to the storage of integers, the storage of a value with a fractional part requires that we store not only the pattern of 0s and 1s representing its binary representation but also the position of the radix point. A popular way of doing this is based on scientific notation and is called **floating-point notation.**

Floating-Point Notation

Let us explain floating-point notation with an example using only one byte of storage. Although machines normally use much longer patterns, this example is representative of actual systems and serves to demonstrate the important concepts without the clutter of long bit patterns. We first designate the high-order bit of the byte as the sign bit. Once again, a 0 in the sign bit will mean that the value stored is nonnegative, and a 1 will mean that the value is negative. Next, we divide the remaining seven bits of the byte into two groups, or fields, the **exponent field** and the **mantissa field.** Let us designate the three bits following the sign bit as the exponent field and the remaining four bits as the mantissa field. The byte is therefore divided as shown in Fig. 1.24.

We can explain the meaning of the fields by considering the following example. Suppose a byte contains the bit pattern 01101011. Analyzing this pattern with the preceding format, we see that the sign bit is 0, the exponent is 110, and the mantissa is 1011. To decode the byte, we first extract the mantissa and place a radix point on its left side, obtaining

.1011

Next, we extract the contents of the exponent field (110) and interpret it as an integer stored using the three-bit excess method (see Fig. 1.20). Thus the pattern in the exponent field in our example represents a positive 2. This tells us to move the radix in our solution to the right by two bits. (A negative exponent would mean to move the radix to the left.) Consequently, we obtain

10.11

which represents 2¾. Next, we note that the sign bit in our example is 0; the value represented is thus nonnegative. We conclude that the byte 01101011 represents 2¾.

As another example, consider the byte 10111100. We extract the mantissa to obtain

.1100

and move the radix one bit to the left, since the exponent field (011) represents the value –1. We therefore have

.01100

which represents ⅜. Since the sign bit in the original pattern is 1, the value stored is negative. We conclude that the pattern 10111100 represents –⅜.

To store a value using floating-point notation, we reverse the preceding process. For example, to code 1⅛, first we express it in binary notation and obtain 1.001. Next, we copy the bit pattern into the mantissa field from left to right, starting with the first nonzero bit in the binary representation. At this point, the byte looks like this:

_ _ _ _ 1 0 0 1

We must now fill in the exponent field. To this end, we imagine the contents of the mantissa field with a radix point at its left and determine the number of bits and the direction the radix must be moved to obtain the original binary number. In our example, we see that the radix in .1001 must be moved one bit to the right to obtain 1.001. Because the exponent should therefore be a positive 1,

Figure 1.24 Floating-point notation components

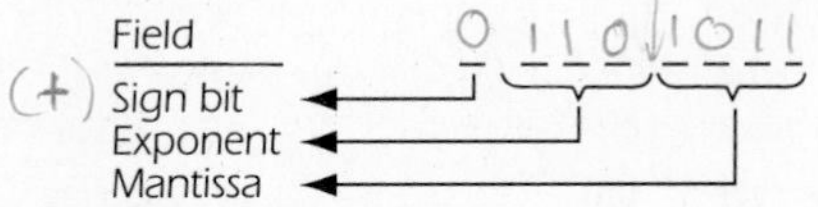

Field
Sign bit
Exponent
Mantissa

we place 101 (which is positive 1 in excess four notation) in the exponent field. Finally, we fill the sign bit with 0 because the value being stored is nonnegative. The finished byte looks like this:

<u>01011001</u>

Before moving on, we should explain why excess notation is used for representing the exponent in floating-point systems. It reduces the task of comparing the relative size of two values to merely scanning their representations from left to right while looking for the first bit in which the two patterns differ. For example, if both sign bits are 0, the larger of the two values being compared is the one containing a 1 in the first bit position from the left in which the two patterns differ. Thus, if 00101010 and 00011001 were floating-point representations, we could conclude that the former represents a larger value without first determining what the values involved actually are.

Round-Off Errors

Let us consider the annoying problem that occurs if we try to store 2⅝ with our one-byte floating-point system. We first write 2⅝ in binary, which gives us 10.101. But when we copy this into the mantissa field, we run out of room, and the last 1 (which represents the last ⅛) is lost (Fig. 1.25). If we ignore this problem for now and continue by filling in the exponent field and the sign bit, we end up with the bit pattern 01101010, which represents 2½ instead of 2⅝. What has occurred is called a **round-off error,** caused in this case by a four-bit mantissa field when a five-bit field is required for accuracy. This suggests the solution of lengthening this field, which is exactly what is done on real machines. As with integer storage, it is common to use at least 32 bits for storing floating-point notation instead of the eight we have used here. This approach also allows for a longer exponent field at the same time. Even with these longer formats, however, there are still times when more accuracy is required. Again we find the concept of double precision being applied when extreme precision is required.

Another source of round-off errors is a phenomenon that you are already accustomed to in decimal notation: the problem of nonterminating expansions,

Figure 1.25 Coding the value 2⅝

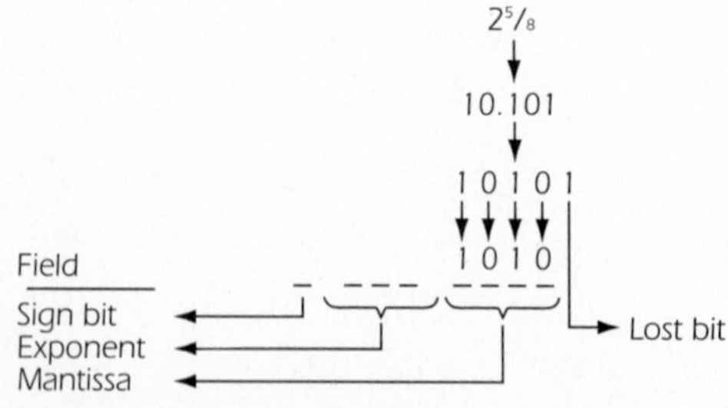

such as those found when trying to express ⅓ in decimal form. Some values cannot be accurately expressed regardless of how many digits we use.

The difference between our normal decimal notation and binary notation is that more values have nonterminating representations in binary than in decimal notation. For example, the value one-tenth is nonterminating when expressed in binary. Imagine the problems this might cause the unwary person using floating-point notation to store and manipulate dollars and cents. In particular, if the dollar is used as the unit of measure, the value of a dime could not be stored accurately.

A solution in this case is to manipulate the data in units of pennies so that all values are integers that can be accurately stored using a method such as two's complement. Such techniques are representative of those used by software packages designed for nontechnical users (such as a spreadsheet system). In these cases, use of a machine's floating-point facilities is usually avoided to shield the user from erroneous results.

Round-off errors and their related problems are an everyday concern for people working in the area of numerical analysis. This branch of mathematics deals with the problems involved when doing actual computations that are often massive and require significant accuracy.

We close this section with an example of a general rule of thumb that would warm the heart of any numerical analyst. Suppose we are asked to add the following three values using our one-byte floating-point notation defined previously:

$$2\tfrac{1}{2} + \tfrac{1}{8} + \tfrac{1}{8}$$

If we add the values in the order listed, we first add 2½ to ⅛ and obtain 2⅝, which in binary is 10.101. Unfortunately, because this value cannot be stored accurately (as seen previously), the result of our first step ends up being stored as 2½ (which is the same as one of the values we were adding). The next step is to add this result to the last ⅛. Here again a round-off error occurs, and our final result turns out to be the incorrect answer 2½.

Now let us add the values in the opposite order. We first add ⅛ to ⅛ to obtain ¼. In binary this is .01; so the result of our first step is stored in a byte as 00111000, which is accurate. We now add this ¼ to the next value in the list, 2½, and obtain 2¾, which we can accurately store in a byte as 01101011. The result this time is the correct answer.

In summary, when adding values in floating-point notation, the order in which they are added can be extremely important. The general rule is to always add the smaller values together first; however, even this process does not guarantee accuracy.

Questions/Exercises

1. Decode the following bit patterns using the floating-point format discussed in the text:

   a. 01001010 b. 01101101 c. 00111001 d. 11011100 e. 10101011

2. Code the following values into the floating-point format discussed in the text. Indicate the occurrence of round-off errors.

   a. 2¾ b. 5¼ c. ¾ d. −3½ e. −4⅜

3. In terms of the floating-point format discussed in the text, which of the patterns 01001001 and 00111101 represents the larger value? Describe a simple procedure for determining which of two patterns represents the larger value.

4. When using the floating-point format discussed in the text, what is the largest value that can be represented? What is the smallest positive value that can be represented?

1.8 Communication Errors

When information is transferred back and forth among the various parts of a computer, or transmitted from the earth to the moon and back, or, for that matter, merely left in storage, a chance exists that the bit pattern finally retrieved may not be identical to the original one. Particles of dirt or grease on a magnetic recording surface or a malfunctioning circuit may cause data to be incorrectly recorded or read. Moreover, in the case of some technologies, background radiation can alter patterns stored in a machine's main memory.

To resolve such problems, a variety of coding techniques have been developed to allow the detection and even the correction of errors. Today, because these techniques are largely built into the internal components of a computer system, they are not apparent to the personnel using the machine. Nonetheless, their presence is important and represents a significant contribution to scientific research. In fact, many of these techniques are prime examples of the contributions made by theoretical mathematics. It is fitting therefore that we investigate some of these techniques that lie behind the reliability of today's equipment.

Parity Bits

A simple method of detecting errors is based on the principle that if each bit pattern being manipulated has an odd number of 1s and a pattern is found with an even number of 1s, an error must have occurred.

To use this principle, we need a system in which each pattern contains an odd number of 1s. This is easily obtained by first adding an additional bit, the **parity bit,** to each pattern in a system already available (usually at the high-order end). (Thus the eight-bit ASCII code becomes a nine-bit code, or a sixteen-bit pattern representing a value in two's complement notation becomes a seventeen-bit pattern.) In each case we assign the value 1 or 0 to this new bit so that the resulting pattern has an odd number of 1s. As Fig. 1.26 shows, the ASCII code for A becomes 101000001 (parity bit 1), and the ASCII for I becomes 001001001 (parity bit 0). Although the eight-bit pattern for A has an even number of 1s and the eight-bit pattern for F has an odd number of 1s, both the nine-bit patterns have an odd number of 1s. Once our coding system has been modified in this way, a pattern with an even number of 1s indicates an error has occurred and the pattern being manipulated is incorrect.

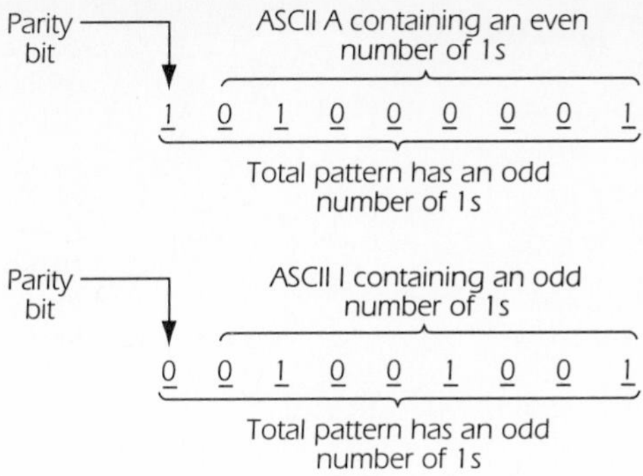

Figure 1.26 The ASCII codes for A and FI adjusted for odd parity

The particular parity system just described is called **odd parity,** because we designed our system so that each pattern would contain an odd number of 1s. Another technique is to use **even parity.** In such a system, each pattern is designed to contain an even number of 1s, and thus an error is signaled by the occurrence of a pattern with an odd number of 1s.

Today, it is not unusual to find parity bits being used in a computer's main memory. Although we envision these machines as having memory cells of eight bits, in reality they may have nine-bit cells, one bit of which is used as a parity bit. Each time an eight-bit pattern is given to the memory circuitry for storage, the circuitry adds a parity bit and stores the resulting nine-bit pattern. When the pattern is later retrieved, the circuitry checks the parity of the nine-bit pattern. If this does not indicate an error, the memory removes the parity bit and confidently returns the remaining eight-bit pattern. Otherwise, the memory returns the eight data bits with a warning that the pattern being returned may not be the same pattern that was originally entrusted to memory.

Long bit patterns are often accompanied by a collection of parity bits making up a **checkbyte.** Each bit within the checkbyte is a parity bit associated with a particular collection of bits scattered throughout the pattern. For instance, one parity bit may be associated with every eighth bit in the pattern starting with the first bit, while another may be associated with every eighth bit starting with the second bit. In this manner, a collection of errors concentrated in one area of the original pattern is more likely to be detected, since it will be in the scope of several parity bits. Variations of this checkbyte concept lead to error detection schemes known as checksums and cyclic redundancy codes (CRC).

Error-Correcting Codes

Although the use of a parity bit allows the detection of an error, it does not provide the information needed to correct the error. Many people are surprised that **error-correcting codes** can be designed so that errors can be not only detected but also corrected. After all, intuition says that we cannot correct errors in a received

Symbol	Code
A	000000
B	001111
C	010011
D	011100
E	100110
F	101001
G	110101
H	111010

Figure 1.27 An error-correcting code

message unless we already know the information in the message. However, a simple code with such a corrective property is presented in Fig. 1.27.

To understand how this code works, we first define the **Hamming distance** (named after R. W. Hamming, who pioneered the search for error-correcting codes after becoming frustrated with the lack of reliability of the early relay machines of the 1940s) between two patterns to be the number of bits in which the two differ. For example, the Hamming distance between A and B in the code in Fig. 1.27 is four, and the Hamming distance between B and C is three. The important feature of the code is that any two patterns are separated by a Hamming distance of at least three. If a single bit is modified by a malfunctioning device, the error can be detected since the result will not be a legal pattern. (We must change at least three bits in any pattern before it will look like another legal pattern.)

If a single error has occurred in a pattern from Fig. 1.27, we can also figure out what the original pattern was. Indeed, the modified pattern will be a Hamming distance of only one from its original form but at least two from any of the other legal patterns. To decode a message, we simply compare each received pattern with the patterns in the code until we find one that is within a distance of one from the received pattern. This we consider to be the correct symbol for decoding. For example, suppose we receive the bit pattern 010100. If we compare this pat-

Figure 1.28 Decoding the pattern 010100 using the code in Figure 1.27

Character	Distance between the received pattern and the character being considered	
A	2	
B	4	
C	3	
D	1	(Smallest distance)
E	3	
F	5	
G	2	
H	4	

tern to the patterns in the code, we obtain the table in Fig. 1.28. Thus we can conclude that the character transmitted must be a D because this is the closest match.

You will observe that using this technique with the code in Fig. 1.27, actually allows us to detect up to two errors per pattern and to correct one error. If we designed the code so that each pattern was a Hamming distance of at least five from each of the others, we would be able to detect up to four errors per pattern and correct up to two. Of course, the design of efficient codes associated with large Hamming distances is not a straightforward task. In fact, it constitutes a part of the branch of mathematics called algebraic coding theory.

Issues of Application

As mentioned earlier, the use of parity bits or error-correcting codes today is almost always a concern handled within the equipment itself and is rarely visible to the machine's user. The average computer user may be concerned with these concepts only when it is necessary to connect two pieces of equipment, such as a printer and a computer. In such cases, most devices have switches whose settings determine the communication technique to be used. Under these circumstances, it is the user's responsibility to adjust the switches so that both pieces of equipment are set for the same technique. For instance, you could imagine that little would be accomplished if a computer sent characters with odd parity to a printer that was expecting even parity.

The decision whether to use parity checks, an error-correcting code, or some other error-handling system depends on the application at hand and to what extent one is willing to go for the added reliability. As already mentioned, parity systems are used in many computer memory systems. Error-correcting codes are often used by high-capacity disk units, where the need for accuracy exceeds the costs introduced by the added complexity.

Of course, no error-handling system is foolproof. Parity systems cannot detect the occurrence of an even number of errors, and too many errors in a single pattern of an error-correcting code can produce another valid but incorrect pattern.

Questions/Exercises

1. The following bytes were originally coded using odd parity. In which of them do you know that an error has occurred?

   a. 10101101 b. 10000001 c. 00000000 d. 11100000 e. 11111111

2. Could errors have occurred in a byte from Question 1 without your knowing it? Explain your answer.
3. How would your answers to Questions 1 and 2 change if you were told that even parity had been used instead of odd?
4. Code these sentences in ASCII using odd parity by adding a parity bit at the high-order end of each character code:

   a. Where are you?

   b. "How?" Cheryl asked.

   c. 2 + 3 = 5.

5. Using the error-correcting code presented in Fig. 1.27, decode the following messages:
   a. 001111 100100 001100
   b. 010001 000000 001011
   c. 011010 110110 100000 011100
6. Construct a code for the characters A, B, C, and D using bit patterns of length five so that the Hamming distance between any two patterns is at least three.

CHAPTER REVIEW PROBLEMS *(Asterisked problems are associated with optional sections.)*

1. Determine the output of each of the following circuits, assuming that the upper input is 1 and the lower input is 0.

   a.

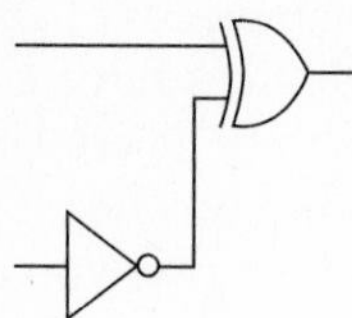

   b.

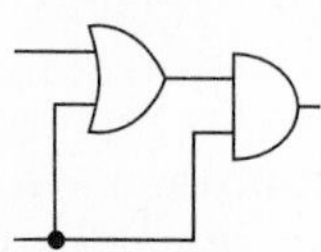

   c.

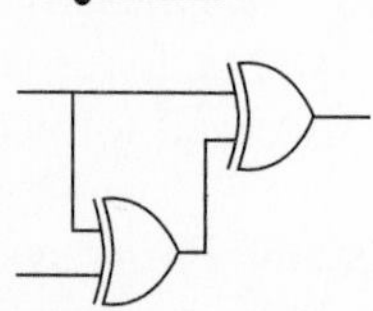

2. For each of the following circuits, identify the input combinations that produce an output of 1.

   a.

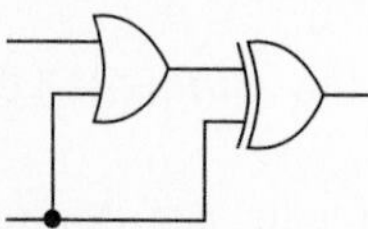

   b.

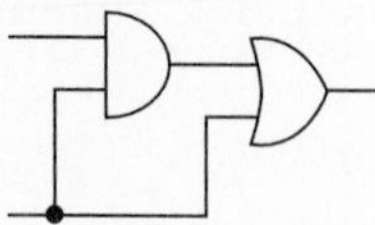

   c.

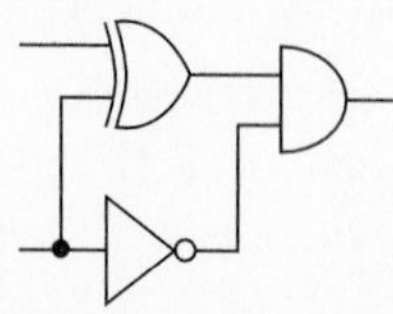

3. Assume that both of the inputs in the next circuit are 1. Describe what would happen if the upper input were temporarily changed to 0. Describe what would happen if the lower input were temporarily changed to 0.

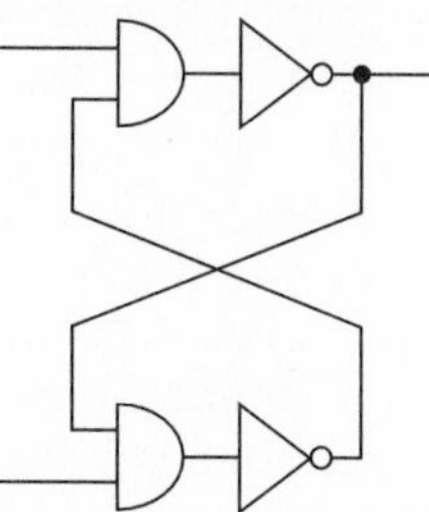

4. The following table represents the addresses and contents of some cells in a machine's main memory using hexadecimal notation. Starting with this memory arrangement, follow the sequence of instructions and record the final contents of each of these memory cells:

Address	*Contents*
00	AB
01	53
02	D6
03	02

Step 1. Move the contents of the cell whose address is 03 to the cell at address 00.
Step 2. Move the value 01 into the cell at address 02.
Step 3. Move the value stored at address 01 into the cell at address 03.

5. How many cells can be in a computer's main memory if each cell's address can be represented by three hexadecimal digits?

6. What bit patterns are represented by the following hexadecimal notations?

   a. BC b. 67 c. 9A d. 10 e. 3F

7. What is the value of the most significant bit in the bit patterns represented by the following hexadecimal notations?

   a. FF b. 7F c. 8F d. 1F

8. Express the following bit patterns in hexadecimal notation:

   a. 101010101010

   b. 110010110111

   c. 000011101011

9. Suppose a monitor screen displayed 24 rows containing 80 text characters each. If the image on the screen were stored in memory by representing each character by its ASCII code (one character per byte), how many bytes of the machine's memory would be required to hold the entire screen image?

10. Suppose a picture is represented on a monitor screen by a rectangular array containing 1024 columns and 768 rows of small dots. If eight bits are required to code the color and intensity of each dot, how many byte-size memory cells are required to hold the entire picture?

11. a. Identify two advantages that a machine's main memory has over disk storage.

    b. Identify two advantages that disk storage has over a machine's main memory.

12. Suppose you are about to use your personal computer to write a term paper that you estimate will be 40 double-spaced typed pages. Your machine has a disk drive for 3½-inch floppy disks with a capacity of 1.44MB per disk. Will your completed term paper fit on one of these disks? If so, how many such papers can be stored on one disk? If not, how many disks are required?

13. Suppose that only 30MB of your personal computer's 500MB hard-disk drive is empty and you are about to replace that drive with a 1GB drive. You want to save all the information stored on the hard drive on 3¼-inch floppy disks while the conversion is made. Is this practical?

14. If each sector on a disk contained 512 bytes, how many sectors are required to store a single double-spaced typed page if each character requires one byte?

15. A typical 3½-inch floppy disk has a capacity of 1.44MB. How does this compare to the size of a 400-page novel in which each page contains 3500 characters?

16. If a floppy disk with 16 sectors per track and 512 bytes per sector spins at the rate of 300 revolutions per minute, at approximately what rate, measured in bytes per second, does data pass by the read/write head?

17. If a microcomputer using the floppy disk in Problem 16 executed ten instructions every microsecond (millionth of a second), how many instructions can it execute in the time between consecutive bytes passing the read/write head?

18. If a floppy disk is rotating at 300 revolutions per minute and the machine can execute ten instructions in a microsecond (millionth of a second), how many instructions can the machine perform during the disk's latency time?

19. Compare the latency time of the typical floppy disk in Problem 18 with that of a typical hard-disk drive spinning at 60 revolutions per second.

20. What is the average access time for a hard disk spinning at 60 revolutions per second with a seek time of 10 milliseconds?

21. Suppose a typist could type 60 words per minute continuously day after day. How long would it take the typist to fill a CD-ROM whose capacity is 1GB? Assume one word is five characters and each character requires one byte of storage.

22. Here is a message in ASCII. What does it say?

    01010111 01101000 01100001 01110100 0100000
    01100100 01101111 01100101 01110011 0010000
    01101001 01110100 00100000 01110011 0110001
    01111001 00111111

23. The following is a message coded in ASCII using one byte per character and then represented in hexadecimal notation. What is the message?
    68657861646563696D616C

24. Code the following sentences in ASCII using one byte per character.

    a. 100/5 = 20

    b. To be or not to be?

    c. The total cost is $7.25.

25. Express your answers to Problem 24 in hexadecimal notation.

26. List the binary representations of the integers from 6 to 16.

27. a. Write the number 13 by representing the 1 and 3 in ASCII.

b. Write the number 13 in binary representation.

28. What values have binary representations in which only one of the bits is 1? List the binary representations for the smallest six values with this property.

***29.** Code the following sentences in ASCII using one byte per character. Use the most significant bit of each byte as a (odd) parity bit.

a. 100/5 = 20

b. To be or not to be?

c. The total cost is $7.25.

***30.** The following message was originally transmitted with odd parity in each short bit string. In which strings have errors definitely occurred?

11011 01011 10110 00000 11111 10101 10001 00100 01110

***31.** Suppose a 24-bit code is generated by representing each symbol by three consecutive copies of its ASCII representation (for example, the symbol A is represented by the bit string 010000010100000101000001). What error-correcting properties does this new code have?

***32.** Using the error-correcting code described in Fig. 1.27, decode the following words:

a. 111010 110110

b. 101000 100110 001100

c. 011101 000110 000000 010100

d. 010010 001000 001110 101111
000000 110111 100110

e. 010011 000000 101001 100110

***33.** Convert each of the following binary representations to its equivalent decimal form:

a. 111 b. 0001 c. 11101
d. 10001 e. 10111 f. 000000
g. 100 h. 1000 i. 10000
j. 11001 k. 11010 l. 11011

***34.** Convert each of the following decimal representations to its equivalent binary form:

a. 7 b. 12 c. 16 d. 15 e. 33

***35.** Convert each of the following excess 16 representations to its equivalent decimal form:

a. 100007 b. 10011 c. 01101
d. 01111 e. 10111

***36.** Convert each of the following decimal representations to its equivalent excess four form:

a. 0 b. 3 c. –3 d. –1 e. 1

***37.** Convert each of the following two's complement representations to its equivalent decimal form:

a. 10000 b. 10011 c. 01101
d. 01111 e. 10111

***38.** Convert each of the following decimal representations to its equivalent two's complement form using patterns of seven bits:

a. 12 b. –12 c. –1 d. 0 e. 8

***39.** Perform each of the following additions assuming the bit strings represent values in two's complement notation. Identify each case in which the answer is incorrect because of overflow.

a. 00101 + 01000
b. 01111 + 00001
c. 11111 + 00001
d. 10111 + 11010
e. 00111 + 00111
f. 00111 + 01100
g. 11111 + 11111
h. 01010 + 10101
i. 01000 + 01000
j. 01010 + 00011

***40.** Solve each of the following problems by translating the values into two's complement notation (using patterns of 5 bits), converting any subtraction problem to an equivalent addition problem, and performing that addition. Check your work by converting your answer to decimal notation. (Watch out for overflow.)

a. 7 + 1
b. 7 – 1
c. 12 – 4
d. 8 – 7
e. 12 + 4
f. 4 + 11

***41.** Convert each of the following binary representations into its equivalent base ten form:

a. 11.001 b. 100.1101 c. .0101
d. 1.0 e. 10.01

***42.** Express each of the following values in binary notation:

a. $5\frac{3}{4}$ b. $\frac{1}{16}$ c. $7\frac{7}{8}$
d. $1\frac{1}{4}$ e. $6\frac{5}{8}$

***43.** Decode the following bit patterns using the floating-point format discussed in this chapter:

a. 01011100 b. 11001000
c. 00101010 d. 10111001

***44.** Code the following values using the floating-point format discussed in this chapter. Indicate each case in which a round-off error occurs.

a. $\frac{1}{2}$ b. $7\frac{1}{2}$ c. $-3\frac{3}{4}$
d. $\frac{3}{32}$ e. $\frac{31}{32}$

***45.** What is the best approximation to the square root of 2 that can be expressed in the floating-point format described in Section 1.7? What value is actually obtained if this approximation is squared by a machine using this floating-point format?

***46.** What is the best approximation to the value one-tenth that can be represented using the floating-point format described in Section 1.7?

***47.** Explain how errors could occur when measurements using the metric system are recorded in floating-point notation. For example, what if 110 cm was recorded in units of meters?

***48.** Using the floating-point format described in Section 1.7, what would be the result of computing the sum $\frac{1}{8} + \frac{1}{8} + \frac{1}{8} + 2\frac{1}{2}$ from left to right? How about from right to left?

***49.** In each of the following addition problems, interpret the bit patterns using the floating-point format discussed in Section 1.7, add the values represented, and code the answer in the same floating-point format. Identify those cases in which round-off errors occur.

a.	01011100 +01101000	b.	01101010 +00111000
c.	01111000 +00011000	d.	01011000 +01011000

***50.** One of the bit patterns 01011 and 11011 represents a value stored in excess 16 notation and the other represents the same value stored in two's complement notation.

a. What can be determined about this common value?

b. What is the relationship between a pattern representing a value stored in two's complement notation and the pattern representing the same value stored in excess notation using the same bit pattern length?

***51.** The three bit patterns 01101000, 10000010, and 00000010 are representations of the same value in two's complement, excess, and the floating-point notation discussed in this chapter, but not necessarily in that order. What is the common value, and which pattern is in which notation?

***52.** In each of the following cases the different bit strings represent the same value but in different numeric coding systems that we have discussed. Identify each value and the coding systems used to represent it.

a. 11111010 0011 1011
b. 11111101 01111101 11101100
c. 1010 0010 01101000

***53.** Which of the following bit patterns are not valid representations in an excess 16 notation system?

a. 01001 b. 101 c. 010101 d. 00000
e. 1000 f. 000000 g. 1111

***54.** Which of the following values cannot be represented accurately in the floating-point format introduced in Section 1.7?

a. $6\frac{1}{2}$ b. 9 c. $1\frac{3}{16}$ d. $\frac{17}{32}$ e. $\frac{15}{16}$

***55.** If you doubled the length of the bit strings being used to represent integers in binary from four bits to eight bits, what change would be made in the value of the largest integer you could represent? What if you were using two's complement notation?

***56.** What would be the hexadecimal representation of the largest memory address in a memory consisting of 4MB if each cell had a one-byte capacity?

***57.** Using gates, design a circuit with few inputs and one output such that the output if 1 if and only if the pattern of four inputs has odd parity.

QUESTIONS OF ETHICS

The following questions are provided to help you understand some of the ethical/social/legal issues associated with the field of computing as well as investigate your own beliefs and their foundations. The goal is not merely to answer these questions. You should also consider why you answered as you did and whether your justifications are consistent from one question to the next.

1. Suppose a round-off error occurs in a critical situation, causing extensive damage and loss of life. Who is liable, if anyone? the designer of the hardware? the designer of the software? the programmer who actually wrote that part of the program? the person who decided to use the software in that particular application? What if the software had been corrected by the company that originally developed it, but that update had not been purchased and applied in the critical application? What if the software had been pirated?
2. Is it acceptable for an individual to ignore the possibility of round-off errors when developing his or her own applications?
3. Many argue that coding information dilutes or otherwise distorts the information, since it essentially forces the information to be quantified. They argue that a questionnaire in which subjects are required to record their opinions by responding within a scale from 1 to 5 is inherently flawed. To what extent is information quantifiable? Can the pros and cons of different locations for a waste disposal plant be quantified? Is the debate over nuclear power and nuclear waste quantifiable? Is it dangerous to base decisions on averages and other statistical analysis? Is it ethical for news agencies to report polling results without including the exact wording of the questions? Is it possible to quantify the value of a human life? Is it acceptable for a company to stop investing in the improvement of a product, even though additional investment could lower the possibility of a fatality relating to the product's use?
4. The concept of public libraries is largely based on the premise that all citizens in a democracy must have access to information. As more and more information is stored and disseminated via computer technology, does access to this technology become a right of every individual? If so, should public libraries be the channel by which this access is provided?

ADDITIONAL ACTIVITIES

1. What is the largest integer your language/machine combination can conveniently handle? As an experiment, write a loop that initializes an integer at 1 and repeatedly multiplies by 2 seventy times while printing the result at each step. Explain the results.
2. What statements does your programming language provide for identifying how the various data items in your programs are to be coded by the machine?
3. Does your programming language provide a convenient technique for handling overflow?
4. Write a program that requests two integers as input, adds them, and displays the result. What happens if the values entered are very large? Can you modify your program so that it prints the message "overflow occurred" when such is the case?
5. What statements in your programming language allow access to data
   a. in main memory?
   b. in mass storage?
6. Write a loop that initializes a real variable at 0.01 and repeatedly increments it by 0.01 up to the value 1, printing its value at each step. Does it print the correct values? Why would you suspect that it may not? Experiment with different initial values and step sizes.
7. Does your programming language allow you to mix data types in the same instruction? For example, can you add an integer value to a floating-point value and store the result as a floating-point value? How about storing the result as an integer value? What activities must be done by the language/machine system to accomplish such a procedure?

8. Write a program to convert binary numerals into Roman numerals. (Recall that 1 = I, 5 = V, 10 = X, 50 = L, 100 = C, 500 = D, and 1000 = M.)

9. Write a program that receives characters from the keyboard and displays the bit patterns representing these characters on the monitor screen. Does your machine use ASCII for character storage?

10. If you are familiar with a spreadsheet system, read its documentation regarding the storage of data and perform experiments in which you ask the software to store and manipulate various numeric values. Write a summary of what you can decipher regarding the manner in which the software handles these tasks. For example, can you detect whether the software uses the machine's floating-point facilities and if so for what tasks does it do so? Does the software present the user with the entire numerical answer, or does it present a shorter, rounded version of the answer? How does the software handle overflow problems when larger and larger values are added together?

Place an extremely large number (such as 10^{26}) in a cell of a spreadsheet and place the value 1 in another cell. Ask the spreadsheet system to add the contents of the two cells and then subtract the contents of the cell containing the large number from that sum. Is the result correct? Explain your findings.

ADDITIONAL READING

Hamacher, V. C., Z. G. Vranesic, and S. G. Zaky. *Computer Organization,* 4th ed. New York: McGraw-Hill, 1996.

Patterson, D. A., and J. L. Hennessy. *Computer Organization and Design.* San Francisco: Morgan Kaufmann, 1994.

Tanenbaum, A. S. *Structured Computer Organization,* 3rd ed. Englewood Cliffs, N.J.: Prentice-Hall, 1990.

CHAPTER TWO

Data Manipulation

2.1 The Central Processing Unit
Registers
CPU/Memory Interface
Machine Instructions

2.2 The Stored-Program Concept
Instructions as Bit Patterns
A Typical Machine Language

2.3 Program Execution
An Example of Program Execution
Programs Versus Data

2.4 Other Architectures
CISC Versus RISC Architectures
Pipelining
Multiprocessor Machines

***2.5 Arithmetic/Logic Instructions**
Logic Operations
Rotation and Shift Operations
Arithmetic Operations

***2.6 Computer–Peripheral Communication**
Controllers
CPU–Controller Communication
Parallel and Serial Communication

In Chapter 1 we studied the concepts relating to the storage of data and a computer's memory. In addition to being able to store data, an algorithmic machine must be able to manipulate the data as directed by an algorithm. Data manipulation requires that the machine have the mechanism for performing operations on data and coordinating the sequence of these operations. In today's typical machine this mechanism is called the central processing unit. It is the study of this unit and related topics on which this chapter concentrates.

*Sections marked by an asterisk are optional in that they provide additional depth of coverage that is not required for an understanding of future chapters.

2.1 The Central Processing Unit

The circuitry in a typical computer that performs operations (such as addition and subtraction) on data is not directly connected to the storage cells in the machine's main memory. Instead, this circuitry is isolated in a part of the computer called the **central processing unit,** or **CPU.** This unit consists of two parts: the **arithmetic/logic unit,** which contains the circuitry that performs data manipulation, and the **control unit,** which contains the circuitry for coordinating the machine's activities.

Registers

For temporary storage of information, the CPU contains cells, or **registers,** that are similar to main memory cells. These registers can be classified as either **general-purpose registers** or **special-purpose registers.** We will meet some of the special-purpose registers in Section 2.3. For now, our concern is the role of the general-purpose registers.

General-purpose registers serve as temporary holding places for data being manipulated by the CPU. These registers hold the inputs to the arithmetic/logic unit's circuitry and provide storage space for results produced by that unit. To perform an operation on data stored in main memory, it is the control unit's responsibility to transfer the data from memory into the general-purpose registers, to inform the arithmetic/logic unit which registers hold the data, to activate the appropriate circuitry within the arithmetic/logic unit, and to tell the arithmetic/logic unit which register should receive the result.

It is instructive to consider registers in the context of a machine's overall memory facilities. Registers are used to hold the data immediately applicable to the operation at hand; main memory is used to hold the data that will be needed in the near future; and mass storage is used to hold data that will likely not be needed in the near future.

In many machines, an additional level, called cache memory, is added to this hierarchy. **Cache memory** is a section of high-speed memory with response times similar to that of the CPU's registers, often located within the CPU itself. In this special memory area, the machine attempts to keep a copy of that portion of main memory that is of current interest. In this setting, data transfers that normally would be made between registers and main memory are made between registers and cache memory. These changes are then transferred collectively to main memory at a more opportune time.

CPU/Memory Interface

For the purpose of transferring bit patterns between a machine's CPU and main memory, these units are connected by a collection of wires called a **bus** (Fig. 2.1). Through this bus the CPU is able to extract, or read, data from main memory by supplying the address of the pertinent memory cell along with a read signal. In a similar manner, the CPU can place, or write, data in memory by providing the address of the destination cell and the data to be stored together with a write signal.

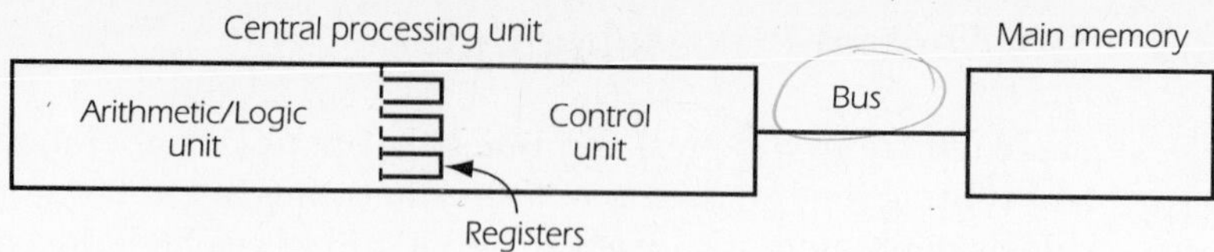

Figure 2.1 A CPU/main memory architecture

With this mechanism in mind, we see that performing an operation such as addition on data stored in main memory involves more than the mere execution of the addition operation itself. The process involves the combined efforts of both the control unit, which coordinates the transfer of information between the registers and main memory, and the arithmetic/logic unit, which performs the operation of addition when instructed to do so by the control unit. The complete process of adding two values stored in memory might be broken down into the steps listed in Fig. 2.2.

Machine Instructions

The steps in Fig. 2.2 provide examples of the types of instructions a typical CPU must be able to follow. Such instructions are called **machine instructions.** You may be surprised to learn that the list of machine instructions is quite short. One of the fascinating aspects of computer science is that once a machine can perform certain elementary but well-chosen tasks, adding more features does not increase the machine's theoretical capabilities. In other words, beyond a certain point, additional features may increase such things as convenience and speed but add nothing to the machine's basic abilities. We discuss these ideas further in Chapter 11.

When discussing the instructions in a machine's repertoire, it is helpful to recognize that they can be classified into three categories: the data transfer group, the arithmetic/logic group, and the control group.

Data Transfer The first group consists of instructions that request the movement of data from one location to another. Steps 1, 2, and 4 in Fig. 2.2 fall into this category. As in the case of main memory, it is unusual for the data being transferred from any location in a machine to be erased from its original

Figure 2.2 Adding values stored in memory

Step 1. Get one of the values to be added from memory and place it in a register.

Step 2. Get the other value to be added from memory and place it in another register.

Step 3. Activate the addition circuitry with the registers used in steps 1 and 2 as inputs and another register designated to hold the result.

Step 4. Store the result in memory.

Step 5. Stop.

location. The process involved in a transfer instruction is more like copying the data into another location rather than moving it. In this sense, the popular *transfer* or *move* terminology is actually a misnomer, with more descriptive terms being *copy* or *clone.* While on the subject of terminology, we should mention that special terms are used when referring to the transfer of data between the CPU and main memory. A request to fill a general-purpose register with the contents of a memory cell is commonly referred to as a LOAD instruction; conversely, a request to transfer the contents of a register to a memory cell is called a STORE instruction. In Fig. 2.2 steps 1 and 2 are LOAD instructions and step 4 is a STORE instruction.

An important group of instructions within the data transfer category consists of the commands for communicating with devices outside the CPU-main memory context. Since these instructions handle the input/output (I/O) activities of the machine, they are classified as the I/O instructions and are sometimes considered as a category in their own right. On the other hand, Section 2.6 describes how these I/O activities are often handled by the same instructions that request data transfers between the CPU and main memory, so placing them in a separate category therefore would be somewhat misleading.

Arithmetic/Logic The arithmetic/logic group consists of the instructions that tell the control unit to request an activity within the arithmetic/logic unit. Step 3 in Fig. 2.2 falls into this group. As its name suggests, the arithmetic/logic unit is capable of performing operations other than the basic arithmetic operations. Some of these additional operations are the common logic operations AND, OR, and XOR, which we introduced in Chapter 1 and will discuss more deeply later in this chapter. These operations are often used for manipulating individual bits within a general-purpose register without disturbing the rest of the register. Another collection of operations available within most arithmetic/logic units allows the contents of registers to be moved to the right or the left within the register. These operations are known as either SHIFT or ROTATE operations, depending on whether the bits that "fall off the end" of the register when its contents are moved are merely discarded (SHIFT) or are used to fill the holes left at the other end (ROTATE).

Control The control group consists of those instructions that direct the execution of the program rather than the manipulation of data. Step 5 in Fig. 2.2 falls into this category, although it is an extremely elementary example. This group contains many of the more interesting instructions in a machine's repertoire, such as the family of JUMP (or BRANCH) instructions used to direct the control unit to execute an instruction other than the next one in the list. These JUMP instructions appear in two varieties: unconditional jumps and conditional jumps. An example of the former would be the instruction "Skip to step number 5"; an example of the latter would be "If the value obtained is 0, then skip to step number 5." The distinction is that a conditional jump results in a "change of venue" only if a certain condition is satisfied. As an example, the sequence of instructions in Fig. 2.3 represents an algorithm for dividing two values where step 3 is a conditional jump that protects against the possibility of division by zero.

Step 1. LOAD a register with a value from memory.

Step 2. LOAD another register with another value from memory.

Step 3. If this second value is zero, JUMP to step 6.

Step 4. Divide the contents of the first register by the second register and leave the result in a third register.

Step 5. STORE the contents of the third register in memory.

Step 6. Stop.

Figure 2.3 Dividing values stored in memory

Questions/Exercises

1. What sequence of events do you think would be required in a machine to move the contents of one memory cell to another?
2. What information must the CPU supply to the main memory circuitry to write a value into a memory cell?
3. Why might the term *move* be considered an incorrect name for the operation of moving data from one location in a machine to another?
4. In the text, JUMP instructions were expressed by identifying the destination explicitly by stating the name (or step number) of the destination within the JUMP instruction (for example, "Jump to step 6"). This technique's drawback is that if an instruction name (number) is later changed, we must be sure to find all jumps to that instruction and change that name also. Describe another way of expressing a JUMP instruction so that the name of the destination is not explicitly stated.
5. Is the instruction "If 0 equals 0, then jump to step 7" a conditional or unconditional jump? Explain your answer.

2.2 The Stored-Program Concept

Early computing devices were not known for their flexibility, as the program that each device executed tended to be built into the control unit as a part of the machine. Such a system is analogous to a music box that always plays the same tune when what is needed is the flexibility of a CD changer. One approach used to gain this flexibility in early electronic computers was to design the control units so they could be conveniently rewired. This flexibility was accomplished by means of a pegboard arrangement similar to old telephone switchboards in which the ends of jumper wires were plugged into holes.

Instructions as Bit Patterns

A breakthrough (credited, perhaps incorrectly,[1] to John von Neumann) came with the realization that a program, just like data, can be coded and stored in main memory. If the control unit is designed to extract the program from

[1] Some people claim that this idea was originally developed by J. P. Eckert, Jr., at the Moore School but that his ideas became a part of a group effort and were ultimately misattributed to von Neumann.

memory, decode the instructions, and execute them, a computer's program can be changed merely by changing the contents of the computer's memory instead of rewiring the control unit. This stored-program concept has become the standard approach used today. To apply it, a machine is designed to recognize certain bit patterns as representing certain instructions. This collection of instructions along with the coding system is called the **machine-language** because it defines the means by which we communicate algorithms to the machine.

The coded version of a machine instruction typically consists of two parts: the **op-code** (short for operation code) field and the **operand** field. The bit pattern appearing in the op-code field indicates which of the elementary operations, such as STORE, SHIFT, XOR, and JUMP, is requested by the instruction. The bit patterns found in the operand field provide more detailed information about the operation specified by the op-code. For example, in the case of a STORE operation, the information in the operand field indicates which register contains the data to be stored and which memory cell is to receive the data.

The concept of storing a program in memory is not difficult at all. What made it difficult to think of originally was that everyone thought of programs and data as different entities: Data were stored in memory; programs were part of the control unit. The result was a prime example of not being able to see the forest for the trees. It is easy to be caught in such ruts, and the development of computer science might well remain in many of them today without our knowing it. Indeed, part of the excitement of the science is that new insights are constantly opening doors to new theories and applications.

A Typical Machine Language

Let us see how the instructions of a typical machine might be coded. The machine that we will use for our discussion is described in Appendix C and summarized in Fig. 2.4. It has 16 general-purpose registers, numbered O through F in hexadecimal. Moreover, the machine has 256 cells in its main memory. Consequently, each memory cell is uniquely addressed, or identified, by an integer in the range from 0 to 255. As we mentioned earlier, memory cells containing eight bits are quite popular, so let us pretend that the memory cells in our machine are that size. Since the general purpose registers are used to hold data from memory cells on a temporary basis, it makes sense to have each register also consists of eight bits.

Op-Codes Referring to the machine language listing in Appendix C, you find that each instruction is coded with a total of 16 bits, represented in the listing by four hexadecimal digits (Fig. 2.5). The op-code for each instruction consists of the first four bits or, equivalently, the first hexadecimal digit. The entire instruction list consists of only 12 basic instructions whose op-codes are represented by the hexadecimal digits 1 through C. Thus any instruction code starting with the hexadecimal digit 3 (bit pattern 0011) refers to a STORE instruction, and any instruction code starting with hexadecimal A refers to a ROTATE instruction.

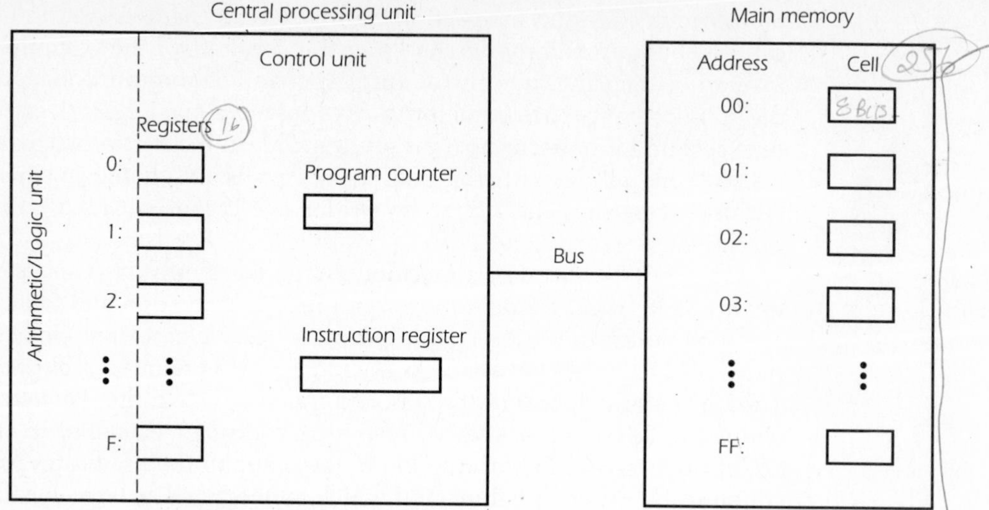

Figure 2.4 The architecture of the machine of Appendix C

The machine has two ADD instructions: one for adding two's complement representations and one for adding floating-point representations. This distinction results from the fact that adding bit patterns that represent values coded in binary notation requires different activities within the arithmetic/logic unit than when adding floating-point notation.

Operands Now we take a look at the operand field. It consists of three hexadecimal digits (12 bits) and in each case (except for the HALT instruction, which needs no further refinement) clarifies the general instruction given by the op-code. For example, if the first hexadecimal digit of an instruction were 1 (the op-code for loading from memory), the next hexadecimal digit of the instruction

Figure 2.5 The format of a machine instruction for the machine in Appendix C

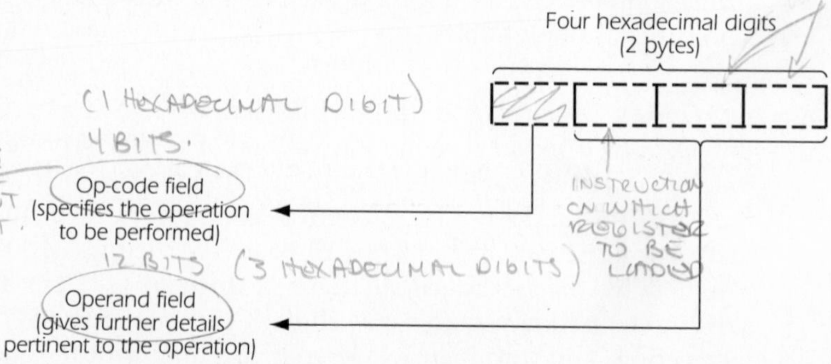

Four hexadecimal digits (2 bytes)

Op-code field (specifies the operation to be performed)

Operand field (gives further details pertinent to the operation)

would indicate which register is to be loaded, and the last two hexadecimal digits would indicate which memory cell is to provide the data. Thus the instruction 1347 (hexadecimal) translates to the statement "LOAD register 3 with the contents of the memory cell at address 47." In the case of the op-code hexadecimal 7, which requests that the contents of two registers be ORed, the next hexadecimal digit indicates where the result should be placed, while the last two hexadecimal digits of the operand field are used to indicate which two registers are to be ORed. Thus the instruction 70C5 translates to the statement "OR the contents of register C with the contents of register 5 and leave the result in register 0."

A subtle distinction exists between our machine's two LOAD instructions. Here we see that the op-code 1 (hexadecimal) refers to the instruction that loads a register with the contents of a memory cell, whereas the op-code 2 (hexadecimal) refers to the instruction that loads a register with a particular value. The difference is that the operand field in an instruction of the first type contains an address, whereas in the second type it contains the bit pattern to be loaded.

An interesting situation occurs in the case of the JUMP instruction (op-code hexadecimal B). The first hexadecimal digit of the operand field indicates which register is to be compared with register 0. If this register contains the same pattern as register 0, the machine jumps to the instruction at the address indicated by the last two hexadecimal digits of the operand. Otherwise, the execution of the program continues as usual. In general, this provides a conditional jump. However, if the first hexadecimal digit of the operand field is 0, the instruction requests that register 0 be compared with register 0. Since a register is always equal to itself, the jump is always taken. Consequently, any instruction whose code starts with the hexadecimal digits B0 translates to an unconditional jump.

A Program Example We close this section with the following coded version of the instructions in Fig. 2.2. We have assumed that the values to be added are stored in two's complement notation at memory addresses 6C and 6D and the sum is to be placed in memory at address 6E.

Step 1. 156C
Step 2. 166D
Step 3. 5056
Step 4. 306E
Step 5. C000

Questions/Exercises

1. Write the instructions at the end of this section in actual bit patterns.
2. The following are instructions written in the machine language described in Appendix C. Rewrite them in English.

   a. 368A   b. BADE   c. 803C   d. 40F4
3. What is the difference between the instructions 15AB and 25AB in the machine language of Appendix C?

4. Here are some instructions in English. Translate each of them into the machine language of Appendix C.
   a. LOAD register number 3 with the hexadecimal value 56.
   b. ROTATE register number 5 three bits to the right.
   c. JUMP to the instruction at location F3 if the contents of register number 7 are equal to the contents of register 0.
   d. AND the contents of register A with the contents of register 5 and leave the result in register 0.

2.3 Program Execution

A computer follows a program stored in its memory by copying the instructions from memory into the control unit as needed. Once in the control unit, each instruction is decoded and obeyed. The order in which the instructions are fetched from memory corresponds to the order in which the instructions are stored in memory unless otherwise specified by a JUMP instruction. To understand how the overall execution process takes place, it is necessary to take a closer look at the control unit inside the CPU. Within this unit are two special-purpose registers: the **program counter** and the **instruction register** (Fig. 2.4). The program counter contains the address of the next instruction to be executed, thereby serving as the machine's way of keeping track of where it is in the program. The instruction register is used to hold the instruction being executed.

The control unit performs its job by continually repeating an algorithm, the **machine cycle,** that consists of three steps: fetch, decode, and execute (Fig. 2.6). During the fetch step, the control unit requests that main memory provide it with the next instruction to be executed. The unit knows where the next instruction is in memory because its address is kept in the program counter. The control

Figure 2.6 The machine cycle

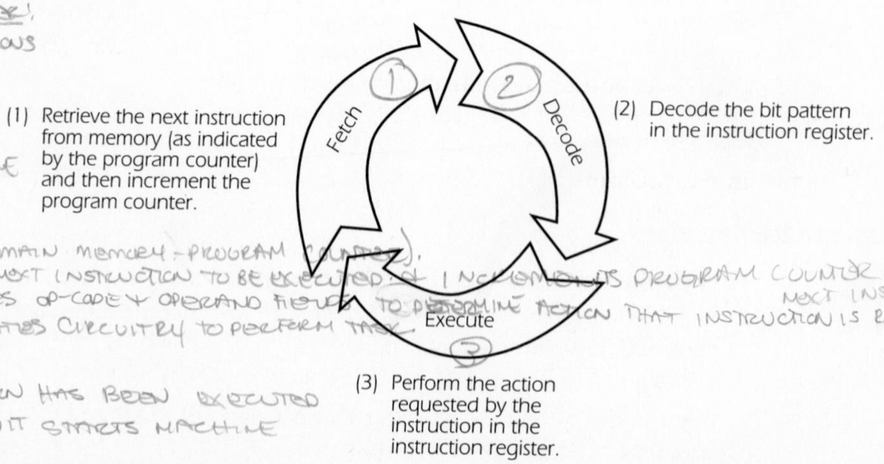

Fetch
Decode
Execute

(1) Retrieve the next instruction from memory (as indicated by the program counter) and then increment the program counter.

(2) Decode the bit pattern in the instruction register.

(3) Perform the action requested by the instruction in the instruction register.

unit places the instruction received from memory in its instruction register and then increments the program counter so that the counter contains the address of the next instruction.

With the instruction now in the instruction register, the control unit begins the decode phase of the machine cycle. At this time, it analyzes the op-code and operand fields to determine what action the instruction is requesting.

Having decoded the instruction, the control unit enters the execute phase, during which it activates the correct circuitry to perform the requested task. For example, if the instruction is a load from memory, the control unit causes the load to occur; if the instruction is for an arithmetic operation, the control unit activates the appropriate circuitry in the arithmetic/logic unit with the correct registers as inputs.

When the instruction has been executed, the control unit again begins the machine cycle with the fetch phase. Observe that since the program counter was incremented at the end of the previous fetch phase, it again provides the control unit with the correct instruction address.

A somewhat special case is the execution of a JUMP instruction. Consider, for example, the instruction B258, which translates into "JUMP to the instruction at address 58 if the contents of register 2 is the same as that of register 0." In this case the execute phase of the machine cycle begins with the comparison of registers 2 and 0. If they are different, the execute phase terminates and the next fetch phase begins. If, however, the contents of these registers are equal, the machine places the value 58 in its program counter before completing the execute phase. In this case, then, the next fetch phase finds 58 in the program counter, so the instruction at that address is the next instruction executed.

An Example of Program Execution

Let us follow the machine cycle applied to the program we coded at the end of Section 2.2. We first need to put the program somewhere in memory. For our example, suppose the program is stored in consecutive addresses, starting at address A0 hexadecimal. A table representing the contents of this area of memory appears in Fig. 2.7. With the program stored in this manner, we can cause the machine to execute it by placing the address (A0) of the first instruction in the program counter and starting the machine.

The control unit begins its fetch phase by extracting the instruction at location A0 and placing this instruction (156C) in its instruction register. Notice that, in our machine, instructions are 16 bits (two bytes) long. Thus the instruction to be fetched occupies the memory cells at both address A0 and A1. The control unit is designed to take this into account so it retrieves the contents of both cells and places these data in the instruction register, which is 16 bits long. The control unit then adds 2 to the program counter so that this register contains the address of the next instruction. At the end of the fetch phase of the first machine cycle, the program counter and instruction register contain the following data:

Program Counter:	A2
Instruction Register:	156C

Address	Contents
A0	15
A1	6C
A2	16
A3	6D
A4	50
A5	56
A6	30
A7	6E
A8	C0
A9	00

Figure 2.7 Our "add" program stored in memory starting at address A0

Next, the control unit analyzes the instruction in its instruction register and concludes that it is to load register 5 with the contents of the memory cell at address 6C. This load activity is performed during the execution phase, and the control unit then returns to the fetch phase of the machine cycle.

During this fetch phase, the control unit obtains the instruction 166D from the two memory cells starting at address A2, places this instruction in its instruction register, and increments the program counter to A4. The values in the program counter and instruction register therefore become the following:

Program Counter: A4
Instruction Register: 166D

Now the control unit decodes the instruction 166D and determines that it is to load register 6 with the contents of memory address 6D. It then enters the execute phase, during which register 6 is actually loaded.

Since the program counter now contains A4, the control unit extracts the next instruction starting at this address. The result is that 5056 is placed in the instruction register, and the program counter is incremented to A6. The control unit now decodes the contents of its instruction register and enters the execution phase by activating the two's complement addition circuitry with inputs being registers 5 and 6.

During this execution phase, the arithmetic/logic unit performs the requested addition, leaves the result in register 0 (as requested by the control unit), and reports to the control unit that it has finished. The control unit then begins another fetch phase of the machine cycle. Once again, with the aid of the program counter, it fetches the next instruction (306E) from the two memory cells starting at memory location A6 and increments the program counter to A8. This instruction is decoded during the next decode phase and executed during the next execute phase. At this point, the sum is placed in memory location 6E.

The next instruction is fetched starting from memory location A8, and the program counter is incremented to AA. The contents of the instruction register (C000) are now decoded as the halt instruction. Consequently, the machine stops during the next execute phase of the machine cycle, and the program is completed.

In summary, we see that the execution of a program stored in memory involves nothing mysterious. In fact, the process is similar to the process you and I might use if we needed to follow a detailed list of instructions. Whereas we might keep our place by checking the instructions off as we do them, the computer keeps its place by using the program counter. After determining which instruction to execute next, we would read the instruction and extract its meaning just as the machine decodes its instructions. Finally, we would perform the task requested and return to the list for the next instruction in the same manner that the machine executes its instructions during the execute phase and then continues with another fetch.

The significant differences between humans and machines when following such a list of instructions are accuracy and speed. The control unit faithfully repeats the machine cycle again and again without any tendency or desire to cut corners and thus without errors. Humans, on the other hand, quickly become bored, think they see what is to be done, and hurry to do it without giving each instruction its fair attention.

As for speed, technology continues to amaze us with faster and faster equipment. Today it is not unusual to find machine speeds measured in units of a million instructions per second (MIPS), with common speeds in the 10-MIPS to 100-MIPS range. There are signs, however, that there will be a limit to the speed with which machines can execute instructions, and technology is already turning toward alternatives. This is the subject of Section 2.4.

Programs Versus Data

Many programs can be stored simultaneously in a computer's main memory, as long as they occupy different locations. Which program will be run when the machine is started can then be determined merely by setting the program counter appropriately.

One must keep in mind, however, that because data are also contained in memory and coded in terms of 0s and 1s, the machine alone has no way of knowing what is data and what is program. If the program counter is assigned the address of data instead of the address of the desired program, the computer, not knowing any better, extracts the data bit patterns as though they were instructions and executes them. The final result depends on the data involved.

Care must be taken at this point not to assume that this feature is all bad. Once again, the concept of programs and data being completely different entities can be severely limiting. In reality, providing programs and data with a common appearance in a machine's memory has proven a useful attribute because it allows one program to manipulate other programs (or even itself) as it would data. Indeed, we will see that what may be data to one program often turns out to be another program.

Questions/Exercises

1. Suppose the memory cells from addresses 00 to 05 in the machine described in Appendix C contain the (hexadecimal) bit patterns given in the following table:

Address	*Contents*
00	14
01	02
02	34
03	17
04	C0
05	00

If we start the machine with its program counter containing 00, what bit pattern is in the memory cell whose address is hexadecimal 17 when the machine halts?

2. Suppose the memory cells at addresses B0 to B8 in the machine described in Appendix C contained the (hexadecimal) bit patterns given in the following table:

Address	*Contents*
B0	13
B1	B8
B2	A3
B3	02
B4	33
B5	B8
B6	C0
B7	00
B8	0F

a. If the program counter starts at B0, what bit pattern is in register number 3 after the first instruction has been executed?

b. What bit pattern is in memory cell B8 when the halt instruction is executed?

3. Suppose the memory cells at addresses A4 to B1 in the machine described in Appendix C contain the (hexadecimal) bit patterns given in the following table:

Address	*Contents*
A4	20
A5	00
A6	21
A7	03
A8	22
A9	01
AA	B1
AB	B0
AC	50
AD	02
AE	B0
AF	AA
B0	C0
B1	00

Answer the following questions assuming that the machine is started with its program counter containing A4:

a. What is in register 0 the first time the instruction at address AA is executed?

b. What is in register 0 the second time the instruction at address AA is executed?

c. How many times is the instruction at address AA executed before the machine halts?

4. Suppose the memory cells at addresses F0 to F9 in the machine described in Appendix C contain the (hexadecimal) bit patterns described in the following table:

Address	*Contents*
F0	20
F1	C0
F2	30
F3	F8
F4	20
F5	00
F6	30
F7	F9
F8	FF
F9	FF

If we start the machine with its program counter containing F0, what does the machine do when it reaches the instruction at address F8?

2.4 Other Architectures

To broaden our perspective, let us consider some alternatives to the machine architecture of the previous sections.

CISC Versus RISC Architectures

The design of a machine's language involves numerous decisions, one of which is whether to build a complex machine that can decode and execute a wide variety of instructions or a simpler machine that has a limited instruction set. The former results in what is called a complex instruction set computer, or **CISC;** the latter produces a reduced instruction set computer, or **RISC.** The more complex machine is easier to program because a single instruction can be used to accomplish a task that requires a multi-instruction sequence in the simpler machine. However, the complex machine is harder and more costly to build and perhaps costs more to operate. Moreover, many of the complex instructions can find limited applications and thus tend merely to increase overhead.

To minimize the amount of circuitry required, CISC processors are often constructed in a two-tiered fashion in which each machine instruction is actually executed as a sequence of simpler instructions. In such designs the CPU contains a block of special memory cells, known as **micromemory,** where a program, called the **microprogram,** is stored. It is this microprogram that directs the fetch–

decode–execute cycle of the CPU. In a sense the CPU is actually a small computer that is programmed to fetch, decode, and execute instructions from the machine's main memory.

In addition to providing a CISC architecture without the complex circuitry that would otherwise be required to support an elaborate instruction repertoire, the microprogram approach allows a single CPU design to be customized to include special machine-language instructions by merely changing its microprogram. However, proponents of RISC architecture argue that these benefits do not outweigh the overhead associated with the microprogram. They argue that a better approach is to design a simple machine with a small, well-designed instruction set. This approach removes the complexity involved with a micromemory and results in a simpler CPU design. On the other hand, it means that programs represented in the machine's language must be longer than those in a CISC architecture, because several instructions are required to perform the complex operations represented by single instructions in a CISC architecture.

Both CISC and RISC processors are commercially available. The Pentium processor, developed by Intel Corporation, is an example of CISC architecture; the PowerPC series of processors, developed by Apple Computer, IBM, and Motorola, are examples of RISC architecture.

Pipelining

In Section 2.3, we indicated that a barrier exists to the development of increasingly faster machines. The reason is because electric pulses travel through a wire no faster than the speed of light. (Optical machines are a current subject of research, but these machines also suffer from the speed-of-light limitation.) Since light travels approximately 1 foot in a nanosecond (one billionth of a second), it requires at least 2 nanoseconds for the control unit in the CPU to fetch an instruction from a memory cell that is 1 foot away. (The read request must be sent to memory, requiring at least 1 nanosecond, and the instruction must be sent back to the control unit, requiring at least another nanosecond.) Consequently, to fetch, decode, and execute an instruction in such a machine requires several nanoseconds. Thus increasing the execution speed of a machine ultimately becomes a miniaturization problem, and although fantastic advances have been made in this area, there appears to be a limit.

In an effort to solve this dilemma, computer scientists have turned to the concept of **throughput** rather than execution speed. Throughput refers to the total amount of work the machine can accomplish in a given amount of time rather than to how long it takes to do one task. One example of how a machine's throughput can be increased without requiring an increase in execution speed is the technique called **pipelining.** This term comes from the analogy of pushing objects—in our case instructions—into a pipe at one end and having them emerge from the other. At any given time, several instructions are in the pipe, each at a different stage of being processed. In particular, while one instruction is being executed, another instruction is being decoded, while still another is being fetched.

With such a system, although each instruction requires the same amount of time to be fetched, decoded, and executed, the total throughput of the machine is increased by a factor of three because three instructions are processed at once. (In reality, an increase of a factor of three is seldom achieved because of the occurrence of JUMP instructions. For example, if an instruction is a jump, the pipe must be emptied because the instructions in it are not the ones needed after all. Thus any gain that would have been obtained by prefetching is not realized.)

Multiprocessor Machines

Other approaches to increasing throughput fall under the classification of **parallel processing,** in which more than one processing unit is applied to the task at hand. One argument in favor of such an approach looks to the human mind as a model. Today's technology is approaching the ability to construct electronic circuitry with roughly as many switching circuits as there are neurons in the human brain (neurons are believed to be nature's switching circuits), yet the capabilities of today's machines still fall far short of those of the human mind. This, so it is claimed, is a result of the inefficient use of a machine's components as dictated by its architecture. After all, if a machine is constructed with a lot of memory circuits but only a single CPU, then most of its circuitry is destined to be idle most of the time. In contrast, much of the human mind can be active at any given moment. For this reason, the proponents of parallel processing argue in favor of a machine with many processing units. This, they argue, results in a configuration with the potential of a much higher utilization factor.

A variety of machines today are designed with this idea in mind. One approach is to attach several processing units, each resembling the CPU in a single processor machine, to the same main memory. In this configuration, the processors can proceed independently of one another yet coordinate their efforts by leaving messages to one another in their common memory cells. For instance, when one processor is faced with a large task, it can store a program for part of that task in the common memory and then request another processor to execute it. The result is a machine in which different instruction sequences are performed on different sets of data, which is called a **MIMD** (multiple-instruction stream, multiple-data stream) architecture, as opposed to the more traditional **SISD** (single-instruction stream, single-data stream) architecture.

A variation of multiple-processor architecture is to link the processors together such that they execute the same sequence of instructions in unison, each with its own set of data. The result is an example of **SIMD** (single-instruction stream, multiple-data stream) architecture. Such machines are useful in applications in which the same task must be applied to each set of similar items within a large block of data.

Another approach to the parallel processing concept is to construct large machines as conglomerates of smaller machines, each with its own memory and CPU. Within such an architecture, each of the small machines is coupled to its neighbors so that tasks assigned to the whole system can be divided among the individual machines. Thus, if a task assigned to one of the internal machines can be broken into independent subtasks, that machine can ask its neighbors to perform these subtasks concurrently. Consequently, the original task can be completed in much less time than would be required by a single processor machine.

Current problems in the development and use of multiprocessor machines involve issues of **load balancing,** that is, dynamically allocating tasks to the various processes so that all processors are used efficiently. Closely associated with this problem is that of scaling, or dividing the present task into a number of subtasks compatible with the number of processors available. Another problem entails handling the complexity of distributed task allocation. Indeed, as the number of tasks increases, the work required to allocate the assignments and to coordinate the interaction between the various tasks grows exponentially. If there are four tasks, then there are six potential pairs of tasks that may need to communicate with one another. If there are five tasks, this number of potential communication paths grows to ten; in the case of six tasks, the number jumps to fifteen.

In Chapter 10 we will study artificial neural networks, whose design is based on our understanding of the human brain. These machines represent another form of multiprocessor architecture in that they consist of many elementary processors, or processing units, each of whose output is merely a simple reaction to its combined inputs. These simple processors are linked to form a network in which the outputs of some processors are used as inputs to others. Such a machine is programmed by adjusting the extent to which each processor's output is allowed to influence the reaction of the other processors to which it is connected. This simulates the way in which we believe our brains learn. Apparently, biological neural networks learn to produce a particular reaction to a given stimulus by adjusting the chemical composition of the junctions (synapses) between neurons, which in turn adjusts the ability of one neuron to affect the action of others.

Questions/Exercises

1. Why does the CPU in a microprogrammed machine require two program counters and two instruction registers?
2. Referring back to Question 3 of Section 2.3, if the machine used the pipeline technique discussed in the text, what will be in "the pipe" when the instruction at address AA is executed? Under what conditions would the pipelining technique not be beneficial at this point in the program?
3. What conflicts must be resolved when running the program in Question 4 of Section 2.3 on a pipeline machine?
4. Suppose there were two "central" processing units attached to the same memory and executing different programs. Furthermore, suppose that one of these processors needs to add one to the contents of a memory cell at roughly the same time that the other needs to subtract one from the same cell. (The net effect should be that the cell ends up with the same value with which it started.)
   a. Describe a sequence in which these activities would result in the cell's ending up with a value one less than its starting value.

b. Describe a sequence in which these activities would result in the cell's ending up with a value one greater than its starting value.

2.5 Arithmetic/Logic Instructions

As indicated earlier, the arithmetic/logic group of instructions consists of instructions requesting arithmetic, logic, and shift operations. In this section we look at these operations more closely.

Logic Operations

We introduced the logic operations AND, OR, and XOR (exclusive or) in Chapter 1 as operations that combine two input bits to produce a single output bit. These operations can be extended to operations that combine two strings of bits to produce a single output string by applying the basic operation to individual columns. For example, the result of ANDing the patterns 10011010 and 11001001 results in

```
    10011010
AND 11001001
    --------
    10001000
```

where we have merely written the result of ANDing the two bits in each column at the bottom of the column. Likewise, ORing and XORing these patterns would produce

```
   10011010        10011010
OR 11001001    XOR 11001001
   --------        --------
   11011011        01010011
```

One of the major uses of the AND operation is for placing 0s in one part of a bit pattern while not disturbing the other part. Consider, for example, what happens if the byte 00001111 is the first operand of an AND operation. Without knowing the contents of the second operand, we still can conclude that the four most significant bits of the result are 0s. Moreover, the four least significant bits of the result are a copy of that part of the second operand, as shown in the following example:

```
    00001111
AND 10101010
    --------
    00001010
```

This use of the AND operation is an example of the process called **masking.** Here one operand, called the **mask,** determines which part of the other operand will affect the result. In the case of the AND operation, masking produces a result that is a partial replica of one of the operands, with 0s occupying the nonduplicated positions.

Such an operation is useful when manipulating a **bit map,** a string of bits in which each bit represents the presence or absence of a particular object. For example, a string of 52 bits, in which each bit is associated with a particular playing card, can be used to represent a poker hand by assigning 1s to those 5 bits associated with the cards in the hand and 0s to all the others. Likewise, a bit map of 52 bits, of which 13 are 1s, can be used to represent a hand of bridge, or a bit map of 32 bits can be used to represent which of 32 ice cream flavors are available.

Suppose, then, that an eight-bit memory cell is being used as a bit map, and we want to find out whether the object associated with the third bit from the high-order end is present. We merely need to AND the entire byte with the mask 00100000, which produces a byte of all 0s if and only if the third bit from the high-order end of the bit map is itself 0. A program can then act accordingly by following the AND operation with a condition branch instruction. Moreover, if the third bit from the high-order end of the bit map is a 1, and we want to change it to a 0 without disturbing the other bits, we can AND the bit map with the mask 11011111 and then store the result in place of the original bit map.

Where the AND operation can be used to duplicate a part of a string while placing 0s in the nonduplicated part, the OR operation can be used to duplicate a part of a bit string while putting 1s in the nonduplicated part. For this we again use a mask, but this time we indicate the bit positions to be duplicated with 0s and use 1s to indicate the nonduplicated positions. For example, ORing any byte with 11110000 produces a result with 1s in its most significant four bits while its remaining bits contain a copy of the least significant four bits of the other operand, as demonstrated by the following example:

```
   11110000
OR 10101010
-----------
   11111010
```

Consequently, whereas the mask 11011111 can be used with the AND operation to force a 0 in the third bit from the high-order end of an eight-bit bit map, the OR the mask 00100000 can be used with the OR operation to force a 1 in that position.

A major use of the XOR operation is in forming the complement of a bit string. For example, note the relationship between the second operand and the result in the following example:

```
    11111111
XOR 10101010
------------
    01010101
```

XORing any byte with a byte of 1s produces the complement of the first byte.

Rotation and Shift Operations

The operations in the class of rotation and shift operations provide a means for the movement of bits within a register and are often used in solving alignment problems, such as preparing a byte for future use in masking operations or manipulating the mantissa of floating-point representations. These operations are classified as to the direction of motion (right or left) and as to whether the process is circular. Within these classification guidelines are numerous variations with mixed terminology. Let us take a quick look at the ideas involved.

If we consider starting with a byte of bits and shifting its contents one bit to the right or the left, we might imagine the bit on one end falling off the edge and a hole appearing at the other end. What happens with this extra bit and the hole is the distinguishing feature among the various shift operations. One technique is to place the extra bit in the hole at the other end. The result is a circular shift, also called a rotation. Thus, if we perform a right circular shift on a byte eight times, we obtain the same bit pattern we started with, and seven right circular shifts are equivalent to a single left circular shift.

Another technique is to discard the bit that falls off the edge and always fill the hole with a 0. The term **logical shift** is often used to refer to these operations. Such shifts to the left can be used for multiplying two's complement representations by 2. After all, shifting binary digits to the left corresponds to multiplication by 2, just as a similar shift of decimal digits corresponds to multiplication by 10. Moreover, division by 2 can be accomplished by shifting the binary string to the right. In either shift, care must be taken to preserve the sign bit when using certain notational systems. Thus we often find right shifts that always fill the hole (which occurs at the sign bit position) with its original value. Shifts that leave the sign bit unchanged are sometimes called **arithmetic shifts.**

Arithmetic Operations

Although we have already mentioned the arithmetic operations of add, subtract, multiply, and divide, a few loose ends must still be connected. First, as we have mentioned, this collection of operations can often be generated from the single add operation and a negation process. For this reason, some small computers are designed with only the add or perhaps only the add and subtract instructions.

We should also mention that for each arithmetic operation, numerous variations exist. We have already alluded to this in relation to the add operations available on our machine in Appendix C. In the case of addition, for example, if the values to be added are stored in two's complement notation, the addition process must be performed as a straightforward binary add. However, if the operands are stored as floating-point values, the addition process must extract the mantissa of each, shift them right or left according to the exponent fields, check the sign bits, perform the addition, and translate the result into floating-point notation. We see, then, that although both operations are considered addition, the action of the machine is not the same. As far as the machine is concerned, the two operations may have no relationship at all.

Questions/Exercises

1. Perform the indicated operations.

a.		b.		c.	
	01001011		10000011		11111111
	AND 10101011		AND 11101100		AND 00101101

d. 01001011
OR 10101011

e. 10000011
OR 11101100

f. 11111111
OR 00101101

g. 01001011
XOR 10101011

h. 10000011
XOR 11101100

i. 11111111
XOR 00101101

2. Suppose you want to isolate the middle three bits of a seven-bit string by placing 0s in the other four bits without disturbing the middle three bits. What mask must you use together with what operation?
3. Suppose you want to complement the three middle bits of a seven-bit string while leaving the other four bits undisturbed. What mask must you use together with what operation?
4. a. Suppose you XOR the first two bits of a string of bits and then continue down the string by successively XORing each result with the next bit in the string. How is your result related to the number of 1s appearing in the string?
   b. How does this problem relate to determining what the appropriate parity bit should be when coding a message?
5. It is often convenient to use a logical operation in place of a numeric one. For example, the logical operation AND combines two bits in the same manner as multiplication. Which logical operation is almost the same as adding two bits, and what goes wrong in this case?
6. What logical operation together with what mask can you use to change ASCII codes of lowercase letters to uppercase? What about uppercase to lowercase?
7. What is the result of performing a three-bit right circular shift on the following bit strings:
   a. 01101010 b. 00001111 c. 01111111
8. What is the result of performing a one-bit left circular shift on the following bytes represented in hexadecimal notation? Give your answer in hexadecimal form.
   a. AB b. 5C c. B7 d. 35
9. A right circular shift of three bits on a string of eight bits is equivalent to a left circular shift of how many bits?
10. What bit pattern represents the sum of 01101010 and 11001100 if the patterns represent values stored in two's complement notation? What if the patterns represent values stored in the floating-point format discussed in Chapter 1?
11. Using the machine language of Appendix C, write a program that places a 1 in the most significant bit of the memory cell whose address is A7 without modifying the remaining bits in the cell.
12. Using the machine language of Appendix C, write a program that copies the middle four bits from memory cell E0 into the least significant four bits of memory cell E1, while placing 0s in the most significant four bits of that same cell.

2.6 Computer–Peripheral Communication

In this section we investigate the communication between a machine's CPU and its peripheral devices and the controllers' role in this communication.

Controllers

Communication between a machine's CPU and a peripheral device is normally handled through an intermediary device known as a **controller.** Each controller handles communication for a particular type of peripheral device. In the case of a personal computer a controller physically corresponds to a circuit board and is often purchased along with the peripheral device it is designed to control. Each of these boards plugs into a slot on the computer's main circuit board (the motherboard) and connects via cables to the peripheral device within the machine or perhaps to a connector on the back of the machine where the peripheral device can be attached.

The controller converts messages and data back and forth between forms compatible with the internal characteristics of the machine and those of the peripheral device, or devices, attached to the controller. These controllers are often small computers within themselves, each with its own memory circuitry and CPU that performs a program directing the activities of the controller.

Controllers are attached to the same bus that connects the machine's CPU and main memory (Fig. 2.8). From this position each controller monitors the signals sent out from the machine's CPU and responds when it detects that the signal is directed to itself. Moreover, the controller can write and read data to and from the machine's main memory during those microseconds in which the CPU is not using the bus. This ability of a controller to access main memory is known as **direct memory access (DMA).** If the controller for a machine's disk drive has

Figure 2.8 Controllers attached to a machine's bus

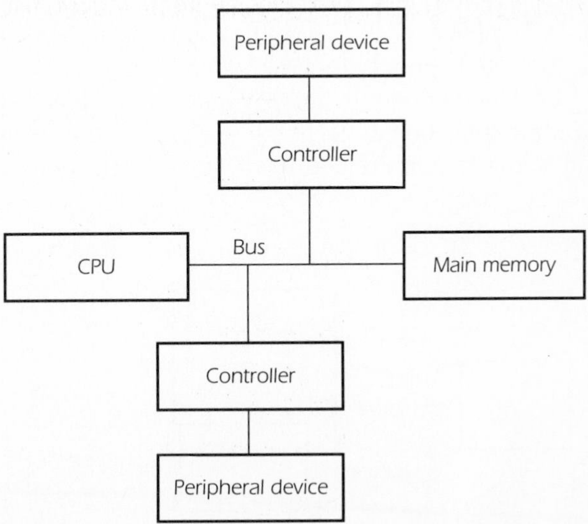

direct memory access, the CPU can send requests coded as bit patterns to the controller asking the controller to read a particular sector from the disk and place the data in a specified block of memory cells. Then the CPU can continue with other tasks while the controller performs the read operation. When the controller completes its task, it can send an appropriate signal to the CPU via the bus. (Such special signals take the form of interrupts, which we discuss in Chapter 3.) Likewise, the CPU can prepare a block of data in main memory, ask the controller to copy that block to a disk, and then proceed with other tasks until the controller indicates that it has completed the assigned task.

A block of memory used for transferring data to and from peripheral devices, as in the previous examples, is called a **buffer.** More generally, a buffer is any location where one system leaves data to be picked up later by another, a process known as **buffering.** The registers in a CPU serve as buffers between the control unit and the arithmetic/logic unit or between the CPU as a whole and the main memory.

Controllers that are attached to a computer's bus significantly increase the level of communication being handled over this central communication path. Bit patterns must move between the CPU and main memory, between the CPU and each controller, and between each controller and main memory. Coordination of this activity is a major design issue. Even with excellent designs, the central bus can become an impediment, known as the **von Neumann bottleneck,** as the CPU and the controllers compete for access to the bus.

CPU–Controller Communication

Communication between a machine's CPU and a controller is handled in much the same way as that between the CPU and main memory. In fact, in many machines the controller is disguised as a block of main memory cells. When the CPU writes a bit pattern to a memory cell within that block, as in a STORE instruction, the bit pattern is really transferred to the controller rather than memory. In a similar fashion, when the CPU tries to read data from one of these memory cells as in a LOAD instruction, what it receives is a bit pattern from the controller. Such a communication system, termed **memory-mapped I/O,** is represented conceptually by Fig. 2.9.

In machines that do not use memory-mapped I/O, each controller is assigned a unique collection of "I/O addresses." For instance, one controller might be assigned the I/O addresses 10 through 1F (hexadecimal), and another controller

Figure 2.9 A conceptual representation of memory-mapped I/O

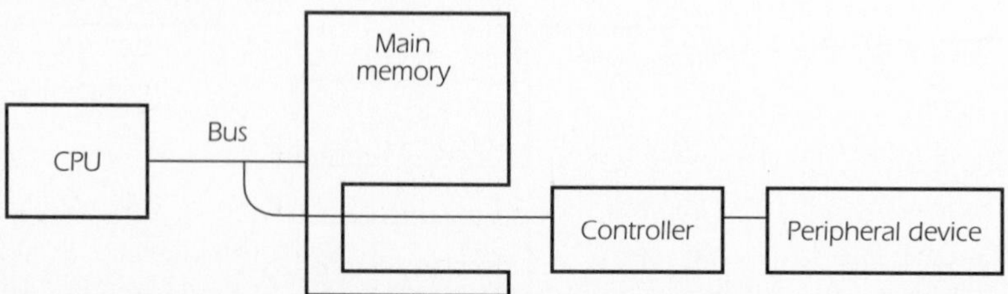

might be assigned the values 20 through 2F. These I/O address blocks play the same role as the address blocks in memory-mapped I/O except that they use two different address systems. If the CPU writes to memory address 12, the bit pattern is accepted by main memory; if the CPU writes to I/O address 12, the bit pattern is accepted by a controller. In turn, the machine language instructions for communicating with controllers must be distinct, although similar in form, from those for communicating with main memory. For example, we might reserve the op-code D in the machine described in Appendix C for writing data to an I/O address. More precisely, whereas the instruction 382A sends the bit pattern in register 8 to memory address 2A, the instruction D82A would send the bit pattern in register 8 to I/O address 2A.

Whether or not memory-mapped I/O is used, the block of addresses associated with a controller is collectively called a **port** in that it represents a "location" through which information enters and leaves the machine. Each address within a port identifies a location in the controller where data can be stored on a temporary basis. These storage locations serve as buffers between the machine and the controller. Some are used to receive data and messages coming from the CPU; others hold bit patterns produced by the controller to be read by the CPU. In turn, two-way communication between the controller and CPU is possible.

The controller's task in this communication is twofold. In some cases the communication consists of messages between the CPU and the controller itself; in other cases the controller serves as an intermediary between the internal machine environment and a peripheral device. In this latter role the controller's task is to translate data and messages back and forth between formats compatible with the internal characteristics of the machine and those of the peripheral device.

Two-way communication also takes place between a controller and the peripheral device being controlled, even though communication in only one direction may be apparent. For example, a computer can produce and send characters through a controller to a printer much faster than the printer can print them. Thus, without two way communication between the machine and printer, the printer would quickly fall behind.

The term **handshaking** refers to the two-way communication that takes place between devices to avoid such coordination problems. In the case of a printer handshaking is usually accomplished by designing the printer so that it not only receives data from the controller but also transmits its status (such as the message, "I cannot handle more data") in the form of a bit pattern (known as a status word) back to the controller. Depending on the system, the controller may respond to this status information itself or make it available to the CPU through the port. In either case either the program within the controller or the program being executed by the CPU can be designed so that the flow of data to the printer is delayed until the appropriate status information from the printer is received.

Parallel and Serial Communication

Communication between portions of a computer system takes one of two basic forms: parallel or serial. These terms refer to the manner in which the bit patterns are transferred with respect to time. With **parallel communication,** all the bits in a bit pattern are transferred at the same time, each on a separate line. Such a technique is capable of transferring data rapidly but requires a relatively complex communication path, which results in the use of large multiwire cables. In contrast, **serial communication** is based on transmitting only one bit at a time. This technique tends to be slower but requires a simpler data path because all the bits are transferred over the same line, one after the other.

The simpler data path required for serial communication allows computer data transfers to take place over existing communication systems that were originally developed for other purposes. One common example is the use of telephone lines where the digital information is converted into audio signals by a **modem** (short for modulator-demodulator), serially transferred via the existing telephone system, and converted back into digital form when it is received. Such communication would not be feasible using parallel techniques because of the inherent properties of the existing telephone system.

The speed of serial communication is measured in bits per second (**bps**) with speeds ranging from a few hundred bits per second to several million bps. Another common (but often misused) measure is **baud rate,** which refers to the rate at which the communication line transfers states. Let us clarify this latter measure with an example. If we apply a tone at one end of a telephone connection, the tone can be detected at the other end. Consequently, we can send messages over the phone system by agreeing that a certain note represents a 0 and another note represents a 1. In such a system, the communication line can be in one of two states: carrying one of the notes or carrying the other. Since each state represents a single bit, the rate in which states are communicated is the same as the rate in which bits are communicated, so the baud rate is the same as the bits per second. However, if we change our protocol to include four possible states (notes), each state can represent two bits. For example, we might agree to use a low pitch to represent the bits 00, a higher pitch to represent the bits 01, a still higher pitch to represent the bits 10, and the highest pitch to represent the bits 11. In this system, the rate at which bits are transferred is twice the rate that states (or notes) are transferred because each state represents two bits. Thus the bits per second is twice the baud rate.

In reality, the simple technique of representing different bit patterns by tones of different frequencies (known as frequency-shift keying) is used only for low-speed communication. To construct modems with data transfer rates of 2400 bps, 9600 bps, and higher, the different states used to represent bit patterns are created by combining changes in tone frequency, amplitude (volume), and phase (the degree to which the transmission of the tone is delayed). But the general theme remains the same: By representing several bits with a single state, the rate in which bits are transferred (measured in bits per second) can significantly exceed the rate in which states are transferred (the baud rate).

Still another method for increasing the efficiency of data transfers (and data storage as well), **data compression,** reduces the number of bits used to represent information. Numerous data compression techniques are available, each with its own best-case and worst-case scenarios. In the case of digitizing a picture as a string of pixels, one may find long strings of identical pixels. Here it is often helpful to code the common color of these pixels along with the length of the string rather than explicitly listing each pixel. When coding a sequence of pictures representing motion, it is often more efficient to code the differences between consecutive pictures than to code each picture in its entirety. This procedure is known as *relative encoding*.

In the case of representing strings of characters, a **Huffman code** (also known as a frequency-dependent code) may be helpful. Such a code is designed so that the length of a bit pattern representing a character is inversely proportional to the frequency of the character's use. Hence the more frequently used characters (the letters *e, t, a,* and *i* in the English language) are represented by short bit patterns, while the less frequently used letters (*z, q,* and *x*) are represented by longer patterns. The result is a shorter representation of an entire text than would be obtained by the use of a uniform length code such as ASCII.

Another technique, **Lempel-Ziv encoding,** that is applicable when coding data representing text is to replace recurring patterns with merely a reference to the previous occurrence rather than repeating the pattern itself. In the case of English text this approach can be used to reduce the space required by repeated copies of such patterns as *ing* and *the.*

Efforts to standardize data compression techniques have resulted in their inclusion in many of the modems on the market today. When modems containing compatible data compression schemes communicate, the transmitting modem compresses the data before transmission and the receiving modem decompresses the data upon reception. Using this approach, modems can obtain apparent transfer rates of 57,600 bps, even though only 14,400 bits are being transferred per second at a baud rate of perhaps 1200 baud.

Questions/Exercises

1. Suppose a serial communication system is capable of transmitting and receiving eight different states. If bit patterns are assigned to each of the eight states so that each state represents a total of three bits, how does the baud rate of the system compare to the measure of bits per second?
2. Suppose the machine described in Appendix C uses memory mapped I/O and the address B5 is the location within the printer port to which data to be printed should be sent.
   a. If register 7 contains the ASCII code for the letter A, what machine language instruction should be used to cause that letter to be printed at the printer?
   b. If the machine executes a million instructions per second, how many times can this character be sent to the printer in one second?
   c. If the printer is capable of printing five traditional pages of text per minute, will it be able to keep up with the characters being sent to it in part (b)?
3. Suppose the hard disk on your personal computer has only 20 MB of storage space available and you want to add another software package. Suppose this software package is shipped to you on 13 floppy disks, each having a capacity of 1.44 MB. Do you have enough room on the hard disk to add the software?
4. Identify three techniques for data compression.

CHAPTER REVIEW PROBLEMS *(Asterisked problems are associated with optional sections.)*

1. Give a brief definition of each of the following:
   a. Register   b. Cache memory
   c. Main memory   d. Mass storage

2. Suppose a block of data is stored in the memory cells of the machine described in Appendix C from address B9 to C1, inclusive. How many memory cells are in this block? List their addresses.

3. What is the value of the program counter in the machine described in Appendix C immediately after executing the instruction B0BA?

4. Suppose the memory cells at addresses 00 through 05 in the machine described in Appendix C contain the following (hexadecimal) bit patterns:

Address	*Contents*
00	21
01	04
02	31
03	00
04	C0
05	00

Assuming that the program counter initially contained 00, record the contents of the program counter, instruction register, and memory cell at address 00 at the end of each fetch phase of the machine cycle until the machine halts.

5. Suppose three values (x, y, and z) are stored in a machine's memory. Describe the sequence of events (loading registers from memory, saving values in memory, and so on) that lead to the computation of $x + y - z$. How about $(2x) + y$?

6. The following are instructions written in the machine language described in Appendix C. Translate them into English.
   a. 407E   b. 9028   c. A302
   d. B3AD   e. 2835

7. Suppose a machine language is designed with an op-code field of four bits. How many different instruction types can the language contain? What if the op-code field is increased to eight bits?

8. Translate the following instructions from English into the machine language described in Appendix C.
   a. LOAD register 8 with the contents of memory cell 55.
   b. LOAD register 8 with the hexadecimal value 55.
   c. ROTATE register 4 three bits to the right.
   d. AND the contents of registers F and 2 leaving the result in register 0.
   e. Jump to the instruction at memory location 31 if the contents of register 0 equals the value in register B.

9. Classify each of the following instructions (in the machine language of Appendix C) in terms of whether its execution changes the contents of the memory cell at location 3B, retrieves the contents of the memory cell at location 3B, or is independent of the contents of the memory cell at location 3B.
   a. 153B   b. 253B   c. 353B
   d. 3B3B   e. 403B

10. Suppose the memory cells at addresses 00 through 03 in the machine described in Appendix C contain the following (hexadecimal) bit patterns:

Address	*Contents*
00	23
01	02
02	C0
03	00

   a. Translate the first instruction into English.
   b. If the machine is started with its program counter containing 00, what bit pattern is in register 3 when the machine halts?

11. Suppose the memory cells at addresses 00 through 05 in the machine described in Appendix C contain the following (hexadecimal) bit patterns:

Address	*Contents*
00	10
01	04
02	30
03	45
04	C0
05	00

Answer the following questions assuming that the machine starts with its program counter equal to 00:

a. Translate the instructions that are executed into English.
b. What bit pattern is in the memory cell at address 45 when the machine stops?
c. What bit pattern is in the program counter when the machine stops?

12. Suppose the memory cells at addresses F0 through FD in the machine described in Appendix C contain the following (hexadecimal) bit patterns:

Address	*Contents*
F0	20
F1	00
F2	21
F3	01
F4	23
F5	05
F6	B3
F7	FC
F8	50
F9	01
FA	B0
FB	F6
FC	C0
FD	00

If we start the machine with its program counter equal to F0, what is the value in register 0 when the machine finally executes the halt instruction at location FC?

13. If the machine in Appendix C executes an instruction every microsecond (a millionth of a second), how long does it take to complete the program in Problem 12?

14. Suppose the memory cells at addresses 00 through 05 in the machine described in Appendix C contain the following (hexadecimal) bit patterns:

Address	*Contents*
00	25
01	B0
02	35
03	04
04	C0
05	00

If we start the machine with its program counter equal to 00, when does the machine halt?

15. In each of the following cases, write a short program in the machine language described in Appendix C to perform the requested activities. Assume that each of your programs is placed in memory starting at address 00.

a. Move the value at memory location 8D to memory location B3.
b. Interchange the values stored at memory locations 8D and B3.
c. If the value stored in memory location 45 is 00, then place the value CC in memory location 88; otherwise, put the value DD in memory location 88.

16. A popular game among computer hobbyists is core wars—a variation of battleship. (The term *core* originates from an early memory technology in which 0s and 1s were represented as magnetic fields in little rings of magnetic material.) The game is played between two opposing programs, each stored in different locations of the same computer's memory. The computer is assumed to alternate between the two programs, executing an instruction from one followed by an instruction from the other. The goal of each program is to destroy the other by writing extraneous data on top of it; however, neither program knows the location of the other.

a. Write a program in the machine language of Appendix C that approaches the game in a defensive manner by being as small as possible.
b. Write a program in the language of Appendix C that tries to avoid any attacks from the opposing program by moving to different locations. More precisely, write your program to start at location 00, copy itself to location 70, and then jump to this new copy.
c. Extend the program in part (b) to continue relocating to new memory locations. In particular, make your program move to location 70, then to E0 (70 + 70), then to 60 (70 + 70 + 70), etc.

17. Write a program in the machine language of Appendix C to compute the sum of the two's complement values stored at memory locations A1, A2, A3, and A4. Your program should store the total at memory location A5.

18. Suppose the memory cells at addresses 00 through 05 in the machine described in Appendix C contain the following (hexadecimal) bit patterns:

Address	*Contents*
00	20
01	C0
02	30
03	04
04	00
05	00

What happens if we start the machine with its program counter equal to 00?

19. What happens if the memory cells at addresses 06 and 07 of the machine described in Appendix C contain the bit patterns B0 and 06, respectively, and the machine is started with its program counter containing the value 06?

20. Suppose the following program, written in the machine language of Appendix C, is stored in main memory beginning at address 30 (hexadecimal). What task will the program perform when executed?

```
2003
2101
2200
2310
1400
3410
A221
A331
3239
333B
B248
B038
C000
```

21. Suppose you are given 32 processors, each capable of finding the sum of two multidigit numbers in a millionth of a second. Describe how concurrent processing techniques can be applied to find the sum of 64 numbers in only six-millionths of a second. How much time does a single processor require to find this same sum?

22. Summarize the difference between a CISC architecture and a RISC architecture.

23. Summarize the distinction between main memory and micromemory.

24. Identify two approaches to increasing throughput.

25. Describe how the average of a collection of numbers can be computed more rapidly with a multiprocessor machine than a single processor machine.

***26.** Suppose the registers 4 and 5 in the machine described in Appendix C contain the bit patterns 3C and C8, respectively. What bit pattern is left in register 0 after executing each of the following instructions:

a. 5045 b. 6045 c. 7045
d. 8045 e. 9045

***27.** Using the machine language described in Appendix C, write programs to perform each of the following tasks:

a. Copy the bit pattern stored in memory location 66 into memory location BB.

b. Change the least significant four bits in the memory cell at location 34 to 0s while leaving the other bits undisturbed.

c. Copy the least significant four bits from memory location A5 into the least significant four bits of location A6 while leaving the other bits at location A6 undisturbed.

d. Copy the least significant four bits from memory location A5 into the most significant four bits of A5. (Thus, the first four bits in A5 will be the same as the last four bits.)

***28.** Perform the indicated operations:

```
a.     111000        b.     000100
   AND 101001           AND 101010

c.     000100        d.     111011
   AND 010101           AND 110101

e.     111000        f.     000100
    OR 101001            OR 101010

g.     000100        h.     111011
    OR 010101            OR 110101

i.     111000        j.     000100
   XOR 101001           XOR 101010

k.     000100        l.     111011
   XOR 010101           XOR 110101
```

***29.** Identify both the mask and the logical operation needed to accomplish each of the following objectives:

a. Put 0s in the middle four bits of an eight-bit pattern without disturbing the other bits.

b. Complement a pattern of eight bits.

c. Complement the most significant bit of an eight-bit pattern without changing the other bits.

d. Put a 1 in the most significant bit of an eight-bit pattern without disturbing the other bits.

e. Put 1s in all but the most significant bit of an eight-bit pattern without disturbing the most significant bit.

***30.** Identify a logical operation (along with a corresponding mask) that, when applied to an input string of eight bits, produces an output string of all 0s if and only if the input string is 10000001.

***31.** Describe a sequence of logical operations (along with their corresponding masks) that, when applied to an input string of eight bits, produces an output byte of all 0s if the input string both begins and ends with 1s. Otherwise, the output should contain at least one 1.

***32.** What would be the result of performing a four-bit left circular shift on the following bit patterns?

a. 10101 b. 11110000 c. 001

d. 101000 e. 00001

***33.** What would be the result of performing a one-bit right circular shift on the following bytes represented in hexadecimal notation (give your answers in hexadecimal notation)?

a. 3F b. 0D c. FF d. 77

***34.** Write a program in the machine language of Appendix C that reverses the contents of the memory cell at address 8C.

***35.** Can a printer, printing 40 characters per second, keep up with a string of ASCII characters (each with a parity bit) arriving serially at the rate of 300 bps? What about 1200 bps?

***36.** Suppose a person is typing 30 words per minute at a keyboard. (A word is considered to be five characters.). If a machine executes one instruction every microsecond (millionth of a second), how many instructions does the machine execute during the time between the typing of two consecutive characters?

***37.** How many bits per second must a keyboard transmit to keep up with a typist typing 30 words per minute? (Assume each character is coded in ASCII along with a parity bit and each word consists of five characters.)

***38.** A communication system capable of transmitting any sequence of eight different states at the rate of at most 300 states per second could be used to transfer information at what rate in bits per second?

***39.** Suppose the machine described in Appendix C communicates with a printer using the technique of memory mapped I/O. Suppose also that address FF is used to send characters to the printer, and address FE is used to receive information about the printer's status. In particular, suppose the least significant bit at the address FE indicates whether the printer is ready to receive another character (with a 0 indicating "not ready" and a 1 indicating "ready"). Starting at address 00, write a machine language routine that waits until the printer is ready for another character and then send the character represented by the bit pattern in register 5 to the printer.

***40.** Write a program in the machine language described in Appendix C that places 0s in all the memory cells from address A0 through C0 but is small enough to fit in the memory cells from address 00 through 13 (hexadecimal).

***41.** Suppose a machine has 500MB of storage space available on a hard disk and receives data over a telephone connection at the rate of 14,400. At this rate, how long would it take to fill the available storage space?

***42.** Suppose a communication line is being used to transmit data serially at 14,400 bps. If a burst of interference lasts .01 second, how many data bits would be affected?

QUESTIONS OF ETHICS

The following questions are provided to help you understand some of the ethical/social/legal issues associated with the field of computing as well as investigate your own beliefs and their foundations. The goal is not merely to answer these questions. You should also consider why you answered as you did and whether your justifications are consistent from one question to the next.

1. Suppose a computer manufacturer develops a new machine architecture. To what extent should the company be allowed to own that architecture? What policy would be best for society?
2. We often think in terms of how computer technology has changed our society. Many argue, however, that this technology has often kept changes from occurring by allowing old systems to survive and, in some cases, become more entrenched. For example, would the dominance of the New York Stock Exchange or the U.S. government's role in society have survived without computer technology? To what extent would centralized authority be present today had computer technology not been available? To what extent would we be better off or worse off without computer technology?
3. Is it ethical for an individual to take the attitude that he or she need not know anything about the internal details of a machine because someone else will build it, maintain it, and fix any problems that arise? Does your answer depend on whether the machine is a computer, automobile, nuclear power plant, or toaster?
4. Suppose a manufacturer produces a computer chip and later discovers a flaw in its design. Suppose further that the manufacturer decides not to recall the chips already shipped but to keep the flaw a secret, reasoning that none of the chips already in use are being used in an application in which the flaw will have consequences. Is anyone hurt by the manufacturer's decision?

ADDITIONAL ACTIVITIES

1. Which statements in your programming language are straightforward applications of the traditional machine-language operations discussed in this chapter? Which are not?
2. Pick a simple statement in a programming language you know and translate it into the machine language of Appendix C.
3. What notation does your programming language use to indicate arithmetic addition? What determines whether this addition ultimately is performed by the machine's floating-point instruction or by its two's complement instruction?
4. Translate each of the following machine language program segments (see Appendix C) into a programming language that you know. Assume that part (c) begins at memory address A0.

a.	b.	c.
1110	1110	2005
1211	1211	1111
6012	5012	B1AE
3012	3012	1201
		5112
		3110
		B0A2

5. Write a program to simulate the machine in Appendix C.

ADDITIONAL READING

Almasi, G. S., and A. Gottlieb. *Highly Parallel Computing*, 2nd ed. Redwood City, Calif.: Benjamin/Cummings, 1994.

Hamacher, V. C., Z. G. Vranesic, and S. G. Zaky. *Computer Organization*, 4th ed. New York: McGraw-Hill, 1996.

Patterson, D. A., and J. L. Hennessy. *Computer Organization and Design*. San Francisco: Morgan Kaufmann, 1994.

Sayood, K. *Introduction to Data Compression*. San Francisco: Morgan Kaufmann, 1996.

Stallings, W. *Computer Organization and Architecture*, 4th ed. Upper Saddle River, N.J.: Prentice-Hall, 1996.

PART TWO

SOFTWARE

In Part One we discussed the major components of a computer. These components, which are tangible, are classified as hardware. In contrast, the programs that the hardware executes are intangible and are classified as software. In Part Two, we turn our attention to topics associated with software, which leads us to the core of computer science—the study of algorithms. In particular, we will investigate the discovery, representation, and communication of algorithms.

We begin by discussing operating systems in Chapter 3. These systems are large, complex software packages that control the overall activities of a machine or group of machines connected as a network. In Chapter 4, we study algorithms, with an emphasis on how algorithms are discovered and represented. In Chapter 5, we turn to the topic of how algorithms are communicated to machines through the programming process and investigate properties of popular programming languages. Finally, in Chapter 6, we look at the entire software development process in the context of software engineering.

CHAPTER THREE

Operating Systems and Networks

3.1 The Evolution of Operating Systems
Single-Processor Systems
Multiprocessor Systems

3.2 Operating System Architecture
A Software Survey
The Shell
The Kernel
Getting It Started

3.3 Coordinating the Machine's Activities
The Concept of a Process
Process Administration
The Client/Server Model

***3.4 Handling Competition Among Processes**
Semaphores
Deadlock

3.5 Networks
Network Classification
The Internet
Security

***3.6 Network Protocols**
Controlling Transmission Privileges
The Layered Approach to Network Software
The TCP/IP Protocol Suite

Today's computer applications often require a single machine to perform activities that may compete with one another for the machine's resources. For example, a machine may be connected to several terminals or workstations from which different users can simultaneously request machine services. Even in a single-user installation the user may require several intertwined activities such as printing a document, modifying another document, and creating a graphical display to be inserted into a document. These demands require a high degree of coordination to ensure that unrelated activities do not interfere with one another and that communication between related activities is efficient and reliable. This coordination is handled by a software system known as an **operating system.**

Similar coordination and communication problems arise when different machines are connected to form a computer network. Solving these problems is a natural extension of the subject of operating systems. In this section we discuss fundamental concepts relating to operating systems and networking.

*Sections marked by an asterisk are optional in that they provide additional depth of coverage that is not required for an understanding of future chapters.

3.1 The Evolution of Operating Systems

We approach our study of operating systems and networking with a historical perspective, from the early single-process systems to the more recent multiprocessor systems.

Single-Processor Systems

The single-processor machines of the 1940s and 1950s were not very flexible or efficient. Program execution required significant preparation of equipment in terms of mounting tapes, placing punched cards in the card reader, setting switches, and so on. Thus, the execution of each program, called a *job*, was handled as an isolated activity. When several users were required to share a machine, sign-up sheets on which the users could reserve the machine for blocks of time were common. During the time period allocated to a user, the machine was totally under that user's control. The session usually began with program setup, was followed by short periods of program execution, and was often completed in a hurried effort to do just one more thing ("It will only take a minute") while the next user was impatiently starting to set up.

In such an environment operating systems began as systems for simplifying program setup and for streamlining the transition between jobs. One early development was the separation of users and equipment, which eliminated the physical transition of people in and out of the computer room. For this purpose a computer operator was hired to perform the actual operation of the machine. Anyone wanting a program run was required to submit it (along with any required data and special directions about the program's requirements) to the operator and return later for the results. The operator in turn loaded these materials into the machine's mass storage where the operating system could access them for execution. This was the beginning of **batch processing**—the execution of jobs by collecting them in a single batch, then executing them without further interaction with the user. The jobs residing in mass storage waited for execution in a **job queue** (Fig. 3.1).

Figure 3.1 Batch processing

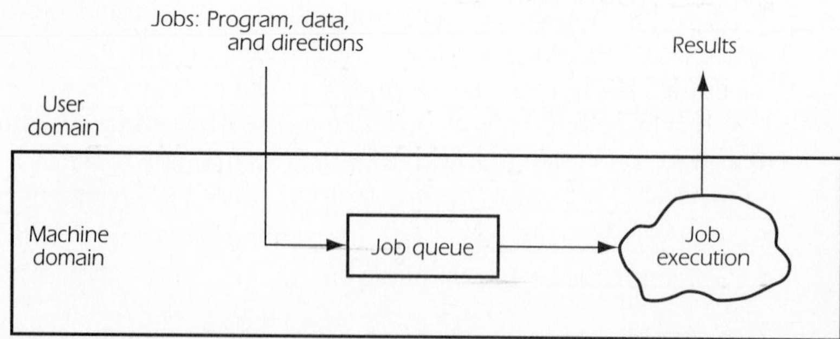

A queue is a storage organization in which objects (in our case, jobs) are ordered in **first-in, first-out (FIFO)** fashion. That is, the objects are removed from the queue in the order in which they arrived. In reality, most job queues do not rigorously follow the FIFO structure, since most operating systems provide for consideration of job priorities. As a result, a job waiting in the job queue can be bumped by a higher-priority job.

In early batch processing systems, each job was accompanied by a set of instructions explaining the steps required to prepare the machine for that particular job. These instructions were coded in a job control language (JCL) and stored with the job in the job queue. When the job was selected for execution, the operating system printed these instructions at a printer where they could be read and followed by the operator. The instructions that required action by the operator dealt mainly with issues of off-line equipment, and since these activities are minimal today, job control languages have become a conduit for communication with the operating system rather than a computer operator. Indeed, the job of computer operator is becoming obsolete. Instead, institutions today hire system administrators to manage the computer system (obtaining and overseeing the installation of new equipment and software, enforcing local regulations such as restricting the disk space consumed by each user to his or her fair share, and coordinating efforts to resolve problems that arise in the system) rather than operating machines in a hands-on manner.

The major drawback to traditional batch processing is that the user has no interaction with the program once it is submitted to the job queue. This approach is acceptable for some applications, such as payroll processing, in which the data and all processing decisions are established in advance. However, it is not acceptable when the user must interact with the program during its execution. Examples include reservation systems in which reservations and cancellations must be reported as they occur, word processing systems in which documents are developed in a dynamic write and rewrite manner, and computer games in which interaction with the machine is the central feature of the game.

To accommodate these needs, new operating systems were developed to provide **interactive processing** (Fig. 3.2). These systems allowed the execution of programs that carried on a dialogue with the user through remote terminals or workstations. These interactive systems gave birth to the concept known as **real-time processing,** which refers to the requirement that the activities taking place in a machine must be coordinated with the activities in the machine's environment. No longer satisfied with waiting overnight to obtain the results of their job, users demanded a timely response as they communicated with the machine through a distant workstation.

If interactive systems had been allowed to address only one user at a time, real-time processing would have been no problem. But, machines were expensive and so each machine had to serve more than one user. In turn, it was common for several users to seek interactive service of a machine at the same time, and real-time considerations presented obstacles. If the operating system for such a multiuser environment insisted on executing only one job at a time, only one user would receive satisfactory real-time service.

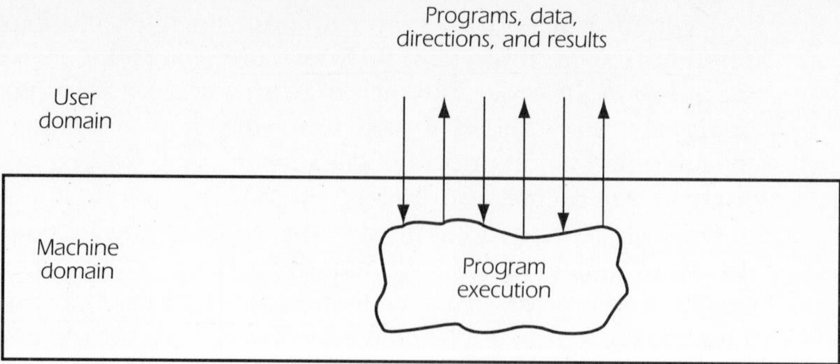

Figure 3.2 Interactive processing

A solution to this problem was to design the operating system so that it rotated the various jobs in and out of execution by a process called time-sharing. More precisely, **time-sharing** refers to the technique of dividing time into intervals, or time slices, and then restricting the execution of a job to only one time slice at a time. At the end of each time slice, the current job is set aside and another is allowed to execute during the next time slice. By rapidly shuffling the jobs in this manner, the illusion of several jobs executing simultaneously is created. Depending on the types of jobs being executed, early time-sharing systems were able to provide acceptable real-time processing to as many as 30 users at the same time.

Today, time-sharing is used in single-user systems as well as multiuser systems, although in the former it is usually called **multitasking,** in reference to the illusion of more than one task being performed simultaneously. Regardless of whether the environment is single-user or multiuser, the use of time-sharing has been found to increase the overall efficiency of a machine. This finding may be surprising when one considers that the shuffling process required by time-sharing introduces a significant overhead. However, without time-sharing a computer system spends much of its time waiting for peripheral devices to complete tasks or for a user to make the next request. Time-sharing allows this lost time to be given to another task. Hence, progress on one task can be made while another task is waiting. In turn, a collection of tasks will often be completed in less time when executed in a time-sharing environment than when executed in a sequential manner.

Multiprocessor Systems

In recent years the need to share information and resources among different machines has spawned the desire to link the machines for the exchange of information. To fill that need, coupled computer systems called **networks** have become popular. Indeed, the concept of a large central machine serving many users has largely given way to the concept of many small machines connected via a network in which users share resources (such as printing capabilities, software packages, data storage facilities, and information) scattered throughout the system. A prime example is the **Internet,** a network of networks that today links millions of machines worldwide. We will study the Internet more closely in Sections 3.5 and 3.6.

Many of the coordination problems that occur in network designs are the same or very similar to those faced by operating systems. In fact, software for controlling a network can be viewed as a networkwide operating system. In this light, network software development is a natural extension of the field of operating systems. Whereas early networks were constructed as loosely coupled individual machines, each under the control of its own operating system, network research is moving toward networkwide systems in which the resources in a network are shared equally among the tasks assigned to the network, and the processors in the network are assigned tasks according to the needs of the network, regardless of the physical location. An example is the name server system used in the Internet, which we will study in Section 3.5. This system allows a variety of machines scattered around the world to work together to translate an Internet address from its human compatible mnemonic form into its network compatible numeric form.

Networks represent only one example of the multiprocessor designs that are inspiring the development of today's operating systems. Whereas a network produces a multiprocessor system by combining machines, each of which may contain only one CPU, other multiprocessor systems are designed as single machines containing more than one processor. An operating system for such a machine must not only coordinate the competition between the various activities that are actually executing simultaneously but also control the assignment of activities to the processors in the machine. This process involves problems of **load balancing** (making sure that the processors are used efficiently) as well as **scaling** (breaking tasks into a number of subtasks compatible with the number of processors in the machine).

We see then that the development of multiprocessor systems has added new dimensions to the subject of operating systems, and the field promises to remain active for years to come.

Questions/Exercises

1. Identify examples of queues. In each case indicate any situations that violate the FIFO structure.
2. Which of the following would require real-time processing?
   a. Printing mailing labels
   b. Playing a computer game
   c. Displaying letters on a monitor screen as they are typed at the keyboard
   d. Executing a program that predicts the state of next year's economy
3. What is the difference between real-time processing and interactive processing?
4. What is the difference between time-sharing and multitasking?

3.2 Operating System Architecture

To understand the architecture of a typical operating system, it is helpful to grasp the complete spectrum of software found within a typical computer system. We begin this task with a software survey in which we group pieces of software according to a classification scheme. Such classifications invariably place similar software units in different classes in the same manner as the assignment of time zones dictates that nearby communities must set their clocks an hour apart even though there is no significant difference between the occurrence of sunrise and sunset. Moreover, in the case of software classification the dynamics of the subject and the lack of a definitive authority lead to contradictory classifications and terminology. The following classification (Fig. 3.3) should therefore be viewed as a means of gaining a foothold in a complex subject rather than as a statement of universally accepted fact.

A Software Survey

Let us first divide a machine's software into two broad categories: **application software** and **system software.** Application software consists of the programs for performing tasks particular to the machine's utilization. A machine used to maintain the inventory for a manufacturing company will contain different application software from that found on a machine used by a textbook author. Examples of application software include spreadsheets, database systems, desktop publishing systems, program development software, and games.

In contrast to application software, system software performs those tasks that are common to computer systems in general. In a sense the system software provides the environment in which the application software resides, in much the same manner as a nation's infrastructure provides the foundation on which its citizens rely for their individual lifestyles.

Within the class of system software are two categories, one being the operating system itself and the other consisting of software units collectively known as **utility software.** The majority of an installation's utility software consists of programs for performing activities that are fundamental to computer installations, yet not included in the operating system. In a sense, utility software consists of software units that extend the capabilities of the operating system. For example, the

Figure 3.3 Software classification

Software
Application
System
Utility
Operating system
Shell
Kernel

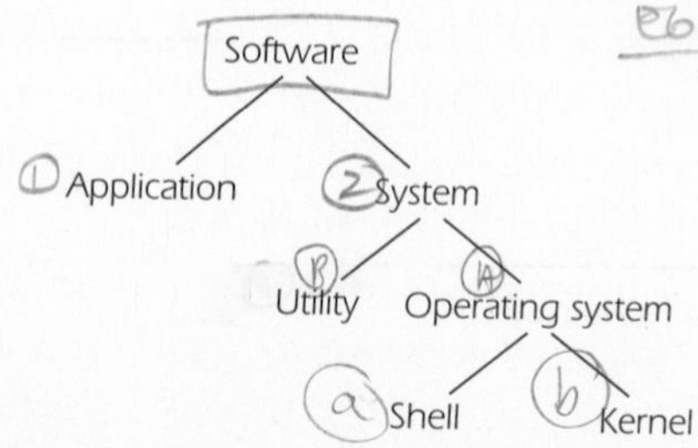

ability to format a disk or to copy a file is often not implemented within the operating system itself but instead is provided by means of a utility program. Other instances of utility software include software for communicating through a modem over telephone lines, software to project the time of day on the monitor screen, and in a growing number of installations, software for handling networking activities.

The distinction between application software and utility software is often vague. Many computer users consider the class of utility software to include any software that accompanies an operating system when the system is purchased. In turn, they tend to think of program development systems as utility software, since such packages have historically been supplied with the purchase of an operating system. The distinction between utility software and the operating system is equally vague. Some systems implement the software for providing such basic services as listing files in mass storage as utility software; others include it within the operating system.

It is easy to see that by implementing certain activities in utility software, an operating system can be simpler than it would be if forced to encompass all the basic features required by a computer system. Moreover, the routines implemented as utility software can be customized more readily to the needs of a particular installation. Indeed, it is not uncommon to find companies or individuals who have modified, or added to, the utility software that was originally provided with their machine's operating system.

The Shell

The portion of an operating system that defines the interface between the operating system and its users is often called the **shell.** The job of the shell is to communicate with the user, or users, of the machine. Modern shells perform this task by means of a **graphical user interface** (GUI) in which objects to be manipulated, such as files and programs, are represented pictorially on the monitor screen as icons. These systems allow users to issue commands by pointing to and pushing these icons on the screen by means of a hand-held device called a mouse. Older shells communicate via users through textual messages using a keyboard and monitor screen.

Although an operating system's shell plays an important role in establishing a machine's functionality, this shell is merely an interface between a user and the real heart of the operating system (Fig. 3.4). This distinction between the shell and the internal parts of the operating system is emphasized by the fact that some operating systems allow a user to select among different shells to obtain the most compatible interface for that particular user. Users of the UNIX operating system, for example, can select among a variety of shells including the Borne shell, the C shell, and the Korn shell. Early versions of Windows® from Microsoft Corporation were essentially replacement shells for MS-DOS. In these cases the operating system remains the same except for the way it communicates with the machine's users.

Alternatively, shells that project similar characteristics can be used in conjunction with operating systems with different internal structures to produce

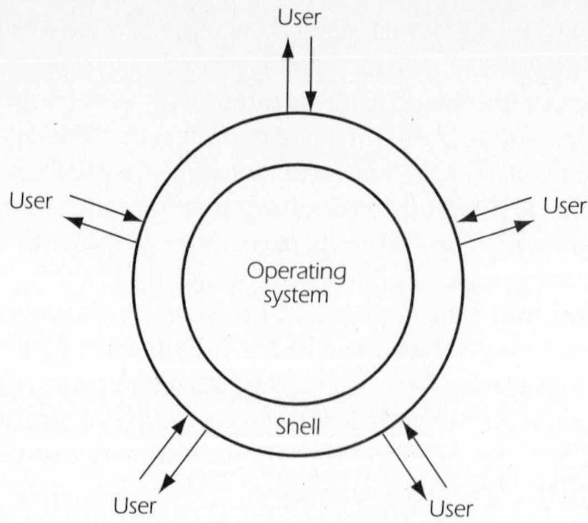

Figure 3.4 The shell as an interface between users and the operating system

uniformity in the human–machine interface across a variety of machines. The first application of this standardizing effect was implemented by IBM with the System/360 series of machines introduced in the 1960s. This series consisted of a variety of machines ranging from designs for small-business applications to large machines for businesses with significant needs. All these machines were supplied with operating systems that communicated with their environments in essentially the same manner. Thus, as a business grew, it could change to a larger machine in the 360 series without major reprogramming and retraining efforts.

Today, the advantages of standardized interfaces are well recognized and sought after throughout the software spectrum. For example, communication with spreadsheet systems and word processors provided by different vendors have similar characteristics, simplifying customers' changing from one product to another. Standardization has led to a multitude of legal questions, however, including the question of who owns an interface. When the interface designed by one company becomes popular, it becomes advantageous for competing companies to design their systems to look like the well-known one. This similarity makes it easier for users of the well-known system to convert to the competitor's system, even though the interior designs of the two systems may be quite different. Of course, the company that designed the original system claims ownership of the "look and feel" of that system, just as it claims ownership of the design of the system itself. How the courts ultimately rule in "look and feel" cases remains an open question.

The Kernel

The internal part of an operating system is often called its **kernel.** An operating system's kernel contains those software components that perform the very basic functions required by the computer installation. One such unit is the **file manager,** whose job is to coordinate the use of the machine's mass storage facilities. More precisely, the file manager keeps records of all the files stored in mass storage, including where each file is located, which users are allowed to access the various files, and what portions of mass storage are available for new or extending files.

For the convenience of the machine's users, most file managers allow files to be grouped into a bundle called a **directory** or **folder.** This approach allows a user to organize his or her files according to their purposes by placing related files in the same directory. Moreover, by allowing directories to contain other directories, called subdirectories, a hierarchical organization can be constructed. For example, a user may create a directory called Records that contains subdirectories called FinancialRecords, MedicalRecords, and HouseholdRecords. Within each of these subdirectories could be files that fall within that particular category. A sequence of directories within directories is called a directory **path.**

Any access to a file by other software units is obtained at the discretion of the file manager. The procedure begins by requesting that the file manager grant access to the file through a procedure known as opening the file. If the file manager approves of the requested access, it provides the information needed to find and manipulate the file. This information is stored in an area of main memory called a **file descriptor.** It is by referencing the information in this file descriptor that individual operations are performed on the file.

Another component of the kernel consists of a collection of **device drivers,** which are the software units that communicate with the controllers (or at times directly with the devices) to carry out operations on the machine's peripheral devices. Each device driver, uniquely designed for its particular type of controller or device (such as a printer, disk drive, magnetic tape unit, or monitor), translates general requests into the more technical steps required by the controller or the device assigned to that driver. In this manner, other software units are shielded from the details of the devices attached to the machine. They need merely make general requests to the device drivers and let the device drivers take care of the details. For example, a device driver for a disk drive might translate a request to write a portion of a file onto a disk into steps involving tracks and sectors (using information in the file descriptor) and pass this information to the appropriate controller. In turn, the controller would take the responsibility of positioning the read/write head and overseeing the actual recording process. In contrast, a device driver for a printer would translate a request to write the same portion of the file at a printer into instructions involving the transfer of fonts, characters, and printer control instructions. In fact, the steps required are even different for different printers, and this is why an owner of a personal computer who buys a new printer often receives a new device driver as well.

Still another component of an operating system's kernel is the **memory manager,** charged with the task of coordinating the machine's use of main memory. Such duties are minimal in an environment in which the machine is asked to perform only one task at a time. In these cases the program for performing the current task is placed in main memory, executed, and then replaced by the program for performing the next task. However, in multiuser or multitasking environments in which the machine is asked to address many needs at the same time, the duties of the memory manager are extensive. In these cases many programs and blocks of data must reside in main memory concurrently, each in an area of memory set aside for it by the memory manager. As the needs of different activities come and go, the memory manager must find places to fulfill their memory requirements and keep track of those memory areas no longer occupied.

The task of the memory manager is complicated further when the total main memory space required exceeds the space actually available in the machine. In this case the memory manager may create the illusion of additional memory space by rotating programs and data back and forth between main memory and mass storage. This illusionary memory space is called **virtual memory.** Suppose, for example, that a main memory of 64 megabytes is required but only 32 megabytes is actually available. To create the illusion of the larger memory space, the memory manager would divide the required space into units called **pages** and store the contents of these pages in mass storage. A typical page size is no more than four kilobytes. As different pages are actually required in main memory, the memory manager would exchange them for pages that are no longer required, and thus the other software units could execute as though there were actually 64 megabytes of main memory in the machine.

Also within the kernel of an operating system are the **scheduler** and **dispatcher,** which we study in the next section. For now we merely note that in a time-sharing system the scheduler determines which activities are to be considered for execution and the dispatcher controls the allocation of time slices to these activities.

Getting It Started

We have seen how an operating system communicates with the machine's users and how the components of the operating system work together to coordinate the execution of activities within the machine, but we have not considered how the operating system gets started. This is accomplished through a procedure known as boot strapping, often shortened to **booting,** that is performed by the machine each time it is turned on. The first step to understanding this procedure is to understand why it is necessary in the first place.

A CPU is designed so that its program counter starts with a particular predetermined address each time the CPU is turned on. It is at this location, then, that the CPU expects to find the program to be executed. To ensure that the desired program is present, this portion of memory is normally constructed in such a way that its content is permanent. Such memory is known as **read-only memory (ROM).** Once bit patterns are placed in ROM by a special process analogous to blowing fuses on a chip, it remains there whether the machine is on or off.

In the case of small computers used as control devices in microwave ovens, automobile ignition systems, and stereo receivers, it is feasible to devote significant portions of main memory to ROM since flexibility is not an issue. The program executed by such devices is the same each time it is turned on. But this is not the case in general-purpose computers, so it is not practical to construct large portions of the main memory in these machines from ROM. In fact, most of the memory in a general-purpose machine is volatile, meaning that the memory's content is lost when the machine is turned off.

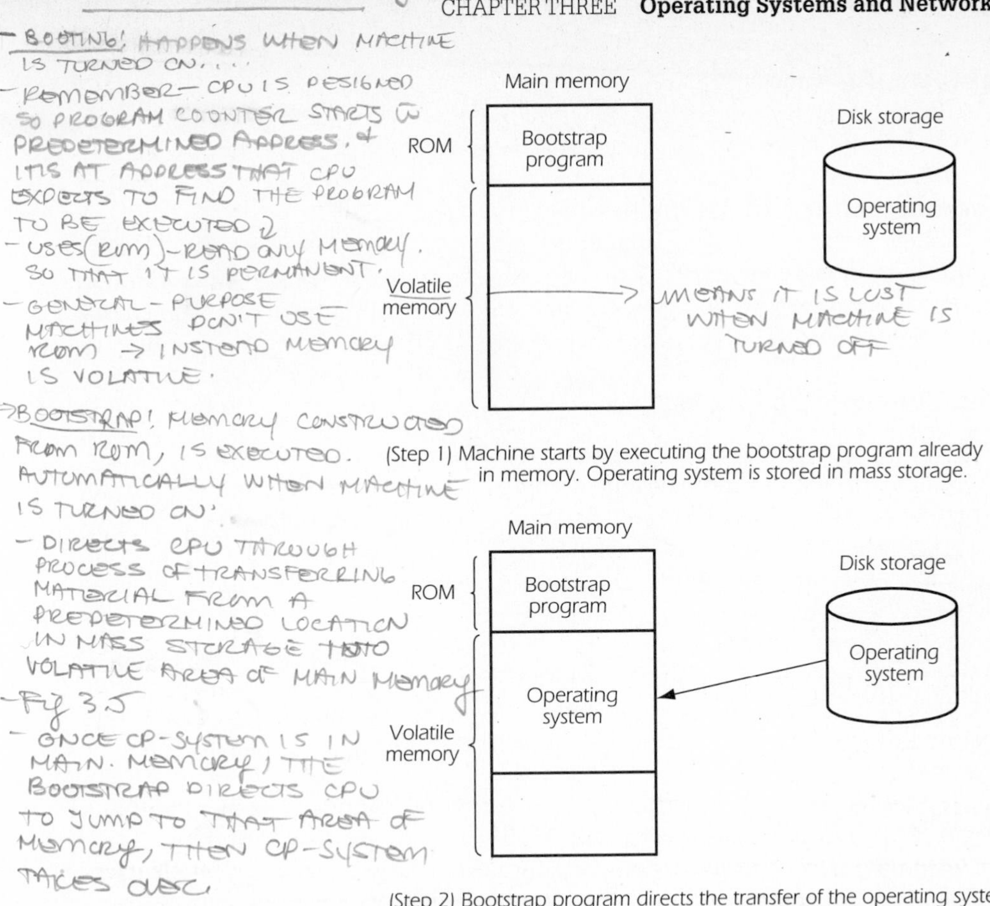
Main memory
ROM
Bootstrap program
Volatile memory
Disk storage
Operating system
(Step 1) Machine starts by executing the bootstrap program already in memory. Operating system is stored in mass storage.
Main memory
ROM
Bootstrap program
Operating system
Volatile memory
Disk storage
Operating system
(Step 2) Bootstrap program directs the transfer of the operating system into main memory and then transfers control to it.

Figure 3.5 The booting process

For the purpose of booting a general-purpose machine, the portion of memory that is constructed from ROM is programmed with a short program, called the **bootstrap.** This is the program that is executed automatically when the machine is turned on. It directs the CPU through the process of transferring material from a predetermined location in mass storage into the volatile area of main memory (Fig. 3.5). In most cases this material is the operating system. Once the operating system has been placed in main memory, the bootstrap directs the CPU to jump to that area of memory. At this point the operating system takes over and begins controlling the machine's activities.

Questions/Exercises

1. List the components of a typical operating system and summarize the role of each in a single phrase.
2. What is the difference between application software and utility software?

3. What is virtual memory?
4. Summarize the booting procedure.

3.3 Coordinating the Machine's Activities

In this section we consider how an operating system coordinates the execution of application software, utility software, and units within the operating system itself. We begin with the concept of a process.

The Concept of a Process

One of the most fundamental concepts of modern operating systems is the distinction between a program and the activity of executing a program. The former is merely a static set of directions, the latter is a dynamic activity whose properties change as time progresses. This activity is known as a **process.** A process encompasses the current status of the activity, called the **process state.** This state includes the current position in the program being executed (the value of the program counter) as well as the values in the other CPU registers and the associated memory cells. Roughly speaking, the process state is a snapshot of the machine at that time. At different times during the execution of a program (at different times in a process) different snapshots (different process states) will be observed.

To emphasize the distinction between a program and a process, note that a single program can be associated with more than one process at the same time. For example, in a multiuser, time-sharing system two users may wish to edit separate documents at the same time. Both activities may use the same editing program, but each would be a separate process with its own set of data and its own rate of progress. In this situation an operating system may keep only one copy of the editor program in main memory and allow each process to use it during its time slice.

In a typical time-sharing computer installation many processes are normally competing for time slices. These processes include the execution of application and utility programs as well as portions of the operating system. It is the task of the operating system to coordinate these processes. Coordination involves assuring that each process has the resources (peripheral devices, space in main memory, access to data, and access to a CPU) that it needs, that independent processes do not interfere with one another, and that processes that need to exchange information are able to do so. Communication between processes is called **interprocess communication.**

Process Administration

The tasks associated with process coordination are handled by the scheduler and dispatcher within the operating system's kernel. As such, the scheduler maintains a record of the processes present in the computer system, introduces new processes to this pool, and removes processes that are complete. To keep track of all the processes, the scheduler maintains a block of information in main memory called the **process table.** Each time a new task is assigned to the machine the scheduler creates a process for that task by placing a new entry in the process table. This entry contains such information as the memory area assigned to the process (obtained from the memory manager), the priority of the process, and whether the process is ready or waiting. A process is **ready** if it is in a state in which its progress can continue; it is **waiting** if its progress is currently delayed until some external event occurs, such as the completion of a disk access or the arrival of a message from another process. The scheduler, then, maintains this information as the process progresses. In particular, a process will most likely shift back and forth between being ready and waiting, the priority of a process changes as time passes, and of course, the scheduler must remove the process from the process table when the process is completed.

The dispatcher is the component of the kernel that ensures that the scheduled processes are actually executed. In a time-sharing system this task is accomplished by dividing time into short segments, each called a **time slice** or **quantum** (typically about 50 milliseconds), and then switching the CPU's attention among the processes as each is allowed to execute for no longer than one time slice (Fig. 3.6). The procedure of changing from one process to another is called a **process switch.** Each time a process begins its time slice the dispatcher initiates a timer circuit that will measure the next quantum. At the end of the quantum the timer circuit generates a signal called an **interrupt.** The CPU reacts to this signal in much the same way that you react when interrupted from a task. You stop what you are doing, record where you are in the task, and take care of the interrupting entity. When the CPU receives an interrupt signal, it completes its current fetch–decode–execute cycle, saves its position in the current process (we will return to this step in a moment), and begins executing a program, called the **interrupt handler,** that is stored at a predetermined location in main memory.

In our time-sharing scenario the interrupt handler is a part of the dispatcher. Thus the effect of the interrupt signal is to preempt the current process and transfer control back to the dispatcher. At this point, the dispatcher allows the

Figure 3.6 Time-sharing between process A and process B

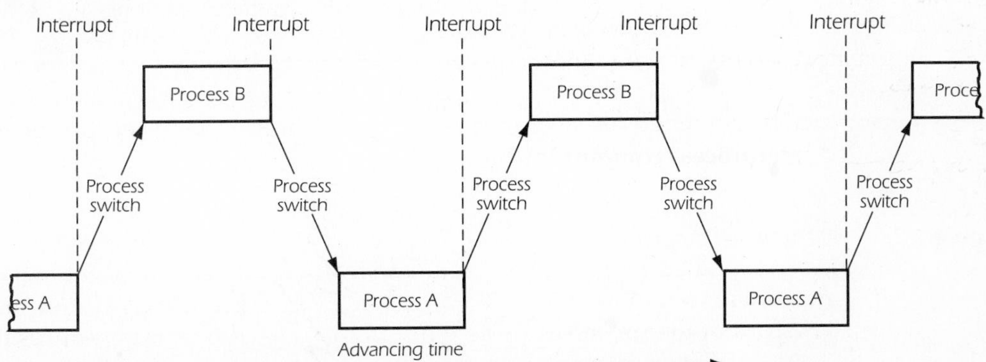

scheduler to update the process table (for instance, the priority of the process that has just completed its time slice may need to be lowered and the priorities of other processes may need to be raised). The dispatcher then selects the process from the process table that has the highest priority among the ready processes, restarts the timer circuit, and allows the selected process to begin its time slice.

Paramount to the success of a time-sharing system is the ability to stop, and later restart, a process. If you are interrupted while reading a book, your ability to continue reading at a later time depends on your ability to remember your location in the book as well as the information that you had accumulated to that point. In short, you must be able to re-create the environment that was present immediately prior to the interruption. Such an environment in the case of a process is the process's state. Recall that this state includes the value of the program counter as well as the contents of the registers and pertinent memory cells. Machines designed for time-sharing systems incorporate the task of saving this information as part of the CPU's reaction to the interrupt signal. These machines also tend to have machine-language instructions for reloading a previously saved state. Such machine features simplify the task of the dispatcher when performing a process switch and exemplify how the design of modern machines is influenced by the needs of today's operating systems.

At times a process's time slice is terminated before the timer has expired. For example, if a process executes an I/O request, such as a request to retrieve data from a disk, that process's time slice will be terminated since the process would merely waste the remaining time waiting for the controller to perform the request. In this case, the scheduler will update the process table to reflect the process's waiting status and the dispatcher will assign a new quantum to a process that is ready. Later (perhaps several hundred milliseconds), when the controller indicates that the I/O request has been completed, the scheduler will reclassify the process as ready and thus that process will again compete for a time slice.

The Client/Server Model

The various units within an operating system normally execute as individual processes that, in a time-sharing system, compete for time slices under control of the dispatcher. To coordinate their activities, these processes must communicate with one another. To schedule a new process, the scheduler must obtain memory space from the memory manager for that process. To access a file in mass storage, any process must first obtain information from the file manager.

To simplify this interprocess communication, the components of an operating system are often designed to conform to the **client/server model** (Fig. 3.7).

Figure 3.7 The client/server model

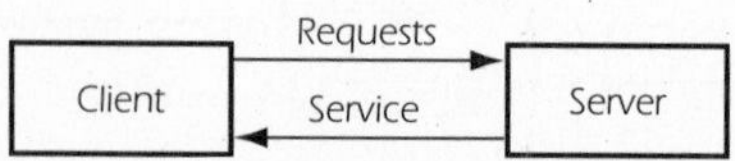

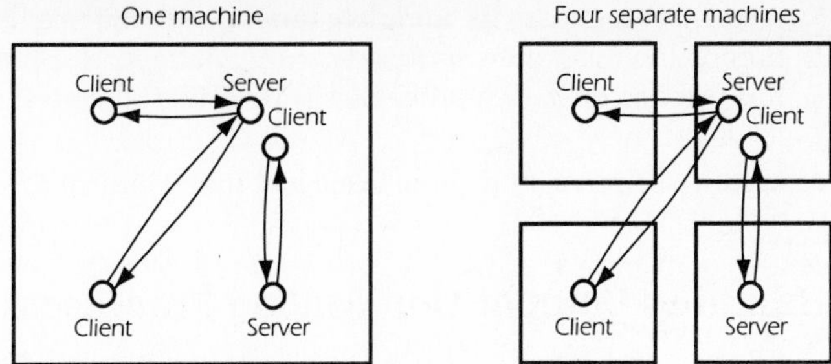

Figure 3.8 Identical communication structure between clients and servers operating on the same machine and distributed among different machines

This model defines the basic roles played by the components as being that of either a **client,** which makes requests of other units, or a **server,** which satisfies the requests made by clients. For example, the file manager would take the form of a server that provides access to files as requested by its clients. Based on this model interprocess communication within an operating system consists of requests from processes playing the client role and replies from processes playing the server role.

Compliance to the client/server model in the design of software leads to uniformity among the types of communication taking place in the system. This is one of the main reasons the model has been widely adopted in operating system design. If the components of an operating system are designed as clients and servers, then the communication between these units takes the same form whether that communication is between components within the same machine or between components on different machines separated by great distances (Fig. 3.8). A client merely sends requests to servers and waits for replies; a server merely performs the services requested and sends replies back to the clients. Thus as long as a network of machines provides a means of sending requests and replies among the machines, a collection of clients and servers can be distributed among the machines in any configuration that is convenient for the network.

Questions/Exercises

1. Summarize the difference between a program and a process.
2. Summarize the steps performed by the CPU when an interrupt occurs.
3. In a time-sharing system, how can high-priority processes be allowed to run faster than others?
4. If each quantum in a time-sharing system is 50 milliseconds and each process switch requires 5 milliseconds, how many processes can the machine service in a single second?

5. If each process uses its complete quantum in the machine in Exercise 4, what fraction of the machine's time is spent actually performing processes? What would this fraction be if each process executes an I/O request after only 5 milliseconds of its quantum?
6. Identify some relationships in society that conform to the client/server model.

3.4 Handling Competition Among Processes

A universal task among the components of an operating system's kernel is the allocation of the machine's resources to the processes in the system. Here we are using the term *resource* in a broad sense, including the machine's peripheral devices as well as features within the machine itself. The file manager allocates both access to current files and disk space for the construction of new files; the memory manager allocates memory space; the scheduler allocates space in the process table; and the dispatcher allocates time slices. As with many problems in computer systems, this allocation task may appear simple on the surface. Below the surface, however, lie several problems that can lead to system malfunctions unless they have been accounted for. Remember, a machine does not think for itself; it merely follows directions. Thus, to construct reliable operating systems, we must develop algorithms that cover every possible issue, regardless of how minuscule it may appear.

Semaphores

Consider a machine with a single printer running a time-sharing operating system. If a process needs to print its results, it must request that the operating system give it access to the printer's device driver. At this point, the operating system must decide whether to grant this request, depending upon whether the printer is already being used by another process. If it is not, the operating system should grant the request and allow the process to continue; otherwise, the operating system should deny the request and perhaps classify the process as a waiting process until the printer becomes available. Indeed, if two processes were given simultaneous access to the machine's printer, the results would be worthless to both.

Access allocation requires that the operating system keep track of whether the printer has been allocated. One approach would be to use a flag, which in this context refers to a bit in memory those states are often referred to as set and clear, rather than 1 and 0. A clear flag indicates that the printer is available and a set flag indicates that the printer is currently allocated. On the surface this approach seems to hold no unforeseen problems. The operating system merely clears the flag to begin, then checks the flag each time a request for printer access is made. If it is clear, the request is granted and the operating system sets the flag. If the flag is set, the operating system makes the requesting process wait. Each time a process finishes with the printer, the operating system either allocates the printer to a waiting process or, if no processes are waiting, merely clears the flag.

Although this solution looks good at first glance, it has a problem. The task of testing and possibly setting the flag requires several machine steps. It is therefore possible for the task to be interrupted after a clear flag has been detected but before the flag has been set. In turn, the following scenario could take place.

Suppose the printer is currently available and a process requests use of it. The corresponding flag is checked and found to be clear, indicating that the printer is available. However, at this point the process is interrupted and another process begins its time slice. It too requests the use of the printer. Again, the flag is checked and found still clear because the previous process was interrupted before the operating system had time to set the flag. Consequently, the operating system allows the second process to begin using the printer. Later, the original process resumes execution where it left off, which is immediately after the operating system found the flag to be clear. Thus the operating system continues by granting the original process access to the printer. Two processes are now using the same printer.

The problem here is that the task of testing and possibly setting the flag must be completed without interruption. One solution is to use the interrupt disable and interrupt enable instructions provided in most machine languages. If the operating system starts the flag-testing routine with a disable interrupt instruction and ends it with an enable interrupt instruction, no other activity can interrupt the routine once it starts.

Another approach is to use the **test-and-set** instruction that is available in many machine languages. This instruction directs the CPU to retrieve the value of a flag, note the value received, and then set the flag all within a single machine instruction. The advantage here is that since the CPU always completes an instruction before recognizing an interrupt, the task of testing and setting the flag cannot be interrupted when it is implemented as a single instruction.

A properly implemented flag, as just described, is called a **semaphore,** in reference to the railroad signals used to control access to sections of track. In fact, semaphores are used in software systems in much the same way as they are in railway systems. Corresponding to the section of track that can contain only one train at a time is a sequence of instructions that can be executed by only one process at a time. Such a sequence of instructions is called a **critical region.** A process must find the semaphore clear and set it before entering the critical region; then it must clear the semaphore once the critical region is completed.

Deadlock

Another problem that can arise during resource allocation is **deadlock,** the condition in which two or more processes are blocked from progressing because each is waiting for access to resources allocated to another. For example, one process may have access to the machine's printer but be waiting for the tape drive, while another process has access to the tape drive but is waiting for the printer. Another example occurs when processes create new processes to perform subtasks. If the scheduler has no space left in the process table and each process in the system must create an additional process before it can complete its task, then no process can continue. Such conditions, as in other settings (Fig. 3.9), can severely degrade a system's performance.

Analysis of deadlock has revealed that it cannot occur unless all three of the following conditions are satisfied:

1. There is competition for nonshareable resources.
2. The resources are requested on a partial basis; that is, having received some resources, a process will return later to request more.
3. Once a resource has been allocated, it cannot be forcibly retrieved.

The point of isolating these conditions is that the deadlock problem can be removed by attacking any one of the three. In general, techniques that attack the third condition tend to fall in the category known as deadlock detection and correction schemes. In these cases the occurrence of deadlock is considered so remote that no effort is made to avoid the problem. Instead, the approach is to detect it should it occur and then correct it by forcibly retrieving some of the allocated resources. Our example of a full process table falls in this class. A system administrator will usually establish a process table that is large enough for that particular installation. If, however, deadlock should occur due to a full table, the administrator merely uses his or her powers as "super user" to remove (the technical term is *kill*) some of the processes, which releases space in the process table, so that the remaining processes can continue their tasks.

Techniques that attack the first two conditions tend to be known as deadlock avoidance schemes. One, for example, attacks the second condition by requiring each process to request all its resources at one time. Another, perhaps more imaginative technique, attacks the first condition, not by removing the competition directly, but by converting nonshareable resources into shareable ones. For example, suppose the resource in question is a printer and a variety of processes

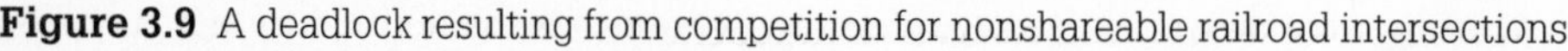

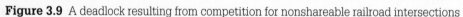

Figure 3.9 A deadlock resulting from competition for nonshareable railroad intersections

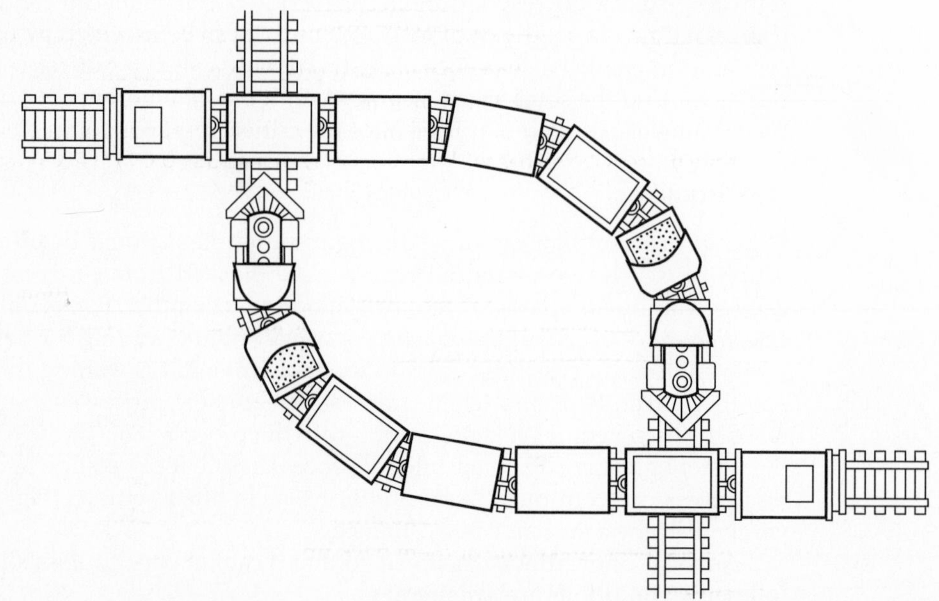

require its use. Each time a process requests the printer, the operating system grants the request. However, instead of connecting the process to the printer's device driver, the operating system connects it to a device driver that stores the information to be printed on a disk rather than sending it to the printer. Thus each process, thinking it has access to the printer, executes in its normal way. Later, when the printer is available, the operating system can transfer the data from the disk to the printer. In this manner the operating system has made the nonshareable resource appear shareable by creating the illusion of more than one printer. This technique of holding data for output at a later but more convenient time is called **spooling** and is quite popular on systems of all sizes.

Of course, when processes compete for a machine's resources, other problems arise. For example, a file manager should normally grant several processes access to the same file if the processes are merely reading data from the file, but conflicts can occur if more than one process tries to alter a file at the same time. Thus a file manager may allocate file access according to the needs of the processes, allowing several processes to have read access but only one having write access at any given time. Other systems may divide the file into pieces so that different processes can alter different parts of the file concurrently. Additional problems must still be resolved, however. How, for example, should those processes with only read access to a file be notified when a process with write access alters the file?

Questions/Exercises

1. Suppose process A and process B are sharing time on the same machine, and each needs the same nonshareable resource for short periods of time. (For example, each process may be printing a series of independent, short reports.) Each process may then repeatedly acquire the resource, release it, and later request it again. What is a drawback to controlling access to the resource in the following manner:

   Begin by assigning a flag the value 0. If process A requests the resource and the flag is 0, grant the request. Otherwise, make process A wait. If process B requests the resource and the flag is 1, grant the request. Otherwise, make process B wait. Each time process A finishes with the resource, change the flag to 1. Each time process B finishes with the resource, change the flag to 0.

2. Suppose a two-lane road converges to one lane to pass through a tunnel. To coordinate the use of the tunnel, the following signal system has been installed:

   A car entering either end of the tunnel causes red lights above the tunnel entrances to be turned on. As the car exits the tunnel, the lights are turned off. If an approaching car finds a red light on, it waits until the light is turned off before entering the tunnel. What is the flaw in this system?

3. Suppose the following solutions have been proposed for removing the deadlock that occurs on a single-lane bridge when two cars meet. Identify which condition for deadlock given in the text is removed by each solution.

   a. Do not let a car onto the bridge until the bridge is empty.

   b. If cars meet, make one of them back up.

   c. Add a second lane to the bridge.

4. Suppose we represent each process in a time-sharing system with a dot and draw an arrow from one dot to another if the process represented by the first dot is waiting for a resource being used by the second. Mathematicians call the resulting picture a directed graph. What property of the directed graph is equivalent to deadlock in the system?

3.5 Networks

A typical early computer network consisted of isolated machines that could do little more than transfer files over temporary telephone connections using software tacked onto the machines' operating systems in the form of utility software. Today, much of the software for handling network functions is still implemented in the utility software form, although modern operating systems, being designed with networking in mind, are beginning to incorporate many of these features. For instance, software implementing the TCP/IP protocol suite (which we will learn about shortly) is supplied today as a part of the UNIX operating system. In this section and the next we address some of the topics associated with this expanded realm of operating systems.

Network Classification

Each computer network falls into one of two broad categories: **local area networks** (**LANs**) and **wide area networks** (**WANs**). A LAN normally consists of a collection of computers in a single building or building complex. For example, the computers used on a university campus or those used in a manufacturing plant might be connected by a LAN. A WAN links machines that may be on opposite sides of a city or the world. The major distinction between LANs and WANs is found in the technologies used to establish communication paths. (Satellite links, for example, are appropriate for WANs, but not for LANs.) Today, the software that deals with these distinctions is usually isolated in a small part of the overall network software package, so, from a software perspective, the distinction between LANs and WANs is becoming less and less important.

Another dichotomy of networks is based on whether the network is comprised of hardware and software from a single vendor or implemented as a conglomerate of products from different manufacturers. Networks of the former type are sometimes called closed networks (or proprietary networks), and networks of the latter variety are known as open networks. (Actually, *open* refers to the fact that the specifications for the network components are open to the public, which leads to compatibility among the products of different vendors and thus indirectly implies that the network consists of equipment and software from competing sources.) Instances of closed networks are most common among LANs because in these cases a single organization is usually in charge of the entire network. In contrast, WANs tend to be open networks because they often involve different organizations, each with its own equipment. The Internet is an open system. Indeed, communication throughout the Internet is governed by an open collection of standards known as the TCP/IP protocol suite,[1] which we discuss in the next section.

Another way of classifying networks is based on the topology of the network, which refers to the pattern in which the machines are connected. Figure 3.10 represents some of the popular topologies including the ring, in which the machines are connected in a circular fashion; the bus, in which the machines are all connected to a common communication line called a bus; the star, in which one machine serves as a hub to which all the others are connected; and the irregular topology, in which the machines are connected in what appears to be a haphazard manner. The irregular topology is common in WANs, whereas the ring and bus topologies are usually found in local environments where the network's construction is more likely to fall under a single authority.

The Internet

The Internet is a network of networks that has evolved and grown over time. Its origins were in a research program initiated in 1973 by the Defense Advanced Research Projects Agency (DARPA). The goal of this program was to develop the ability to connect a variety of computer networks so that they could function as a single, reliable network. Today, the Internet is a combination of WANs and LANs containing a "backbone" network constructed from high-speed, high-capacity communication paths that span the United States. To this backbone, other networks, which tend to be more centrally located, connect at designated machines, known as **routers.** These networks, in turn, connect through other routers to other networks. In this manner, a worldwide network of millions of machines, each called a **host,** has evolved and continues to evolve on a daily basis.

Internet Addressing Conceptually, the Internet can be viewed as a collection of network clusters known as **domains** (Fig. 3.11), each of which normally consists of those networks operated by a single organization such as a university, company, or government institution. Each domain is an autonomous system that can be configured as the local authority desires, perhaps even as a global collection of WANs.

The address of a machine (a host) on the Internet is a bit pattern (currently 32 bits long) consisting of two parts—a pattern identifying the domain in which the host resides and a pattern identifying the particular host within the domain. The part of the address identifying the domain, the **network identifier,** is assigned by the InterNIC (Internet Network Information Center) at the time the domain is established and registered with the InterNIC. It is this registration process that ensures that each domain in the Internet has a unique network identifier. The portion

[1] This common thread technically defines the boundary of the Internet. However, this definition is being challenged by the fact that organizations with existing proprietary networks are connecting to the Internet through machines known as gateways that convert between the TCP/IP protocol standards and those used by the proprietary network. Thus the term *the Internet* is sometimes used in reference to a broader system than that included in the technical sense.

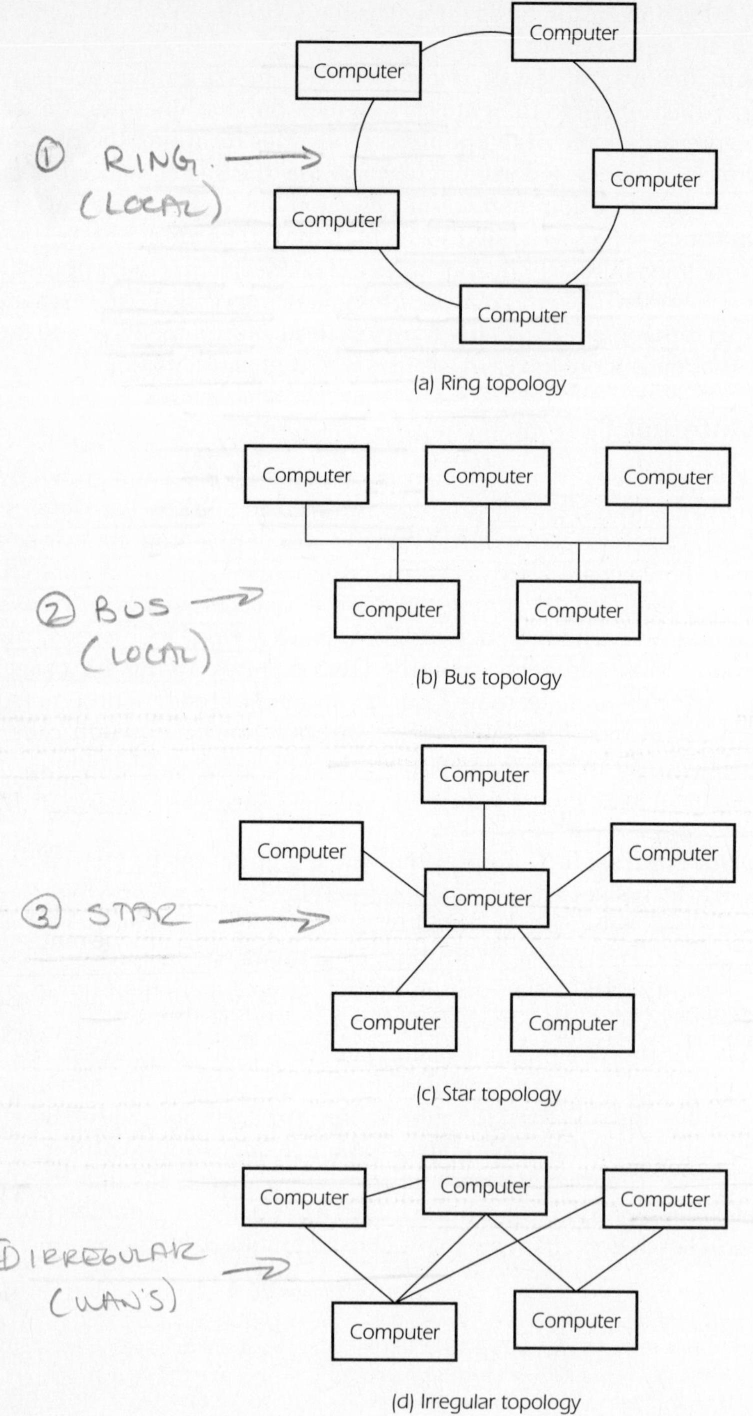

Figure 3.10 Network topologies

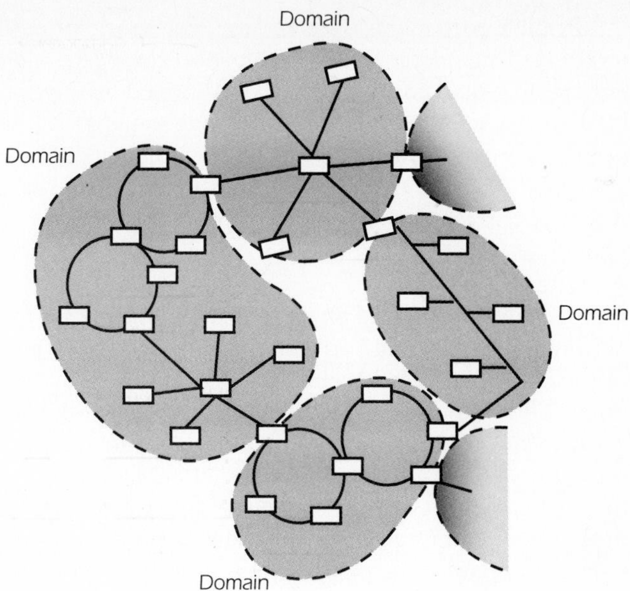

Figure 3.11 Local networks grouped into domains

of the address that identifies a particular host within a domain, the **host address,** is assigned by the domain's local authority. For example, the network identifier of Addison Wesley Longman, Inc. is `192.207.177` (network identifiers are traditionally written in dotted decimal notation; see Exercise 8 at the end of Section 1.4). In turn, a machine within this domain would have an address such as `192.207.177.133`, the last byte of which is the host address.

Addresses in bit pattern form are rarely conducive to human consumption. For this reason the InterNIC also assigns each domain a unique mnemonic address known as a **domain name.** Each local authority is then free to extend this domain name to obtain mnemonic names for the hosts within its domain. For example, the domain name of Addison Wesley Longman, Inc. is `aw.com`. An individual machine within that domain may be identified as `mozart.aw.com`.

The dotted notation used in mnemonic addresses is not related to the dotted decimal notation used to represent addresses in bit pattern form. Instead, the sections in a mnemonic address identify the host's location within a hierarchical classification system. In particular, the address `mozart.aw.com` indicates a host known as `mozart` within the institution `aw` within the class of commercial institutions `com`. In the case of large domains, a local authority may break its domain into subdomains, in which case the mnemonic addresses of the hosts within the domain may be longer. For example, suppose Nowhere University was assigned the domain name `nu.edu` and chose to divide its domain into subdomains. Then, a host at Nowhere University could have an address such as `laststop.compsc.nu.edu`, meaning that the host `laststop` is in the subdomain `compsc` within the institution `nu` within the class of educational domains `edu`.

For the purpose of transferring messages among individual users of the Internet (a system known as **e-mail,** short for electronic mail), each local authority assigns an e-mail address to each authorized user within its domain. This address consists of a character string identifying the user, followed by a `@`, and finally the domain name for the machine assigned the task of handling the domain's e-mail activities. Thus the e-mail address of an individual at Addison Wesley Longman, Inc. might appear as `wshakespeare@mozart.aw.com`. In other words, the host known as `mozart` within the domain `aw.com` handles e-mail for the user `wshakespeare`.

Each domain's local authority is responsible for maintaining a directory containing the mnemonic address and the corresponding numeric Internet address of those hosts within its domain that are to be accessible from outside the domain. This directory is implemented on a designated machine within the domain in the form of a server, called a **name server,** that responds to requests regarding address information. Together, all of the name servers throughout the Internet constitute an Internet-wide directory system that is used to convert addresses in mnemonic form into their equivalent numeric forms. In particular, when a human requests that a message be sent to a destination given in mnemonic form, this system of name servers is used to convert that mnemonic address into its equivalent bit-pattern form that is compatible with the Internet software. Normally, such a task is completed in a fraction of a second.

When an organization decides to join the Internet, it can either become a part of an existing domain or find a point in the Internet at which it can place a router and establish its own domain. The advantage of establishing a new domain is that the organization has local authority over its facilities rather than being subject to the authority of another organization. To establish a new domain, the organization must register with the InterNIC to obtain a network identifier and a domain name.

An individual normally obtains access to the Internet through membership in an organization with a domain. Several companies offer Internet access to individuals on a commercial basis. These companies, which normally have established their own domain in the Internet, provide software on their machines that allows their customers to establish telephone connections. Through such a connection a customer can access the Internet services to which he or she has subscribed.

The World Wide Web In addition to being a means of communicating via e-mail, the Internet has become a means of propagating information via **hypertext** documents. Hypertext documents contain specific words, phrases, or images that are linked to other documents. A reader of a hypertext document can access these related documents as desired, usually by pointing and clicking with the mouse or using the arrow keys on the keyboard. For example, suppose the sentence "The orchestra's performance of 'Bolero' by Maurice Ravel was outstanding" appeared in a hypertext document and the name *Maurice Ravel* was linked to another document—perhaps giving information about the composer. A reader might choose to view that associated material by pointing to the name *Maurice Ravel* with the mouse and pressing the mouse button.

In this manner, a reader of hypertext documents can explore related documents or follow a train of thought from document to document. As portions of various documents are linked to other documents, an intertwined web of related information is formed. When implemented on a network, the documents within such a web can reside on different machines, forming a network-wide web. Similarly, the web that has evolved on the Internet spans the entire globe and is known as the **World Wide Web.**

Software packages that assist readers of hypertext with the task of traversing hypertext links tend to fall into one of two categories: programs that play the role of clients and programs that play the role of servers. A client resides on the reader's machine and is charged with the tasks of obtaining materials requested by the user and presenting these materials to the user in an organized manner. It is the client that provides the user interface that allows a user to browse within the Web. In turn, a client is often referred to as a **browser,** or sometimes as a Web browser. A server resides on a machine containing documents to be accessed. Its task is to provide access to the documents on its machine as requested by a client. In summary, a user gains access to hypertext documents by communicating with a browser residing on the user's machine, and this browser fulfills the reader's requests by soliciting the services of the hypertext servers scattered throughout the Internet.

The collection of browsers available today include Lynx, Mosaic, and Netscape Navigator. They vary with the types of documents they can handle. Lynx, for example, is designed to handle only traditional hypertext documents consisting of text. Other browsers are capable of handling documents consisting of sound, photographs, and video. Such documents are sometimes referred to as **hypermedia** to distinguish them from traditional hypertext.

Creating hypertext requires a method of establishing links between documents. For this purpose, each document is identified by a unique address, a **uniform resource locator (URL),** through which a browser can contact the proper server and request the desired document. A typical URL is described in Fig. 3.12. At many hosts in the Internet, a particular document is designated as

Figure 3.12 A typical URL

```
http://mozart.aw.com/authors/Shakespeare/Julius_Caesar.html
```

Document name

Directory path indicating the location of the document within the host's file system

Mnemonic name of host holding the document

Protocol required to access the document. In this case it is the hypertext transfer protocol (http).

the default document. In these cases, this default document can be referenced by a short URL that contains only the protocol and the mnemonic name of the host.

A hypertext document is similar to a traditional text document in that its text is coded character by character using a system such as ASCII. The distinction is that a hypertext document also contains special markers that, among other things, allow the document's author to indicate which items within the document are to be linked to other documents and to provide the URLs required for these links. This system of markers is known as **Hypertext Markup Language (HTML).** Thus it is in terms of HTML that a hypertext author describes the information that a browser needs to perform its task.

Security

When a machine is connected to a network, it becomes accessible to many potential users. The problems encountered fall into two general categories: unauthorized access to information and vandalism. One approach to solving the problem of unauthorized access is to use passwords, either to control access to the machine itself or to control access to particular items of data. Unfortunately, passwords can be obtained by trickery. The most common method is to try the most obvious passwords and see whether they work. For example, users who fear forgetting their passwords may use their own names as passwords. Dates such as birthdays are also popular passwords.

In an effort to thwart those playing the guess-the-password game, operating systems can be designed to report any avalanche of incorrect passwords. Operating systems are also designed to tell each user when his or her account was last used each time the user starts a new session. This method allows users to detect any unauthorized use of their accounts. A more sophisticated defense against password guessers is to create the illusion of success (called a trapdoor) when false passwords are given and to proceed to give the intruder misinformation while recording the intruder's origin.

Another approach to protecting data from unauthorized access is to encrypt the data, the idea being that even if the data are obtained by an intruder, the information remains safe. For this purpose a variety of encryption techniques have been developed and continue to be developed.

The problem of vandalism is exemplified by the occurrence of such afflictions as computer viruses and network worms, both terms designed to awake the popular interest more than technically identify a particular type of vandalism. In general, a **virus** is a program segment that attaches itself to other programs in the computer system. For example, a virus may insert itself at the beginning of a program already in the system, so each time the host program is executed, the virus is performed first. When executed, the virus may perform malicious acts that are readily noticeable or merely search for other programs to which it can attach copies of itself. If an infected program is transferred to a new machine, either via a network or via a floppy disk, the virus will begin to infect programs on the new machine as soon as the transferred program is executed. In this manner, the virus moves from machine to machine. In some cases, viruses are designed to spread themselves to other programs until a predetermined condition, such as the arrival of a particular date, is met and then perform more malicious vandalism. This increases the likelihood that the virus will be spread to numerous machines before it is detected.

The term **worm** normally refers to an autonomous program that transfers itself through a network, taking up residence in machines and forwarding copies of itself through the network. As in the case of viruses, these programs can be designed merely to replicate themselves or to perform additional vandalism.

As the popularity of networks increases, the potential for damage from unauthorized access to information and vandalism also grows. This leads to a multitude of questions regarding the wisdom of placing sensitive information on a networked machine, the liability for the release of inadequately protected information, and the liability for vandalism. In turn, the ethical and legal questions associated with these issues promise to lead to extensive debate in the future.

Questions/Exercises

1. What is an open network?
2. What is a router?
3. What are the components of the complete Internet address of a host machine?
4. What is a URL? a browser?
5. In a LAN based on the ring topology, what is a disadvantage of restricting the transfer of messages to a single direction?

3.6 Network Protocols

The rules that govern the communication between different components within a computer system are called **protocols** in recognition of the protocols used in society to govern the interactions among people. Within a computer network protocols define the details of each activity, including how messages are addressed, how the right to transmit messages is delegated among the machines, and how the duties of packaging messages for transmission and unpacking received messages are to be handled. Let us begin by considering protocols for controlling the right of a machine to transmit its own messages over the network.

Controlling Transmission Privileges

One approach to coordinating the right to transmit messages is the token ring protocol for networks with the ring topology. In this protocol, each machine transmits messages only to its "right" and receives messages only from its "left," as shown in Fig. 3.13. A message from one machine to another must therefore be forwarded counterclockwise around the network until it reaches its destination. When the message reaches its destination, the destination machine keeps a copy of it and forwards a copy around the ring. When the forwarded copy reaches the originating

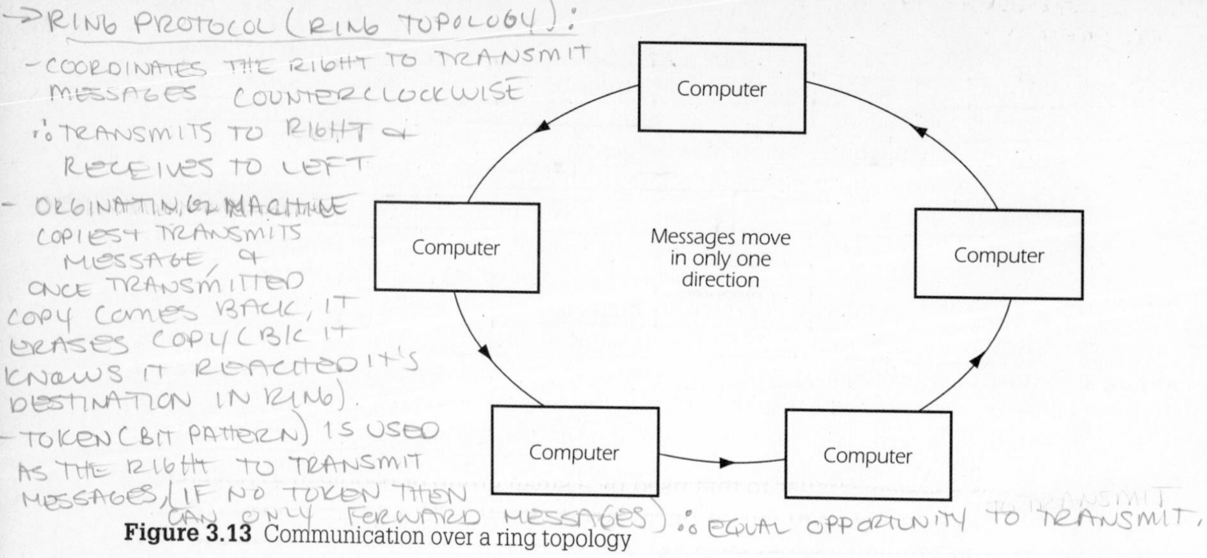

Figure 3.13 Communication over a ring topology

machine, that machine knows that the message must have reached its destination and removes the message from the ring. Of course, this system depends on intermachines cooperation. If each machine insists on constantly transmitting messages of its own rather than forwarding those of the other machines, nothing will be accomplished.

To solve this problem, a unique bit pattern, called a token, is passed around the ring. Possession of this token gives a machine the authority to transmit its own message; without the token, a machine is only allowed to forward messages. Normally, each machine merely relays the token from left to right in the same manner in which it relays messages. If, however, the machine receiving the token has messages of its own to introduce to the network, it transmits one message while holding the token. When this message has completed its cycle around the ring, the machine forwards the token to the next machine in the ring. Likewise, when the next machine receives the token, it can either forward the token immediately or transmit its own new message before sending the token on to the next machine. In this manner, each machine in the network has equal opportunity to introduce messages of its own as the token circles around the ring.

Another protocol for coordinating the right to transmit is found in an Ethernet, which is a popular version of a bus topology network. In an Ethernet the right to transmit messages is controlled by a protocol known as CSMA/CD (Carrier Sense, Multiple Access with Collision Detection). This protocol dictates that each message transmitted by any machine be broadcast to all the machines on the bus (Fig. 3.14). Each machine monitors all the messages but keeps only those addressed to itself. To transmit a message, a machine waits until the bus is silent, at which time it begins transmitting while continuing to monitor the bus. If another machine also begins transmitting, both machines detect the clash and pause for a brief random period of time before trying to transmit again. The re-

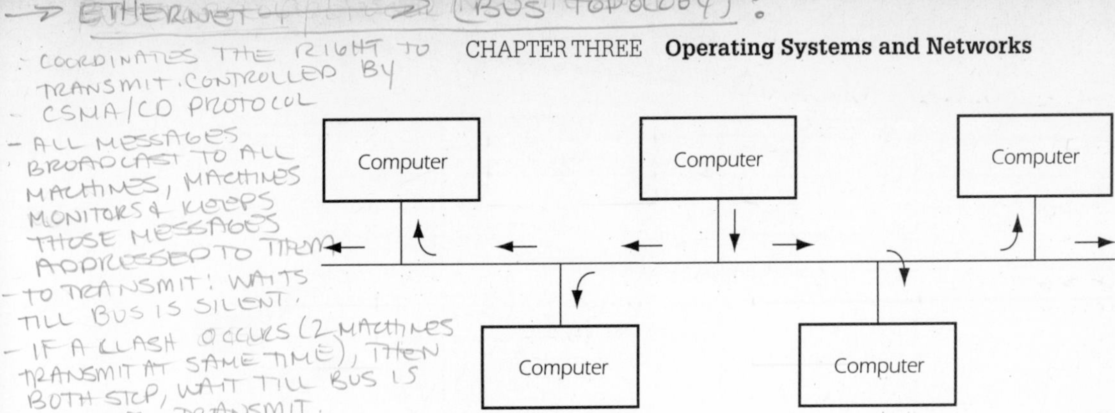

Figure 3.14 Communication over a bus topology

sult is a system similar to that used by a small group of people in a conversation. If two people start to talk at once, they both stop. The difference is that people may go through a series such as, "I'm sorry, what were you going to say." "No, no. You go first," whereas under the CSMA/CD protocol each machine merely tries again.

The Layered Approach to Network Software

A major task of network software is to provide the abstract tools required for transferring messages across the network. Indeed, such tools form the infrastructure on which the client/server model is based. Our goal in studying the structure of this software is twofold: A basic understanding of this structure is beneficial to understanding the Internet, and the layered approach exemplifies many of the principles on which large software systems are based.

An Analogy We first consider the following analogy: Suppose your company wants to send replacement parts to a customer in a distant city. Your task is to collect the parts and to package them according to the specifications of a shipping company. You then deliver the package, appropriately addressed, to the shipping company of your choice. At this point, your job is complete; responsibility for the parts has been passed to the shipper.

Of course, the shipping company does not view its task as transporting replacement parts. Instead, its task is to transport a package of a certain weight and certain dimensions to a designated location by a designated time. The shipper can choose to send the package by train, truck, ship, or airplane as long as these specifications are met. Hence, your package, along with others, may be placed in a container conforming to airline requirements. Having conformed to the specifications of the airline, the shipping company transfers the responsibility for the parts to the airline.

At this point, the airline has the task of transporting a large container from one airport to another. Depending on its particular cargo load, it may choose to place that container on a direct flight, send it through an intermediate stop, or perhaps subcontract the transportation of the container to another airline.

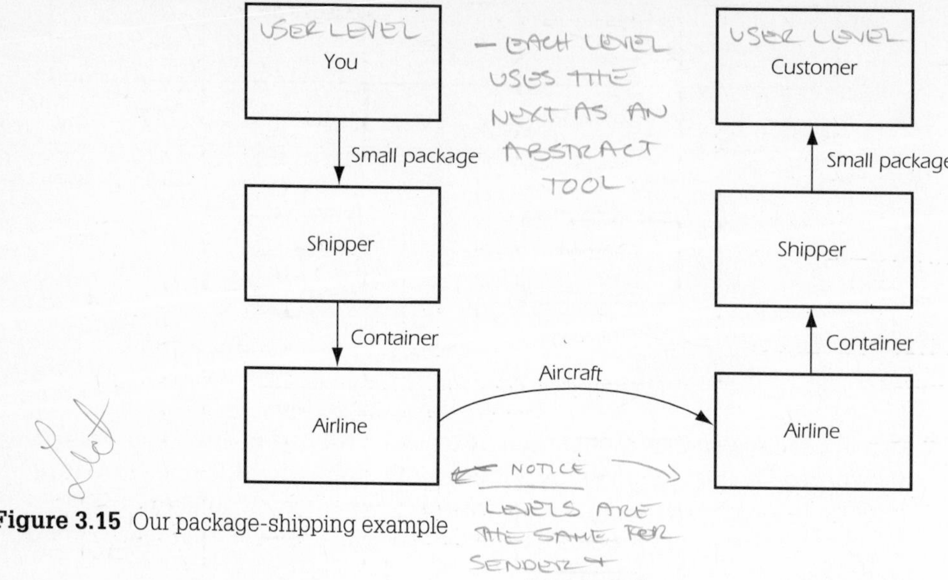

Figure 3.15 Our package-shipping example

In any case, the airline ultimately delivers the container to the shipping company in the destination city according to the directions provided by the shipping company. The shipping company unpacks the container and delivers your package to your customer according to the address you provided.

In summary, the transportation of the parts is carried out by a three-level hierarchy (Fig. 3.15): the user level (consisting of you and your customer), the shipping company, and the airline. Each level uses the next lower level as an abstract tool. (You are not concerned with the details of the shipping company, and the shipping company is not concerned with the internal operations of the airline.) Each level in the hierarchy has representatives at both the origin and the destination, with the representatives at the destination tending to do the reverse of their counterparts at the origin. Such is the case with software for controlling communication over a network, except that there are normally more than three levels and each level, called a layer, consists of a collection of software routines rather than people and businesses.

This division of labor into a hierarchy of layers has two important consequences that are common objectives in any hierarchical design. First, it breaks the overall task into manageable subtasks, each with it specific goals. Second, the hierarchy establishes well-defined boundaries between the subtasks at which standard interfaces can be implemented. By conforming to these standard interfaces, different solutions for the same subtask can be substituted for one another without disrupting the rest of the system. Indeed, the solution of each subtask can be used as an abstract tool in the solution of higher-level tasks.

The Internet Software Hierarchy The four layers of the Internet software are summarized in Fig. 3.16. The column on the left represents the software layers

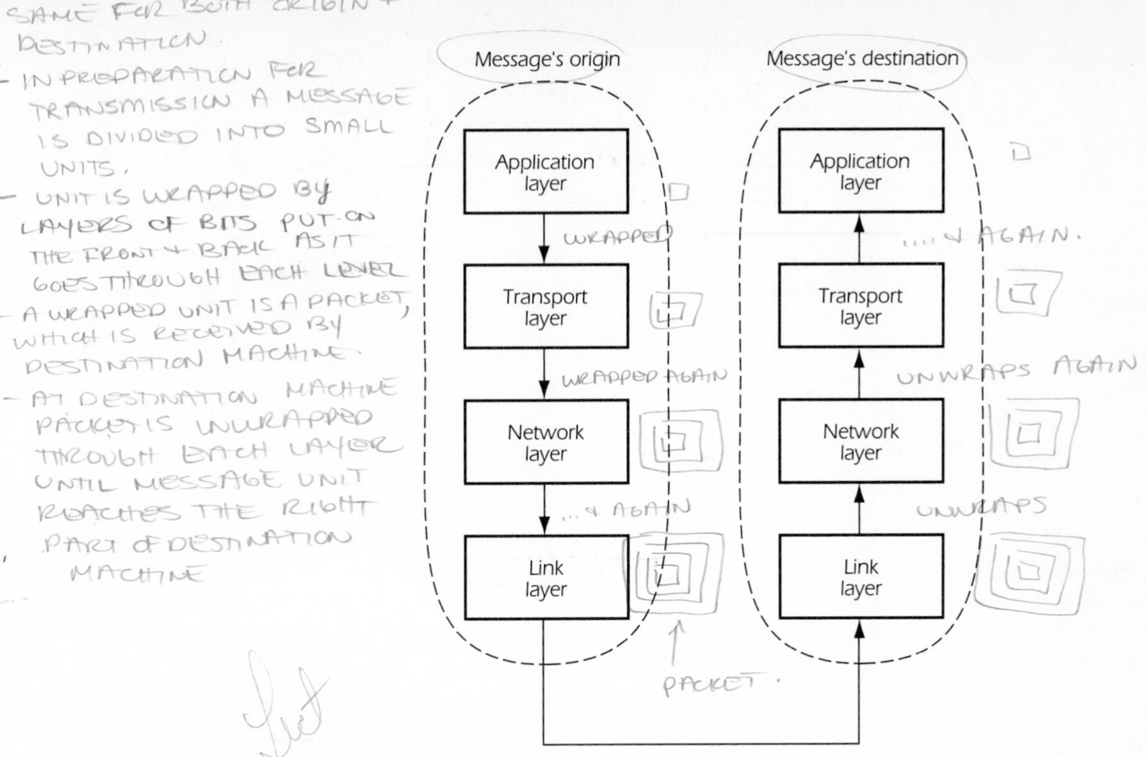

Figure 3.16 The Internet software layers

used by the machine at a message's origin; the column on the right represents the layers used by the machine at a message's destination. As in our shipping analogy, the software layers at the origin and destination are the same. The arrows in Fig. 3.16 represent the path traversed by a message. In preparation for transmission, a message may be divided into small units. Then, each message unit is repeatedly "wrapped" by the software layers as the unit works its way down the left column. This wrapping consists of additional bits appended to the front and back of the unit. A wrapped unit is referred to as a **packet.** Thus the packets that are received at the destination machine are actually packets within packets. These nested packets are unwrapped, layer by layer, as the message unit works its way up the right column of Fig. 3.16 until the units are finally reassembled and delivered to the appropriate software unit at the destination machine.

It is not unusual for the size of a packet's wrapping to exceed the size of the message unit found within. Message units consisting of single bytes are common, whereas each packet contains more than 50 bytes of wrapping. Although this appears to be inefficient, the system works quite well.

The uppermost layer in the Internet software hierarchy is the application layer. It contains the software that handles the activities unique to a particular application. For example, in the case of electronic mail, the application layer software stores messages that have been received and oversees the transmission of messages. In the case of transferring files from one machine to another, the application layer software communicates with the system's file manager to obtain access to the file being transferred and likewise communicates with the file manager at the destination machine to place the transferred file in the new machine's file system.

We should distinguish between software contained in the Internet's application layer and software viewed as application software in our classification scheme in Section 3.2. Although the names are similar, the Internet's application layer software is usually implemented as utility software and consists of routines that are used as abstract tools by traditional applications. The various software packages that allow a user to receive and send e-mail via a GUI fall within the traditional class of application software but are not themselves part of the Internet's application layer. They do, however, use the abstract tools provided by the Internet's application layer to accomplish their tasks. Other examples of application software that rely on the services of the Internet's application layer include the Web browsers used for accessing hypertext documents.

The transport layer is used by the application layer in much the same way that you use the shipping company when sending the replacement parts. That is, the application layer hands to the transport layer the message to be sent along with the address of the destination. Just as it is your responsibility to provide an address compatible with the specifications of the shipping company, it is the application layer's responsibility to provide an address that is compatible with the transport layer. It is to fulfill this need that the application layer requires the services of the name servers within the Internet to translate mnemonic addresses used by humans into network-compatible addresses.

Having received the message and its address, the transport layer divides the message into segments of a size compatible with the transport layer's design, adds sequence numbers to these segments so that the original message can be reconstructed, attaches the destination address to each of these segments, and hands the resulting packets to the network layer.

The network layer is responsible for seeing that the packets it receives are properly forwarded through the Internet to their final destinations. It does so by appending an intermediate destination address to each packet that is determined as follows: If the final destination of the packet is within the current network, the appended address will be a duplicate of the ultimate destination address; otherwise, the appended address will be that of a router in the current network. In this way, a packet destined for a machine within the current network will be sent to that machine, whereas a packet destined for a machine outside the current network will be sent to a router where it will be transferred into an adjacent network. The network layer, then, wraps the packets it receives from the transport layer with additional wrapping that reflects the intermediate address rather than the original address. These extended packets are then handed to the link layer.

The link layer's responsibility is to deal with the communication details particular to the individual network in which the machine resides. If that network is a token ring, the link layer must wait for possession of the token before transmitting. If the network uses CSMA/CD, the link layer must listen for a silent bus before transmitting. Moreover, each individual network within the Internet has its own addressing system that is independent from the addressing system used by the Internet. After all, many of these networks functioned on their own long before their owners decided to attach them to the Internet. Thus the link layer must translate the Internet addresses appearing on the outside of the packets into the appropriate local addressing system and add these translated addresses to the packet in the form of an additional layer of wrapping.

As in our replacement parts analogy, each layer in the Internet software hierarchy also plays a role in the process of receiving messages, which is roughly that of undoing the task performed by its counterpart at the message's origin. Thus the link layer receives packets from the network communication, strips off the outer wrapping (the address in local network compatible form) that was placed there by the link layer at the message's origin, and hands the underlying packets to its network layer.

Each time the network layer receives a packet from its link layer, it strips off the intermediate Internet address that was previously appended by its counterpart and considers the ultimate destination address that it finds underneath. If this is its own address, the network layer hands the underlying packet to its transport layer; otherwise, the network layer knows that the underlying packet should be forwarded on through the Internet. In this case, it must rewrap the underlying packet by appending a new intermediate address to the segment and send the rewrapped packet on its way by returning it to the link layer. In this manner, packets hop from one machine to another until they reach their final destinations. At each intermediate step, it is the network layer that is charged with determining the destination of the next hop.

To assist with this readdressing process, the network layer maintains a routing table that contains the final destination addresses that it has dealt with recently and the intermediate addresses to which it forwarded each of those packets. The various network layers within the Internet routinely exchange the data in their routing tables so that information about forwarding addresses tends to propagate through the Internet. Each network layer keeps only that information that it thinks it may need and also deletes stale entries from its routing table on a routine basis so that the table does not grow too large. The contents of the routing tables throughout the Internet are therefore dynamic, and it is possible for packets representing different parts of the same message to find their way through the Internet along different paths.

If the network layer unwraps a packet and discovers that the underlying packet is addressed to its own machine, it hands the underlying packet to its transport layer. Thus it is only the link and network layers that are involved in the forwarding of packets destined to other machines. The transport layer, as well as the application layer, are shielded from this distraction and see only those packets addressed to their machine (Fig. 3.17). As the transport layer receives packets from the network layer, it extracts the underlying message segments and reconstructs the original message according to the sequence numbers supplied by the transport layer at the message's origin. Once the message is

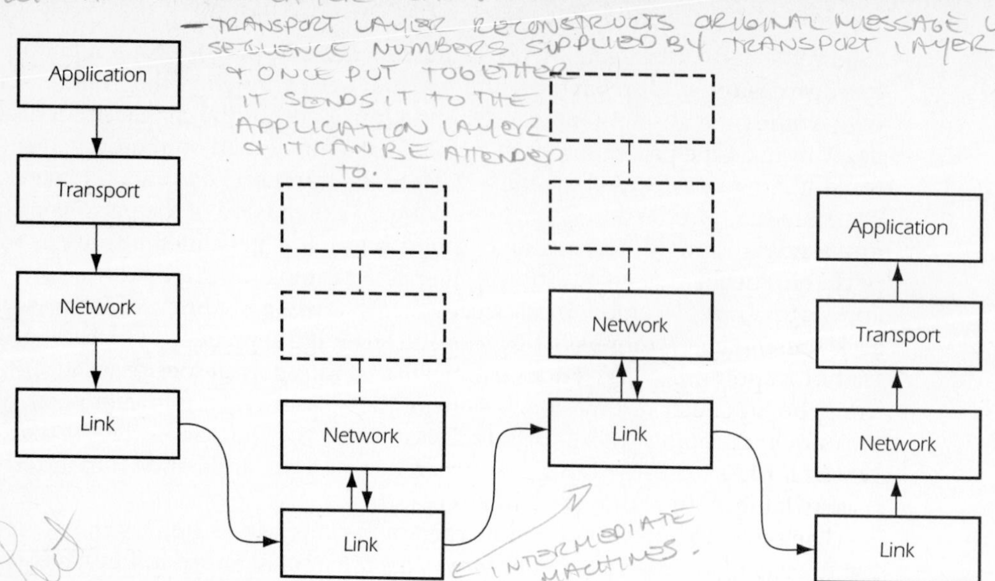

Figure 3.17 A path of a data unit through the Internet involving two intermediate machines

complete, the transport layer hands it to its application layer, where it can be properly attended to.

In conclusion, communication over the Internet involves the interaction of several layers of software residing on many machines throughout the system. In this context, it is amazing that the response time of the Internet is measured in milliseconds. Indeed, most transactions appear to take place instantaneously.

The TCP/IP Protocol Suite

The demand for open networks has generated a need for published standards by which manufacturers can supply equipment and software that function properly with products from other vendors. One standard that has resulted is the Open System Interconnection (OSI) reference model, produced by the International Standards Organization (ISO). This standard is based on a seven-level hierarchy as opposed to the four-level system used by the Internet. It has become an often-quoted model because it carries the authority of the International Standards Organization, but it has not been readily implemented, mainly because before it was established the TCP/IP protocol suite had already been developed, implemented, widely publicized, and proven reliable as the protocol system for the Internet.

The TCP/IP protocol suite is a collection of protocols defining the four-level hierarchy used by the Internet. Actually, TCP (Transmission Control Protocol) and IP (Internet Protocol) are the names of only two of the protocols in this collection—so the fact that the entire collection is referred to as the TCP/IP protocol suite is rather misleading. More precisely, TCP defines a version of the transport layer. We say a *version* because the TCP/IP protocol suite provides for two ways of implementing the transport layer, the second being defined by UDP (User Datagram

Protocol). This is analogous to the fact that when shipping the replacement parts to your customer, you have a choice of different shipping companies, each of which offers the same basic service but with its own unique characteristics. Thus, depending on the particular quality of service required, the application layer software may choose to send data via a TCP or UDP version of the transport layer.

There are two basic differences between TCP and UDP. The first is that before sending data, a transport layer based on TCP sends a message to the transport layer at the destination telling it that data are about to be sent and which application layer software is to receive the data. It then waits for this message to be acknowledged before starting to send message segments. In this manner, a TCP transport layer is said to establish a connection before sending data. A transport layer based on UDP does not establish such a connection prior to sending data. It merely sends the data to the address it was given and forgets about it. For all it knows, the destination machine may not even be operational. For this reason, UDP is called a connectionless protocol.

The second basic difference between TCP and UDP is that TCP transport layers at the origin and destination work together by means of acknowledgments and segment retransmissions to confirm that all segments of a message are successfully transferred to the destination. In turn, TCP is called a reliable protocol, whereas UDP, which does not offer such retransmission services, is said to be an unreliable protocol. This does not mean that UDP is a poor choice. Indeed, a transport layer based on UDP is more streamlined than a layer based on TCP, and thus if an application is prepared to handle the potential consequences of UDP, that option is the better choice.

IP is the Internet's standard for the network layer. Among its features is that each time an IP network layer prepares a packet to be handed to the link layer, it appends a value called a hop count, or time to live, to that packet. This value is the limit to the number times the packet should be forwarded as it tries to find its way through the Internet. Each time an IP network layer forwards a packet, it decrements that packet's hop count by one. With this information the network layer can protect the Internet from packets circling endlessly within the system. Although the Internet continues to grow on a daily basis, an initial hop count of 64 remains more than sufficient to allow a packet to find its way through the maze of LANs, WANs, and routers.

Questions/Exercises

1. What layers of the Internet software hierarchy are used to forward an incoming message to another machine?
2. What are some differences between a transport layer based on the TCP protocol and another based on the UDP protocol?
3. How does the Internet software ensure that messages are not relayed within the Internet forever?
4. What keeps a host on the Internet from recording copies of all the messages passing through it?

CHAPTER REVIEW PROBLEMS *(Asterisked problems are associated with optional sections.)*

1. Explain how operating systems can be used to make different machines appear to have the same characteristics.
2. List four activities of a typical operating system.
3. Summarize the distinction between batch processing and interactive processing.
4. What is the difference between interactive processing and real-time processing?
5. What is a multitasking operating system?
6. What information is contained in a process table within an operating system?
7. What is the difference between a process that is ready and a process that is waiting?
8. What is the difference between virtual memory and the main memory actually in a computer?
9. What complications could arise in a time-sharing system if two processes require access to the same file at the same time? Are there cases in which the file manager should grant such requests? Are there cases in which the file manager should deny such requests?
10. Define load balancing and scaling in the context of multiprocessor architectures.
11. Summarize the booting process.
12. Suppose a time-sharing operating system is allotting time slices of 50 milliseconds. If it normally takes 8 milliseconds to position a disk's read/write head over the desired track and another 17 milliseconds for the desired data to rotate around to the read/write head, how much of a program's time slice can be spent waiting for a read operation from a disk to take place? If the machine is capable of executing one instruction each microsecond, how many instructions can be executed during this waiting period? (This is why a time-sharing system normally allows another process to run while the first process is waiting for the services of a peripheral device.)
13. List five resources whose use a multitasking operating system might have to coordinate.
14. A process is said to be I/O-bound if it requires a lot of I/O operations, whereas a process that consists of mostly computations within the CPU/memory system is said to be compute-bound. If both a compute-bound process and an I/O-bound process are waiting for a time slice, which should be given priority? Why?
15. Would greater throughput be achieved by a system running two processes in a time-sharing environment if both processes were I/O-bound (refer to Problem 14) or if one was I/O-bound and the other was compute-bound? Why?
16. Identify the components of a process's state.
17. Identify a situation in a time-sharing system in which a process does not consume the entire time slice allocated to it.
18. List in chronological order the major events that take place when a process is interrupted.
19. Describe the client/server model.
20. Identify two ways of classifying computer networks.
21. Describe the components of the e-mail address `kermit@frogs.animals.com`.
22. Define each of the following:
    a. Name server
    b. Domain
    c. Router
    d. Host
23. The text referred to the length of each host address on the Internet as "currently 32 bits." This wording is intended to imply that longer addresses will soon be required to provide a unique address to each host on the Internet. What is the maximum number of unique addresses possible in the current system?
24. What is the difference between an open network and a closed network?
25. Define each of the following:
    a. Hypertext
    b. HTML
    c. Browser
26. What is the World Wide Web?
27. Identify the components of the following URL and describe the meaning of each.
    `http://frogs.animals.com/animals/moviestars/kermit.html`

28. In the context of computer networks, what is the difference between a worm and a virus?

***29.** Explain an important use for the test-and-set instruction found in many machine languages. Why is it important for the entire test-and-set process to be implemented as a single instruction?

***30.** A banker with only $100,000 loans $50,000 to each of two customers. Later, both customers return with the story that before they can repay their loans they must each borrow another $10,000 to complete the business deals in which their previous loans are involved. The banker resolves this deadlock by borrowing the additional funds from another source and passing on this loan (with an increase in the interest rate) to the two customers. Which of the three conditions for deadlock has the banker removed?

***31.** Students who want to enroll in Model Railroading II at the local university are required to obtain permission from the instructor and pay a laboratory fee. The two requirements are fulfilled independently in either order and at different locations on campus. Enrollment is limited to 20 students; this limit is maintained by both the instructor, who will grant permission to only 20 students, and the financial office, which will allow only 20 students to pay the laboratory fee. Suppose that this registration system has resulted in 19 students having successfully registered for the course, but with the final space being claimed by two students—one who has only obtained permission from the instructor and another who has only paid the fee. Which requirement for deadlock is removed by each of the following solutions to the problem:

a. Both students are allowed in the course.

b. The class size is reduced to 19, so neither of the two students is allowed to register for the course.

c. The competing students are both denied entry to the class and a third student is given the 20th space.

d. It is decided that the only requirement for entry into the course is the payment of the fee. Thus the student who has paid the fee gets into the course, and entry is denied to the other student.

***32.** Explain how deadlock can occur as two pawns approach each other in a chess game. What nonshareable resources are involved? How is such deadlock normally broken?

***33.** Suppose each nonshareable resource in a computer system is classified as a level 1, level 2, or level 3 resource. Moreover, suppose each process in the system is required to request the resources it needs according to this classification. That is, it must request all the required level 1 resources at once before requesting any level 2 resources. Once it receives the level 1 resources, it can request all the required level 2 resources, and so on. Can deadlock occur in such a system? Why or why not?

***34.** Each of two robot arms is programmed to lift assemblies from a conveyor belt, test them for tolerances, and place them in one of two bins depending on the results of the test. The assemblies arrive one at a time with a sufficient interval between them. To keep both arms from trying to grab the same assembly, the computers controlling the arms share a common memory cell. If an arm is available as an assembly approaches, its controlling computer reads the value of the common cell. If the value is nonzero, the arm lets the assembly pass. Otherwise, the controlling computer places a nonzero value in the memory cell, directs the arm to pick up the assembly, and places the value 0 back into the memory cell. What sequence of events could lead to a tug-of-war between the two arms?

***35.** Suppose each computer in a ring network is programmed to transmit simultaneously in both directions those messages that originate at that station and are addressed to all the other stations belonging to the network. Moreover, suppose this is done by first acquiring access to the communication path to the machine's left, retaining this access until access to the path to the right is acquired, and then transmitting the message. Identify the deadlock that occurs if all the machines in the network tried to originate such a message at the same time.

*36. Identify the use of a queue in the process of spooling output to a printer.

*37. The pavement in the middle of an intersection can be considered as a nonshareable resource for which cars approaching the intersection compete. A traffic light rather than an operating system is used to control the allocation of the resource. If the light is able to sense the amount of traffic arriving from each direction and is programmed to give the green light to the heavier traffic, the lighter traffic might suffer from what is called starvation. What is meant by starvation? What could happen in a multiuser computer system where routines are assigned priorities and competition for resources is always resolved strictly by priority?

*38. What problem can occur in a time-sharing system if the dispatcher always assigns time slices according to a priority system in which the priority of each task sharing time remains fixed? (*Hint:* What is the priority of the routine that just completed its time slice in comparison to the routines that are waiting, and consequently which routine gets the next time slice?)

*39. What is the similarity between deadlock and starvation? (Refer to Problem 37.) What is the difference between deadlock and starvation?

*40. What problem arises as the length of the time slices in a time-sharing system are made smaller and smaller? What about as they become longer and longer?

*41. What is the OSI reference model?

*42. In a network based on the bus topology, the bus is a nonshareable resource for which the machines must compete in order to transmit messages. How is deadlock controlled in this context?

*43. Suppose the machines in Figure 3.10(a) are called A, B, C, D, and E (starting at the top center and moving clockwise) and that the privilege to transmit a new message is controlled by a token. If machine D has a message to transmit, and the token is currently between machines B and C, which machines will have an opportunity to transmit before machine D?

*44. Token-based protocols can be used to control the right to transmit in networks that do not have a ring topology. Design a token-based protocol to control the right to transmit in a LAN with a bus topology.

*45. List the four layers in the Internet software hierarchy and identify a task performed by each layer.

*46. In what way could TCP be considered a better protocol for implementing the transport layer than UDP? In what way could UDP be considered better than TCP?

*47. What does it mean to say that UDP is a connectionless protocol?

QUESTIONS OF ETHICS

The following questions are provided to help you understand some of the ethical/social/legal issues associated with the field of computing as well as investigate your own beliefs and their foundations. The goal is not merely to answer these questions. You should also consider why you answered as you did and whether your justifications are consistent from one question to the next.

1. Suppose you are using a multiuser operating system that allows you to view the names of the files belonging to other users as well as to view the contents of those files that are not otherwise protected. Would viewing such information without permission be similar to wandering through someone's unlocked house without permission, or would it be more like reading materials placed in a common lounge?
2. When you have access to a multiuser system, what responsibilities do you have when selecting your password?
3. To what extent do you believe that a company should be allowed to own the "look and feel" of a software package that it has produced? Would the implementation of your opinions encourage or hinder progress in software development?

4. What ethical concerns arise in a society that relies on the use of abstract tools? Are there cases in which it is unethical to use a product or service without knowing how it is produced?
5. Electronic bulletin boards allow users of networks to post messages (often anonymously) and read messages posted by others. Should the manager of such a bulletin board be held responsible for its contents? Should a telephone company be held responsible for the contents of telephone conversations? Should the manager of a grocery store be held responsible for the contents of a community bulletin board located in the store?
6. Should the use of the Internet be monitored? Should it be regulated? If so, by whom?

ADDITIONAL ACTIVITIES

1. If you know a programming language, identify the utility/application software that you use to prepare and execute a program written in that language. Can you request the execution of utility software from within a program written in that language? If so, what are those utilities and how are they requested?
2. If you have access to two operating systems, experiment with them to identify their similarities and differences. For example, you should find that both provide access to routines for formatting disks, creating and editing text files, and manipulating (copying, renaming, and deleting) files in general, but how these routines are accessed may differ. Do the routines appear to be a part of the operating system itself or implemented as utility (or application) software?
3. If you have access to an interactive multiuser operating system, how can you find out how many users are also using the system and who they are? Does the system's response become sluggish as the number of users increases? Why would you expect it to? Does the system's response seem to depend on what the various users are doing? Why would you expect it to?
4. If you have access to a multitasking operating system, experiment with different tasks to see whether you can generate a deadlock between two competing tasks. Summarize your findings in a short report.
5. Write two programs that simulate the allocation of resources to various processes as directed by you from the keyboard. One of your programs should merely detect the occurrence of deadlocks and report their occurrences to you. The other version should avoid deadlocks. Summarize the method you use in your programs to detect and avoid deadlocks.
6. If you have access to the Internet, investigate the e-mail features available to you. How can you obtain another person's address? Can you detect whether another person has read all his or her e-mail? What happens if you send e-mail to a nonexisting address?
7. If you have access to a network, investigate the topology of your LAN and any nearby LANs to which your LAN may be connected. Are these LANs a part of the Internet? If so, are they all a part of the same domain and, if so, how are their Internet addresses related?

ADDITIONAL READING

Dietel, H. M. *An Introduction to Operating Systems,* 3rd ed. Reading, Mass.: Addison-Wesley, 1994.

Shay, W. A. *Understanding Data Communications and Networks.* Boston: PWS, 1994.

Stevens, W. R. *TCP/IP Illustrated,* Volume 1. Reading, Mass: Addison-Wesley, 1994.

Tanenbaum, A. S. *Distributed Operating Systems.* Upper Saddle River, N.J.: Prentice-Hall, 1995.

Tanenbaum, A. S. *Modern Operating Systems.* Englewood Cliffs, N.J.: Prentice-Hall, 1992.

CHAPTER FOUR

Algorithms

4.1 The Concept of an Algorithm

4.2 Algorithm Representation
Primitives
Pseudocode

4.3 Algorithm Discovery
The Theory of Problem Solving
Getting a Foot in the Door

4.4 Iterative Structures
The Sequential Search Algorithm
Loop Control
The Insertion Sort Algorithm

4.5 Recursive Structures
The Binary Search Algorithm
Recursive Control
The Quick Sort Algorithm

4.6 Efficiency and Correctness
Algorithm Efficiency
Software Verification

We have seen that, before a computer can perform a task, it must be given an algorithm telling it precisely what to do; consequently, the study of algorithms is the cornerstone of computer science. In this chapter we introduce many of the fundamental concepts of this study, including the issues of algorithm discovery and representation as well as the major control concepts of iteration and recursion. In so doing we also present a few well-known algorithms for searching and sorting.

4.1 The Concept of an Algorithm

In the introductory chapter we informally defined an algorithm as a set of steps that defines how a task is performed. In this section we look more closely at this fundamental concept. We begin by emphasizing the distinction between an algorithm and its representation—a distinction that is analogous to that between a story and a book. A story is abstract, or conceptual, in nature; a book is a physical representation of a story. If a book is translated into another language or republished in a different format, it is merely the representation of the story that changes—the story itself remains the same.

In the same manner, an algorithm is abstract and distinct from its representation. A single algorithm can be represented in many ways. As an example, the algorithm for converting temperature readings from Celsius to Fahrenheit is traditionally represented as the algebraic formula

$$F = (9/5)C + 32$$

But it could be represented by the instruction

Multiply the temperature reading in Celsius by 9/5 and then add 32 to the product

or even in the form of an electronic circuit. In all these cases the underlying algorithm is the same; only the representations differ.

In the context of distinguishing between algorithms and their representations, we should also clarify the distinction between two other related concepts—programs and processes. A program is a representation of an algorithm. In fact, computer scientists use the term *program* to refer to a formal representation of an algorithm designed for computer application. We defined a process in Chapter 3 to be the activity of executing a program. Note, however, that to execute a program is to execute the algorithm represented by the program, so a process could equivalently be defined as the activity of executing an algorithm. We conclude that processes, algorithms, and programs are distinct, yet related, entities.

Consider now the formal definition of an algorithm given in Fig. 4.1, beginning with the requirement that the set of steps in an algorithm be ordered. This means that the steps in an algorithm must have a well-established structure in terms of the order in which its steps are executed. This does not mean that the steps must be executed in a sequence consisting of a first step, followed by a second, and so on. Some algorithms, known as **parallel algorithms,** for example, contain more than one sequence of steps, each designed to be executed by different processors in a multiprocessor machine. In such cases the overall algorithm does not possess a single thread of steps that conforms to the first-step, second-step scenario. Instead, the algorithm's structure is that of multiple threads that branch and reconnect as different processors perform different parts of the overall task. Other examples include algorithms executed by circuits such as the flip-flop in Section 1.1, in which each gate performs a single step of the overall algorithm. Here the steps are ordered by cause and effect, as the action of each gate propogates throughout the circuit.

An algorithm is an ordered set of unambiguous, executable steps, defining a terminating process.

Figure 4.1 The definition of an algorithm

Next, consider the requirement that an algorithm must consist of executable steps. To appreciate this condition, consider the instructions

Step 1. Make a list of all positive integers.
Step 2. Arrange this list in descending order (from largest to smallest).
Step 3. Extract the first integer from the resulting list.

These instructions do not describe an algorithm, because steps 1 and 2 are impossible to perform. One cannot make a list of all the positive integers, and the positive integers cannot be arranged in descending order. Computer scientists use the term *effective* to capture the concept of being executable. That is, to say that a step is effective means that it is doable.

Another requirement imposed by the definition in Fig. 4.1 is that the steps in an algorithm be unambiguous. This means that during execution of an algorithm, the information in the state of the process must be sufficient to determine uniquely and completely the actions required by each step. In other words, the execution of each step in an algorithm does not require creative skills. Rather, it requires only the ability to follow directions.

The distinction between an algorithm and its representation is significant. Ambiguities in an algorithm's representation are often misinterpreted as ambiguities within the underlying algorithm. A common example involves the level of detail at which an algorithm must be described. Among meteorologists the instruction "Convert the Celsius reading to its Fahrenheit equivalent" may suffice, but a layperson, requiring a more detailed description, would argue that the instruction is ambiguous. Note that the problem is not that the underlying algorithm is ambiguous but that the algorithm is not represented in enough detail for the layperson. Thus the ambiguity is in the algorithm's representation rather than in the algorithm. In the next section we will see how the concept of primitives can be used to eliminate such ambiguity problems in an algorithm's representation.

The requirement that an algorithm define a terminating process means that the execution of an algorithm must lead to an end. The origin of this requirement is in theoretical computer science, where the goal is to answer such questions as "What are the ultimate limitations of algorithmic machines?" Here computer science seeks to distinguish between problems whose answers can be obtained algorithmically and problems whose answers lie beyond the capabilities of algorithmic systems. In this context a line is drawn between processes that culminate with an answer and those that merely proceed forever without producing a result.

In more applied settings the requirement that an algorithm define a terminating process is useful in that it rules out endless processes that never produce meaningful results. For example, following the instruction "Do this step again" is of little value. There are, however, meaningful applications for nonterminating processes, including monitoring the vital signs of a hospital patient and maintaining an aircraft's attitude in flight. Some would argue that these applications involve merely the repetition of algorithms, each of which reaches an end and then automatically repeats. Others would counter that such arguments are simply attempts to cling to an overly restrictive formal definition.

Regardless of which side is correct, the fact is that the term *algorithm* is often used in applied, informal settings in reference to sets of steps that do not necessarily define terminating processes. An example is the long-division algorithm, which does not define a terminating process when dividing 1 by 3.

* LONG DIVISION ALGORITHM DOES NOT END FOR 1 ÷ BY 3 *

Questions/Exercises

1. Summarize the distinction among a process, an algorithm, and a program.
2. Give some examples of algorithms with which you are familiar. Are they really algorithms in the precise sense?
3. Identify some points of vagueness in our informal definition of an algorithm introduced in Section 0.1.
4. In what sense do the steps described by the following list of instructions fail to constitute an algorithm?

   Step 1. Take a coin out of your pocket and put it on the table.

   Step 2. Return to step 1.

4.2 Algorithm Representation

In this section we consider issues relating to an algorithm's representation. Our goal is to introduce the basic concepts of primitives and pseudocode as well as to establish a representation system for our own use.

Primitives

The representation of an algorithm requires some form of language. In the case of humans this may be a traditional natural language (English, Russian, Japanese) or perhaps the language of pictures, as demonstrated in Fig. 4.2, which describes an algorithm for folding a bird from a square piece of paper. Often, however, such natural channels of communication lead to misunderstandings, sometimes because the terminology used may have more than one meaning. The sentence, "Visiting grandchildren can be nerve-racking," could mean either that the grandchildren cause problems when they come to visit or that going to see them is problematic. Problems also arise over misunderstandings regarding the level of detail required. Few readers could successfully fold a bird from the directions given in Fig. 4.2, yet a student of origami would probably have little

Figure 4.2 Folding a bird from a square piece of paper

difficulty. In short, communication problems arise when the language used for an algorithm's representation is not precisely defined or when information is not given in adequate detail.

Computer science approaches these problems by establishing a well-defined set of building blocks from which algorithm representations can be constructed. Such a building block is called a **primitive.** Assigning precise definitions to these primitives removes many problems of ambiguity, and requiring algorithms to be described in terms of these primitives establishes a uniform level of detail. A collection of primitives along with a collection of rules stating how the primitives can be combined to represent more complex ideas constitutes a **programming language.**

Each primitive consists of two parts: its syntax and its semantics. **Syntax** refers to the primitive's symbolic representation, and **semantics** refers to the concept represented, or the meaning of the primitive. The syntax of *air* consists of three symbols, whereas the semantics is a gaseous substance surrounding the world. As an example, Fig. 4.3 presents some of the primitives used in origami,

Figure 4.3 Origami primitives

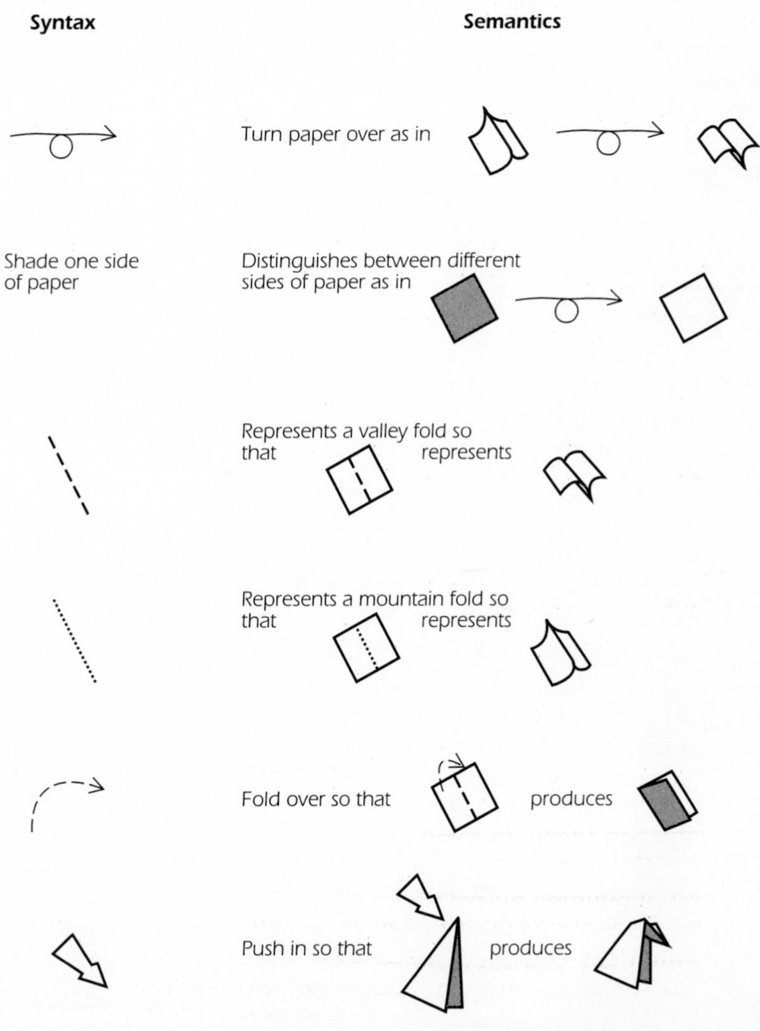

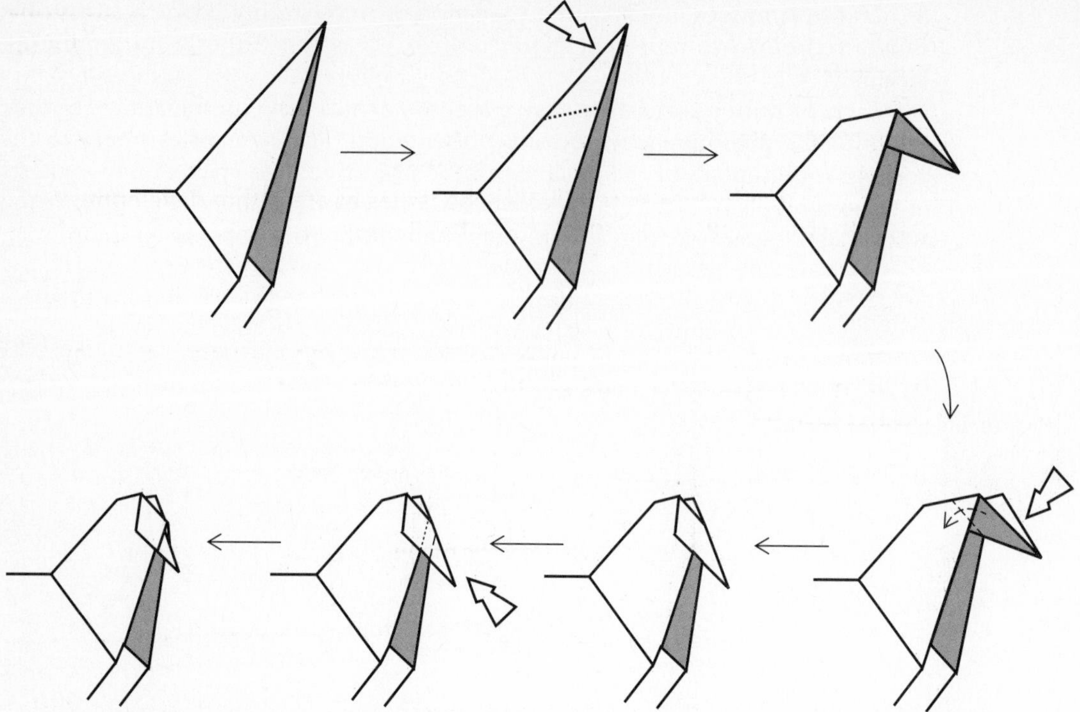

Figure 4.4 Forming the bird's head

and Fig. 4.4 shows how a portion of the bird-folding algorithm could be expressed in terms of those primitives.

To obtain a collection of primitives to use in representing algorithms for computer execution, we could turn to the individual instructions that the machine is designed to execute. If an algorithm is expressed at this level of detail, we will certainly have a program suitable for machine execution. However, expressing algorithms at this level is tedious, and so one normally uses a collection of "higher-level" primitives, each being an abstract tool constructed from the lower-level primitives provided in the machine's language. The result is a formal programming language in which algorithms can be expressed in a conceptually higher form than in the actual machine language. We discuss such programming languages in the next chapter.

Pseudocode

For now, we forego the introduction of a formal programming language in favor of a less formal, more intuitive notational system known as pseudocode. In general, a **pseudocode** is a notational system in which ideas can be expressed informally during the algorithm development process.

One way to obtain a pseudocode is simply to loosen the rules of the formal language in which the final version of the algorithm is to be expressed. This approach is commonly used when the target programming language is known in advance. There the pseudocode used during the early stages of program development consists of syntax-semantic structures similar to, but less formal than, those used in the target programming language.

Our goal, however, is to consider the issues of algorithm development and representation without confining our discussion to a particular programming language. Thus our approach to pseudocode is to develop a consistent, concise notation for representing recurring semantic structures. In turn, these structures will become the primitives in which we attempt to express future ideas.

For example, the need to select one of two possible activities depending on the truth or falseness of some condition is a common algorithmic structure. Examples include:

> If the gross domestic product has increased, buy common stock; otherwise, sell common stock.
>
> Buy common stock if the gross domestic product has increased and sell it otherwise.
>
> Buy or sell common stock depending on whether the gross domestic product has increased or decreased, respectively.

Each of these statements could be rewritten to conform to the structure

```
if (condition) then (activity)
               else (activity)
```

where we have used the key words if, then, and else to announce the different substructures within the main structure and parentheses to delimit the boundaries of these substructures. By adopting this syntactic structure for our pseudocode, we acquire a uniform way in which to express this common semantic structure. This, then, is what we do.

Whereas the statement

> Depending on whether or not the year is a leap year, divide the total by 366 or 365, respectively.

may possess a more creative literary style, we will consistently opt for the straightforward

```
if (year is leap year)
   then (divide total by 366)
   else (divide total by 365)
```

We also adopt the shorter syntax

```
if (condition) then (activity)
```

for those cases not involving an else activity. Using this notation, the statement

> Should it be the case that sales have decreased, lower the price by 5%.

will be reduced to

```
if (sales have decreased) then (lower the price by 5%)
```

Another common algorithmic structure involves the need to continue executing a statement or sequence of statements as long as some condition remains true. Informal examples include

As long as there are tickets to sell, continue selling tickets.

and

While there are tickets to sell, keep selling tickets.

For such cases, we adopt the uniform pattern

```
while (condition) do (activity)
```

for our pseudocode. In short, such a statement means to check the *condition* and, if it is true, perform the *activity* and return to check the *condition* again. If the *condition* is ever found to be false, move on to the next instruction following the while structure. Thus both of the preceding statements are reduced to

```
while (tickets remain to be sold) do (sell a ticket)
```

We will often want to refer to values by descriptive names. To make such associations, we will use the form

```
assign name the value expression
```

where *name* is the descriptive name and *expression* describes the value to be associated with the name. For example, the statement

```
assign Total the value Price + Tax
```

associates the result of adding the values of Price and Tax with the name Total.

Indentation often enhances the readability of a program. For example, the statement

```
if (item is taxable)
   then [if (price > limit)
            then (pay x)
            else (pay y)]
   else (pay z)
```

is easier to comprehend than the otherwise equivalent

```
if (item is taxable) then [if (price > limit) then (pay x)
else (pay y)] else (pay z)
```

Thus we will adopt the use of indentation in our pseudocode. (Note that we have also introduced the use of brackets to alleviate the confusion of nested parentheses.)

We want to use our pseudocode to describe activities that can be used as abstract tools in other applications. Computer science has a variety of terms for such program units, including subprogram, subroutine, procedure, module, and function, each with its own variation of meaning. We will adopt the term *procedure* for our pseudocode and use this term to announce the title by which the pseudocode unit will be known. More precisely, we will begin a pseudocode unit with a statement of the form

procedure *name*

where *name* is the particular name of the unit. We will then follow this introductory statement with the statements that define the unit's action. For example, Fig. 4.5 is a pseudocode representation of a procedure called Greetings that prints the message "Hello" three times.

When the task performed by a procedure is required elsewhere in our pseudocode, we will merely request it by name. For example, if two procedures were named ProcessLoan and RejectApplication, then we could request their services within an if-then-else structure by writing

```
if (. . .) then (Execute the procedure ProcessLoan)
       else (Execute the procedure RejectApplication)
```

which would result in the execution of the procedure ProcessLoan if the tested condition were true or in the execution of RejectApplication if the condition were false.

Procedures should be designed to be as generic as possible. A procedure for sorting lists of names should be designed to sort any list—not a particular one—so it should be written in such a way that the list to be sorted is not specified in the procedure itself. Instead, the list should be referred to by a generic name within the procedure's representation.

In our pseudocode we will adopt the convention of listing these generic names in parentheses on the same line on which we identify the procedure's name. In particular, a procedure named Sort, which is designed to sort any list of names, would begin with the statement

procedure Sort (List)

Later in the representation where a reference to the list being sorted is required, the generic name List would be used. In turn, when the services of Sort are required, we will identify which list is to be substituted for List in the procedure Sort. Thus we will write something such as

Apply the procedure Sort to the organization's membership list

Figure 4.5 The procedure Greetings in pseudocode

```
procedure Greetings

assign Count the value 3;
while Count > 0 do
(print the message "Hello" and
assign Count the value Count − 1)
```

and

Apply the procedure Sort to the wedding guest list

depending on our needs.

Keep in mind that the purpose of our pseudocode is to provide a means of jotting down rough outlines of algorithms—not the writing of finished, formal programs. Thus we will feel free to insert informal phrases that request activities whose details are not rigorously specified. (How these details are resolved is not so much a feature of the algorithm being expressed as it is a property of the language in which the formal program is ultimately written.) If, however, we find a particular idea recurring in our outlines, we will adopt a consistent syntax for representing it and thus extend our pseudocode.

Questions/Exercises

1. A primitive in one context may turn out to be a composite of primitives in another. For instance, our while statement is a primitive in our pseudocode, yet it is implemented as a composite of machine-language instructions. Give two examples of this phenomenon in a noncomputer setting.
2. In what sense is the construction of procedures the construction of primitives?
3. The Euclidean algorithm finds the greatest common divisor of two positive integers *X* and *Y* by the following process:

   As long as the value of neither *X* nor *Y* is zero, continue dividing the larger of the values by the smaller and assigning *X* and *Y* the values of the divisor and remainder, respectively. (The final value of *X* is the greatest common divisor.)

   Express this algorithm in our pseudocode.
4. Describe a collection of primitives that are used in a subject other than computer programming.

4.3 Algorithm Discovery

The development of a program consists of two activities—discovering the underlying algorithm and representing that algorithm as a program. Up to this point we have been concerned with the issues of algorithm representation without considering the question of how algorithms are found in the first place. Yet algorithm discovery is usually the more challenging step in the software development process. After all, to discover an algorithm is to find a method of solving that problem whose solution the algorithm is to compute. Thus to understand how algorithms are discovered is to understand the problem-solving process.

The Theory of Problem Solving

The techniques of problem solving and the need to learn more about them are not unique to computer science, but rather they are topics pertinent to almost any field. The close association between the process of algorithm discovery and that of general problem solving has caused computer scientists to join with those of other disciplines in the search for better problem-solving techniques. Ultimately, one would like to reduce the process of problem solving to an algorithm in itself, but this has been shown to be impossible. (This is a result of the material in Chapter 11, where we show that there are problems that do not have algorithmic solutions.) Thus the ability to solve problems remains more of an artistic skill to be developed than a precise science to be learned.

As evidence of the illusive, artistic nature of problem solving, the following loosely defined problem-solving phases presented by the mathematician G. Polya in 1945 remain the basic principles on which attempts to teach problem-solving skills are based today.

Phase 1. Understand the problem.
Phase 2. Devise a plan for solving the problem.
Phase 3. Carry out the plan.
Phase 4. Evaluate the solution for accuracy and for its potential as a tool for solving other problems.

Translated into the context of program development, these phases become

Phase 1. Understand the problem.
Phase 2. Get an idea as to how an algorithmic procedure might solve the problem.
Phase 3. Formulate the algorithm and represent it as a program.
Phase 4. Evaluate the program for accuracy and for its potential as a tool for solving other problems.

Having presented Polya's list, we should emphasize that these phases are not steps to be followed when trying to solve a problem but rather phases that will be completed sometime during the solution process. The key word here is *followed.* You do not solve problems by following. Rather, to solve a problem, you must take the initiative and lead. If you approach the task of solving a problem in the frame of mind depicted by "Now I've finished phase 1, it's time to move on to phase 2," you are not likely to be successful. However, if you become involved with the problem and ultimately solve it, you most likely can look back at what you did and realize that Polya's four phases had been completed.

Another important observation is that Polya's four phases are not necessarily completed in sequence. Contrary to the claim made by many authors, successful problem solvers often start formulating strategies for solving a problem (phase 2) before the problem itself is entirely understood (phase 1). Then, if these strategies fail (during phases 3 or 4), the potential problem solver gains a deeper understanding of the intricacies of the problem and, based on this deeper understanding, can return to form other and hopefully more successful strategies.

Keep in mind that we are discussing how problems are solved—not how we would like them to be solved. Ideally, we would like to eliminate the waste inherent in the trial-and-error process just described. In the case of developing large software systems, discovering a misunderstanding as late as phase 4 can represent a tremendous loss in resources. Avoiding such catastrophes is a major goal of software engineers (Chapter 6), who have traditionally insisted on a thorough understanding of a problem before proceeding with a solution. One could argue, however, that a true understanding of a problem is not obtained until a solution has been found, that the mere fact that a problem is unsolved implies a lack of understanding. To insist on a complete understanding of the problem before proposing any solutions is therefore somewhat idealistic.

As an example, consider the following problem:

> Person A is charged with the task of determining the ages of person B's three children. B tells A that the product of the children's ages is 36. After considering this clue, A replies that another clue is required, so B tells A the sum of the children's ages. Again, A replies that another clue is needed, so B tells A that the oldest child plays the piano. After hearing this clue, A tells B the ages of the three children. How old are the three children?

At first glance the last clue seems to be totally unrelated to the problem, yet it is this clue that allows A to finally determine the ages of the children. How can this be? Let us proceed by formulating a plan of attack and following this plan, even though we still have many questions about the problem. Our plan will be to trace the steps described by the problem statement while keeping track of the information available to person A as the story progresses.

The first clue given A is that the product of the children's ages is 36. This means that the triple representing the three ages is one of those listed in Fig. 4.6(a). The next clue is the sum of the desired triple. We are not told what this sum is, but we are told that this information is not enough for A to isolate the correct triple; therefore the desired triple must be one whose sum appears at least twice in the table of Fig. 4.6(b). But the only triples appearing in Fig. 4.6(b) with identical sums are (1,6,6) and (2,2,9), both of which produce the sum 13. This is the information available to A at the time the last clue is given. It is at this point that we finally understand the significance of the last clue. It has nothing to do with playing the piano; rather it is the fact that there is an oldest child. This rules out the triple (1,6,6) and thus allows us to conclude that the children's ages are 2, 2, and 9.

In this case, then, it is not until we attempt to implement our plan for solving the problem (phase 3) that we gain a complete understanding of the problem

Figure 4.6

(1,1,36)	(1,6,6)
(1,2,18)	(2,2,9)
(1,3,12)	(2,3,6)
(1,4,9)	(3,3,4)

(a) Triples whose product is 36

1 + 1 + 36 = 38	1 + 6 + 6 = 13
1 + 2 + 18 = 21	2 + 2 + 9 = 13
1 + 3 + 12 = 16	2 + 3 + 6 = 11
1 + 4 + 9 = 14	3 + 3 + 4 = 10

(b) Sums of triples from part (a)

(phase 1). Had we insisted on completing phase 1 before proceeding, we would probably never have found the children's ages. Such irregularities in the problem-solving process are fundamental to the difficulties in developing systematic approaches to problem solving.

Another irregularity is the mysterious inspiration that may come to a potential problem solver who, having worked on a problem without apparent success, may at a later time suddenly see the solution while doing another task. This phenomenon was identified by H. von Helmholtz as early as 1896 and was discussed by the mathematician Henri Poincaré in a lecture before the Psychological Society in Paris. There Poincaré described his experiences of realizing the solution to a problem he had worked on after he had set it aside and begun other projects. The phenomenon is as though a subconscious part of the mind continues working and, if successful, immediately forces the solution into the conscious mind. Today, the period between conscious work on a problem and the sudden inspiration is known as an incubation period, and its understanding remains a goal of current research.

Getting a Foot in the Door

We have been discussing problem solving from a somewhat philosophical point of view while avoiding a direct confrontation with the question of how we should go about trying to solve a problem. There are, of course, numerous problem-solving approaches, each of which can be successful in certain settings. We will identify some of them shortly. For now, we note that there seems to be a common thread running through these techniques, which simply stated is "get your foot in the door." As an example, let us consider the following simple problem:

> Before A, B, C, and D ran a race they made the following predictions:
>
> A predicted that B would win.
> B predicted that D would be last.
> C predicted that A would be third.
> D predicted that A's prediction would be correct.
>
> Only one of these predictions was true, and this was the prediction made by the winner. In what order did A, B, C, and D finish the race?

After reading the problem and analyzing the data, it should not take long to realize that since the predictions of A and D were equivalent and only one prediction was true, the predictions of both A and D must be false. Thus neither A nor D were winners. At this point we have our foot in the door, and obtaining the complete solution to our problem is merely a matter of extending our knowledge from here. If A's prediction was false, then B did not win either. The only remaining choice for the winner is C. Thus, C won the race, and C's prediction was true. Consequently, we know that A came in third. That means that the finishing order was either CBAD or CDAB. But the former is ruled out because B's prediction must be false. Therefore the finishing order was CDAB.

Of course, being told to get our foot in the door is not the same as being told how to do it. Obtaining this toehold, as well as realizing how to expand this initial thrust into a complete solution to the problem, requires creative input from the would-be problem solver. There are, however, several general approaches that have been proposed by Polya and others for how one might go about getting a foot in the door. One is to try working the problem backward. For instance, if the problem is to find a way of producing a particular output from a given input, one might start with that output and attempt to back up to the given input. This approach is typical of someone trying to discover the bird-folding algorithm in the previous section. They tend to unfold a completed bird in an attempt to see how it is constructed.

Another general problem-solving approach is to look for a related problem that is either easier to solve or has been solved before and then try to apply its solution to the current problem. This technique is of particular value in the context of program development. Often the major difficulty in program development is not that of solving a particular instance of a problem but rather of finding a general algorithm that can be used to solve all instances of the problem. More precisely, if we were faced with the task of developing a program for alphabetizing lists of names, our task would not be to sort a particular list but to find a general algorithm that could be used to sort any list of names. Thus, although the instructions

```
Interchange the names David and Alice.
Move the name Carol to the position between Alice and David.
Move the name Bob to the position between Alice and Carol.
```

correctly sort the list David, Alice, Carol, and Bob, they do not constitute the general-purpose algorithm we desire. What we need is an algorithm that can sort this list as well as other lists we may encounter. This is not to say that our solution for sorting a particular list is totally worthless in our search for a general-purpose algorithm. We might, for instance, get our foot in the door by considering such special cases in an attempt to find general principles that can in turn be used to develop the desired general-purpose algorithm. In this case, then, our solution is obtained by the technique of solving a collection of related problems.

Still another approach to getting a foot in the door is to apply **stepwise refinement,** which is essentially the technique of not trying to conquer an entire task (in all its gory detail) at once. Rather, stepwise refinement proposes that one first view the problem at hand in terms of several subproblems. The idea is that by breaking the original problem into subproblems, one is able to approach the overall solution in terms of steps, each of which is easier to solve than the entire original problem. In turn, stepwise refinement proposes that these steps be decomposed into smaller steps and these smaller steps be broken into still smaller ones until the entire problem has been reduced to a collection of easily solved subproblems.

In this light, stepwise refinement is a top-down methodology in that it progresses from the general to the specific. In contrast, bottom-up methodologies progress from the specific to the general. Although contrasting in theory, the two approaches actually complement each other in practice. For instance, the decomposition of a problem proposed by the top-down methodology of stepwise refinement is often guided by the problem solver's intuition, which is working in a bottom-up mode.

Solutions produced by stepwise refinement possess a natural modular structure, and herein lies a major reason for the popularity of stepwise refinement in algorithm design. If an algorithm has a natural modular structure, then it is easily adapted to a modular representation, which is conducive to the development of a manageable program. Furthermore, the modules produced by stepwise refinement are compatible with the concept of team programming, in which several people are assigned the task of developing a software product as a team. After all, once the task of the software has been broken into subproblems (or potential modules), the personnel on the team can work independently on these subtasks without getting in each other's way.

These advantages of stepwise refinement in the context of software development have produced many followers of the technique. However, with all its good points, stepwise refinement is not the final word in algorithm discovery. Rather, it is essentially an organizational tool whose problem-solving attributes are consequences of this organization. Stepwise refinement is a natural methodology to use when organizing a nationwide political campaign, writing a term paper, or planning a sales convention. Similarly, most software development projects in the data processing community have a large organizational component. The task is not so much that of discovering a startling new algorithm as it is a problem of organizing the tasks to be performed into a coherent package. For these reasons, stepwise refinement has correctly become a major design methodology in data processing.

But stepwise refinement remains only one of many design methodologies of interest to computer scientists, and thus one should not be misled into believing that all algorithm discoveries can be achieved by means of stepwise refinement. In fact, bringing preconceived notions and preselected tools to the problem-solving task can sometimes mask a problem's simplicity. Consider the following problem:

> As you step from a pier into a boat, your hat falls into the water, unbeknownst to you. The river is flowing at 2.5 miles per hour so your hat begins to float downstream. In the meantime, you begin traveling upstream in the boat at a speed of 4.75 miles per hour relative to the water. After 10 minutes you realize that your hat is missing, turn the boat around, and begin to chase your hat down the river. How long will it take to catch up with your hat?

Most students of high school algebra as well as pocket calculator enthusiasts approach this problem by first determining how far upstream the boat will have traveled in 10 minutes as well as how far downstream the hat will have traveled during that same time. Then, they try to determine how long it will take for the boat to travel downstream to this position. But, when the boat reaches this position, the hat will have floated farther downstream! Thus, the would-be problem solver becomes trapped in a cycle of computing where the hat will be each time the boat goes to where the hat was.

The problem is much simpler than this, however. The trick is to resist the urge to begin writing formulas and making calculations. Instead, we need to put these skills aside and adjust our perspective. The entire problem takes place in the river. The fact that the water is moving in relation to the shore is irrelevant. Think of the same problem posed on a large conveyer belt instead of a river. First, solve the problem with the conveyer belt stopped. If you place your hat at your feet while standing on the belt and then walk away from your hat for 10 minutes, it will take 10 minutes to return to your hat. Now turn on the conveyer belt. This means that the scenery will begin to move past the belt, but, because you are on the belt, this does not change your relationship to the belt or your hat. It will still take 10 minutes to return to your hat.

We conclude that algorithm discovery remains a challenging art that must be developed over a period of time rather than taught as a subject consisting of well-defined methodologies. Indeed, to train a potential problem solver to follow certain methodologies is to squash those creative skills that should instead be nurtured.

Questions/Exercises

1. a. Find an algorithm for solving the following program: Given a positive integer n, find the list of positive integers whose product is the largest among all the lists of positive integers whose sum is n. For example, if n is 4, the desired list is 2, 2 because 2×2 is larger than $1 \times 1 \times 1 \times 1$, $2 \times 1 \times 1$, and 3×1. If n is 5, the desired list is 2, 3.
   b. What is the desired list if $n = 2001$?
   c. Explain how you got your foot in the door.
2. a. Suppose we are given a checkerboard consisting of 2^n rows and 2^n columns of squares, for some positive integer n, and a box of L-shaped tiles, each of which can cover exactly three squares on the board. If any single square is cut out of the board, can we cover the remaining board with tiles such that tiles do not overlap or hang off the edge of the board?
   b. Explain how your solution to part (a) can be used to show that $2^{2n} - 1$ is divisible by 3 for all positive integers n.
   c. How are parts (a) and (b) related to Polya's phases of problem solving?
3. Decode the following message. Then, explain how you got your foot in the door.

   Pdeo eo pda yknnayp wjosan.

4.4 Iterative Structures

Our goal now is to study some of the repetitive structures used in describing algorithmic processes. In this section we discuss **iterative structures** in which a collection of instructions is repeated in a looping manner, and in the next section we introduce the technique of recursion. Moreover, as examples, we introduce some popular algorithms for searching and sorting—the sequential and binary searches and the insertion and quick sorts—since they involve applications of the repetitive structures being considered. We begin by introducing the sequential search algorithm.

The Sequential Search Algorithm

Consider the problem of searching a list for the occurrence of a particular target value. We want to develop an algorithm that determines whether that value is in the list. If the value is in the list, we consider the search a success; otherwise, we consider it a failure. We assume that the list is sorted according to some rule for ordering its entries. For example, if the list is a list of names, we assume the names appear in alphabetical order, or if the list is a list of numbers, we assume its entries appear in order of increasing magnitude.

To get our foot in the door, we imagine how we might search a guest list of perhaps 20 entries for a particular name. In this setting we might scan the list from its beginning, comparing each entry with the target name. If we find the target name, the search terminates as a success. However, if we reach the end of the list or reach a name greater than (alphabetically) the target name, our search terminates as a failure. (Remember, the list is arranged in alphabetical order, so reaching a name greater than the target name indicates that the target does not appear in the list.) In summary, our rough idea is to continue searching down the list as long as there are more names to be investigated and the target name is less than the name currently being considered.

In our pseudocode this process can be represented as

```
Select the first entry in the list as the test entry.
while (target value > test entry and
          there remain entries to be considered)
          do (Select the next entry in the list as the test entry)
```

Upon terminating the while structure, either the test entry is no less than the target name or it is the last name in the list. In either case we can detect a successful search by comparing the test entry to the target value. If they are equal, the search has been successful. Thus we add the statement

```
if (target value = test entry)
   then (Declare the search a success.)
   else (Declare the search a failure.)
```

to the end of our pseudocode routine.

Finally, we observe that the first statement in our search routine is based on the assumption that the list in question contains at least one entry. We might reason that this is a safe guess, but just to be sure we can position our routine as the else option of the statement

```
if (List empty)
   then (Declare search a failure.)
   else (. . .)
```

which produces the procedure shown in Fig. 4.7. Note that this procedure can be used to perform searches in other procedures by statements such as

```
Apply the procedure Search to the passenger list to look for the name Darrel Baker.
```

to find out if Darrel Baker is a passenger and

```
procedure Search (List, TargetValue)

if (List empty)
  then
    (Declare search a failure.)
  else
    [Select the first entry in List as the test entry;
     while (TargetValue > test entry and
       there remain entries to be considered)
       do (Select the next entry in List as the test entry.);
     if (TargetValue = test entry)
        then (Declare search a success.)
        else (Declare search a failure.)]
```

Figure 4.7 The sequential search algorithm in pseudocode

```
Apply the procedure Search to the list of ingredients using nutmeg as the target value.
```

to find out if nutmeg appears in the list of ingredients.

In summary, the algorithm represented by Fig. 4.7 sequentially considers the entries in the order in which they occur in the list. For this reason, the algorithm is called the **sequential search algorithm.** Because of its simplicity, it is often used for short lists or when other concerns dictate its use. However, in the case of long lists, sequential searches are not as efficient as other techniques (as we shall soon see).

Loop Control

The repetitive use of an instruction or sequence of instructions is an important algorithmic concept. One method of implementing such repetition is the iterative structure known as the **loop,** in which a collection of instructions, called the body of the loop, is executed in a repetitive fashion under the direction of some control process. A typical example is found in the sequential search algorithm represented in Fig. 4.7. Here we use a while statement to control the repetition of the single statement Select the next entry in List as the test entry. Indeed, the while statement

```
while (condition) do (body)
```

exemplifies the concept of a loop structure in that its execution traces the cyclic pattern

check the *condition*
execute the *body*
check the *condition*
execute the *body*
.
.
.
check the *condition*

until the condition fails.

As a general rule the use of a loop structure produces a higher degree of flexibility than would be obtained merely by writing the body several times. For example, although the loop structure

Execute the statement "Add a drop of sulfuric acid" three times.

is equivalent to the sequence

Add a drop of sulfuric acid.
Add a drop of sulfuric acid.
Add a drop of sulfuric acid.

we cannot produce a similar sequence that is equivalent to the loop described by

```
while (the pH level is greater than 4) do
  (add a drop of sulfuric acid)
```

because we do not know in advance how many drops of acid will be required.

Let us now take a closer look at the composition of loop control. You may be tempted to view this part of a loop structure as having minor importance. After all, it is typically the body of the loop that actually performs the task at hand (for example, adding drops of acid)—the control activities appear merely as the overhead involved because we chose to execute the body in a repetitive fashion. However, experience has shown that the control of a loop is the more error-prone part of the structure and therefore deserves our attention.

The control of a loop consists of the three activities initialize, test, and modify (Fig. 4.8), with the presence of each being required for successful loop control. The test activity has the obligation of causing the termination of the looping process by watching for a condition that indicates termination should take place. It is for the purpose of this test activity that we provide a condition within each while statement of our pseudocode. This is the condition under which the body of the loop should be executed. Thus the termination condition is the negation of the condition stated in the while structure.

The other two activities in the loop control assure the termination condition will ultimately occur. The initialization step establishes a starting condition, and the modification step moves this condition toward the termination condition. For instance, in Fig. 4.7 initialization takes place in the statement preceding the while statement, where the current test entry is established as the first list entry. The modification step in this case is actually accomplished within the loop body, where our position of interest is moved toward the end of the list. Thus, having

Figure 4.8 Components of repetitive control

Initialize:	Establish an initial state that will be modified toward the termination condition
Test:	Compare the current state to the termination condition and terminate the repetition if equal
Modify:	Change the state in such a way that it moves toward the termination condition

executed the initialization step, repeated application of the modification step results in the termination condition being reached. (If we never find the target value, we ultimately reach the end of the list.)

We should emphasize that the initialization and modification steps must lead to the appropriate termination condition. This characteristic is critical for proper loop control, and thus one should always double-check for its presence when designing a loop structure. Failure to make such an evaluation can lead to errors even in the simplest cases. A typical example is the use of a termination condition, such as testing a location for the value 6, initializing the location at 1, and then using the addition of 2 as the modification step. In this case, as the loop cycles the location in question contains the values 1, 3, 5, 7, 9, and so on, but never the value 6. Thus the loop never terminates.

There are two popular loop structures that differ merely in the order in which the loop control components are executed. The first is exemplified by our pseudocode statement

while (*condition*) **do** (*activity*)

whose semantics is represented in Fig. 4.9 in the form of a **flowchart.** Such charts use various shapes to represent individual steps and arrows to indicate the sequence of steps. The distinction between the shapes indicates the type of action involved in the associated step. A diamond indicates a decision and a rectangle indicates an arbitrary statement or sequence of statements. Note that the test for termination in the while structure occurs before the loop's body is executed.

In contrast, the structure in Fig. 4.10 requests that the body of the loop be executed before the test for termination is performed. In this alternative structure, the loop's body is always performed at least once, whereas in the while structure

Figure 4.9 The while loop structure

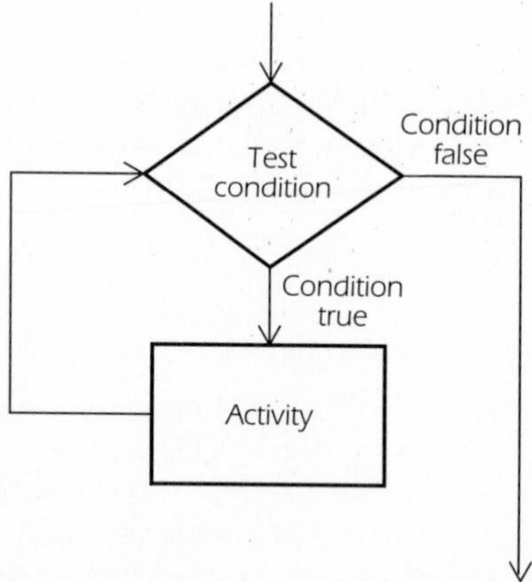

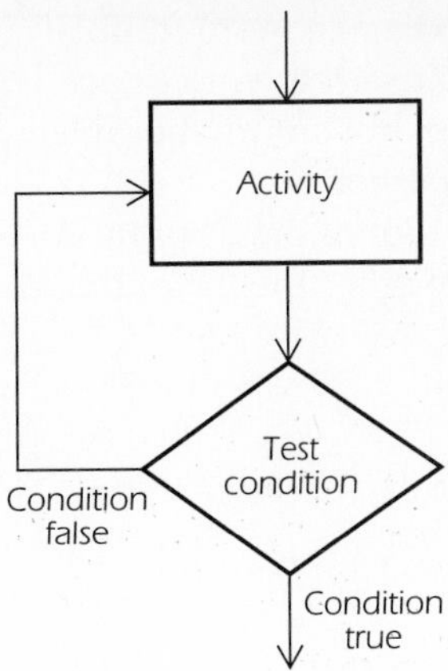

Figure 4.10 The repeat loop structure

the body is never executed if the termination condition is satisfied the first time it is tested.

We use the syntactic form

repeat (*activity*) **until** (*condition*)

in our pseudocode to represent the structure shown in Fig. 4.10. The statement

repeat (take a coin from your pocket)
until (there are no coins in your pocket)

assumes there is a coin in your pocket at the beginning, but

while (there is a coin in your pocket)
do (take a coin from your pocket)

does not.

The Insertion Sort Algorithm

As an additional example of the use of iterative structures, let us consider the problem of sorting a list of names into alphabetical order. But before proceeding, we should identify the constraints under which we will work. Simply stated, our goal is to sort the list "within itself." In other words, we want to sort the list by shuffling its entries as opposed to moving the list to another location. This rules out the technique of reconstructing the list in another location in such a way that the new version is sorted.

Our situation is analogous to the problem of sorting a list whose entries are recorded on separate index cards spread out on a crowded desk top. We have cleared off enough space for the cards but are not allowed to push additional materials back to make more room. This restriction is typical in computer applications, not because the work space within the machine is necessarily crowded like our desk top, but simply because we want to use the storage space available in an efficient manner.

Let us get a foot in the door by considering how we might sort the names on the desk top. Consider the list of names

Fred
Alice
David
Bill
Carol

One approach to sorting this list is to note that the sublist consisting of only the top name, Fred, is sorted but the sublist consisting of the top two names, Fred and Alice, is not. Thus we might pick up the card containing the name Alice, slide the name Fred down into the space where Alice was, and then place the name Alice in the hole at the top of the list, as represented by the first row in Fig. 4.11. At this point our list would be

Alice
Fred
David
Bill
Carol

Now the top two names form a sorted sublist, but the top three do not. Thus we might pick up the third name, David, slide the name Fred down into the hole where David was, and then insert David in the hole left by Fred, as summarized in the second row of Fig. 4.11. The top three entries in the list would now be sorted. Continuing in this fashion, we could obtain a list in which the top four entries are sorted by picking up the fourth name, Bill, sliding the names Fred and David down, and then inserting Bill in the hole (see the third row of Fig. 4.11). Finally, we can complete the sorting process by picking up Carol, sliding Fred and David down, and then inserting Carol in the remaining hole (see the fourth row of Fig. 4.11).

Having analyzed the process of sorting a particular list, our task now is to generalize this process to obtain an algorithm for sorting general lists. To this end, we observe that each row of Fig. 4.11 represents the same general process: Pick up the first name in the unsorted portion of the list, slide the names greater than the extracted name down, and insert the extracted name back in the list where the hole appears. If we identify the extracted name as the pivot entry, this process can be expressed in our pseudocode as

```
Move the pivot entry to a temporary location leaving a hole in List;
while (there is a name above the hole and that name is greater than the pivot) do
   (move the name above the hole down into the hole leaving a hole above the name)
Move the pivot entry into the hole in List
```

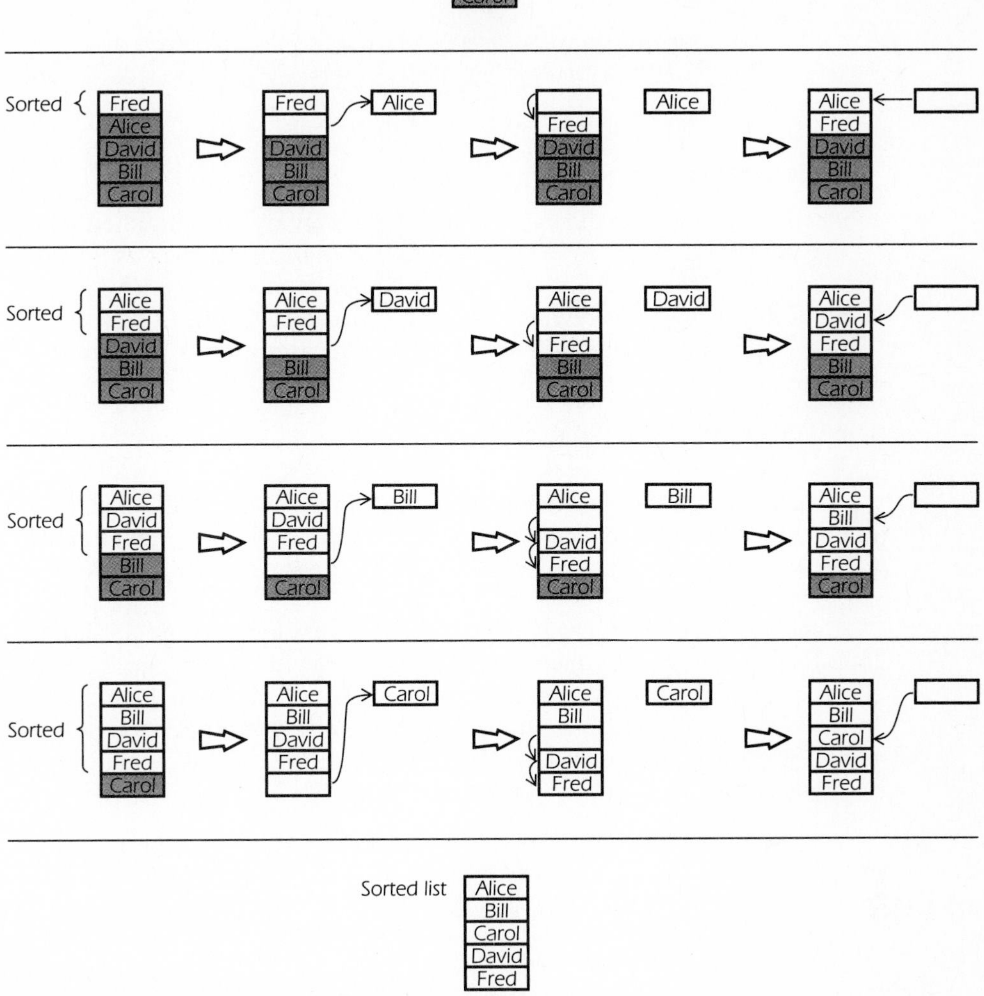

Figure 4.11 Sorting the list Fred, Alice, David, Bill, and Carol

Next, we observe that this process should be executed repeatedly. At first, the pivot should be the second entry in the list and then, before each additional execution, the pivot selection should be moved one entry down the list until the last entry has been positioned. This advancement of the pivot assignment is indicated in Fig. 4.11 by means of shading. At any point in the figure, the portion of the list below the last pivot assignment is shaded. Each row in the figure begins by picking the top entry from the shaded portion to be the pivot and removing the shading from this position in the list. Thus, we can control the repetition of the preceding pseudocode routine with the statements

```
Shade the portion of List from the second entry through the last entry;
repeat
 (Remove the shading from the first name in the shaded portion of List and
   identify this name as the pivot entry
              .
              .
              .   )
until (entire List is unshaded)
```

where the dots indicate the location where the previous routine should be placed.

Of course, our routine so far assumes that there are at least two entries in the list to be sorted, an assumption that should not be made in general. On the other hand, if the list in question has fewer than two entries, it must be sorted already. Thus we can extend our routine to handle such cases merely by starting with the statement

```
if (there are two or more entries in List)
   then (. . .)
```

Our complete pseudocode program is shown in Fig. 4.12. In short, the program sorts a list by repeatedly removing an entry and inserting it into its proper place. It is because of this repeated insertion process that the underlying algorithm is called the **insertion sort.**

Note that the structure of Fig. 4.12 is that of a loop within a loop, the outer loop being expressed by the repeat statement and the inner loop represented by the while statement. Each execution of the body of the outer loop results in the inner loop being initialized and executed until its termination condition is obtained. Thus a single execution of the outer loop's body will result in several executions of the inner loop's body.

Figure 4.12 The insertion sort expressed in pseudocode

```
procedure Sort (List)

if (there are two or more entries in List) then
  [Shade the portion of List from the second entry
     through the last entry;
   repeat
     (Remove the shading from the first name in the shaded
        portion of List and identify this name as the
        pivot entry;
      Move the pivot entry to a temporary location leaving
        a hole in List;
      while (there is a name above the hole and that name
        is greater than the pivot) do
        (Move the name above the hole down into the hole
           leaving a hole above the name)
      Move the pivot entry into the hole in List)
   until (entire List is unshaded)]
```

The initialization component of the outer loop's control consists of shading the portion of the list from the second entry to the last. The modification component is handled by the statement

```
Remove the shading from the first name in the shaded
  portion of List and identify this name as the
  pivot entry;
```

The termination condition occurs when the shaded portion of the list becomes empty, as indicated by the until clause.

The inner loop's control is initialized by removing the pivot entry from the list that creates a hole. The loop's modification step is accomplished by moving entries above the hole down, thus moving the hole up. The termination condition consists of the hole being immediately below a name that is not greater than the pivot or of the hole reaching the top of the list.

Questions/Exercises

1. Modify the sequential search program in Fig. 4.7 to allow for lists that are not sorted.
2. Convert the pseudocode routine:

```
assign Z the value 0;
assign X the value 1;
while (X < 6) do
   (assign Z the value Z + X;
    assign X the value X + 1)
```

   to an equivalent routine using a repeat statement.
3. Suppose the insertion sort as presented in Fig. 4.12 was applied to the list George, Cheryl, Alice, and Bob. Describe the organization of the list at the end of each execution of the body of the repeat structure.
4. Why would we not want to change the phrase *greater than* in the while statement in Fig. 4.12 to *greater than or equal to?*

4.5 Recursive Structures

Recursive structures provide an alternative to the loop paradigm for repetitive structures. As an introduction to the technique, we consider the **binary search** algorithm that applies a divide-and-conquer methodology to the search process.

The Binary Search Algorithm

Let us again tackle the problem of searching a sorted list to see whether it contains a particular entry, but this time we get our foot in the door by considering the procedure we follow when searching a dictionary. We do not search a dictionary by performing a sequential word-by-word or even a page-by-page procedure. Rather, we begin by opening the dictionary to a page in the area where we believe the target entry is located. If we are lucky, we will find the target entry there; otherwise, we must continue searching. But at this point we will have narrowed our search either to that portion of the dictionary preceding our current position or to that portion following our current position.

Figure 4.13 is a pseudocode representation of this approach applied to a generic sorted list. In this general setting we do not have the advantage of knowing approximate locations of entries, so the directions in the figure tell us to begin by opening the list to the "middle" entry.

We have placed the word *middle* in quotation marks to indicate the possibility that a list with an even number of entries has no middle entry. In this case, the middle entry refers to the first entry in the second half of the list.

If the selected entry is not the target of the search, the routine in Fig. 4.13 provides two options, both of which require a secondary search performed by a procedure named Search. To complete our program, therefore we must provide such a procedure, describing how this secondary search is to be performed. Note that this procedure must be robust enough to handle a request to search an empty list. For instance, if the routine in Fig. 4.13 is given a list containing only one entry that is not the target value, then the procedure is requested to search either the sublist above or below the single entry, both of which are empty.

We could use the sequential search developed in the previous section as the required procedure, but this is not the technique we probably would use when searching a dictionary. Rather, we probably would repeat the same process on the restricted portion of the dictionary that we used for the whole dictionary. That is, we would select an entry toward the middle of that portion of the dictionary and use it to narrow our search further.

We can implement this procedure in our pseudocode by first modifying the routine in Fig. 4.13 to handle the case of an empty list and then giving the resulting procedure the name Search to obtain the pseudocode program shown in Fig. 4.14. If we were following this routine and came to the instruction "Apply the mod-

Figure 4.13 The core of the binary search

```
Select the "middle" entry in List as the test entry;
Execute one of the following blocks of instructions
   depending on whether TargetValue is equal to, less
   than, or greater than the test entry.
   TargetValue = test entry:

      (Declare the search a success.)
   TargetValue < test entry:

      [Apply the procedure Search to see whether TargetValue is
            in the portion of List preceding the test entry, and
      if (that search is successful)
            then (Declare this search a success.)
            else (Declare this search a failure.)]
   TargetValue > test entry:

      [Apply the procedure Search to see whether TargetValue is
         in the portion of List following the test entry, and
      if (that search is successful)
         then (Declare this search a success.)
         else (Declare this search a failure.)]
```

```
procedure Search (List, TargetValue)

if (list empty)
  then
    (Declare the search a failure.)
  else
    [Select the "middle" entry in List as the test entry;
    Execute one of the following blocks of instructions
      depending on whether TargetValue is equal to, less
      than, or greater than the test entry.
      TargetValue = test entry;
        (Declare the search a success.)
      TargetValue < test entry;
        [Apply the procedure Search to see whether TargetValue is
           in the portion of List preceding the test entry, and
         if (that search is successful)
            then (Declare this search a success.)
            else (Declare this search a failure.)]
      TargetValue > test entry;
        [Apply the procedure Search to see whether TargetValue is
           in the portion of List following the test entry, and
         if (that search is successful)
            then (Declare this search a success.)
            else (Declare this search a failure.)]]
```

Figure 4.14 The binary search algorithm in pseudocode

ule Search . . .," we would apply the same search technique to the smaller list that we were applying to the original one. If that search succeeded, we would return to declare our original search successful; if this secondary search failed, we would declare our original search a failure.

To clarify this process, let us apply the algorithm represented in Fig. 4.14 to the list Alice, Bill, Carol, David, Evelyn, Fred, and George, with the target value being Bill. Our search begins by selecting David (the middle entry) as the test entry under consideration. Since the target value (Bill) must precede this test entry, we are instructed to apply the procedure Search to the list of entries preceding David—that is, the list Alice, Bill, and Carol. In so doing we create a second copy of the search procedure and assign it to this secondary task.

For a while we have two copies of our search procedure being executed, as summarized in Fig. 4.15. Progress in the original copy is temporarily suspended at the instruction

```
Apply the procedure Search to see whether TargetValue is
  in the portion of List preceding the test entry
```

while we apply the second copy to the task of searching the list Alice, Bill, and Carol. When we complete this secondary search, we will discard the second copy of the procedure, report its findings to the original copy, and continue progress in the original. In this way the second copy of the procedure executes as a subordinate to the original, performing the task requested by the original module and then disappearing.

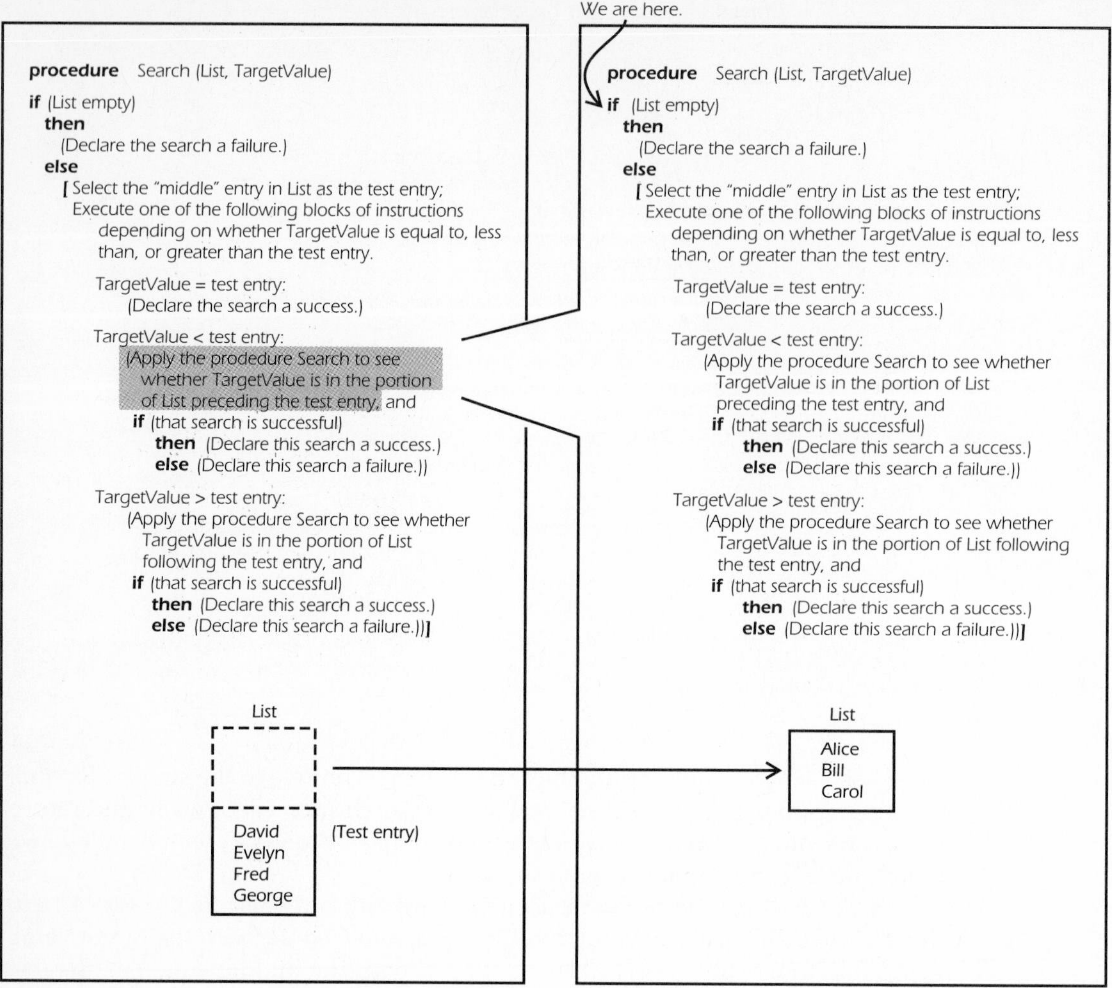

Figure 4.15

The secondary search selects Bill as its test entry because that is the middle entry in the list Alice, Bill, and Carol. Since this is the same as the target value, it declares its search to be a success and terminates.

At this point, we have completed the secondary search as requested by the original copy of the procedure, so we are able to continue the execution of that original copy. Here we are told that if the secondary search was successful, we should declare the original search a success. Our process has correctly determined that Bill is a member of the list Alice, Bill, Carol, David, Evelyn, Fred, and George.

Let us now consider what happens if we ask our routine to search the list Alice, Carol, Evelyn, Fred, and George for the entry David. This time the original copy of the procedure selects Evelyn as its test entry and concludes that the target value must reside in the preceding portion of the list. It therefore requests another copy of the procedure to search the list of entries appearing in front of Evelyn—that is, the two-entry list consisting of Alice and Carol. At this stage our situation is as represented in Fig. 4.16.

The second copy of the procedure selects Carol as its current entry and concludes that the target value must lie in the latter portion of its list. It then requests a third copy of the procedure to search the list of names following Carol in the list Alice and Carol. This sublist is empty, so the third copy of the procedure has the task of searching the empty list for the target value David. Our situation at this point is represented by Fig. 4.17. The original copy of the procedure

Figure 4.16

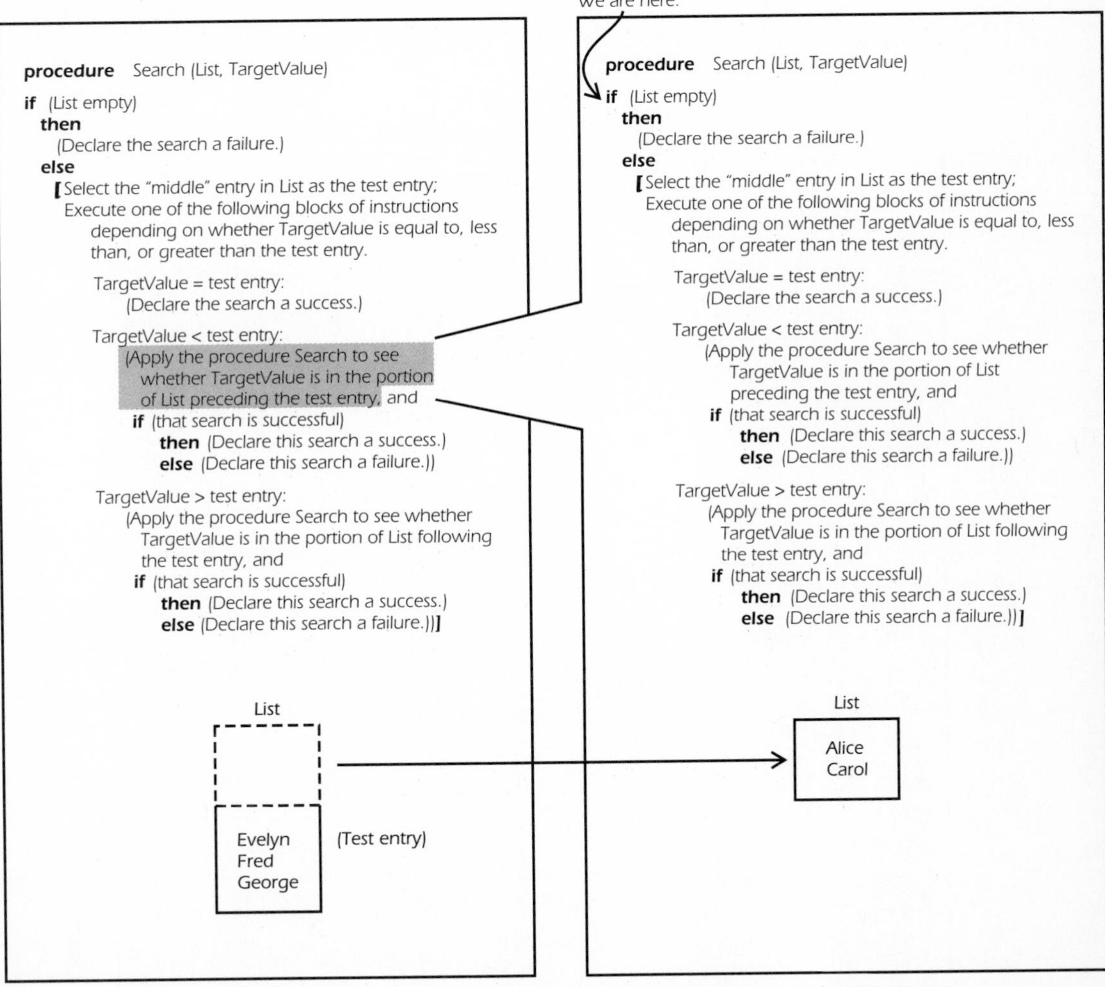

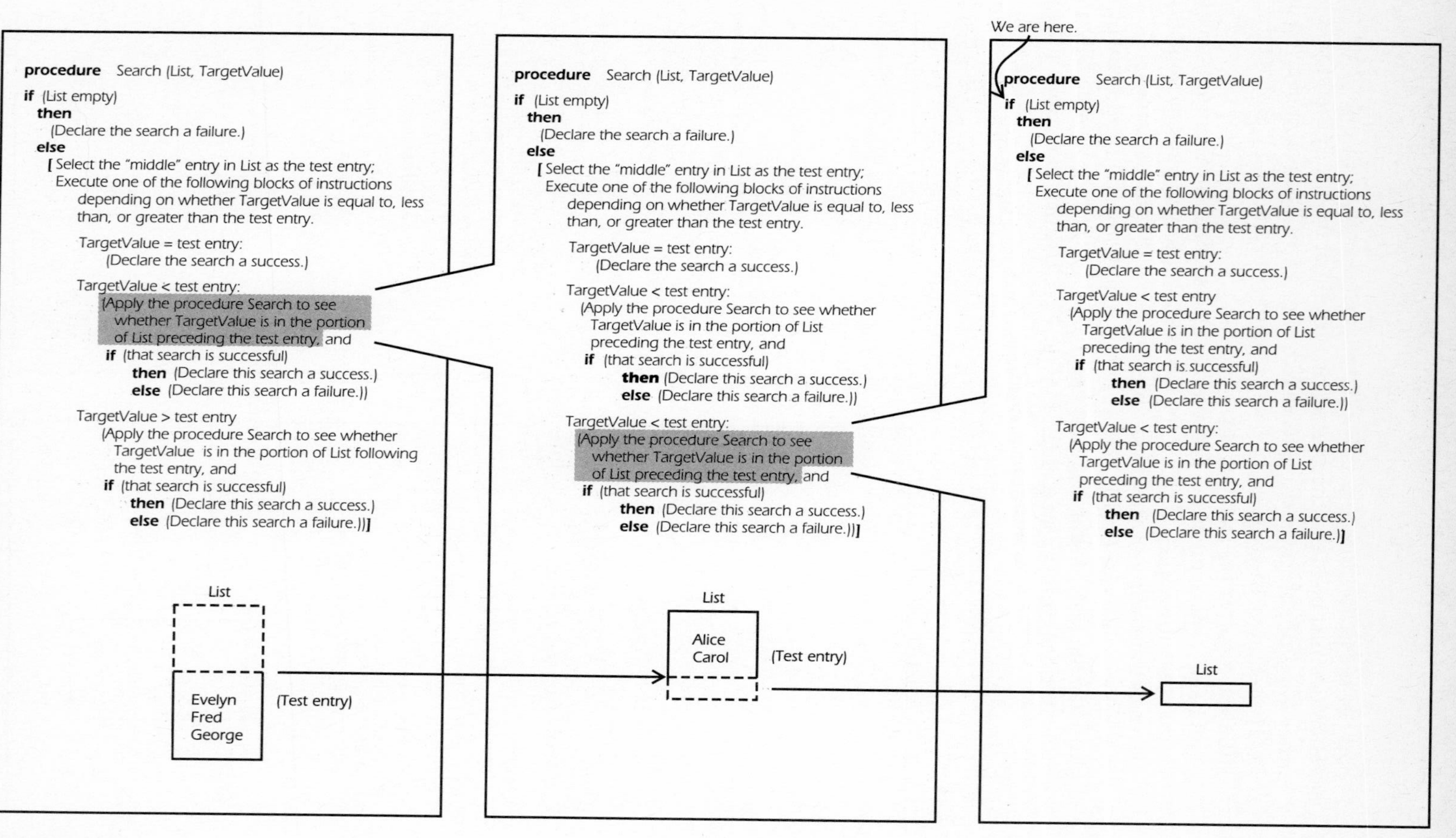

procedure Search (List, TargetValue)
if (List empty)
then
(Declare the search a failure.)
else
[Select the "middle" entry in List as the test entry;
Execute one of the following blocks of instructions depending on whether TargetValue is equal to, less than, or greater than the test entry.
TargetValue = test entry:
(Declare the search a success.)
TargetValue < test entry:
(Apply the procedure Search to see whether TargetValue is in the portion of List preceding the test entry, and
if (that search is successful)
then (Declare this search a success.)
else (Declare this search a failure.))
TargetValue > test entry
(Apply the procedure Search to see whether TargetValue is in the portion of List following the test entry, and
if (that search is successful)
then (Declare this search a success.)
else (Declare this search a failure.))]
List
Evelyn
Fred
George
(Test entry)
procedure Search (List, TargetValue)
if (List empty)
then
(Declare the search a failure.)
else
[Select the "middle" entry in List as the test entry;
Execute one of the following blocks of instructions depending on whether TargetValue is equal to, less than, or greater than the test entry.
TargetValue = test entry:
(Declare the search a success.)
TargetValue < test entry:
(Apply the procedure Search to see whether TargetValue is in the portion of List preceding the test entry, and
if (that search is successful)
then (Declare this search a success.)
else (Declare this search a failure.))
TargetValue < test entry:
(Apply the procedure Search to see whether TargetValue is in the portion of List preceding the test entry, and
if (that search is successful)
then (Declare this search a success.)
else (Declare this search a failure.))]
List
Alice
Carol
(Test entry)
We are here.
procedure Search (List, TargetValue)
if (List empty)
then
(Declare the search a failure.)
else
[Select the "middle" entry in List as the test entry;
Execute one of the following blocks of instructions depending on whether TargetValue is equal to, less than, or greater than the test entry.
TargetValue = test entry:
(Declare the search a success.)
TargetValue < test entry
(Apply the procedure Search to see whether TargetValue is in the portion of List preceding the test entry, and
if (that search is successful)
then (Declare this search a success.)
else (Declare this search a failure.))
TargetValue < test entry:
(Apply the procedure Search to see whether TargetValue is in the portion of List preceding the test entry, and
if (that search is successful)
then (Declare this search a success.)
else (Declare this search a failure.)]
List

Figure 4.17

has the task of searching the list Alice, Carol, Evelyn, Fred, and George, with the test entry being Evelyn; the second copy is searching the list Alice and Carol, with its test entry being Carol; and the third copy is about to begin searching the empty list.

Of course, the third copy of the procedure quickly declares its search to be a failure and terminates. The completion of the third copy's task allows the second copy to continue its task. It notes that the search it requested was unsuccessful, declares its own task to be a failure, and terminates. This report is what the original copy of the procedure has been waiting for, so it can now proceed. Since the search it requested failed, it declares its own search to have failed and terminates. Our routine has correctly concluded that David is not contained in the list Alice, Carol, Evelyn, Fred, and George.

In summary, if we were to look back at the previous examples, we could see that the process employed by the algorithm represented into Fig. 4.14 is to repeatedly divide the list in question into two smaller pieces in such a way that the remaining search can be restricted to only one of these pieces. This divide-by-two approach is the reason why the algorithm is known as the binary search.

Recursive Control

The binary search algorithm is similar to the sequential search in that each algorithm requests the execution of a repetitive process. However, the implementation of this repetition is significantly different. Whereas the sequential search involves a circular form of repetition, the binary search executes each stage of the repetition as a subtask of the previous stage. This technique is known as **recursion.**

As we have seen, the illusion created by the execution of a recursive algorithm is the existence of multiple copies of itself, called *activations,* that appear and disappear as the algorithm advances. Of those activations existing at any given time, only one is actively progressing. The others are effectively in limbo, each waiting for another activation to terminate before it can continue.

Being a repetitive process, recursive systems are just as dependent on proper control as are loop structures. For example, just as in loop control, recursive systems are dependent on testing for a termination condition and on a design that assures this condition will be reached. In fact, proper recursive control involves the same three ingredients—initialization, modification, and test for termination—that are required in loop control.

In general, a recursive routine is designed to test for the termination condition (often called the base or degenerative case) before requesting further activations. If this condition is not met, the routine assigns an activation to the task of solving a revised problem that is closer to the termination condition than that assigned to the current activation. However, if the termination condition is met, a path is taken that avoids further recursive action, causing the current activation to terminate without creating additional activations. This means that one of the activations in limbo is allowed to continue execution, complete its task, and in turn allow yet another activation to continue. In this fashion, all the activations that are generated ultimately terminate, leaving the original task completed.

Let us see how the initialization and modification phases of repetitive control are implemented in our recursive binary search routine of Fig. 4.14. In this case the creation of additional activations is terminated once the target value is found or the task is reduced to that of searching an empty list. The process is initialized implicitly by being given an initial list and a target value. From this initial configuration the routine modifies the task it is assigned to that of searching a smaller list. Since the original list is of finite length and each modification step reduces the length of the list in question, we are assured that the target value ultimately is found or the task is reduced to that of searching the empty list. We can therefore conclude that the repetitive process is guaranteed to cease.

Having seen both iterative and recursive control structures, you may wonder whether the two are equivalent in power. That is, if an algorithm were designed using a loop structure, could another algorithm using only recursive techniques be designed that would solve the same problem and vice versa? Such questions are important in computer science because their answers tell us what features should be provided in a programming language in order to obtain the most powerful programming system possible. We return to these ideas in Chapter 11, where we consider some of the more theoretical aspects of computer science and its mathematical foundations. With this background, we then can prove the equivalence of iterative and recursive structures in Appendix E.

The Quick Sort Algorithm

For another application of recursion, we reconsider the problem of sorting a list of names. Once again, we work within the constraints of sorting the list within itself, as dictated by the crowded desktop analogy described in our introduction to the insertion sort in Section 4.4.

We approach our sorting task this time by selecting one name, which we call the pivot entry, finding this name's correct position, and placing the name in that position. To find the correct position for the pivot, we essentially divide the list into two smaller lists, the first consisting of the names that should precede the pivot in the final order and the second consisting of the names that should follow the pivot. Consequently, the correct location for the pivot entry is between these two sublists.

To start the process, we must select a list entry as the pivot. Not knowing anything about the list, we might as well pick the name currently at the top. Next, we must divide the list into the two sublists just described. For this purpose we place an arrow, which we call a pointer, at the first name in the list (which is the pivot entry) and another pointer at the last name. Our algorithm directs the movement of these pointers toward each other in such a way that the following assertion is always satisfied:

> **Assertion 1:** The names above the top pointer are less than (alphabetically) or equal to the pivot entry, and those below the bottom pointer are greater than the pivot.

This assertion states that the pointers identify two groups within the list. One group contains only entries that should precede the pivot entry (the names above the top pointer) in the final sorted list, while the other group contains only entries that should follow the pivot (the names below the bottom pointer).

To describe how the pointers are moved, we consider the problem of sorting the list:

Jane
Bob
Alice
Tom
Carol
Bill
George
Cheryl
Sue
John

We begin with the configuration

→ Jane (Pivot entry)
Bob
Alice
Tom
Carol
Bill
George
Cheryl
Sue
→ John

Next, we move the bottom pointer up the list, comparing the name pointed to with the pivot entry at each step. As long as this name is greater than the pivot entry, we keep moving the pointer. Ultimately we must reach a name less than or equal to the pivot entry, because the top name certainly fits this criterion. Once such a name has been reached, we stop moving the pointer. In our example, because this happens when the pointer reaches Cheryl, we stop moving the pointer at that position, producing the following configuration:

→ Jane (Pivot entry)
Bob
Alice
Tom
Carol
Bill
George
→ Cheryl

Greater-than pivot {
Sue
John

Now we begin moving the top pointer down the list, comparing the names pointed to with the pivot entry. This time, however, we keep moving the pointer as long as the name in the list is less than or equal to the pivot entry or until the two pointers coincide. As we will see, the latter condition indicates that the correct location for the pivot has been found. On the other hand, the former condition would present us with a dilemma, because any further movement of either pointer would destroy the validity of Assertion 1. This is demonstrated in our example, which at this stage appears as follows:

```
Less-than-        {  Jane      (Pivot entry)
or-equal-to       {  Bob
pivot             {  Alice
                  ------------
                  → Tom
                    Carol
                    Bill
                    George
                  → Cheryl
                  ------------
Greater-than      {  Sue
pivot             {  John
```

Observe that this deadlock can be broken by interchanging the names designated by the pointers, after which we can again move the bottom pointer up (and then the top pointer down) without violating Assertion 1. This, then, is what we do. Immediately after the interchange, our example has the following configuration:

```
Less-than-        {  Jane      (Pivot entry)
or-equal-to       {  Bob
pivot             {  Alice
                  { → Cheryl
                  ------------
                    Carol
                    Bill
                    George
                  ------------
Greater-than      { → Tom
pivot             {  Sue
                  {  John
```

By continuing the process of moving the pointers and then interchanging names to break the deadlock, the two pointers must at some point coincide. In our example, this meeting occurs after the bottom pointer has stopped at George and the top pointer has moved down to it, producing the situation that appears as follows:

```
                  {  Jane      (Pivot entry)
                  {  Bob
Less-than-        {  Alice
or-equal-to       {  Cheryl
pivot             {  Carol
                  {  Bill
                  ------------
                  → George
                  ------------
Greater-than      {  Tom
pivot             {  Sue
                  {  John
```

Once the pointers coincide, how does the identified entry compare to the pivot? To answer this question, we first justify the following assertion:

> **Assertion 2:** At the beginning of the sort process and after each interchange for breaking a deadlock, the top pointer points to a name less than or equal to the pivot.

This assertion is certainly true at the beginning of the sort, because at that time the top pointer points to the pivot entry itself. Furthermore, since each time a deadlock occurs the bottom pointer must point to a name less than or equal to the pivot entry, the interchange performed to break the deadlock leaves the top pointer pointing to an entry that is less than or equal to the pivot. We conclude that Assertion 2 holds.

Based on Assertion 2, we claim

> **Assertion 3:** If the pointers coincide, the entry they identify is less than or equal to the pivot.

To justify this claim, we consider the two processes that can lead to the coincidence of the pointers. First, the bottom pointer can move up to the top pointer. In this case Assertion 2 confirms that the top pointer must point to an entry less than or equal to the pivot before the bottom pointer can begin to move. Thus, if the bottom pointer reaches the top one, Assertion 3 is satisfied. The other process that can lead to common pointer positions is for the top pointer to move down to the bottom one. But in this case, the bottom pointer has previously stopped at an entry that is less than or equal to the pivot, so again, Assertion 3 is satisfied.

Combining Assertions 1 and 3, we conclude that once the pointers coincide, the entries in the list below the pointers are all greater than the pivot, and those entries at or above the common pointers are all less than or equal to the pivot. Indeed, in our example, we find the following configuration:

Less-than-or-equal-to pivot	Jane	(Pivot entry)
	Bob	
	Alice	
	Cheryl	
	Carol	
	Bill	
	→ George	
Greater-than pivot	Tom	
	Sue	
	John	

We are now ready to position the pivot entry; it belongs between the two sublists we have formed. To place it there, we could remove the pivot from the list, repeatedly move names up one notch in the list until a hole is generated at the position of the common pointers, and then insert the pivot in this hole. This action would generate a tremendous amount of motion on our desk top as we pushed cards up to make room for the pivot. Therefore, we prefer to simply interchange the pivot with the entry identified by the common pointers. After all, this entry belongs in front of the pivot (by Assertion 3), and this interchange involves the movement of only two names instead of many. After this interchange, our example takes on the following appearance:

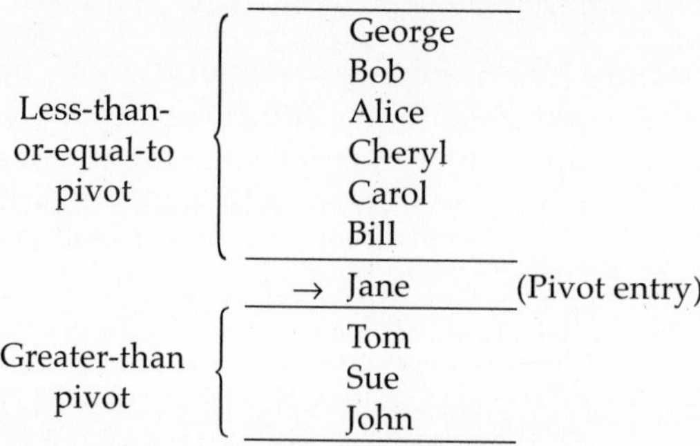

What we have accomplished at this stage is the correct positioning of one name. Admittedly, this does not sound like much, but the fact is that we are almost done from the algorithm-development point of view. Indeed, if the portions of the list above and below the name just positioned were sorted, the entire list would now be sorted. As a result, the problem is reduced to sorting these two portions as though they were two separate lists.

Having started with the problem of sorting one list, we have arrived at the problem of sorting two lists. You might conclude that we are getting further from the solution rather than closer, but such a conclusion overlooks the fact that each of the two lists that must now be sorted is shorter than the original one. This observation leads to the conclusion that by applying this same algorithmic process to these shorter lists, we obtain even more but still shorter lists to sort. Successive applications of the process ultimately reduce the initial sort problem to the problem of sorting numerous lists, each of which contain no more than one name. (We use the phrase *no more than one* to allow for the occurrence of a list with no names in it. Such a case arises, for instance, if the pivot entry turns out to belong at the first of the list, resulting in the list of names above it being empty.) Since such lists are already sorted by default, we see that repeated applications of the process are, at some stage, no longer required; at that point the original list is sorted.

Our completed solution, which is known as the **quick sort**[1] **algorithm,** is shown in Fig. 4.18. We implement our solution as a procedure called Sort, which begins by testing the length of the list it is asked to sort. If that list has two or more entries, the procedure branches to the else portion of its if-then-else structure. There the procedure positions the pivot entry as we have described and then requests that the portions of the list above and below the pivot be sorted. These requests appear in the last two lines of the procedure as additional applications of the procedure Sort.

[1]The quick sort algorithm presented here differs slightly from the traditional version in the manner in which the pivot is handled. Interested readers are encouraged to consult the additional readings at the end of this chapter for other discussions of the quick sort algorithm.

```
procedure Sort (List)
if (List contains fewer than two entries)
   then (Declare List to be sorted.)
   else
     [Select the first entry in List as the pivot;
      Place pointers at the first and last entries of List;
      while (the pointers do not coincide) do
        (Move the bottom pointer up to the nearest
           entry less than or equal to the pivot
           but not beyond the top pointer;
         Move the top pointer down to the nearest entry
           greater than the pivot but not beyond the
           bottom pointer;
         If (the pointers do not coincide)
           then (interchange the entries indicated by the
              pointers.))
     Interchange the pivot with the entry indicated by the
        common pointers;
     Apply the procedure Sort to the portion of List above the pivot.
     Apply the procedure Sort to the portion of List below the pivot.]
```

Figure 4.18 The quick sort algorithm in pseudocode

Let us apply the quick sort algorithm to the list

Bob
Elaine
David
Alice
Cheryl

We check the length of the list, establish Bob as the pivot entry, position pointers at the top and bottom of the list, move the bottom pointer up to the name Alice, move the top pointer down to the name Elaine, and interchange Elaine and Alice. Our situation now becomes

	Bob	(Pivot entry)
→	Alice	
	David	
→	Elaine	
	Cheryl	

Now we move the bottom pointer up to Alice but cannot move the top pointer down because the pointers already coincide. Thus we interchange the names Bob and Alice. At this point our list appears as follows:

Alice	
Bob	(Pivot entry)
David	
Elaine	
Cheryl	

We are now requested to sort the portion of the list above the pivot, which is the list containing the single name Alice. It is important to keep in mind that for a while we have two activations of our algorithm. One is temporarily suspended at the instruction

Apply the procedure Sort to the portion of List above the pivot.

while the second is charged with the task of sorting the list Alice. Our situation is analogous to that represented in Fig. 4.19.

Actually, the second activation of the algorithm does not last long. It recognizes that its list has fewer than two entries and declares its task complete. We

Figure 4.19

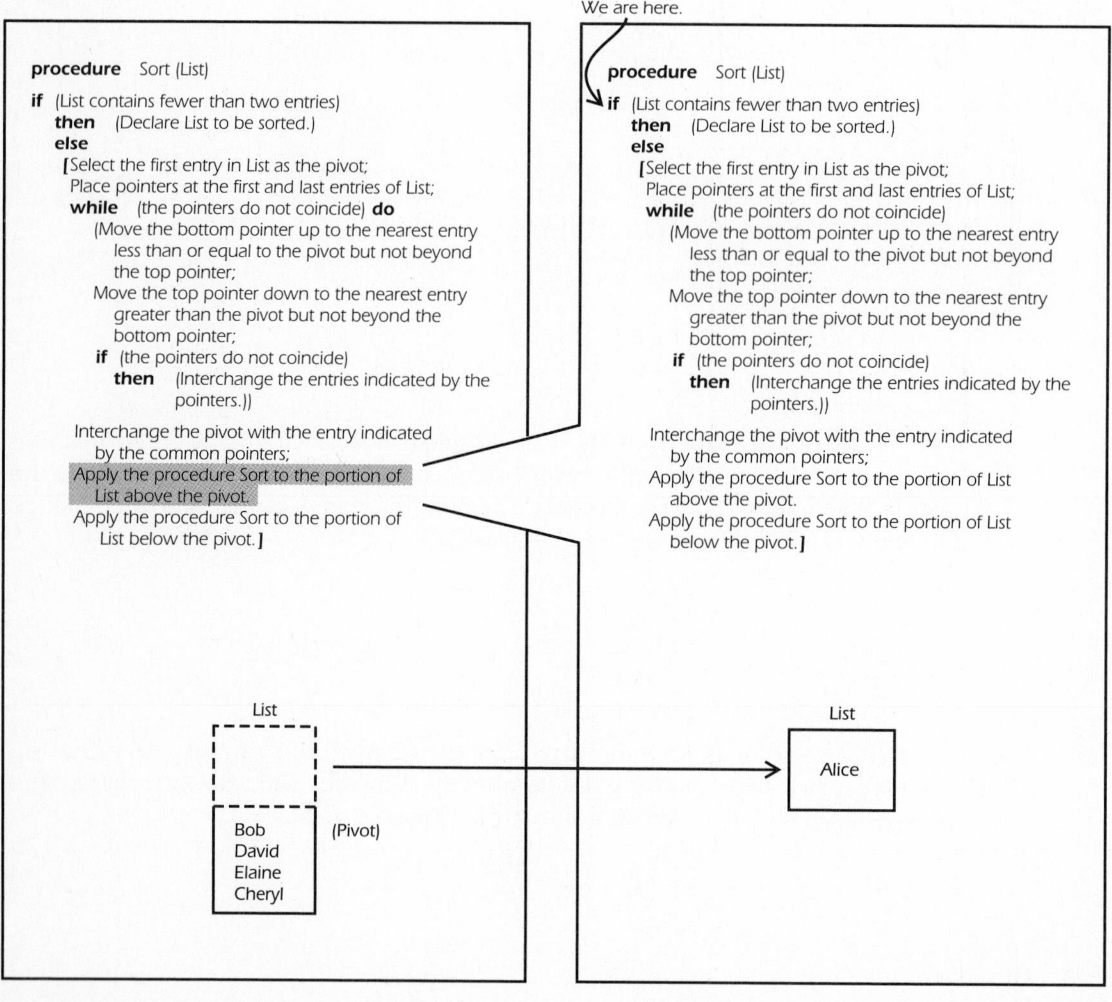

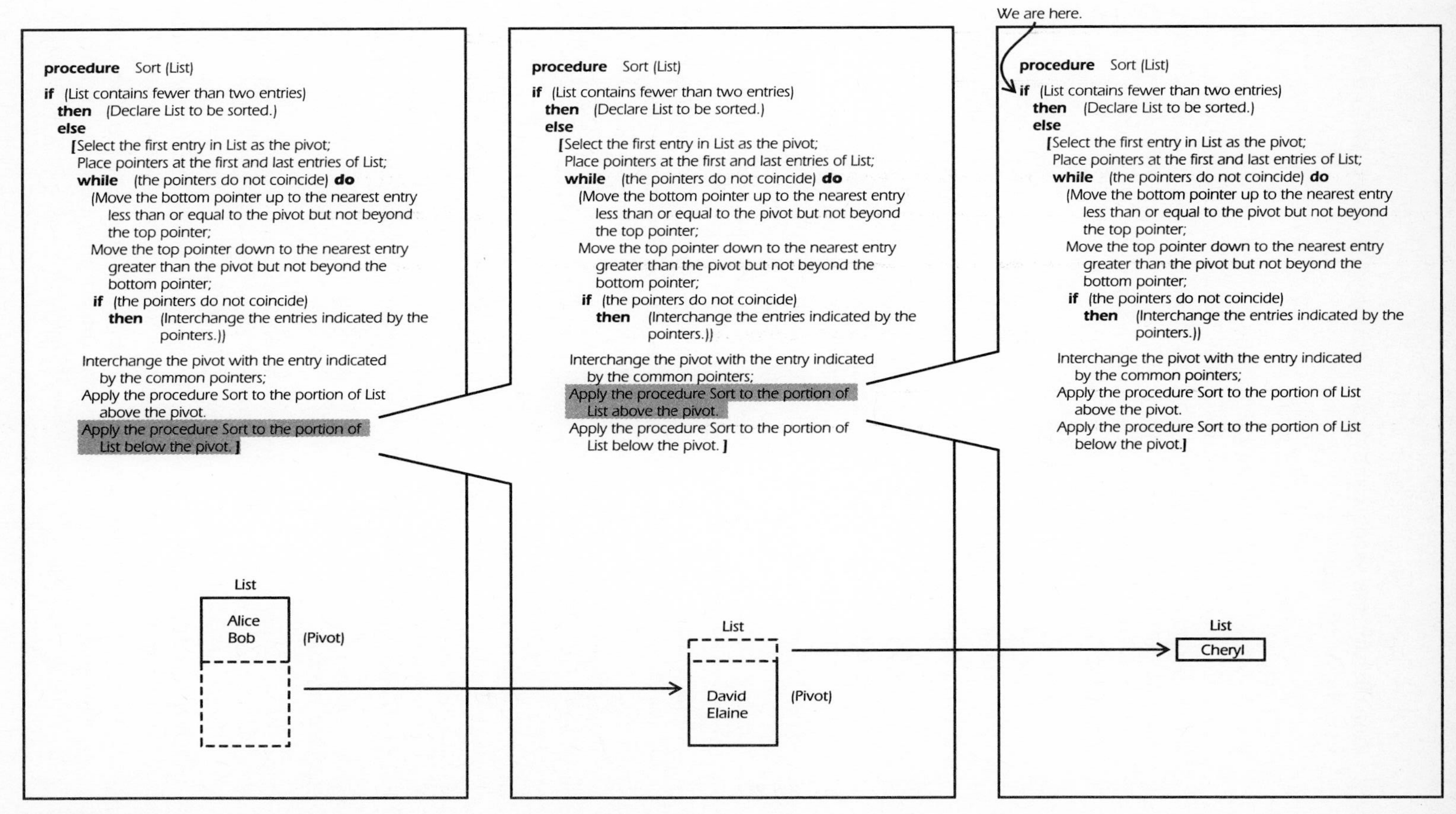

procedure Sort (List)
if (List contains fewer than two entries)
then (Declare List to be sorted.)
else
[Select the first entry in List as the pivot;
Place pointers at the first and last entries of List;
while (the pointers do not coincide) do
(Move the bottom pointer up to the nearest entry less than or equal to the pivot but not beyond the top pointer;
Move the top pointer down to the nearest entry greater than the pivot but not beyond the bottom pointer;
if (the pointers do not coincide)
then (Interchange the entries indicated by the pointers.))
Interchange the pivot with the entry indicated by the common pointers;
Apply the procedure Sort to the portion of List above the pivot.
Apply the procedure Sort to the portion of List below the pivot.]
List
Alice
Bob
(Pivot)
procedure Sort (List)
if (List contains fewer than two entries)
then (Declare List to be sorted.)
else
[Select the first entry in List as the pivot;
Place pointers at the first and last entries of List;
while (the pointers do not coincide) do
(Move the bottom pointer up to the nearest entry less than or equal to the pivot but not beyond the top pointer;
Move the top pointer down to the nearest entry greater than the pivot but not beyond the bottom pointer;
if (the pointers do not coincide)
then (Interchange the entries indicated by the pointers.))
Interchange the pivot with the entry indicated by the common pointers;
Apply the procedure Sort to the portion of List above the pivot.
Apply the procedure Sort to the portion of List below the pivot.]
List
David
Elaine
(Pivot)
We are here.
procedure Sort (List)
if (List contains fewer than two entries)
then (Declare List to be sorted.)
else
[Select the first entry in List as the pivot;
Place pointers at the first and last entries of List;
while (the pointers do not coincide) do
(Move the bottom pointer up to the nearest entry less than or equal to the pivot but not beyond the top pointer;
Move the top pointer down to the nearest entry greater than the pivot but not beyond the bottom pointer;
if (the pointers do not coincide)
then (Interchange the entries indicated by the pointers.))
Interchange the pivot with the entry indicated by the common pointers;
Apply the procedure Sort to the portion of List above the pivot.
Apply the procedure Sort to the portion of List below the pivot.]
List
Cheryl

Figure 4.20

then discard the second activation and return to continue in the first, where we find the instruction

> Apply the procedure Sort to the portion of List below the pivot.

which requests that we establish another activation of the sort algorithm and assign it the task of sorting the list David, Elaine, and Cheryl. This activation establishes David as its pivot entry, interchanges Elaine and Cheryl, and then interchanges David (the pivot) and Cheryl (the name identified by the common pointers). The list under consideration by this activation of the algorithm has the structure

Cheryl
David (Pivot entry)
Elaine

At this point the current activation reaches the instruction

> Apply the procedure Sort to the portion of List above the pivot.

so it requests yet another activation to sort the list Cheryl. This results in a total of three activations currently underway. As the third of these activations begins, our situation is that of Fig. 4.20. The original activation is waiting for the lower portion of its list to be sorted by the second activation. The second activation is waiting for the upper portion of its list to be sorted by the third activation. The third activation is about to begin its task.

Here again, the task of sorting a one-entry list does not take long. The third activation simply declares its list to be sorted and terminates. Thus the second activation can proceed by requesting that the lower portion of its list be sorted. This, of course, creates a third activation charged with the task of sorting the list Elaine. This third activation does its job, terminates, and allows the second activation to continue once more.

At this stage, having completed its task, the second activation terminates and allows the original activation to continue. The original activation had been suspended at its last instruction, which requested the lower portion of its list to be sorted. Since that request has now been fulfilled, the original activation is finished and terminates. Indeed, the entire list has now been sorted.

Questions/Exercises

1. What names are interrogated by the binary search (Fig. 4.14) when searching for the name Joe in the list Alice, Bob, Carol, David, Evelyn, Fred, George, Henry, Irene, Joe, Karl, Larry, Mary, Nancy, and Oliver?
2. What is the maximum number of entries that must be interrogated when applying the binary search to a list of 200 entries? What about 100,000 entries?
3. If we apply the quick sort (Fig. 4.18) to the list Carol, Alice, Bob, Larry, and John, what is the order of the names immediately after the first interchange of names? What about after executing the next-to-the-last instruction in the first activation of the program?

4. What happens if we apply the quick sort to a list that is already sorted? What if the list is in exactly reverse order?
5. What happens if we apply the quick sort to a list in which all the names are the same?

4.6 Efficiency and Correctness

Of the remaining topics we could discuss as a part of our formal introduction to algorithms, this section discusses two that should linger in your mind as you develop programs on your own. The first of these is efficiency, and the second is correctness.

Algorithm Efficiency

We discuss the issues of algorithm efficiency more thoroughly in Chapter 11. For now, however, we emphasize the importance of this topic by taking a few paragraphs to introduce the idea of comparative efficiency. Even though today's machines are capable of executing millions of instructions each second, efficiency remains a major concern in algorithm design. Often the choice between efficient and inefficient algorithms can make the difference between a practical solution to a problem and an impractical one.

Let us consider the problem of a university registrar faced with the task of retrieving and updating student records. Although the university has an actual enrollment of approximately 10,000 students during any one semester, its "current student file" contains the records of more than 30,000 students who are considered current students in the sense that they have registered for at least one course in the past few years but have not completed a degree. We envision these records as being stored in the registrar's computer in a list ordered by student identification numbers. To find any student record, the registrar would essentially search this sorted list for a particular identification number.

We have presented two algorithms for searching such a list: the sequential search and the binary search. Our question now is whether the choice between these two algorithms makes any difference in the case of the registrar. We consider the sequential search first.

Given a student identification number, the sequential search algorithm starts at the beginning of the list and compares the entries it finds to the number desired. Not knowing anything about the source of the target value, we cannot conclude how far into the list this search must go. We can say, though, that after many searches we expect the average depth of the searches to be halfway through the list; some will be shorter, but others will be longer. We conclude that over a period of time, the sequential search will investigate roughly 15,000 records per search. If retrieving and checking a record for its identification number requires a millisecond (one thousandth of a second), such a search will require an average of 15 seconds. Because an eight-hour workday contains 28,800 seconds, the sequential search allows the registrar to perform an average of no more than 2000 searches during a day. This means that retrieving each of the 10,000 active student records represents more than a week's work. Moreover, this does not allow time for using or updating the information retrieved.

In contrast, the binary search proceeds by comparing the target value to the middle entry in the list. If this is not the desired entry, then at least the remaining search is restricted to only half of the original list. Thus, after interrogating the middle entry in the list of 30,000 student records, the binary search has at most 15,000 records still to consider. After the second inquiry, at most 7500 remain, and after the third retrieval, the list in question has dropped to no more than 3750 entries. Continuing in this fashion, we see that if the target record is in the list, it will be found after retrieving at most 15 entries from the list of 30,000 records. Thus, if each of these retrievals can be performed in one millisecond, the process of searching for a particular record requires only 0.015 second. This means that the process of searching for each of the 10,000 active student records one at a time consumes at most 2.5 minutes—a substantial improvement over the sequential search algorithm.

Of course, to reap the benefits of the binary search algorithm, the student records must be stored in a manner that allows the middle entries of successively smaller sublists to be retrieved without undue hardship. In short, the ultimate efficiency of the algorithm is closely associated with the details of its implementation. Our example is rather typical in that a major concern regarding the algorithm's implementation is data organization. The relationship between algorithms and data organization is the underlying theme of Part Three of this text.

We conclude that the issue of efficiency is quite important. In fact, the search for efficient solutions to problems and for techniques of measuring efficiency is a major topic in the area of complexity theory. We discuss this topic in Chapter 11.

Software Verification

Recall that the fourth phase in Polya's analysis of problem solving (Section 4.3) is to evaluate the solution for accuracy and for its potential as a tool for solving other problems. The significance of the first part of this phase is exemplified by the following example:

> A traveler with a gold chain of seven links must stay in an isolated hotel for seven nights. The rent each night consists of one link from the chain. What is the fewest number of links that must be cut so that the traveler can pay the hotel one link of the chain each morning without paying for lodging in advance?

We first realize that not every link in the chain must be cut. If we cut only the second link, we could free both the first and second links from the other five. Following this insight we are led to the solution of cutting only the second, fourth, and sixth links in the chain, a process that releases each link while cutting only three (Fig. 4.21). Furthermore, any fewer cuts leaves two links connected, so we conclude that the correct answer to our problem is three.

Upon reconsidering the problem, however, we might make the observation that when only the third link in the chain is cut, we obtain three pieces of chain of

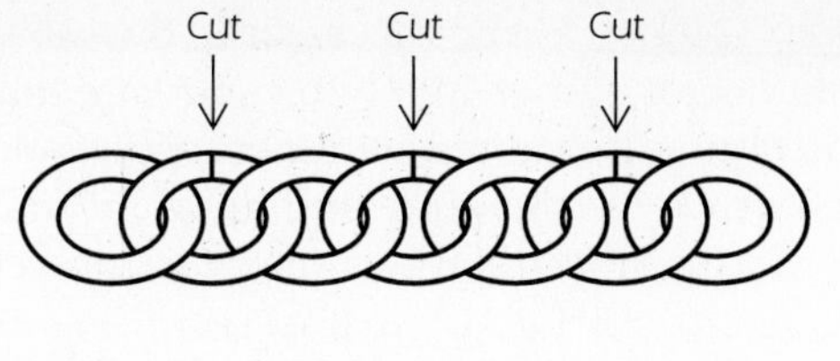

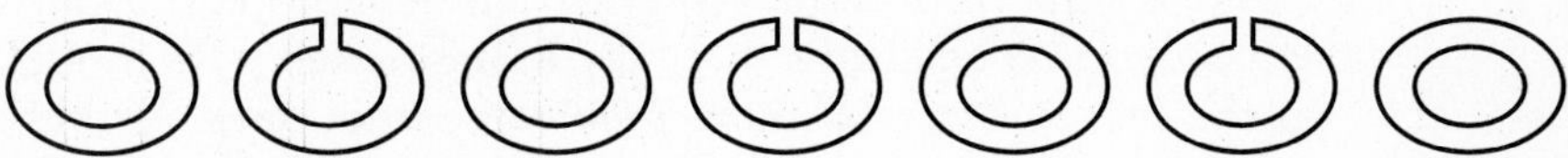

Figure 4.21 Separating the chain using only three cuts

lengths one, two, and four (Fig. 4.22). With these pieces we can proceed as follows:

On the first morning, give the hotel the single link.
On the second morning, retrieve the single link and give the hotel the two-link piece.
On the third morning, give the hotel the single link.
On the fourth morning, retrieve the three links held by the hotel and give the hotel the four-link piece.
On the fifth morning, give the hotel the single link.
On the sixth morning, retrieve the single link and give the hotel the double-link piece.
On the seventh morning, give the hotel the single link.

Consequently, our first answer, which we were sure was correct, is incorrect. How, then, can we be sure that our new solution is correct? We might argue as follows: Since a single link must be given to the hotel on the first morning, at least one link of the chain must be cut, and since our new solution requires only one cut, it must be optimal.

Translated into the programming environment, this example emphasizes the distinction between a program that is believed to be correct and a program that

Figure 4.22 Solving the problem with only one cut

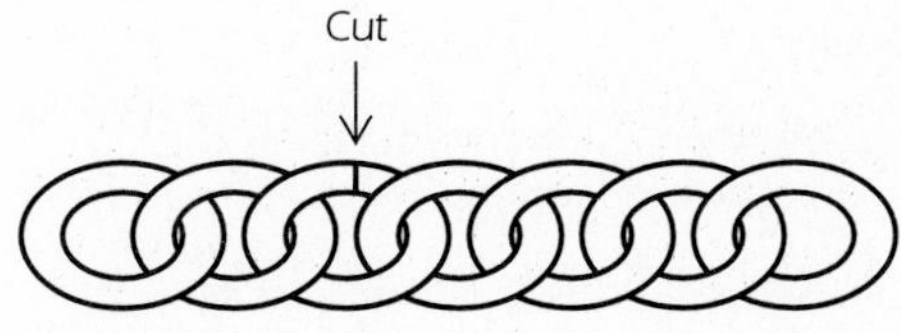

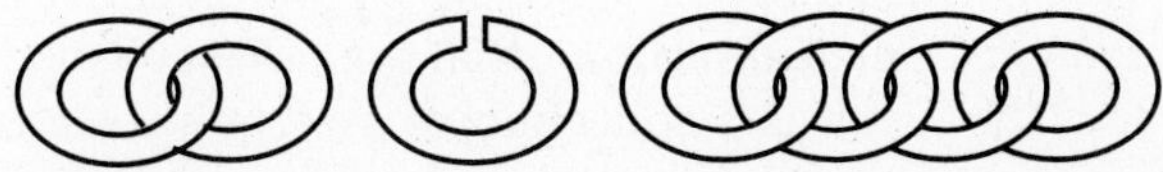

is correct. The two are not necessarily the same. The data processing community is rich in horror stories involving software that although "known" to be correct still failed at a critical moment because of some unforeseen situation. Verification of software is therefore an important undertaking, and the search for efficient verification techniques constitutes an active field of research in computer science.

One current line of research in this area attempts to apply the techniques of formal logic to prove the correctness of a program. The underlying thesis is that by reducing the verification process to a formal procedure, one is protected from the inaccurate conclusions that may be associated with intuitive arguments, as was the case in the gold chain problem. Let us consider this approach to program verification in more detail.

Just as a formal mathematical proof is based on axioms (geometric proofs are often founded on the axioms of Euclidean geometry, whereas other proofs may be based on the axioms of set theory), a formal proof of a program's correctness is based on the specifications under which the program was designed. To prove that a program correctly sorts lists of names, we are allowed to begin with the assumption that the program's input is a list of names, or if the program is designed to compute the average of one or more positive numbers, we can assume that the input does, in fact, consist of one or more positive numbers. In short, a proof of correctness begins with the assumption that certain conditions, called **preconditions,** are satisfied at the beginning of program execution.

The next step in a proof of correctness is to consider how the consequences of these preconditions propagate through the program. For this purpose, researchers have analyzed various program structures to determine how a statement, known to be true before the structure is executed, is affected by executing the structure. As a simple example, if a certain statement about the value of Y is known to hold prior to executing the instruction

```
assign X the value of Y
```

then that same statement can be made about X after the instruction has been executed. More precisely, if the value of Y is not 0 before the instruction is executed, then we can conclude that the value of X will not be 0 after the instruction is executed.

A slightly more involved example occurs in the case of an if-then-else structure such as

```
if (condition) then (instruction 1)
               else (instruction 2)
```

Here, if some statement is known to hold before execution of the structure, then immediately before executing *instruction 1,* we know that both that statement and the condition tested are true, whereas if *instruction* 2 is to be executed, we know the statement and the negation of the condition must hold.

Following rules such as these, a proof of correctness proceeds by identifying statements, called **assertions,** that can be established at various points in the program. The result is a collection of assertions, each being a consequence of the program's preconditions and the sequence of instructions that lead to the point in the program at which the assertion is established. If the assertion so established at the end of the program corresponds to the desired output specifications, we can conclude that the program is correct.

For example, consider the typical repeat loop structure represented in Fig. 4.23. Suppose, as a consequence of the preconditions given at point A, we can establish that a particular assertion is true each time point B is reached during the repetitive process. (Such an assertion within a loop is known as a **loop invariant.**) Then, if the repetition ever terminates, execution moves to point C, where we can conclude that both the loop invariant and the termination condition hold. (The loop invariant still holds because the test for termination does not alter any values in the program, and the termination condition holds because otherwise the loop does not terminate.) If these combined statements imply the desired output, our proof of correctness can be completed merely by showing that the initialization and modification components of the loop ultimately lead to the termination condition.

You should compare this analysis to our example of the insertion sort shown in Fig. 4.12. Indeed, the development of that program was based on the loop invariant

> Each time the loop body is completed the names in the unshaded portion of the list are sorted.

Figure 4.23 The assertions associated with a typical repeat structure

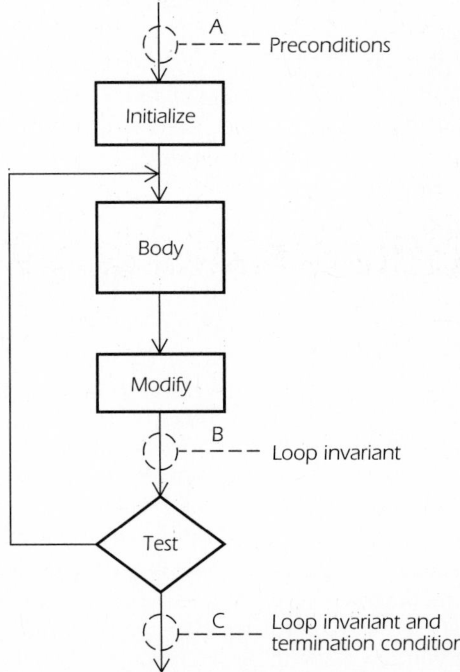

the termination condition

> The entire list is unshaded.

and the fact that by repeatedly unshading an additional name, the entire list ultimately is unshaded.

The fact that we informally identified the loop invariant in the process of developing the insertion sort program is not an uncommon phenomenon. It turns out that the assertions obtained when proving a program correct are often essentially the insights that led to the program in the first place. This, in turn, has caused many researchers to propose an assertion approach to program development. That is, they propose that the assertions for the various stages of a program be developed first, before the instructions that lead to these assertions are inserted. This is similar to our development of the quick sort algorithm represented in Fig. 4.18, where we used the assertion approach to record various relationships among the list entries during program development.

Unfortunately, formal program verification techniques have not been refined to the point that they can be easily applied in general data processing applications. The result is that in most cases today, software is "verified" by applying it to test data—a process that is shaky at best. After all, verification by test data proves nothing more than that the program runs correctly for the test data. Any additional conclusions are merely projections based on statistical analysis. Thus obtaining test data for use in program verification should be given the same careful consideration as obtaining a random sample for a statistically based survey. It is this analogy that clarifies one of the major (yet often violated) rules of thumb in verification by test data: Test data should not be designed by a person closely involved in the software's development. A person so involved would tend to overlook the same possibilities when designing the test data that were overlooked when designing the software. The test data produced in these circumstances would be anything but a random sample, and consequently errors in the software, just as our error in the gold chain problem, could go undetected.

Questions/Exercises

1. Following are a problem and a proposed answer. Is the proposed answer correct? Why or why not?

   Problem: Suppose a box contains three cards. One of three cards is painted black on both sides, one is painted red on both sides, and the third is painted red on one side and black on the other. One of the cards is drawn from the box, and you are allowed to see one side of it. What is the probability that the other side of the card is the same color as the side you see?

   Proposed answer: One-half. Suppose the side of the card you can see is red. (The argument would be symmetric with this one if the side were black.) Only two cards among the three have a red side. Thus the card you see must be one of these two. One of these two cards is red on the other side, while the other is black. Thus the card you can see is just as likely to be red on the other side as it is to be black.

2. The following program segment is an attempt to compute the quotient (forgetting any remainder) of two positive integers by counting the number of times the divisor can be subtracted from the dividend before what is left becomes less than the divisor. For instance, 7/3 should produce 2 because 3 can be subtracted from 7 twice. Is the program correct? Justify your answer.

```
assign Count the value 0;
assign Remainder the value of the dividend;
repeat (assign Remainder the value of Remainder − divisor;
        assign Count the value of Count + 1)
until (Remainder < the divisor)
assign Quotient the value of Count
```

3. The following program segment is designed to compute the product of two nonnegative integers *X* and *Y* by accumulating the sum of *X* copies of *Y*—that is, 3 times 4 is computed by accumulating the sum of three 4s. Is the program correct? Justify your answer.

```
assign Product the value of Y;
assign Count the value 1;
while (Count < X) do
   (assign Product the value Product + Y;
    assign Count the value Count + 1)
```

4. Assuming the precondition that the value associated with *N* is a positive integer, establish a loop invariant that leads to the conclusion that if the following routine terminates, then Sum is assigned the value $0 + 1 + \ldots + N$.

```
assign Sum the value 0;
assign I the value 0;
while (I < N) do
   (assign I the value I + 1;
    assign Sum the value Sum + I)
```

Give an argument to the effect that the routine does, in fact, terminate.

CHAPTER REVIEW PROBLEMS

1. Give an example of a set of steps that conforms to the informal definition of an algorithm given in the opening paragraph of Section 4.1 but does not conform to the definition given in Fig. 4.1.
2. Explain the distinction between an ambiguity in a proposed algorithm and an ambiguity in the representation of an algorithm.
3. Describe how the use of primitives helps remove ambiguities in an algorithm's representation.
4. Does the following program represent an algorithm in the strict sense? Why or why not?

```
assign Count the value 0;
while (Count not 5) do
   (assign Count the value of Count + 2)
```

5. In what sense do the following steps not constitute an algorithm?

   Draw a straight line segment between the points with rectangular coordinates (2,5) and (6,11).
   Draw a straight line segment between the points with rectangular coordinates (1,3) and (3,6).
   Draw a circle with radius two and center at the intersection of the previous line segments.

6. Rewrite the following program segment using a repeat structure rather than a while structure.

Be sure the new version prints the same values as the original.

```
assign Count the value 2;
while (Count < 7) do
  (print the value assigned to Count and
  assign Count the value Count + 1)
```

7. Rewrite the following program segment using a while structure rather than a repeat structure. Be sure the new version prints the same values as the original.

```
assign Count the value 1;
repeat (print the value assigned to Count and
  assign Count the value Count + 1)
until (Count = 5)
```

8. Draw flowcharts representing the structure of each of the following pseudocode sequences.

a.
```
if (X = 5) then
  (if (Y = 6) then assign Z the value 7)
```
b.
```
assign X the value 0;
while (X < 3) do
  (assign Y the value 0;
   while (Y < 2) do
     (assign Y the value Y + 1;)
   assign X the value X + 1)
```
c.
```
assign X the value 0;
repeat
  (if (X < 5) then assign X the value X + 1)
until (X > 3)
```

9. Design an algorithm that, when given an arrangement of the digits 0, 1, 2, 3, 4, 5, 6, 7, 8, 9, rearranges the digits so that the new arrangement represents the next larger value that can be represented by these digits (or reports that no such rearrangement exists if no rearrangement produces a larger value). Thus 5647382901 would produce 5647382910.

10. What is the difference between a formal programming language and a pseudocode?

11. What is the difference between syntax and semantics?

12. Design an algorithm that, given two strings of characters, tests whether the first string appears as a substring somewhere in the second.

13. The following algorithm is designed to print the beginning of what is known as the Fibonacci sequence. Identify the body of the loop. Where is the initialization step for the loop control? the modification step? the test step? What list of numbers is produced?

```
assign Last the value 0;
assign Current the value 1;
while (Current < 100) do
  (print the value assigned to Current;
   assign Temp the value of Last;
   assign Last the value of Current; and
   assign Current the value of Last + Temp)
```

14. What sequence of numbers is printed by the following algorithm if it is started with input values 0 and 1?

```
procedure MysteryWrite (Last, Current)
if (Current < 100)
  then (print the value assigned to Current;
  assign Temp the value of Current + Last;
  apply MysteryWrite to the values Current and
    Temp)
```

15. Modify the procedure MysteryWrite in the preceding problem so that the values are printed in reverse order.

16. What letters are interrogated by the binary search (Fig. 4.14) if it is applied to the list A, B, C, D, E, F, G, H, I, J, K, L, M, N, O when searching for the value J? What about the value Z?

17. What name is interchanged with the pivot in the first activation of the quick sort (Fig. 4.18) if it is applied to the list consisting of only Bill and Carol? What if the list is Carol and Bill?

18. On the average, how many times must two names be compared when searching a list of 6000 entries using the sequential search? What can be said about the binary search?

19. Identify the body of the following loop structure and count the number of times it will be executed. What happens if the test is changed to read "while (Count not 6)"?

```
assign Count the value 1;
while (Count not 7) do
  (print the value assigned to Count and
   assign Count the value Count + 3)
```

20. What problems do you expect to arise if the following program is implemented on a computer? (*Hint:* Remember the problem of round-off errors associated with floating-point arithmetic.)

```
assign Count the value one-tenth;
repeat (print the value assigned to Count and
  assign Count the value Count + one-tenth)
until (Count equals 1)
```

21. Design a recursive version of the Euclidean algorithm (question 3 of Section 4.2).

22. Suppose we apply both Test1 and Test2 (defined below) to the input value 1. What is the difference in the printed output of the two routines?

```
procedure Test1 (Count)
  assign Count the value the input number;
  if (Count not 5)
    then (print the value assigned to Count
          and apply Test1 to the value Count + 1)

procedure Test2 (Count)
  if (Count not 5)
    then (apply Test2 to the value Count + 1
          and print the value assigned to Count)
```

23. Identify the important constituents of the control mechanism in the routines of the previous problem. In particular, what condition causes the process to terminate? Where is the state of the process modified toward this termination condition? Where is the state of the control process initialized?

24. Design an algorithm to generate the sequence of positive integers (in increasing order) whose only prime divisors are 2 and 3; that is, your program should produce the sequence 2, 3, 4, 6, 9, 12, 16, 18, 24, 27, ... Does your program represent an algorithm in the strict sense?

25. Redesign the quick sort algorithm using the last name in the list as the pivot entry.

26. Does the quick sort algorithm represented in Fig. 4.18 still sort lists correctly if the last line is changed to read as follows:

    Apply the module Sort to the portion of the list consisting of the pivot entry and all entries below the pivot.

    Explain your answer.

27. Answer the following questions in terms of the list: Alice, Byron, Carol, Duane, Elaine, Floyd, Gene, Henry, Iris.
    a. Which search algorithm (sequential or binary) will find the name Gene more quickly?
    b. Which search algorithm (sequential or binary) will find the name Alice more quickly?
    c. Which search algorithm (sequential or binary) will detect the absence of the name Bruce more quickly?
    d. Which search algorithm (sequential or binary) will detect the absence of the name Sue more quickly?
    e. How many entries will be interrogated when searching for the name Elaine when using the sequential search? How many will be interrogated when using the binary search?

28. The factorial of 0 is defined to be 1. The factorial of a positive integer is defined to be the product of that integer times the factorial of the next smaller nonnegative integer. We use the notation $n!$ to express the factorial of the integer n. Thus the factorial of 3 (written 3!) is $3 \times (2!) = 3 \times (2 \times (1!)) = 3 \times (2 \times (1 \times (0!))) = 3 \times (2 \times (1 \times (1))) = 6$. Design a recursive algorithm that computes the factorial of a given value.

29. What sequence of steps is executed if the quick sort algorithm (Fig. 4.18) is applied to a list containing only one name?

30. a. Suppose you must sort a list of five names, and you have already designed an algorithm that sorts a list of four names. Design an algorithm to sort the list of five names by taking advantage of the previously designed algorithm.
    b. Design a recursive algorithm to sort arbitrary lists of names based on the technique of part a.

31. The puzzle called the Towers of Hanoi consists of three pegs, one of which contains several rings stacked in order of descending diameter from bottom to top. The problem is to move the stack of rings to another peg. You are allowed to move only one ring at a time, and at no time is a ring to be placed on top of a smaller one. Observe that if the puzzle involved only one ring, it would be extremely easy. Moreover, when faced with the problem of moving several rings, if you could move all but the largest ring to another peg, the largest ring could then be placed on the third peg, and then the problem would be to move the remaining rings on top of it. Using this observation, develop a recursive algorithm for solving the Towers of Hanoi puzzle for an arbitrary number of rings.

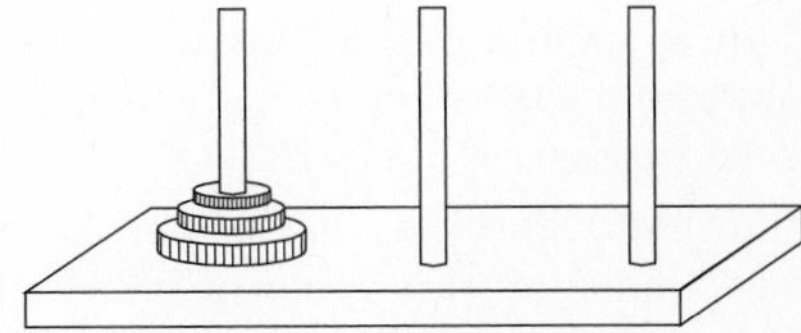

32. Another approach to solving the Towers of Hanoi puzzle (Problem 31) is to imagine the pegs arranged on a circular stand with a peg mounted at each of the positions of 4, 8, and 12 o'clock. The rings, which begin on one of the pegs, are numbered 1, 2, 3, and so on, starting with the smallest ring being 1. Odd-numbered rings, when on top of a stack, are allowed to move clockwise to the next peg; likewise, even-numbered rings are allowed to move counterclockwise (as long as that move does not place a ring on a smaller one). Under this restriction, always move the largest numbered ring that can be moved. Based on this observation, develop a nonrecursive algorithm for solving the Towers of Hanoi puzzle.

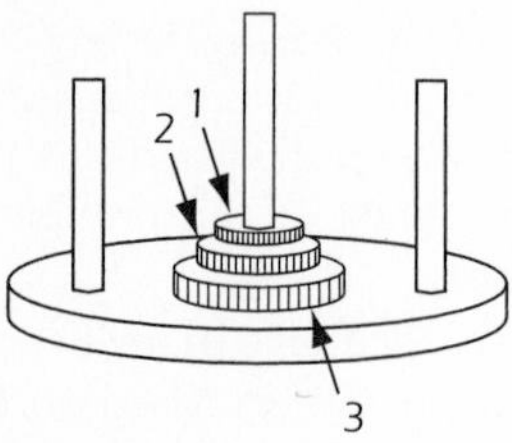

33. Develop two algorithms, one based on a loop structure and the other on a recursive structure, to print the daily salary of a worker who each day is paid twice the previous day's salary (starting with one penny for the first day's work) for a 30-day period. What problems relating to number storage are you likely to encounter if you implement your solutions on an actual machine?

34. Design an algorithm to find the square root of a positive number by starting with the number itself as the first guess and repeatedly producing a new guess from the previous one by averaging the previous guess with the result of dividing the original number by the previous guess. Analyze the control of this repetitive process. In particular, what condition should terminate the repetition?

35. Design an algorithm that lists all possible rearrangements of the symbols in a string of five distinct characters.

36. Design an algorithm that, given a list of names, finds the longest name in the list. Determine what your solution does if there are several "longest" names in the list. In particular, what would your algorithm do if all the names had the same length?

37. Design an algorithm that, given a list of five or more numbers, finds the five smallest and five largest numbers in the list without sorting the entire list.

38. Does the loop in the following routine terminate? Explain your answer. Explain what might happen if this routine is actually executed by a computer (refer to Section 1.7)

```
assign X the value 0;
assign Y the value 1/2;
while (X not equal 1) do
  (assign X the value X + Y;
   assign Y the value Y ÷2)
```

39. The following program segment is designed to compute the product of two nonnegative integers *X* and *Y* by accumulating the sum of *X* copies of *Y*; that is, 3 times 4 is computed by accumulating the sum of three 4s. Is the program segment correct? Explain your answer.

```
assign Product the value 0;
assign Count the value 0;
repeat (assign Product the value Product + Y,
        assign Count the value Count + 1)
until (Count = X)
```

40. The following program segment is designed to report which of the positive integers X and Y is larger. Is the program segment correct? Explain your answer.

```
assign Difference the value of X −Y;
if (Difference is positive)
  then (print "X is bigger than Y")
  else (print "Y is bigger than X")
```

41. The following program segment is designed to find the largest entry in a nonempty list of integers. Is it correct? Explain your answer.

```
assign TestValue the value the first list entry;
assign CurrentEntry the value the first list entry;
while (CurrentEntry is not the last entry) do
  (if (CurrentEntry > TestValue)
     then (assign TestValue the value CurrentEntry)
   assign CurrentEntry the value of the next list entry)
```

42. a. Identify the preconditions for the sequential search as represented in Fig. 4.7. Establish a loop invariant for the while structure in that program that, when combined with the termination condition, implies that upon termination of the loop, the following if statement reports success or failure correctly.

b. Give an argument showing that the while loop in Fig. 4.7 does, in fact, terminate.

43. Based on the preconditions that X and Y are assigned nonnegative integers, identify a loop invariant for the following while structure that, when combined with the termination condition, implies that the value associated with Z upon loop termination must be $X - Y$.

```
assign Z the value of X;
assign J the value 0;
while (J < Y) do
  (assign Z the value Z − 1;
   assign J the value J + 1)
```

QUESTIONS OF ETHICS

The following questions are provided to help you understand some of the ethical/social/legal issues associated with the field of computing as well as investigate your own beliefs and their foundations. The goal is not merely to answer these questions. You should also consider why you answered as you did and whether your justifications are consistent from one question to the next.

1. Since it is currently impossible to verify completely the accuracy of complex programs, under what circumstances, if any, should the creator of a program be liable for errors?

2. a. Suppose you have an idea and develop it into a product that many people can use. It is truly a brilliant idea that no one else has had, but it has required a year of work and your investment of $50,000 to develop into a form that is useful to the general public. In its final form, however, the product, once its existence is known, can be implemented by most people without buying anything from you. What right do you have for compensation?

b. Is it ethical to pirate computer software?

3. Suppose a software package is so expensive that it is totally out of your price range. Is it ethical to copy it for your own use? (After all, you are not cheating the supplier out of a sale because you would not have bought the package anyway.)

4. Suppose Jake Programmer discovers a startling new algorithm for breaking security systems. Should Jake be entitled to ownership rights to that algorithm? If so, what rights should he have? Should his rights be dependent on the subject of the algorithm?

ADDITIONAL ACTIVITIES

1. Compare the pseudocode in this chapter to a programming language you know. In what respects are the two similar? Identify some points at which the programming language requires more precision than the pseudocode.

2. Identify some of the primitives in a programming language you know.

3. Implement the sequential search and insertion sort algorithms in a programming language you know.

4. Identify the statements in a programming language you know that are designed for loop control. In each case, identify what parts of the loop control are provided automatically and what parts you must still specify explicity.

5. Write two programs to compute the factorial of nonnegative integers (Problem 28)—one using recursion, the other using a loop structure. Execute the programs with large input values. Which program requires more memory space? Why?

6. Implement your solutions to Problem 33 so that the length of the pay period can be easily altered. For what length pay period are your answers computed correctly?

ADDITIONAL READING

Brassard, G., and P. Bratley. *Fundamentals of Algorithmics.* Englewood Cliffs, N.J.: Prentice-Hall, 1996.

Gries, D. *The Science of Programming.* New York: Springer-Verlag, 1981.

Harbin, R. *Origami—The Art of Paper Folding.* London: Hodder Paperbacks, 1973.

Harel, D. *Algorithmics: The Spirit of Computing,* 2nd ed. Reading, Mass.: Addison-Wesley, 1992.

Polya, G. *How to Solve It.* Princeton, N.J.: Princeton University Press, 1973.

Rawlins, G. J. E. *Compared to What? An Introduction to the Analysis of Algorithms.* New York: Computer Science Press, 1992.

Roberts, E. S. *Thinking Recursively.* New York: John Wiley and Sons, 1986.

Sedgewick, R., and P. Flajolet. *An Introduction to the Analysis of Algorithms.* Reading, Mass.: Addison-Wesley, 1996.

CHAPTER FIVE

Programming Languages

5.1 Historical Perspective
Early Generations
Machine Independence and Beyond
Programming Paradigms

5.2 Traditional Programming Concepts
Variables, Constants, and Literals
Data Type
Data Structure
Assignment Statements
Control Statements
Comments

5.3 Program Units
Procedures
Parameters
Functions
I/O Statements
Program Examples

***5.4 Language Implementation**
The Translation Process
Linking and Loading
Software Development Packages

***5.5 Parallel Computing**

***5.6 Declarative Programming**
Logical Deduction
Prolog

The development of complex software systems such as operating systems and network software would likely be impossible if humans were forced to express the algorithms involved directly in machine language. Dealing with the massive amount of intricate detail would be a taxing experience, to say the least. Consequently, programming languages similar to our pseudocode have been developed that allow algorithms to be expressed in a form that is both palatable to humans and easily convertible into machine language instructions. These languages allow humans to avoid the intricacies of registers, memory addresses, and machine cycles during the program development process and, instead, to concentrate on the properties of the problem being solved. In this chapter we investigate the subject of programming languages.

*Sections marked by an asterisk are optional in that they provide additional depth of coverage that is not required for an understanding of future chapters.

5.1 Historical Perspective

We begin our study by tracing the historical development of today's programming languages.

Early Generations

Originally the programming process was accomplished by the arduous method of requiring the programmer to express all algorithms in the machine's language. This approach added significantly to the already exacting task of an algorithm's design and more often than not led to errors that had to be located and corrected (a process known as debugging) before the job was finished.

The first step toward removing these complexities from the programming process was to do away with the use of numeric digits for representing the op-codes and operands found in a machine's language. To this end, it became popular to assign mnemonics to the various op-codes and to use them in place of hexadecimal representation during the design process. In place of the op-code for loading a register, for example, a programmer might write LD, or to store the contents of a register, ST might be used. In the case of operands, rules were designed by which the programmer could assign descriptive names (often called identifiers) to locations in memory and use these names in place of the memory cell addresses in an instruction. A special case of this idea was the assignment of names such as R0, R1, R2, . . . to the registers in the CPU.

By choosing descriptive names for the memory cells and using mnemonics for representing op-codes, programmers could greatly increase the readability of a sequence of machine instructions. As an example, let us return to the machine-language routine at the end of Section 2.2 that added the contents of memory cells 6C and 6D and placed the result in location 6E. Recall that the instructions in hexadecimal notation appeared as follows:

```
156C
166D
5056
306E
C000
```

If we assign the name PRICE to location 6C, TAX to 6D, and TOTAL to 6E, we can express the same routine as follows using the mnemonic technique:

```
LD R5,PRICE
LD R6,TAX
ADDI R0,R5 R6
ST R0,TOTAL
HLT
```

Most would agree that the second form, although still lacking, does a much better job of representing the meaning of the routine than does the first. (Note that the mnemonic ADDI is used to represent the op-code for adding integers, to distinguish it from the op-code for adding floating-point numbers, which might be represented by ADDF.)

When these techniques were first introduced, programmers used such notation when designing a program on paper and later translated it into machine-usable form. It was not long, however, before this translation process was recognized as a procedure that could be performed by the machine itself. Consequently, the use of mnemonics was formalized into a programming language, an **assembly language,** and a program, an **assembler,** was developed to translate other programs written in the assembly language into machine-compatible form. (The program was called an assembler because its task was to assemble machine instructions out of the op-codes and operands obtained by translating mnemonics and identifiers. The term *assembly language* followed this lead.)

Today, with such a system, a programmer can type a program in mnemonic form using the system's editor and then ask the operating system to use the assembler to translate the program and save the translated version as a file for later execution.

At the time assembly languages were first developed, they appeared as a giant step forward in the search for better programming environments. In fact, many considered them to represent a totally new generation of programming languages. In time, assembly languages came to be known as second-generation languages, the first generation being the machine languages themselves.

Although second-generation languages had many advantages over their machine-language counterparts, they still fell short of providing the ultimate programming environment. After all, the primitives used in an assembly language were essentially the same as those found in the corresponding machine language. The difference was simply in the syntax used to represent them.

A consequence of this close association between assembly and machine languages is that any program written in an assembly language is inherently machine dependent. That is, the instructions within the program are expressed in terms of a particular machine's attributes. In turn, a program written in assembly language is not easily transported to another machine because it must be rewritten to conform to the new machine's register configuration and instruction set.

Another disadvantage of an assembly language is that a programmer, although not required to code instructions in bit pattern form, is still forced to think in terms of the small, incremental steps of the machine's language rather than being allowed to concentrate on the overall solution of the task at hand. The situation is analogous to designing a house in terms of boards, glass, nails, bricks, and so on. It is true that the actual construction of the house ultimately requires a description based on these elementary pieces, but the design process is easier if we think in terms of rooms, basements, windows, roofs, and so on.

In short, the elementary primitives in which a product must ultimately be expressed are not necessarily the primitives that should be used during the product's design. The design process is better suited to the use of high-level primitives, each representing a concept associated with a major feature of the product. Once the design is complete, these primitives can be translated to lower-level concepts relating to the details of implementation, just as a contractor ultimately translates a building's design into a bill of materials.

Following this philosophy, computer scientists began developing programming languages that were more conducive to software development than were the low-level assembly languages. The result was the emergence of a third generation of programming languages that differed from previous generations in that their primitives were both higher level and machine independent.

In general, the approach to third-generation programming languages was to identify a collection of high-level primitives (in essentially the same spirit as that in which we developed our pseudocode in Chapter 4) in which software could be developed. Each of these primitives was designed so that it could be implemented as a sequence of the low-level primitives available in machine languages. For example, the statement

assign Total **the value** Price + Tax

expresses a high-level activity without reference to how a particular machine should perform the task, yet it can be implemented by the sequence of machine instructions discussed earlier. Thus the structure

assign *identifier* **the value** *expression*

is a potential high-level primitive.

Once this collection of high-level primitives had been identified, a program, called a **translator,** was written that translated programs expressed in these high-level primitives into machine-language programs. Such a translator was similar to the second-generation assemblers, except that it often had to compile several machine instructions into short sequences to simulate the activity requested by a single high-level primitive. Thus, these translator programs came to be known as **compilers.**

Machine Independence and Beyond

With the development of third-generation languages, the goal of machine independence was largely achieved. Since the statements in a third-generation language did not refer to the attributes of any particular machine, they could be compiled as easily for one machine as for another. A program written in a third-generation language could theoretically be used on any machine simply by applying the appropriate compiler.

Reality, however, has not proven to be this simple. When a compiler is designed, certain restrictions imposed by the underlying machine are ultimately reflected as conditions on the language being translated. For example, the size of a machine's registers and memory cells limits the maximum size of integers that can be manipulated conveniently. Such conditions result in the fact that the "same" language tends to have different characteristics, or dialects, on different machines; consequently, it is often necessary to make at least minor modifications to a program to move it from one machine to another.

Compounding this problem of portability is the lack of agreement in some cases as to what constitutes the correct definition of a particular language. To aid in this regard, the American National Standards Institute (ANSI) and the International Standards Organization (ISO) have adopted and published standards for many of the popular languages. In other cases informal standards have evolved due to the popularity of a certain dialect of a language and the desire of other compiler writers to produce compatible products.

In the overall history of programming languages, the fact that third-generation languages fell short of true machine independence is actually of little significance for two reasons. First, they were close enough to being machine-independent that software could be transported from one machine to another with relative ease. Second, the goal of machine independence turned out to be only a seed for more demanding goals. By the time machine independence was within reach, in fact, its significance had been diluted in comparison to the loftier ambitions of the time. Indeed, the realization that machines could respond to such high-level statements as

assign Total **the value** Price + Tax

led computer scientists to dream of programming environments that would allow humans to communicate with machines in terms of the abstract concepts in which humans naturally view problems rather than forcing humans to translate these concepts into machine-compatible form. Moreover, computer scientists want machines that can perform much of the algorithm discovery process rather than just algorithm execution. The result has been an ever-expanding spectrum of programming languages that challenges a clear-cut classification in terms of generations.

As a general rule, however, the term *fourth-generation language* is used in reference to software packages that allow users to customize computer software to their applications without needing technical expertise. Programming in such languages normally involves selecting from choices presented on the monitor's screen in sentence or icon form. Such packages include spreadsheet systems that assist in maintaining tables of data in a form reminiscent of traditional accounting records; database systems that assist in the maintenance and recall of information; graphics packages that assist in the development of graphs, charts, and other pictorial representations of information; and powerful word processors that allow documents to be merged, rearranged, and reformatted. Moreover, packages such as these are often bundled (as integrated software) to form one coherent system. With such a system an economist can construct and modify economic models, analyze the effects various changes might have on the economy in general or a given business in particular, and present the results in a written document using graphs and charts as visual aids. In contrast, a small-business manager might customize the same package to develop a system for maintaining inventory and predicting the effects of stocking certain slow-moving items.

The term *fifth-generation language* is often used in reference to the concept of declarative programming, with an emphasis on the more specialized approach known as logic programming. We define these ideas more thoroughly later in this section. For now we merely note that the idea of declarative programming is to allow the computer user to solve a problem by concentrating on the problem's characteristics rather than on how the problem is to be solved. At this point, such a goal probably seems outrageous to you. How can we hope to solve a problem without ultimately concentrating on how to solve it? The answer is that we do not solve the problem; rather, we let the computer system, with its underlying software, solve it. With this approach, then, our task is merely to describe the problem while the machine tackles the issues of its solution.

Programming Paradigms

The concept of declarative programming brings us to the major problem encountered when trying to push the generation analysis of programming languages beyond the third generation. This problem is that the generation approach insists on classifying programming languages on a linear scale (Fig. 5.1) according to the degree to which the user of the language is freed from the world of computer gibberish and allowed to think in terms associated with the problem. In reality, the development of programming languages has not progressed entirely in this manner but has branched as different approaches to the programming process (different paradigms) have surfaced and been pursued. Consequently, the historical development of programming languages is better represented by a multiple-track diagram as shown in Fig. 5.2, in which different paths resulting from different paradigms are shown to emerge and progress independently. In particular, Fig. 5.2 presents four paths representing the functional, object-oriented, imperative, and declarative paradigms, with various languages associated with each paradigm positioned in a manner that indicates their births relative to other languages. It does not imply that one language necessarily evolved from a previous one.

The different programming paradigms are of interest from both research and application points of view. From a research perspective they have stimulated activity in the development, refinement, and comparison of alternative programming languages. From an application perspective the languages that have emerged from the research arena offer contrasting tools that software developers can apply to a project. Each of these tools encourages an alternative, often insightful, approach to the problem at hand. The significance of such varied approaches was observed in our discussion of the hat-in-the-river problem in Section 4.3, where we saw that adherence to preconceived ideas and preselected tools can degrade our problem-solving ability. An understanding of the princi-

Figure 5.1 Generations of programming languages

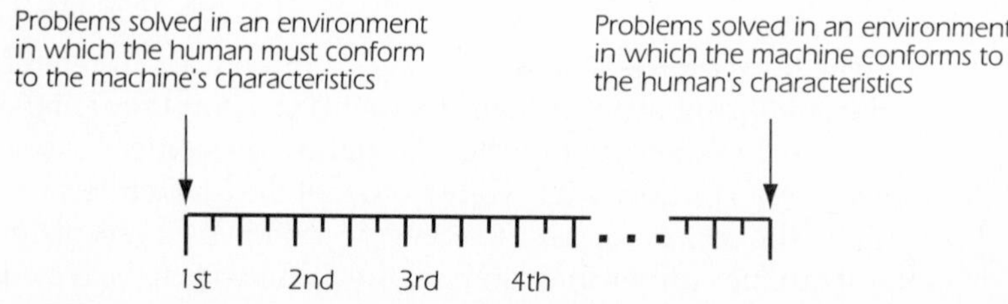

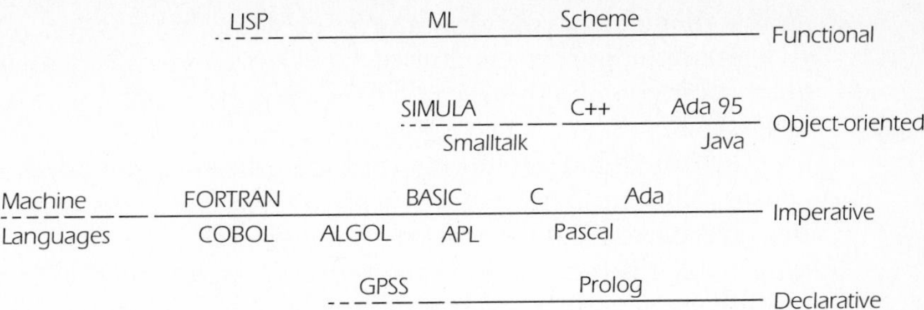

Figure 5.2 The evolution of programming paradigms

pal programming paradigms is not only of academic significance, therefore, but also is important background for any computer practitioner.

The **imperative paradigm,** also known as the **procedural paradigm,** represents the traditional approach to the programming process. Indeed, the imperative paradigm is the one on which a CPU's fetch–decode–execute cycle is based. As the name suggests, the imperative paradigm defines the programming process to be the development of a sequence of commands that when followed manipulate data to produce the desired result. Thus the imperative paradigm tells us to approach a problem by trying to find a method for solving it.

In contrast, consider the **declarative paradigm.** As already mentioned, this paradigm emphasizes the question "What is the problem?" rather than "What procedure is required to solve the problem?" The trick here is to discover and implement a general problem-solving algorithm. Once this is done, problems can be solved merely by stating them in a form compatible with this algorithm and then applying the algorithm. In this context the task of the programmer becomes that of developing a precise statement of the problem rather than of discovering an algorithm for solving the problem.

A major obstacle in developing a programming language based on the declarative paradigm is the discovery of the underlying problem-solving algorithm. For this reason early declarative languages tended to be special-purpose in nature, designed for use in particular applications. For example, the declarative approach has been used for many years in simulation languages with which computer technology is used to simulate a system (economic, physical, political, and so on) in order to test hypotheses. In these settings the underlying algorithm is essentially the process of simulating the passage of time by repeatedly recomputing values of parameters (gross domestic product, trade deficit, and so on) based on the previously computed ones. Implementing a declarative language for such simulations therefore requires that one implement an algorithm that performs this repetitive procedure. Following this, the only task required of a programmer using the language is to describe the relationships among the parameters to be simulated. Then the simulation algorithm merely simulates the passage of time using these relationships to perform its calculations.

More recently, the declarative paradigm has been given a tremendous boost by the discovery that the subject of formal logic within mathematics provides a simple problem-solving algorithm suitable for use in a general-purpose declarative programming system. The result has been increased attention to the declarative paradigm and the emergence of logic programming, a subject discussed in Section 5.6.

The **functional paradigm** views the process of program development as the construction of "black boxes," each of which accepts inputs (at the top) and products outputs (at the bottom). Mathematicians refer to such "boxes" as functions, which is the reason this approach is called the functional paradigm. The primitives of a functional programming language consist of elementary functions (boxes) from which the programmer must construct the more elaborate functions required to solve the problem at hand. Thus a programmer using the functional paradigm approaches a problem by considering the input that is given, the output that is desired, and the transformation that is required to produce that output from the given input. The solution would probably be obtained by dividing this transformation into smaller transformations that produce intermediate outputs that serve as inputs to other small transformations.

As an example, Fig. 5.3 shows how a function for computing the average of a list of numbers can be constructed from three simpler functions: One, `Sum`, finds the sum of the entries in the list, another, `Count`, counts the number of entries in

Figure 5.3 A function that computes the average of a list of numbers constructed from the simpler functions `Sum`, `Count`, and `Divide`

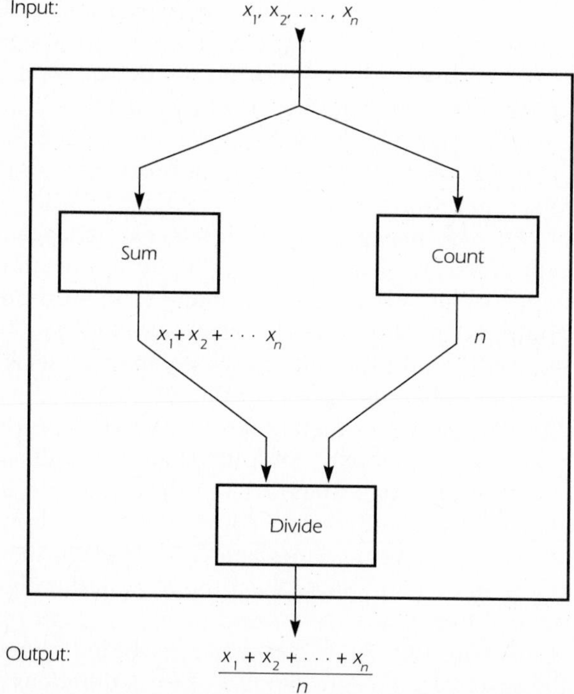

the list, and the third, `Divide`, determines the quotient of the preceding values. This construction can be represented in the syntax of LISP, a prominent functional programming language, by the expression

```
(Divide (Sum Numbers) (Count Numbers))
```

whose nested structure reflects the fact that the function `Divide` operates on the results of `Sum` and `Count`. As another example, an alphabetized list of the words in a document can be constructed by nesting three functions: `DropPunc`, which removes punctuation symbols from its input; `DropDups`, which removes duplicate words from its input; and `Sort`, which sorts its input, by the expression

```
(Sort (DropDups (DropPunc document)))
```

In short, the programming process under the functional paradigm is that of constructing functions as nested complexes of simpler functions.

An advantage of the functional programming paradigm over the imperative model is that it encourages a modular approach to program construction. Indeed, the fact that programs are viewed as functions that must be constructed from other functions forces one to think in modular terms. For this reason, proponents of functional programming argue that their approach leads to well-organized programs more naturally than the imperative paradigm. Moreover, many argue that the functional paradigm is a natural environment for the "building block" approach to the construction of programs. This is the approach of constructing new programs from previously established pieces rather than from scratch, a technique generally accepted by computer scientists as a preferred approach to the development of large software packages.

Another approach to program development is the **object-oriented paradigm,** which leads to the programming process called **object-oriented programming (OOP)**. Using this approach, units of data are viewed as active "objects" rather than the passive units envisioned by the traditional imperative paradigm. To clarify this, consider a list of names. In the traditional imperative paradigm, this list is considered merely a collection of data. Any program accessing this list must contain the algorithms for performing the required manipulations. Thus the list is passive in the sense that it is maintained by a controlling program rather than having the responsibility of maintaining itself. In the object-oriented approach, however, the list is considered an object consisting of the list together with a collection of routines for manipulating the list. They may include routines for entering a new entry in the list, detecting if the list is empty, and sorting the list. In turn, a program accessing this list does not need to contain algorithms for performing these tasks. Instead, it makes use of the routines provided in the object. In a sense, rather than sorting the list as in the imperative paradigm, the program asks the list to sort itself.

As another example of the object-oriented approach, consider the task of developing a graphical user interface. Here the icons on the monitor screen are implemented as objects. Each of these objects encompasses a collection of routines describing how that object is to respond to the occurrence of various events such as being selected by a click of the mouse button or being dragged across the screen by the mouse. The result is an example of an **event-driven system** in which software units are activated by the occurrence of events rather than by explicit requests from other software units. Although we will not study them in this text, Visual Basic (a product of Microsoft Corporation) and Delphi (a product of Borland International) are popular object-oriented programming languages that apply the event-driven approach to the development of GUIs.

Many of the advantages of an object-oriented design are consequences of the modular structure that emerges as a natural by-product of the object-oriented philosophy. Each object is implemented as a separate, well-defined unit. Once the properties of an entity have been defined in this manner, that definition can be reused each time an occurrence of that entity is required. In turn, proponents of object-oriented programming argue that the object-oriented paradigm provides a natural environment for the "building block" approach to software development. They envision software libraries of object definitions from which new software systems can be constructed in the same way that many traditional products are constructed from off-the-shelf components.

The object-oriented paradigm is rapidly growing in popularity, and many believe it will be a major influence well into the future. In fact, the following chapters will repeatedly demonstrate the role of object-oriented methods throughout computer science. In particular, we will witness the influence of the object-oriented paradigm in the fields of software engineering (Chapter 6) and database design (Chapter 9). And in Chapter 7 our study of data structures will lead to a more in-depth study of object-oriented programming, including such related concepts as encapsulation, classes, inheritance, and polymorphism.

In closing, the subject of programming languages is a vast discipline, consisting of multiple generations and paradigms. It is also dynamic. New languages continue to evolve as computer science searches for more convenient ways to communicate with machines. With each step in the evolution, the human–machine communication becomes less technical and hence more conducive to application-minded users. Today, most computer users either buy prewritten software that performs the tasks required or use fourth-generation packages to construct the customized software they need. These prewritten systems and fourth-generation packages tend to be written in third-generation languages by more technically oriented software developers (usually applying either the imperative or object-oriented paradigms). In turn, second-generation languages, once considered the utopia of software development environments, are used only in the most technical applications. To project what the status will be in the future would be highly speculative.

Questions/Exercises

1. In what sense is a program in a third-generation language machine independent? In what sense is it still machine dependent?
2. What is the difference between an assembler and a compiler?
3. We can summarize the imperative programming paradigm by saying that it places emphasis on describing a process that leads to the solution of the prob-

lem at hand. Give a similar summary of the declarative, functional, and object-oriented paradigms.

4. In what sense are the later-generation programming languages at a higher level than the earlier generations?

5.2 Traditional Programming Concepts

In this section we consider some of the generic concepts found in imperative and object-oriented programming languages. For this purpose, and in future sections, we will draw examples from the languages Ada, C, C++, FORTRAN, Java, and Pascal. FORTRAN, Pascal, and C are third-generation imperative languages. C++ is an object-oriented language that was developed as an extension of the language C. Java is an object-oriented language that was derived from C and C++. Ada was originally designed as a third-generation imperative language containing many object-oriented characteristics. Its newest version, however, more fully embraces the object-oriented paradigm. Appendix E contains a brief introduction to each of these languages as well as an example of how the insertion sort algorithm could be implemented in each. Our purpose here is not to learn details of any of these languages but merely to demonstrate how the concepts discussed may appear in actual languages.

Statements in programming languages tend to fall into three categories: declarative statements, imperative statements, and comments. **Declarative statements** define customized terminology that is used later in the program, such as the names used to reference data items; **imperative statements** describe steps in the underlying algorithms; and **comments** enhance the readability of a program by explaining its esoteric features in a more human compatible form. Each program unit tends to begin with a **declarative part,** in which declarative statements are used to describe terminology, followed by a **procedural part,** in which imperative statements are used to describe actions to be performed (Fig. 5.4). Comments are used throughout the program as needed.

Figure 5.4 The underlying organization of a traditional program unit

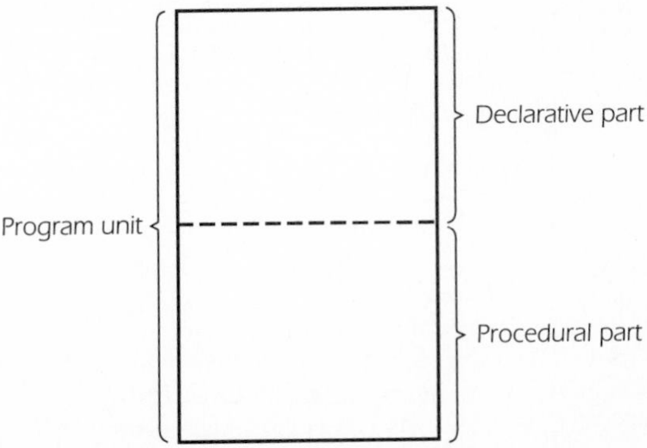

Our discussion will develop along similar lines—beginning with concepts associated with declarative statements, followed by those of imperative statements, and closing with issues of documentation.

Variables, Constants, and Literals

In Section 5.1 we witnessed the advantage of identifying memory locations by means of descriptive names rather than by numeric addresses. Such identifiers are known as **variables,** in reference to the fact that by changing the value stored at the location, the value associated with the identifier changes as the program executes.

In contrast, in some cases a fixed, predetermined value is referenced in a program. For example, a program for controlling air traffic in the vicinity of a particular airport may contain numerous references to that airport's altitude above sea level. When writing such a program, one can include this value, say 645 feet, literally each time it is required. Such an explicit appearance of a value is called a **literal.** The use of literals leads to program statements such as

```
assign EffectiveAlt the value (Altimeter − 645)
```

where EffectiveAlt and Altimeter are assumed to be variables and 645 is a literal.

Often, the use of literals is not good programming practice because literals can mask the meaning of the statements in which they appear. How, for instance, can a reader of the preceding statement know what the value 645 represents? Moreover, literals can complicate the task of modifying the program should it become necessary. If our air traffic program is moved to another airport, all references to the airport's altitude must be changed. If the literal 645 is used in each reference to that altitude, each such reference throughout the program must be located and changed. The problem is compounded if the literal 645 also occurs in reference to a quantity other than the airport's altitude. How do we know which occurrences of 645 to change and which to leave alone?

To solve these problems, programming languages allow descriptive names to be assigned to specific, nonchangeable values. Such a name is called a **constant.** As an example, in the language Pascal, the declarative statement[1]

```
const AirportAlt = 645;
```

associates the constant `AirportAlt` with the value 645. Following this declaration the descriptive name `AirportAlt` can be used in lieu of the literal 645. Using such a constant in our pseudocode, the statement

```
assign EffectiveAlt the value (Altimeter − 645)
```

could be rewritten as

```
assign EffectiveAlt the value (Altimeter − AirportAlt)
```

[1]As in the case of natural languages, programming languages are often associated with a culture of their own. An example is that in the languages Pascal and Ada it is customary to typeset key words in bold, as we did in our pseudocode. This practice is not widely adopted among users of FORTRAN, C, C++, and Java. We adopt such cultural traditions in our examples.

which better represents the meaning of the statement. Moreover, if such constants are used in place of literals and the program is moved to another airport whose altitude is 267 feet, then changing the single declarative statement to read

```
const AirportAlt = 267;
```

is all that is needed to convert all references to the airport's altitude to the new value.

Data Type

Declarative statements that assign descriptive names to data items often identify the type of that data as well. **Data type** refers to both the interpretation given a bit pattern and the operations that can be performed on that pattern. Common types include integer, real, character, and Boolean. The type **integer** refers to numeric data consisting of whole numbers, probably stored using two's complement notation. Operations that can be performed on integer data include the traditional arithmetic operations and comparison of relative size, such as determining whether one value is greater than another. The type **real** refers to numeric data that may contain values other than whole numbers, probably stored in floating-point notation. Operations performed on data of type real are similar to those performed on data of type integer. Note, however, that the activity required for adding two items of type real differs from that for adding two items of type integer.

The type **character** refers to data consisting of symbols, probably stored using ASCII. Operations performed on such data include comparison such as determining whether one symbol occurs before another in alphabetical order, testing to see whether one string of symbols appears inside another, and concatenating one string of symbols at the end of another to form one long string.

The type **Boolean** refers to data items that can take on only the values true or false. Examples occur as the result of comparisons such as Is Tax equal to withholding? Operations on data of type Boolean include inquiries as to whether the current value is true or false.

Most programming languages require that a declarative statement that introduces a variable also specify the type of data that will be referenced by that variable. Figure 5.5 gives examples of such declarative statements in Pascal, C, C++, Java, and FORTRAN. In each case the variables `Length` and `Width` are declared to be of type real, and `Price`, `Tax`, and `Total` are declared to be of type integer. Note that C, C++, and Java use the term *float* to refer to the type real, since data of this type are represented in floating-point notation.

In the Section 5.4 we will see how a translator uses knowledge of data types when translating a program from a high-level language into machine language. For now we note that such information can be used to identify errors. For example, an attempt to add two values of type character or to perform an operation that combines data of different types should arouse suspicion.

Variable declarations in Pascal

```
var
   Length, width:      real;
   Price, Tax, Total:  integer;
```

Variable declarations in C, C++, and Java

```
float Length, Width;
int Price, Tax, Total;
```

Variable declarations in FORTRAN

```
REAL Length, Width
INTEGER Price, Tax, Total
```

Figure 5.5 Variable declarations in Pascal, C, C++, Java, and FORTRAN

Data Structure

Another concept associated with many declarative statements is **data structure,** which relates to the conceptual shape of the data. When using a string of characters to represent an employee's name or a part identification number, it is not sufficient to declare that the data item is of type character. One must also declare the number of symbols that make up the item. (For a translator to translate an instruction to move an employee's name from one location to another, it must know how many memory cells must be copied.) Thus the item has both type and length.

Viewed in this light, a string of characters is a special case of a generic data structure known as a **homogeneous array.** A homogeneous array is a block of values of the same type such as a one-dimensional list, a two-dimensional table with rows and columns, or tables with higher dimensions. To declare such an array, most programming languages use a declaration statement in which the length of each dimension of the array is specified. For example, Fig. 5.6 displays declaration statements in C and Pascal that declare `Name` to be a one-dimensional array of type character with length eight, and `Scores` to be a two-dimensional array of type integer with two rows and nine columns.

In contrast to a homogeneous array in which all data items are the same type, a **heterogeneous array** is a block of data in which different elements can have different types. For example, a block of data referring to an employee may consist of an entry called `Name` of type character, an entry called `Age` of type integer, and an entry called `SkillRating` of type real. Figure 5.7 shows how such an array would be declared in the languages C and Pascal.

Once an array has been declared, it can be referenced in its entirety by its name, or an individual component can be referenced by its position. In the case of a homogeneous array components are identified via indices that specify the row, column, and so on, desired. For example, in a Pascal program the entry in the second row and fourth column of the array `Scores` could be referenced as `Scores[2,4]`; in C the same entry would be identified by `Scores[1][3]`. (Row and column numbers start at zero in C; for example, the entry in the first row and first column would be referenced by `Scores[0][0]`.)

The arrays declared in Pascal

```
var
  Name:   packet array[1..8] of char;
  Scores: array[1..2,1..9] of integer;
```

The arrays declared in C

```
char Name[8];
int Scores[2][9];
```

The conceptual structure of the arrays

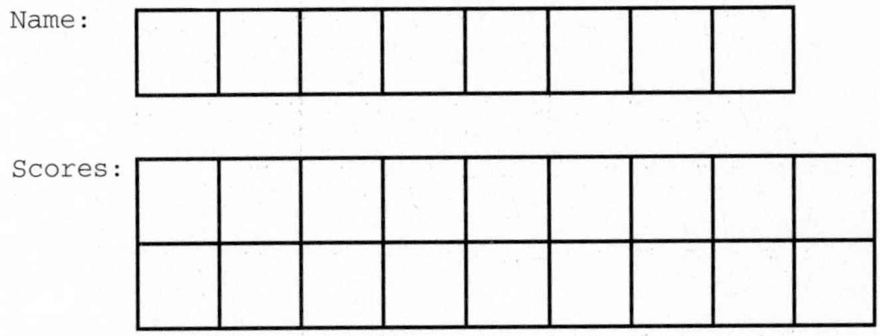

Figure 5.6 Declaration of homogeneous arrays in Pascal and C

Entries in a heterogeneous array are usually referenced by identifying the array, followed by the component name separated by a period. For example, the `Age` component of the array `Employee` in Fig. 5.7 would be referenced by `Employee.Age` in both C and Pascal.

In Chapter 7 we will see that the shape associated with a data structure actually exists only in the programmer's mind, not in the machine. In reality, the data contained in an array may be scattered over a wide area of main memory or mass storage. This is why we refer to data structure as being the conceptual shape of data.

Assignment Statements

Perhaps the most basic imperative statement is the assignment statement, which requests that a value be assigned to a variable. Such a statement normally takes the syntactic form of variable, followed by a symbol representing the assignment operation, followed by an expression indicating the value to be assigned. The semantics of such a statement is that the expression is to be evaluated and the result assigned as the value of the variable. For example, the statement

```
Total = Price + Tax;
```

in C and C++ requests that the sum of `Price` and `Tax` be assigned to the variable `Total`. In Ada and Pascal the equivalent statement would appear as

```
Total := Price + Tax;
```

The array declaration in Pascal

```
var
   Employee: record
                  Name: packed array[1..8] of char;
                  Age: integer;
                  SkillRating: real
                end
```

The array declaration in C

```
struct
{char Name [8];
 int Age;
 float SkillRating;
} Employee;
```

The conceptual organization of array

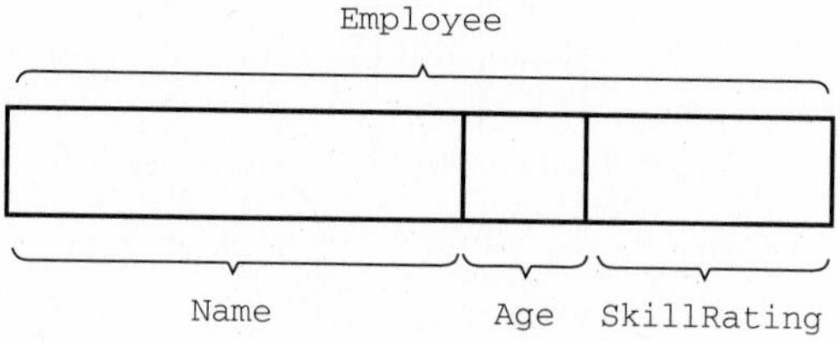

Figure 5.7 Declaration of heterogeneous arrays in Pascal and C

Note that these statements differ only in the syntax of the assignment operator, which in C and C++ is merely an equals sign but in Ada and Pascal is a colon followed by an equals sign.

In the imperative and object-oriented programming paradigms, the assignment statement is the major workhorse. Indeed, it is mainly by means of assignment statements that data items are manipulated and moved about. In a sense the purpose of declaration statements is to establish terminology for use in assignment statements, and the purpose of control statements, which we will study shortly, is to direct the order in which the assignment statements will be executed.

Much of the power of assignment statements comes from the scope of expressions that can appear on the right side of the statement. In general, any algebraic expression can be used, with the arithmetic operations of addition, subtraction, multiplication, and division typically represented by the symbols +, −, *, and /, respectively. Languages differ, however, in the manner in which these expressions are interpreted. For example, the expression 2 * 4 + 6 / 2 could produce the value 14 if it is evaluated from right to left, or 7 if evaluated from left to right. These ambiguities are normally resolved by rules of **operator precedence,** meaning that certain operations are given precedence over others. The traditional rules of algebra dictate that multiplication and division have precedence over addition and subtraction. That is, multiplications and divisions are performed before additions and subtractions. Following this convention, the preceding expression would produce the value 11. In most languages parentheses can be used to override the language's operator precedence. Thus 2 * (4 + 6) / 2 would produce the value 10.

Expressions in assignment statements can also involve operations other than the traditional algebraic ones. For instance, if `First` and `Last` are variables associated with character strings, the FORTRAN statement

```
Both = First // Last
```

causes the variable `Both` to be assigned the string produced by concatenating the values of `First` and `Last`. Thus if `First` and `Last` are associated with the strings *abra* and *cadabra,* respectively, then `Both` would be assigned the string *abracadabra.*

Many programming languages allow the use of one symbol to represent more than one type of operation. In these cases the meaning of the symbol is determined by the data type of the operands. For example, the symbol + traditionally indicates addition when its operands are numeric, but in some languages, such as Java, the symbol indicates concatenation when its operands are character strings. Such multiple use of a symbol is called **overloading.**

Control Statements

Control statements are imperative statements that alter the execution sequence of the program. Of all the programming statements, those from this group have probably received the most attention and generated the most controversy. The major villain is the simplest control statement of all, the goto statement. It provides a means of directing the execution sequence to another location that has been labeled for this purpose by a name or number. It is therefore nothing more than a direct application of the machine-level jump instruction. The problem with such a feature in a high-level programming language is it allows programmers to write rat's nests like

```
      goto 40
20    Total = Price + 10
      goto 70
40    if Price < 50 goto 60
      goto 20
60    Total = Price + 5
70    stop
```

when a two-statement program like this does the job:

```
if Price < 50 then Total = Price + 5
              else Total = Price + 10
stop
```

To avoid such complexities, modern languages are designed with more elaborate control statements, such as if-then-else, that allow a certain branching pattern to be expressed within a single syntactic structure. The choice of which control

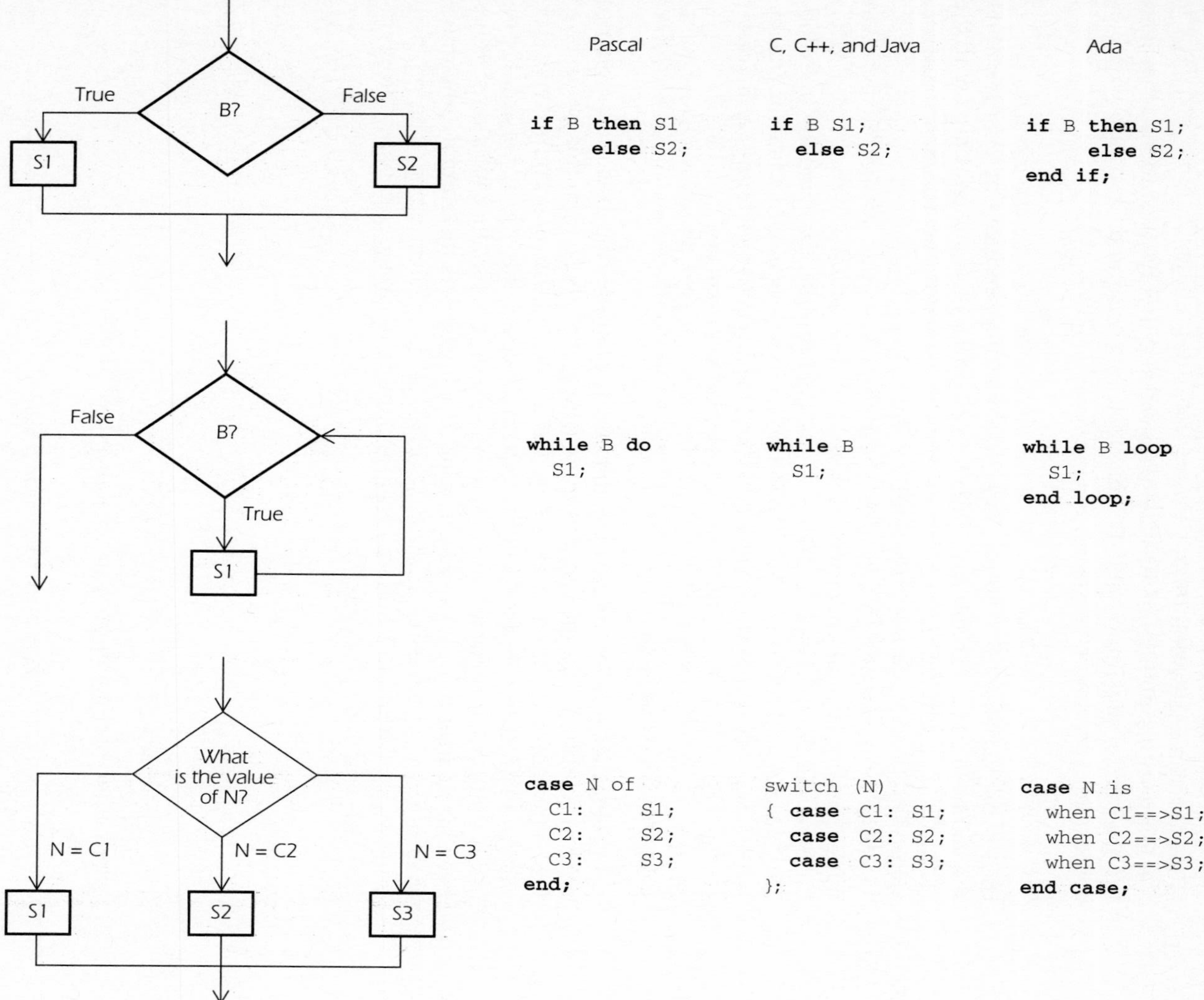

Figure 5.8 Control structures and their representations in Pascal, C, C++, Java, and Ada

structures to incorporate into a language is a significant design decision. The object is to provide a language that not only allows algorithms to be expressed in a readable form but also assists the programmer in obtaining such readability. This is done by restricting the use of those features that have historically led to sloppy programming while encouraging the use of better-designed features. The result is the often misunderstood practice known as **structured programming,** which encompasses an organized design methodology combined with the appropriate use of the language's control statements. The idea is to produce a program that can be readily comprehended and shown to meet its specifications.

Figure 5.8 presents some common branching structures and the control statements provided in various programming languages for representing those structures. Note that the first two structures are those that we have already encountered in Chapter 4. They are represented by the if-then-else and while statements in our pseudocode. The third structure, known as the case structure, can be viewed as an extension of the if-then-else structure. Whereas the if-then-else structure allows a choice between two options, the case structure allows a selection between many options.

Another common structure, often called the for structure, and its representation in various languages is shown in Fig. 5.9. This is a looping structure similar to that of the while statement in our pseudocode. The difference is that all the initialization, modification, and termination of the loop structure is incorporated into a single statement. Such a statement is convenient when the body of the

Figure 5.9 The for structure and its representation in Pascal, C, C++, and Java

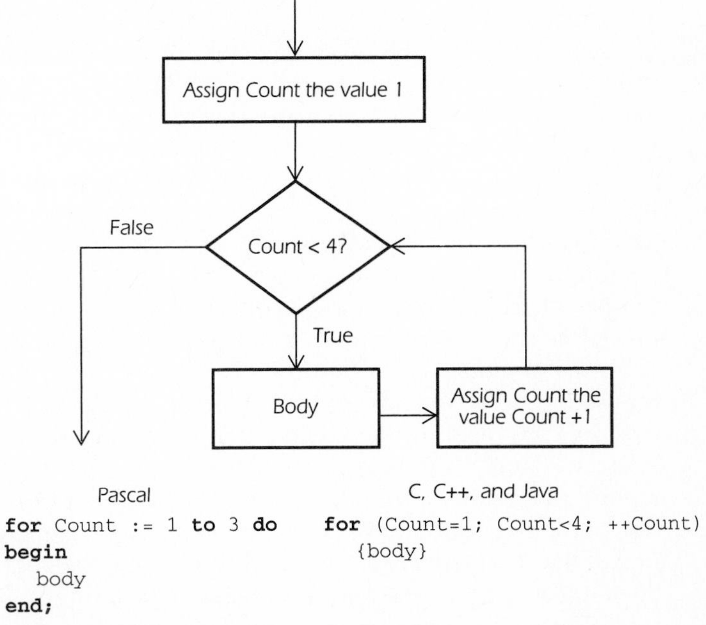


```
for Count := 1 to 3 do
begin
   body
end;
```

```
for (Count=1; Count<4; ++Count)
   {body}
```

loop is to be performed once for each value within a range of values that is ordered. In particular, the statements in Fig. 5.9 direct that the loop body be performed with the value of `Count` being 1, then again with the value of `Count` being 2, and again with the value of `Count` being 3.

The purpose of these examples is to demonstrate that generic branching structures appear, with slight variations, throughout the gamut of imperative and object-oriented programming languages. A somewhat surprising result from theoretical computer science is that the ability to express only a few of these structures ensures that a programming language provides a means of expressing a solution to any problem that has an algorithmic solution. We investigate this claim in Chapter 11. For now, we merely point out that learning a programming language is not an endless task of learning different control statements. Indeed, the major control statements available in a programming language can often be counted on the fingers of one hand.

Comments

Experience has shown that no matter how well a programming language is designed and how well the language's features are used, additional information is either helpful or mandatory when a human tries to understand a program of any significant size. For this reason, programming languages provide syntax for inserting explanatory statements, called *comments,* within a program. The documentation provided by these comments is called **internal documentation,** since it appears within the program itself rather than in a separate document.

Such internal documentation is ignored by a translator, and therefore its presence or absence does not affect the program from a machine's point of view. The machine-language version of the program produced by a translator will be the same with or without comments, but the information provided by these statements constitutes an important part of the program from a human's point of view. Without such documentation large, complex programs can easily thwart the comprehensive powers of a human programmer.

To allow for comments within a program, programming languages provide two common means of delimiting the comments from the rest of the program. One is to bracket the entire comment by special markers, one at the beginning of the comment and one at the end. The other is to mark the beginning of the comment and allow the comment to occupy the remainder of the line to the right of the marker. In this case the beginning of the next line terminates the comment. Pascal and C use the former of these methods. In Pascal the beginning of a comment is marked by the symbol `{`and the end is marked by`}`. In C the beginning of a comment is indicated by `/*` and the end by `*/`. Ada and FORTRAN use the other technique. In Ada the beginning of a comment is marked by a double hyphen (`--`), and in FORTRAN with an explanation mark. In each of these cases the comment extends for the remainder of the line. If the comment continues on the next line, the beginning of that line must be marked as well. C++ and Java use both techniques. Being a derivative of C, they allow comments to be bracketed by `/*` and `*/`, but they also allow a comment to begin with `//` and extend through the remainder of the line. Thus in

C++ and Java both

```
/* This is a comment. */
```

and

```
// This is a comment.
```

are valid comment statements.

A few words are in order about what constitutes a meaningful comment. Beginning programmers, when told to use comments for internal documentation, tend to follow a program statement such as:

```
Total := Price + Tax;
```

with a comment such as "Calculate `Total` by adding `Price` and `Tax.`" Such redundancy adds length rather than clarity to a program. Remember that the purpose of internal documentation is to explain the program, not to repeat it. A more appropriate comment associated with the preceding statement might be to explain why the total is being calculated if that is not obvious. For example, the comment, "`Total` is used later to compute `GrandTotal` and not needed after that" is more helpful than the previous one.

Additionally, a program in which comments are scattered among the program statements can be harder to comprehend than a program with no comments at all. A good approach is to collect comments that relate to a single program unit into one place, perhaps at the beginning of the unit. This provides a central place where the reader of the program unit can look for explanations. It also provides a location in which the purpose and general characteristics of the program unit can be described. If this format is adopted for all program units, the written program is given a degree of uniformity in which each unit consists of a block of explanatory statements followed by the formal presentation of the program unit. Such uniformities in a program enhance its readability.

Questions/Exercises

1. Why is the use of a constant considered better programming style than the use of a literal?
2. What is the difference between a declarative statement and an imperative statement?
3. List some common data types.
4. Identify some common control structures found in imperative and object-oriented programming languages.
5. What is the difference between a homogeneous array and a heterogeneous array?

5.3 Program Units

In previous chapters we have seen advantages to breaking large programs into manageable units. Programming languages are rich in methods for accomplishing this decomposition. Languages based on the functional paradigm naturally break programs into functions; languages based on the object-oriented paradigm lead to program units representing objects.

In this section we focus on methods for obtaining a modular representation of an algorithm. Here the approach is to group steps in the algorithm to form short, simple portions of the overall algorithm and to use these portions as abstract tools to express the final product. The result is the subprogram structure that we expressed in our pseudocode as a procedure.

Procedures

A **procedure,** in its generic sense, is a program unit written independently of the main program yet associated with it through a transfer/return process (Fig. 5.10). Control is transferred to the procedure (by means of a machine language JUMP instruction) at the time its services are required and then returned to the original program unit after the procedure has finished. The process of transferring control to a procedure is often referred to as calling or invoking the procedure. We will refer to a program unit that requests the execution of a procedure as the *calling unit.*

In our example programming languages, procedures are defined in much the same way as in our pseudocode in Chapter 4. In many respects a procedure is a miniature program, consisting of declaration statements that describe such things as variables and constants used in the procedure as well as imperative statements that describe the steps to be performed when the procedure is executed. The definition begins with a statement, known as the **procedure's header,** that identifies, among other things, the name of the procedure. Following this header are the declaration and imperative statements that define the procedure.

As a general rule, variables declared within a procedure are **local variables,** meaning that they can be referenced only within that procedure. This rule eliminates any possible confusion that might occur if two procedures, written independently, happened to use variables of the same name. There are times,

Figure 5.10 The flow of control involving a subprogram

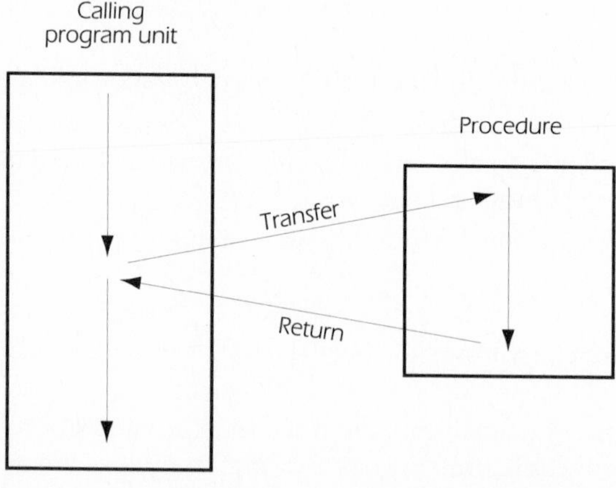

however, when an item of data should be shared by all units within a program. A variable representing such an item is called a **global variable.** Most languages provide a means of declaring both local and global variables.

The syntax used to request the execution of a procedure from another part of a program varies little from language to language. FORTRAN uses the term `CALL` to announce such a request. Ada, C, C++, Java, and Pascal merely state the procedure's name. Thus, if `GetNames`, `SortNames`, and `WriteNames` were procedures for acquiring, sorting, and printing a list of names (identified by a global variable), we could use them to obtain a program to get, sort, and print the list in FORTRAN by the statement sequence

```
CALL GetNames
CALL SortNames
CALL WriteNames
```

or in Ada, C, C++, Java, and Pascal by

```
GetNames;
SortNames;
WriteNames;
```

Note that the result of this approach is a program consisting of three instructions, each of which requests the services of an abstract tool. The details of how each tool performs its task are isolated within the definition of the respective procedure.

Parameters

We will learn in the next chapter that sharing information by means of global variables is not a recommended technique. Briefly, such an approach tends to disguise the activities of the program units sharing the data. A better approach is to identify data being shared among program units in a more explicit manner. This can be done by expanding the statement requesting the execution of a procedure to include an explicit list of the data items to be shared. In turn, the procedure's header contains a list of variables it expects to be assigned values when the procedure is called. The items in both lists are called **parameters.**

When the procedure is called, the parameter list appearing in the calling program unit is associated, entry by entry, with the parameter list in the procedure's header. In the most general case, the values of the parameters in the calling unit are effectively transferred to their corresponding parameters in the procedure. The procedure is then executed, and the (possibly modified) values are transferred back to the original program unit. In other cases the transfer can take place in only one direction: either to the procedure before it is executed or to the calling program unit after the procedure's execution. Languages that provide more than one of these transfer techniques also provide a means by which the programmer can specify which option is desired.

Perhaps the most straightforward example among our example languages is found in Ada. Here the key words `in`, `out`, and `in out` are used to indicate the direction in which data are transferred. For example, consider a procedure named Larger, defined with three parameters named I, J, and K in such a way that, when called, the procedure compares the numbers assigned to I and J and places the larger one in location K. Such a procedure can be written in Ada as

```
procedure Larger(I,J: In INTEGER; K: out INTEGER) is
begin
  if I < J then K := J
           else K := I
end Larger;
```

Here the parameters I and J are designated as in parameters, while the parameter K is designated as an out parameter. These designations described the direction in which information is to be transferred in relation to the procedure. That is, information is to be transferred into the parameters I and J but out of the parameter K.

Once our procedure has been defined, it can be used from within another program unit to place the larger of the two numbers associated with locations Num1 and Num2 in location L using the statement

```
Larger(Num1, Num2, L);
```

When this statement is executed, the following sequence of events is performed (see Fig. 5.11):

1. The values associated with Num1 and Num2 in the main program are effectively copied[2] into the locations I and J, respectively, in the procedure.
2. The procedure is executed, leaving the larger value in location K.
3. The value in K (in the procedure) is copied into the location L in the main program.
4. Execution of the main program continues with the statement following the statement that invoked the procedure.

From this sequence of events we see that the names used for the parameters within the procedure can be thought of as merely standing in for the actual data values that are supplied when the procedure is requested. As a result, you often hear them called **formal parameters,** whereas the data values supplied from the other program unit are referred to as **actual parameters.**

A significant benefit of this substitution system is that the same procedure can be asked to perform its task on different sets of data at different times. In particular, our Larger procedure can be used at one point to find the larger of the two values Num1 and Num2 with the statement

```
Larger(Num1, Num2, L);
```

[2]We use the words *effectively copied* to reflect the fact that different programming languages transfer parameters in different ways. In some cases, the data are actually copied from their location in the main program into memory cells associated with the procedure. This technique is inefficient when the amount of data associated with the parameters being passed is large. A more efficient method is to transfer only the address of the memory cells that contain the required data. This gives the procedure access to the data without the overhead of producing a duplicate copy. In the latter case the information in the memory cells is said to be passed to the procedure by reference. If, however, the information is actually copied, it is said to be passed by value.

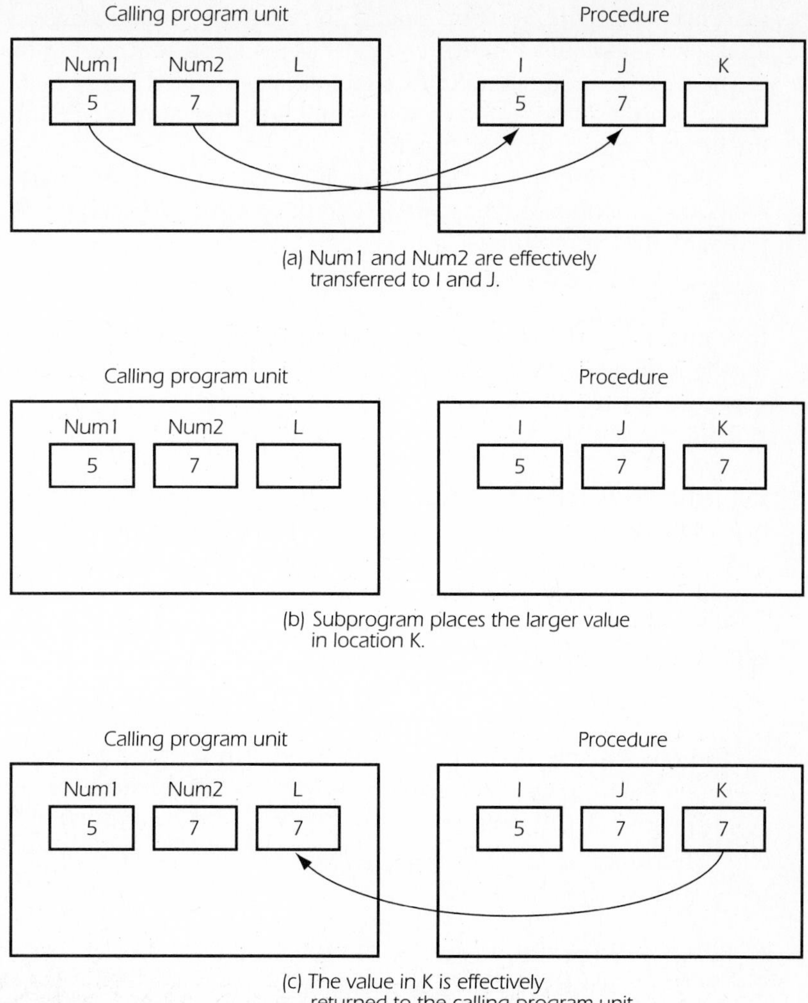

Figure 5.11 An example of parameter passing

and later to find the larger of the values X and Y with the statement

```
Larger(X, Y, L);
```

Functions

The purpose of a program unit is often to perform an action and/or to produce a value. When the emphasis is on producing a value, the program unit may be implemented as a function. Here the term **function** refers to a program unit similar to a procedure except that a value is transferred back to the main program as "the value of the function" rather than via the parameter list. That is, the value is associated with the function's name in much the same way as a value is associated with a variable. The difference is in the effort required to obtain the value. In the case of a reference to a variable the associated value is usually obtained from main memory; in the case of a function the value is obtained by executing the instructions within the function.

As an example, if `Total` is a variable that has been assigned the total cost of an item (price plus purchase tax), then the cost of two such items could be computed by the expression

```
2 * Total
```

In contrast, if `TotalCost` is a function that computes the cost of an item based on the item's price and the sales tax rate, then the cost of two items could be computed by the expression

```
2 * TotalCost(Price, TaxRate)
```

In the first case the value associated with `Total` would be retrieved from memory and multiplied by 2. In the second case the function `TotalCost` would be executed with the input values `Price` and `TaxRate`, and the value produced would be multiplied by 2.

If we implement our Ada procedure `Larger` as a function called `Max`, we can store the larger of `Num1` and `Num2` in `L` using the statement

```
L := Max(Num1, Num2);
```

More precisely, the meaning of this statement is that the larger of the values `Num1` and `Num2` is returned as the value associated with `Max`, and this value is then assigned to `L`. Moreover, if we define `Min` to be a function that returns the smaller of its two parameters, then the statement

```
Z := Max(Num1, Num2) - Min(Num3, Num4);
```

assigns to the variable `Z` the largest difference that can be obtained by subtracting either `Num3` or `Num4` from `Num1` or `Num2`. Accomplishing this same task using program units in the traditional procedure form requires a sequence of statements, such as

```
Larger(Num1, Num2, L);
Smaller(Num3, Num4, S);
Z := L - S;
```

I/O Statements

Procedures and functions provide a means of expanding the features of a programming language. If the language does not provide a particular operation as a primitive, one can write a procedure or function to perform that task and then call upon that program unit when the operation is required. This is the manner in which most languages implement I/O operations except that the procedures and functions being called are actually routines within the machine's operating system.

As an example, to retrieve a value from the keyboard and assign it as the value of a variable named `Value`, a Pascal programmer writes

```
readln (Value);
```

and to write the value on the monitor,

```
writeln (Value);
```

Note that the syntax is that of calling a procedure with a parameter list. (`readln` and `writeln` are pronounced "read line" and "write line," respectively.)

In a similar manner, a C programmer could use the functions `scanf` and `printf` for performing input and output. These functions use parameters for communicating both the data to be transferred and the organization of that data in its printed form. The result is known as formatted input and output. For example, a C programmer writes

```
printf("%d %d\n", Value1, Value2);
```

to cause the values of the variables Value1, and Value2 to be printed in decimal notation on a single line. The string in quotation marks indicates the data's format. Each %d indicates a position that is to be filled by a value in decimal notation. The values are supplied by the remaining parameters. The pattern \n indicates that a new line should be started after these values have been printed. Assuming the values of Age1 and Age2 are 16 and 25, respectively, the statement

```
printf("The ages are %d and %d.\n", Age1, Age2);
```

causes the message

The ages are 16 and 25.

to appear on the monitor.

Being an object-oriented language, C++ approaches I/O operations in a different way. It provides ready-made objects known as `cin` and `cout` to represent the standard input device (probably the keyboard) and output device (probably the monitor), respectively. Data items are then transferred to and from these objects in the form of messages. For example, a value could be retrieved from the keyboard and assigned to the variable `Value` with the statement

```
cin >> Value;
```

and the value assigned to the variable `Value` could be sent to the monitor with the statement

```
cout << Value;
```

Program Examples

At this point we have introduced enough language features to understand the major portions of some simple programs written in our example languages. In particular, Fig. 5.12 displays two complete programs, one written in Pascal and

(a) A complete program in Pascal

```
{A program to compute the area of a circle.}
program CircleArea (Input, Output);
const Pi = 3.1416;
var
  Radius: real;
  Area: real;
begin
  writeln("Enter the radius of a circle.");
  readln(Radius);
  Area := Pi * Radius * Radius;
  writeln("The area of the circle is", Radius)
end.
```

(b) A complete program in C

```
/*A program to compute the area of a circle*/
 #include <stdio.h>
void main(void)
{const float Pi = 3.1416;
 float Radius;
 float Area;

 printf("Enter the radius of a circle.\n");
 scanf(&Radius);
 Area = Pi * Radius * Radius;
 printf("The area of the circle is %f\n", Area);
}
```

Figure 5.12 Complete programs in Pascal and C

the other in C. Both programs are designed to compute and report the area of a circle whose radius is typed by a user at a keyboard.

Each program begins with a comment identifying the purpose of the program. The C program then requests the inclusion of a file called `stdio.h` that contains some "bookkeeping" details required to allow the use of the functions `scanf` and `printf`. This need not concern us here.

Both programs take the form of program units similar to procedures. In the Pascal example this program unit is named `CircleArea` and has two parameters, `Input` and `Output`. In the C program the unit is called `main` and has no parameters, indicated by the term `void` within the parentheses. The term `void` preceding the word `main` indicates that the "function" `main` does not return a value; that is, the "function" is really just a procedure.

From here on the programs are quite similar. They each establish the identifier `Pi` to represent the constant value 3.1416 and define `Radius` and `Area` to be variables of type real. Each program then requests that the user type a value at the keyboard. It accepts this value as the radius of the circle in question, computes the area of that circle, and presents this result on the monitor screen.

Questions/Exercises

1. What is the difference between a global variable and a local variable?
2. What is the difference between a procedure and a function?
3. Why do many programming languages implement I/O operations as if they were calls to procedures?
4. What is the difference between a formal parameter and an actual parameter?

5.4 Language Implementation

In this section we investigate the process of converting a program written in a high-level language into a machine-executable form.

The Translation Process

The process of converting a program from one language to another is called **translation.** The program in its original form is the **source program;** the translated version is the **object program.** The translation process consists of three activities—lexical analysis, parsing, and code generation—that are performed by units in the translator known as the **lexical analyzer, parser,** and **code generator** (Fig. 5.13).

Lexical analysis is the process of recognizing which strings of symbols from the source program represent a single entity. For example, the three symbols 153 should not be interpreted as a 1 followed by a 5 followed by a 3 but should be recognized as representing a single numeric value. Likewise, a word appearing in the program, although composed of individual symbols, should be interpreted as a single unit. Most humans perform lexical analysis with little conscious effort. When asked to read aloud, we pronounce words rather than individual characters.

As the lexical analyzer identifies a group of symbols that represent a single unit, it classifies that unit according to whether it is a numeric value, a word, an arithmetic operator, and so on, and generates a bit pattern known as a **token** that indicates the unit's class. These tokens are the input data for the parser.

Parsing is the process of identifying the grammatical structure of the program and recognizing the role of each component. It is the technicalities of parsing that cause one to hesitate when reading the sentence

The man the horse that won the race threw was not hurt.

To simplify the parsing process, early programming languages insisted that each program statement be positioned in a particular manner on the printed page. Such languages were known as **fixed-format languages.** Today, most programming languages are **free-format languages,** meaning that the positioning of statements is not critical. Their advantage lies in programmers' ability to organize the written program in a way that enhances readability, that is, in a way that simplify humans' task of parsing the program. In these cases it is common to use indentation to help a reader grasp the structure of a statement. Rather than writing

```
if Cost < Cash on hand then pay with cash else use credit card
```

Figure 5.13 The translation process

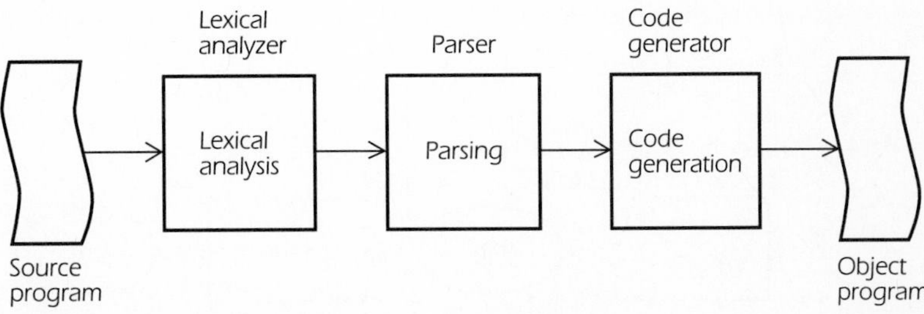

a programmer might write

```
if Cost < Cash on hand
  then pay with cash
  else use credit card
```

For a machine to parse a program written in a free-format language, the syntax of the language must be designed so that the structure of a program can be identified regardless of the spacing used in the source program. To this end, most free-format languages use punctuation marks such as semicolons to mark the end of a program statement, as well as **key words** such as if, then, and else to mark the beginning of individual phrases. These key words are often **reserved words,** meaning that they cannot be used by the programmer for other purposes within the program.

The parsing process is based on a set of syntax rules that define the syntax of the programming language. One way of expressing these rules is by means of **syntax diagrams**, which are pictorial representations of a program's grammatical structure. Figure 5.14 shows a syntax diagram of the if-then-else statement from our pseudocode in Chapter 4. This diagram indicates that an if-then-else structure begins with the word if, followed by a Boolean expression, followed by the word then, followed by a statement. This combination may or may not be followed by the word else and a statement. Notice that terms that actually appear in an if-then-else statement are enclosed in ovals, whereas terms that require further description, such as Boolean expression and Statement, are enclosed in rectangles. Terms that require further description (those in rectangles) are called **nonterminals**; terms that appear in ovals are called **terminals.** In a complete description of a language's syntax the nonterminals are described by additional diagrams.

As a more complete example, Fig. 5.15 presents a set of syntax diagrams that describes the syntax of a structure called Expression. The first diagram describes an Expression as consisting of a Term that may or may not be followed by a + or − symbol and another z, or else a Term followed by a * or / symbol, followed by another Expression.

The manner in which a particular string conforms to a set of syntax diagrams can be represented in a pictorial form by a **parse tree,** as demonstrated in Fig. 5.16 that presents a parse tree for the string

```
x + y * z
```

based on the set of diagrams in Fig. 5.15. Note that the tree starts at the top with the nonterminal Expression and at each level shows how the nonterminals at that level are decomposed until the symbols in the string itself are obtained.

Figure 5.14 A syntax diagram of our if-then-else pseudocode statement

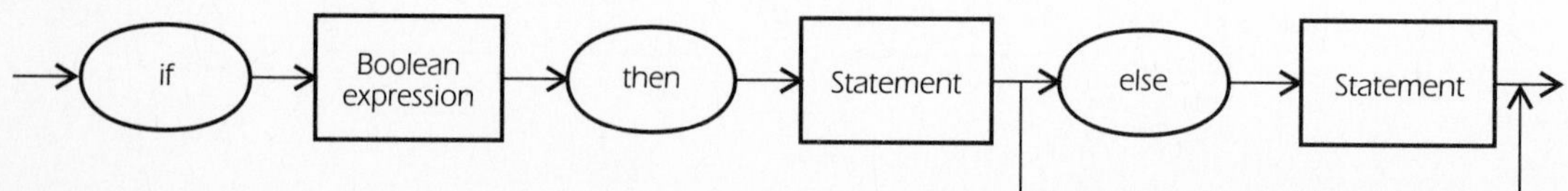

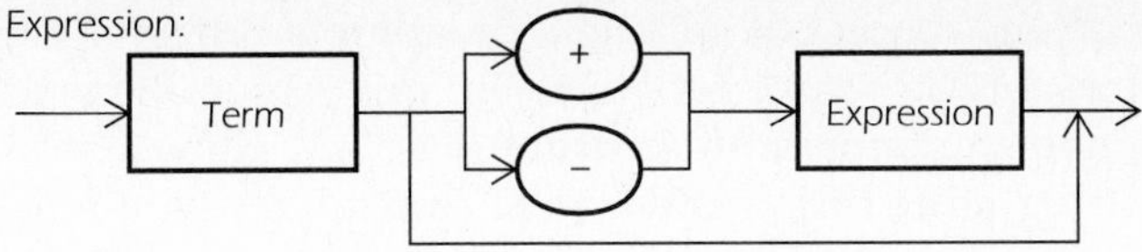

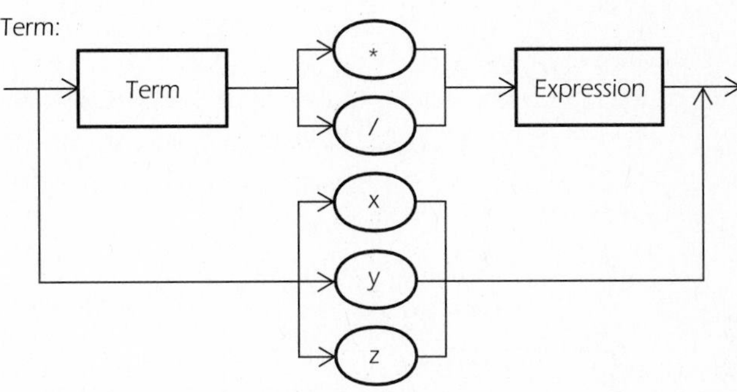

Figure 5.15 Syntax diagrams describing the structure of a simple algebraic expression

Figure 5.16 The parse tree for the string x + y * z based on the syntax diagrams in Fig. 5.15

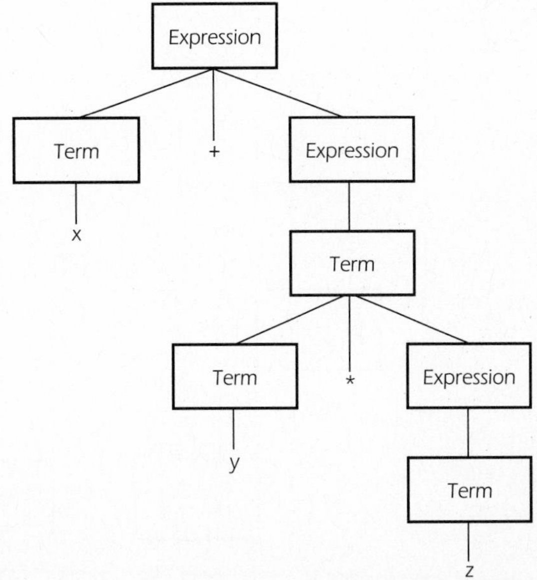

The process of parsing a program is essentially that of constructing a parse tree for the source program. For this reason the syntax rules describing a program's grammatical structure must not allow two distinct parse trees for one string, since this would lead to ambiguities within the parser. Such flaws can be quite subtle. Indeed, the rule in Fig. 5.14 contains such a flaw. It allows both the parse trees in Fig. 5.17 for the single statement

if B1 **then if** B2 **then** S1 **else** S2

Note that these interpretations are significantly different. The first implies that statement S2 is to execute if B1 is false; the second implies that S2 is to execute only if B1 is true and B2 is false.

Figure 5.17 Two distinct parse trees for the statement **if** B1 **then if** B2 **then** S1 **else** S2

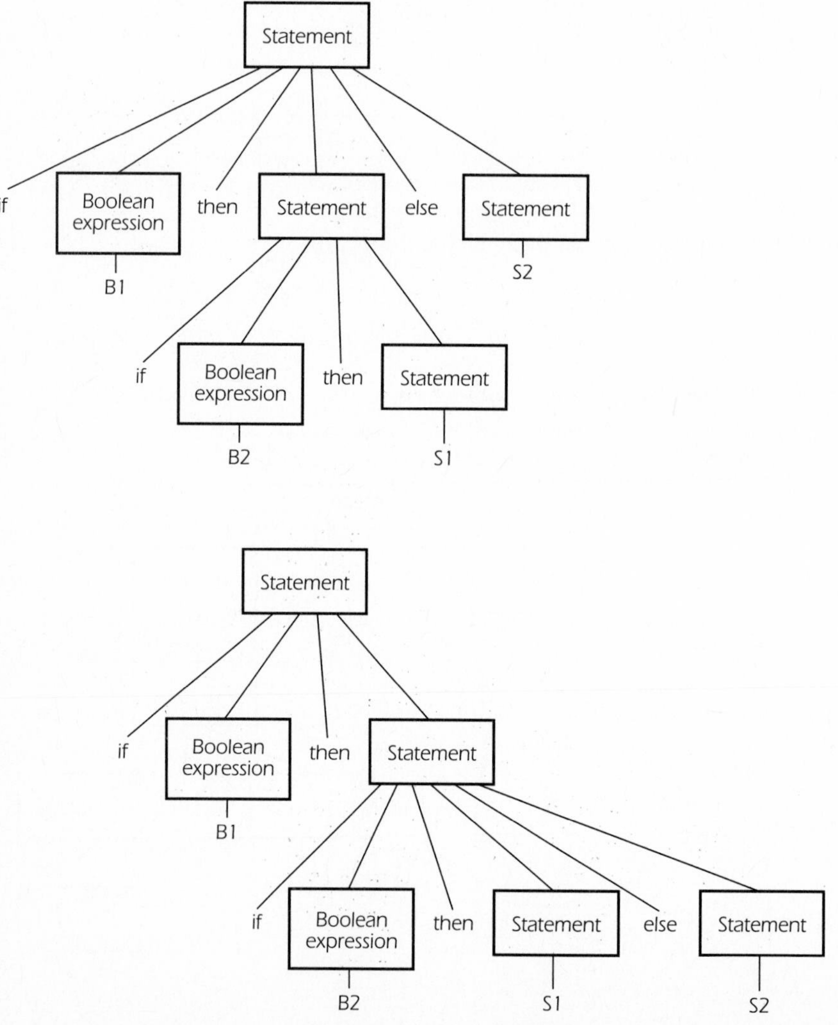

The syntax definitions of formal programming languages are designed to avoid such ambiguities. In our pseudocode we avoid such problems by using parentheses. In particular, we might write

```
if B1
  then (if B2 then S1)
  else S2
```

and

```
if B1
  then (if B2 then S1
              else S2)
```

to distinguish between the two possible interpretations.

As a parser receives tokens from the lexical analyzer, it analyzes the declarative and imperative statements and ignores the comments. The information extracted from the declaration statements is recorded in a table called the **symbol table.** Thus the symbol table contains such information as which variables have been declared and what data types and data structures are associated with those variables. The parser then relies on this information when analyzing imperative statements such as

```
assign Total the value Price + Tax;
```

Indeed, to determine the meaning of the symbol +, the parser must know the data type associated with Price and Tax. If Price is of type real and Tax is of type character, then adding Price and Tax makes little sense and should be reported as an error. If Price and Tax are both of type integer, then the parser will request that the code generator build a machine-language instruction using the machine's integer addition op-code; if both are of type real, the parser will request that floating-point addition op-code be used.

The preceding statement is also meaningful when the data types involved are not the same. For instance, if Price is integer and Tax is real, the concept of addition is still applicable. In this case the parser may choose to have the code generator build the instructions to convert one value to the other type and then perform the addition. Such implicit conversion between types is called **coercion.**

Coercion is frowned on by many language designers. They argue that the need for coercion usually indicates a flaw in the program's design and therefore should not be accommodated by the parser. The result is that most modern languages are **strongly typed,** which means that all activities requested by a program must involve data of agreeable types without coercion. Parsers for these languages report all type conflicts as errors.

The final activity in the translation process, **code generation,** is the process of constructing the machine-language instructions to simulate the statements recognized by the parser. This process involves numerous issues, one being that of producing efficient code. For example, consider the task of translating the two-statement sequence

```
assign x the value y + z;
assign w the value x + z;
```

These statements could be translated as individual statements. Such a single-statement approach, however, would not produce an efficient product. The code generator should be designed to recognize that upon completing the first statement the values of x and z are already in the CPU's general-purpose registers and therefore should not be loaded from memory before computing the value of w. The implementation of insights such as this is called **code optimization** and is an important task of the code generator.

We should note that lexical analysis, parsing, and code generation are not carried out in a strict sequential order. Instead, these activities are intertwined. The lexical analyzer begins by identifying the first token and handing it to the parser. This gives the parser a clue as to what structure may be following and it asks the analyzer for the next token. As the parser recognizes phrases or complete statements, it calls on the code generator to produce the proper machine instructions.

Linking and Loading

The object program produced by the translation process, although expressed in machine language, is rarely in a form that can be executed directly by the machine. One reason is that most programming environments allow the modules of a program to be developed and translated as individual units at different times (which supports the modular construction of software). Thus the object program produced from a single translation process is often only one of several pieces of a complete program, each piece of which requests services from the others in order to accomplish the task of the entire system. Even when a complete program is developed and translated as a single unit, its object program is rarely prepared to stand alone at execution time because it most likely contains requests for services from utility software available through the operating system or from the operating system itself. Thus an object program is actually a machine-language program containing several loose ends that must be connected to other object programs before an executable program is obtained.

The task of making these connections is performed by a program called a **linker.** Its job is to link several object programs (the result of previous and separate translations), operating system routines, and other utility software to produce a complete, executable program (sometimes called a **load module**) that is in turn stored as a file in the machine's mass storage system.

Finally, to execute a translated program, the load module must be placed in memory by a program called a **loader** that is usually part of the operating system's scheduler (Section 3.4). The significance of this step is most pronounced in the case of multitasking systems, in which the exact memory area available to the program is not known until it is time to execute the program (since it must share memory with other processes being executed) and varies from one execution to the next. In this setting the task of the loader is to place the program in the memory area identified by the operating system and make any last-minute (last-microsecond) adjustments that might be needed once the exact memory location of the program is known. (A jump instruction in the program must jump to the

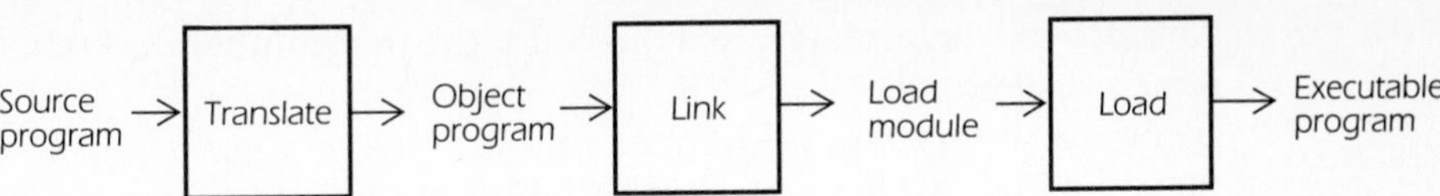

Figure 5.18 The complete program preparation process

correct address within the program.) It is the desire to minimize these last-minute adjustments by the loader that has encouraged the development of techniques by which explicit references to memory addresses within a program can be avoided, resulting in a program (called a relocatable module) that, without modification, executes correctly regardless of where it is placed in memory.

In summary, the complete task of preparing a high-level-language program for execution consists of the three-step sequence of translate, link, and load, as represented in Fig. 5.18. Once the translate and link steps have been completed, the program can be repeatedly loaded and executed without returning to the source version. If, however, a change is necessary to the program, it is made to the source program, and then the modified source program is translated and linked to produce a new load module containing the change.

Software Development Packages

The current trend is to group a translator along with other software units used in the software development process in a package that functions as one integrated software system. Such a system would be classified as application software in the classification scheme of Section 3.4. By executing this application package, a programmer gains ready access to an editor for writing programs, a translator for converting the programs into machine language, and a variety of debugging tools that allow the programmer to trace the execution of a malfunctioning program to discover where it goes astray.

The advantages of using such an integrated system are numerous. Perhaps the most obvious is that a programmer can move back and forth between the editor and debugging tools with ease, as changes to the program are made and tested. Moreover, many software development packages allow related program units that are under development to be linked in such a way that access to related units is simplified. Some packages maintain records regarding which program units within a group of related units have been altered since the last benchmark was made. Such capabilities are quite advantageous in the development of large software systems in which many interrelated units are developed by different programmers.

On a smaller scale, the editors in software development packages are often customized to the programming language being used. For example, an editor in a software development package will usually provide line indentation that is the de facto standard for the target language and in some cases may recognize and automatically complete key words after the programmer has typed only the first few characters.

Some software development packages are moving beyond the use of traditional editors and are using graphical interface systems instead. These packages allow programs to be constructed from prewritten blocks that are represented as icons and selected by the programmer as they are needed in the program construction process. Such packages mark the continuing evolution of the programming process. Indeed, the programming process in the near future is likely to be that of constructing software from large, prefabricated blocks rather than writing them instruction by instruction.

Questions/Exercises

1. Describe the three major steps in the translation process.
2. What is a symbol table?
3. Draw the parse tree for the expression

   x * y + x + z

   based on the syntax diagrams in Fig. 5.15.
4. Describe the strings that conform to the structure Chacha according to the following syntax diagrams.

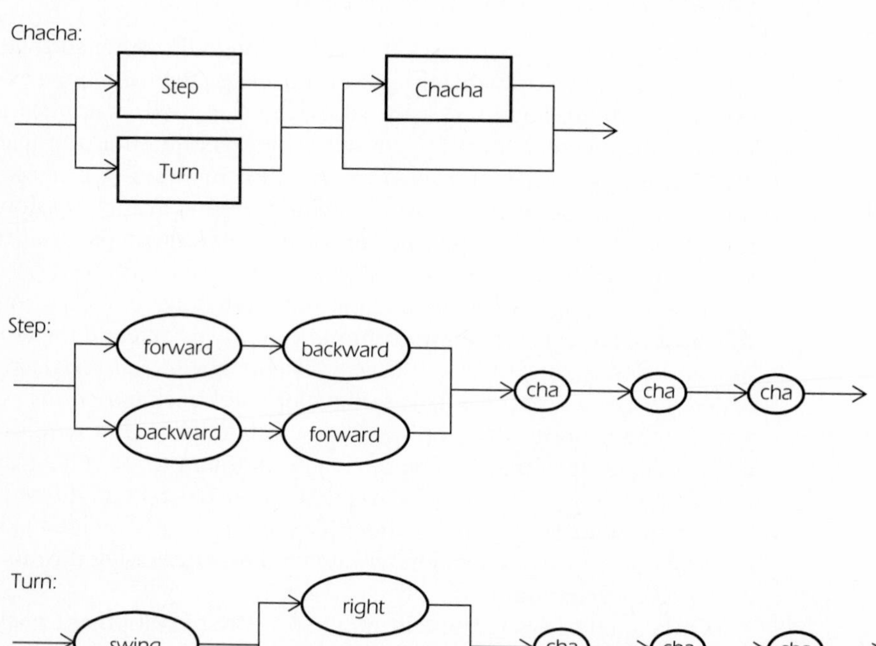

5.5 Parallel Computing

A growing area of research in the field of programming languages involves the development of languages for describing processes that execute simultaneously. In reality, these processes might actually execute at the same time on different processors (in a multiprocessor environment) or perhaps only appear to execute simultaneously (in a time-sharing environment).

An example might be a program for weather forecasting based on a two-level model of the atmosphere. One process might be given the task of predicting conditions in the upper atmosphere (such as the path and strength of the jet stream), while another process would be charged with predicting the conditions in the lower atmosphere. Of course, these two tasks would not be totally independent, so it would be necessary for the two processes to communicate with each other. To fulfill this need, the system could be designed so that each process would begin by independently projecting the current conditions one hour into the future; once these predictions had been made, the processes would share their predictions before making their independent predictions for the next one-hour period. In this manner, the two processes would produce a 24-hour forecast by coordinating their efforts over 24 steps.

To write programs for such parallel computing applications, language features are needed that allow programmers to express the activities involved in coordinating the actions of the various processes in the system. In some cases, these features have been incorporated as primitives in a language; in others, they are implemented as extensions to an existing language. Ada is an example of the former approach. Indeed, a major goal in the design of Ada was to produce a language that could be used for expressing programs for use in parallel processing environments.

An example of the language extension approach is based on the collection of features known as Linda. Linda is not a programming language but rather a collection of primitives that, when added to an existing language, produces an extended language with parallel computing capabilities. Using Linda, researchers have created and experimented with parallel extensions of such languages as C, FORTRAN, LISP, Pascal, and Prolog.

The central concept of Linda is that of a shared storage area called the tuple space, in which each process in the system can deposit and retrieve data bundles called tuples. A process can deposit a tuple in the tuple space at any time. It can also attempt to remove a tuple from the tuple space at any time, but an attempt to remove a nonexistent tuple results in the process being forced to wait until a tuple with the desired properties is deposited by another process.

A tuple is a collection of one or more data items with an associated order. We often represent a tuple by listing its data items within parentheses. Thus the tuple containing the values 5, 3.2, and Fred is written

```
(5, 3.2, "Fred")
```

which is not the same as the tuple

(3.2, "Fred", 5)

because the order is different.

Linda provides the primitives named out and in for expressing the basic operations of depositing and retrieving tuples to and from the tuple space. The primitive in is used to retrieve tuples from the tuple space; out is used to deposit tuples. The terms *in* and *out* express the action from the context of the process, not the tuple space. Thus the primitive out is used to transfer a tuple out of the process into the tuple space, whereas in is used to transfer a tuple into the process from the tuple space (Fig. 5.19). For example, the statement

```
out (5, 17)
```

is used by a process to deposit the tuple (5, 17) into the tuple space, and the statement

```
in (5, 17)
```

is used to retrieve such a tuple.

Variables preceded by a question mark can be used to save components of the tuple being retrieved. In particular, if Value is a variable of type integer, then the statement

```
in ("final cost", ?Value)
```

can be used to retrieve any tuple whose first component is the character string final cost and whose second component is an integer. The integer value occurring

Figure 5.19 Direction of tuple movement associated with the in and out primitives

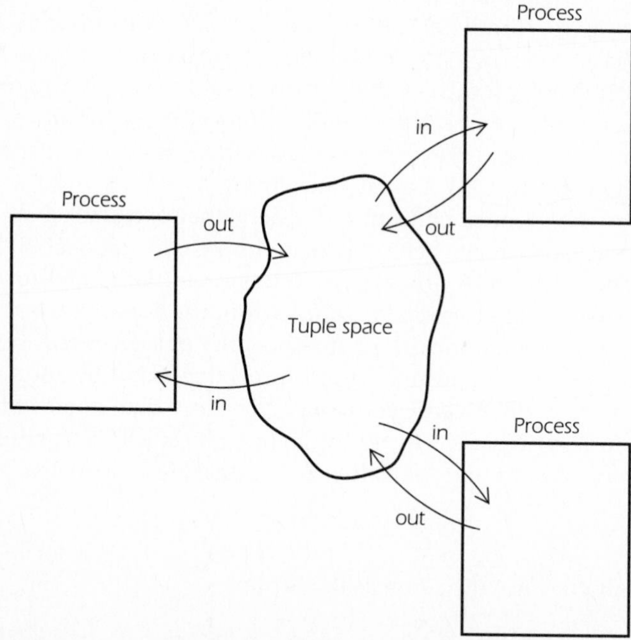

in the chosen tuple is then assigned to the variable Value. If no such tuple exists in the tuple space, the process is forced to wait until such a tuple is deposited. When such a deposit is finally made, the tuple is removed from the tuple space, the assignment is made to Value, and the process is allowed to continue.

We should note that the operations in and out must be implemented as atomic routines; that is, each must be executed as an indivisible unit in the sense of a critical region. Indeed, if a process begins an in operation and finds a tuple of the desired type, it must be allowed to retrieve that tuple before another process is allowed to find the same tuple. Remember, in a multiprocessing environment, many processes can be rummaging through the tuple space at the same time.

Figure 5.20 shows how the processes in our weather-forecasting example can be expressed if we extend our pseudocode to include the Linda primitives. Here the two processes are represented by the procedures LowLevel and HighLevel. If LowLevel completes its forecast for the next one-hour period first, it deposits the tuple ("low-level done") in the tuple space and tries to retrieve the tuple ("high-level done"). But that tuple is not present, so the LowLevel process is forced to wait. When the HighLevel process completes its forecast for the first one-hour period, it deposits the tuple that the LowLevel process is waiting for and then retrieves the tuple deposited by the LowLevel process. At that time, both processes continue their tasks by beginning their forecasts for the next one-hour period. Note that the results of each process's one-hour forecast could also be exchanged by adding that information to the tuples.

We close by identifying the other primitives found in most Linda implementations. These include rd (short for read), which is the same as in except that the tuple is not removed from the tuple space. A major use of rd is to allow several processes to detect the presence of the same tuple in the tuple space. The primitives inp and rdp are similar to in and rd; the difference is that these primitives do not require the process to wait if the desired tuple is not present in the tuple space. Finally, the primitive eval is used to start the execution of processes that are executed in parallel. For example, the statements

```
eval (LowLevel)
eval (HighLevel)
```

can be used to start our weather-forecasting processes.

Figure 5.20 A pseudocode representation of our weather-forecasting program

```
procedure LowLevel
assign Count the value 1;
while (Count ≤ 24) do
      (Prepare the low-level forecast
         for the next one-hour period;
       out ("low-level done");
       in ("high-level done");
       assign Count the value Count + 1)
```

```
procedure HighLevel
assign Count the value 1;
while (Count ≤ 24) do
      (Prepare the high-level forecast
         for the next one-hour period;
       out ("high-level done");
       in ("low-level done");
       assign Count the value Count + 1)
```

Questions/Exercises

1. If ValueA and ValueB are variables declared to be of type integer, which of the following tuples can be retrieved by the statement

   ```
   in (?ValueA, ?ValueB)
   ```

   a. (5.3, 6) b. (6, 7, 8) c. (5, 12) d. (3)
2. Explain how a critical region can be implemented using the Linda primitives in and out.
3. Suppose the tuple space contains only the tuple (5, 7), and Value is a variable of type integer. What would be the result of each of the following commands?

   a. in (4, 2) b. out (8, 3.4) c. rd (?Value, 7) d. in (?Value, 7)

5.6 Declarative Programming

Earlier we claimed that formal logic provides a general problem-solving algorithm around which a declarative programming system can be constructed. In this section we investigate this claim by first introducing the rudiments of the algorithm and then taking a brief look at a declarative programming language based on it.

Logical Deduction

Suppose we know that either Kermit is on stage or Kermit is sick, and we are told that Kermit is not on stage. We could then conclude that Kermit must be sick. This is an example of a deductive-reasoning principle called **resolution.**

To better understand this principle, let us first agree to represent simple statements by single letters and the negation of a statement by the symbol ¬. For instance, we might represent the statement "Kermit is a prince" by *A* and "Miss Piggy is an actress" by *B*. Then, the expression

$A \text{ OR } B$

would mean "Kermit is a prince or Miss Piggy is an actress" and

$B \text{ AND } \neg A$

would mean "Miss Piggy is an actress and Kermit is not a prince." We will use an arrow to indicate "implies." For example, the expression

$A \rightarrow B$

means "If Kermit is a prince, then Miss Piggy is an actress."

In its general form, the resolution principle states that from two statements of the form

$P \text{ OR } Q$

and

$R \text{ OR } \neg Q$

we can conclude the statement

P OR R

In this case, we say that the two original statements resolve to form the third statement, which we call the **resolvent.** It is important to observe that the resolvent is a logical consequence of the original statements. That is, if the original statements are true, the resolvent must also be true. (If Q is true, then R must be true; but if Q is false, then P must be true. Thus regardless of the truth or falseness of Q, either P or R must be true.)

We will represent the resolution of two statements pictorially as shown in Fig. 5.21, where we write the original statements with lines projecting down to their resolvent. Note that resolution can be applied only to pairs of statements that appear in **clause form**—that is, statements whose elementary components are connected by the Boolean operation OR. Thus

P OR Q

is in clause form, whereas

$P \rightarrow Q$

is not. The fact that this potential problem poses no serious concern is a consequence of a theorem in mathematical logic to the effect that any statement expressed in the first-order predicate logic (a system for representing statements with extensive expressive powers) can be expressed in clause form. We will not pursue this important theorem here, but for future reference we observe that the statement

$P \rightarrow Q$

is equivalent to the clause form statement

Q OR $\neg P$

A collection of statements is said to be **inconsistent** if it is impossible for all the statements to be true at the same time. In other words, an inconsistent collection of statements is a collection of statements that are self-contradictory. A simple example would be a statement of the form P combined with the statement $\neg P$. Logicians have shown that repeated resolution provides a systematic method of confirming the inconsistency of a set of self-contradictory clauses. The rule is that if repeated application of resolution produces the empty clause (the result of resolving a clause of the form P with a clause of the form $\neg P$), then

Figure 5.21 Resolving the statements (P OR Q) and (R OR ¬ Q) to produce (P OR R)

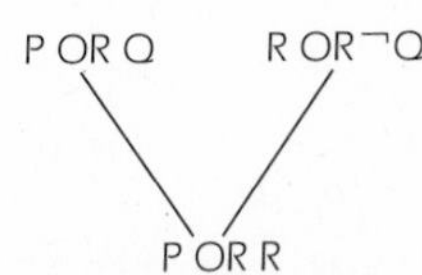

the original collection of statements must be inconsistent. As an example, Fig. 5.22 demonstrates that the collection of statements

P OR *Q*   *R* OR ¬*Q*   ¬*R*   ¬*P*

is inconsistent.

Suppose now that we want to confirm that a collection of statements implies another statement, which we denote by *P*. Implying the statement *P* is the same as contradicting the statement ¬*P*. Thus, to demonstrate that the original collection of statements implies *P*, all we need to do is express the original statements as well as the statement ¬*P* in clause form, and then apply resolution until an empty clause occurs. Upon obtaining an empty clause, we can conclude that statement ¬*P* is inconsistent with the original statements, and thus the original statements must imply *P*.

One final point remains before we are ready to apply resolution in an actual programming environment. Suppose we have the two statements

(Mary is at *X*) → (Mary's lamb is at *X*)

where X represents any location and

Mary is at home

In clause form the two statements become

(Mary's lamb is at *X*) OR ¬(Mary is at *X*)

and

(Mary is at home)

which at first glance do not have components that can be resolved. On the other hand, the components (Mary is at home) and ¬(Mary is at *X*) are quite close to being opposites of each other. The problem is to recognize that *X*, being a statement about locations in general, is a statement about home in particular. Thus a special case of the first statement is

Figure 5.22 Resolving the statements (P OR Q), (R OR ¬Q), ¬R, and ¬P

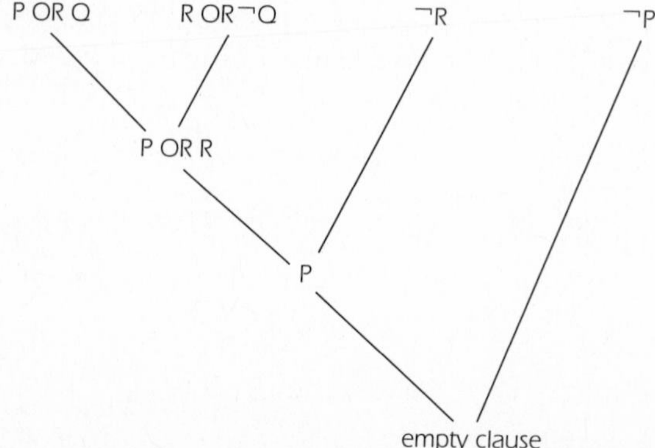

(Mary's lamb is at home) OR ¬(Mary is at home)

which can be resolved with the statement

(Mary is at home)

to produce the statement

(Mary's lamb is at home)

The process of assigning values to variables (such as assigning the value *home* to X) so that resolution can be performed is called unification. It is this process that allows general statements to be applied to specific applications in a deduction system.

Prolog

The language Prolog (short for PROgramming in LOGic) is a declarative programming language whose underlying problem-solving algorithm is based on repeated resolution. A program in Prolog consists of a collection of initial statements upon which the underlying algorithm bases its deductive reasoning. The components from which these statements are constructed are called predicates. A predicate consists of a predicate identifier followed by a parenthetical statement listing the predicate's arguments. A single predicate represents a fact about its arguments, and its identifier is usually chosen to reflect this underlying semantics. Thus, if we want to express the fact that Bill is Mary's parent, we can use the predicate form

```
parent(bill, mary).
```

Note that the arguments in this predicate start with lowercase letters, even though they represent proper nouns. This is because Prolog distinguishes between constants and variables by insisting that constants begin with lowercase letters and variables begin with uppercase letters.

Statements in a Prolog program are either facts or rules, each of which is terminated by a period. A fact consists of a single predicate. For example, the fact that a turtle is faster than a snail could be represented by the Prolog statement

```
faster(turtle, snail).
```

and the fact that a rabbit is faster than a turtle could be represented by

```
faster(rabbit, turtle).
```

A Prolog rule is an "implies" statement. Instead of writing such a statement in the form $X \rightarrow Y$, a Prolog programmer writes Y if X, except that the symbol :- is used to in place of the word *if*. Thus the rule "X is faster than some Y and that Y is faster than Z implies that X is faster than Z" may be expressed by a logician as

(faster(X, Y) AND faster(Y, Z)) → faster(X, Z)

but would be expressed in Prolog as

```
faster(X, Z) :- faster(X, Y), faster(Y, Z).
```

The comma separating `faster(X, Y)` and `faster(Y, Z)` represents the conjunction AND. Such rules can be converted easily to clause form by the Prolog software.

Keep in mind that the Prolog system does not know the meaning of the predicates in a program; it simply manipulates the statements in a totally symbolic manner according to the resolution inference rule. Thus, it is up to the programmer to describe all the pertinent features of a predicate in terms of facts and rules. In this light, Prolog facts tend to be used to identify specific instances of a predicate, whereas rules are used to describe general principles. This is the approach followed by the preceding statements regarding the predicate `faster`. The two facts describe particular instances of "fasterness" while the rule describes a general property. Note that the fact that a rabbit is faster than a snail, though not explicitly stated, is a consequence of the two facts combined with the rule.

Most Prolog implementations are designed to be used interactively. In this context the task of a programmer is to develop the collection of facts and rules that constitute the set of initial statements to be used in the deductive system. Once this collection of statements is established, conjectures (called *goals* in Prolog terminology) can be proposed to the system by typing them at a computer's keyboard. When such a goal is presented to a Prolog system, the system applies resolution to try to confirm that the goal is a consequence of the initial statements. Based on our collection of statements describing the relationship faster, each of the goals

```
faster(turtle, snail).
faster(rabbit, turtle).
faster(rabbit, snail).
```

could be so confirmed because each is a logical consequence of the initial statements. The first two are identical to facts appearing in the initial statements, whereas the third requires a certain degree of deduction by the system.

More interesting examples are obtained if we provide goals whose arguments are variables rather than constants. In these cases Prolog tries to derive the goal from the initial statements while keeping track of the unifications required to do so. Then, if the goal is obtained, Prolog reports these unifications. For example, consider the goal

```
faster(W, snail).
```

In response to this, Prolog reports

```
faster(turtle, snail).
```

Indeed, this is a consequence of the initial statements and agrees with the goal via unification. Furthermore, if we asked Prolog to tell us more, it finds and reports the consequence

```
faster(rabbit, snail).
```

In contrast, we can ask Prolog to find instances of animals that are slower than a rabbit by proposing the goal

```
faster(rabbit, W).
```

In fact, if we started with the goal

```
faster(V, W).
```

Prolog ultimately reports all the `faster` relationships that can be derived from the initial statements. Thus a single Prolog program can be used to confirm that a particular animal is faster than another, to find those animals that are faster than a given animal, to find those animals that are slower than a given animal, or to find all faster relationships. This versatility is one of the features that has captured the imagination of computer scientists.

Questions/Exercises

1. Which of the statements R, S, T, U, and V are logical consequences of the collection of statements ($\neg R$ OR T OR S), ($\neg S$ OR V), ($\neg V$ OR R), (U OR $\neg S$), (T OR $\neg U$), and (S OR V)?
2. Is the following collection of statements consistent? Explain your answer.

   P OR Q OR R
   $\neg R$ OR Q
   R OR $\neg P$
   $\neg Q$

3. Suppose a Prolog program consisted of the statements

   ```
   thriftier(carol, john).
   thriftier(bill, sue).
   thriftier(sue, carol).
   thriftier(X,Z) :- thriftier(X,Y), thriftier(Y,Z).
   ```

   List the results that can be produced from each of the following goals:

   a. `thriftier(sue, V).`

   b. `thriftier(U, carol).`

   c. `thriftier(U,V).`

CHAPTER REVIEW PROBLEMS *(Asterisked problems are associated with optional sections.)*

1. What does it mean to say that a programming language is machine independent?
2. Translate the following pseudocode program into the machine language described in Appendix C.

   assign x **the value** 0;
   while (x ≠ 3) **do**
   (**assign** x **the value** x + 1)

3. Translate the statement

   assign Halfway **the value** Length + Width

   into the machine language of Appendix C, assuming that Length, Width, and Halfway are all represented in floating-point notation.
4. Translate the high-level statement

   if X equals 0 **then** move Y plus W into Z
   else move Y plus X into Z

   into the machine language of Appendix C, assuming that W, X, Y, and Z are all represented as binary values occupying one byte of memory each.

5. Why was it necessary to identify the type of data associated with the variables in Problem 4 in order to translate the statements? Why do many high-level programming languages require the programmer to identify the type of each variable at the beginning of a program?
6. Name and describe four different programming paradigms.
7. Suppose the function f expects two numeric values as its parameters and returns the smaller of the two values as its output value. If w, x, y, and z represent numeric values, what is the result returned by f(f(w,x),f(y,z))?
8. Suppose f is a function that returns the result of reversing the string of symbols given as its input, and g is a function that returns the concatenation of the two strings given as its input. If x is the string *abcd*, what is returned by g(f(x),x)?
9. Suppose your checking account is represented as an object in an object-oriented program for maintaining your financial records. What data is stored inside this object? What messages can that object receive and how does it respond to each? What are other objects that might be used in the program?
10. Summarize the distinction between a machine language and an assembly language.
11. Design an assembly language for the machine described in Appendix C.
12. John Programmer argues that the ability to declare constants within a program is not necessary because variables can be used instead. For example, our example of AirportAlt in Section 5.2 can be handled by declaring AirportAlt to be a variable and then assigning it the required variable at the beginning of the program. Why is this not as good as using a constant?
13. Summarize the distinction between the declarative and procedural parts of a program written in a procedural programming language.
14. Explain the differences among a literal, a constant, and a variable.
15. What is operator precedence?
16. What is structured programming?
17. Draw a flowchart representing the structure expressed by the following Pascal statement:

```
for X := 2 to 7 do
begin . . . end
```

18. Draw a flowchart representing the structure expressed by the following C, C++, and Java statement.

```
for (x = 2; x < 8; ++ x)
{. . . }
```

19. Draw a flowchart representing the structure expressed by the following C, C++, and Java statement.

```
switch (suite)
  {case "clubes": bid(1);
   case "diamonds": bid(2);
   case "hearts": bid(3);
   case "spades": bid(4);
  }
```

20. If you are familiar with written music, analyze musical notation as a programming language. What are the control structures? What is the syntax for inserting comments? What music notation is similar to the for statements in Fig. 5.9?
21. Summarize the following rat's-nest routine with a single if-then-else statement:

```
   if X > 5 goto 80
   X = X + 1
   goto 90
80 X = X + 2
90 stop
```

22. Identify the declarative and procedural parts of the programs in Fig. 5.12.
23. Describe the differences among in, out, and in out parameters in the Ada programming language. Which ones allow the calling program unit to pass information to the procedure? Which ones allow the procedure to pass information to the calling unit?
24. The following Ada program sequence is designed to make use of the subprogram Larger discussed in this chapter. What values are assigned to the variables A, B, and C at the end of the routine?

```
A := 5;
B := 6;
C := 7;
Larger(A, B, C);
Larger(C, B, A)
```

25. Why would a large array probably not be passed to a subroutine by value?

26. Using the subprogram `Larger` from the text, describe a sequence of instructions that accomplishes the same objective as the single statement

```
Z = Max(I,J) + Max(A,B)
```

where `Max` is the function introduced in the text.

27. What ambiguity exists in the statement

assign X **the value** of 3 + 2 * 5

28. Suppose a small company has five employees and is planning to increase the number to six. The following are excerpts from two equivalent programs used by the company that must be altered to reflect the change in the number of employees. Both programs are written in a Pascal-like language. Indicate what changes must be made to each program. What complications arise in the case of program 1 that are avoided by the use of constants in program 2?

Program 1

```
        .
        .
        .
DailySalary := TotalSal/5;
AvgSalary := TotalSal/5;
DailySales := TotalSales/5;
AvgSales := TotalSales/5;
        .
        .
        .
```

Program 2

```
        .
        .
        .
const
  NumEmpl = 5;
  DaysWk = 5;
        .
        .
        .
DailySalary := TotalSal/DaysWk;
AvgSalary := TotalSal/NumEmpl;
DailySales := TotalSales/DaysWk;
AvgSales := TotalSales/NumEmpl;
        .
        .
        .
```

29. Draw a syntax diagram representing the structure of the while statement in the pseudocode of Chapter 4.

***30.** Design a set of syntax diagrams to describe the syntax of telephone numbers written in the form such as (444) 555-1234.

***31.** Design a set of syntax diagrams to describe simple English sentences.

***32.** Describe the syntax of a string as defined by the syntax diagram below and draw the parse tree for the string xxyxx.

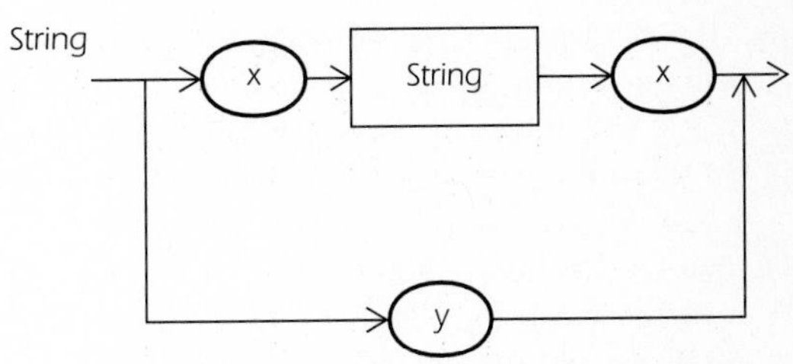

***33.** Add syntax diagrams to those in Question 4 of Section 5.4 to obtain a set of diagrams that defines the structure Dance to be either a Chacha or a Waltz, where a Waltz consists of one or more copies of the pattern

forward diagonal close

or

backward diagonal close

***34.** Draw the parse tree for the expression

x * y + y / x

based on the syntax diagrams in Fig. 5.15.

***35.** What code optimization could be performed by a code generator when building the machine code representing the statement

if (X > 5) **then** (**assign** Z **the value** X + 2)
else (**assign** Z **the value** X + 4)

***36.** Using the Linda primitives in and out as a way of extending the pseudocode in Chapter 4, describe two parallel processes A and B such that A generates widgets that B then checks for defects before it declares them finished.

***37.** Using the Linda primitives in and out as a way of extending the pseudocode in Chapter 4, describe two parallel processes A and B such that each generates widgets that are inspected by the other for defects before receiving final approval.

***38.** Give an example in which the Linda primitive rd is used rather than the primitive in.

***39.** Give an example in which the Linda primitive inp is used rather than the primitive in.

***40.** Draw a diagram (similar to Fig. 5.22) representing the resolutions needed to show that the collection of statements (Q or ¬R), (T or R), ¬P, (P or ¬T), and (P or ¬Q) are inconsistent.

***41.** Is the collection of statements ¬R, (T or R), (P or ¬Q), (Q or ¬T), and (R or ¬P) consistent? Explain your answer.

***42.** What conclusions can Prolog find if faced with the goal

```
bigger(X, lassie).
```

and the initial statements

```
bigger(rex, lassie).
bigger(fido, rex).
bigger(spot, rex).
bigger(X,Z) :— bigger(X,Y), bigger
(Y,Z).
```

***43.** What conclusions can Prolog find if faced with the goal

```
eq(X,Y).
```

and the initial statements

```
grteq(a,b).
grteq(b,c).
grteq(c,a).
grteq(U,W) :- grteq(U,V), grteq(V,W).
eq(X,Y) :- grteq(X,Y), grteq(Y,X).
```

QUESTIONS OF ETHICS

The following questions are provided to help you understand some of the ethical/social/legal issues associated with the field of computing as well as investigate your own beliefs and their foundations. The goal is not merely to answer these questions. You should also consider why you answered as you did and whether your justifications are consistent from one question to the next.

1. In general, copyright laws support ownership rights associated with the expression of an idea but not for the idea itself. As a result, a paragraph in a book is copyrightable but the ideas expressed in the paragraph are not. How should this right extend to source programs and the algorithms they express? To what extent do you believe a person who knows the algorithms used in a commercial software package should be allowed to write his or her own program expressing those algorithms and market this version of the software?
2. Should a person who develops a new and useful programming language have a right to profit from the use of that language? If so, how can that right be protected? To what extent can a language be owned?
3. To what extent is a programmer who helps develop a violent computer game responsible for any consequences of that game? Should children's access to violent computer games be restricted? If so, how and by whom? What about other groups in society, such as convicted criminals?
4. To what extent should a computer professional be knowledgeable in the various programming paradigms? Some companies insist that all software developed in that company be written in the same, predetermined programming language. Does your answer to the original question change if the professional works for such a company?
5. With a deadline approaching, is it acceptable for a programmer to forgo documentation via comment statements to get a program running on time? (Beginning students are often surprised to learn how important documentation is considered among professional software developers.)

ADDITIONAL ACTIVITIES

1. In a programming language you know, what features allow a translator to isolate the various statements in a program? How are potential ambiguities resolved?
2. Identify the data types and structures that are available as primitives in a programming language you know. What features are provided for extending these primitive types?
3. Investigate the statements used in a programming language you know for receiving data from the keyboard and writing data on the monitor screen. What notational conversion features do they provide? Explain what is required to convert the digits 3, 5, and 6 typed at the keyboard into the two's complement representation of the value 356 used for internal storage.
4. In the context of a programming language you know, at what locations in a program can new variables be declared? How is the scope of a variable dependent on the location at which it is declared?
5. Identify the control structures available in a programming language you know. Which ones control branching, iteration, recursion?
6. Investigate the geneology of a programming language you know. When, where, and why was it developed? Does it have any direct ancestors or descendants?
7. Design and implement an assembly language for the machine described in Appendix C.

ADDITIONAL READING

Aho, A. V., R. Sethi, and J. D. Ullman. *Compilers: Principles, Techniques, and Tools.* Reading, Mass.: Addison-Wesley, 1986.

Barnes, J. *Programming in Ada 95.* Reading, Mass.: Addison-Wesley, 1996.

Bergin, T. J., and R. G. Gibson. *History of Programming Languages.* New York: ACM Press, 1996.

Clocksin, W. F., and C. S. Mellish. *Programming in Prolog,* 3rd ed. New York: Springer-Verlag, 1987.

Fisher, C. N., and R. J. LeBlanc, Jr. *Crafting a Compiler with C.* Menlo Park, Calif.: Benjamin/Cummings, 1991.

Graham, P. *ANSI Common Lisp.* Englewood Cliffs, N.J.: Prentice-Hall, 1996.

Holub, A. *Compiler Design in C.* Englewood Cliffs, N.J.: Prentice-Hall, 1990.

Lemay, L., and C. L. Perkins. *Teach Yourself Java in 21 Days.* Indianapolis, Ind.: Sams.net, 1996.

Metcalf, M., and J. Reid. *Fortran 90 Explained.* Oxford: Oxford University Press, 1990.

Pohl, I., and A. Kelley. *A Book on C,* 2nd ed. Redwood City, Calif.: Benjamin/Cummings, 1990.

Pratt, T. W., and M. V. Zelkowitz. *Programming Languages, Design and Implementation,* 3rd ed. Englewood Cliffs, N.J.: Prentice-Hall, 1996.

Savitch, W. *Problem Solving with C++.* Reading, Mass.: Addison-Wesley, 1996.

Sebesta, R. W. *Concepts of Programming Languages,* 3rd ed. Reading, Mass.: Addison-Wesley, 1996.

CHAPTER SIX

Software Engineering

6.1 The Software Engineering Discipline

6.2 The Software Life Cycle
- The Cycle as a Whole
- The Traditional Development Phase
- More Recent Trends

6.3 Modularity
- Modular Implementation
- Coupling
- Side Effects
- Cohesion

6.4 Development Tools and Techniques
- Top-Down Design
- Bottom-Up Design
- Dataflow Diagrams
- Entity-Relationship Diagrams
- Data Dictionaries

6.5 Documentation

6.6 Software Ownership and Liability

In this chapter we consider topics relating to the overall process of software development and maintenance. Many of the techniques applied here are similar to those applied by engineers in the development of automobiles, bridges, and television sets. In fact, the topic is called software engineering.

Our discussion concerns large software systems, the complete comprehension of which exceeds the short-term memory capabilities of the human mind. Examples might include business inventory systems, telephone switching control systems, or environment/security control systems for office buildings. The problems faced when developing such systems are more than enlarged versions of those problems faced when writing small programs. For instance, the development of such systems requires the efforts of more than one person over an extended period of time during which the requirements of the proposed system may be altered and the personnel assigned to the project may change, due to promotions, job transfers, and so on. Consequently, the subject of software engineering includes topics, such as personnel and project management, that are more readily associated with business management than computer science. We do not follow these leads in this chapter, although we do close the chapter with legal topics relating to software ownership and liability.

6.1 The Software Engineering Discipline

Beginning computer science students are somewhat disadvantaged when approaching the study of software engineering. They have never participated in the development of large software systems and therefore cannot fully comprehend the problems involved. Their experiences most likely encompass programming projects that can be completed in a few days. Moreover, they have probably not been required to live with and maintain the programs they have written.

It might be helpful therefore to begin our study of software engineering by selecting any large complex device you want (an automobile, a multistory office building, or perhaps a cathedral) and imagine being asked to design it and then to supervise its construction. How can you estimate the cost in time, money, and other resources to complete the project? How can you divide the project into manageable pieces? How can you assure that the pieces produced are compatible? How can those working on the various pieces communicate? How can you measure progress? How can you cope with the wide range of detail (the selection of the door knobs, the design of the gargoyles, the availability of blue glass for the stained glass windows, the strength of the pillars, the design of the duct work for the heating system)? Questions of the same scope must be answered during the development of a large software system.

Since engineering is a well-established field, you might think that there is a wealth of previously developed engineering techniques that can be useful in answering such questions. This reasoning, however, overlooks the many distinctions between the properties of software and those of other fields of engineering.

One of these distinctions deals with the role of tolerances. Traditional areas of engineering deal with the development of products that are acceptable as long as they perform their task within certain bounds. A washing machine that cycles through its wash–rinse–spin cycle within a 2% tolerance of the desired time is acceptable. Software, in contrast, performs either correctly or incorrectly. An accounting system that is accurate only to within a 2% tolerance is not acceptable.

Another distinction relates to the lack of quantitative systems, called **metrics,** for measuring the properties of software. What metric, for example, can be used for measuring the quality of software? The quality of a mechanical device is often measured in terms of the mean time between failures, which is a measurement of how well the device endures wear and tear. Software, in contrast, does not wear out, so this method of measuring quality does not carry over into software engineering.

The inability to measure software properties in a quantitative manner is one of the major reasons that software engineering has not yet found a rigorous footing in the same sense as mechanical and electrical engineering. Whereas these subjects are founded on the established science of physics, software engineering is still searching for its roots.

Thus research in software engineering is currently progressing on two levels: Some researchers work toward developing techniques for immediate application, while others search for underlying principles and theories on which more stable techniques can someday be constructed. Being based on a subjective foundation, many methodologies developed on the first level, which were preached as fact in the past, have been replaced by other approaches that may themselves become obsolete with time. Meanwhile, progress on the other level continues to be evasive.

The need for progress on both levels is enormous. Our society has become addicted to computer systems and their associated software. Our economy, health care, government, law enforcement, transportation, and defense depend on large software systems. Yet there continue to be major problems with the reliability of these systems. Software errors have caused such disasters and near disasters as the rising moon being interpreted as a nuclear attack, the loss of $5 million by the Bank of New York in only one day, the loss of the *Mariner 18* space probe, radiation overdoses that have killed and paralyzed, and the simultaneous disruption of telephone communications over large regions.

While science continues to search for methods of developing better-quality software, professional organizations have contributed their efforts indirectly by promoting high standards of ethics and professional conduct among their membership. The Association of Computing Machinery (ACM) has adopted a code of professional conduct, while the Data Processing Management Association (DPMA) and the Institute of Electrical and Electronics Engineers (IEEE) have each adopted their own codes of ethics. Such codes enhance the professionalism of software developers and counter nonchalant attitudes toward each individual's responsibilities.

In this chapter we introduce some of the results of software engineering research, including some of the basic principles of software engineering (the software life cycle, modularity, coupling, and cohesion) as well as some of the development tools and techniques that are used today.

Questions/Exercises

1. Why is the number of lines in a program not a good measure of the complexity of the program?
2. What technique can be used for determining how many errors are in a piece of software?
3. Suggest a metric for measuring software quality. What weaknesses does your metric have?

6.2 The Software Life Cycle

The most fundamental concept in software engineering is the software life cycle.

The Cycle as a Whole

The software life cycle is shown in Fig. 6.1. This figure represents the fact that once software is developed, it enters a cycle of being used and modified that continues for the rest of the software's life. Such a pattern is common for many manufactured products as well. The difference is that, in the case of other prod-

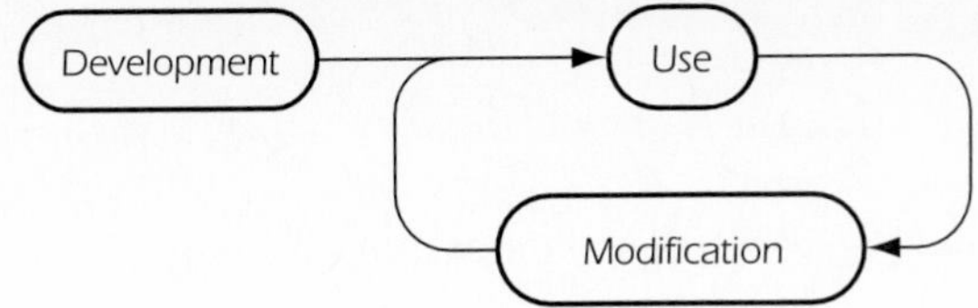

Figure 6.1 The software life cycle

ucts, the modification phase is more accurately called a repair or maintenance phase because other products tend to move from being used to being modified as their parts become worn.

Software, on the other hand, does not wear out. Instead, a piece of software moves into the modification phase because errors that were not discovered earlier in the development phase force changes to be made, because changes in the program's application occur that require corresponding changes in the software, or because changes made during a previous modification are found to induce problems elsewhere in the software. For example, changes in tax laws often require modifications to payroll programs that calculate withholding taxes, and all too often these changes have adverse effects in other areas of the program that may not be discovered until some time later.

Regardless of why a piece of software enters the modification phase, this process requires that a person (often not the original author) study the program and its documentation until the program, or at least the pertinent part of the program, is understood. Otherwise, any modification could introduce more problems than it solves. Acquiring this understanding can be a difficult task even when the software is well designed and documented. It is often within this phase that a piece of software is finally discarded under the pretense (too often true) that it is easier to develop a new system from scratch than to modify the existing package successfully.

Experience has shown that a little effort during the development of software can make a tremendous difference when modifications in the software are required. For example, in our discussion of data description statements in Chapter 5 we saw how the name `AirportAlt` might be used in lieu of the nondescriptive value 645 in a program and reasoned that if a change became necessary, it would be easier to change the value associated with the name instead of finding and changing numerous occurrences of the value 645. In turn, most of the research in software engineering focuses on the development stage of the software life cycle, with the goal being to benefit from this effort/benefit leverage.

The Traditional Development Phase

Let us, then, take a closer look at the stages within the development phase of the software life cycle (Fig. 6.2). They consist of analysis, design, implementation, and testing.

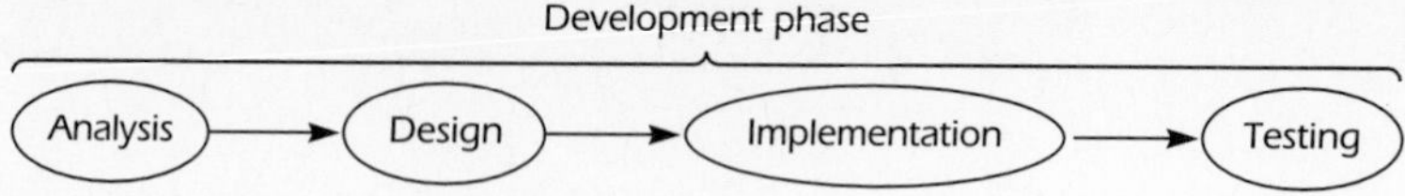

Figure 6.2 The development phase of the software life cycle

Analysis It is in the early stage of analysis that the potential for a computer application is recognized and the decision is made to develop a software system. Recognition may be in the context of a need and a market for a generic software product or the need for a customized software system for use within a particular organization. In either case, much of this part of the analysis phase involves business management and perhaps marketing decisions rather than topics associated with the study of algorithms.

Once the decision is made to develop an automated system, the true analysis phase begins. The major goal of this process is to identify the needs of the user of the proposed system. For example, if the system is to be generic software sold in a competitive market, then the needs of the target audience must be identified. If the system is to be an in-house product such as an inventory maintenance system for the company's purchasing department, then the needs and expectations of the purchasing department must be identified.

One of the formal results of the analysis phase is a set of requirements that the new system must satisfy. These requirements are stated in terms of the application rather than in the technical terminology of the data processing community. One requirement might be that access to data must be restricted to authorized personnel. Another might be that the data must reflect the current state of the inventory as of the end of the last business day or that the arrangement of the data as displayed on the computer screen must adhere to the format of the paper forms currently in use.

After the system requirements are identified, they are converted into more technical system specifications. For example, the requirement that data be restricted to authorized personnel might become the specification that the system will not respond until an approved five-digit password has been typed at the keyboard or that data will be displayed in coded form unless preprocessed by a routine known only to authorized personnel.

Design It is in the design phase that the technical details of the proposed system are developed. It is here that the system is broken into manageable units called modules, with each module constituting a small part of the overall system.

It is by means of this modular decomposition that the implementation of large systems becomes a possibility. Without such a breakdown, the technical details required in the implementation of a large system would exceed a human's comprehensive powers. With a modular design, however, only the details pertaining to the module under consideration need be mastered. This same modular design is also conducive to future maintenance because it allows changes to be made on a modular basis. (If a change is to be made to the way each employee's health benefits are calculated, then only modules dealing with health benefits need be considered.)

We see, then, that a good modular structure is important to the implementation as well as later modification of the system. This is a major reason that the object-oriented paradigm is gaining popularity. Indeed, an object-oriented design is inherently a modular design.

Implementation This phase involves the actual writing of programs, creation of data files, and development of databases.

Testing This phase is closely associated with the previous one, because each module of the system is normally tested as it is implemented. Indeed, each module in a well-designed system can be tested independently of the other modules by using simplified versions of the other modules, called stubs, to simulate the interaction between the target module and the rest of the system. Of course, this individual testing gives way to overall system testing as the various modules are completed and combined.

Unfortunately, the testing and debugging of a system is extremely difficult to perform successfully. Experience has shown that large software systems can contain numerous errors, even after significant testing. Many of these errors may go undetected for the life of the system, and others may cause major malfunctions, such as opened train doors between stations and false alerts from automated national defense systems. The elimination of such errors is one of the goals of software engineering. The fact that they are still prevalent means that a lot of research remains to be done.

Early approaches to software engineering were based on a strict adherence to the analysis, design, implementation, and testing sequence of software development. The feeling was that too much was at risk during the development of a large software system to allow for trial-and-error techniques. As a result, software engineers insisted that the entire analysis of the system be completed before beginning the design and, likewise, that the design be completed before beginning implementation. The result was a development process now referred to as the **waterfall model,** an analogy to the fact that the development process was allowed to flow in only one direction.

More Recent Trends

You will notice a similarity between the four problem-solving phases identified by Polya (Section 4.3) and the analysis, design, implementation, and testing phases of software development. After all, to develop a large software system is to solve a problem. On the other hand, the traditional waterfall approach to software development is in stark contrast to the "free-wheeling," trial-and-error process that is often vital to creative problem solving. Whereas the waterfall approach seeks to establish a highly structured environment in which development progresses in a sequential fashion, creative problem solving seeks a nonstructured environment in which one can drop previous plans of attack to pursue sparks of intuition without explaining why.

In recent years software engineering techniques have begun to reflect this underlying contradiction. A major force behind this shift in philosophy has been the development of **computer-aided software engineering (CASE)** tools. These tools include software systems that assist in the development and updating of documents such as dataflow diagrams, entity-relationship diagrams, and data dictionaries (all of which we discuss later) that are used to model the projected system. Some CASE systems even include code generators that, when given specifications for a part of a system, produce high-level language programs that implement that part of the system. The use of these automated tools significantly reduces the effort required in the analysis, design, and implementation phases of software development so that it is much easier to back up and change previous decisions found to be wrong. The result has been a relaxation of the strict waterfall approach to software engineering.

One of the more prominent consequences of this newer approach to software development has been the use of prototyping, a technique that is also supported by many CASE tools. **Prototyping** refers to the construction of simplified versions or parts of the proposed system that can be analyzed before further development is done.

As a result of prototyping, software development ceases to be a strictly sequential process in which one phase is completed before the next begins. Instead, it becomes a process in which analysis, design, and prototyping are intertwined so that the design may change as results from prototyping are obtained. In many cases the prototypes that are constructed during this iterative process are discarded in favor of a fresh implementation of the final design. This approach is known as throwaway prototyping. In contrast, the process of evolutionary prototyping continually refines the prototype until it, itself, becomes the final system.

Another development that is affecting the field of software engineering is the emergence of the object-oriented paradigm. The software engineering techniques that evolved in the 1970s and 1980s are essentially tools to aid in the construction of software based on the imperative programming paradigm. Thus these techniques view the software development process as developing a collection of procedures that collectively solve the problem at hand. However, when software is based on the object-oriented paradigm, the fundamental structure is that of a collection of objects rather than procedures. Consequently, the object-oriented paradigm has led researchers to search for new development techniques. We will witness some of this phenomenon in the following sections.

Questions/Exercises

1. What is the difference between system requirements and system specifications?
2. Summarize each of the four stages (analysis, design, implementation, and testing) within the development phase of the software life cycle.
3. Summarize the distinction between the traditional waterfall model of software development and the newer prototyping paradigm.

6.3 Modularity

One of the key statements in Section 6.2 was that to modify software one must understand the program or at least the pertinent parts of the program. Such an understanding is often difficult enough to obtain in the case of small programs and would be close to impossible when dealing with large software systems if it were not for the concept of **modularity.** This refers to the practice of dividing the software into manageable units, with each unit designed to perform only a part of the overall task.

Modular Implementation

We have already encountered the concept of modularity in this chapter as well as in Chapters 4 and 5. There we observed that by isolating the details of certain activities within procedures we could obtain a program that more readily expresses its purpose and methods than would be available if we insisted on including complete descriptions of the activities in a single program unit.

We have also met modularity in the context of the object-oriented paradigm (Chapter 5). In this case modules take the form of objects, each with its own internal structures that are independent of the contents of other objects. It is this inherent modular structure that has led to the rise in popularity of the object-oriented approach to software development.

The **structure chart** is a major tool for representing the modular structure of a software system based on the imperative paradigm. In such a chart each module is represented by a rectangle, and dependencies between modules are represented by arrows connecting the rectangles. The structure chart in Fig. 6.3 represents a simple payroll system for a small business. This chart indicates that the module ProcessPayroll is dependent on the module ComputeTax; that is, module ProcessPayroll uses module ComputeTax (most likely in the context of calling it as a procedure) to accomplish its task.

In a sense, a structure chart is a way of representing the division of labor within a software system. In our example this division of labor is as follows:

ProcessPayroll is the controlling module charged with the task of computing the appropriate pay for each employee.

ComputeEarnings queries the record of an employee to determine the employee's earnings for the current pay period.

ComputePretaxWithholding determines the amount a given employee should contribute to the company's retirement program.

ComputeTax determines how much should be withheld from an employee's pay for state and federal taxes. It uses the modules ComputeFederalTaxes and ComputeStateTaxes to accomplish its task.

ComputePosttaxWithholding determines how much additional money should be withheld from an employee's income to cover company charges such as child care, parking, and cafeteria bills.

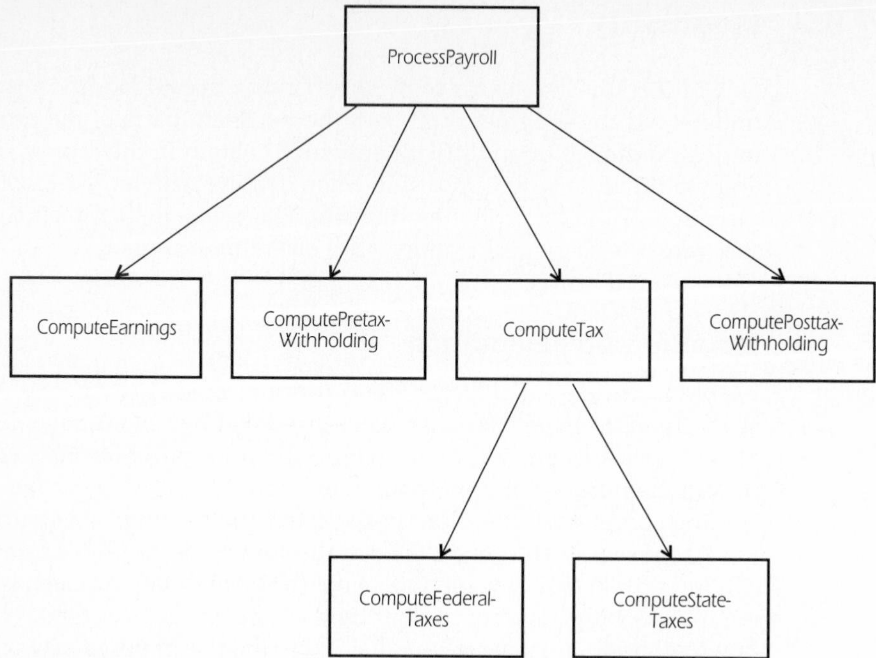

Figure 6.3 A structure chart of a simple payroll system

Although structure charts have been a major software engineering tool in the past, the fact that they represent a division of labor is likely to lead them to extinction in the future. The reason is that the design of an object-oriented system is not based on a division of labor but on an identification of entities. The fundamental goal when designing an object-oriented system is to identify the objects required rather than the procedures to be followed. Procedural analysis does not occur in an object-oriented design until it is time to design how each object will perform its internal tasks.

As an example of an object-oriented design, let us reconsider our payroll example. The system is to produce paychecks for the employees based on their time sheets, while updating tax records and employee benefit records. In turn, our first attempt at identifying the objects that should be found in our final system would include Paycheck, Employee, TimeSheet, TaxRecord and BenefitRecord. What we have done is extract the nouns from the description of the proposed system. This noun extraction process is, in fact, a popular object-oriented design methodology. The next step in the design would be to begin to identify what communication between these objects would be required to obtain the proposed system's goals. During this process the proposed collection of objects may be refined and expanded. Once the objects have been established and the tasks each object will be required to perform have been identified, the internal design of each object can begin.

Coupling

We have introduced modularity as a way of obtaining manageable software. The idea is that a future modification will likely apply to only a few of the modules so that one's attention can be restricted to that portion of the system during the modification process. This, of course, depends on the assumption that changes in one module will not unknowingly affect other modules in the system. Consequently, one's goal when designing a modular system should be to maximize independence between modules.

Working against this objective is the fact that some connection between modules is necessary for them to form a coherent system. This connection is referred to as **coupling.** The goal of maximizing independence therefore corresponds to minimizing coupling.

Intermodule coupling actually occurs in several forms. One form is **control coupling,** which occurs when one module passes control to another, as in the transfer/return relationship associated with procedures. Another form is **data coupling,** which refers to the sharing of data between modules.

The structure chart in Fig. 6.3 already represents the control coupling in our simple payroll system based on the imperative paradigm. Data coupling is traditionally represented in a structure chart with additional arrows, as represented in Fig. 6.4. This chart indicates the data items that are passed to a module when its services are first requested and those data items that are passed back to the original module when the requested task is completed. In particular, when ProcessPayroll requests action from ComputePretaxWithholding, it passes the pertinent EmployeeID and TotalEarnings to ComputePretaxWithholding; and upon completing its task, ComputePretaxWithholding reports its conclusions to ProcessPayroll through the data item Withholding. In the imperative paradigm, this intermodule data coupling is traditionally implemented by means of procedure parameter lists, as introduced in Chapter 5.

In an object-oriented system most intermodule coupling takes the form of interobject communication, which is usually implemented as control coupling. A request for an object to perform a task is essentially a request for the execution of a routine within the object. In turn, the request results in control being passed to the object in a manner similar to control being passed to a procedure. The minimalization of data coupling is one of the main features of the object-oriented approach. Indeed, the concept of an object is that of collecting the routines that manipulate a particular item of data into a single module.

Regardless of the type of coupling involved, one should strive to make that coupling apparent in the written version of the program. Coupling that is disguised is known as **implicit coupling** and is the cause of many software errors. A common form of implicit coupling is obtained by the use of global data. **Global data** refers to data elements that are automatically available to the modules throughout a system, as opposed to local data elements that are accessible only within a particular module unless explicitly passed to another. Most high-level languages provide methods for implementing both global and local data.

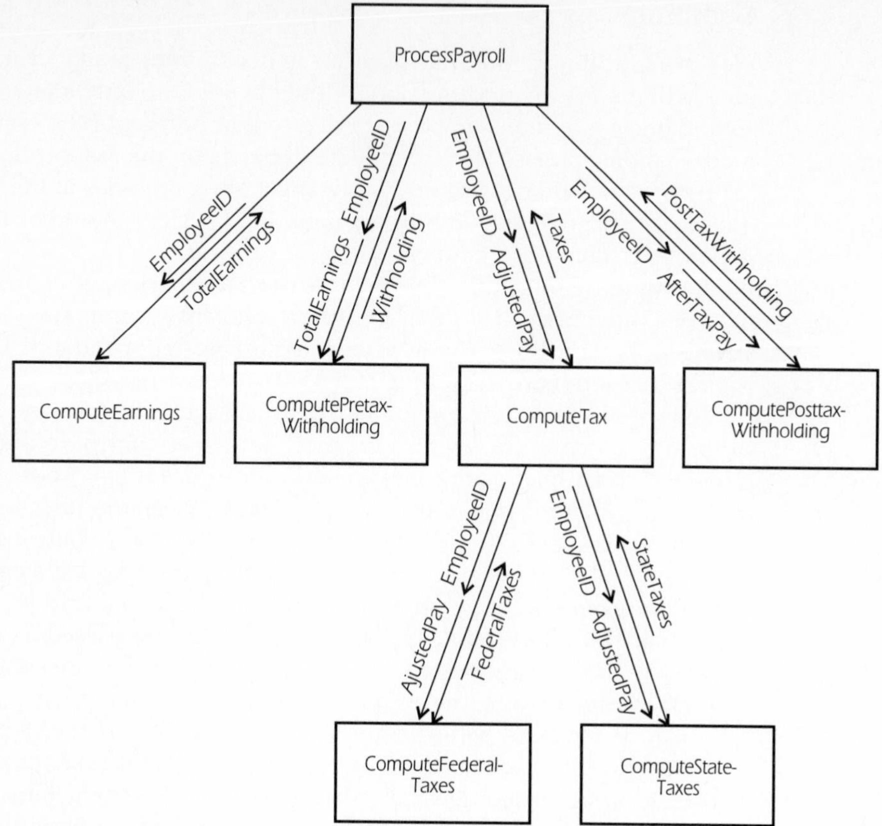

Figure 6.4 A structure chart showing data coupling

In our imperative-based payroll example, implicit data coupling may occur through the use of a global employee database to which each module may refer without being granted explicit permission. More precisely, ComputeEarnings may interrogate this database to find the total number of hours worked by an employee, while ComputePretaxWithholding might consult the same database to confirm that the employee in question participates in the company's retirement program.

The potential problem here is that one module may alter information used by other modules in a manner that is not anticipated by the rest of the system. This is especially likely after the system has been modified over a period of time. The result is that an apparently straightforward change to the system can have unforeseen and possibly disastrous side effects.

Side Effects

In a programming environment, the term **side effect** refers to an action performed by a program that is not readily represented by the program's syntax. Consider, for example, a module called CheckPassword whose task is to determine the privileges associated with different passwords. (Some users of the system may have passwords that allow the user to change data, while others may have passwords that allow only data retrieval.) If the privilege information were implemented as local data and passed through the parameter list, a request for services from the module CheckPassword might appear as

```
CheckPassword(Password, Privilege)
```

In contrast, if Privilege were implemented as a global data element, then a request for CheckPassword might appear as

```
CheckPassword(Password)
```

which does not explicitly reflect the fact that Privilege is involved. Indeed, in this case the action of CheckPassword has been demoted to a side effect.

Being inherently transparent, side effects constitute a major source of programming errors, and because implicit data coupling is one of the major sources of side effects, its use is sometimes scorned by software engineers. On the other hand, the proper use of global data can often simplify a program's presentation and hence increase its reliability. This, then, is an example of when the use of comment statements in the source program can be helpful. In particular, good programming style encourages the use of comments to identify any global data used by a module.

Cohesion

Just as important as minimizing the coupling between modules is maximizing the internal binding within each module. The term **cohesion** has been adopted for referring to this internal binding, or the degree of relatedness of a module's internal parts. Intuitively, one would expect an imperative-based module that projects future income from real estate investments to be more cohesive than a module that projects income from a variety of investments.

To appreciate the importance of cohesion, we must look beyond the initial development of the system and consider the entire software life cycle. If it becomes necessary to make changes in a module, the existence of a variety of activities within it can easily confuse what would otherwise be a simple process. Thus, in addition to seeking low intermodule coupling, software designers strive for high intramodule cohesion.

A weak form of cohesion is known as **logical cohesion.** This is the cohesion within a module induced by the fact that its internal elements perform activities logically similar in nature. For example, consider a module that performs all of a system's communication with the outside world. The "glue" that holds such a module together is that all the activities within the module deal with communication. However, the subjects of the communication can vary greatly. Some may deal with obtaining data, while others deal with reporting errors.

A stronger form of cohesion is known as **functional cohesion,** which means that all the parts of the module are geared toward the performance of a single activity. What constitutes a single activity depends on the tools available. The module ProcessPayroll in Fig. 6.3 is not functionally cohesive if the details of computing taxes and determining retirement contributions are included. However, by isolating these activities in other modules and using them as abstract tools, each step in the ProcessPayroll module can be focused on performing a single task (processing payroll) among all the other activities involved in the company's operation.

In an object-oriented environment the cohesion within each object is a type of logical cohesion in that the object is the collection of all program elements relating to the object. A software designer, however, strives to make the components within the object functionally cohesive. For example, each routine within an object should be designed to perform a functionally cohesive task.

Questions/Exercises

1. How does a novel differ from an encyclopedia in terms of the degree of coupling between its units such as chapters, sections, or entries? What about cohesion?
2. A hand of bridge is divided into two phases: the bidding and the actual playing of the cards. Analyze the coupling between these phases by identifying the information that is passed from the first phase to the second explicitly. What is passed implicitly?
3. Is the goal of maximizing cohesion compatible with minimizing coupling? That is, as cohesion increases, does coupling naturally tend to decrease?
4. Identify the cohesive property that binds the various parts together in each of the following settings. Also identify how the natural divisions in each setting are related to cohesion:

   a. A club
   b. A university registration system
   c. A department store
   d. A newspaper

6.4 Development Tools and Techniques

In this section we consider how modular designs are obtained. The development of design techniques is a major topic within software engineering, and its study has resulted in the development of design strategies general enough to be applied uniformly over a wide range of applications. In fact, the concepts discussed in this section are often applicable whether the system being designed is to be automated or not.

Top-Down Design

Perhaps the most common concept associated with system design is the top-down design methodology. The point of this concept is that one's first step when performing a task, such as a system design or the programming of a module, should be to produce a short, undetailed summary of the solution rather than a final detailed version of the solution. This summary often takes the form of little more than a restatement of the problem itself.

The next step is to refine the solution produced in the preceding step. Here one considers the solution in slightly more detail and divides the preceding summarized activity into its major units. The important point is that each of these units, although being more detailed, encompasses only a part of the overall task. The original problem thus gets divided into several smaller and simpler problems whose solutions collectively provide a solution to the original problem. This refinement process continues successively until manageable solutions are obtained.

In the traditional imperative approach the result of top-down design is a hierarchical system of refinements that often can be translated directly into a modular structure. That is, the smallest units in the hierarchy become modules that perform simple tasks, while the superior units become modules that perform more complex tasks using the lower modules as abstract tools. In contrast, object-oriented environments often use top-down design when establishing the types of objects that are required and designing the internal components of the objects.

Bottom-Up Design

In contrast to the top-down design methodology is the bottom-up approach, in which one starts the design of a system by identifying individual tasks within the system and then considers how solutions to these tasks can be used as abstract tools in the solution to more complex problems.

For many years, this approach has been considered inferior to the top-down design paradigm. Today, however, the bottom-up design methodology is gaining support. One reason for this shift in opinion is that the top-down methodology tends to seek a solution with a hierarchical structure. Indeed, the process of dividing tasks into subtasks naturally leads to a design consisting of a dominant module that uses submodules, each of which relies on subsubmodules, and so on. On the other hand, the best design for some systems is not of a hierarchical nature. A design consisting of two modules interacting as equals (Fig. 6.5a) may be a better solution than a design consisting of a superior module that relies on subordinates to perform its task (Fig. 6.5b). For example, a multinational economic model might be implemented as several modules, one for each nation, that communicate directly with one another to simulate the interaction between nations.

Another problem with top-down design is that it tends to lock one into a specific structure early in the software design process. If the original decomposition of the proposed system proves to be problematic, modifying that decomposition can cause much of the design effort already invested to be lost.

Still another reason for the increased interest in bottom-up design rests in the emphasis on constructing abstract tools that can be used as building blocks in a variety of applications. Much of the momentum for this approach stems from the popularity of object-oriented programming, in which programs are often constructed from stand-alone objects, each having the ability to interact with other objects directly rather than through a supervising module. In turn, these objects are also available as ready-made units for use in other designs. In this atmosphere, then, the design of a new system conforms more closely to the process of building complex solutions from pieces than to the process of refining global approaches into subtasks.

(a) Modules interacting as equals

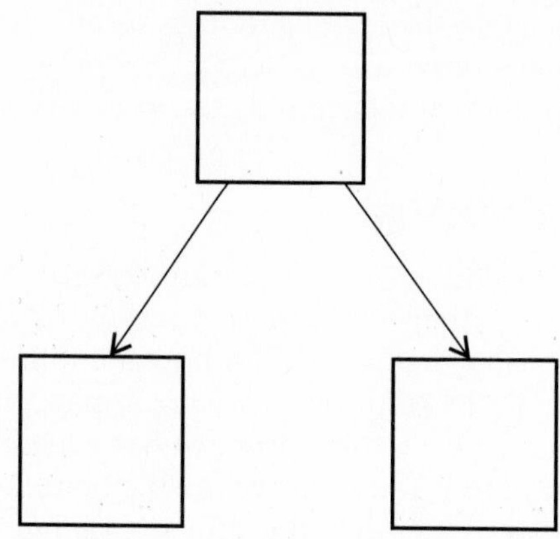

(b) Modules under control of a supervising module

Figure 6.5 Contrasting modular designs

Dataflow Diagrams

Software engineering has produced a variety of notational systems to aid in the system analysis and design process, many of which are applicable in either top-down or bottom-up paradigms. One of these, the dataflow approach, emphasizes the data, or information, that will flow through the proposed system as opposed to the procedures, or algorithms, that will be executed. The dataflow approach to software development originated in the context of the imperative programming paradigm. The idea was that by following the data paths through the proposed system, we discover where data units merge, split, or are otherwise altered. Because computational activity is needed at these locations in the system, such activities, or groupings of activities, should form the modules of the system. Consequently, concentrating on flow of data helps us discover a modular structure for a system instead of forcing us to break it into pieces according to intuition.

Although developed with the imperative programming paradigm in mind, dataflow analysis has found some use in object-oriented environments, where it can help identify the objects required by the system and the tasks those objects must perform.

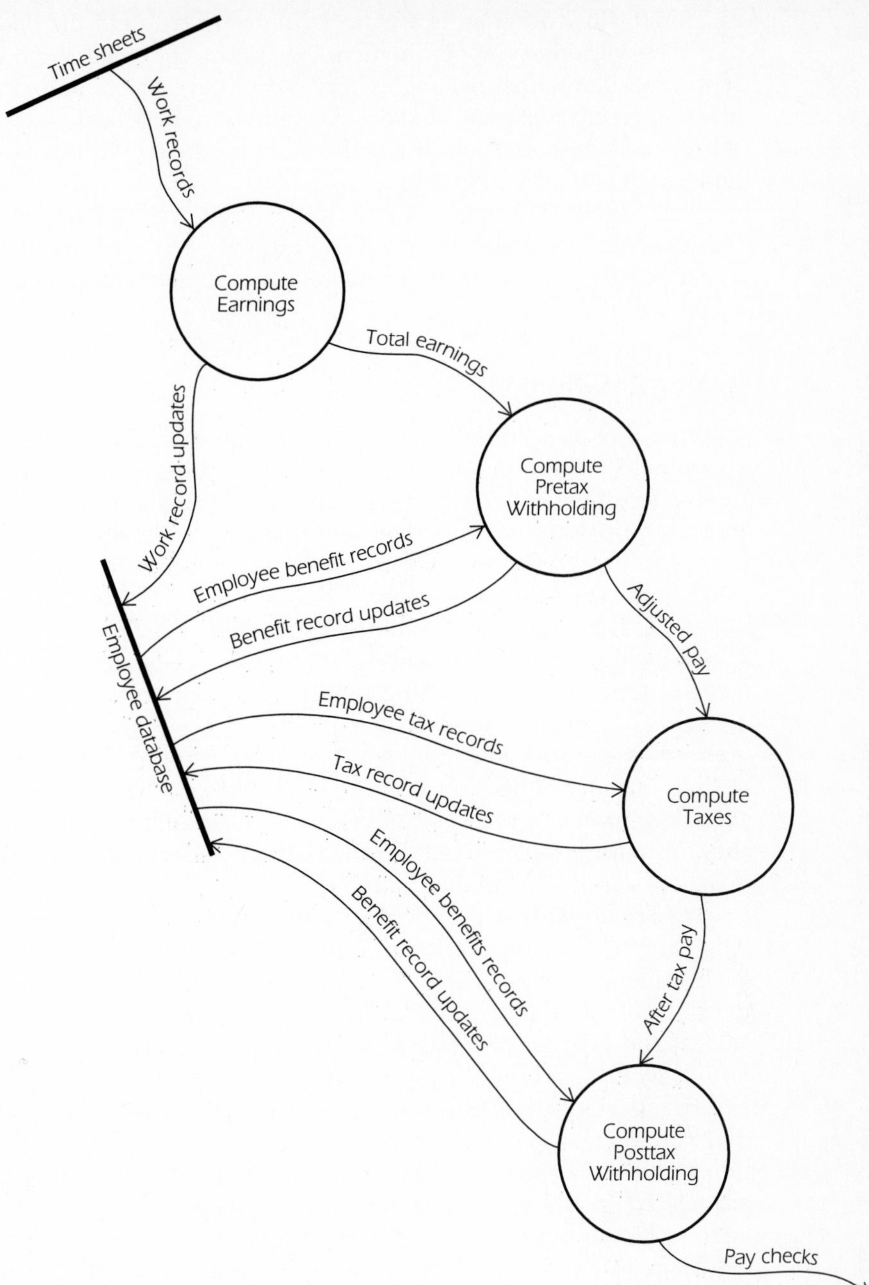

Figure 6.6 A dataflow diagram of a simple payroll system

A **dataflow diagram** is a pictorial representation of the data paths in a system. The various symbols in such a diagram have specific meanings: Arrows represent data paths, rectangles represent data sources and sinks, circles (bubbles) represent locations of data manipulation, and heavy straight lines represent data storage. In each case the symbol is labeled with the name of the object represented either within it or alongside it.

A dataflow diagram for our simple payroll system is shown in Fig. 6.6. Note that the dataflow diagram, in which emphasis is placed on the data, more readily reflects the role of the underlying employee database than the structure chart in Fig. 6.4.

Entity-Relationship Diagrams

Another tool used in the analysis and design of software systems is the **entity-relationship diagram,** which is a pictorial representation of the items of information (entities) within the system and the relationships between these pieces of information. As an example, let us consider part of an entity-relationship diagram for a software system for maintaining information about professors, students, and classes at a university.

We first identify the data entities involved. They include the entity Professor, which we think of as representing a single professor at the university; the entity Student, which represents a single student; and the entity Class, which represents a section of a given course. With each occurrence of the Professor entity is associated a name, address, employee identification number, salary, and so on; with each occurrence of the Student entity is associated a name, address, student identification number, grade point average, and so on; and with each occurrence of the Class entity is associated a course identification (History 101), semester and year, classroom, time of day, and so on.

Having identified the entities in our system, we now consider the relationships among the entities. We first note that each professor teaches classes and each student attends classes. We therefore identify the relationship between the entities Professor and Class as the relationship Teaches and that between the entities Student and Class as the relationship Attends. (Note that entities are referred to by nouns, whereas relationships are referenced by verbs.)

To represent these entities and relationships, we use the entity-relationship diagram in Fig. 6.7. Here each entity is represented by a rectangle and each relationship is represented by a diamond. The diagram clearly shows that professors are related to classes by means of the relationship Teaches and students are related to classes by means of the relationship Attends.

There is, however, a different structure associated with the two relationships in our example. The relationship between Professor and Class is a one-to-many relationship in that each professor teaches several classes but each class is taught by only one professor. In contrast, the relationship between Student and Class is a many-to-many relationship because each student attends several classes and each class is attended by several students. This additional information is represented in Fig. 6.7 by the presence of pointers on the lines connecting

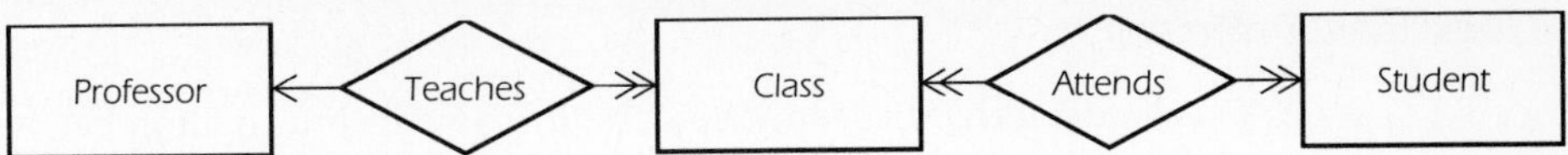

Figure 6.7 An entity-relationship diagram

relationships to entities. In particular, a single pointer toward an entity indicates that only one occurrence of that entity is involved in each occurrence of the relationship, whereas a double pointer indicates that more than one occurrence of the entity may be involved.[1] Thus the pointer toward the entity Professor in Fig. 6.7 indicates that only one professor teaches a class, while the double pointer toward the entity Class in the Teaches relationship indicates that each professor may teach more than one class.

Among the various tools used by software engineers in the past, entity-relationship diagrams appear to be the most likely to survive the shift to object-oriented methodologies. This is because the identification of entities is essentially the identification of objects, and the classification of entity relationships is the first step toward identifying the relationships and communication paths required between objects.

Data Dictionaries

Still another tool in the development of a software system is the **data dictionary**—a central depository of information about the data items appearing throughout the system. This information includes the identifier used to reference each item, what constitutes valid entries in each item (Will the item always be numeric or perhaps always alphabetic? What will be the range of values that might be assigned to this item?); where the item is stored (Will the item be stored in a file or a database and, if so, which one?); and where the item is referenced in the software (Which modules will refer to the item?).

Several goals are associated with the development of a data dictionary. One is to enhance communication between the potential user of the system and the analyst charged with the task of converting the user's needs into requirements and specifications. It would be discouraging to find, after the system has been implemented, that part numbers are not really numeric or that the size of the inventory exceeds the maximum allowed by the system. The process of constructing a data dictionary helps avoid such misunderstandings.

Another goal associated with the data dictionary is to establish uniformity throughout the system. It is usually by means of constructing the dictionary that redundancies and contradictions surface. For example, the item referred to as PartNumber in the inventory records may be the same as the PartId in the sales records. Moreover, the personnel department may use the item Name to refer to an employee while inventory records may contain the item Name in reference to a part.

[1]No universal standard exists for representing multiplicity within an entity-relationship diagram. The single/double pointer system used here may not agree with other material you will read.

Questions/Exercises

1. Draw a dataflow diagram depicting the flow of information between an instructor, a student, and a textbook. Include the fact that quizzes are given.
2. Suppose that a certain receptionist receives requests for appointments. The response to a request is either a schedule for a future appointment or an immediate appointment. Draw a dataflow diagram representing this part of the receptionist's job.
3. Give a short definition of a dataflow diagram, an entity-relationship diagram, and a data dictionary.
4. Draw an entity-relationship diagram representing airline companies, flights flown by each company, and the passengers on the various flights.

6.5 Documentation

A software system is of little use unless people can learn to use and maintain it. Hence, documentation is an important part of a software package, and in turn its development is an important topic in software engineering.

Documentation of a software package is normally produced for two purposes. One is to explain the features of the software and describe how to use them. This is known as **user documentation** because it is designed to be read by the user of the software. Hence, user documentation tends to be nontechnical.

Today, user documentation is recognized as an important marketing tool. Good user documentation (combined with a well-designed user interface) makes a software package accessible and thus increases its sales. Recognizing this, many software developers hire technical writers to produce this part of their product, or they provide preliminary versions of their products to independent manual writers so that how-to books are available in book stores when the software itself is released to the public.

User documentation traditionally takes the form of a manual that presents an introduction to the most commonly used features of the software (often in the form of a tutorial), a section explaining how to install the software, and a reference section describing the details of each feature of the software.

This manual is often available in book form, but in many cases it is provided as a file that is stored on the same medium as the software. This allows a user of the software to review portions of the manual at the computer monitor while using the software. In this case the information may be broken into small units, sometimes called help packages, that are presented as a part of the software system itself. That is, the ability to request access to one of the help packages is an option built into the software system. In some systems help packages may appear on the monitor screen automatically if the user dallies too long between commands.

The other purpose for documentation is to describe the software itself so that the system can be maintained later in its life cycle. Documentation of this type is known as **system documentation** and is inherently more technical than user documentation. In the past system documentation consisted of the final source programs and some sketchy explanations that were written after the software was developed—an approach with which most beginning programmers can identify. However, such haphazard documentation is simply not acceptable for today's large software systems.

Today, system documentation begins with the development of the original system specifications and continues throughout the software's life cycle. Ultimately, it consists of all the documents that were prepared during the software's development, including the specifications by which the system was verified, the dataflow and entity-relationship diagrams from which the software was designed, the data dictionary, and the structure charts representing the modular structure of the system.

Of major importance is the source version of all the programs in the system. It is important that these programs be presented in a readable format, which is why software engineers support the use of well-designed, high-level programming languages, the use of comment statements for annotating a program, and a modular design that allows each module to be presented as a coherent unit.

The fact that the development of system documentation is an ongoing process leads to a conflict between the goals of software engineering and human nature. It is highly unlikely that the initial specifications, dataflow diagrams, entity-relationship diagrams, or structure charts will remain unchanged as the system development progresses. It is more likely that changes will be made as the people involved in the project recognize problems that were not foreseen. (This phenomenon is the driving force behind the development of prototyping techniques.) At issue in this case is the temptation to make ongoing changes in the system's design without going back to update the earlier design documents. The result is a strong possibility that these documents will be incorrect and hence their use in the final documentation misleading.

Herein lies another argument in favor of CASE tools. They make the tasks of redrawing diagrams and updating dictionaries much easier than they were with the older manual methods. Moreover, combining this advantage with the newer prototyping methodologies, which accept the idea of analysis and design being iterative processes involving implementation, brings the task of document alteration into the realm of accepted practice rather than that of discouraged exception. In turn, updates are more likely to be made in this environment, and the final documentation is more likely to be accurate.

We close by emphasizing that the example of updating documents is only one of many instances in which software engineering must encompass both the cold, hard facts of a science and the realistic understanding of human nature. Others include the inevitable personality conflicts, jealousies, and ego clashes that arise when people work together. Thus, as we have mentioned before, the subject of software engineering covers much more than those subjects directly associated with computer science.

Questions/Exercises

1. In what forms can software be documented?
2. At what phase (or phases) in the software life cycle is documentation prepared?
3. Which is more important, a program or its documentation?

6.6 Software Ownership and Liability

We close this chapter by considering some legal issues that are closely related to the software engineering discipline. One might think that previously established legal principles would be sufficient to resolve disputes in the evolving software industry, but this has not always been the case. In particular, a method is required by which a company or individual can recoup, and profit from, the massive investment needed to develop quality software, because without a means of protecting this investment, few would be willing to undertake the task of producing the software our society desires. But questions of software ownership and ownership rights often fall between the cracks of well-established copyright and patent laws. Although these laws were developed to allow the developer of a "product" to release that product to the public while protecting his or her ownership rights, which is certainly the goal of the software industry, the characteristics of software have repeatedly challenged the courts in their efforts to apply copyright and patent principles to issues of software ownership.

Copyright laws were originally established to protect an author's ownership of literary works. In this case the value is in how ideas are expressed rather than in the ideas themselves. The value in a poem is in the rhythm, style, and format of the poem rather than the subject matter; the value of a novel is in the author's presentation of the story rather than the story itself. Thus a poet's or an author's investment can be protected by giving him or her ownership of that particular expression of the idea, but not the idea itself. Another person is free to express the same idea as long as that expression does not have "substantial similarity" to that of the original.

In the case of software the idea expressed is the algorithm. In contrast to a poem or novel, the value of software is not in the particular manner in which an algorithm is expressed. Instead, it is in the algorithm. Indeed, in many cases, the cost of software development is concentrated in the discovery of the algorithms rather than in their representations. In turn, a straightforward application of copyright laws tends not to protect a software developer's investment. Instead, it allows an algorithm that the developer discovered as a result of major investments to be used by a competitor as long as that competitor's representation is not substantially similar to the original.

In a sense, copyright laws were developed to protect implementation rather than function, but the value of a program is often in its function rather than its form. As a result, copyright laws are better suited for protecting programs that implement well-known, unoriginal algorithms than they are at protecting investments that lead to new algorithms. If the algorithm is well known, the only value in the program is its expression; if, however, the algorithm expressed is new and creative, the major value of the program is the algorithm, which copyrights do not protect. This is somewhat paradoxical; the more that creative efforts are required to produce a program, the less likely it is that copyright laws will protect the investment of those efforts.

The use of patents for protecting software ownership rights is hampered by several obstacles, one being the longstanding principle that no one can own a natural phenomenon such as laws of physics, mathematical formulas, and thoughts. Courts have generally ruled that algorithms fall within this category. Thus, as in the case of copyright, patent laws tend not to protect the major item of value within a program—the algorithm. Moreover, obtaining a patent is an expensive and time-consuming process, often involving several years. During this time a software product could become obsolete, and until the patent is granted the applicant has no right to exclude others from appropriating the product.

Copyright and patent laws are designed to allow, and even encourage, the dissemination of inventions and to encourage the free exchange of ideas for the betterment of society. The reasoning is that when ownership rights are protected, creators and inventors are more likely to make their achievements known to the public. In contrast, trade secret laws provide a means of restricting the distribution of ideas. Designed to maintain ethical conduct between competing businesses, these laws protect against improper disclosure or wrongful appropriation of a company's internal accomplishments. The question of improper disclosure is often formalized as nondisclosure agreements, in which a company requires those with access to company secrets to agree not to disclose their knowledge to others. Courts have generally upheld such agreements.

To protect against liability, software developers often accompany their product with disclaimers, in which they state the limitations of their liability. Such statements as "In no event will Company X be liable for any damages arising out of the use of this software" and "Company X does not warrant that this software will meet your needs" are common. Courts, however, rarely consider a disclaimer if the plaintiff can show negligence on the part of the defendant. Thus liability cases tend to focus on whether the defendant used a level of care compatible with the product being produced. A level of care that might be deemed acceptable in the case of developing a word processing system may be considered negligent when developing software to control a nuclear reactor. In turn, the best defense against liability claims in software development is a concerted approach to the software development process.

Questions/Exercises

1. What test can be applied to decide whether one program is substantially similar to another?
2. In what ways are copyright, patent, and trade secret laws designed to benefit society?
3. To what extent are disclaimers not recognized by the courts?

CHAPTER REVIEW PROBLEMS

1. Give an example of how efforts in the development of software can pay dividends later in software maintenance.
2. What is evolutionary prototyping?
3. Summarize how the use of CASE tools has changed the software development process.
4. Explain how the lack of metrics for measuring certain software properties affects software engineering discipline.

5. How does software engineering differ from other, more traditional fields of engineering.
6. a. Identify a disadvantage of the traditional waterfall model for software development.
   b. Identify an advantage of the traditional waterfall model for software development.
7. How does the establishment of codes of ethics and professional conduct aid in the development of quality software?
8. What is the difference between explicit and implicit data coupling? Give an example of each.
9. What is the difference between coupling and cohesion? Which should be minimized and which should be maximized? Why?
10. Which of the following statements is an argument for coupling, and which is an argument for cohesion:
    a. For a student to learn, the subject should be presented in well-organized units with specific goals.
    b. A student doesn't really understand a subject until the subject's overall scope and relationship with other subjects has been grasped.
11. In the text, we mentioned control coupling but did not pursue it. Contrast the coupling between two program units obtained by a simple goto statement with the coupling obtained by a procedure call.
12. Answer the following questions in relation to the accompanying structure chart:

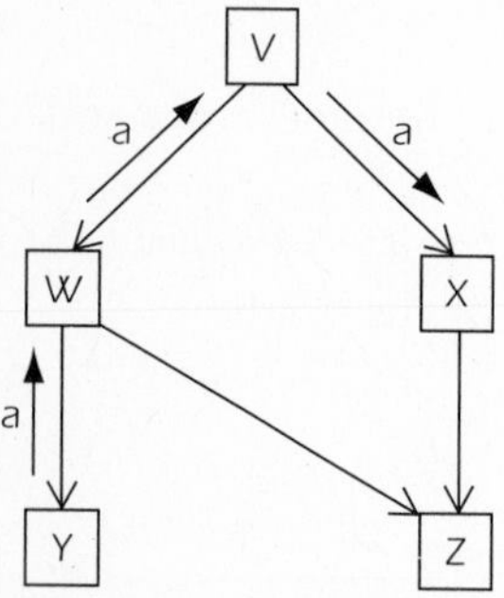

    a. To which module does module Y return control?
    b. To which module does module Z return control?
    c. Are modules W and X linked via control coupling?
    d. Are modules W and X linked via data coupling?
    e. What data is shared by both module W and module Y?
    f. In what way are modules Y and X related?
13. In relation to the structure chart in Problem 12, what stubs are necessary to test module V? What characteristics might these stubs have?
14. Answer the following questions in relation to the accompanying structure chart:

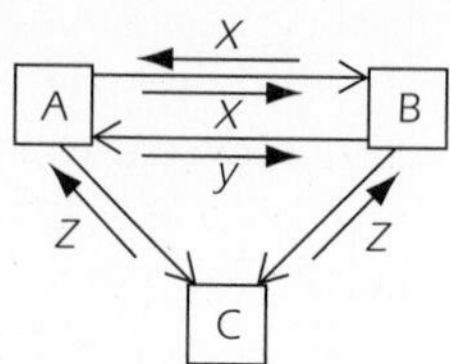

    a. What is different between the way modules A and B use data items *x* and *y*?
    b. If one of the modules was in charge of obtaining data item *z* from a user at a remote terminal, which module would that apparently be?
15. Here are sketches of procedures A, B, C, D, E, and F expressed in an Ada-like syntax. Draw a structure chart representing the control and data coupling indicated by these sketches. Within which module is a person's address apparently determined? What about a person's age? The skills required for a job?

```
procedure A(Name: in String;
            Addr: out String);
      .
      .
end;
procedure B(Job: in String);
      .
      .
  F(Job, Skills);
      .
      .
end;
procedure C(Name: in String);
      .
      .
  D(Name, Age);
```

```
      .
      .
  A(Name, Addr):
      .
      .
end;
procedure D(Name: in String;
            Age: out int);
      .
      .
end;
procedure E(EmplID: in String);
      .
      .
  C(Name);
      .
      .
  B(Job);
      .
      .
end;
procedure F(Job: in String;
            Skills: out SkillType);
      .
      .
end;
```

16. Here are sketches of procedures A, B, and C expressed in an Ada-like syntax. Draw a structure chart representing the control and data coupling among them.

```
procedure A(x: in integer;
            y: in out integer);
  .
  .
end;
procedure B(z: out integer);
  .
  .
end;
procedure C;
  .
  .
  B(z);
  A(x, y);
  .
  .
end;
```

17. Design a modular structure for an on-line inventory/customer records system for a mail-order business and represent it with a structure chart. What modules in your system must be modified because of changes in sales tax laws? What if the length of the postal system's ZIP code changes?

18. Suppose the function Handicap were designed to compute and return the handicap of the golfer identified in the parameter list, but in so doing suppose it also adds one to the value of a global variable called Par. If the value of Par is initially 4 and Bill's handicap is 2, how will the result of the computation

    Par + Handicap(Bill)

    vary depending on the order in which the values needed in the computation are obtained?

19. Give a definition for the term *side effect.*

20. What potentially disastrous side effects are lurking in a software system whose modules use global rather than local variables?

21. What effect does the order of execution have in performing the calculation 4 / 2 + 6?

22. Draw a dataflow diagram depicting the registration process at a university.

23. Contrast the information represented in dataflow diagrams with that given in structure charts.

24. What is the difference between a one-to-many relationship and a many-to-many relationship?

25. Draw an entity-relationship diagram representing the relationships between the cooks, waitresses, customers, and cashiers in a restaurant.

26. Draw an entity-relationship diagram representing the relationships between magazines, publishers of magazines, and subscribers to magazines.

27. In each of the following cases, identify whether the activity relates to a structure chart, a dataflow diagram, an entity-relationship diagram, or a data dictionary.
    a. Identifying the data pertinent to the system to be developed.
    b. Identifying the relationship between the various items of data appearing in the system.
    c. Identifying the characteristics of each item of data in the system.
    d. Identifying which items of data are shared among the various parts of the system.

28. Summarize the distinction between top-down and bottom-up design strategies.
29. What is the difference between user documentation and system documentation?
30. Suppose that 100 errors were intentionally placed in a large software system before the system was subjected to final testing. Moreover, suppose that a total of 200 errors were discovered and corrected during this final testing, of which 50 errors were from the group intentionally placed in the system. If the remaining 50 known errors are then corrected, how many unknown errors would you estimate are still in the system?
31. Why would it not be desirable for the same person who wrote a program to also design the test data?
32. In what way do traditional copyright laws fail to safeguard the rights of software developers?
33. In what way to traditional patent laws fail to safeguard the rights of software developers?

QUESTIONS OF ETHICS

The following questions are provided to help you understand some of the ethical/social/legal issues associated with the field of computing as well as investigate your own beliefs and their foundations. The goal is not merely to answer these questions. You should also consider why you answered as you did and whether your justifications are consistent from one question to the next.

1. a. Mary Analyst has been assigned the task of designing a system with which medical records will be stored on a machine that is connected to a large network. Her concerns regarding security have been overruled for financial reasons, and she has been told to proceed with the project using a security system that she feels is inadequate. What should she do? Why?
   b. Suppose that Mary Analyst developed the system as she was told, and now she is aware that the medical records are being observed by unauthorized personnel. What should she do? To what extent is she liable for the breach of security?
   c. Suppose that instead of obeying her employer, Mary Analyst refuses to proceed with the system and blows the whistle by making the flawed design public, resulting in a financial hardship for the company and the loss of many innocent employees' jobs. Was Mary Analyst's actions correct? What if it turns out that, being only a part of the overall design team, Mary Analyst was unaware that sincere efforts were being made elsewhere within the company to develop a valid security system that would be applied to the system on which Mary was working. How does this change your judgment of Mary's actions? (Remember, Mary's view of the situation is the same as before.)
2. When large software systems are developed by many people, how should liabilities be assigned? Is there a hierarchy of responsibility? Are there degrees of liability?
3. We have seen that large, complex software systems are often developed by many individuals, few of which may have a complete picture of the entire project. Is it proper for an employee to contribute to a project without full knowledge of its function?
4. To what extent is someone responsible for how his or her accomplishments are ultimately applied by others?
5. In the relationship between a computer professional and a client, is it the professional's responsibility to implement the client's desires or rather to direct the client's desires? What if the professional foresees that a client's desires could lead to unethical consequences? For example, the client may wish to cut corners for the sake of efficiency, but the professional may foresee a potential source of erroneous data or misuse of the system if those shortcuts are taken. If the client insists, is the professional free of responsibility?

ADDITIONAL ACTIVITIES

1. Draw a structure chart for a software system that simulates the machine described in Appendix C. Assume that the software will be written using the imperative paradigm.
2. Design an object-oriented software system that simulates the machine described in Appendix C.
3. What features are provided by a programming language you know for implementing data coupling between modules? How can data be implicitly passed between modules? How can data be explicitly passed between modules?
4. What features are provided by a programming language you know to encourage well-designed programs?
5. Companies involved in software development often insist that all programmers conform to a uniform programming style. Design a style for writing programs in a language you know that could serve as a companywide standard. Your proposal should consider such items as indentation, documentation, spacing, and naming of variables and types.

ADDITIONAL READING

Arthur, L. J. *Rapid Evolutionary Development.* New York: John Wiley, 1992.

Booch, G. *Object-Oriented Analysis and Design with Applications,* 2nd ed. Redwood City, Calif.: Benjamin/Cummings, 1994.

Conte, S. D., H. E. Dunsmore, and V. Y. Shen. *Software Engineering Metrics and Models.* Redwood City, Calif.: Benjamin/Cummings, 1986.

Pressman, R. S. *Software Engineering: Practitioner's Approach,* 3rd ed. New York: McGraw-Hill, 1992.

Schach, S. R. *Classical and Object-Oriented Software Engineering,* 3rd ed. Chicago: Irwin, 1996.

Sommerville, I. *Software Engineering,* 4th ed. Reading, Mass.: Addison-Wesley, 1992.

PART THREE

DATA ORGANIZATION

We have seen that the information stored inside a machine is represented in coded form and stored either in memory cells or in some mass storage system. The information in this form is rarely conducive for use in an application. Rather, the application normally suggests that we imagine the data as being organized in an alternative manner. For example, data representing the weekly sales of a company's sales force might be envisioned in tabular form, with a separate column for each day of the week and a separate row for each member of the sales force; the names and positions of a company's employees might be pictured in the form of an organization chart; or a company may want its inventory records organized by part number for one application and by cost for another.

Part Three introduces the study of how a machine can be programmed to present its internal data to a user as though it were stored in these conceptual and more useful forms and how this goal affects the way the data items are actually stored within the machine. In Chapter 7 we concentrate on data stored in a machine's main memory; in Chapter 8 we consider data stored in mass storage; and in Chapter 9 we introduce the topic of database systems.

CHAPTER SEVEN

Data Structures

7.1 Arrays
One-Dimensional Arrays
Multidimensional Arrays

7.2 Lists
Pointers
Contiguous Lists
Linked Lists
Supporting the Conceptual List

7.3 Stacks
Stack Applications
Stack Implementation
A Particular Stack Application

7.4 Queues
Queue Implementation
A Particular Queue Application

7.5 Trees
Terminology
Tree Implementation
A Binary Tree Package

***7.6 Customized Data Types**
User-Defined Types
Abstract Data Types
Encapsulation

***7.7 Object-Oriented Programming**

A machine's main memory is organized as individual cells with consecutive addresses. However, it is often convenient to associate other data arrangements in these cells. For example, weekly sales records are more naturally viewed in a tabular form in which sales of different items on different days are arranged in rows and columns. In this chapter we consider how such abstract data organizations are simulated. The goal is to allow the data user to think in terms of abstract organizations rather than being concerned with the actual organization within a machine's main memory.

*Sections marked by an asterisk are optional in that they represent additional depth of coverage that is not required for an understanding of future chapters. (Section 7.7 is a minor exception. It is required background for Section 9.4.)

7.1 Arrays

We begin our study of data structures by considering the organizations known as arrays encountered earlier in our discussion of high-level programming languages. There we saw that many high-level languages allow a programmer to express an algorithm as though the data being manipulated were stored in a rectangular arrangement; the programmer might refer to the fifth element in a one-dimensional array or the element in the third row and sixth column of a two-dimensional array. Since the array is actually stored in the memory cells of the machine, it becomes the job of the translator to convert such references into the terminology of memory cells and addresses.

One-Dimensional Arrays

Suppose an algorithm for manipulating a series of 24 hourly temperature readings is expressed in a high-level language. The programmer would probably find it convenient to think of these readings arranged as a one-dimensional array, that is, as a list called Readings whose various entries are referenced in terms of their position in the list. This position is often called an index. The first reading might be referenced by Readings[1], the second by Readings[2], and so on.[1]

The conversion from the conceptual one-dimensional array organization to the actual arrangement within the machine can be rather straightforward. The data can be stored in a sequence of 24 memory cells with consecutive addresses in the same order envisioned by the programmer. Knowing the address of the first cell in this sequence, a translator can then convert terms such as Readings[4] into the proper memory terminology. To find the actual address, one merely subtracts one from the position of the desired entry and then adds the result to the address of the first cell in the sequence. (If the first cell in the sequence is at address 13, the fourth entry in the array is located at location 13 + (4 − 1) = 16, as shown in Fig. 7.1.)

Multidimensional Arrays

The conversion is not quite as simple with multidimensional arrays. Consider, for example, a record of the sales made by a company's sales force during a one-week period. We can think of such data arranged in tabular form, with the names of the sales personnel listed down the left side and the days of the week listed across the top. Hence we can think of the data being arranged in rows and columns; the values across each row indicate the sales made by a particular employee, while the values down a column represent all the sales made during a particular day. Extracting information from the table therefore involves finding the value common to both a given row and a given column.

[1]Recall that some languages, such as C, C++, and Java, use 0 as the index of the first entry in an array. In these cases the programmer would refer to the readings as Readings[0], Readings[1], and so on.

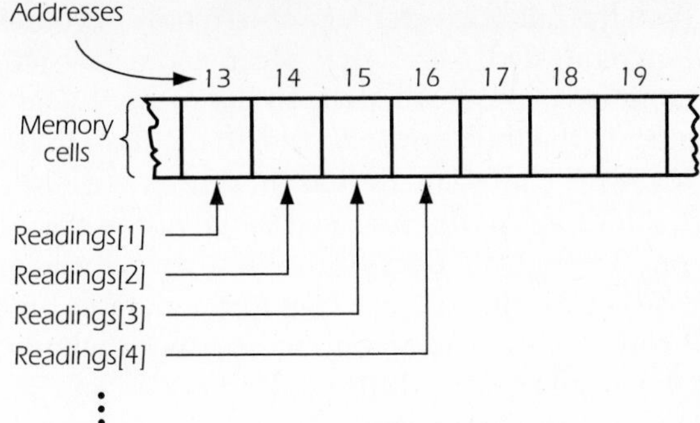

Figure 7.1 The array of Readings stored in memory starting at address 13

A machine's memory is not organized in this rectangular fashion but rather as individual cells with consecutive addresses. Thus the rectangular structure required by the sales table must be simulated. To do this, we first recognize that the size of the array does not vary as updates are made. We can therefore calculate the amount of storage area needed and reserve a block of contiguous memory cells of that size. Next, we store the data in the cells row by row. That is, starting at the first cell of the reserved block, we copy the values from the first row of the table into consecutive memory locations; following this we copy the next row, then the next, and so on (Fig. 7.2). Such a storage system is said to use **row major order** in contrast to **column major order,** in which the array is stored column by column.

Figure 7.2 A two-dimensional array with four rows and five columns stored in row major order

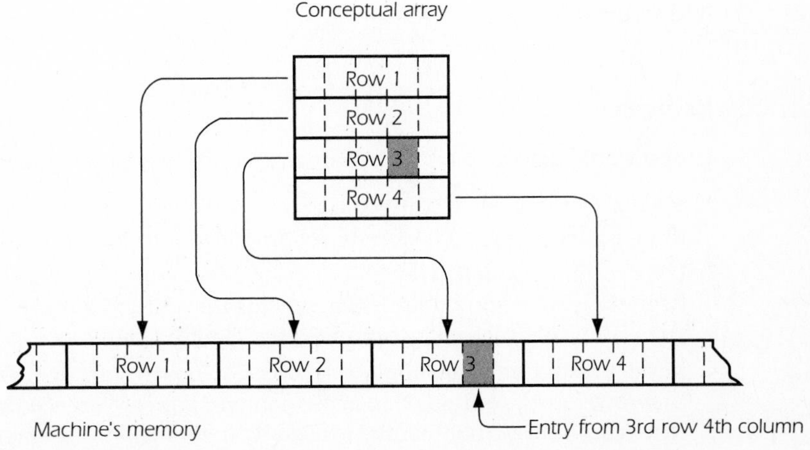

With the data stored, the problem now becomes locating particular entries as they are requested. Recall that because the user will be thinking in terms of rows and columns, a request will be in the form of wanting, for example, the value of the entry in the third row and fourth column, that is, the sales made by the third employee on Thursday. To find this entry, we first envision ourselves as being at the first location in the reserved block of the machine's memory. From this location on, we find the data in the first row of the array followed by the second, then the third, and so on. To get to the data in the third row, we must move beyond both the first and second rows. Since each row contains five entries (one for each day from Monday through Friday), we must move beyond a total of ten entries to reach the first entry of the third row. From the beginning of the third row, we must move beyond another three entries to reach the entry in the fourth column of the array. Altogether, to reach the entry in the third row and fourth column, we must move beyond 13 entries from the beginning of the block.

The preceding calculation is a special case of a general process that can be used for finding entries in a two-dimensional array when it is stored in row major order. In particular, if we let C represent the number of columns in the array (which is the number of entries in each row), to find the entry in the Ith row and Jth column, we must move beyond.

$$(\mathrm{C} \times (I-1)) + (J-1)$$

entries from the beginning of the array. (This expression is sometimes called the **address polynomial.**) That is, we must move beyond $I - 1$ rows, each of which contains C entries, to reach the Ith row and then $J - 1$ more entries to reach the Jth entry in this row. In our prior example C was equal to 5, I to 3, and J to 4: $(5 \times (3-1)) + (4-1)$ equals 13.

With this information, software routines can be written to convert requests in terms of rows and columns into locations within the block of memory containing the array. A translator, for example, uses this technique to convert a reference such as Sales[2,4] into an actual memory address. A programmer can therefore enjoy the luxury of thinking of the data in tabular form (the conceptual structure) even though it is actually stored in a single row (the actual structure) within the machine.

Questions/Exercises

1. Show how the array $\begin{matrix} 5 & 3 & 7 \\ 4 & 2 & 8 \\ 1 & 9 & 6 \end{matrix}$ appears in memory when stored in row major order.
2. Give a formula for finding the entry in the Ith row and Jth column of a two-dimensional array if it is stored in column major order rather than row major order.
3. If a two-dimensional array of 8 rows and 11 columns is stored in row major order beginning at memory address 25, what is the address of the entry in the third row, sixth column if each entry occupies two memory cells?
4. In the C programming language indices of arrays start at 0. Thus the entry in the first row, fourth column of an array named Array is referenced by Array[0][3]. In this case what address polynomial is used by the translator to convert references of the form Array[I][J] into memory addresses?

7.2 Lists

An important property of arrays is the constancy of their size and shape, so simulating them in a machine's memory is essentially a process of converting the conceptual location of an element into the actual location. In contrast are dynamic structures, which vary in size and shape. For instance, an organization's membership list grows as new members join and shrinks as old members leave. In such cases we find that in addition to locating elements in the structure, we must accommodate variations in the structure itself.

Pointers

A prominent concept in the maintenance of dynamic structures is that of a pointer, so let us introduce this idea before proceeding. Recall that the various storage locations in a machine's memory are identified by numeric addresses. If we know the address of a piece of data, we can find that item with little difficulty. Being merely numeric values, these addresses themselves are easily stored in a machine's memory. Thus, having stored an item of data in one cell of memory, we can store the address of that data in another memory cell. Later, if we want to retrieve the data item and we have access to the cell containing its address, we can find the data by referring to its address.

In a sense, then, a memory cell containing the address of a data item can be thought of as pointing to that data item. Such cells are called **pointers.** We have already encountered the idea of a pointer in our discussion of a machine's fetch–decode–execute cycle, in which a program counter is used to hold the address of the next instruction to be executed. In fact, another but somewhat outdated term for program counter is **instruction pointer.** The URLs used to link hypertext comments are also examples of the pointer concept except that URLs are pointers to locations in the Internet rather than to locations in main memory.

Many programming languages today allow for the declaration, allocation, and manipulation of pointers, just as they allow for such operations for integers or character strings. Using such a language, a programmer can design elaborate networks of data items within a machine's memory. For example, suppose a library has its holdings represented in a machine's memory in alphabetical order by title. Although convenient in many applications, this arrangements makes it difficult to find all the books by a particular author, because the books are scattered throughout the list. To solve this problem we can reserve an additional memory cell of type pointer within the block of cells representing each book. In each of these pointer cells we can place the address of another block representing a book by the same author so that each collection of books with common authorship is linked in a loop (Fig. 7.3). Once we find one book by a given author, we can then find all the others by following the pointers from one book to another.

Let us now return to our discussion of dynamic data structures by considering two methods of maintaining a list of names within a machine's memory. The first of these methods (contiguous list) is similar to array storage systems and does not use pointers; the other method (linked list) uses pointers to overcome some of the disadvantages encountered with a contiguous list.

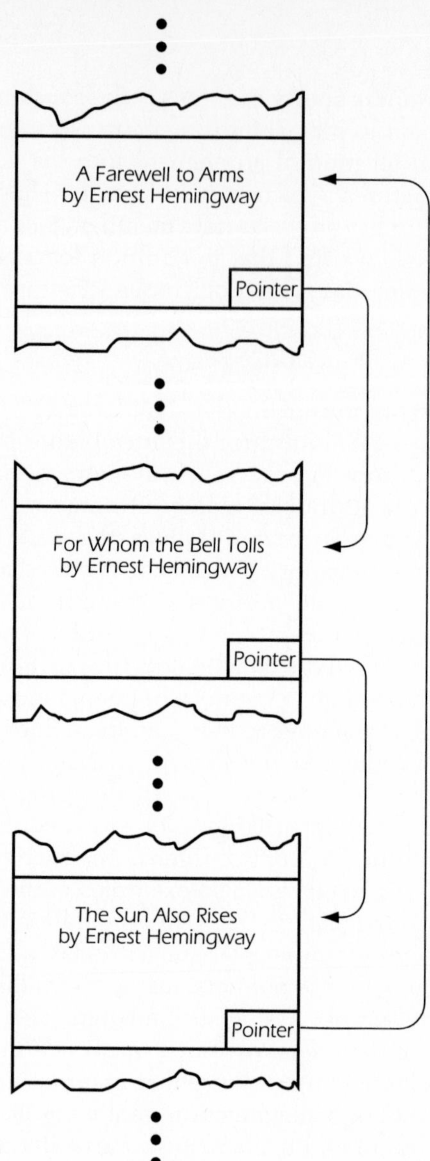

Figure 7.3 Library holdings arranged by title but linked according to authorship

Contiguous Lists

One technique for storing a list of names in a machine's memory is to store the entire list in a single block of memory cells with consecutive addresses. Assuming that each name is no longer than eight letters, we can divide this large block of cells into a collection of subblocks, each containing eight cells. Into

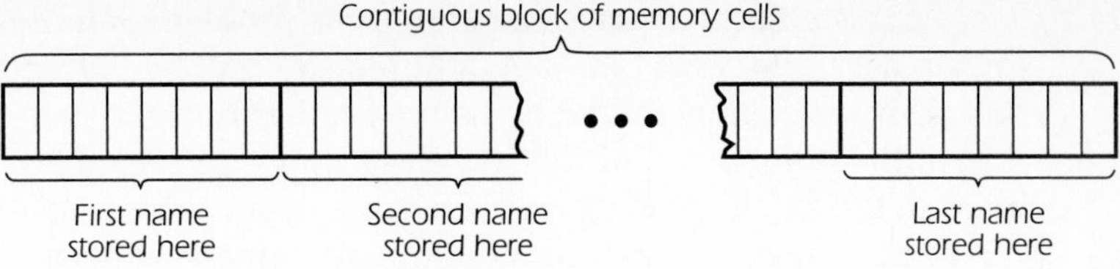

Figure 7.4 Names stored in memory as a continguous list

each subblock we can store a name by recording its ASCII code using one cell per letter (Fig. 7.4). If the name alone does not fill all the cells in the subblock allocated to it, we can merely fill the remaining cells with the ASCII code for a space. Using this system requires a block of 80 consecutive memory cells to store a list of ten names.

Such an organization is referred to as a **contiguous list** and is typical of the storage system obtained when a programmer stores a list in an array. In particular, the Pascal programming language statement

```
var
  list packed array [1..8,1..10] of char;
```

which requests a two-dimensional array with eight rows and ten columns, produces the main memory storage system just described.

Such a storage structure is convenient in its simplicity but has several disadvantages. Suppose we need to delete a name. If this name is currently toward the beginning of the list and we need to keep the list in the same (possibly alphabetical) order, we must move all the names occurring later in the list forward in memory to fill the hole left by the deleted entry. A more serious problem occurs if we need to add names, since there may not be adequate space in memory.

Linked Lists

Such problems can be avoided if we allow the individual names in the list to be stored in different areas of memory rather than together in one large, contiguous block. To do this, we store each name in a string of nine memory cells. The first eight of these cells are used to hold the name itself, and the last cell is used as a pointer to the next name in the list. In this form the list can be scattered among several small nine-cell blocks linked together by pointers. Because of this linkage system, such an organization is called a **linked list.**

To keep track of where the first entry of a linked list is located, we set aside a memory cell in which we save the address of the first entry. This cell points to the beginning of the list and is normally called the **head pointer.** To read the list, we start at the location indicated by this head pointer and find the first name along with the pointer to the next entry. Following this pointer, we can find the second entry and so forth throughout the list. In this manner, we can traverse the entire list by hopping from one name to the next.

At this point, we have considered the problem of moving from one member of the list to the next but have ignored the problem of detecting the end of the list. This problem is solved by using a **NIL pointer,** a special bit pattern appearing in the pointer cell of the last entry that indicates that no further entries appear in the list. For example, if we agree never to start an entry at address 0, the value zero never appears as a legitimate pointer value, and we can use it as the NIL pointer in the list storage. Thus we place the value zero in the pointer cell of the last entry in the list. Later, when the list is traversed, this special value can be interpreted as marking the end of the list rather than as being the address of yet another entry.

The final linked list storage organization is represented by the diagram in Fig. 7.5. We depict the scattered blocks of memory used for the list by individual rectangles. Each rectangle is labeled to indicate its composition. Note that the information stored in each pointer is represented by an arrow that leads from the pointer itself to the pointer's addressee.

Let us return now to the problem of deleting and inserting entries in the list to see how the use of pointers alleviates the movement of names encountered when storing the list in a single contiguous block. First we note that a name can be deleted by changing a single pointer. This is done by changing the pointer that formerly pointed to the name being deleted so that it points to the name following the deleted entry (Fig. 7.6). From then on, when the list is traversed, the deleted name is passed by because it no longer is part of the chain.

Inserting a new name is only a little more involved. We first find an unused block of nine memory cells, store the new name in the first eight cells, and fill the ninth cell with the address of the name in the list that should follow the new name. Finally, we change the pointer associated with the name that should precede the new name so that it points to the new name (Fig. 7.7). Observe that after this is done, the new entry is found in the proper place anytime the list is traversed.

In reality, the deletion or insertion of an entry in a linked list is not quite as simple as our description implies, because we might want to keep track of those

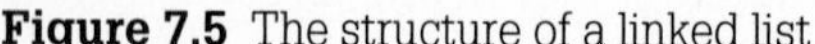

Figure 7.5 The structure of a linked list

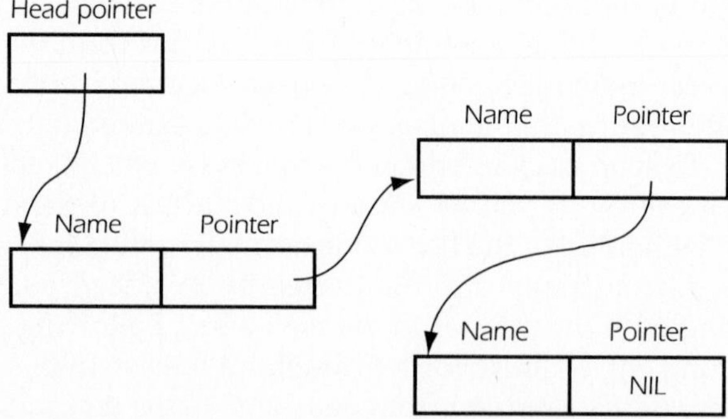

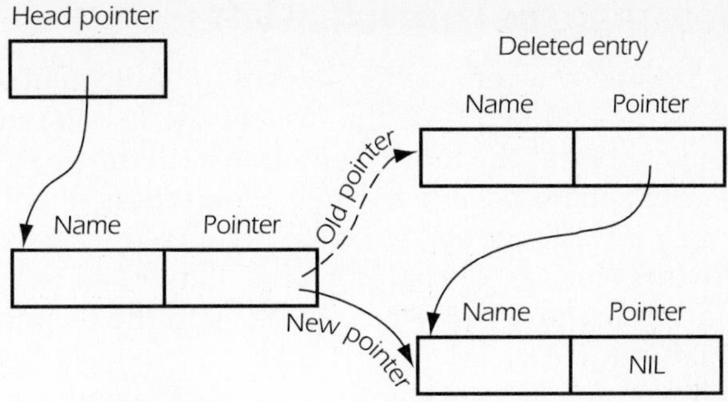

Figure 7.6 Deleting an entry from a linked list

blocks of cells that have been removed from the list. The information in these blocks is no longer needed, so these blocks of cells can be reused at a later date to hold new entries in the list. One technique for keeping track of blocks available for reuse is to maintain a record of pointers to reusable blocks or perhaps maintain another linked list consisting of these blocks. When a block is removed from the main list, it is added to the list of available storage blocks. As new entries are needed, blocks to contain them can be removed from the list of available blocks and inserted in the list.

The process of collecting reusable memory space, known as **garbage collection,** is an important component of a dynamic storage system. If the space occupied by deleted data is not identified and made reusable, the space available erodes as items are stored and deleted, until no more data can be entered. Such a loss of memory space is known as a **memory leak.**

Figure 7.7 Inserting an entry into a linked list

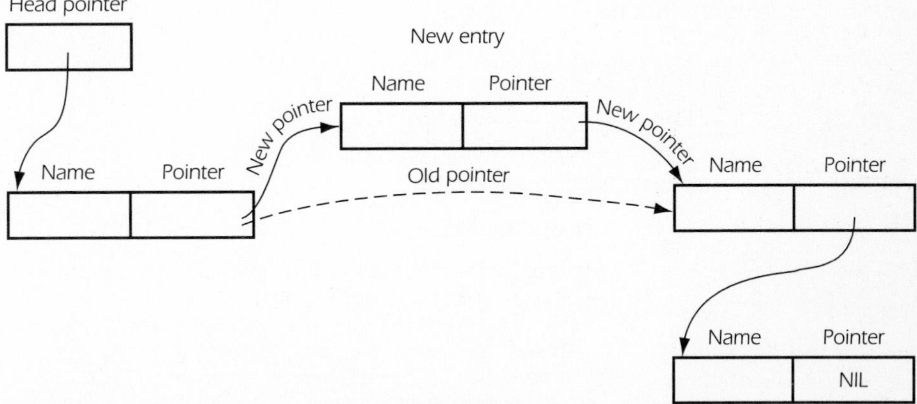

Supporting the Conceptual List

Regardless of whether one chooses to implement a list as a contiguous structure or as a linked one, the user of the list should not have to consider the technicalities of the implementation each time a list access is required. Rather, the user should be able to forget about these details and merely use the list as though the storage system were organized in the same way as the conceptual structure (just as a programmer is allowed to refer to a particular element in an array without being concerned with the technicalities of how the array is actually stored).

For example, consider the task of developing a software package for maintaining the class enrollments for a university registrar. The person developing this package might approach the problem by establishing a separate list structure for each class, with each list containing an alphabetically ordered list of the students in that class. Once this is done, the programmer's attention should be allowed to shift to the more general concerns of the problem and not be repeatedly distracted by the details of how data might be moved within a contiguous list or what shifting of pointers is required in a linked list.

What we need is a collection of procedures for performing the activities, such as inserting a new entry, deleting an old entry, searching for an entry, or printing the list. These procedures together with the actual storage cells being used, fill the needs of the remaining software package while hiding the technicalities of how the list is actually implemented. For example, to place J. W. Brown in the course Physics 208, the programmer can write a statement such as

```
insert ("Brown, J.W.", "Physics 208")
```

and rely on the procedure to carry out the details of the insertion.

As an example of such a routine, a procedure named PrintList for printing a linked list of names is shown in Fig. 7.8. Recall that the first entry of the list is pointed to by a pointer called the head pointer, and each entry in the list consists of two pieces: a name and a pointer. Once this procedure has been developed, it can be used as an abstract tool to print the list without concern for how the list is actually stored. For example, to obtain a printed class list for Economics 301, a programmer need only write

```
PrintList ("Economics 301")
```

Figure 7.8 A procedure for printing a linked list

```
procedure PrintList (List)

Assign CurrentPointer the value in the head pointer of List.
while (CurrentPointer is not NIL) do
   (Print the name in the entry pointed to by CurrentPointer;
    Observe the value in the pointer cell of the List entry
      pointed to by CurrentPointer, and reassign CurrentPointer
      to be that value.)
```

Questions/Exercises

1. If you know the address of the beginning of the first entry in a contiguous list, how can you find the address of the fifth entry? What about the case of a linked list?
2. What condition indicates that a linked list is empty?
3. Modify the procedure in Fig. 7.8 so it stops printing once a particular name has been printed.
4. Design an algorithm for finding a particular entry in a linked list and then deleting it.

7.3 Stacks

One of the properties of a list that makes a linked structure more inviting than a contiguous one is the need to insert and delete entries inside the list. Recall that it was such operations that had the potential of forcing the massive movement of names to fill or create holes in the case of a contiguous list. If we restrict such operations to the ends of the structure, we find that the use of a contiguous structure becomes a more convenient system. An example of this phenomenon is a **stack,** which is a list in which all insertions and deletions are performed at the same end of the structure. The end at which these operations occur is called the **top** of the stack. The other end is sometimes called the stack's base.

To reflect the fact that access to a stack is restricted to the topmost entry, we use special terminology when referring to the insertion and deletion operations. The process of inserting an object on the stack is called a **push** operation, and the process of deleting an object is called a **pop** operation. Thus we speak of pushing an entry onto a stack and popping an entry off a stack.

We are quite familiar with stack structures in everyday life. For example, consider a stack of books on a table. Such an organization yields itself to the particular insertion and deletion operations of placing books on top of the stack (a push operation) and lifting books off the top (a pop operation). Disaster can result, however, from an attempt to remove or insert a book in the middle of a tall stack. Indeed, the structure of a stack dictates that the last object inserted must be the first one removed. This observation results in a stack often being referred to as a **last-in, first-out (LIFO)** structure.

Stack Applications

Before considering how a stack can be implemented in a computer's memory, let us take a moment to see where such structures might be useful. A common application involves the execution of program units such as the procedures found in our pseudocode. When the execution of a procedure is requested, the machine must transfer its attention to the procedure; yet later, when the procedure is completed, it must return to the original location before continuing (Fig. 7.9). This means that, when the initial transfer is made, there must be a mechanism for remembering the location to which execution ultimately returns.

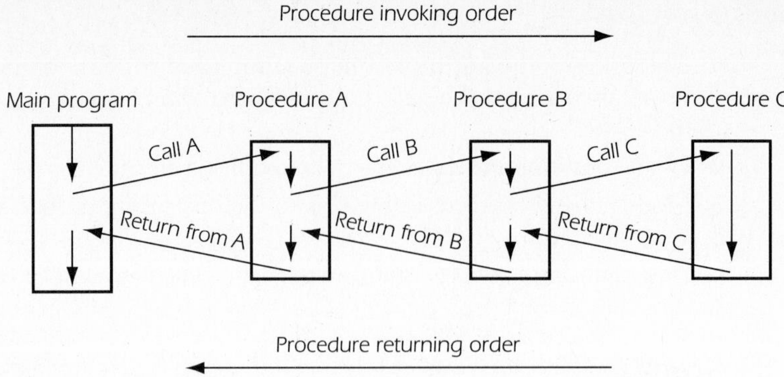

Figure 7.9 Nested procedures terminating in the opposite order to that in which they were requested

The situation is further complicated by the fact that the procedure may itself request the execution of another procedure, which may request still another, and so on. Consequently, the return locations being remembered begin to pile up. Later, as each of these procedures is completed, execution must be returned to the proper place within the program unit that called the completed procedure. A system is therefore needed to save the return locations and later retrieve them in the proper order.

A stack is an ideal structure for such a system. As each procedure is called a pointer to the pertinent return location is pushed on top of a stack, and as each procedure is completed the top entry from the stack is extracted with the assurance of obtaining a pointer to the proper return location. Indeed, the return locations are required in exactly the opposite order from which the procedure calls were made.

This example is representative of stack applications in general because it demonstrates the relationship between stacks and the process of backtracking. The concept of a stack is inherent in any process that entails backing out of a system in the opposite order from which it was entered.

Stack Implementation

We turn now to the problem of implementing a stack structure in a computer's memory. It is customary to reserve a block of contiguous memory cells large enough to accommodate the stack as it grows and shrinks. Determining the size of this block can often be a critical design problem. If too little room is reserved, the stack ultimately exceeds the allotted storage space.

Having reserved a block of memory, we select one end to serve as the stack's base. This is where we place the first entry that is pushed on the stack, with each additional entry being placed next to its predecessor as the stack grows toward the other end of the reserved block.

One additional tool is needed in our system: a way of keeping track of the top of the stack. After all, as entries are pushed and popped the stack top moves

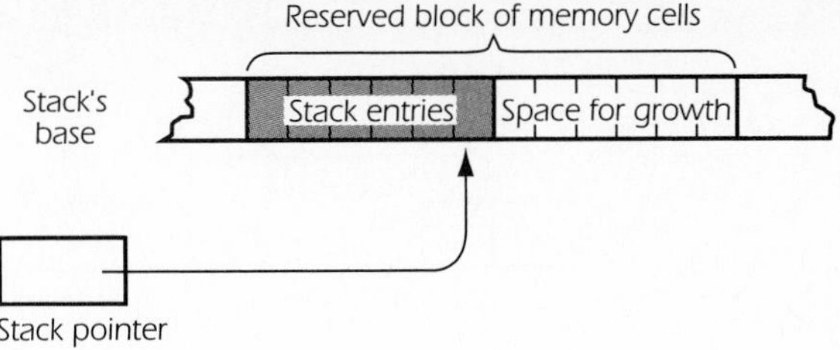

Figure 7.10 A stack in memory

back and forth within the reserved block of memory cells. We must therefore maintain a record of the location of the top entry. For this purpose we set aside another memory cell in which we store the address of the cell currently residing at the top of the stack. This additional cell is known as the **stack pointer.** The complete system, as illustrated in Fig. 7.10, works as follows: To push a new entry on the stack, we first adjust the stack pointer to point to the vacancy just beyond the top of the stack and then place the new entry at this location. To pop an entry from the stack, we read the data pointed to by the stack pointer and then adjust the pointer to point to the next entry down on the stack.

A stack organized in this manner exhibits little difference between the conceptual structure and the actual structure of the data in memory. Suppose, however, that we cannot reserve a fixed block of memory and be assured that the stack will always fit. A solution is to implement the stack as a linked structure similar to that discussed in Section 7.2. This avoids the limitations of restricting the stack to a fixed-size block, since it allows the entries in the stack to be stuffed into small pieces of available space anywhere in memory. In such a situation the conceptual stack structure will be quite different from the actual arrangement of the data in memory.

To complete the implementation of a stack, one must develop routines to perform the push and pop operations as well as a routine to test whether the stack is empty. These three routines would allow the stack to be used by a programmer without demanding that the programmer pay attention to the internal implementation of the stack itself.

A Particular Stack Application

As a closing example, we return to the list-printing problem considered at the end of Section 7.2. Suppose that now we want the names in the linked list printed in the opposite order. The problem is that the only way we can access the names is by following the linked structure, in which the first name accessed must be the last one printed. We need a way of holding each name retrieved until all the following names have been retrieved and printed. Our solution is to traverse the list from its beginning to its end while pushing the names we find onto a stack (Fig. 7.11). After reaching the end of the list, we print the names as we pop them off the stack. The procedure for this process is presented in Fig. 7.12.

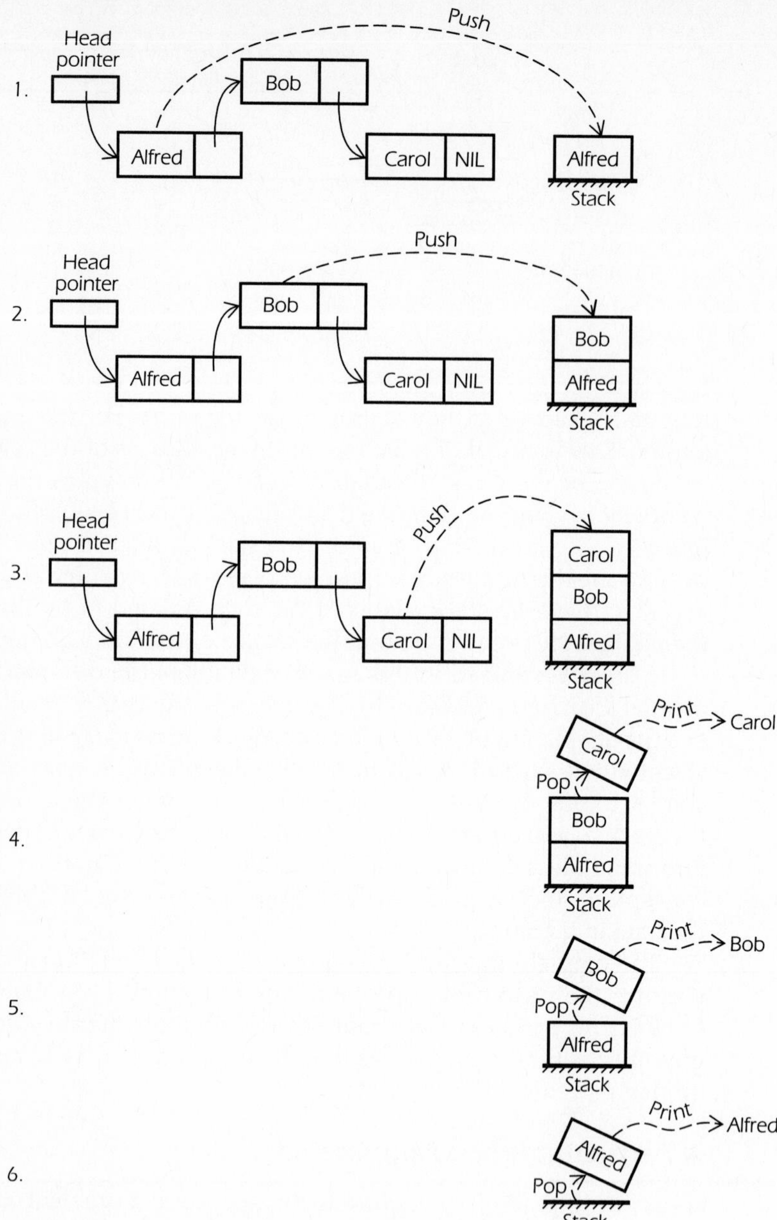

Figure 7.11 Using a stack to print a linked list in reverse order

```
procedure ReversePrint (List)

Assign CurrentPointer the value in the head pointer of List.
while (CurrentPointer is not NIL) do
     (Push the name pointed to by CurrentPointer onto the stack;
      Observe the value in the pointer cell of the List entry
         pointed to by CurrentPointer, and reassign CurrentPointer
         to be that value.)
while (the stack is not empty) do
     (Pop a name off the stack and print it.)
```

Figure 7.12 A procedure (using an auxiliary stack) for printing a linked list in reverse order

Questions/Exercises

1. List some additional occurrences of stacks in everyday life.
2. Suppose a main program calls procedure A, which in turn calls procedure B, and after B is completed procedure A calls procedure C. Follow this scenario, maintaining the stack of return locations.
3. Based on the technique of this section for implementing a stack in a contiguous block of cells, what condition indicates that the stack is empty?
4. Design an algorithm for popping an entry off a stack that is implemented with a stack pointer. Your algorithm should print an error message if the stack is empty.
5. Describe how a stack can be implemented in a high-level language in terms of a one-dimensional array.

7.4 Queues

A queue is another form of a restricted access list. In contrast to a stack in which both insertions and deletions are performed at the same end, a queue restricts all insertions to one end while all deletions are made at the other. We have already met and discussed this structure in relation to waiting lines in Chapter 3, where we recognized it as being a first-in, first-out (FIFO) storage system. Actually, the concept of a queue is inherent in any system in which objects are served in the same order in which they arrive.

The ends of a queue get their names from this waiting-line relationship. More precisely, the end at which entries are removed is called the **head** (or sometimes the front) of the queue just as we say that the next person to be served in a cafeteria is at the head (or front) of the line. Similarly, the end of the queue at which new entries are added is called the **tail** (or rear).

As we have mentioned before, terminology tends to evolve over time. Our definition of a queue as a strictly FIFO structure is traditional, but you will also hear the term *queue* used to refer to any structure in which each entry is removed from the head, regardless of when it entered the structure. This more relaxed definition includes structures in which new entries may be inserted in front of previous entries to maintain alphabetical order or to give certain entries higher priority than others. It also allows a stack to be considered as a particular type of queue.

Queue Implementation

Let us consider how we can implement a queue in a computer's memory. We can do this within a block of contiguous cells in a way similar to our storage of a stack. We need to perform operations at both ends of the structure, so it makes sense to set aside two memory cells to use as pointers instead of just one, as we did for a stack. We therefore establish one pointer, the **head pointer** that always points to the head of the queue, and another pointer, the **tail pointer** that keeps track of the tail. We begin with an empty queue by setting both these pointers to the same location (Fig. 7.13). Each time an entry is inserted we place it in the location pointed to by the tail pointer and then adjust the pointer to point toward the next unused location. In this manner, we see that the tail pointer is always pointing to the first vacancy at the tail of the queue. To remove an entry, we extract the object occupying the location pointed to by the head pointer and then adjust this pointer to point toward the entry that followed the removed one.

A problem remains with the storage system as described thus far. If left unchecked, the queue crawls slowly through memory like a glacier, destroying any other data in its path (Fig. 7.14). This movement is the result of the rather egocentric policy of inserting each new entry by merely placing it next to the previous one and repositioning the tail pointer accordingly. If we add enough entries, the tail of the queue ultimately extends all the way to the end of the machine's memory.

This greed for memory is not the result of the queue's size but is a side effect of the queue's access procedure. (A small yet active queue can easily require more of a machine's memory resources than a large, inactive one.) One solution

Figure 7.13 A queue implemented with head and tail pointers

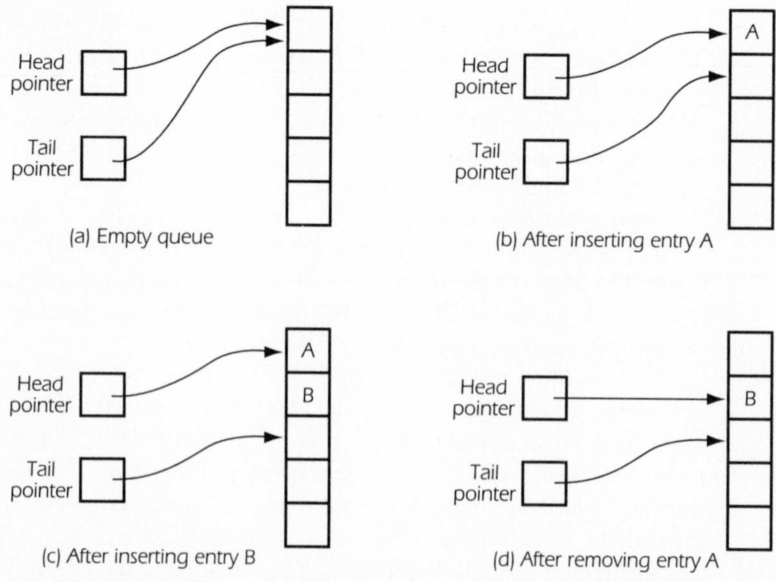

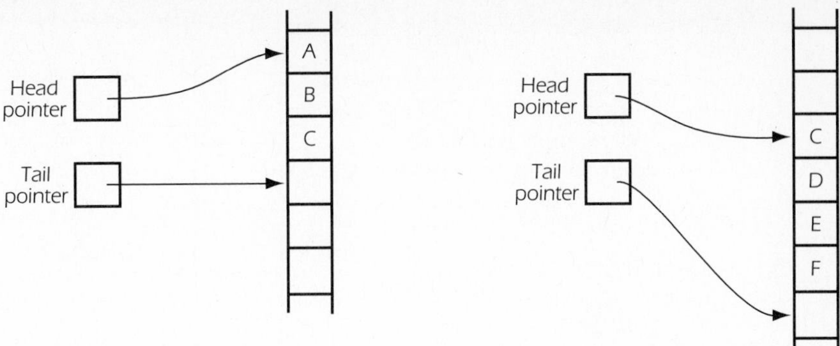

Figure 7.14 A queue "crawling" through memory, shown here containing entries A, B, and C and later containing C, D, E, and F

to this memory space problem is to move the entries in a queue forward as the leading ones are removed, in the same manner as people waiting to buy theater tickets step forward each time a person has been served. However, it was such mass movement of data that drove us to the concept of linked structures in the discussion of lists. What we want is a way of confining the queue to one area of memory without being forced to perform major rearrangements of data.

A common solution to this dilemma is to set aside a block of memory for the queue, start the queue at one end of the block, and let the queue migrate toward the other end of the block. When the tail of the queue reaches the end of the block, we merely start inserting additional entries back at the original end of the block, which by this time is vacant. Likewise, when the last entry in the block finally becomes the head of the queue and is removed, we adjust the head pointer back to the beginning of the block where other entries are by this time waiting. In this manner, the queue chases itself around within the block rather than wandering off through memory.

Such a technique results in an implementation that is called a **circular queue** because the effect is that of forming a loop out of the block of memory cells allotted to the queue (Fig. 7.15). As far as the queue is concerned, the last cell in the block is adjacent to the first cell.

Once again, we should recognize the difference between the conceptual structure envisioned by the user of a queue and the actual cyclic structure implemented in the machine's memory. As in the case of the previous structures, these differences are bridged by software. That is, along with the collection of memory cells used for data storage, the queue implementation includes a collection of procedures that interpret the stored data according to the rules of a queue. These procedures consist of routines to insert and remove entries from the queue as well as routines to detect whether the queue is empty or full. Then, by means of these routines, a programmer can request that entries be inserted or removed by executing prewritten software routines that perform these operations without reflecting the details of the actual storage system in memory.

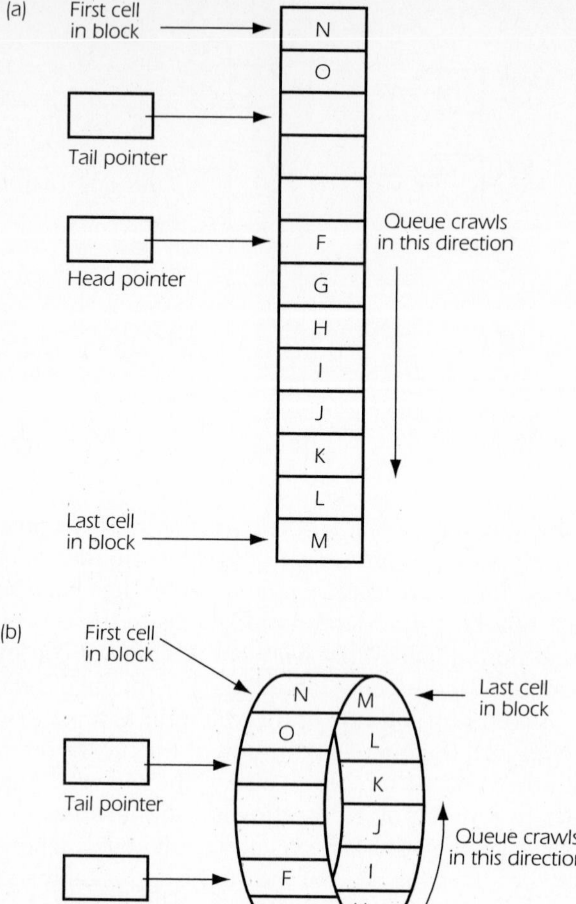

Figure 7.15 A circular queue (a) containing the letters F through O as actually stored in memory, and (b) in its conceptual form in which the last cell in the block is "adjacent" to the first cell

A Particular Queue Application

In closing, we return to the idea of manipulating a linked list of names, but this time we assume the list represents a combined alphabetized listing of both undergraduate and graduate students at a university. Moreover, we assume that with each name in the list is an additional item of data indicating whether the student is an undergraduate or a graduate student. Our task is to produce an alphabetized listing of the undergraduate students followed by an alphabetized listing of the graduate students.

```
procedure PrintSeparateListings (List)

Assign CurrentPointer the value in the head pointer of List.
while (CurrentPointer is not NIL) do
    [If (CurrentPointer points to the name of an undergraduate)
       then (Print the name.)
       else (Insert the name in the queue called Graduates.)
     Observe the value in the pointer cell of the List entry
       pointed to by CurrentPointer, and reassign CurrentPointer
       to be that value.]
while (the queue called Graduates is not empty) do
  (Remove an entry from the queue and print it.)
```

Figure 7.16 A procedure (using an auxiliary queue) for printing separate listings of undergraduates and graduates

One technique would be to traverse the linked list twice, producing the undergraduate list the first time and the graduate list the second. However, the second pass through the list can be avoided by storing the names of the graduate students found during the first pass (while the undergraduate names are being printed) and then producing the graduate list from the auxiliary storage. Note that once we are ready to produce the list of graduate students, we want to retrieve the names from the auxiliary storage system in the same order in which they were inserted so that the final listing is in alphabetical order. Thus this auxiliary system is organized as a queue. An algorithm for solving the printing problem takes the form shown in Fig. 7.16.

Questions/Exercises

1. Using paper and pencil, keep a record of the circular queue structure described in this section during the following scenario (assume the block reserved for the queue can contain four entries):

   Insert entry A.
   Insert entry B.
   Insert entry C.
   Remove an entry.
   Remove an entry.
   Insert entry D.
   Insert entry E.
   Remove an entry.
   Insert entry F.
   Remove an entry.

2. When a queue is implemented in a circular fashion as described in this section, what is the relationship between the head and tail pointers when the queue is empty? What about when the queue is full? How can one detect whether a queue is full or empty?
3. Design an algorithm for inserting an entry in a circular queue.

7.5 Trees

The last data structure that we will consider is the **tree,** which is the structure reflected by an organization chart of a typical company (Fig. 7.17). Here, the president is represented at the top, with lines branching down to the vice-presidents, who are followed by regional managers, and so on. To this intuitive definition of a tree structure we impose one additional constraint, which (in terms of an organization chart) is that no individual in the company reports to two different people. That is, different branches of the organization do not merge at a lower level.

Terminology

In the terminology of tree structures, each position in the tree is called a **node.** The single node at the top is called the **root node** (since if we turned the drawing upside down, this node would represent the base or root of the tree). The nodes at the other extreme are called **terminal nodes** (or **leaf nodes**). A line connecting two nodes is called an **arc.**

If we position ourselves at any node in a tree, we find that this node together with those nodes below it again have the structure of a tree. This, in fact, is a major advantage of such an organizational structure, because it divides a company into different suborganizations, each of which has the same type of structure. (A regional manager is effectively the president of that region.) We call these smaller structures **subtrees.**

Additional terminology has its origins in the concept of each node giving birth to those nodes immediately below it. We often speak of a node's ancestors or descendants. We refer to its immediate descendants as its **children** and its immediate superior as its **parent.** Moreover, we speak of nodes with the same parent as being **twins** or **siblings.**

Finally, we often refer to the **depth** of a tree, which is nothing more than the number of nodes in the longest path from the root to a leaf. In other words, the depth of a tree is the number of horizontal layers within it.

Figure 7.17 An example of an organization chart

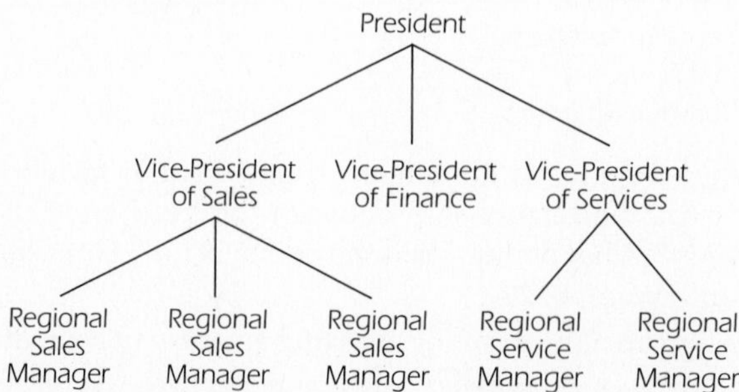

We encounter tree structures repeatedly in subsequent chapters, so we will not elaborate on applications now. Later in this section, as well as in our discussion of index organization in Chapter 8 we will find that information that must be searched quickly for data retrieval is often organized as a tree; and in Chapter 10 we see how games can be analyzed in terms of trees.

Tree Implementation

In our discussion of the storage of a tree structure in a machine's memory, we restrict our attention to **binary trees**—trees in which each node has at most two children. Such trees normally are stored in memory using a linked structure similar to that of linked lists. However, rather than each entry consisting of two components (the data followed by a next-entry pointer), each entry (or node) of the binary tree contains three components: the data, a pointer to the node's first child, and a pointer to the node's second child. Although there is no left or right inside a machine, it is helpful to refer to the first pointer as the **left child pointer** and the other pointer as the **right child pointer** in reference to the way we would draw the tree on paper. Each node of the tree is represented by a short, contiguous block of memory cells with the format shown in Fig. 7.18.

Storing the tree in memory involves finding available blocks of memory cells to hold the nodes and linking these nodes according to the desired tree structure. That is, each pointer must be set to point to the left or right child of the pertinent node or assigned the NIL value if there are no more nodes in that direction of the tree. This means that a terminal node is characterized by having both of its pointers assigned NIL. Finally we set aside a special memory location where we store the address of the root node. We call this the **root pointer.**

An example of this linked storage system is presented in Fig. 7.19, where a conceptual binary tree structure is exhibited along with a representation of how that tree might actually appear in a computer's memory. With this system we can always find the root node by means of the root pointer and then trace any path down the tree by following the appropriate pointers from node to node.

An alternative to a linked storage system for binary trees is the technique of setting aside a contiguous block of memory cells, storing the root node in the first of these cells (for simplicity, we assume that each node of the tree requires only one memory cell), storing the left child of the root in the second cell, storing the right child of the root in the third cell, and in general storing the left and right children of the node found in cell n in the cells $2n$ and $2n + 1$, respectively. Cells within the block that represent locations not used by the current tree structure are marked with a unique bit pattern that indicates the absence of data. Following this technique, the conceptual tree shown in Fig. 7.19 is stored as shown in

Figure 7.18 The structure of a node in a binary tree

Cells containing the data	Left child pointer	Right child pointer

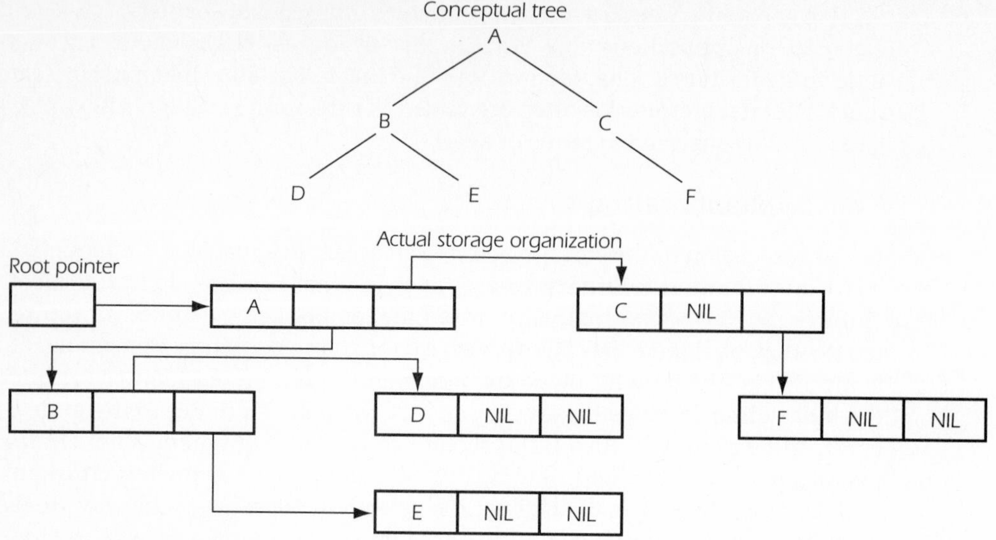

Figure 7.19 The conceptual and actual organization of a binary tree using a linked storage system

Fig. 7.20. Note that the system is essentially that of storing the nodes across successively lower levels of the tree as segments, one after the other. That is, the first entry in the block is the root node, followed by the root's children, followed by the root's grandchildren, and so on.

In contrast to the linked structure described earlier, this alternative storage system provides a convenient method for finding the parent or sibling of any node. (Of course, this can be done in the linked structure at the expense of additional pointers.) Indeed, the location of a node's parent can be found by dividing the node's position in the block by 2 while discarding any remainder (the parent of the node in position 7 would be the node in position 3), and a node's sibling can be found by adding 1 to the location of a node in an even-numbered position or subtracting 1 from the location of a node in an odd-numbered position (the sibling of the node in position 4 is the node in position 5, while the sibling of the node in position 3 is the node in position 2). Moreover, this storage system makes efficient use of space in the case of binary trees that are approximately balanced (in the sense that both subtrees tend to have the same depth) and full (in the sense that they do not have long, thin branches). For trees without these characteristics, though, the system can become quite inefficient, as shown in Fig. 7.21.

Figure 7.20 The tree of Fig. 7.19 stored without pointers

1	2	3	4	5	6	7
A	B	C	D	E		F

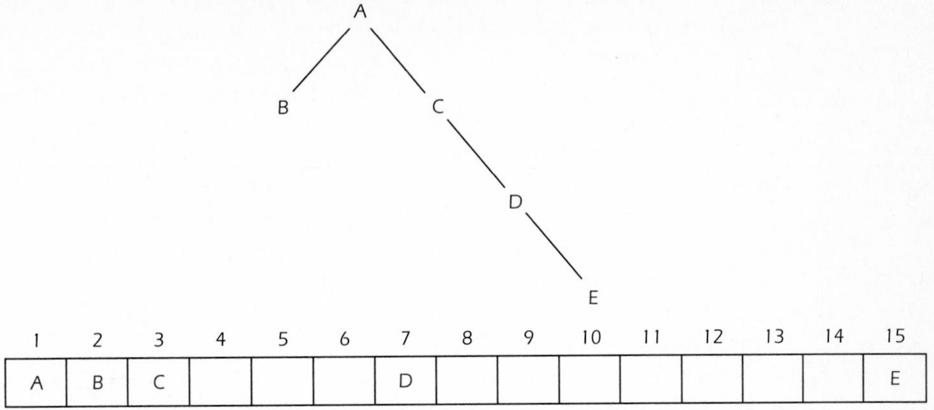

Figure 7.21 A sparse, unbalanced tree shown in its conceptual form and as it would be stored without pointers

We see then that, as in the case of the other structures we have studied, there are a variety of systems for storing binary trees, each with its advantages and disadvantages, and once again we find it advantageous to shield the user of the tree from the technicalities of the implementation chosen. Consequently, one normally identifies the activities that will be performed on a tree by the external software and then writes procedures to accomplish these activities while hiding the technicalities of the actual storage system. These procedures together with the storage area then form a package that allows a programmer to use the tree without being distracted by the details of the implementation.

A Binary Tree Package

To demonstrate such a package, let us return to the problem of storing a list of names in alphabetical order. We assume that the operations to be performed on this list are the following:

search for the presence of an entry,
print the list in alphabetical order, and
insert a new entry

Our goal is to develop a storage system along with a collection of procedures to perform these operations.

We begin by considering options regarding the procedure for searching the list. If the list were stored according to the linked list model in Section 7.2, we would be forced to search the list in a sequential fashion, a process that, as we discussed in Chapter 4, could be very inefficient if the list should become long. We will therefore seek an implementation that allows us to use the binary search algorithm (Chapter 4) for our search procedure. To apply this algorithm, our storage system must allow us to find the middle entry of successively smaller portions of the list. Such an operation is possible when using a contiguous list, since we can compute the address of the middle entry in much the same manner as we can compute the locations of entries in an array. But using a contiguous list introduces problems when making insertions, as observed in Section 7.2.

Our problem can be solved by implementing the list as a binary tree rather than using one of the traditional list systems. We make the middle list entry the root node, the middle of the remaining first half of the list the root's left child, and the middle of the remaining second half the root's right child. The middle entries of each remaining fourth of the list become the children of the root's children and so forth. For example, under this process, the tree in Fig. 7.22 can represent the list of letters A, B, C, D, E, F, G, H, I, J, K, L, and M. (We consider the larger of the middle two entries as the middle when the part of the list in question contains an even number of entries.)

To search the list stored in this manner, we compare the target value to the root node. If the two are equal, our search has succeeded. If they are not equal, we move to the left or right child of the root, depending on whether the target is less than or greater than the root, respectively. There we find the middle of the portion of the list necessary to continue the search. This process of comparing and moving to a child continues until we find the target (meaning that our search was successful) or we reach the bottom of the tree without finding the target (meaning that our search was a failure). Figure 7.23 shows how this search process can be implemented in the case of a linked tree structure. (Annotative comments are bracketed by asterisks.)

Having altered the natural sequential order of our stored list for the sake of search efficiency, you may think that the process of printing the list in alphabetical order would now be difficult. This hypothesis, however, proves to be false. To print the list in alphabetical order, we merely need to print the left subtree in alphabetical order, print the root node, and then print the right subtree in alphabetical order (Fig. 7.24). After all, the left subtree contains those elements that are less than the root node, while the right subtree contains the elements larger than the root. A sketch of our resulting print routine looks like this:

```
if (tree not empty)
   then (Print the left subtree in alphabetical order;
         Print the root node;
         Print the right subtree in alphabetical order)
```

You may argue that this outline achieves little toward our goal of developing a complete print procedure, because it involves the tasks of printing the left sub-

Figure 7.22 The letters A through M arranged in an ordered tree

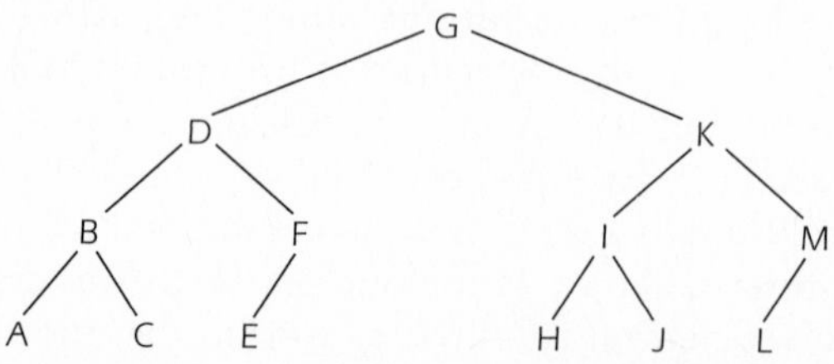

```
**  The variable CurrentPointer is used to hold a pointer   **
**  to the current position in the tree. The node at        **
**  this location is called the current node.               **

procedure BinarySearch (Tree, TargetValue)

Assign CurrentPointer the value in the root pointer of Tree.
Assign Found the value "false."
while (Found is "false" and CurrentPointer is not NIL) do
  [Select the applicable case from those listed below and
  perform the associated activity:
    TargetValue = current node:
      (Assign Found the value "true.")
    TargetValue < current node:
      (Assign CurrentPointer the value in the current
         node's left child pointer.)
    TargetValue > current node:
      (Assign CurrentPointer the value in the current
         node's right child pointer.)]
If (Found = "false") then (Declare the search a failure.)
                     else (Declare the search a success.)
```

Figure 7.23 The binary search applied to a linked binary tree

tree and the right subtree in alphabetical order, both of which are essentially the same as our original task. The only difference in the task of printing the entire tree and that of printing the left or right subtree is in the size of the trees involved. Consequently, solving the problem of printing a tree involves the smaller task of printing subtrees. This suggests a recursive system in which our procedure is applied to smaller and smaller trees.

Following this lead, we can expand our outline into a complete pseudocode procedure for printing our tree in alphabetical order as shown in Fig. 7.25. We have assigned the routine the name PrintTree and then requested the services of

Figure 7.24 Printing a search tree in alphabetical order

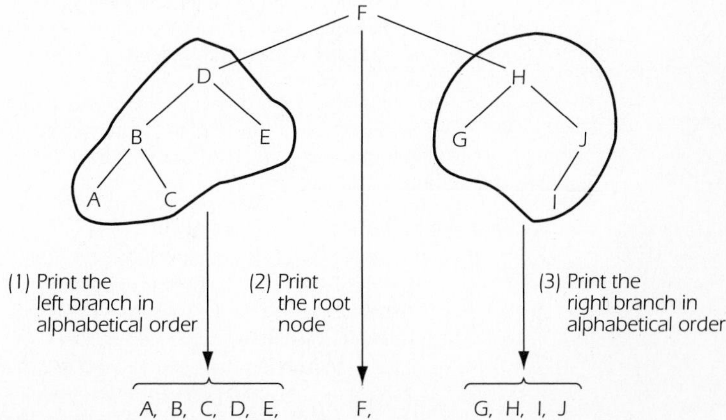

```
procedure PrintTree (Tree)

If (Tree is not empty)
  then (Apply the procedure PrintTree to the tree that
          appears as the left branch in Tree;
        Print the root node of Tree;
        Apply the procedure PrintTree to the tree that
          appears as the right branch in Tree.)
```

Figure 7.25 A procedure for printing a linked tree in alphabetical order

Figure 7.26 A procedure for inserting an entry in a linked ordered tree

```
**  The variable CurrentPointer is used to hold a pointer    **
**  to the current position in the tree. The node at         **
**  this location is called the current node. Likewise,      **
**  PreviousPointer holds a pointer to the parent of the     **
**  current node, which is called the previous node.         **

procedure Insert (Tree, TargetValue)

**  First, find the current location for the new node.      **

Assign CurrentPointer the value in the root pointer of Tree.
Assign Found the value "false."
while (Found is "false" and CurrentPointer is not NIL) do
    [Select the applicable case from those listed below and
     perform the associated activity:
      TargetValue = current node:
          (Assign Found the value "true.")
      TargetValue < current node:
          (Assign PreviousPointer the value of CurrentPointer;
           Assign CurrentPointer the value of the current
             node's left child pointer.)
      TargetValue > current node:
          (Assign PreviousPointer the value of CurrentPointer;
           Assign CurrentPointer the value of the current
             node's right child pointer.)]

**  Now, insert the new node as a child of the current node. **
**  A special case occurs if CurrentPointer is still the same    **
**  as the root pointer, meaning that the original Tree was      **
**  empty.                                                       **

If (Found = "false")
  then [Create a new node containing TargetValue;
        If (CurrentPointer equals the root pointer)
          then (Establish the new node as the root node of Tree.)
          else (If (TargetValue < previous node)
                  then (Establish the new node as the left
                          child of the previous node.)
                  else (Establish the new node as the right child of
                          the previous node.))]
```

PrintTree for printing the left and right subtrees. You should confirm for yourself that the termination condition of the recursive process (reaching an empty subtree) is guaranteed to be reached, because each activation of the routine operates on a smaller tree than the one causing the activation.

The task of inserting a new entry in the tree is also easier than it may at first appear. You may guess that certain insertions would require cutting the tree open to allow room for the new entry, but actually the new node can always be attached to the bottom of the tree as a leaf, regardless of the value involved. To find the proper place for this new leaf, we move down the tree along the path that we would follow if we were searching for the value to be inserted. Then, when we reach the bottom of the tree, we have found the proper location for the new node. Indeed, we have found the location to which a search for the new data would lead.

A procedure expressing this process in the case of a linked tree structure is shown in Fig. 7.26. It first searches the tree for the value being inserted and then places the new node at the proper location. Note that a slightly special case occurs if the tree is empty in the first place. This case is detected by testing for the condition of CurrentPointer still being the same as the root pointer after the search process has been completed. Moreover, if the data being inserted are actually found in the tree during the search, no insertion is made.

We see, then, that a software package consisting of a linked tree together with our procedures for searching, printing, and inserting provides an excellent system for implementing the list required by our hypothetical application.

Questions/Exercises

1. Identify the root and leaf nodes in the following tree. Identify the subtrees below node 9. Identify the groups of siblings within the tree.

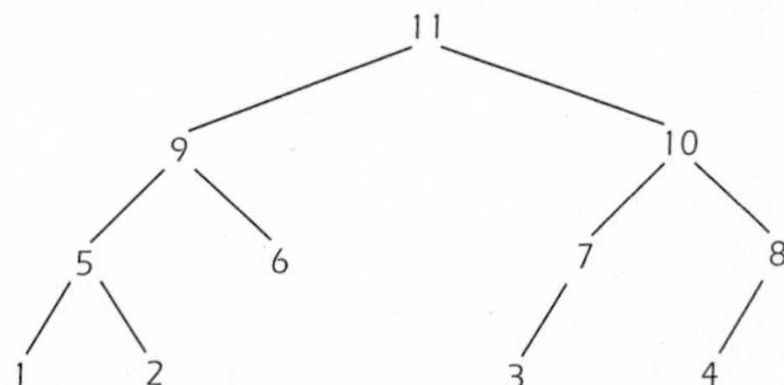

2. What condition indicates that a linked tree in a machine's memory is empty?
3. Draw a diagram representing how the tree

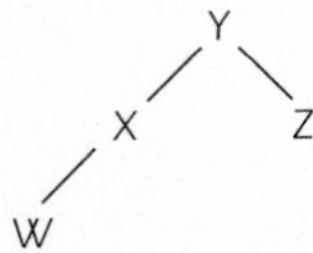

appears in memory when stored using the left and right child pointers, as described in this section. Then, draw another diagram showing how the tree would appear in contiguous storage using the alternative storage system described in this section.

4. Draw a binary tree structure you can use to store the list R, S, T, U, V, W, X, Y, and Z for future searching.
5. Indicate the path traversed by the binary search algorithm in Fig. 7.23 when applied to the tree in Fig. 7.22 when searching for the entry J. What about the entry P?
6. Draw a diagram representing the status of activations of the recursive tree-printing algorithm in Fig. 7.25 at the time node K is printed within the ordered tree in Fig. 7.22.

7.6 Customized Data Types

In Chapter 5 we introduced the concept of a data type and discussed such elementary types as integer, real, character, and Boolean that most programming languages provide as primitives. In this section we consider ways in which a programmer can define his or her own data types that more closely fit the needs of the application.

User-Defined Types

The task of expressing an algorithm is often more convenient if types other than those provided as primitives in the programming language are available. For this reason, most modern programming languages allow programmers to define additional data types, using the primitive types and structures as building blocks. These additional data types are known as **user-defined types.**

As an example, suppose we want to develop a program involving numerous variables, each with the same heterogeneous structure consisting of a name, age, and skill rating. One approach would be to restate the composition of the structure each time a reference to that structure is required. For example, to establish the variable `Employee` with such a heterogeneous structure, a C programmer would write

```
struct
  {char   Name[8];
   int    Age;
   float  SkillRating;
  } Employee;
```

as introduced in Fig. 5.7 of Chapter 5.

A problem with this approach is that the program can become bulky and hard to read if this structure is repeated often. A better method is to describe the structure only once by assigning it a descriptive name and then using that name each time a reference to the structure is required. The C language allows a programmer to accomplish this with the statement

```
typedef struct
  {char   Name[8];
   int    Age;
   float  SkillRating;
  } EmployeeType;
```

This statement defines a new type, `EmployeeType`, that can be used to declare variables in the same way as a primitive type. For example, the variable `Employee` can be declared with the statement

```
EmployeeType  Employee;
```

The benefits of such a user-defined type are more pronounced when multiple variables must be declared. Just as a C programmer can declare the variables `Sleeve`, `Waist`, and `Neck` to be of the primitive type real with the statement

```
float  Sleeve, Waist, Neck;
```

the statement

```
EmployeeType  DistManager, SalesRep1, SalesRep2;
```

declares the three variables `DistManager`, `SalesRep1`, and `SalesRep2` to be of type `EmployeeType`.

It is important to distinguish between a user-defined type and an actual data structure with that type, the latter being referred to as an **instance** of the type. A user-defined type is essentially a template (or a cookie cutter) that is used in constructing instances of the type. It describes the properties that all instances of that type have but does not itself constitute an actual occurrence of that type. In the preceding example the user-defined type `EmployeeType` was used to construct three instances of that type, known as `DistManager`, `SalesRep1`, and `SalesRep2`.

Abstract Data Types

Although the concept of a user-defined type is advantageous, it falls short of allowing the creation of new data types in the full sense. Recall that a data type consists of two parts: a predetermined storage system (such as a two's complement system in the case of the type integer and a floating-point system in the case of type real) and a collection of predefined operations (such as addition and subtraction). Traditional user-defined types, however, merely allow programmers to define new storage systems. They do not provide a means of defining operations to be performed on data with these structures.

An **abstract data type** is a more complete way of extending the types available in a programming language. As with a user-defined type, an abstract data type is a template that is distinct from instances of the type. But an abstract data type encompasses both the storage system and the associated operations. As such, an abstract data type consists of a description of a data storage system as well as a collection of routines that define the operations that can be performed on an instance of the type.

Figure 7.27 shows how an abstract data type known as `StackOfIntegers` can be defined in the Ada programming language. Loosely translated, this figure defines a program unit (a package, in Ada terminology), `StackPackage`, that contains the description of a new type named `StackOfIntegers` and identifies two procedures, `push` and `pop`. `StackOfIntegers` is described as an array (called `StackEntries`) of 25 integers together with an additional integer,

```
package StackPackage is
  type StackOfIntegers is
    record
      StackEntries: array(1..25) of integer;
      StackPointer: integer;
    end record;
  procedure push(Value: in integer; Stack: in out StackOfIntegers);
  procedure pop(Value: out integer; Stack: in out StackOfIntegers);
end StackPackage;
```

Figure 7.27 An abstract data type in Ada

`StackPointer`, used to hold the position within the array of the stack's top (see Exercise 5 in Section 7.3). The details of the procedures `push` and `pop` must be described in another program unit called a package body. It is there that the instructions for actually pushing and popping entries (as well as initializing the `StackPointer`) would be described.

Using this package as a template, actual stacks of integers (instances of the type `StackOfIntegers`) can be declared by statements, such as

```
StackOne: StackOfIntegers;
```

and

```
StackTwo: StackOfIntegers;
```

that declare the variables `StackOne` and `StackTwo` to be of type `StackOfIntegers`. Later, the value 106 can be pushed onto `StackOne` using the statement

```
push(106, StackOne);
```

or the top entry from `StackTwo` can be retrieved in the variable `OldValue` using the statement

```
pop(OldValue, StackTwo);
```

Encapsulation

In this chapter we have repeatedly seen how a software package, consisting of a data structure (or structures) and a collection of routines that manipulate that structure, can be used to represent an otherwise abstract object such as a stack, queue, list, or tree. We have not, however, emphasized the importance of assuring that all operations on the structure within the package be performed by the routines provided. Such assurance is important since to allow direct access to the internal composition of the package often opens the door to unforeseen complications.

For example, suppose a programmer needs to reference the third entry on a stack of type `StackOfIntegers` (Fig. 7.27). The programmer, who knows how the stack is actually implemented, might be tempted to violate the stack's integrity by referencing the array `StackEntry` directly, rather than going through the formal process of popping the first two entries. Such a tactic usually leads to complications later in the software's life cycle and is considered to be one of the worst of evils by software engineers.

The problem is that future maintenance programmers, seeing that the object is described as a stack of integers, could make changes that are not compatible with the "short-cut" reference hidden elsewhere in the program. For instance, to extend the maximum size of the stack, the internal structure of the type `StackOfIntegers` could be changed from an array to a linked structure, which would not be compatible with the "short-cut" reference that assumes the stack is implemented as an array.

To prevent such circumvention of abstract data types, Ada and other newer programming languages provide techniques by which a software package can be **encapsulated,** meaning that the package is constructed in such a manner that its internal structure can be accessed only by means of the approved package routines. If instances of the abstract data types occurring in a software system are encapsulated, the integrity of these data types is protected from poorly conceived modifications.

Figure 7.28 shows a modified version of the abstract data type `StackOfIntegers`, originally presented in Fig. 7.27. The difference is that the new version takes advantage of Ada's encapsulation features. Note that we have moved the details of the stack's structure to the private part (the part following the key word `private`) of the package. Only the information in the public part (the part preceding the key word `private`) of the package is accessible outside the package. The information in the private part is local to the package. In our example, then, only the existence of a type called `StackOfIntegers` and the procedures `push` and `pop` are known outside the package; the fact that such a stack is implemented as an array called `StackEntries` is encapsulated within the package. In turn, statements such as

```
StackOne: StackOfIntegers;
StackTwo: StackOfIntegers;
push(106, StackOne);
```

and

```
pop(OldValue, StackTwo);
```

Figure 7.28 An abstract data type in Ada using encapsulation

```
package StackPackage is
  type StackOfIntegers is private;
  procedure push(Value: in integer; Stack: in out StackOfIntegers);
  procedure pop(Value: out integer; Stack: in out StackOfIntegers);
private
  type StackOfIntegers is
    record
      StackEntries: array(1..25) of integer;
      StackPointer: integer;
    end record;
end StackPackage;
```

are still valid outside the package, but direct references to the array `StackEntries` or the integer `StackPointer` are not.

Of course, if an abstract data type is properly designed and implemented, a programmer will not need to violate the type's integrity nor even want to be aware of its internal details. Such is the essence of abstract tools.

In closing, we observe that the use of abstract data types along with encapsulation allows general-purpose programming languages to be customized to particular applications. A programmer charged with the task of developing a university registration system might start by defining an abstract type similar to a list in which the students enrolled in a course are stored, whereas a biologist studying the nervous system might develop and encapsulate a package whose internal data structures and routines simulate the pertinent characteristics of a single neuron. In either case, once these abstract types have been defined, the programmer can use them as building blocks as though they were primitives in the language. Despite each programmer's having started with the same language, the end result is that each has access to a language providing those primitives particular to the task at hand.

Questions/Exercises

1. In what way is a checking account at a bank encapsulated?
2. What is the difference between an abstract data type and an instance of that type?
3. What is the difference between a traditional program module and an instance of an abstract data type?
4. Describe two underlying structures that might be used to implement an object of type queue-of-integers.

7.7 Object-Oriented Programming

A list implemented in the traditional imperative paradigm can be represented as a simple data structure, such as a linked or contiguous list. The routines for manipulating this list (for example, inserting entries, deleting entries, and so on) appear in the procedural part of the program. When using an abstract data type, however, the routines for manipulating the list are bundled with the list structure to form a package (an abstract data type). This, in effect, shifts the task of performing list manipulations from the user of the list to the package representing the list: Rather than manipulating the list, the user requests that the package do the manipulation.

We see, then, that the concept of abstract data types involves converting passive data structures that are manipulated by other program units into active units that manipulate themselves. This shift from passive to active units captures much of the philosophy of the object-oriented paradigm, which we introduced in Chapter 4.

In the object-oriented paradigm, such active units are called **objects** and the routines within them are called **methods** (or **member functions** in the C++ vernacular). The object-oriented approach to a problem is to identify the objects involved and implement them as self-contained units. At this point, the task of solving the problem is well underway. Since the objects are active rather than passive, all that remains is to activate the objects in the proper manner.

As an example, consider the problem of constructing a model for worldwide economic forecasting. In the traditional imperative paradigm, each nation is represented as a collection of data structures containing that nation's gross domestic product, trade surplus/deficit, monetary exchange rate, and so on. The imperative statements of the program define a controlling algorithm that simulates the passage of time by repeatedly interrogating the various data items, deciding how the values found in each affect those of other nations, and making the changes it determines are appropriate (Fig. 7.29). Because all decisions and actions are performed by the controlling algorithm, the data structures in the system are passive.

In contrast, consider solving this same problem in an object-oriented environment. Each nation is represented by an object. Each object is an encapsulated package containing the appropriate data structures (for holding that nation's gross domestic product and so on) as well as a collection of methods defining how that object (that nation) reacts to various stimuli (messages it receives from other objects or changes occurring within itself). For instance, an object may contain a method describing how that object reacts to receiving an offer of trade from another object. Similarly, it may contain a method that, when an increase in the object's trade deficit is detected, may increase tariffs on incoming goods or try to increase exports to other objects. The result is a collection of self-governing objects that solve the problem by communicating among themselves rather than being manipulated by a supervisory algorithm (Fig. 7.30).

The development of an object in an object-oriented program may not be a simple task, because the object may need to respond in complex ways to many different stimuli. For this reason, most programming languages designed for object-oriented applications provide features to reduce the burden of object

Figure 7.29 The imperative approach to an economic model: a controlling algorithm that makes decisions and manipulates values in the data structures representing nations

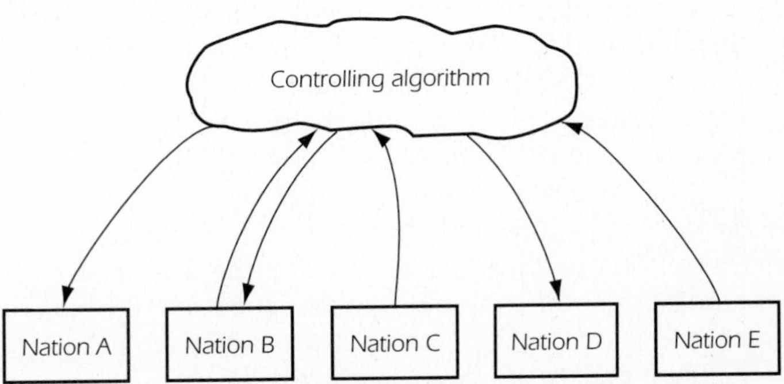

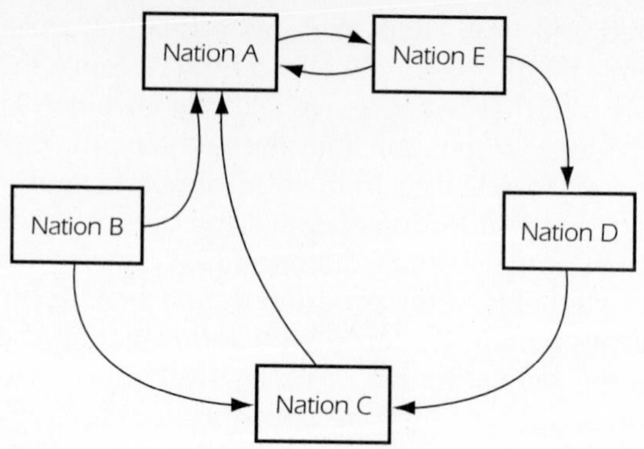

Figure 7.30 The object-oriented approach to an economic model: objects (nations) communicating among themselves

description. One such feature is a template system with which the common properties of an entire collection of similar objects can be described. Such a template, called a **class,** is similar to an abstract data type in that it is a template from which objects are created. However, a class is more general than an abstract data type. For example, a class need not involve a data structure; it could consist entirely of methods. (The term *class* is used sometimes to refer to the collection of objects created from a single template, but we avoid such use here.)

In addition to a system for describing classes, object-oriented programming languages also provide for **inheritance,** which allows classes to be described in a hierarchical manner, with each class inheriting the properties of those higher in the hierarchy. Using inheritance, a biologist can develop a class describing objects that simulate the basic properties of a biological cell. Then the biologist can define additional classes to simulate different types of cells, such as muscle cells, bone cells, and neurons. Each of these more specialized classes can be described as a subclass of the original class and thus inherit the properties of a general cell but include additional features specific to the particular type of cell. (Inheritance also allows new features to override those of a previously defined class, so that the properties of a subclass may not be a true extension of those found in its parents.) Continuing in this fashion, the biologist can define additional subclasses to simulate particular types of neurons, such as those leading from the retina as distinguished from the motor neurons leading to muscles in the legs and arms. At each level of this hierarchy, the classes become more complex, but by applying inheritance, the effort already invested in defining simple classes need not be repeated when defining more specialized ones.

The existence of a variety of objects with similar yet different characteristics leads to a phenomenon reminiscent of overloading, which we met in Chapter 5. (Recall that overloading referred to the use of a single symbol, such as +, for representing different operations depending on the type of its operands.) Suppose that we develop an object-oriented graphics package. In this package, we define a variety of objects, each representing a shape (circle, rectangle, triangle, and so on). A particular image consists of a collection of these objects. Each object knows its size, location, and color as well as how to respond to messages telling it, for example, to move to a new location or to draw itself on the monitor screen. To draw this image, we merely send each object in the collection the message to draw itself.

However, the routine used to perform the draw operation varies depending on the shape of the object—drawing a square is not the same process as drawing

Figure 7.31 A stack of integers implemented (a) in C++ and (b) in Java

(a) Stack of integers described in C++

```
const int MaxStack = 25;

class StackOfIntegers
  {int StackPointer;                          //Data structures are private.
   int StackEntries[MaxStack];

   public:                                    //Access to methods is public.

   void StackOfIntegers ()                    //This is a constructor. It
    {StackPointer = 0;                        //initializes the stack as empty.
    }

    void push (int *Entry)
    {if (StackPointer <MaxStack)
       StackEntries[StackPointer++]= *Entry;
    }

    void pop(int *Entry)
    {if (StackPointer > 0)
       *Entry = StackEntries[StackPointer—];
    }
}
```

(b) Stack of integers described in Java

```
class StackOfIntegers
  {final int MaxStack = 25;
   private int StackPointer;                  //Data structures are private.
   private int[]StackEntries;

   public void StackOfIntegers()              //This is a constructor. It
    {StackEntries = new int[MaxStack];        //establishes an array of integers
     StackPointer = 0;                        //to hold the stack.
    }

   public void push (int *Entry)
    {if (StackPointer < MaxStack)
     StackEntries[StackPointer++]= *Entry;
    }

   public void pop(int *Entry)
    {if (StackPointer > 0)
     *Entry = StackEntries[StackPointer—];
    }
}
```

a circle. This customized interpretation of a message is known as **polymorphism;** the message is said to be polymorphic. In our biological example it is polymorphism that allows cells of different types to respond differently to the same stimulus, and in our economic model it allows capitalistic countries and socialistic countries to respond differently to the initiation of tariffs by another country in the system. In short, polymorphism determines the meaning of a command in terms of the entity that is asked to perform it.

Figure 7.31 demonstrates how a stack of integers might be implemented in the object-oriented languages C++ and Java. Observe that `StackOfIntegers` is defined as a class, meaning that the code here merely defines the properties of a `StackOfIntegers`—actual instances are established elsewhere in the program as they are required. The routine named `StackOfIntegers`, having the same name as the class itself, is a special routine known as a **constructor.** A constructor within a class is executed automatically each time a new instance of the class is established. In our examples, the constructor handles issues associated with establishing a new stack such as setting the stack pointer to indicate that the stack is empty. Note that only those portions of the class that are designated public can be referenced outside an instance of the class. Thus, in both examples, the array holding the stack within an object is accessible only from within that object. Any manipulation of that array must be performed by means of the methods that are declared public.

Questions/Exercises

1. Identify the objects that might be used in an object-oriented simulation of the pedestrian traffic in a shopping mall. What actions should each of these objects be able to perform?
2. In what sense are the objects in an object-oriented system functionally cohesive?
3. In what sense is a single object in an object-oriented system divided into submodules?

CHAPTER REVIEW PROBLEMS *(Asterisked problems are associated with optional sections.)*

1. Draw pictures showing how the following array appears in a machine's memory when stored in row major order and in column major order:

A	B	C	D
E	F	G	H
I	J	K	L

2. Suppose an array with 6 rows and 8 columns is stored in row major order starting at address 20 (decimal). If each entry in the array requires only one memory cell, what is the address of the entry in the third row and fourth column? What if each entry requires two memory cells?
3. Work Problem 2 assuming column major order rather than row major order.
4. Suppose the list of letters A, B, C, E, F, and G is stored in a contiguous block of memory cells. What activities are required to insert the letter D in the list if the alphabetical order is to be maintained?
5. The following table represents the contents of some cells in a computer's main memory along

with the address of each cell represented. Note that some of the cells contain letters of the alphabet, and each such cell is followed by an empty cell. Place addresses in these empty cells so that each cell containing a letter together with the following cell form an entry in a linked list in which the letters appear in alphabetical order. (Use zero for the NIL pointer.) What address should the head pointer contain?

Address	*Contents*
11	C
12	
13	G
14	
15	E
16	
17	B
18	
19	U
20	
21	F
22	

6. The following table represents a portion of a linked list in a computer's main memory. Each entry in the list consists of two cells: The first contains a letter of the alphabet; the second contains a pointer to the next list entry. Alter the pointers so that the letter N is no longer in the list. Then replace the letter N with the letter G and alter the pointers so that the new letter appears in the list in its proper place in alphabetical order.

Address	*Contents*
30	J
31	38
32	B
33	30
34	X
35	46
36	N
37	40
38	K
39	36
40	P
41	34

7. The following table represents a linked list using the same format as in the preceding problems. If the head pointer contains the value 44, what name is represented by the list? Change the pointers so that the list contains the name Jean.

Address	*Contents*
40	N
41	46
42	I
43	40
44	J
45	50
46	E
47	00
48	M
49	42
50	A
51	40

8. Which of the following routines correctly inserts New Entry immediately after the entry called Previous Entry in a linked list? What is wrong with the other routine?

Routine 1

1. Copy the value in the pointer field of Previous Entry into the pointer field of New Entry.
2. Change the value in the pointer field of Previous Entry to the address of New Entry.

Routine 2

1. Change the value in the pointer field of Previous Entry to the address of New Entry.
2. Copy the value in the pointer field of Previous Entry into the pointer field of New Entry.

9. Design an algorithm for concatenating two linked lists (that is, placing one before the other to form a single list).

10. Design an algorithm for combining two sorted contiguous lists into a single sorted contiguous list. What if the lists are linked?

11. Design an algorithm for reversing the order of a linked list.

12. In Fig. 7.12 we presented an algorithm for printing a linked list in reverse order using a stack as an auxiliary storage structure. Design a recursive algorithm to perform this same task without making explicit use of a stack. In what form is a stack still involved in your recursive solution?

13. Sometimes a single linked list is provided with two different orders by following each entry with two pointers rather than one. Fill in the following table so that by following the first pointer after each letter one finds the name

Carol, but by following the second pointer after each letter one finds the letters in alphabetical order. What values belong in the head pointer of each of the two lists represented?

Address	*Contents*
60	O
61	
62	
63	C
64	
65	
66	A
67	
68	
69	L
70	
71	
72	R
73	
74	

14. The following table represents a stack stored in a contiguous block of memory cells, as discussed in the text. If the base of the stack is at address 10 and the stack pointer contains the value 12, what value is retrieved by a pop instruction? What value is then in the stack pointer?

Address	*Contents*
10	F
11	C
12	A
13	B
14	E

15. a. Draw a table showing the final contents of the memory cells if the instruction in problem 14 had been to push the letter D on the stack rather than to pop it. What would the value in the stack pointer be after the push instruction?

b. How would your answer to part (a) change if the base of the stack had been at address 14 rather than 10 (that is, if the cells used for the stack precede the stack rather than follow it)?

16. Design an algorithm to remove the bottom entry from a stack.

17. Design an algorithm to compare the contents of two stacks.

18. Suppose we want to create a stack of names that vary in length. Why is it advantageous to store the names in separate areas of memory and then build the stack out of pointers to these names rather than allowing the stack to contain the names themselves?

19. Does a queue crawl through memory in the direction of its head or its tail?

20. Suppose the entries in a queue require one memory cell each, the head pointer contains the value 11, and the tail pointer contains the value 17. What are the values of these pointers after one entry is inserted and two are removed?

21. a. Suppose a queue implemented in a circular fashion is in the state shown in the following diagram. Draw a diagram showing the structure after the letters G and R are inserted, three letters are removed, and the letters D and P are inserted.

b. What error occurs in part (a) if the letters G, R, D, and P are inserted before any letters are removed?

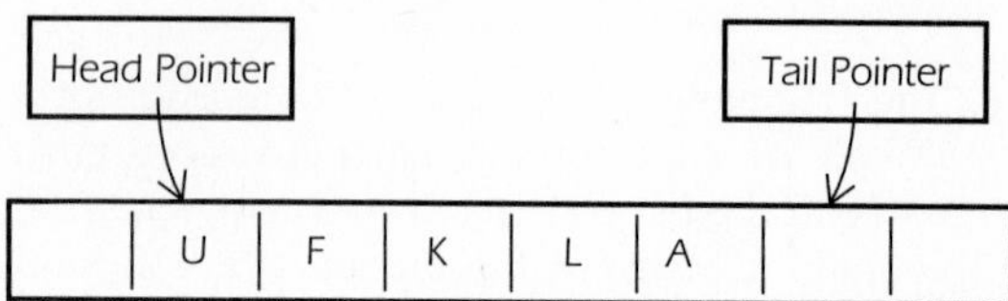

22. Describe how an array can be used to implement a queue in a high-level language.

23. The following table represents a tree stored in a machine's memory. Each node of the tree consists of three cells. The first cell contains the data (a letter), the second contains a pointer to the node's left child, and the third contains a pointer to the node's right child. A value of 0 represents a NIL pointer. If the value of the root pointer is 55, draw a picture of the tree represented.

Address	*Contents*
40	G
41	0
42	0
43	X
44	0
45	0
46	J
47	49
48	0

49	M
50	0
51	0
52	F
53	43
54	40
55	W
56	46
57	52

24. The following table represents the contents of a block of cells in a computer's main memory. Note that some of the cells contain letters of the alphabet, and each such cell is followed by two blank cells. Fill in the blank cells so that the memory block represents the tree following the table. Use the first cell following a letter as the pointer to that node's left child and the next cell as the pointer to the right child. Use 0 for NIL pointers. What value should be in the root pointer?

Address	*Contents*
30	C
31	
32	
33	H
34	
35	
36	K
37	
38	
39	E
40	
41	
42	G
43	
44	
45	P
46	
47	

G
C K
E H P

25. Design a nonrecursive algorithm to replace the recursive one represented in Fig. 7.25. Use a stack to control any backtracking that may be necessary.

26. Apply the recursive tree-printing algorithm of Fig. 7.25 to the tree represented in Problem 23. Draw a diagram representing the nested activations of the algorithm (and the current position in each) at the time node X is printed.

27. While keeping the root node the same and without changing the physical location of the data elements, change the pointers in the tree of Problem 23 so the tree-printing algorithm of Fig. 7.25 prints the nodes alphabetically.

28. Draw a diagram showing how the following binary tree appears in memory when stored without pointers using the alternative storage system presented in this chapter.

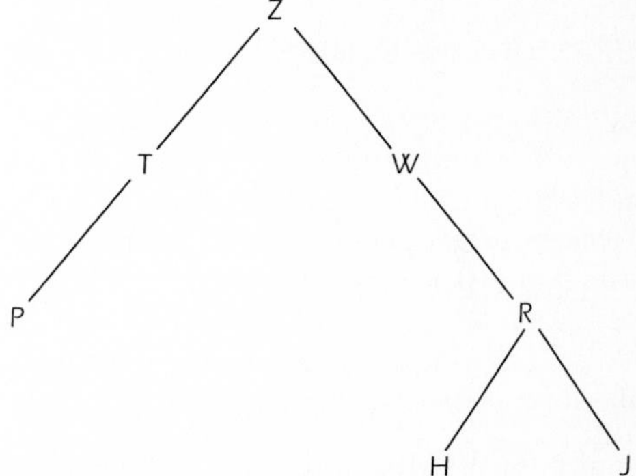

29. Describe a data structure suitable for representing a board configuration during a chess game.

30. Describe a data structure suitable for representing a Rubik's cube. What subprograms should be provided to support the conceptual image?

31. Modify the subprogram in Fig. 7.25 to print the list in reverse order.

32. Describe a tree structure that can be used to store the genealogical history of a family. What operations are performed on the tree? If the tree is implemented as a linked structure, what pointers are associated with each node? Design subprograms to perform the operations you identified above, assuming that the tree is implemented as a linked structure with the pointers you just described.

33. Design an algorithm for finding and deleting a given value from a tree ordered in the fashion of Fig. 7.22.

*34. What is the difference between a user-defined type and an abstract data type?

*35. What is the difference between an abstract data type and an instance of that type?

*36. Give a definition of *encapsulation*.

*37. What is the difference between the public and private parts of an abstract data type?

*38. Identify the data structures and procedures you can include in an abstract data type representing an address book.

*39. Identify the data structures and procedures you can include in an abstract data type representing a spacecraft in a video game.

*40. Define each of the following:
   a. Class
   b. Object
   c. Inheritance
   d. Polymorphism

*41. Summarize the distinction between the object-oriented programming paradigm and the procedural programming paradigm.

*42. Identify some of the objects you would use to develop an object-oriented program for a checker-playing program. What data structures would be in each object? What actions would each of these objects perform?

QUESTIONS OF ETHICS

The following questions are provided to help you understand some of the ethical/social/legal issues associated with the field of computing as well as investigate your own beliefs and their foundations. The goal is not merely to answer these questions. You should also consider why you answered as you did and whether your justifications are consistent from one question to the next.

1. Suppose a software analyst, while working for a particular company, develops a data organization that allows for extremely efficient manipulation of that data in a particular application. He or she is then hired by another company and assigned a similar project. Should the analyst be allowed to implement the same data organization for the second company? How can a company protect itself against its competitors regarding such developments?
2. Many consider the use of coercion in programs to be bad programming style that leads to programming errors. Other programmers, however, continue to use coercion as an acceptable technique. Should these circumstances affect the liability of those programmers who use coercion? In general, to what extent should opinions of some members in a profession affect the actions of others in the profession who may not have the same opinions?
3. Proponents of the object-oriented paradigm encourage the development of "object libraries," consisting of predeveloped objects that can be used as building blocks when constructing large software systems. In such a context, how should issues of liability be resolved? What about compensation? If an object that has been developed and sold to another party later turns out to have enormous value, is the original developer entitled to additional compensation?
4. In a data structure based on a pointer system the deletion of an item usually consists of changing a pointer rather than erasing memory cells. For example, when an entry in a linked list is deleted, the deleted entry actually remains in memory until its memory space is required by other data. What ethical and security issues result from this endurance of deleted data?

ADDITIONAL ACTIVITIES

1. Select a programming language that you know and identify the features it provides for implementing linked data structures.
2. Select a programming language that you know and identify the features it provides for allocating and deallocating memory space. What

garbage-collection features must be provided by the underlying software to support such dynamic memory allocation?

3. Describe different ways in which a stack could be implemented in a programming language you know. Write routines to perform the push and pop operations for each implementation.

4. Describe different ways in which a binary tree could be implemented in a programming language you know.

5. If you know an imperative programming language, describe the extent to which the concept of an object can be implemented in that language.

ADDITIONAL READING

Budd, T. *A Little Smalltalk.* Reading, Mass.: Addison-Wesley, 1987.

Decker, R., and S. Hirshfield. The Object Concept. Boston: PWS, 1994.

Helman, P., and R. Veroff. *Intermediate Problem Solving and Data Structures,* 2nd ed. Redwood City, Calif.: Benjamin/Cummings, 1991.

Kruse, R. L. *Data Structures and Program Design,* 3rd ed. Englewood Cliffs, N.J.: Prentice-Hall, 1994.

CHAPTER EIGHT

File Structures

8.1 Sequential Files
Rudiments of Sequential Files
Programming Concerns

8.2 Text Files
Manipulating Text Files
Programming Concerns

8.3 Indexed Files
Index Fundamentals
Index Organization
Programming Concerns

8.4 Hashed Files
A Particular Hashing Technique
Distribution Problems
Handling Section Overflow
Programming Concerns

8.5 The Role of the Operating System

In Chapter 7 we discussed various ways of organizing data within a machine's main memory. In this chapter we concentrate on data storage techniques used in mass storage. A major theme is the study of the relationship between the way in which the information is to be accessed and the way in which it should be stored.

Recall that a collection of data stored in mass storage is called a file, which in turn is subdivided into records. The subject of this chapter concerns how these records can be organized in mass storage to provide convenient user access. As in the case of data structures, we find that the format ultimately presented to the user may not be the same as that in the actual storage system. Thus, as in Chapter 7, we find ourselves discussing and comparing both conceptual and real organizations.

8.1 Sequential Files

Suppose we want to maintain information about the employees in a business. The information consists of such items as name, address, employee identification number, Social Security number, pay scale, hours worked, date hired, and job title. We may want this employee information stored in mass storage space rather than in main memory for several reasons. One is that there probably is not enough space in main memory. Another might be that the memory in our machine is volatile and the data would be lost if power were disconnected. Still another is that we want to keep a copy of our data in off-line storage (perhaps even at another location) for backup purposes.

For whatever reason, we assume that the information about the employees is to be recorded in mass storage with one logical record for each employee. Each record in turn consists of units, called **fields,** that contain the individual items of information about the employee.

Suppose our employee file is used for payroll processing, for which the entire file must be accessed each pay period. As each employee record is retrieved, that employee's pay is calculated and the appropriate check produced. Since all records are processed, it makes little difference which records are processed first. The most straightforward technique therefore is to consider the records as organized in a list and then to retrieve and process them one at a time from the beginning to the end. Such an organization is called a **sequential file.**

Rudiments of Sequential Files

This sequential organization may, of course, be only conceptual in nature. Depending on the physical characteristics of the storage device being used, we may choose to store the file in another form and present it to the user as a sequential system. If the storage device is a tape system, we normally remain faithful to the conceptual sequential order because of the sequential nature of the tape itself. However, if the device is a disk system, we might choose to disperse the records of the file over the disk to take advantage of available sectors (Fig. 8.1). In this case we could link the records with a pointer system similar to the linked list system in Chapter 7, except that here the pointers would represent locations on the disk rather than in main memory. In reality, however, most operating systems eliminate the need for such pointers by maintaining a record of the sectors in which the file is stored and the order in which these sectors should be read when retrieving the file.

Regardless of the storage system used, the end of a sequential file usually is indicated by an **EOF (end-of-file) mark.** In the linked structure, this mark might be similar to the NIL pointer in a linked list. Another approach is to store a special record, called a **sentinel,** as the last record of the file to mark the end. Of course, to avoid confusion, the fields in such a record must contain values that will never occur as data in the application. Still other implementations record the length of the file at its beginning and then use this information to detect the end of the file.

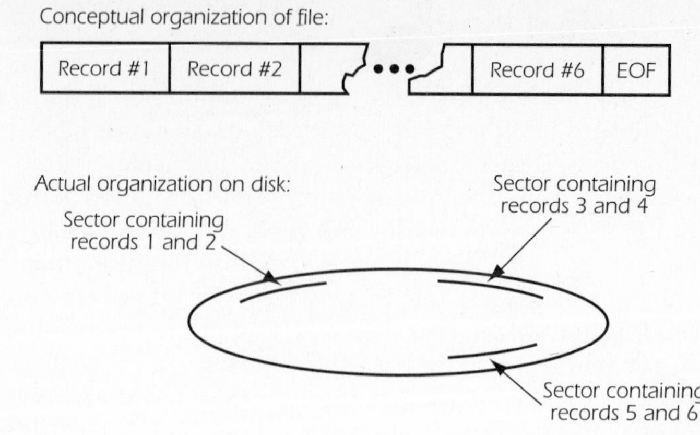

Figure 8.1 A sequential file storage on a disk

The user of a sequential file is allowed (or from another point of view, forced) to view the records in a simple sequential order. The only way to retrieve records is to start at the beginning of the file and extract them in the order provided.

Although convenient for the processing of payroll checks, this sequential nature has some undesirable aspects. For example, suppose that before processing the payroll from the employee file, we must update the records to reflect the amount of time worked by each employee during the current pay period. To accomplish this, we note the time worked by a particular employee, search through the file to find the employee's record, and update the record. Next we select another employee's time sheet and search for the corresponding record.

This process is simplified if the order in which the time sheets are selected agrees with the order of the employee records in the file. This means that after updating an employee record, we need not return to the beginning of the file to initiate the search for the next record to be updated. Instead, we initiate the search from our current position in the file. For this reason sequential files are normally stored in alphabetical or numerical order according to the contents of a selected field, known as the **key field.** For example, we might choose to store the employee file in alphabetical order by last name or, since two employees may have the same last name, we may choose numerical order by Social Security number or employee identification number. If we then arrange the time sheets according to this same key field, updating the payroll file reduces the process to merely updating the records one after the other as they appear in the sequential file.

Having seen the advantage of order, you probably will not be surprised that a lot of sorting takes place in relation to processing sequential files. To update a sequential file, the new information (such as the collection of time sheets) is first recorded in the form of a sequential file known as a transaction file. Then, this transaction file is sorted to match the order of the file to be updated. Finally, the records in the original file are updated in the order in which they appear.

Programming Concerns

Now that we have discussed the rudiments of sequential files, we need to take a brief look at how such files are manipulated from the programmer's point of view. This we do in the context of programming in a high-level language. These languages tend to express file manipulation through procedures that are either defined as a part of the formal language itself or provided as language extensions supplied in an adjoining library. In either case the parameters of these procedures identify the target file and the area of main memory that is to receive or supply the data in the record being manipulated. For example, in Pascal, statements such as

```
read (MailList, MailRecord)
```

and

```
write (MailList, MailRecord)
```

are used to retrieve and deposit information relative to a sequential file identified as `MailList`. Note that along with the file identifier within the parameter list, we find the name `MailRecord` (probably a heterogenous array) that is used within the program to identify the block of data being transferred.

To obtain similar results, a C++ programmer could write

```
MailList >> FirstName >> LastName;
```

and

```
MailList << FirstName << " " << LastName << " ";
```

The first of these statements reads two strings of characters from the file identified as `MailList`, the first being assigned to the array named `FirstName`, the second to the array named `LastName`. The second statement writes the strings identified as `FirstName` and `LastName`, each followed by a blank for separation purposes, in the file identified by `MailList`.

In a similar manner, a C programmer can use the statements

```
fscanf(MailList, "%s%s", FirstName, LastName);
```

and

```
fprintf(MailList, "%s %s ", FirstName, LastName);
```

to read and write names to and from a file identified as `GuestList`. Here `fscanf` and `fprintf` are functions found in C's standard library. These functions apply what is called **formatted I/O,** meaning that the I/O statement includes a description of the data's format (organization) within the file. This is the purpose of the quoted expressions in the preceding statements. In particular, the expression "`%s%s`" in the `fscanf` statement indicates that the format of the data is that of a character string followed by another character string. The expression "`%s %s `" in the `fprintf` statement indicates that the output is to have the form of two character strings with blanks interspersed. The presence of these blanks allows the `fscanf` function to distinguish between the individual strings when reading the file. The variables following the format expression indicate the destination (in the case of `fscanf`) or the source (in the case of `fprintf`) of the data being transferred.

We should note that the program statements introduced here do more than merely transfer bit patterns between main memory and mass storage. In many cases they convert between coding systems. For example, suppose `Reading` is a variable of type integer that is assigned the value 35. Then, the bit pattern in main memory would be the two's complement representation of 35, but the Pascal and C++ statements

```
write(Temperatures, Reading);
```

and

```
Temperatures << Reading;
```

would each cause the ASCII representations of the characters 3 and 5 to be placed in the file `Temperatures`. In C this conversion is more explicitly expressed by the statement

```
fprintf(Temperatures, "%d", Reading);
```

where the expression "`%d`" indicates that the bit pattern placed in the file should be the ASCII code for the digits obtained by converting the value assigned to `Reading` into decimal (base ten) notation. In a similar manner the statements

```
read(Temperatures, Reading);

Temperatures >> Reading;
```

and

```
fscanf(Temperatures, "%d", &Reading);
```

convert the ASCII coded digits found in the file into two's complement notation for storage in main memory.

Note that these statements include no explicit information as to the location in the file of the record being manipulated. Because the file is sequential, there is no choice to be made. The record being read is the one immediately following the current position in the file or the record being written is placed immediately following the current position.

In addition to subroutines for the manipulation of records in a sequential file, most high-level language systems provide features that assist with the problem of detecting the EOF mark. In Pascal, for example, one can test for the EOF mark on the file identified as `EmplData` with the expression `eof(EmplData)`. The result is the value true if the EOF mark has been reached and false if not. Thus a program sequence of the form

```
while (not eof(EmplData)) do
    (read the next record and
    process the appropriate check)
```

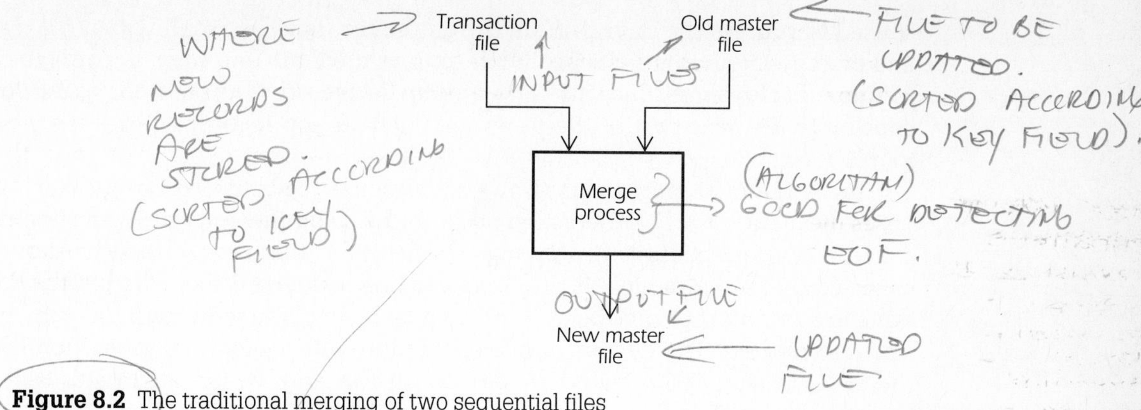

Figure 8.2 The traditional merging of two sequential files

Figure 8.3 The sequential file update (or merge) algorithm represented in pseudocode

```
procedure Merge

if (EOF on the old master file)
   then (declare old master file empty)
   else (read a record from the old master file)
if (EOF on transaction file)
   then (declare transaction file empty)
   else (read a record from the transaction file)
while (neither file declared empty) do
   [if (key field of current master record is less than key field
    of current transaction record)
      then (write the current master record on the new master file;
               if (EOF on old master file)
                  then (declare old master file empty)
                  else (read the next record from the old master file))
      else (write the current transaction record on the new master file;
               if (EOF on transaction file)
                  then (declare transaction file empty)
                  else (read the next record from the transaction file))]
while (old master file not declared empty) do
   (write the current master record on the new master file;
    if (EOF on old master file)
       then (declare old master file empty)
       else (read the next record from the old master file))
while (transaction file not declared empty) do
   (write the current transaction record on the new master file;
    if (EOF on transaction file)
       then (declare transaction file empty)
       else (read the next record from the transaction file))
```

is used to process the payroll from the employee file. The result is that the read and process statements are repeated as long as there are employee records to be processed. However, once the last employee record is processed, execution goes on to the next part of the program. Such an application typifies the while loop structure.

The traditional merge algorithm provides an excellent medium in which to observe the need for EOF detection while at the same time presenting a classical example of sequential file processing. The setting is that new records have been collected that are to be inserted into an existing sequential file. This insertion is done in the context of producing a totally new copy of the sequential file with the updates inserted. The new records are stored in a file called the transaction file, the file to be updated is called the old master file, and the updated file is called the new master file (Fig. 8.2). Both the transaction file and the old master file are assumed to be sorted according to a field referred to as the key field. We assume that all new records are indeed new; that is, no record in the transaction file can be found with an identical key field to that of a record in the old master file.

Observe that with these assumptions the problem becomes one of merging the two existing files, which we call the input files, into one large output file (the new master file). The algorithm accomplishes this by starting at the beginning of the two input files, accessing a record from each file, comparing the records, writing the smaller one into the new master file, and then reading another record from the appropriate input file before returning to compare again.

Within this basic framework we must also maintain a vigil for the end of either input file and, if this is found, respond accordingly. This leads to the algorithm represented in Fig. 8.3.

Questions/Exercises

1. Follow the merge algorithm presented in Fig. 8.3, assuming that the transaction file contains records with key field values equal to B and E while the old master file contains A, C, D, and F.
2. The merge algorithm is the heart of a popular sort algorithm called the merge sort. Can you discover this algorithm? (*Hint:* A file containing only one record is sorted.)
3. Redesign the merge algorithm in Fig. 8.3, assuming that sentinel records are used to mark the end of each file.

8.2 Text Files

By restricting the size of the logical records in a sequential file to a single byte, we obtain another file type known as a **text file.**[1] The name *text file* reflects the fact that files of this type are commonly used for storing documents consisting of

[1]Some refer to these files as stream files, but others reserve the term *stream* to refer to a series of bytes that are passed from one process to another without necessarily being stored as a file in mass storage. Others reserve the term *text file* to refer to a stream whose bytes contain only ASCII codes.

text, with each logical record consisting of a single symbol or control code (such as a carriage return, line feed, or font indicator). When reading a text file, one receives the characters of the document in the sequential order in which they appear when the document is displayed in printed form.

An alternative to viewing a text file as a stream of individual bytes is to view the file as a sequence of lines separated by end-of-line markers. This conceptual image is a consequence of document storage applications and is promoted by the Pascal programming language.

Manipulating Text Files

For storage purposes a text file is broken into multiple-byte units that form physical records of a size compatible with the mass storage system being used. The manipulation of physical records is normally handled by the underlying software, so when either reading from or writing to a text file, the user has the image of a file consisting of a sequence of individual bytes or lines as desired.

In reality, when the first byte or line is requested from the file, the underlying software retrieves one or more entire physical records from the mass storage device and holds these records in a buffer in main memory. From this buffer, the request for a portion of the file as well as future requests are honored. As the underlying software passes the contents of the buffer to the user, additional physical records are retrieved into the buffer until the end of the file is reached.

As a user writes to a text file, the underlying software collects the individual bytes in a buffer until a complete physical record accumulates, or until the user indicates that the end of the file has been reached. It is only at these times that a physical record is transferred to mass storage.

In some cases the underlying software disguises the strict sequential nature of a text file. A word processor, for example, might store documents as text files but not limit the processing of the file strictly to its sequential form. Instead, a word processor normally reads several physical records into main memory and displays this text on the monitor as it would appear in the printed form of the document. Then the processor allows the user to move back and forth within this block of text while making changes. As the user moves farther down the text, more physical records are retrieved from mass storage and displayed on the screen, while the earlier updated portions of the document are redivided into physical records and placed back into mass storage. In this way the word processor provides random access to that portion of the file that is currently held in main memory.

Programming Concerns

Text files are among the most common file structures supported by high-level programming languages. As with sequential files, this support takes the form of prewritten procedures that may be included as a part of the formal definition of the language or as offered in libraries as extensions to the language.

Pascal is an example of the first case. It includes the routines `read` and `write` for accessing text files. In particular, if `Symbol` is declared as a variable of type character, then the statement

```
read(OldManuscript, Symbol);
```

retrieves one byte from the text file identified as `OldManuscript` and assigns that byte to the variable `Symbol`. Similarly, the statement

```
write(NewManuscript, Symbol);
```

places the byte currently assigned to `Symbol` at the current location in the file `NewManuscript`.

Commands for manipulating text files in a C language environment are provided as a language extension by means of prewritten routines within a library. These routines include `getc` and `putc` for retrieving and depositing bytes in a text file. Hence, in a C program the statements

```
getc(OldManuscript, Symbol);
```

and

```
putc(NewManuscript, Symbol);
```

would be used to accomplish the same goals as the preceding `read` and `write` Pascal statements.

In C++, the statement

```
OldManuscript.get(Symbol);
```

which sends the `get` message to the object `OldManuscript`, could be used to accomplish the equivalent of the preceding `getc` command. Likewise, the statement

```
NewManuscript.put(Symbol);
```

would instruct the object `NewManuscript` to `put` the contents of `Symbol` in its file.

To support the line-by-line image of a text file, Pascal provides routines called `readln` and `writeln` that manipulate text files by lines rather than individual characters. For example, the command

```
readln(OldManuscript);
```

advances the current position in the file `OldManuscript` to the beginning of the next line and

```
writeln(NewManuscript);
```

places an end-of-line marker at the current position in the file `NewManuscript`.

Questions/Exercises

1. In what sense is a text file a special case of a sequential file?
2. Identify two applications in which the use of text files is appropriate.
3. Suppose a word processor stores documents in a strict text file format. What problems might be encountered when the word processor is required to backtrack a long distance within a document that is being updated?

8.3 Indexed Files

Let us suppose now that in addition to processing payroll with the employee file, we want to use the file in an interactive query system. For instance, we may want to have a workstation available in the personnel office on which employee records can be displayed to answer questions regarding time in service, available skills, past promotions, and so on. In this atmosphere, records in the file are requested in an arbitrary order throughout the day.

This is a significant departure from the naturally sequential payroll application of Section 8.1. If we store the employee data as a sequential file and attempt to use it in this interactive application, we could easily find a lengthy delay between a request for a record and the displaying of that record. Indeed, to satisfy each request, the program handling the retrieval must apply a sequential search from the beginning of the file.

We have already discussed the disadvantages of such a process in the context of searching a list data structure. Compounding the problem in the present application is that the accessing of records from mass storage requires the additional time-consuming, mechanical motion associated with the storage device being used. The result is that sequential search techniques are even more sluggish when applied to mass storage than when applied to main memory.

What we need is a way of storing the employee file that reduces this search time. One approach is based on the same idea used in a textbook in which an index allows a topic to be located more directly than through a sequential search of the entire book. This index concept is easily applied to file storage, resulting in an **indexed file.**

Index Fundamentals

An index for a file consists of a listing of the key field values occurring in the file along with the location in mass storage of the corresponding record. For example, in an employee file, we might build an index listing all the employee identification numbers. Finding the record for a particular employee in such a file requires searching for the pertinent employee number in the file's index and then retrieving the record stored in the indicated mass storage location.

Of course, this approach requires that we know the key field value (employee identification number) of the desired record. In some cases, it may be necessary for our file to be accessible by more than one key field, perhaps by either Social Security number or employee identification number. In such cases, a multiple index system is often the solution. In particular, in addition to constructing an index listing employee identification numbers, we might build a second index based on the key field being Social Security numbers (Fig. 8.4). Then, regardless of whether one starts with an employee number or a Social Security number, the desired record can be accessed quickly by interrogating the appropriate index. (You sometimes hear such a file referred to as an **inverted file**, with one key field designated as the **primary key** and the other as the **secondary key**.) The luxury of multiple indexes is not without its disadvantages, however. Indeed, as records are inserted and deleted, all indexes must be up-

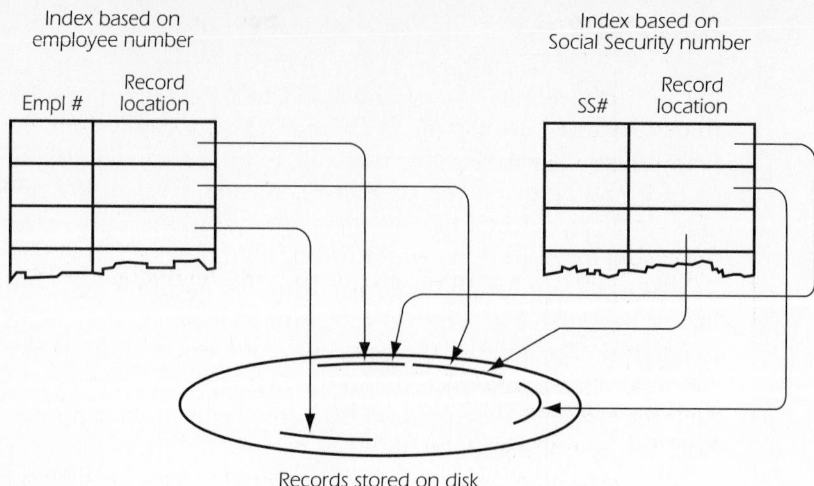

Figure 8.4 An inverted file

dated, so the existence of additional indexes can increase the time required to update the file.

Although we have introduced the topic of indexed files in the context of an employee file, most computer users are more familiar with file indexes in the context of file directory systems maintained by operating systems. These directory systems are essentially indexes in which entries represent files rather than records. In a sense, the operating system considers the entire collection of files stored on a disk as one large file. This directory (index) is stored on the disk and used by the operating system to find files as they are requested. Users of personal computers can usually hear the directory (index) being accessed when they request a listing of the files contained on a floppy disk. Moreover, if the directory is not yet in main memory, they may detect the two-step access process (read the directory from the disk, then read the desired data) when requesting access to a particular file.

Index Organization

Consider now the question of index size. Since the index must be moved to main memory to be searched, it (or perhaps sections of it) must remain small enough to fit within a reasonable memory area. This requirement can produce problems if the number of records in the file becomes large. One technique used to overcome such a growth problem is to use the index to find an approximate, rather than the precise, location of the desired record. Such a search can be accomplished by first organizing the file in a sorted sequential order and then chopping it into short, multirecord segments. Each segment (consisting of several records) is then represented in the index by a single entry, which is normally the last key field value in the segment. The result is a partial index containing only a few of the key field values appearing in the file.

The partial-index structure is summarized in Fig. 8.5, in which we have indicated only the key field entry in each record and have assumed that these entries are single, alphabetic letters. The retrieval of a record from this system consists of finding the first entry in the index that is equal to or greater than the desired entry and then searching the corresponding sequential segment for the target record. For example, to find the record with key field entry E in the file in Fig. 8.5, we follow the pointer associated with the index entry F and then search that segment to find the desired record.

Another approach to the large-index problem is to divide the index into pieces using the concept of an index to the index. Thus the overall index takes on a layered or tree structure. We might envision such a system as an extension of the partial-index idea. More precisely, if the sequential segments represented by the index entries were to become inefficiently large, we could construct a separate index for each of them. The original index would no longer direct the search to a file segment but rather to the correct segment index, which then would be used to find the location of the record in question (Fig. 8.6). A prominent example of such an index structure is the hierarchical directory system used by most operating systems for maintaining files. In these cases each directory (index) is heterogeneous, in that some entries refer to individual files whereas others refer to subdirectories (subindexes).

Figure 8.5 A file with a partial index

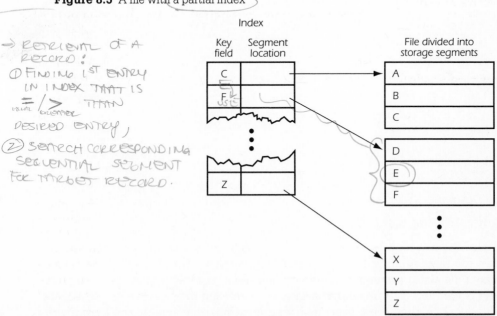

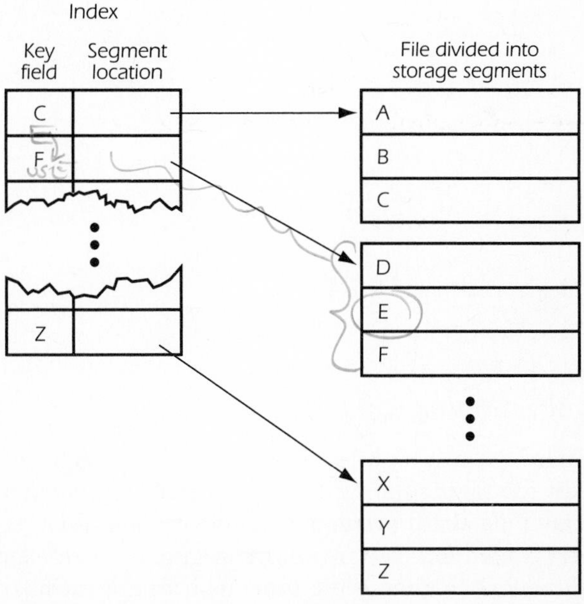

Index

Key field	Segment location
C	
F	
⋮	
Z	

File divided into storage segments

A
B
C

D
E
F

⋮

X
Y
Z

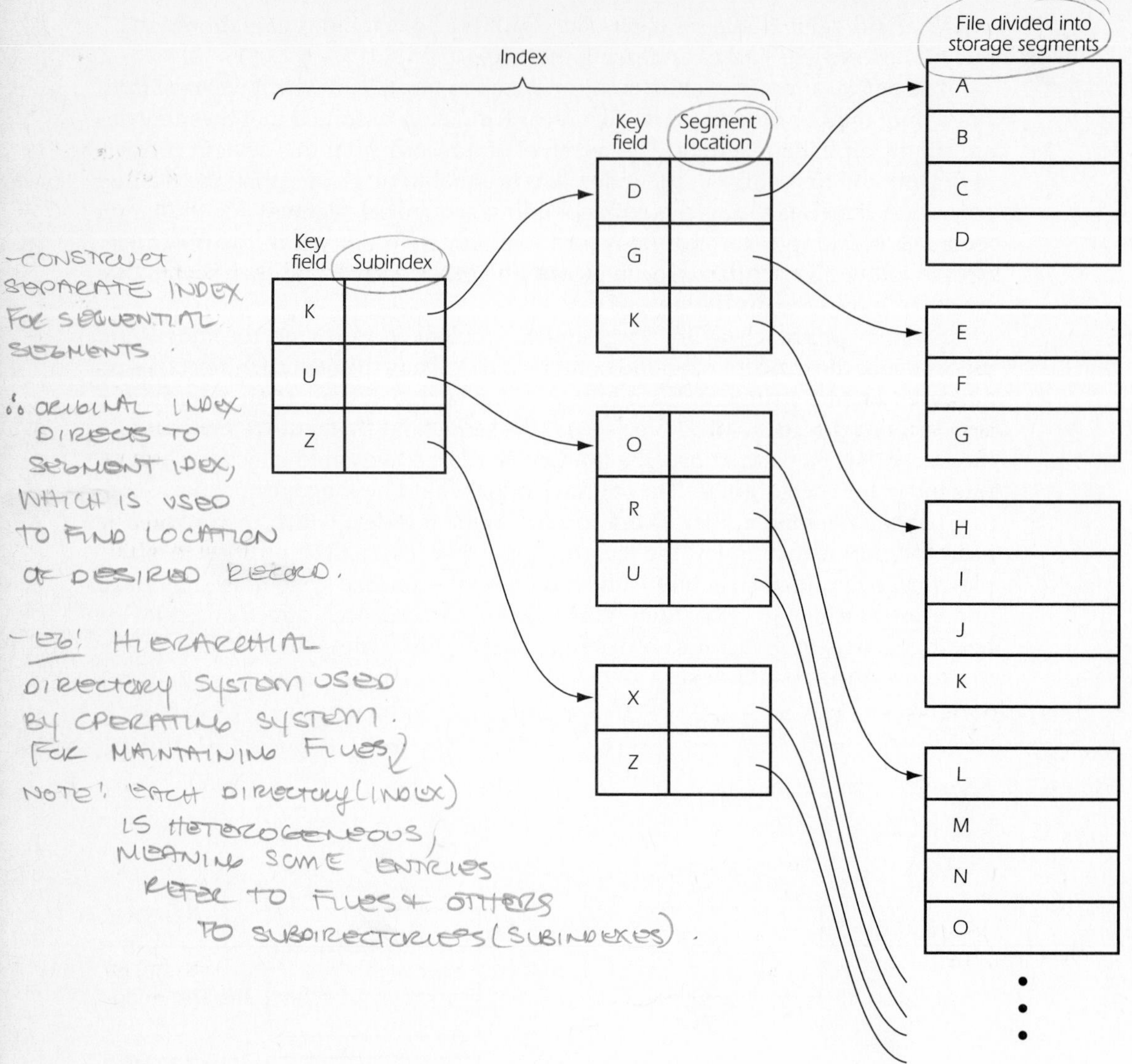

Figure 8.6 A hierarchical index

Programming Concerns

Few of today's high-level programming languages contain commands specifically for manipulating files by means of an index. This reflects the fact that today's database systems usually provide abstract tools that relieve programmers from the task of maintaining their own indexed file systems. As we will see in the next chapter, these tools tend to appear as extensions to the formal programming language, rather than being a part of the language itself.

Many programming languages, however, offer the building blocks required to construct an indexed file system when such an undertaking is necessary. In a C program, for example, the function `fsetpos` can be used to establish a current position within a file. More precisely, the statement

```
fsetpos(Personnel, &Position);
```

requests that the current position in the file `Personnel` be established at the location identified by the value of the variable `Position`. (Exactly how this position is indicated varies from system to system.) If we followed this statement with

```
fscanf(Personnel, "%s", Name);
```

we would retrieve the name of that location in the file.

By maintaining an index consisting of the various key field values and their associated positions in the file, a C programmer can construct an indexed file. To obtain a particular record, the program can first find the appropriate position in the index and then use `fsetpos` and `fscanf` to obtain the record.

To assist in obtaining the locations to be entered in the index, the standard C library contains a function, `fgetpos`, that identifies the current position in a file. In particular, the statement

```
fgetpos(Personnel, &Position);
```

assigns the current position in the file (the location at which the next read or write operation will be performed) to the variable `Position`. Thus `fgetpos` provides the information required to build the index as the file is being created.

Questions/Exercises

1. Within a partial index, why is it advantageous to represent each segment of the file with its largest key field rather than its smallest? (*Hint:* Compare the algorithms needed to search the index in each case.)
2. The concepts of sequential and indexed files are often combined by supplying an index to an otherwise sequential file, producing what is called an indexed sequential file. What advantages does such an organization have?
3. Identify some pros and cons to organizing a file's index as a list rather than as a tree.
4. In the case of an inverted file, can both the primary and secondary indexes be organized as partial indexes using the technique presented in this section?

8.4 Hashed Files

At this point we have discussed examples of two general approaches to file organization. The first, known as sequential access, is represented by sequential and text files. It insists that the file be processed according to a particular serial order. The second is called direct access (sometimes called random access) and allows individual records to be retrieved without interrogating other records in the file. Indexed files provide an example of this paradigm.

Note that by properly traversing the index, one can obtain sequential access to an indexed file. Hence an index system is a way of obtaining both sequential and direct access to a file, a duality obtained at the expense of index maintenance.

Hashed files represent a file storage system that provides direct access only, without the overhead encountered with indexed maintenance. The idea behind a hashed file is to compute the location of a record in mass storage by applying an algorithm (known as the hash algorithm) to the value of the key field in question. The result is a system that, given the desired key field, can determine the location of a record quickly without the use of auxiliary tables that must be maintained by indexed files.

A Particular Hashing Technique

Let us apply the hashing concept to our employee file. First, we divide the mass storage area allotted to the file into several sections called buckets. How many buckets we use is a design decision that we return to later. For now, let us assume that we have divided the storage region into 40 buckets. Next, assuming that records in the file will always be requested in terms of the employee identification number, we establish that field in each record as the key field.

Our first task is to convert any key field value into a numeric value. This step may seem meaningless to you since the key field is, in fact, the employee identification number. However, the actual value of this field may not be numeric. That is, identification "numbers" may take the form 25X3Z or J2-X35. On the other hand, recall that any information stored in the machine is represented in terms of a string of 0s and 1s. Thus, we can always interpret an item of data simply as a binary number whether or not that was the original intention when the information was coded.

Using this numeric interpretation, we can divide any key field value stored in memory by the number of buckets, which in our case is 40. Note that the result of this division process is an integer value, called the quotient, and another integer value known as the remainder. The important point is that this remainder is always in the range from 0 to 39. That is, if we consider only the remainder from the division, we always find one of the 40 possible values 0, 1, 2, 3, . . . 39. Thus, we can relate exactly one of the 40 buckets to each of these possible remainders (Fig. 8.7).

With this system we can convert any key field value into an integer (the remainder of the division) that identifies one of the buckets in mass storage, and we can use this system to determine the bucket in which to store the corresponding record. That is, we can consider each record individually, convert its key field value to an integer, apply our hash algorithm to identify a bucket in mass storage, and then store the record in that bucket as summarized in Fig. 8.8. Later, if we need to retrieve a record with a certain key field value, we can simply transform this value to a bucket number as before, retrieve the records in that bucket, and then search the retrieved records for the one in question.

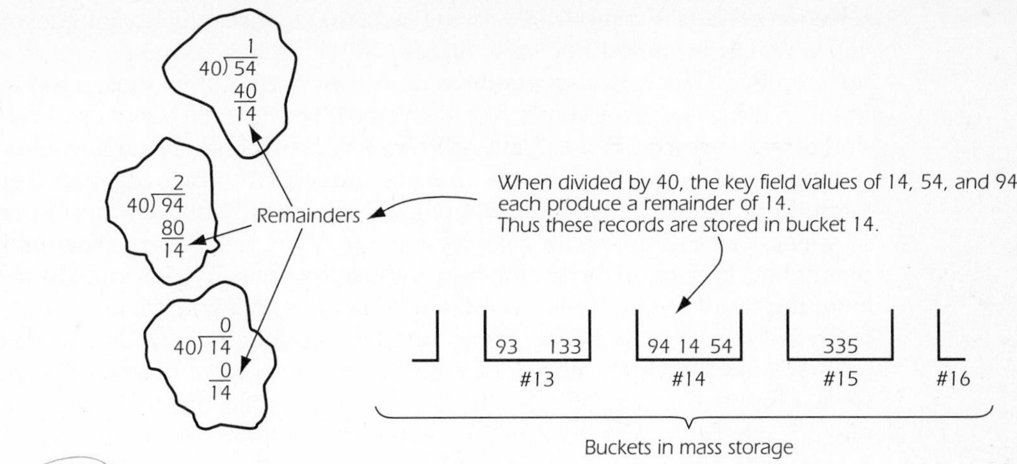

Figure 8.7 The rudiments of a hashing system, in which each bucket holds those records that hash to that bucket number

Distribution Problems

Our simplified explanation has thus far overlooked a few complications inherent in a hashed file. At the root of these complications is the fact that once we have chosen the hash algorithm, we have no more control over the distribution of records in mass storage. For instance, if we use the divide-by-40 algorithm previously presented, and if the numeric interpretation of the key field values tends to be multiples of 40, a disproportionate number of the records are placed in the bucket assigned to the remainder zero. The result is that searching through that bucket approximates a search through the entire file, resulting in little advantage over a sequential file structure. Moreover, unless the buckets are extremely large, a system must be provided for handling buckets that overflow.

It is therefore to our advantage to select a hash algorithm that evenly distributes the records among the buckets provided in mass storage. However, the

Figure 8.8 Hashing the key field value 25X3Z to one of 40 buckets

Key field value:	25X3Z
	↓
ASCII representation:	0011001000110101010110000011001101011010
	↓
Equivalent base ten value:	215,643,337,562
	↓
Remainder after division by 40:	2
	↓
Bucket number:	2

selection process is complicated by the fact that we normally do not know in advance exactly what the key field values will be because of employee turnover, the employee identification numbers used today will not be those used tomorrow. For this reason, the choice of a hash algorithm must be based on a combination of one's artistic abilities, statistical analysis, and rules of thumb.

One such rule of thumb concerns our decision to divide mass storage into 40 buckets, which is generally not a good choice. To see why, recall that if a dividend and a divisor both have a common factor, this factor is present in the remainder. In turn, the remainders produced by the division process tend to be multiples of this common factor, while other values are ignored. We have already seen this effect when we conjectured the possibility of the key fields being multiples of 40, which consistently produced remainders of zero. However, a similar problem exists if the key fields are multiples of 5. Since 40 is also a multiple of 5, the factor of 5 appears in the remainder of our division process, and the records in the file cluster in those buckets associated with the remainders 0, 5, 10, 15, 20, 25, 30, and 35.

Similar situations occur in the case of key field values that are multiples of 2, 4, 8, 10, and 20, because they are all also factors of 40. Of course, the observation of this fact suggests a partial solution. That is, the chance of clustering due to this phenomenon can be minimized by selecting the number of buckets to have as few factors as possible. Thus one usually selects the number of buckets to be a prime number. For instance, the chance of clustering in the employee file example can be greatly reduced by dividing mass storage into 41 buckets rather than 40, because the only factors of 41 are 1 and 41.

Sometimes clustering can be reduced by selecting a hash algorithm based on principles other than division. One suggested technique, called the midsquare method, is to multiply the key field value by itself and select the middle digits from the product to represent the bucket number. Still another, called the extraction method, is to select the digits appearing in certain positions within the key field and construct the bucket number by combining these selected digits using some predetermined process. In any case, one often tests the performance of several hash algorithms on sample records before settling on a final choice.

Unfortunately, regardless of the hash algorithm we ultimately use, clustering of records will most likely occur as a file is modified over a period of time. We can gain an understanding of how quickly this might occur by considering what happens as we initially insert records into the modified 41-bucket employee file.

Assume that we have found a hash algorithm that arbitrarily distributes records among the buckets, that our file is empty, and that we are going to insert records one at a time. When we insert the first record, that record must go into an empty bucket. However, when we insert the next record, only 40 of the 41 buckets are empty and so the probability that the second record will be placed in an empty bucket is only 40/41. Assuming that the second record is placed in an empty bucket, the third finds only 39 empty buckets, and the probability of its being placed in one of them is 39/41. Continuing this process, we find that if the first seven records are placed in empty buckets, the eighth record then has a 34/41 probability of being placed in one of the remaining empty buckets.

This analysis allows us to compute the probability of the first eight records being placed in empty buckets, because it is the product of the probabilities of each record being placed in an empty bucket, assuming that the preceding records were so placed. This probability is therefore

$$(41/41)(40/41)(39/41)(38/41) \cdots (34/41) = .482$$

The point is that the result is less than one-half. That is, it is more likely than not that at least two of the first eight records will hash to the same bucket, a phenomenon called a collision. Thus clustering probably begins with only eight records stored among 41 buckets.

Handling Section Overflow

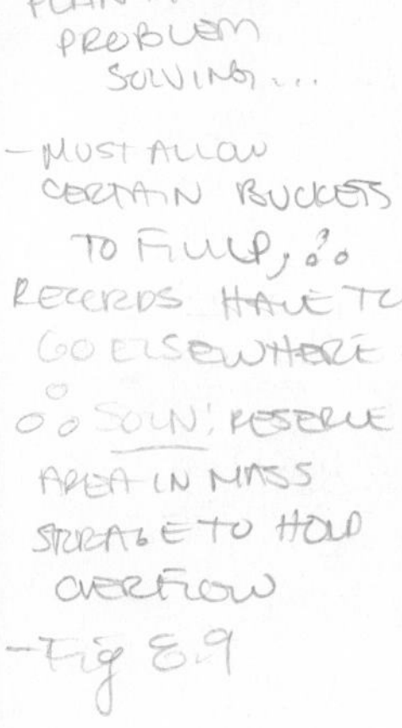

The high probability of collisions indicates that a hashed file should never be implemented under the assumption that clustering will not occur; thus, some plan must be established for handling the associated problems.

In particular, we must allow for the fact that certain buckets might fill up and that records that should go into these buckets must then be placed elsewhere. A typical technique for handling this case is to reserve an additional area of mass storage to hold overflow records. Then, if a bucket fills up, records that normally are added to it are placed in the overflow area and linked to the appropriate bucket through an organization analogous to a linked list. With such a system a hashed file stored in five buckets might have the structure shown in Fig. 8.9, in which the storage area actually occupied by records is indicated by shading. (Note that buckets 1 and 4 have spilled into the overflow area, whereas one additional record in bucket 2 will cause bucket 2 to do the same.)

When trying to retrieve a record from such a file, one would first extract the proper bucket using the hash algorithm. If, however, the desired record was not found there, one would search the overflow records linked to that bucket. We conclude that if a lot of overflowing takes place, the efficiency of searching the file can drop significantly. The design of a hashed file therefore requires a careful

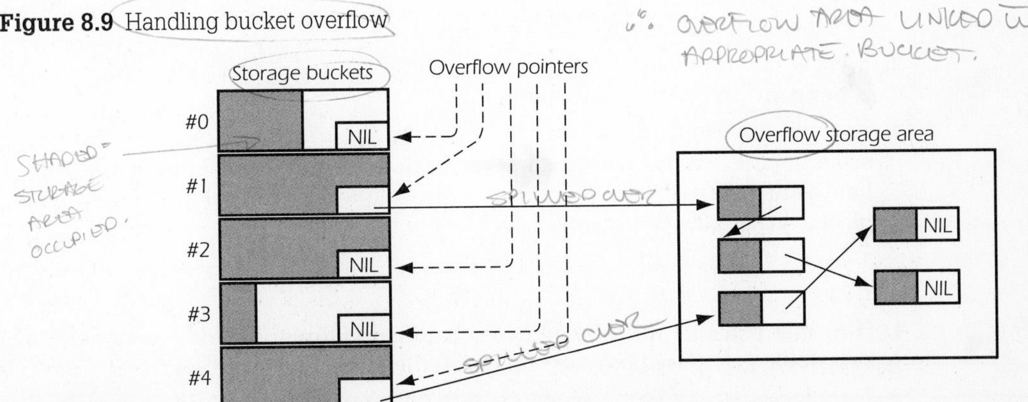

Figure 8.9 Handling bucket overflow

analysis involving the choice of the hash algorithm, the number and size of the buckets in mass storage, and the size and structure of the overflow area.

Programming Concerns

Few, if any, high-level procedural programming languages in use today offer direct implementations of hashed files. This is due to the application-dependent issues (hash algorithm, number of buckets, size of buckets) involved in the design of these files as well as the fact that, as in the case of indexed files, modern database management systems often relieve a programmer from the chore of implementing a hashed file.

When a customized hashed file is required, the same building blocks described in the previous section for implementing indexed files can be used. In the C programming language, for example, one needs merely to maintain a record of the positions at which the various buckets are stored and then use the `fsetpos` function to locate the bucket indicated by the hash function.

Although we have introduced hashing techniques in their traditional file context, hashing is not restricted to systems involving mass storage. Today hashing is often used to distribute data within areas of main memory. For example, a large one-dimensional array can be established in which each component has the capacity to hold several data entries. These components play the role of buckets, and a hash algorithm is used to identify the components in which each data entry belongs.

This expansion in the application of hashing techniques from mass storage systems into main memory systems is exemplary of the continuing evolution in data processing that is a problem for those who attempt to classify topics in the field. Indeed, hashing, which traditionally has been a topic of file structures, may soon be more accurately classified within the subject of data structures.

Questions/Exercises

1. Suppose an employee record system is implemented as a hashed file using 1000 buckets of mass storage with the Social Security number field as the key field. Observe that one possible hash algorithm is to select the first three digits from the Social Security number, because this would always result in a value between 0 and 999, inclusive. Why is this not a good choice?
2. Explain how a poorly chosen hash algorithm can result in a hashed file system becoming little more than a sequential file.
3. Suppose a hashed file is constructed using the division hash algorithm as presented in the text but with six mass storage buckets. For each of the following key field values, identify the bucket in which the record with that key field value is placed. What goes wrong and why?

   a. 24 b. 30 c. 3 d. 18 e. 15
   f. 21 g. 9 h. 39 i. 27 j. 0
4. How many people must be gathered together before the odds are that two members of the group will have birthdays on the same day of the year?

8.5 The Role of the Operating System

We have seen that associated with each file structure is a variety of details relating to the retrieval or insertion of records. However, we concluded our discussion of each structure by indicating that such details are often of no concern when accessing the file from within a high-level programming language environment, because these environments tend to provide prewritten routines for manipulating files. These routines, in turn, communicate with the operating system to perform their assigned tasks. Thus much of the obligation for file manipulation ultimately falls on the operating system.

To fulfill this obligation, the operating system must have access to information about the file being manipulated. For example, it must know the structure of the file, which item within a record is the key field (if applicable), and whether the file is to be saved after the program using it is finished. Furthermore, some items of information must be remembered by the operating system between the retrieval of one record and the next. Depending on the type of file being manipulated, this information may include the current position in the file, which physical record is currently in a buffer in main memory, and whether any abnormal conditions occurred during the previous access. For example, in an indexed file, was the requested record actually found?

To manage this information, the operating system maintains a table, often called a **file descriptor** or file control block, for each file being processed. All the information relating to the processing of a single file is kept there in an organized manner and made available to the various routines in the operating system as needed. Thus, if a program involves the processing of three files, the operating system must construct three file descriptors to assist in the file management.

In a high-level programming language, the construction of a file descriptor normally is initiated by a prewritten routine named `open`. A typical statement in FORTRAN has a form similar to

```
OPEN(UNIT = 10, FILE = 'EmplFile', STATUS = OLD, ACCESS = SEQUENTIAL)
```

which requests the operating system to construct a file descriptor for the file named `EmplFile`. The parameters indicate that the file is referred to later in the program as unit number 10 (`UNIT = 10`), the name of the file is `EmplFile` (`File = 'EmplFile'`), the operating system should find this file already in mass storage (`STATUS = OLD`), and the structure of the file is sequential (`ACCESS = SEQUENTIAL`).

In Turbo Pascal (a popular dialect of Pascal provided by Borland International), file descriptors can be created by means of the predefined procedures called `assign` and `reset`. For example, the statements

```
assign(DocFile, 'document.txt');
reset(DocFile);
```

cause the operating system to construct a file descriptor for the file named `document.txt` and tell the translator that this file is referred to throughout the program by the name `DocFile`.

In C the equivalent process would be requested by the statement

```
DocFile = fopen("document.txt", "r");
```

where the `r` stands for *read,* meaning that the file is to be read from rather than written to.

Note that our examples have shown that a file can be referenced later in a program by an identifier other than the file's proper name; future references to the file `EmplFile` in our FORTRAN example are in terms of the unit number 10, whereas in our Pascal and C examples the `document.txt` file is referred to as `DocFile`. This distinction between a file's external name and the term used to reference it within a program reflects the distinction between the syntax rules of operating systems and programming languages. A name used to identify a file in the context of an operating system may not be a syntactically valid identifier in the programming language being used. Thus a means of name conversion is required. Once established, this distinction between internal and external file identification also provides flexibility because a procedure designed to manipulate a file by means of an internal identifier can be used as a generic routine to process different files. All one must do is open the desired file using the proper internal identifier and then apply the procedure.

In an object-oriented programming language, files are treated as objects. Thus opening a file is done in the context of establishing the object that will play the role of the file. In C++ the file named `document.txt` can be opened by the statement

```
fstream DocFile("document.txt", ios::out);
```

which creates an object called `DocFile` having the characteristics of an `fstream` (a predefined class for manipulating text files). More precisely, this statement not only opens the file but also bundles the file with the routines (found in `fstream`), creating an object known as `DocFile` with the ability to respond to messages. (The notation `ios::out` sends the new object the message that the file is to be used as an output file.) Later in the program, data can be written to the file by sending the appropriate message to the object `DocFile`. For example,

```
DocFile.put('K');
```

tells the object `DocFile` to put the character `K` in its file.

Having been directed to construct a file descriptor, the operating system must also be told when it is no longer needed. After a file has been processed, many programming languages require the use of a routine named `close`. Basically this routine informs the operating system that the memory space used for the file descriptor can be used for something else; however, in some settings, the statement initiates more than this simple release of memory space. For instance, in the case of a text file that has been created by the program, the close routine causes the operating system to transfer the last physical record to mass storage. In any case, the syntax of the close statement is rarely anything more than a simple instruction, such as

```
CLOSE (UNIT = 10)
```

which, in FORTRAN, means the file identified as file number 10 can no longer be used in the program (or if it is used again, it must be reopened); the equivalent statement in Pascal is

```
close(DocFile);
```

and in C it is

```
fclose(DocFile);
```

Closing a file in an object-oriented environment is done by sending the appropriate object a message instructing the object to close its file. For example, in C++ the statement

```
DocFile.close();
```

sends the object called `DocFile` the message to close its file.

Questions/Exercises

1. Identify the sequence of events followed by an operating system when retrieving a record from a partially indexed file.
2. What might be added to your answer to Exercise 1 if the operating system is also controlling a time-sharing system?
3. Could a file that was originally built as a sequential file be opened as an indexed file?

CHAPTER REVIEW PROBLEMS

1. Suppose a sequential file contains 50,000 records and 5 milliseconds (a millisecond is equal to one-thousandth of a second) is required to interrogate an entry. If records are retrieved in random order, what will be the average retrieval time per record?
2. If the merge algorithm in Fig. 8.3 is to be applied to two sequential files, does it matter which file plays the role of the master file and which plays the role of the transaction file?
3. List the steps that are executed in the merge algorithm in Fig. 8.3 if the transaction file is empty at the start.
4. Modify the algorithm in Fig. 8.3 to handle the case in which a transaction record has a key field value equal to a record already in the old master file. In this case, the transaction record should appear in the new master file and the old master record should be omitted.
5. Explain how a single file can be implemented on a disk so that it can be processed as a sequential file with either of two different sequential orderings.
6. Why is a company-assigned employer identification number a better choice for a key field than the last name of each employee?
7. In what sense is the advantage of an index lost if, to keep the index small, the segments used for a partial-index system are made extremely large?
8. The following table represents the contents of a partial index. Indicate which segment should be retrieved when searching for the record with each of the following key field values:

   a. 24X17 b. 12N67
   c. 32E75 d. 26X28

Key field	*Segment number*
13C08	1
23G19	2
26X28	3
36Z05	4

9. Based on the index in Problem 8, what is the largest key field value in the file? What do you know about the smallest?
10. Give an advantage and a disadvantage of using a partial index rather than an index that contains all the key fields in a file.
11. What is the difference between a sequential file and an indexed sequential file?
12. What problems arise if all the indexes for an inverted file are partial indexes?
13. The chapter drew parallels between a traditional file index and the file directory system maintained by an operating system. In what ways does an operating system's file directory differ from a traditional index?
14. What file structure do you recommend for a file containing descriptions of a library's holdings, assuming that books must be referenced by author's name, book title, and subject? Support your recommendation.
15. If the only way to extract information from a hashed file is by actually hashing the key of each record, what information is required to obtain a complete listing of all the records?
16. If a hashed file is partitioned into 10 buckets, what is the probability of at least two of three arbitrary records hashing to the same section? (Assume the hash algorithm gives no bucket priority over the others.) How many records must be stored in the file until it is more likely for collisions to occur than not?
17. Solve the previous problem, assuming that the file is partitioned into 100 buckets instead of 10.
18. If we are using the division technique discussed in this chapter as a hash algorithm and the file storage area is divided into 23 buckets, which section should we search to find the record whose key field value, when interpreted as a binary value, reduces to the integer 124?
19. Compare the implementation of a hashed file to that of a homogeneous array. How are the roles of the hash function and the address polynomial similar?
20. Design a hashed file of words that could be used as a spell checker. What would you use as a hash function? Would your choice of a hash function depend on the language from which the words are chosen? Why should such a file not be stored as a sequential file?
21. Estimate the size of the file in the previous problem, assuming that it contains 50,000 words. Would such a file fit in an 8MB main memory? If so, why would it be advantageous to move the whole file to main memory and use it from there?
22. Design an indexed file of words that could be used as a spell checker. Why should such a file not be stored as a sequential file?
23. If the division hash algorithm as presented in the text is being used, why is clustering more likely to occur when the file storage space is divided into 60 sections rather than 61?
24. Why is it advantageous to keep the list of overflow records (from a bucket in a hashed file) sorted according to key field values?
25. If we divided the storage area for a hashed file into 41 buckets that can each hold exactly one record, we expect at least one section to overflow after only eight records are stored. On the other hand, if we combine the same storage area into one section that can hold 41 records, we can always store 41 records before overflow occurs. What keeps us from deciding to implement hashed files using this latter configuration?
26. Suppose a record's key field value is XY. Using the division technique for hashing discussed in the text, convert this value into the section number that should contain the record in a hashed file consisting of 41 buckets. (Assume characters are stored using ASCII, one byte per character, with a zero in the most significant bit of each byte.)
27. Suppose a hashed file is to be constructed containing information about the residents of a local community in the United States. If the key field of this file is to consist of seven-digit telephone numbers, why would it not be a good idea to base the hashing algorithm on the first three digits in the key field?
28. A hashed file using the division hash algorithm discussed in the text is to be constructed with 50, 51, 52, or 53 buckets. Which of these choices is best? Why?
29. Suppose a hashed file was constructed using the division technique discussed in this chapter as the hash algorithm. Moreover, suppose that a record from bucket 3 is found to have a key field value that, when interpreted as a

binary value, reduces to the integer 26. Into how many buckets was the mass storage area for this file divided?

30. Give an advantage that
 a. a sequential file has over an indexed file.
 b. a sequential file has over a hashed file.
 c. an indexed file has over a sequential file.
 d. an indexed file has over a hashed file.
 e. a hashed file has over a sequential file.
 f. a hashed file has over an indexed file.

31. In each of the following cases, indicate which file structure (sequential, text, indexed, or hashed) you recommend. Support your recommendations.
 a. A rough draft of a speech
 b. A file of a dentist's patient records
 c. A mailing list
 d. A reference file of 50,000 words and their definitions

32. What problems can arise when a large number of new records having similar key field values is inserted into an indexed file?

33. In what way is a sequential file similar to a linked list?

34. Identify two techniques that might be used for identifying the end of a text file.

35. Explain how a sequential file of employee records can be implemented using a programming language's primitives for manipulating text files?

36. Define each of the following:
 a. Text file
 b. Indexed file
 c. Hashed file

37. Why would a programmer need to write a program using an internal identifier to refer to a file rather than the file's actual external name?

38. Identify three items of information that might be found in a file descriptor.

39. What is the purpose of opening a file? What is the purpose of closing a file?

40. How does the implementation of a sequential file differ if it is stored on tape rather than disk?

41. Suppose a sequential file contains 2000 records. If, over an extended period, various records are retrieved from the file, what do you expect to be the average number of records interrogated per retrieval? Explain your answer.

42. Estimate the amount of space required to store a term paper consisting of 40 double-spaced typed pages represented as a text file.

QUESTIONS OF ETHICS

The following questions are provided to help you understand some of the ethical/social/legal issues associated with the field of computing as well as investigate your own beliefs and their foundations. The goal is not merely to answer these questions. You should also consider why you answered as you did and whether your justifications are consistent from one question to the next.

1. To what extent should organizations be allowed to combine files to obtain information that would not otherwise be available? For example, should income tax records be combined with welfare records? Should medical records be combined with insurance records?

2. Due to a heavy workload, a social worker copies some of the files regarding current cases onto floppy disks and takes them home so that he can work on those cases in the evenings. Is this acceptable behavior? Would your answer change if the materials taken home were printed records rather than magnetic records?

3. As a joke, suppose a programmer added an additional field to each record of a personnel file and programmed the associated software to place facetious comments in this field. If only the programmer knows how to access this additional information, is any harm done?

4. When a file is deleted from a disk, it is usually not erased but merely marked as deleted. The information contained in such a file may remain on the disk for some time before that portion of the disk is finally reused for another file. Is it ethical to reconstruct deleted files from disks that were previously used by others?

ADDITIONAL ACTIVITIES

1. Using a programming language you know, implement a sequential file of employee records.
2. What primitives are provided in your programming language for implementing an indexed file? Use these primitives to implement an indexed file consisting of employee records.
3. What primitives are provided in your programming language for implementing a hashed file? Use these primitives to implement a hashed file consisting of employee records.
4. Convert the merge algorithm shown in Fig. 8.3 into a program using a programming language that you know.

ADDITIONAL READING

Bradley, J. *File and Data Base Techniques.* New York: Holt, Rinehart and Winston, 1982.

Folk, M. J., and B. Zoellick. *File Structures: A Conceptual Toolkit,* 2nd ed. Reading, Mass.: Addison-Wesley, 1992.

Hanson, O. *Design of Computer Data Files.* Rockville, MD.: Computer Science Press, 1982.

Miller, N. E., and Charles G. Petersen. *File Structures with Ada.* Redwood City, Calif.: Benjamin / Cummings, 1990.

Miller, N. E. *File Structures Using Pascal.* Redwood City, Calif.: Benjamin / Cummings, 1987.

Smith, P. D., and G. M. Barnes. *Files and Databases.* Reading, Mass.: Addison-Wesley, 1987.

CHAPTER NINE

Database Structures

9.1 **General Issues**

9.2 **The Layered Approach to Database Implementation**

9.3 **The Relational Model**
- Relational Design
- Relational Operations
- SQL

*9.4 **Object-Oriented Databases**

*9.5 **Maintaining Database Integrity**
- The Commit/Rollback Protocol
- Locking

This final chapter about data organization represents a combination of data structures and file structures discussed previously. Indeed, a database is formed by combining techniques from both of these areas to obtain a single mass storage data system that can appear to have a multitude of organizations for serving a variety of applications. Such structures eliminate the duplication (providing separate data systems for each application even though these applications may require much of the same information) found in the file-oriented approach.

*Sections marked by an asterisk are optional in that they provide additional depth of coverage that is not required for an understanding of future chapters.

9.1 General Issues

The term **database** has evolved through its use in the popular press, in the business world, and among computer scientists. It is not surprising therefore to find varying definitions of the term, depending on whom you ask. Loosely speaking, any collection of data can be considered a database, although the term is usually reserved to mean a collection of data stored in mass storage that can take on a variety of appearances depending on the requirements at the time and can thus serve as the data source for a variety of applications.

We have already seen an elementary example of this phenomenon in our discussion of employee records in Chapter 8. There we envisioned times, such as during payroll processing, when we would want the data to appear as a sequential file, while on other occasions, as in general employee information retrieval, a direct access configuration would be more convenient. We discovered that an indexed system can provide this dual appearance, and some argue that such indexed files are simple databases. Others, citing the diversity achievable through large modern databases, say that this example is merely an amoeba in the evolution of databases. After all, databases in use today contain information encompassing the full spectrum of business activities and can provide access to selected portions of those data in a large number of formats.

To grasp a fuller meaning of the term *database,* we might look at the concept from the opposite direction. That is, we have just introduced a database as a data collection injected with the ability to emulate a variety of organizational forms depending on the needs of the application. From the other point of view, one often considers a database as the result of combining a variety of data collections (each of which was originally designed for a particular application) into a single integrated collection.

This consolidation approach to the database concept reflects the historical development of automated data storage and maintenance. As computing machinery found wider and wider uses in information management, each application tended to be implemented as a separate system with its own collection of data. Typically, the need to process payroll gave rise to a sequential file, and later the need for interactive data retrieval produced an entirely different system using a direct access file.

Although each of these systems represented an improvement over the corresponding manual techniques previously used, taken as a whole the collection of individual automated systems still constituted a limited and inefficient use of resources when compared to the possibilities of a combined database system. For example, different departments were not able to share the data they all needed, so much of the information required by an organization was duplicated in storage. The result was that when an employee moved, visits were required to numerous departments throughout the organization where address change cards were filed. Typographical errors, misplaced cards, and employee apathy could soon result in erroneous and conflicting data within the various data systems. After a move, an employee's newsletter might begin to arrive at the new address but with the wrong name, while the payroll records could continue to reflect the old address. In this setting, database systems emerged as a means of consolidating the information stored and maintained by a particular organization (Fig. 9.1). With such a system, both payroll and the mailing of newsletters could be processed from a single integrated data system.

Another advantage of a consolidated data system is the control achieved by an organization when the information it owns is placed in one common pot. As long as each department has complete control over its own data, those data tend to be used for the good of the department rather than for the good of the organization. In contrast, when a central database is implemented in a large organization, the control of information is normally concentrated in the administrative position known as the **database administrator (DBA),** which may or may not be held by a single individual. This central administrator (or administrative position) is cognizant of both the data available within the organization and the needs of the various departments. It is thus within this structure that decisions regarding data organization and access can be made with the entire organization in mind.

Figure 9.1 A file versus a database organization

File-oriented information system:

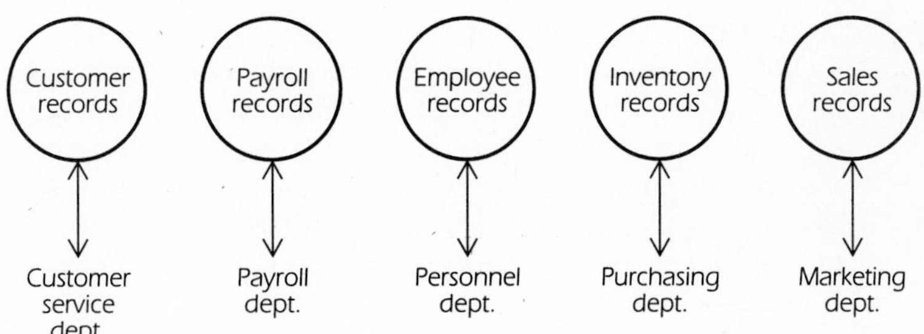

Database-oriented information system:

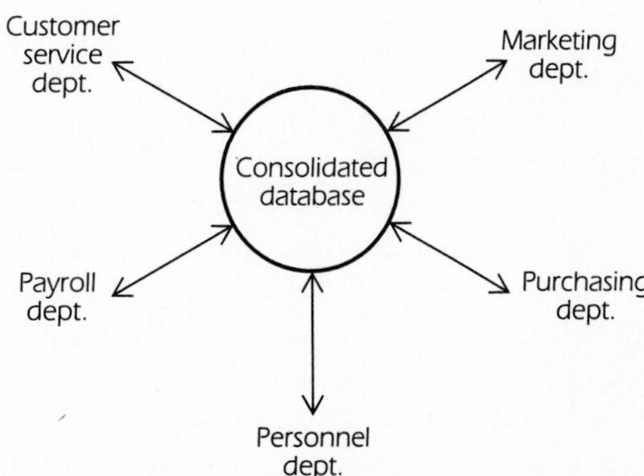

Along with the benefits of data consolidation come disadvantages. One significant concern is the control of access to sensitive data. For example, someone working on the organization's newsletter might need access to employee names and addresses but should not have access to payroll data; similarly, an employee processing payroll should not have access to the other financial records of the corporation. Thus the ability to control access to the information in the database is often as important as the ability to share it.

To provide for this distinction of access privileges, database systems often rely on schemas and subschemas. A **schema** is a description of the entire database structure that is used by the database software to maintain the database. A **subschema** is a description of only that portion of the database pertinent to a particular user's needs. For example, consider a schema for a university database that indicates that each student record contains such items as the current address and phone number of that student in addition to that student's academic record. Moreover, it indicates that each student record is linked to the record of that student's faculty adviser. In turn, the record for each faculty member contains that person's address, employment history, and so on. Based on this schema, a pointer system is maintained that ultimately links the information about a student to the employment history of a faculty member.

To keep the university's registrar from using this linkage to obtain privileged information about the faculty, the registrar's access to the database must be restricted to a subschema whose description of the faculty records does not include employment history. Under this subschema a user can find out which faculty member is a particular student's adviser but cannot obtain access to additional information about that faculty member. In contrast, the subschema for the payroll department provides the employment history of each faculty member but does not include the linkage between students and advisers. Thus the payroll department can modify a faculty member's salary but cannot find the students advised by that person.

There are other disadvantages connected to the evolution of database technology in addition to those directly associated with security. The size and scope of databases have increased rapidly. Today, extremely large collections of data can be assembled and interrogated with little effort over wide geographic areas, and with this increase in magnitude comes an increase in misinformation and misapplications of information. Incidents abound of injustices due to inaccurate credit reports, faulty criminal records, and discrimination resulting from unauthorized or unethical access to personal information.

In other cases, the underlying problem deals with the right to collect and hold information in the first place. What kind of information does an insurance company have a right to collect regarding its clients? Does a government have the right to maintain accounts of an individual citizen's voting record? Does a credit card company have the right to sell records of its customers' purchasing patterns to marketing firms? These questions represent some of the issues with which society must deal as a result of the influx of database technology.

Questions/Exercises

1. Identify two departments in a manufacturing plant that would have different uses for the same or similar inventory information.
2. Identify a variety of data collections found in a university environment that might be collected into one common database.
3. Describe how the subschema for the two departments in Question 1 might differ.

9.2 The Layered Approach to Database Implementation

A person using a database is called the user, or at times the end user. You may imagine this person being an airline reservation clerk who interrogates the database from a terminal at an airport counter or perhaps an executive who retrieves information from the database at a workstation in an office. In either case the user is most likely not trained in computer science and should not be required to consider the details of computer technology and techniques. Instead, the user should be allowed to concentrate on the problems of the application at hand. It is therefore the duty of the overall database system to present its information in terms of the application and not in computer gibberish.

To accomplish this goal in an organized manner, a database system is constructed from layers of abstraction (Fig. 9.2). The image of the data given to the end user is produced by the application software that communicates with the user in an interactive manner and in the application's terminology. In a large company this software might be written by the programming staff within the business, but in the personal computing environment it is often developed by the end users themselves, using fourth-generation programming languages. It is in the design of this software that the overall system is given its personality. It may, for example, communicate with the user through such means as a question-and-answer dialogue or a fill-in-the-blanks scenario. Regardless of the user interface ultimately adopted, the application software communicates with the user to learn what information is required and later, having obtained the requested information, presents it to the user in a meaningful format.

Figure 9.2 The conceptual layers of a database

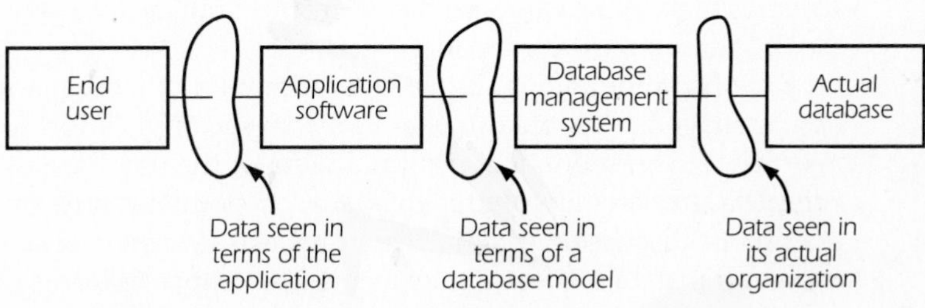

Note that we did not say that the application software retrieves the information from the database. The actual manipulation of the database is accomplished by another software package called the **database management system (DBMS).** This dichotomy has several benefits. One is that the division of duties simplifies the design process. Just as the end user's task would be complicated by the requirement to consider computer concepts along with the task of solving a problem in the application world, the application programmer's task would be more complex if the actual data manipulation were a part of the application software. This is particularly true in the context of a **distributed database** (a database spread over several machines in a network). Without the services of a database management system the application program must contain routines for keeping up with the actual location of the various portions of the database. With a well-designed database management system the application software can be written as though the database were stored on a single machine.

A second advantage of separating the application software from the database management system is that such an organization provides a means for controlling access to the database. By dictating that all access to the database be performed by a central database management system, that system is placed in a position to enforce the restrictions imposed by the various subschemas. In particular, the database management system can use the entire database schema for its internal needs but require that each user remain within the bounds described by that user's subschema.

Still another reason for separating the user interface and actual data manipulation into two different software packages is to achieve **data independence.** This refers to the ability to change the organization of the database itself without changing the application software. For example, the personnel department might need to add an additional field to each employee's record to indicate whether the corresponding employee chose to participate in the company's new health insurance program. If the application software dealt directly with the database, such a change in the data's format would require modifications to all application programs dealing with the same database. As a result, the change instigated by the personnel department would cause changes to the payroll program as well as to the program for printing mailing labels for the company's newsletter.

The distinction between application software and the database management system removes the need for such reprogramming. To implement a change required by a single user, one needs to change only the schema used by the central system and the subschemas of those users involved in the change. All other subschemas remain the same, so the corresponding application software executes as though no changes were made.

One final advantage of the separation of application software and the database management system is that it allows the application software to be written in terms of a simplified, conceptual view of the database rather than the actual, complex structure involving disk tracks, pointers, and overflow areas. Recall that in our discussion of data structures, we saw that software routines could be used to translate requests (such as push and pop) in terms of a conceptual structure (a stack) into the proper activities in the actual storage organization. In a similar manner a database management system contains routines that can be used as abstract tools in the application software to convert commands in terms of a conceptual view of the database, called the **database model,** into terms of the actual database storage.

More precisely, application software is often written in general-purpose programming languages, such as those discussed in Chapter 5. These languages provide the basic ingredients for algorithm expression but lack the operations that make manipulation of the database convenient. The routines provided by the database management system in effect extend the capabilities of the language being used (as we will see in the following sections) in a manner that supports the conceptual image of the database model. This concept of the general-purpose language being the original system to which the capabilities of the database management system are added results in the original language being referred to as the **host language.** (Many commercial database management system packages today are actually combinations of the traditional database system and a host language. This tends to disguise the two as one, although the distinction still exists within.)

To develop application software for a database installation, a programmer must understand the abstract tools provided by the database management system being used. This is the subject of the next section where we look through the eyes of the application programmer at the relational database model. This is the model provided by most of today's database management systems. It allows the application software to be written as though the data in the database were stored in tables with rows and columns.

The search for better database models is an ongoing process. The goal is to find models that allow complex data systems to be conceptualized easily, lead to concise ways of expressing requests for information, and can be implemented efficiently through database management systems to provide abstract tools for use in application programming.

Questions/Exercises

1. Does the use of a common indexed file for both payroll processing and interactive data retrieval provide data independence?
2. In a form similar to Fig. 9.2, draw a diagram representing the machine language, high-level language, and end-user views of a computer.
3. Summarize the roles of the application software, the database management system, and the actual data-manipulating routines in retrieving information from a database.

9.3 The Relational Model

In this section we introduce the relational database model, which is the most popular model today. Its popularity stems from the simplicity of its structure. It portrays data as being stored in tables called **relations.** As an example, the

EmplId	Name	Address	SSNum
25X15	Joe E. Baker	33 Nowhere St.	111223333
34Y70	Cheryl H. Clark	563 Downtown Ave.	999009999
23Y34	G. Jerry Smith	1555 Circle Dr.	111005555
.	.	.	.
.	.	.	.
.	.	.	.

Figure 9.3 A relation containing employee information

relational model allows information regarding the employees of a firm to be represented by a relation such as that in Fig. 9.3.

A row in a relation is called a **tuple.** In the relation of Fig. 9.3 tuples consist of the information about a particular employee. Columns in a relation are referred to as **attributes** because each entry in a column describes some characteristic, or attribute, of the entity represented by the corresponding tuple.

Relational Design

The design of a database in terms of the relational model centers on the design of the relations making up the database. Although this may appear to be a simple task, many subtleties are waiting to trap the unwary designer.

Suppose that, in addition to the information contained in the relation of Fig. 9.3, we want to include information about the jobs held by the employees. Associated with each employee, we may want to include a job history, consisting of such attributes as job title (secretary, office manager, floor supervisor), a job identification code (unique to each job), the skill code associated with each job, the department in which the job exists, and the period during which the employee held the job in terms of a starting date and termination date. (We use an asterisk as the termination date if the job represents the employee's current position.)

One approach to this problem is to extend the relation in Fig. 9.3 to include these attributes as additional columns in the table, as shown in Fig. 9.4. However, close examination of the result reveals several problems. One is a lack of efficiency. Indeed, the relation no longer contains one tuple for each employee but rather one tuple for each assignment of an employee to a job. If an employee has advanced in the company through a sequence of several jobs, several tuples in the new relation are dedicated to that single employee. The problem is that the information contained in the original relation (each employee's name, address, identification number, and Social Security number) must be repeated. Moreover, if a particular job has been held by numerous employees, the department associated with that job along with the appropriate skill code must be identified in each tuple representing an assignment of the job. Of course, this duplication of data need not be present in the actual storage system because it can be simulated from a single source by the database management system. But if the need for this repetition is avoided in the first place, the overall database system is more efficient.

EmplId	Name	Address	SSN	JobId	JobTitle	SkillCode	Dept	StartDate	TermDate
25X15	Joe E. Baker	33 Nowhere St.	111223333	F5	Floor manager	FM3	Sales	9-1-95	9-30-96
25X15	Joe E. Baker	33 Nowhere St.	111223333	D7	Dept. head	D2	Sales	10-1-96	*
34Y70	Cheryl H. Clark	563 Downtown Ave.	999009999	F5	Floor manager	FM3	Sales	10-1-95	*
23Y34	G. Jerry Smith	1555 Circle Dr.	111005555	S25X	Secretary	T5	Personnel	3-1-93	4-30-95
23Y34	G. Jerry Smith	1555 Circle Dr.	111005555	S25Z	Secretary	T6	Accounting	5-1-95	*
⋮	⋮	⋮	⋮	⋮	⋮	⋮	⋮	⋮	⋮

Figure 9.4 A relation containing redundancy
(*Note:* The personal information about Baker and Smith is repeated because they have held more than one job. Also duplicated is the description of the floor manager job because it has been held by more than one person.)

Another, perhaps more serious problem with our extended relation surfaces when we consider deleting information from the database. Suppose, for example, that Joe E. Baker is the only employee to hold the job identified as D7. If he were to leave the company and be deleted from the database represented in Fig. 9.4, we would lose the information about job D7. Indeed, the only tuple containing the fact that job D7 requires a skill level of D2 is the tuple relating to Joe Baker. If we were then to delete all references to Joe Baker and return to the database to retrieve information about the job D7, we would not find the needed data.

You might argue that the ability to erase only a portion of a tuple could solve the problem, but this would in turn introduce other complications. (Should the information relating to job F5 also be retained in a partial tuple, or does this information reside elsewhere in the relation?) Moreover, the temptation to use partial tuples is a strong indication that the design of the relation is not compatible with the application.

The source of these problems is that we have combined more than one concept into a single relation. As it is proposed, the extended relation contains information dealing directly with employees (name, identification number, address, Social Security number), information about the jobs available in the company (job identification, job title, department, skill code), and information regarding the relationship between employees and jobs (start date, termination date). Having made this observation, we find that our problems can be solved by redesigning the system using three relations—one for each of the preceding topics. Using our new system, we can keep the original relation (which we now call the EMPLOYEE relation) as it is and insert the additional information in the form of the two new relations called JOB and ASSIGNMENT, which produces the database in Fig. 9.5.

EMPLOYEE relation

EmplId	Name	Address	SSNum
25X15	Joe E. Baker	33 Nowhere St.	111223333
34Y70	Cheryl H. Clark	563 Downtown Ave.	999009999
23Y34	G. Jerry Smith	1555 Circle Dr.	111005555
.	.	.	.
.	.	.	.
.	.	.	.

JOB relation

JobId	Job Title	SkillCode	Dept
S25X	Secretary	T5	Personnel
S26Z	Secretary	T6	Accounting
F5	Floor manager	FM3	Sales
.	.	.	.
.	.	.	.
.	.	.	.

ASSIGNMENT relation

EmplId	JobId	StartDate	TermDate
23Y34	S25X	3-1-93	4-30-95
34Y70	F5	10-1-95	*
23Y34	S25Z	5-1-95	*
.	.	.	.
.	.	.	.
.	.	.	.

Figure 9.5 An employee database consisting of three relations

A database consisting of these three relations contains the pertinent information about employees through the EMPLOYEE relation, about available jobs through the JOB relation, and about job history through the ASSIGNMENT relation. Additional information is implicitly available by combining the information from different relations. For instance, we can find the departments in which a given employee has worked by first finding all the jobs that employee has held using the ASSIGNMENT relation and then finding the departments associated with those jobs by means of the JOB relation. Through processes such as this any information that could be obtained from the single large relation can be obtained from the three smaller relations without the problems previously cited.

Unfortunately, dividing information into various relations is not always as trouble-free as in the preceding example. For instance, compare the relation in Fig. 9.6, having attributes EmplId, JobTitle, and Dept, to its decomposition into two relations in Fig. 9.7.

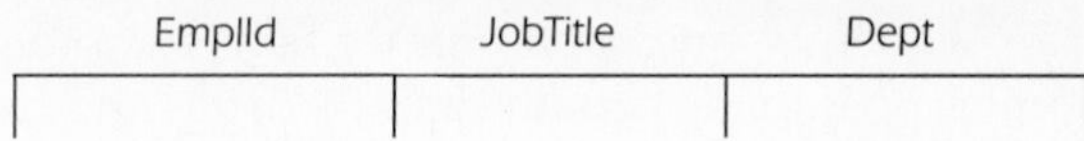

Figure 9.6 A three-attribute relation of employees, jobs, and departments

At first glance, the two-relation system may appear to contain the same information as the single-relation system, but in fact it does not. Consider, for example, the problem of finding the department in which a given employee works. This is easily done in the single-relation system by interrogating the tuple containing the employee identification number of the target employee and extracting the corresponding department. However, in the two-relation system, the desired information is not necessarily available. We can find the job title of the target employee and a department having such a job but this does not necessarily mean that the target employee works in that particular department, because several departments may have jobs with the same title.

In some cases a relation can be decomposed into smaller relations without losing information (called a **nonloss decomposition**), and at other times information is lost. The classification of such characteristics has been, and still is, a concern in computer science. Such questions concerning the properties of relations have resulted in a hierarchy of relation classes called first normal form, second normal form, third normal form, and so on, with the relations in each class being more conducive to use in a database than those in the preceding class.

Relational Operations

Now that you have a basic understanding of the structure involved in the relational model, it is time to see how such an organization can be used from a programmer's point of view. We begin with a look at some operations that we may want to perform on relations.

At times we need to select certain tuples from a relation. To retrieve the information about an employee, we must select the tuple with the appropriate identification attribute value from the EMPLOYEE relation, or to obtain a list of the job titles in a certain department, we must select the tuples from the JOB relation having that department as their department attribute. The result of this selection is another relation (another table) consisting of the tuples selected from the parent relation. The outcome of selecting information about a particular employee results in a relation containing only one tuple from the EMPLOYEE relation. The outcome of selecting the tuples associated with a certain department probably results in several tuples from the JOB relation.

Figure 9.7 Two relations containing information about employees, jobs, and departments

EmplId JobTitle JobTitle Dept

Consequently, one operation we may want to perform on a relation is to select tuples possessing certain characteristics and to place these selected tuples in a new relation. To express this operation, we adopt the syntax

```
NEW ← SELECT from EMPLOYEE where EmplId = "34Y70"
```

The semantics of this statement is to create a new relation called NEW containing those tuples (there should be only one in this case) from the relation EMPLOYEE whose EmplId attribute equals 34Y70 (see Fig. 9.8).

In contrast to the SELECT operation, which extracts rows from a relation, the PROJECT operation extracts columns. Suppose, for example, that in searching for the job titles in a certain department, we had already SELECTed the tuples from the JOB relation that pertained to the target department and placed these tuples in a new relation called NEW1. The list we are seeking is the JobTitle column within this new relation. The PROJECT operation allows us to extract this column (or columns if required) and place the result in a new relation. We express such an operation as

```
NEW2 ← PROJECT JobTitle from NEW1
```

The result is the creation of another new relation (called NEW2) that contains the single column of values from the JobTitle column of relation NEW1.

As another example of the PROJECT operation, the statement

```
MAIL ← PROJECT Name, Address from EMPLOYEE
```

can be used to obtain a listing of the names and addresses of all employees. This list is in the newly created (two-column) relation called MAIL (see Fig. 9.9).

Figure 9.8 The SELECT operation

EMPLOYEE relation

EmplId	Name	Address	SSN
25X15	Joe E. Baker	33 Nowhere St.	111223333
34Y70	Cheryl H. Clark	563 Downtown Ave.	999009999
23Y34	G. Jerry Smith	1555 Circle Dr.	111005555
.	.	.	.
.	.	.	.
.	.	.	.

↓

NEW ← SELECT from EMPLOYEE where EmplId = "34Y70"

↓

NEW relation

EmplId	Name	Address	SSN
34Y70	Cheryl H. Clark	563 Downtown Ave.	999009999

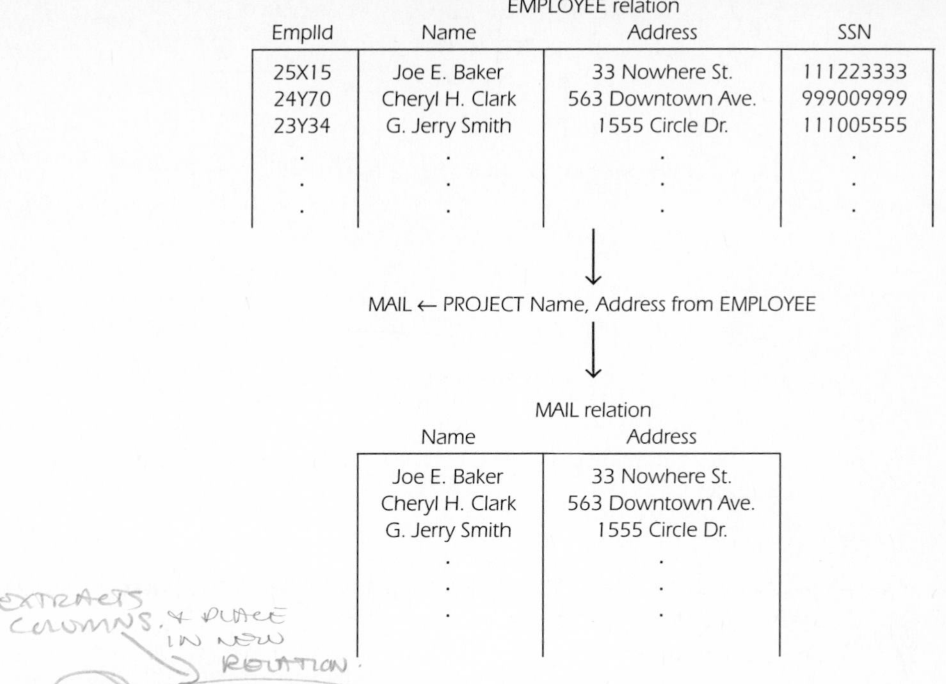

Figure 9.9 The PROJECT operation

The third operation we introduce is the JOIN operation. It is used to combine different relations into one. The JOIN of two relations produces a new relation whose attributes consist of the attributes from the original relations (see Fig. 9.10). The names of these attributes are the same as those in the original relations except that each is prefixed by the relation of its origin. (If relation A containing attributes V and W is JOINed with relation B containing attributes X, Y, and Z, then the result has five attributes named A.V, A.W, B.X, B.Y, and B.Z.) This naming convention ensures that the attributes in the new relation have unique names, even though the original relations may have attribute names in common.

The tuples (rows) of the new relation are produced by concatenating tuples from the two original relations (Fig. 9.10). Which tuples are actually joined to form tuples in the new relation is determined by the condition under which the JOIN is constructed. One such condition is that designated attributes have the same value. This, in fact, is the case represented in Fig. 9.10, where we demonstrate the result of executing the statement

```
C ← JOIN A and B where A.W = B.X
```

In this example a tuple from relation A should be concatenated with a tuple from relation B if and only if the attributes W and X in the two tuples are equal. Thus the concatenation of the tuple (r, 2) from relation A with the tuple (2, m, q) from relation B appears in the result because the value of attribute W in the first equals

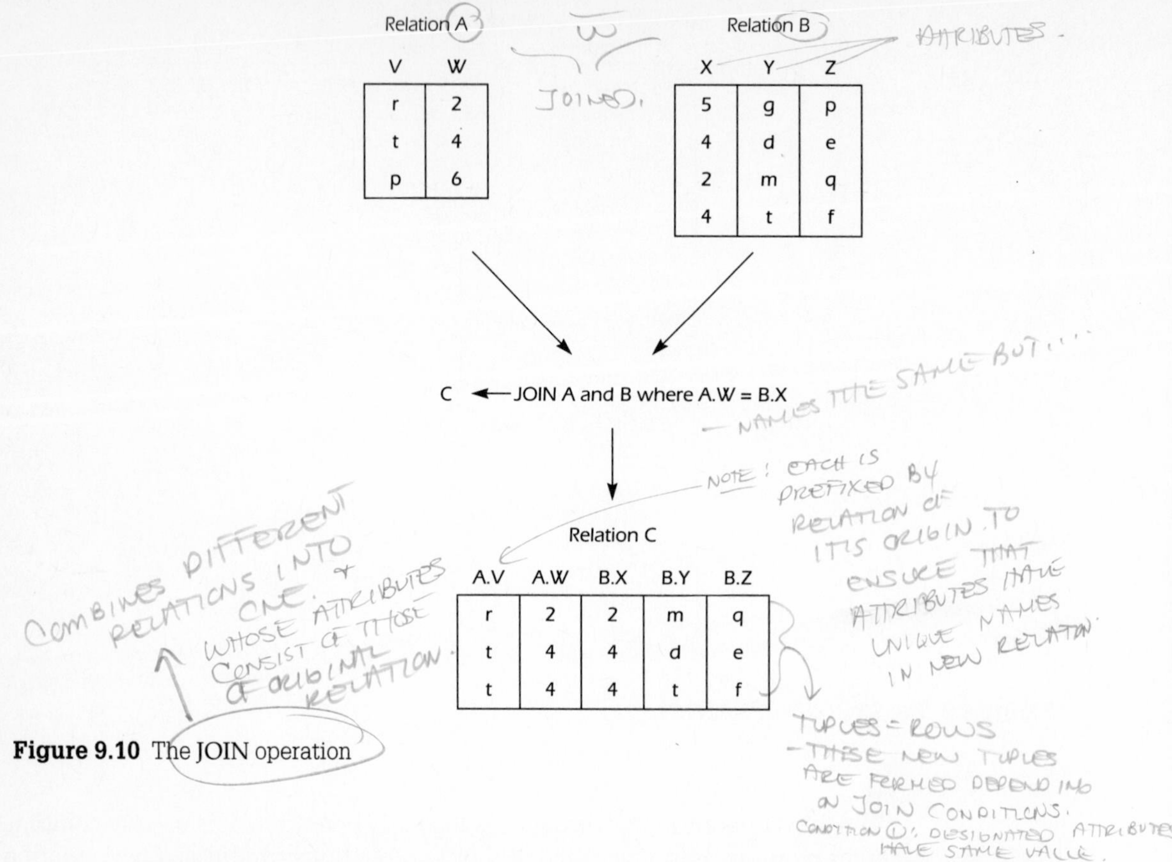

Figure 9.10 The JOIN operation

the value of attribute X in the second. On the other hand, the result of concatenating the tuple (r, 2) from relation A with the tuple (5, g, p) from relation B does not appear in the final relation because these tuples do not share common values in attributes W and X.

As another example, Fig. 9.11 represents the result of executing the statement

```
C ← JOIN A and B where A.W < B.X
```

Note that the tuples in the result are exactly those in which attribute W in relation A is less than attribute X in relation B.

Let us now see how the JOIN operation can be used in the database of Fig. 9.5 to obtain a listing of all employee identification numbers along with the department in which each employee works. Our first observation is that the data required are distributed over more than one relation, and thus the process of retrieving the information must entail more than SELECTions and PROJECTions. In fact, the weapon we need is the statement

```
NEW1 ← JOIN ASSIGNMENT and JOB where ASSIGNMENT.JobId = JOB.JobId
```

that produces the relation NEW1, as shown in Fig. 9.12. From this relation, our problem can be solved by first SELECTing those tuples in which ASSIGNMENT.Term-

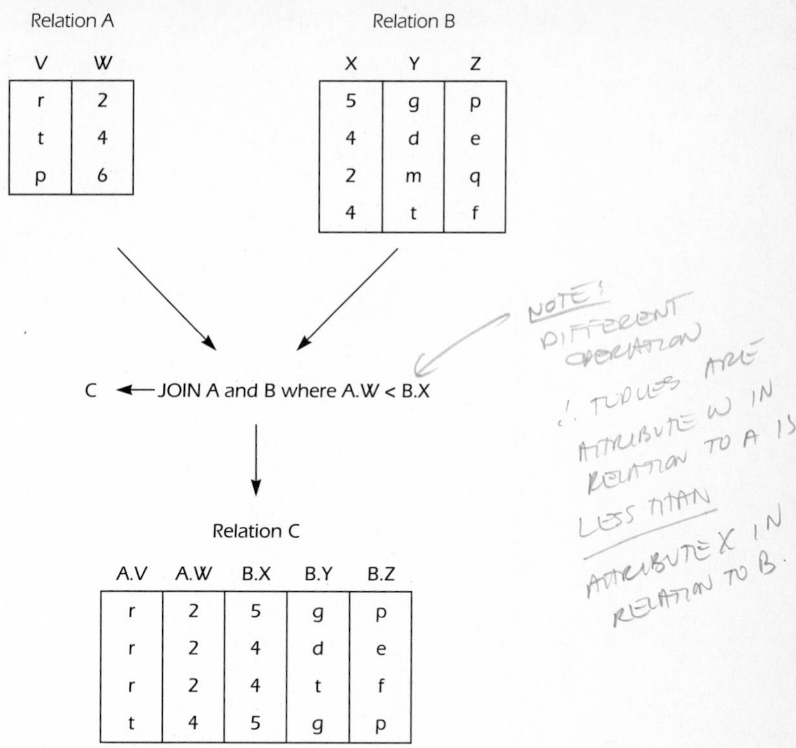

Figure 9.11 Another example of the JOIN operation

Date equals "*" and then PROJECTing the attributes ASSIGNMENT.EmplId and JOB.Dept. In short, the information we need can be obtained from the database in Fig. 9.5 by executing the statements

```
NEW1 ← JOIN ASSIGNMENT and JOB
          where ASSIGNMENT.JobId = JOB.JobId
NEW2 ← SELECT from NEW1 where ASSIGNMENT.TermDate = "*"
  LIST ← PROJECT ASSIGNMENT.EmplId, JOB.Dept from NEW2
```

Let us return to the overall picture of a database system to see where the relational model fits. Remember that the data in a database are actually stored in terms of a mass storage system. To relieve the application programmer from these concerns as well as for other reasons, a database management system is provided that allows the application software to be written in terms of a database model, such as the relational system we have been discussing. It is the duty of the database management system to accept commands in terms of the relational model and convert them into actions relative to the actual storage structure. This is done by providing a collection of routines that can be used within the application software. Thus a database management system using the relational model might include routines to perform the SELECT, PROJECT, and

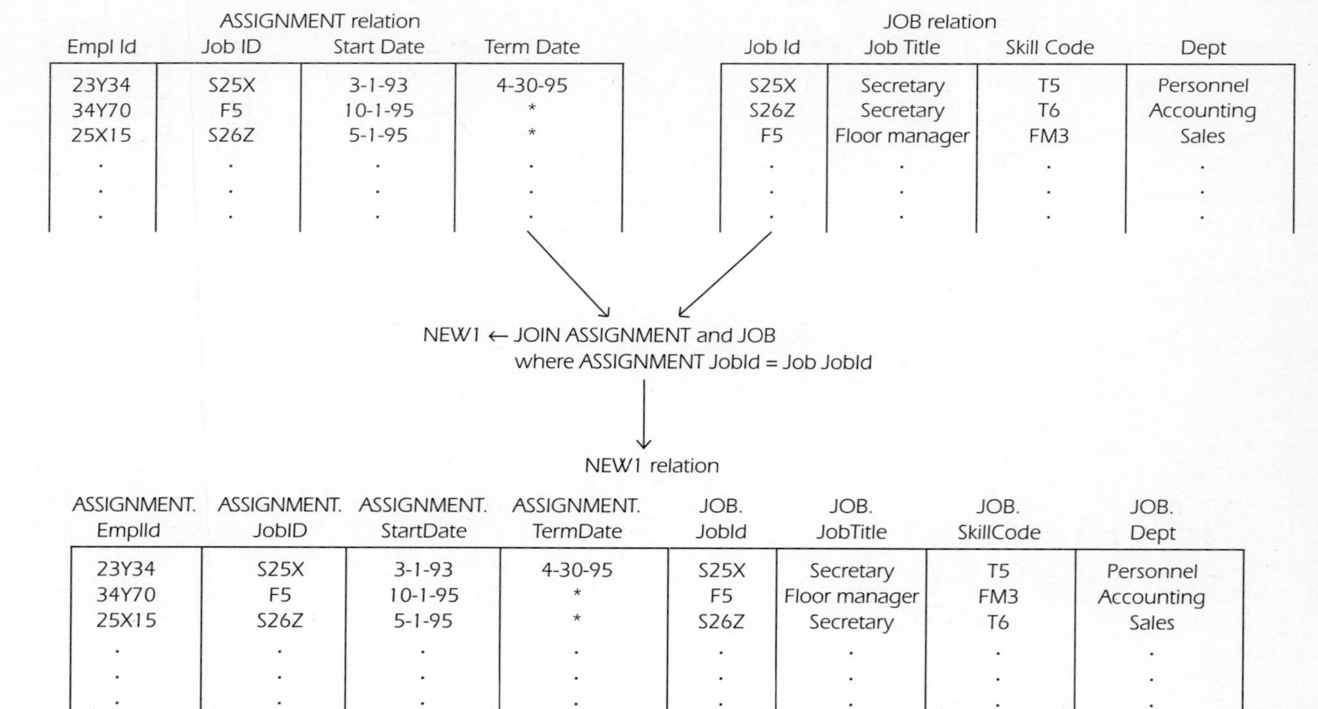

ASSIGNMENT relation

Empl Id	Job ID	Start Date	Term Date
23Y34	S25X	3-1-93	4-30-95
34Y70	F5	10-1-95	*
25X15	S26Z	5-1-95	*
.	.	.	.
.	.	.	.
.	.	.	.

JOB relation

Job Id	Job Title	Skill Code	Dept
S25X	Secretary	T5	Personnel
S26Z	Secretary	T6	Accounting
F5	Floor manager	FM3	Sales
.	.	.	.
.	.	.	.
.	.	.	.

NEW1 relation

ASSIGNMENT. EmplId	ASSIGNMENT. JobID	ASSIGNMENT. StartDate	ASSIGNMENT. TermDate	JOB. JobId	JOB. JobTitle	JOB. SkillCode	JOB. Dept
23Y34	S25X	3-1-93	4-30-95	S25X	Secretary	T5	Personnel
34Y70	F5	10-1-95	*	F5	Floor manager	FM3	Accounting
25X15	S26Z	5-1-95	*	S26Z	Secretary	T6	Sales
.	.	.	.	.	.	.	.
.	.	.	.	.	.	.	.
.	.	.	.	.	.	.	.

Figure 9.12 An application of the JOIN operation

JOIN operations, which could then be called from the application software using a syntactic structure compatible with the host language. In this manner, the application software can be written as though the data were actually stored in the simple tabular form of the relational model.

In reality, today's database management systems do not present the SELECT, PROJECT, and JOIN operations in their raw form. Rather, they provide operations that may be combinations of these basic steps in a form that is more palatable for users. An example is the language SQL.

SQL

The language called SQL (Structured Query Language) is used extensively in the data processing community for manipulating databases that are viewed in terms of the relational model. One reason for its popularity is that it has been standardized by the American National Standards Institute. Another is that it was originally developed and marketed by IBM and has thus benefited from a high level of exposure. In this section we explain how database queries are expressed in SQL.

Our first observation is that a query involving a sequence of SELECT, PROJECT, and JOIN operations can be expressed as a single SQL statement. More important, however, is that SQL statements do not specify a particular sequence of operations. Although a query stated in SQL is expressed in an imperative-sounding form, the reality is that it is essentially a declarative statement. The significance of this is that SQL relieves the database user from the burden of developing a sequence of steps needed to obtain the information desired. He or she needs merely to describe that information. For example, our last query in which we developed a three-step process for obtaining all employee identification numbers along with their corresponding departments could be stated in SQL by the single statement

```
select EmplId, Dept
from ASSIGNMENT, JOB
where ASSIGNMENT.JobId = JOB.JobId
  and ASSIGNMENT.TermDate = '*'
```

As indicated by this example, each SQL query statement can contain three clauses—a `select` clause, a `from` clause, and a `where` clause. Roughly speaking, such a statement is a request for the result of forming the JOIN of all the relations listed in the `from` clause, SELECTing those tuples that satisfy the conditions in the `where` clause, and then PROJECTing those tuples listed in the `select` clause. (Note that the terminology is somewhat reversed, in that the `select` clause in an SQL statement identifies the attributes used in the PROJECT operation.) Let us consider some simple examples.

The statement

```
select Name, Address
from EMPLOYEE
```

produces a listing of all employee names and addresses contained in the relation EMPLOYEE. Note that this is merely a PROJECT operation.

The statement

```
select EmplId, Name, Address, SSNum
from EMPLOYEE
where Name = 'Cheryl H. Clark'
```

produces all the information from the tuple associated with Cheryl H. Clark in the EMPLOYEE relation. This is essentially a SELECT operation.

The statement

```
select Name, Address
from EMPLOYEE
where Name = 'Cheryl H. Clark"
```

produces the name and address of Cheryl H. Clark as contained in the EMPLOYEE relation. This is a combination of SELECT and PROJECT operations.

The statement

```
select EMPLOYEE.Name, ASSIGNMENT.StartDate
from EMPLOYEE, ASSIGNMENT
where EMPLOYEE.EmplId = ASSIGNMENT.EmplId
```

produces a listing of all employee names and their dates of initial employment. Note that this is the result of JOINing the relations EMPLOYEE and ASSIGNMENT and then SELECTing and PROJECTing the appropriate tuples and attributes as identified in the `where` and `select` clauses.

We close by noting that SQL encompasses statements for defining the structure of relations, creating relations, and modifying the contents of relations as well as performing queries. For example, the following are examples of the `insert into`, `delete from`, and `update` statements.

The statement

```
insert into EMPLOYEE
values ('42Z12', 'Lloyd A. Burt', '333 Endless Ave.', '444661111')
```

adds a tuple to the EMPLOYEE relation containing the values given;

```
delete from EMPLOYEE
where Name = 'G. Jerry Smith'
```

removes the tuple relating to G. Jerry Smith from the EMPLOYEE relation; and

```
update EMPLOYEE
set Address = '1812 Napoleon Ave.'
where Name = 'Joe E. Baker'
```

changes the address in the tuple associated with Joe E. Baker in the EMPLOYEE relation.

Questions/Exercises

1. Answer the following questions based on the partial information given in the EMPLOYEE, JOB, and ASSIGNMENT relations in Fig. 9.5:
   a. Who is the secretary in the accounting department with experience in the personnel department?

b. Who is the floor manager in the sales department?
c. What job does G. Jerry Smith currently hold?

2. Based on the EMPLOYEE, JOB, and ASSIGNMENT relations presented in Fig. 9.5 write a sequence of relational operations to obtain a list of all job titles within the personnel department.
3. Based on the EMPLOYEE, JOB, and ASSIGNMENT relations presented in Fig. 9.5, write a sequence of relational operations to obtain a list of employee names along with the employees' departments.
4. Convert your answers to Questions 2 and 3 into SQL.
5. How does the relational model provide for data independence?
6. How are the different relations in a relational database tied together?

9.4 Object-Oriented Databases

One of the newer areas in database research involves applying the object-oriented paradigm to the construction of a database, resulting in an **object-oriented database.** The motivation behind this movement is at least fourfold. First, data independence can be achieved by means of encapsulation. Second, the concepts of classes and inheritance appear ready-made for describing schemas and subschemas of databases. Third, the image of a database consisting of intelligent data objects that can answer questions themselves rather than being interrogated by a supervisory program is inviting. Fourth, early research indicates that the object-oriented approach may overcome some of the restrictions inherent in other database models.[1]

Let us consider an object-oriented implementation of the employee database from the previous section. We have three classes (types of objects): EMPLOYEE, JOB, and ASSIGNMENT. An object from the EMPLOYEE class contains subobjects for such entries as EmplId, Name, Address, and SSNum; an object from the class JOB contains subobjects for the items JobId, JobTitle, SkillCode, and Dept; and each object from the class ASSIGNMENT contains subobjects for StartDate and TermDate. Each of these subobjects consists of a storage structure encapsulated with a collection of methods describing how that subobject responds to messages regarding its contents. In turn, each object from the classes EMPLOYEE, JOB, and ASSIGNMENT contains methods describing how that object responds to requests for information and commands to update data.

For example, each object from the class EMPLOYEE might have a method for reporting that employee's job history and perhaps a method for changing that employee's job assignment. Likewise, each object from the JOB class might have a method for reporting those employees who have held that particular job. Note that these methods accomplish their tasks by sending messages to the appropriate subobjects and other objects in the system. Thus retrieving an employee's job

[1]For example, if a person's entire name is stored as a single attribute in a relational database, then inquiries regarding only last names are awkward. However, if the name is stored as three separate attributes (FirstName, MiddleName, LastName), then it becomes awkward to deal with people who do not have exactly three names. An object, however, can store a person's name in an internal linked list and have the ability to report the entire name as one long string, only the last name, or even as many names as the person has.

history would not require a procedure involving such operators as SELECT or PROJECT. Instead, we would merely ask the appropriate employee object to report its job history.

Proponents of object-oriented database technology argue that the image presented by a database consisting of objects representing employees and jobs more closely represents the user's environment than a database consisting of relations containing tuples and attributes. For example, to add a new employee to an object-oriented database, the user actually adds a new employee object rather than inserting a tuple into a relation.

For the methods within objects to perform their tasks in an efficient manner, some form of linkage between different objects must be maintained. How, for example, does an object from the EMPLOYEE class know which objects from the ASSIGNMENT class represent assignments pertaining to its employee?

One approach toward providing this linkage is to extend the composition of objects beyond that found in traditional object-oriented environments. Traditional objects are composed of data structures and methods. For the purposes of constructing an object-oriented database, this composition can be extended to include a third kind of component, a list of other objects. Objects in such a system therefore consist of data structures, methods, and lists of objects.

If such an approach is applied to our employee database, an object from the class EMPLOYEE can encompass and maintain a list of those objects from the class ASSIGNMENT that relate to the pertinent employee. Methods within the object then can use this list when responding to inquiries about the object's job history. The result is a database consisting of objects that maintain records about the existence of other objects and are therefore able to identify the appropriate objects and communicate with them when responding to requests for information.

Questions/Exercises

1. What methods can be contained in an instance of an object from the ASSIGNMENT class in the employee database discussed in this section?
2. Identify some classes, as well as some of their internal characteristics, that can be used in an object-oriented database dealing with a warehouse inventory.
3. Identify an advantage that an object-oriented database can have over a relational database.

9.5 Maintaining Database Integrity

Inexpensive database management systems for personal use are relatively simple systems. They tend to have a single objective—to shield the user from the technical details of the database implementation. The databases maintained by these systems are relatively small and generally contain information whose loss or corruption would be inconvenient rather than disastrous. When a problem does arise, the user can usually correct the erroneous items directly or reload the database from a backup copy and manually make the modifications required to bring that copy up to date. This process may be inconvenient, but the cost of avoiding the inconvenience tends to be greater than the inconvenience itself. In any case, the inconvenience is restricted to only a few people and any financial loss is generally limited.

In the case of large, multiuser, commercial database systems, however, the stakes are much higher. The cost of incorrect or lost data can be enormous and can have devastating consequences. In these environments a major role of the database management system is to maintain the database's integrity by guarding against problems such as operations that for some reason are only partially completed or different operations that may interact inadvertently to cause inaccurate information in the database. It is this role of a database management system that we address in this section.

The Commit/Rollback Protocol

A single transaction, such as the transfer of funds from one bank account to another, the cancellation of an airline reservation, and the registration of a student in a university course, may involve multiple steps at the database level. For example, a transfer of funds between bank accounts requires that the balance in one account be decremented and the balance in the other be incremented. Between such steps the information in the database may be inconsistent. Indeed, funds are missing during the brief period after the first account has been decremented but before the other has been incremented. Likewise, when reassigning a passenger's seat on a flight there may be an instant when the passenger has no seat or an instant when the passenger list appears to be one passenger greater than it actually is.

In the case of large databases that are subject to heavy transaction loads, it is highly likely that a random snapshot will find the database in the middle of some transaction. A request for the execution of a transaction or an equipment malfunction will therefore likely occur at a time when the database is in an inconsistent state.

Let us first consider the problem of a malfunction. The goal of the database management system is to assure that such a problem will not freeze the database in an inconsistent state. This is often accomplished by maintaining a log containing a record of each transaction's activities in a nonvolatile storage system, such as a disk. Before a transaction is allowed to alter the database the alteration to be performed is first recorded in the log. In fact, some databases use a *deferred update protocol,* in which all of a transaction's proposed alterations must be recorded in the log before any action is taken on the database itself.

The point at which all the steps in a transaction have been recorded in the log is called the **commit point.** It is at this point that the database management system has the information it needs to reconstruct the transaction on its own if that should become necessary. At this point the database management system becomes committed to the transaction in the sense that it accepts the responsibility of guaranteeing that the transaction's activities will be reflected in the database. In the case of an equipment malfunction the database management system can use the information in its log to reconstruct the transactions that have been completed (committed) since the last backup was made.

If problems should arise before a transaction has reached its commit point, the database management system may find itself with a partially executed transaction that cannot be completed. In this case the log can be used to **roll back** (undo) the activities actually performed by the transaction. In the case of a malfunction, for instance, the database management system could recover by rolling back those transactions that were incomplete (noncommitted) at the time of the malfunction.

Rollbacks of transactions are not restricted, however, to the process of recovering from equipment malfunctions. They are often a part of a database management system's normal operation. For example, a transaction may be terminated before it has completed all its steps due to an attempt to access privileged information, or it may be involved in a deadlock in which competing transactions find themselves waiting for data being used by the other. In these cases the database management system can use the log to roll back a transaction and thus avoid an erroneous database due to incomplete transactions.

To emphasize the delicate nature of database management system design, we should note that there are subtle problems lurking within the rollback process. The rolling back of one transaction may affect database entries that have been used by other transactions. For example, the transaction being rolled back may have updated an account balance, and another transaction may have already based its activities on this updated value. This may mean that these additional transactions must also be rolled back, which may adversely affect still other transactions. The result is the problem known as **cascading rollback.**

Locking

We now consider the problem of a transaction being executed while the database is in a state of flux from another transaction, a situation that can lead to inadvertent interaction between the transactions and produce erroneous results. For instance, the problem known as the **incorrect summary problem** can arise if one transaction is in the middle of transferring funds from one account to another when another transaction tries to compute the total deposits in the bank. This could result in a total that is either too large or too small depending on the order in which the transfer steps are performed. Another possibility is known as the **lost update problem**, which is exemplified by two transactions, each of which makes a deduction from the same account. If one transaction reads the account's current balance at the point when the other has just read the balance but has not yet calculated the new balance, then both transactions will base their deductions on the same initial balance. In turn, the effect of one of the deductions will not be reflected in the database.

To solve such problems, a database management system could force transactions to execute in their entirety on a one-at-a-time basis by holding each new transaction in a queue until those preceding it have completed. But, a transaction often spends a lot of time waiting for disk operations to be performed. By interweaving the execution of transactions, the time during which one transaction is waiting can be used by another transaction to process data it has already retrieved. Most large database management systems therefore contain a scheduler to coordinate time-sharing among transactions in much the same way that a time-sharing operating system coordinates interweaving of processes.

To guard against such anomalies as the incorrect summary problem and the lost update problem, such schedulers incorporate a **locking protocol** in which the items within a database that are currently being used by some transaction are marked as such. These marks are called locks; marked items are said to be locked. Two types of locks are common—**shared locks** and **exclusive locks.** They correspond to the two types of access a transaction may require to a data item—shared access and exclusive access. If a transaction is not going to alter the data item, then it requires shared access, meaning that other transactions are also allowed to view the data item. However, if the transaction is going to alter the item, it must have exclusive access, meaning that it must be the only transaction with access to the item.

In a locking protocol, each time a transaction requests access to a data item it must also tell the database management system the type of access it requires. If a transaction requests shared access to a data item that is either unlocked or locked with a shared lock, that access is granted and the item is marked with a shared lock. If, however, the requested item is already marked with an exclusive lock, the additional access is denied. If a transaction requests exclusive access to a data item, that request is granted only if the item has no lock associated with it. In this manner, a transaction that is going to alter a data item protects that item from other transactions by obtaining exclusive access. At the same time, several transactions can share access to a data item if none of them are going to change it. Of course, once a transaction is finished with an item, it notifies the database management system and the associated lock is removed.

Various algorithms are used to handle the case when a transaction's access request is rejected. One is that the transaction is merely forced to wait until the requested item becomes available. This approach, however, can lead to deadlock, since two transactions that require exclusive access to the same two data items could block each other's progress if each obtains exclusive access to one of the items and then insists on waiting for the other. To avoid such deadlocks, some database management systems give priority to older transactions. That is, if an older transaction requires access to a data item that is locked by a younger transaction, the younger transaction is forced to release all of its data items, its activities are rolled back (based on the log), the older transaction is given access to the data item, and the younger transaction is forced to start again. If a younger transaction is repeatedly preempted, it will grow older in the process and ultimately become one of the older transactions. This protocol, known as the **wound-wait protocol** (old transactions wound young transactions, young transactions wait for old ones), assures that every transaction will ultimately be allowed to complete its task.

Questions/Exercises

1. What is the difference between a transaction that has reached its commit point and one that has not?
2. How could a database management system guard against extensive cascading rollback?

3. Show how the uncontrolled interweaving of two transactions, one of which deducts $100 from an account and the other which deducts $200 from the same account, could produce final balances of $100, $200, and $300, assuming that the initial balance is $400.
4. a. Summarize the possible results of a transaction requesting shared access to an item in a database.
   b. Summarize the possible results of a transaction requesting exclusive access to an item in a database.
5. Describe a sequence of events that would lead to deadlock among transactions performing operations on a database system.
6. Describe how the deadlock in your answer to Question 5 could be broken. Would your solution require use of the database management system's log? Explain your answer.

CHAPTER REVIEW PROBLEMS

1. Summarize the distinction between a simple file and a database.
2. What is meant by data independence?
3. What is the role of a database management system in the layered approach to a database implementation?
4. What is the difference between a schema and a subschema?
5. Identify two benefits of separating application software from the database management system.
6. Identify the level within a database system (end user, programmer of application software, designer of the database management system software) at which each of the following concerns or activities occur:
   a. How should the data be stored on a disk to maximize efficiency?
   b. Is there a vacancy on flight 243?
   c. Could a relation be stored as a sequential file?
   d. How many times should a user be allowed to mistype a password before the conversation is terminated?
   e. Should the user/machine interface be menu driven?
   f. How can the PROJECT operation be implemented?
   g. How many packages of sardines were accidentally shipped without ice?
7. Describe how the following information about airlines, flights (for a particular day), and passengers would be represented in a relational database.

   Airlines: Clear Sky, Long Hop, and Tree Top

   Flights for Clear Sky: CS205, CS37, and CS102

   Flights for Long Hop: LH67 and LH89

   Flights for Tree Top: TT331 and TT809

   Smith has reservations on CS205 (seat 12B), CS37 (seat 18C), and LH 89 (seat 14A).

   Baker has reservations on CS37 (seat 18B) and LH89 (seat 14B).

   Clark has reservations on LH67 (seat 5A) and TT331 (seat 4B).
8. In terms of the following relations, what is the appearance of the relation RESULT after executing each of these instructions:

X relation

U	V	W
A	Z	5
B	D	3
C	Q	5

Y relation

R	S
3	J
4	K

   a. RESULT ← PROJECT W from X
   b. RESULT ← SELECT from X where W = 5
   c. RESULT ← PROJECT S from Y
   d. RESULT ← JOIN X and Y where X.W ≥ Y.R

9. Using the commands SELECT, PROJECT, and JOIN, write a sequence of instructions to answer each of the following questions about parts and their manufacturers in terms of the following database:

PART relation

PartName	Weight
Bolt 2X	1
Bolt 2Z	1.5
Nut V5	0.5

MANUFACTURER relation

CompanyName	PartName	Cost
Company X	Bolt 2Z	.03
Company X	Nut V5	.01
Company Y	Bolt 2X	.02
Company Y	Nut V5	.01
Company Y	Bolt 2Z	.04
Company Z	Nut V5	.01

   a. Which companies make Bolt 2Z?
   b. Obtain a list of the parts made by Company X along with each part's cost.
   c. Which companies make a part with weight 1?

10. Answer Problem 9 using SQL.

11. What redundancy is introduced if the information in the PART and MANUFACTURER relations in Problem 9 are combined into one single relation?

12. Using commands such as SELECT, PROJECT, and JOIN, write sequences to answer the following questions about the information in the EMPLOYEE, JOB, and ASSIGNMENT relations in Fig. 9.5:
   a. Obtain a list of the names and addresses of the company's employees.
   b. Obtain a list of the names and addresses of those who have worked or are working in the personnel department.
   c. Obtain a list of the names and addresses of those who are working in the personnel department.

13. Answer Problem 12 using SQL.

14. Design a relational database containing information about music composers, their lives, and their compositions.

15. Design a relational database containing information about manufacturers of computing equipment and their products.

16. Design a relational database containing information about publishers, magazines, and subscribers, in which the relationships between these entities are represented by the following entity-relationship diagram.

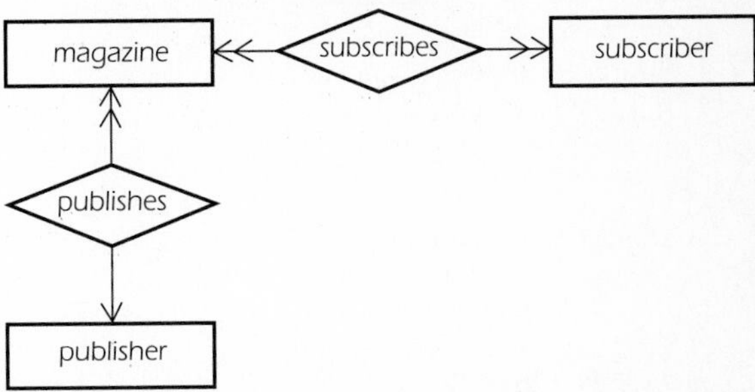

17. Design a relational database containing information about parts, suppliers, and customers. Each part may be supplied by several suppliers and ordered by many customers. Each supplier may supply many parts and have many customers. Each customer may order many parts from many suppliers; in fact, the same part may be ordered from more than one supplier.

18. What changes are required in the design of the relational database shown in Fig. 9.5 to allow one to obtain a list of all employees with the last name Smith using only the SELECT operation?

19. What inconvenience may arise because of our decision to combine the month, day, and year into a single attribute in the relational database in Fig. 9.5?

20. Write a sequence of instructions (using the operations SELECT, PROJECT, and JOIN) to retrieve the JobId, StartDate, and TermDate for each job in the accounting department from the relational database described in Fig. 9.6.

21. Answer Problem 20 using SQL.

22. Write a sequence of instructions (using the operations SELECT, PROJECT, and JOIN) to retrieve the Name, Address, JobTitle, and Dept of every current employee from the relational database described in Fig. 9.5.

23. Answer Problem 22 using SQL.
24. Write a sequence of instructions (using the operations SELECT, PROJECT, and JOIN) to retrieve the Name and JobTitle of each current employee from the relational database described in Fig. 9.5.
25. Answer Problem 24 using SQL.
26. What is the difference in the information supplied by the single relation

Name	Department	TelephoneNumber
Jones	Sales	111-2222
Smith	Sales	111-3333
Baker	Personnel	111-4444

and the two relations

Name	Department
Jones	Sales
Smith	Sales
Baker	Personnel

Department	TelephoneNumber
Sales	111-2222
Sales	111-3333
Personnel	111-4444

27. Design a relational database containing information about automobile parts and their subparts. Be sure to allow for the fact that one part may contain smaller parts and at the same time be contained in still larger parts.
28. Based on the database represented in Fig. 9.5, state the question that is answered by the following program segment:

```
TEMP ← SELECT from ASSIGNMENT
        where TermDate = "*"
RESULT ← PROJECT JobId, StartDate from TEMP
```

29. Translate the query in Problem 28 into SQL.
30. Based on the database represented in Fig. 9.5, state the question that is answered by the following program segment:

```
TEMP1 ← JOIN EMPLOYEE and ASSIGNMENT
        where EMPLOYEE.EmplId =
        ASSIGNMENT.EmplId
TEMP2 ← SELECT from TEMP1
        where TermDate = "*"
RESULT ← PROJECT name, StartDate
        from TEMP2
```

31. Translate the query in Problem 30 into SQL.
32. Based on the database represented in Fig. 9.5, state the question that is answered by the following program segment:

```
TEMP1 ← JOIN EMPLOYEE and JOB
        where EMPLOYEE.EmplId =
        JOB.EmplId
TEMP2 ← SELECT from TEMP1
        where Dept = "SALES"
RESULT ← PROJECT Name from TEMP2
```

33. Translate the query in Problem 32 into SQL.
34. Translate the SQL statement

```
select JOB.JobTitle
from ASSIGNMENT, JOB
where ASSIGNMENT.JoblId = JOB.JobId
      and ASSIGNMENT.EmplId = "34Y70"
```

into a sequence of SELECT, PROJECT, and JOIN operations.
35. Translate the SQL statement

```
select ASSIGNMENT.StartDate
from ASSIGNMENT, EMPLOYEE
where ASSIGNMENT.EmplId = EMPLOYEE.EmplId
      and EMPLOYEE.Name = "Joe E. Baker"
```

into a sequence of SELECT, PROJECT, and JOIN operations.
36. Describe the effect that the following SQL statement would have on the database in Problem 9.

```
insert into MANUFACTURER
values ('Company Z', 'Bolt 2X', .03)
```

37. Describe the effect that the following SQL statement would have on the database in Problem 9.

```
update MANUFACTURER
set Cost = .03
where CompanyName = 'Company Y'
      and PartName = 'Bolt 2X'
```

38. Identify some of the objects that you would expect to find in an object-oriented database used to maintain a grocery store's inventory. What methods would you expect to find within each of these objects?
39. Identify some of the objects that you would expect to find in an object-oriented database

used to maintain records of a library's holdings. What methods would you expect to find within each of these objects?

40. Compare the relationship between a class and an object (in an object-oriented environment) to that between a database schema and an actual database.

41. What incorrect information is generated by the following schedule of transactions T1 and T2? T1 is designed to compute the sum of accounts A and B; T2 is designed to transfer $100 from account A to account B. T1 begins by retrieving the balance of account A; then, T2 performs its transfer; and finally, T1 retrieves the balance of account B and reports the sum of the values it has retrieved.

42. Explain how the locking protocol described in the text would resolve the error produced in Problem 41.

43. What effect would the wound-wait protocol have on the sequence of events in Problem 41 if T1 was the younger transaction? If T2 was the younger transaction?

44. Suppose one transaction tries to add $100 to an account whose balance is $200 while another tries to withdraw $100 from the same account. Describe an interweaving of these transactions that would lead to a final balance of $100. Describe an interweaving of these transactions that would lead to a final balance of $300.

QUESTIONS OF ETHICS

The following questions are provided to help you understand some of the ethical/social/legal issues associated with the field of computing as well as investigate your own beliefs and their foundations. The goal is not merely to answer these questions. You should also consider why you answered as you did and whether your justifications are consistent from one question to the next.

1. What restrictions are appropriate regarding the construction of databases about individuals? What information does a government have a right to hold regarding its citizens? What information does an insurance company have a right to hold regarding its clients? What information does a company have a right to hold regarding its employees? Should controls in these settings be implemented and, if so, how?

2. Is it proper for a credit card company to sell the purchasing patterns of its clients to marketing firms? Is it acceptable for a sports car mail order business to sell its mailing list to a sports car magazine? Is it acceptable for the Internal Revenue Service to sell the names and addresses of those taxpayers with significant capital gains to stockbrokers?

3. To what extent is the designer of a database responsible for how the information in that database is used?

4. Suppose a database mistakenly allows unapproved access to information in the database. If that information is obtained and used adversely, to what degree do the database designers share responsibility for the misuse of the information? Does your answer depend on the amount of effort required by the perpetrator to discover the flaw in the database design and obtain the unauthorized information?

ADDITIONAL ACTIVITIES

1. Using sequential files to represent relations with each record representing one tuple, write a system of subprograms to perform the operations of SELECT, PROJECT, and JOIN appearing in the relational model.

2. Using the routines developed in Activity 1, write a program to answer a specific question about the information in the database. What part of this software would normally be part of

a database management system? What part would be classified as application software?

3. If you know an object-oriented language, describe how you might implement an object-oriented version of the database in Fig. 9.5.

4. Analyze one of the commercial database systems for personal computers. On which database model is it based? If it is the relational model, identify the way in which the SELECT, PROJECT, and JOIN operations are implemented.

ADDITIONAL READING

Cattell, R. G. G. *Object Data Management.* Reading, Mass.: Addison-Wesley, 1991.

Date, C. J. *An Introduction to Database Systems,* 6th ed. Reading, Mass.: Addison-Wesley, 1995.

Elmasri, R., and S. B. Navathe. *Fundamentals of Database Systems,* 2nd ed. Redwood City, Calif.: Benjamin/Cummings, 1994.

Teorey, T. J. *Database Modeling and Design: An Entity-Relationship Approach.* San Mateo, Calif.: Morgan Kaufmann, 1990.

PART FOUR

THE POTENTIAL OF ALGORITHMIC MACHINES

In Part Four we consider the potential of algorithmic machines. We begin by investigating the subject of artificial intelligence in Chapter 10. There we find that major advances are being made in the production of machines that mimic the activities of humans and thus project the image of intelligent behavior. This technology raises the question as to what, if any, the limitations of machines are.

We address this question in Chapter 11, where we study the theory of computation. There we learn that there are, in fact, bounds on the tasks that algorithmic machines can accomplish. Moreover, we find that issues of practicality limit these tasks even further. That is, we find that there are tasks that, although within the theoretical powers of computers, would require so much time that they are infeasible in reality, even with advances in technology.

CHAPTER TEN

Artificial Intelligence

10.1 Some Philosophical Issues
Machines Versus Humans
Performance Versus Simulation
Intelligence as an Interior Characteristic
An "Intelligent" Machine

10.2 Image Analysis

10.3 Reasoning
Production Systems
Other Applications

10.4 Control System Activities
Search Trees
Problems of Efficiency

10.5 Using Heuristics
Designing Heuristics
Applying Heuristics

10.6 Artificial Neural Networks
Basic Properties
A Specific Application

10.7 Applications of Artificial Intelligence
Language Processing
Robotics
Database Systems
Expert Systems

A major goal among computer scientists is to develop machines that communicate with their environments through traditionally human sensory means and proceed intelligently without human intervention. Such a goal often requires that the machine "understand," or perceive, the input received and be able to draw conclusions through some form of a reasoning process.

Both perception and reasoning fall within the category of commonsense activities that, although natural for the human mind, are apparently quite difficult for machines. The result is that the area of research associated with this pursuit, known as artificial intelligence, is still in its infancy when compared to its goals and expectations.

The subject of artificial intelligence can be discussed in two contexts. One is in a philosophical sense in which one considers questions regarding intelligence itself and whether machines can possess actual intelligence or merely simulate its presence. The other is the more scientific sense in which one asks how technology can be applied to produce machines that behave in intelligent ways.

10.1 Some Philosophical Issues

Perhaps one of the more difficult tasks for a beginner in computer science involves the separation of science fiction from science, and nowhere is this distinction more clouded than in the area of artificial intelligence. Although the major thrust behind the subject is merely to build machines that are able to forge ahead in uncontrolled environments without relying on human backup (and thus better serve the human race), the popular press would have us believe that computer scientists are striving to build mechanical humans.[1] Of course, the aura of mystery is only enhanced by calling the subject artificial intelligence. Let us begin then by considering the distinction between today's algorithmic machines and human minds.

Machines Versus Humans

Although the computer is often personified, an important distinction exists between its properties and the properties of the human mind. Algorithmic machines are designed to perform precisely defined tasks with speed and accuracy, and they do this extremely well. However, machines are not gifted with common sense. When faced with a situation not foreseen by the programmer, a machine's performance is likely to deteriorate rapidly. The human mind, although often floundering on complex computations, is capable of understanding and reasoning. Consequently, whereas a machine might outperform a human in computing solutions to problems in nuclear physics, the human is much more likely to understand the results and determine what the next computation should be.

If we are to build machines that are able to continue when faced with unforeseen or unpredictable situations, the machines must become more humanlike in the sense that they must possess (or at least simulate) the ability to reason. Recognizing this requirement, computer scientists have turned to psychologists and their models of the human mind in hopes of finding principles that can be applied to the construction of more flexible machines and programs. The result is that it is often difficult to distinguish between the research of a psychologist and that of a computer scientist. The distinction is not in what they do but rather in their goals. The psychologist is trying to learn more about the human mind; the computer scientist is trying to build more useful machines.

Performance Versus Simulation

Suppose that a mathematician and a psychologist each embark independently on projects to develop a poker-playing program. The mathematician would most likely design a program based on the foundations of probability and statistics. The result would be a program that would play the odds, bluff at random, show no

[1] There are those, of course, who dream of building models of the human mind. John von Neumann and other early researchers even discussed the components of early machines in terms of organs. Major breakthroughs must still be made, however, before such dreams have a chance of becoming realities.

emotion, and consequently maximize its chances of winning. The psychologist, on the other hand, might develop a program based on theories of human thought and behavior. The project could even result in the production of several different programs; one might play aggressively while another might be easily intimidated. In contrast to the mathematician's program, the psychologist's program might become "emotionally involved" in the game and lose everything it owned.

Reconsidering, we hypothesize that the mathematician's main concern while developing the program would be the program's final performance. Such an approach is said to be **performance oriented.** In contrast, the psychologist would be more interested in understanding the processes of natural intelligence and so would approach the project as an opportunity to test theories by building computer models based on those theories. From this point of view, the development of the "intelligent" program is actually a side effect of another pursuit—progress in understanding human thought and behavior. This approach is said to be **simulation oriented.**

Both approaches are sound and make significant contributions to the field of artificial intelligence. However, they also raise elusive philosophical questions within the discipline. Consider, for example, the discussion that might ensue if a group is asked to decide whether the programs possess intelligence and if so which program is more intelligent. (Is intelligence measured by the ability to win or the ability to be humanlike?)

Intelligence as an Interior Characteristic

The difficulty in determining whether or not a program possesses intelligence is rooted in the difficulty of distinguishing between the mere appearance of intelligence and its actual existence. In the final analysis intelligence is an interior characteristic whose existence is detected from the outside only indirectly in the context of a stimulus/reaction dialogue.

This illusive nature of intelligence was recognized by Alan Turing in 1950 when he proposed a test (now known as the **Turing test**) for detecting intelligence within a machine. Turing's proposal was to allow a human, whom we call the interrogator, to communicate with a test subject by means of a typewriter system, without being told whether the test subject was a human or a machine. In this environment a machine would be declared intelligent in the event that the interrogator was not able to distinguish it from a human. As yet, machines have not been able to pass the Turing test, although surprising results have been achieved.

A well-known example arose as a result of the program DOCTOR (a version of the more general system called ELIZA) developed by Joseph Weizenbaum in the mid-1960s. This interactive program was designed to project the image of a Rogerian analyst conducting a psychological interview; the computer played the role of analyst while the user played the patient. Internally, all that DOCTOR did was restructure the statements made by the patient according to some well-defined rules and direct them back to the terminal screen. For example, in response to a statement such as "I am tired today," DOCTOR might have replied with "Why do you think you're tired today?" If DOCTOR was unable to recognize the sentence structure, it merely responded with something like "Go on" or "That's very interesting."

Weizenbaum's purpose in developing DOCTOR dealt with the study of natural language communication. From this point of view, the subject of psychotherapy played the secondary role of providing an environment (or a domain of discourse) in which the program could function. To Weizenbaum's dismay, however, several psychologists proposed using the program for actual psychotherapy. (The Rogerian thesis is that the patient, not the analyst, should lead the discussion during the therapeutic session, and thus, they argued, a computer could possibly conduct a discussion as well as a therapist could.) Moreover, DOCTOR projected the image of comprehension so strongly that many who "communicated" with it found themselves relating intimate thoughts and feelings and, in many cases, actually becoming subservient to the machine's question-and-answer dialogue. The result was that moral, as well as technical, issues were raised.

An "Intelligent" Machine

With such philosophical questions residing at the very foundation of artificial intelligence, it is not surprising that much of the subject is accompanied by an aura of mystery often exploited by both the news media and fiction writers. In an effort to get our feet firmly on the ground, let us consider the design of a machine having elementary "intelligence" properties.

Our machine takes the form of a metal box equipped with a gripper, a video camera, and a finger with a rubber end so that it does not slip when pushing something (Fig. 10.1).

Figure 10.1 Our puzzle-solving machine

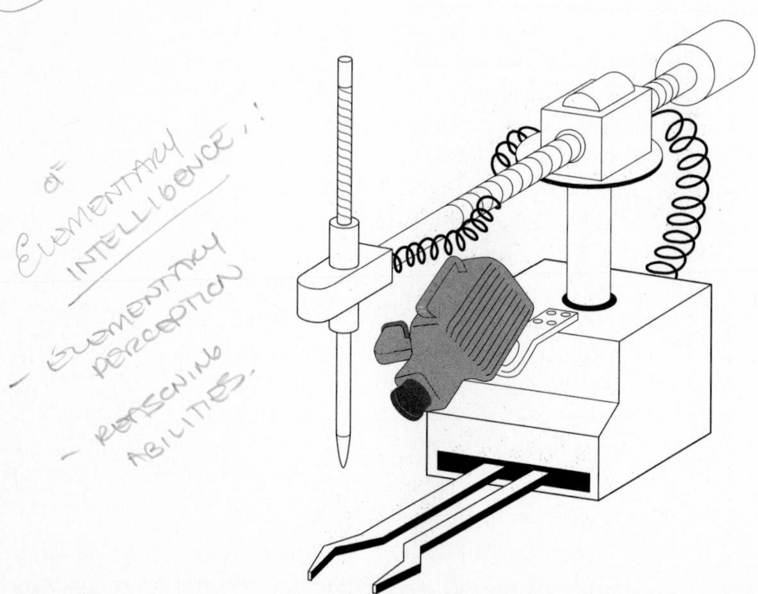

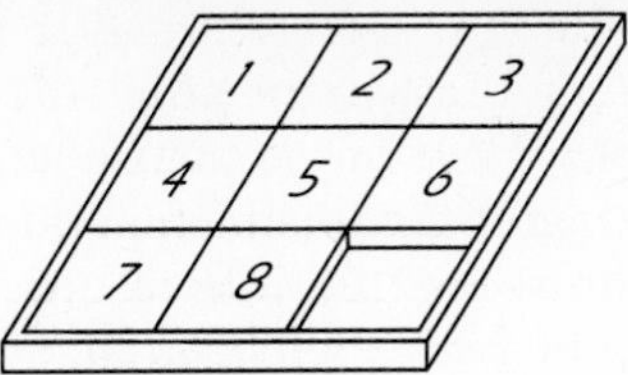

Figure 10.2 The eight-puzzle in its solved configuration

Imagine such a machine next to a table on which an eight-puzzle is placed. This is a puzzle consisting of eight square tiles labeled 1 through 8 mounted in a frame capable of holding a total of nine such tiles in three rows and three columns. Among the tiles in the frame then is a vacancy into which any of the adjacent tiles can be pushed. The tiles are currently arranged as shown in Fig. 10.2.

We begin by picking up the puzzle and rearranging it by repeatedly pushing arbitrarily chosen tiles into the vacancy. We then turn on the machine, and the gripper begins to open and close as if asking for the puzzle. We place the puzzle in the gripper, and the gripper closes on the puzzle. After a short time the finger lowers and begins pushing the tiles around in the frame (in an orderly fashion) until they are back in their original order. At this point the machine places the puzzle back on the table and turns itself off. Because such a machine involves elementary perception as well as reasoning abilities, its design provides a basis for presenting the topics of the following four sections.

Questions/Exercises

1. A plant placed in a dark room with a single light source grows toward the light. Is this an intelligent response? Does the plant possess intelligence?
2. Suppose a vending machine is designed to dispense various products depending on which lever is pulled. Would you say that such a machine is "aware" of which lever is pulled?

10.2 Image Analysis

The opening and closing of the gripper on our machine presents no serious problem, and the ability to detect the presence of the puzzle in the gripper during this process is straightforward because our application requires very little precision. (Automatic garage door openers are able to detect and react to the presence of an obstacle in the doorway when closing.) Even the problem of focusing the camera on the puzzle can be handled simply by designing the arm to position the puzzle at a particular predetermined position for viewing. Consequently, the first intelligent behavior required by our puzzle-solving machine is the extraction of information through a visual medium.

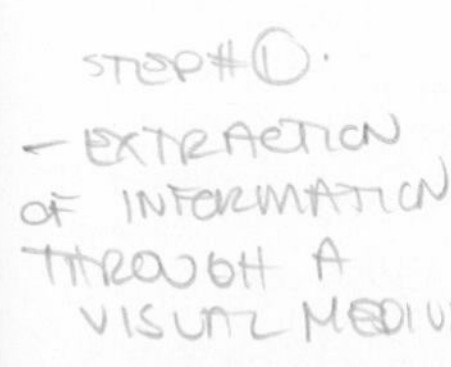

It is important to realize that the problem faced by our machine when looking at the puzzle is not that of merely producing and storing an image. Technology has been able to do this for years as in the case of traditional photography and television systems. Rather, the problem is to understand the image in order to extract the current status of the puzzle (and later to monitor the movement of the tiles). This is a significant distinction from the activity of a television receiver that simply transforms the image from one medium to another with no conceptual understanding of the image. In short, our machine must demonstrate the ability to perceive.

In the case of our puzzle-solving machine, the options as to what the images might be are relatively limited. We can assume that what appears is always an image of the puzzle containing the digits 1 through 8 in a well-organized pattern. The problem is merely to extract the arrangement of these digits. For this, we imagine that the picture of the puzzle has been coded in terms of bits in the computer's memory, with each bit representing the brightness level of a particular part of the picture called a pixel. Assuming a uniform size of the image (the machine holds the puzzle at a predetermined location in front of the camera), we can detect which tile is in which position by comparing the different sections of the picture to prerecorded templates consisting of the bit patterns produced by the individual digits used in the puzzle. As matches are found, the condition of the puzzle is revealed.

This technique of recognizing images is one method used in optical character readers. It has the drawback, however, of requiring a certain degree of uniformity among the style, size, and orientation of the symbols being read. In particular, the bit pattern produced by a physically large character does not match the template for a smaller version of the same symbol, even though the shapes are the same, and you can imagine how such problems increase when trying to process handwritten material.

Another approach to the problem of character recognition is based on matching the geometric characteristics rather than the exact appearance of the symbols. In such cases the digit 1 might be characterized as a single vertical line, 2 might be an opened curved line joined with a horizontal straight line across the bottom, and so on. This recognition of the symbols turns out to be the process of extracting the features from the image being processed (called **feature extraction**) and comparing them to those of known symbols (**feature evaluation**). This technique is not foolproof either, because minor errors in the image can produce a set of entirely different geometric features, as in the case of distinguishing between an O and a C or, in the case of the eight-puzzle, a 3 and an 8.

We are fortunate in our puzzle application that we do not need to recognize and understand images of general three-dimensional scenes. Consider, for example, the advantage we have by being assured that the shapes to be recognized (the digits 1 through 8) are isolated in different parts of the picture rather than appearing as overlapping images, as is common in more general settings. In a general photograph, for instance, one is faced not only with the problem of recognizing an object from different angles but also with the fact that some portions of the object may be hidden from view.

In short, the problems associated with general image analysis are enormous. Tasks that are performed quickly and apparently easily by the human mind continue to lie beyond the capabilities of machines. On the other hand, there are indications that alternative machine architectures may someday overcome the problems that elude us today (see Section 10.6).

Questions/Exercises

1. How do the requirements of a video system on a robot differ if the pictures are used by the robot itself to control its activities as opposed to being relayed to a human who controls the robot remotely?
2. What tells you that the following drawing is nonsense? How can this insight be programmed into a machine?

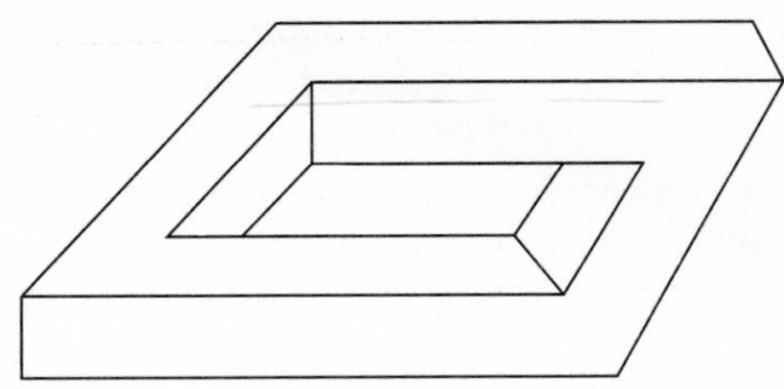

10.3 Reasoning

Once our puzzle-solving machine has deciphered the positions of the tiles from the visual image, its task becomes that of actually solving the puzzle. One technique that might come to mind is to preprogram the machine with solutions to all possible arrangements of the tiles. Then, the machine's task is merely to select and execute the proper program. However, because even this simple puzzle provides a total of 181,440 different configurations, the idea of providing an explicit solution for each is certainly not inviting and probably not even possible when time and storage constraints are considered.

We are thus forced to approach the problem in terms of programming our machine to solve the problem itself. Consequently, the program we develop must provide the machine with the ability to make decisions, draw conclusions, and in short, perform elementary reasoning activities.

Production Systems

The development of reasoning abilities within a machine is a current topic of research, and as with any subject of current research debate exists over which technique or theory is the correct one to pursue. For our purposes, we approach the subject in the context of production systems. A **production system** consists of three main components:

1. *A collection of states.* Each **state** is a situation that might occur in the application environment. The beginning state is called the **start** (or initial) **state;** the

desired state (or states) is called the **goal state.** (In our case, the start state is the configuration of the puzzle when handed to the machine; the goal state is the configuration of the solved puzzle, as shown in Fig. 10.2.)

2. *A collection of productions (or rules).* A **production** is an operation that can be performed in the application environment to move from one state to another. Each production may be associated with preconditions; that is, conditions may exist that must be present in the environment before a production can be applied. (Productions in our case are the movements of tiles. Each movement of a tile has the precondition that the vacancy must be next to the tile in question.)
3. *A control system.* The **control system** consists of the logic that solves the problem of moving from the start state to the goal state. At each step in the process the control system must decide which of those productions whose preconditions are satisfied should be applied next. (Given a particular state in our eight-puzzle example, there would be several tiles next to the vacancy and therefore several applicable productions. The control system must decide which tile to move.)

From the point of view of production systems, the task of developing an intelligent machine is to implement the control system as a program stored in the machine. This program inspects the current state of the target system, identifies a sequence of productions that leads to the goal state, and executes this sequence. To this end, the control system constructs an algorithm to solve the initial problem using productions as building blocks. The main obstacle to designing our puzzle-solving machine is the development of this control program. This we do in the following sections.

For now we should present the concept of a **state graph,** which is a convenient way of representing, or at least conceptualizing, all the states, productions, and preconditions in a production system. Here we use the term **graph** in its mathematical sense, meaning a collection of locations called **nodes** connected by arrows, or **arcs.** A state graph consists of a collection of nodes representing the states in the system connected by arcs representing the productions that produce movement from one state to another. Two nodes can be connected by an arc in the state graph if and only if a production is in the system that can be used to transform the system from the state at the origin of the arc to the state at the destination of the arc. Preconditions are implicitly represented by the absence of arcs between certain nodes.

We might emphasize here that just as the number of possible states prevented us from explicitly providing predesigned solutions to the eight-puzzle, the problem of magnitude prevents us from explicitly representing the entire state graph. A state graph is then a way of conceptualizing the problem at hand but not something that we would consider expressing in its entirety. Nonetheless, you may find it helpful to consider (and possibly extend) the portion of the state graph for the eight-puzzle displayed in Fig. 10.3.

Note that in terms of the state graph the problem faced by the control system becomes one of finding a sequence of arcs that leads from the start state to the

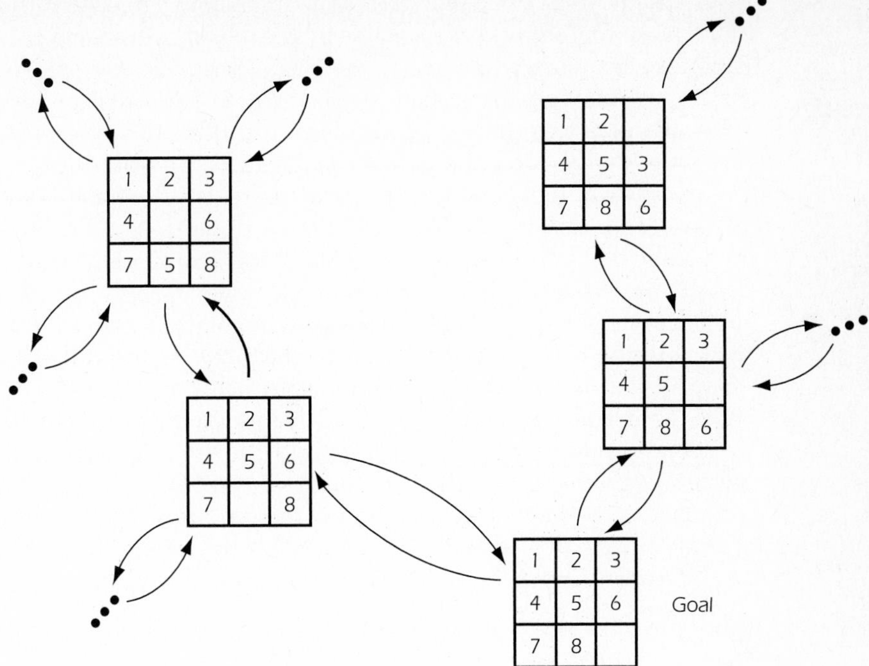

Figure 10.3 A small portion of the eight-puzzle's state graph

goal state, because this sequence of arcs represents a sequence of productions that solves the original problem. This is the context in which our control system functions. Moreover, observe that there is nothing unique about the eight-puzzle that allows us to conceptualize the production system in terms of a state graph. Such a representation is applicable in any production system, and thus the formulation of problems in terms of production systems provides a uniform approach to the problem-solving process. That is, regardless of the application, the control system involved always reduces to the problem of finding a path through a state graph. To emphasize this point, we close this section by observing how some popular tasks can be formulated in terms of production systems and thus of state graphs.

Other Applications

One of the old standbys in the area of artificial intelligence is the playing of games such as chess. Such games involve moderate complexity in a well-defined context and hence provide an ideal environment for testing theories. In chess the states are the possible board configurations, the productions are the moves of the pieces, and the control system is embodied in the players (human or otherwise). The start node of the state graph represents the board with the pieces in their initial positions. Branching from this node are arcs leading to those board configurations that can be reached after the first move in a game; branching from each of these nodes one finds those configurations reachable by the next move; and so on. With this formulation we can imagine a game of chess as consisting of two players, each trying to find a path through a large state graph to a goal node of his or her own choosing.

Perhaps a less obvious example of a production system is the problem of drawing logical conclusions from given facts. The productions in this context are the rules of logic that allow new statements to be formed from old ones. For example, the statements "All students work hard" and "John is a student" can be combined to produce "John works hard." Similarly, "Mary and George are smart" can be reworded as "Neither Mary nor George is not smart." States in such a system consist of collections of statements known to be true at particular points in the deduction process: The start state is the collection of basic statements (often called axioms) from which conclusions are to be drawn, and a goal state is any collection of statements that contain the proposed conclusion.

As an example, Fig. 10.4 shows the portion of a state graph that might be traversed when the conclusion "Socrates is mortal" is drawn from the collection of statements "Socrates is a man," "All men are humans," and "All humans are mortal." There we see the body of knowledge shifting from one state to another as the reasoning process applies appropriate productions to generate additional statements.

Figure 10.4 Deductive reasoning in the context of a production system

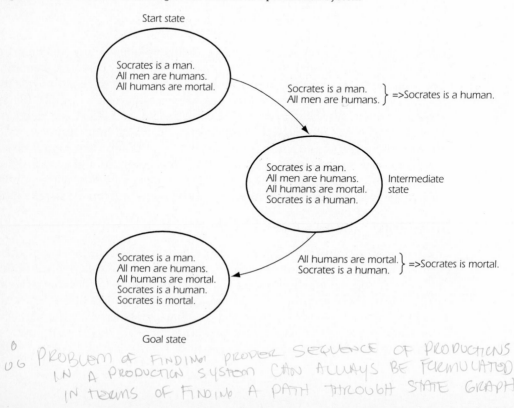

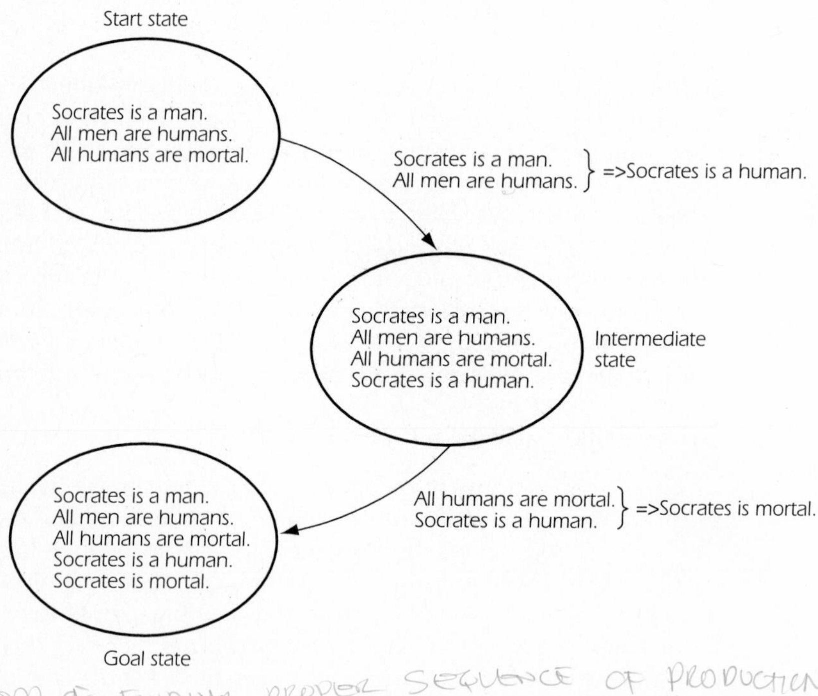
Start state
Socrates is a man.
All men are humans.
All humans are mortal.
Socrates is a man.
All men are humans.
=>Socrates is a human.
Socrates is a man.
All men are humans.
All humans are mortal.
Socrates is a human.
Intermediate state
All humans are mortal.
Socrates is a human.
=>Socrates is mortal.
Socrates is a man.
All men are humans.
All humans are mortal.
Socrates is a human.
Socrates is mortal.
Goal state

Questions/Exercises

1. What is the significance of production systems in artificial intelligence?
2. Draw a portion of the state graph for the eight-puzzle surrounding the node representing the following state:

4	1	3
	2	6
7	5	8

3. Formulate the problem of traversing the following maze in terms of a production system:

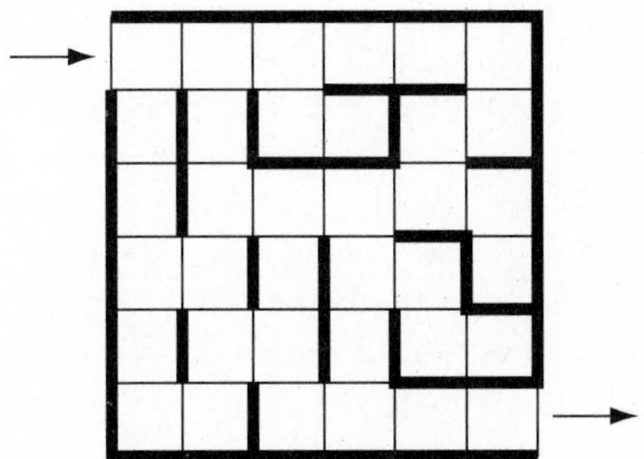

10.4 Control System Activities

A major point of Section 10.3 is that the problem of finding the proper sequence of productions in a production system can always be formulated in terms of finding a path through a state graph. This is important to computer scientists because it means that any knowledge gained about finding paths through graphs has immediate application to a multitude of problems. This means that, by designing control systems from the state-graph point of view, one is effectively working on numerous applications at the same time.

Our consideration of control systems therefore centers on the problem of graph traversals along with a look at how paths in a state graph (or actually in what we call the search tree) can be converted into solutions to the original problem. In terms of the graph traversal problem we present in this section a rather brute-force technique and see in the next section how a degree of intuition can be added to provide a more efficient (or more intelligent) system.

Search Trees

The major part of the control system's job of developing a solution to the target problem requires little more than an algorithm for searching the state graph to find a path from the start node to the goal. A common method of performing this search is to traverse each of the arcs leading from the start state and in each case record the destination state, then traverse the arcs leaving these new states and again record the results, and so on. Our search for the goal spreads out from the start state like a drop of dye in water. This process continues until one of the new states is the goal, at which point a solution has been found. The control system needs merely to apply the productions along the discovered path from the start state to the goal.

The effect of this strategy is to build a tree, called a **search tree,** that consists of the part of the state graph that has been investigated by the control system. The root node of the search tree is the start state, and the children of each node are those states reachable from the parent by applying one production. Each arc between nodes in a search tree represents the application of a single production, and each path from the root to a leaf represents a path between the corresponding states in the state graph.

If the eight-puzzle were originally configured as in Fig. 10.5, Fig. 10.6 represents the search tree that might result. The leftmost branch of this tree represents an attempt to solve the problem by first moving the 6 tile up, the center branch represents the approach of moving the 2 tile to the right, and the rightmost branch represents moving the 5 tile down. Furthermore, the search tree shows that if we do begin by moving the 6 tile up, the only production allowable next is to move the 8 tile to the right. (Actually, at that point we could also move the 6 tile down but that would return us to the state represented by the root node and thus be an extraneous move.)

The goal state occurs in the last level of the search tree of Fig. 10.6. Since this represents the completion of the search, the control system does not need to construct additional levels of the tree once this point is reached. As soon as this node is discovered, the control system can terminate its search procedure and begin constructing the instruction sequence that will be used to solve the puzzle in the external environment. This turns out to be the simple process of walking up the search tree from the location of the goal node while pushing the productions represented by the tree arcs on a stack as they are encountered. Applying this technique to the search tree in Fig. 10.6 produces the stack of productions in Fig. 10.7. Note that the control system can now solve the puzzle in the outside world by executing the instructions as they are popped from this stack.

Figure 10.5 An unsolved eight-puzzle

1	3	5
4	2	
7	8	6

Figure 10.6 A sample search tree

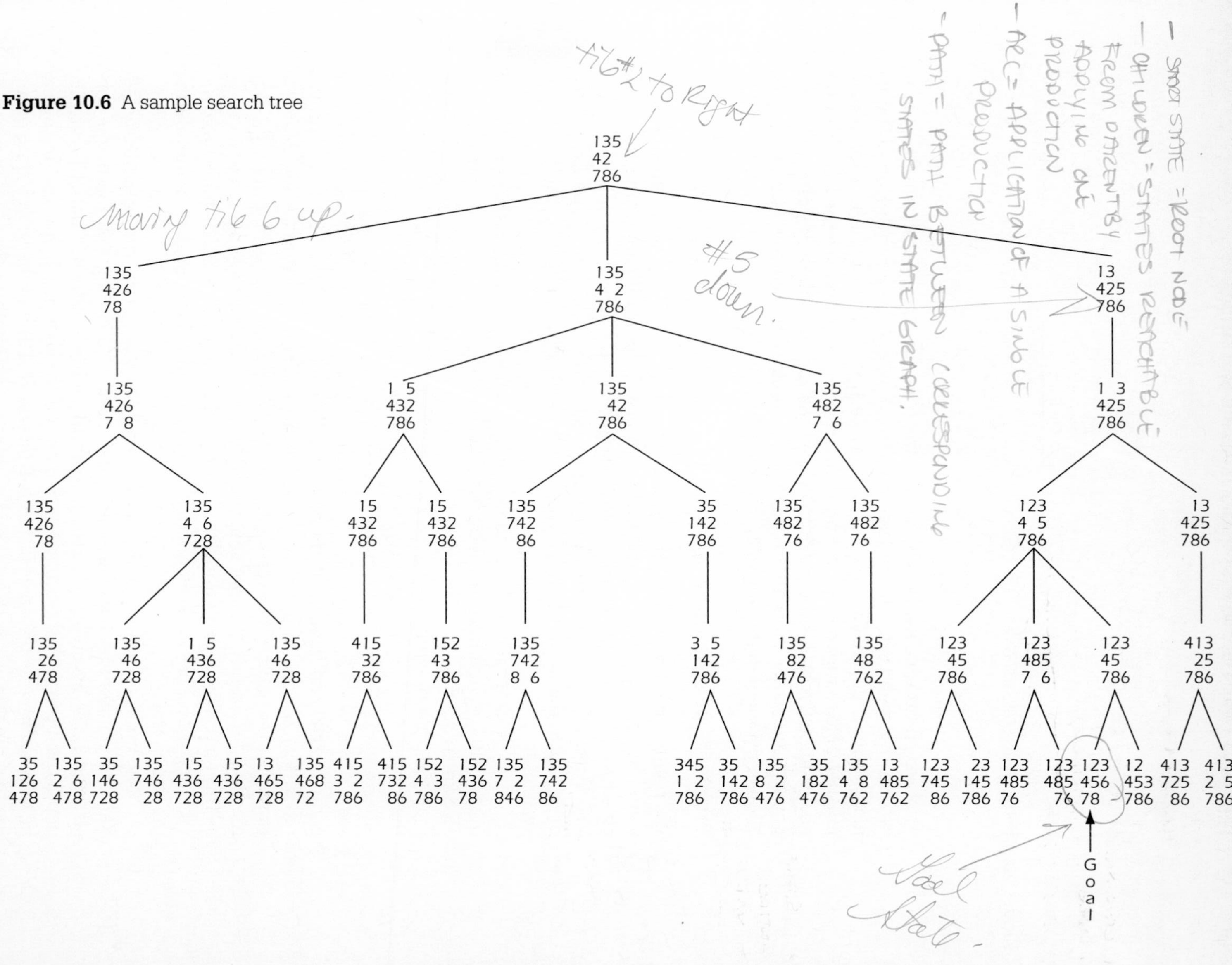

Top of stack →

Move the 5 tile down.
Move the 3 tile right.
Move the 2 tile up.
Move the 5 tile left.
Move the 6 tile up.

Figure 10.7 Productions stacked for later execution

One point remains. Recall that the trees we discussed earlier use a pointer system that points down the tree, thereby allowing us to move from a parent node to its children. In the case of a search tree, however, the control system must be able to move from a child to its parent as it moves up the tree from the goal state to the start state. Such trees are constructed with their pointer systems pointing up rather than down (or in some cases, with two sets of pointers that allow movement in the tree in both directions).

Problems of Efficiency

We pointed out earlier that the size of the state graph normally precludes its actual representation in a machine's memory. Thus, while analyzing the available productions, the control system usually creates and stores only the search tree. After all, the search tree represents that part of the state graph considered pertinent to the task at hand and is therefore all that is required by the control system.

For our example in this section, we have chosen a problem that produces a manageable search tree. In contrast, you can imagine that the search tree generated in an attempt to solve a more complex problem would grow much larger than the preceding one because of a larger number of options at each stage and the greater depth required in the tree before the goal is found. For example, consider a game of chess that has 20 possible first moves: The root node of the search tree in such a case has 20 children rather than the 3 in the case of the eight-puzzle; and a game of chess can easily consist of 30 to 35 pairs of moves rather than the 5 straightforward ones in our example. Even in the eight-puzzle example, the search tree can become quite large if the goal is not quickly reached. As a result, it is not surprising that developing a full search tree can be as impractical as representing the entire state graph in terms of both time and memory space. These cases require more economical methods of manipulating the search tree.

One approach changes the order in which the search tree is constructed. Rather than building it in a **breadth-first** manner (meaning that the tree is constructed layer by layer), we can pursue the more promising paths to greater depths and consider the other options only if these original choices turn out to be false leads. This results in a **depth-first** construction of the search tree, meaning that the tree is constructed by building vertical paths rather than horizontal layers. This approach is the subject of the next section.

An additional approach to reducing the size of a search tree is to avoid redundancy. For example, the same state need not have multiple occurrences in the tree, because the occurrence of a node in the search tree indicates that the search process has discovered a path in the state graph leading to that node, and little is gained by maintaining records of several ways to reach the same state. Yet, had we not reached the goal in our example early in the search process, we would have soon found many duplications in the tree, and ultimately the search tree would have become plagued with repetitions. We should therefore consider changing our search procedure so that the search tree retains records of only one path to each node.

In the case of the eight-puzzle this can be accomplished simply by adopting the policy of not attaching a new node to the tree if that state is already represented elsewhere. This restriction certainly removes the chance for repeated entries but is too simplistic as a general rule in other applications. For instance, in other problems, it might well be the case that the new occurrence of the node in some way represents a more advantageous or efficient solution than the previous one and consequently should be added while the older occurrence is removed. In a game of chess, for example, trying to reach a certain board configuration via one path of moves may rely on the opponent's overlooking an opportunity to take control of the game, whereas pursuing another (perhaps longer) path might assure that the advantage remains at home. The more conservative path should therefore be kept in the search tree, regardless of whether it was the first one discovered.

Consequently, many control systems use more complex methods for eliminating redundancy in the search tree than the simple technique previously proposed. These systems normally associate a cost to the various paths represented in the tree and pursue the paths with the smallest cost. Redundancy in the search tree is eliminated because, as repetitions of states are encountered, only the occurrence associated with the smallest cost is retained.

We can adopt this cost-evaluating approach in the eight-puzzle by considering the cost of any path to be the number of moves in the path. As repetitions of states occur in the search tree, we always keep the occurrence on the less expensive path. Of course, the less expensive path is the shorter one, so we always keep the occurrence of the state appearing highest in the tree. If we develop the tree level by level, as previously discussed, the node retained is always the older one, and the effect of adopting this cost system for our application is the same as applying the rule of always retaining the older node.

Questions/Exercises

1. Using a breadth-first approach, draw the search tree that is constructed by a control system when solving the eight-puzzle from the following start state:

1	2	3
4	8	5
7	6	

2. In what way can a depth-first approach to the construction of a search tree prove more efficient than a breadth-first approach?
3. Use pencil, paper, and the breadth-first approach to try to construct the search tree that is produced when solving the eight-puzzle from the following start state. (You do not have to finish.) What problems do you encounter?

4	3	
2	1	8
7	6	5

10.5 Using Heuristics

We closed Section 10.4 by briefly discussing ways in which the size of a search tree can be controlled through the use of elementary techniques. In this section we look at this problem in more detail and discover that the equivalent of intuition can be added to our system to increase efficiency.

We might begin by considering how we as humans would proceed when faced with the eight-puzzle. We would rarely pursue several options at the same time, as our previous control system did. Instead, we probably would select the option that appeared most promising and follow it. Note that we said *appeared* most promising. After all, we usually do not know for sure which option is best at a particular point but follow our intuition, which may, of course, lead us into a trap. Nonetheless, the use of such intuitive information seems to give humans an advantage over the brute-force methods of Section 10.4, where each option was given equal attention.

It is customary to refer to such untested and empirical information (which humans gain by the use of intuition) as heuristic information. More specifically, we define a heuristic policy as one that leads in a direction that appears to be the best but offers no assurance that it will turn out to be the correct direction. Thus, whereas a human might follow a rule of thumb, we speak of a program applying a heuristic policy.

Designing Heuristics

The first step is to identify those characteristics for which we as humans look when deciding which option to pursue. In general, we can argue that humans tend to keep the goal state in mind and pick the option that appears to lead toward that state. In the case of the eight-puzzle this means that a human, when given a choice, tends to select the option that moves a tile in the direction of its final position.

To apply this technique in a programming environment, we must first develop a quantitative measure by which a program can determine which of several states is considered closest to the goal. Such a measure is called a **heuristic.**

1	5	2
4	8	
7	6	3

Figure 10.8 An unsolved eight-puzzle

One heuristic might be to associate with each state the value equal to the number of tiles out of position and consider the state with the smallest value to be closest to the goal. However, this value does not take into account how far out of position the tiles are, so we might want to adopt a slightly more complicated measure that accounts for this distance as well. One technique is to measure the distance each tile is from its destination and add these values to obtain a single quantity. The distance in this case can be taken as the minimum number of moves a tile must make to reach its goal position, disregarding any complexities introduced by the location of the other tiles. Thus a tile immediately adjacent to its final destination is associated with a distance of one, whereas a tile whose corner touches the square of its final destination is associated with a distance of two (because it must move at least one position vertically and another position horizontally).

Adopting this system, we observe that the quantity associated with each state is actually an approximation of the number of moves required to reach the goal from that state, which we refer to as the projected cost. For instance, the total projected cost associated with the configuration in Fig. 10.8 is seven (because tiles 2, 5, and 8 are each a distance of one from their final destinations while tiles 3 and 6 are each a distance of two from home). In fact, it actually takes seven moves to return this puzzle configuration to the solved configuration.

The projected cost has two important characteristics. First, as just noted, it constitutes a reasonable estimate of the amount of work remaining in the solution if that state were reached. This means that it should be helpful in decision making. Second, it can be calculated easily. This means that its use has a chance of benefiting the search process rather than of becoming a burden. (In contrast, although the actual number of moves required to reach the goal from the given state is an excellent piece of information to have when making decisions, computing this information involves finding the actual solution first.)

Applying Heuristics

Now that we have a heuristic for the eight-puzzle, the next step is to incorporate it into our decision-making process. To this end, we recall that a human faced with a decision tends to select the option that appears closest to the goal. We then alter our search procedure of Section 10.4 to consider the projected cost of each leaf node in the tree and pursue the search from a leaf node associated with the smallest such cost. Based on this principle, we present the algorithm of Fig. 10.9 for developing a search tree and executing the solution obtained.

```
Establish the start node of the state graph as the root of the
  search tree and record its projected cost.
while (the goal node has not been reached) do
  [Select the leftmost leaf node with the smallest projected
     cost of all leaf nodes, and attach as children to the
     selected node those nodes that can be reached by a
     single production from the selected node.
   Record the projected cost of each of these new nodes next
     to the node in the search tree.]
Traverse the search tree from the goal node up to the root,
  pushing the production associated with each arc traversed onto a stack.
Solve the original problem by executing the productions as they
  are popped off the stack.
```

Figure 10.9 An algorithm for a control system using heuristics

Let us walk through this algorithm as it applies to the eight-puzzle, starting from the initial configuration in Fig. 10.5. First, we establish this initial state as the root node and record its projected cost, which is five. Then, the first pass through the body of the while structure instructs the addition of the three nodes, as in Fig. 10.10. Note that we have recorded in parentheses the projected cost of each leaf node beneath it.

The goal node has not been reached, so we again pass through the body of the while structure, this time extending our search from the leftmost node ("the leftmost leaf node with the smallest projected cost"). After this, the search tree has taken the form displayed in Fig. 10.11.

Note that the projected cost of the leftmost leaf node is now five, indicating that this is perhaps not a good choice to pursue after all. The algorithm picks up on this and in the next pass through the loop instructs us to expand the tree from the rightmost node (which now is the "leftmost leaf node with the smallest projected cost"). Having been expanded in this fashion, the search tree appears as in Fig. 10.12.

Figure 10.10 The beginning of our heuristic search

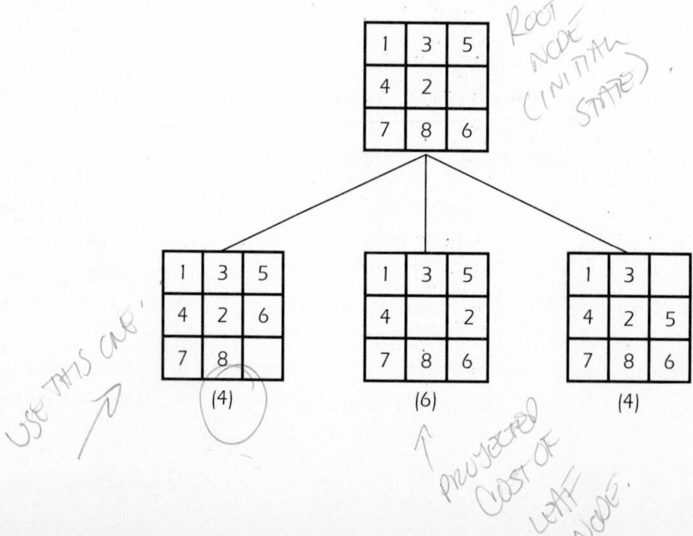

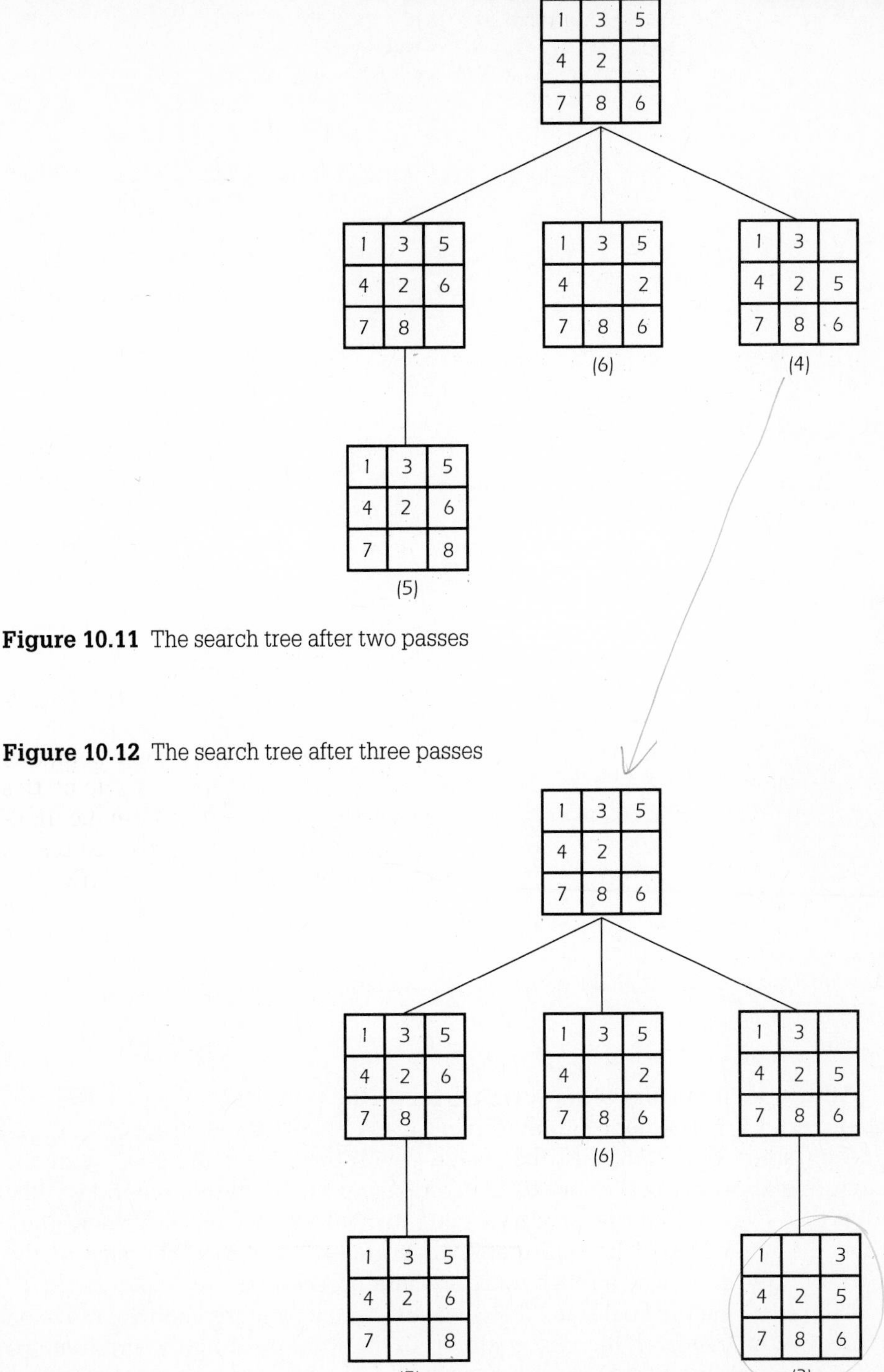

Figure 10.11 The search tree after two passes

Figure 10.12 The search tree after three passes

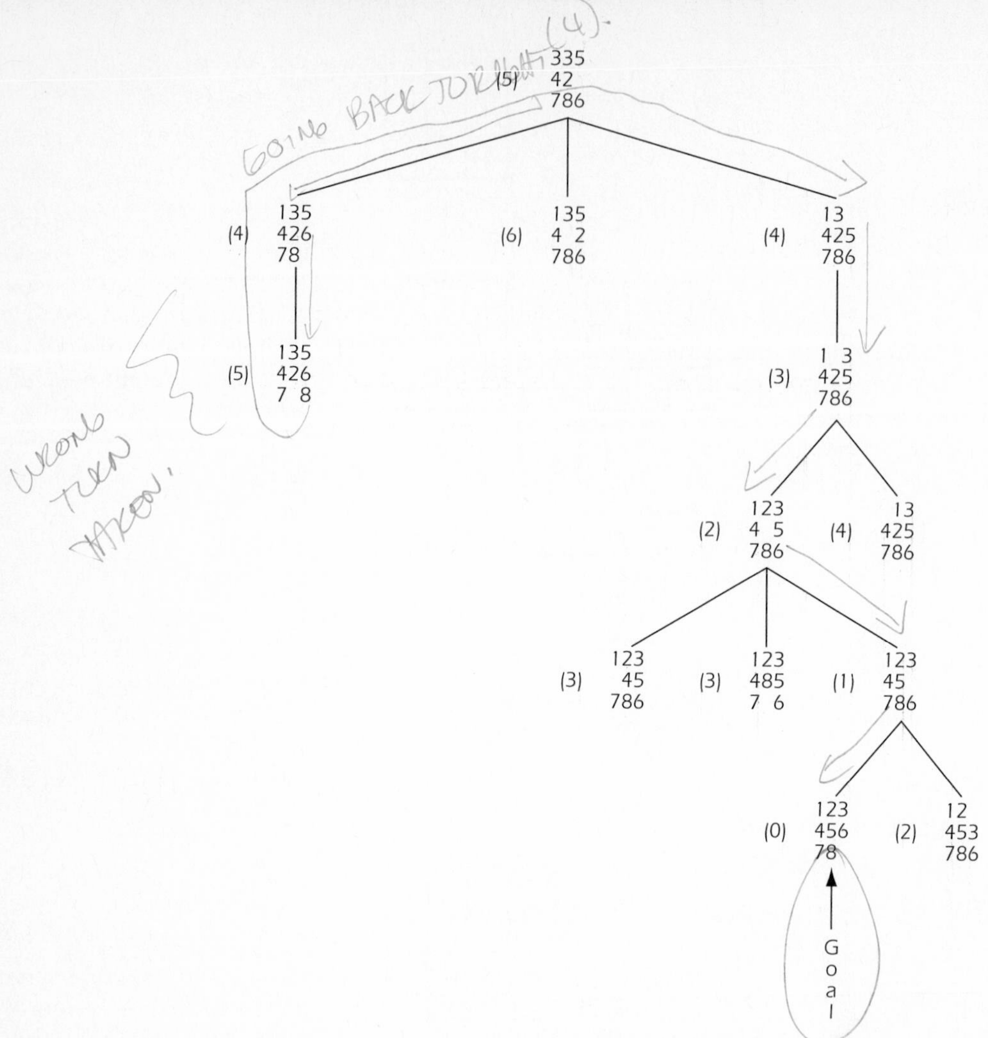

Figure 10.13 The complete search tree formed by our heuristic system

At this point the algorithm seems to be on the right track. Because the projected cost of this last node is only three, the while structure instructs us to continue pursuing this path, and the search finally arrives at the goal, with the search tree appearing as in Fig. 10.13. Comparing this with the tree in Fig. 10.6 shows that, even with the temporary wrong turn taken early on by the new algorithm, the use of heuristic information has greatly decreased the size of the search tree and produced a much more efficient process.

After reaching the goal state, the while structure terminates, and we move on to traverse the tree from the goal node up to the root, pushing the productions encountered onto a stack as we go. The resultant stack appears as depicted earlier, in Fig. 10.7.

Finally, we are instructed to execute these productions as they are popped from the stack. At this point, we would observe the puzzle-solving machine lower its finger and begin to move the tiles.

Questions/Exercises

1. What analogy can be drawn between our heuristic system for solving the eight-puzzle and a mountain climber who attempts to reach the peak by considering only the local terrain and always proceeding in the direction of steepest ascent?
2. Using the heuristic information as presented in this section, apply the control-system algorithm of Fig. 10.9 to the problem of solving the following eight-puzzle.

1	2	3
4		8
7	6	5

3. Refine our method of computing the projected cost for a state so that the search algorithm of Fig. 10.9 does not make the wrong choice, as it did in the example in this section. Can you find an example in which your system still causes the search to go astray?
4. What would be the shape of the search tree produced by the algorithm in Fig. 10.9 if the projected cost of all states is the same?

10.6 Artificial Neural Networks

With all the progress that has been made in artificial intelligence, many problems in the field continue to tax the abilities of today's traditional computers. Central processing units that execute single sequences of instructions do not seem capable of perceiving and reasoning at levels comparable to those of the multiprocessor human mind. For this reason, many researchers are turning to machines with multiprocessing architectures. One of these is the artificial neural network.

Basic Properties

As introduced in Chapter 2, artificial neural networks are constructed from many individual processors, which we will call processing units (or just units for short), in a manner that models networks of neurons in living biological systems. Each processing unit is a simple device that produces an output of 1 or 0, depending on whether the effective input of that unit exceeds a given threshold value. This effective input is a weighted sum of the actual inputs, as represented in Fig. 10.14. In this figure the outputs of three processing units (denoted by v_1, v_2, and v_3) are used as inputs to another unit. The inputs to this fourth unit are

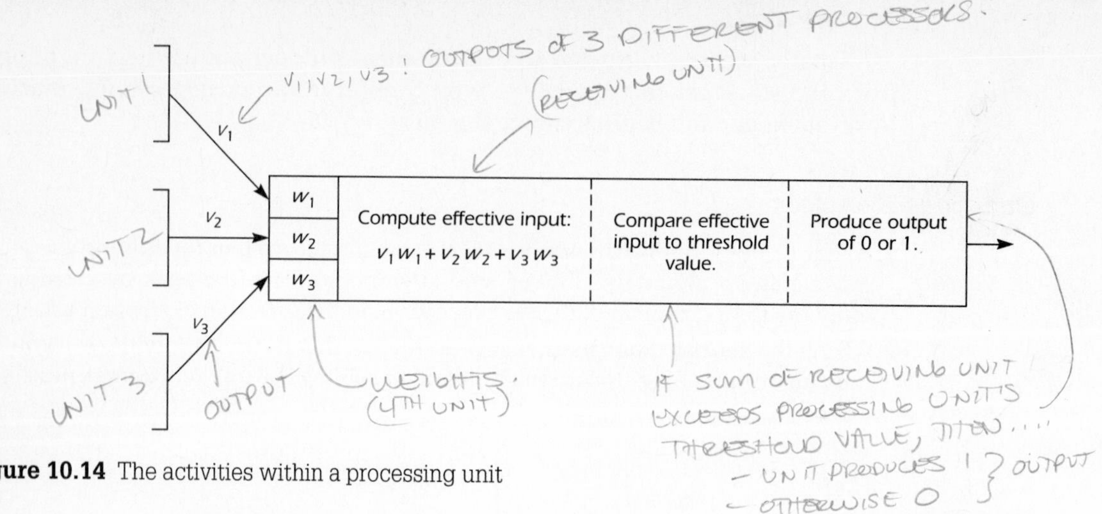

Figure 10.14 The activities within a processing unit

associated with values called weights (denoted by w_1, w_2, and w_3). The receiving unit multiplies each of its input values by the weight associated with that particular input position and then adds these products to form the effective input ($v_1w_1 + v_2w_2 + v_3w_3$). If this sum exceeds the processing unit's threshold value, the unit produces an output of 1; otherwise the unit produces a 0 as its output.

Following the lead of Fig. 10.14, we adopt the convention of representing processing units as rectangles. At the input end of the unit we place a smaller rectangle for each input, and in this rectangle we write the weight associated with that input. Finally, we write the unit's threshold value in the middle of the large rectangle. As an example, Fig. 10.15 represents a processing unit with three inputs and a threshold value of 1.5. The first input is weighted by the value -2, the second is weighted by 3, and the third is weighted by -1. Therefore, if the unit receives the inputs 1, 1, and 0, its effective input is $(1)(-2) + (1)(3) + (0)(-1) = 1$, and thus its output is 0. But, if the unit receives 0, 1, and 1, its effective input is $(0)(-2) + (1)(3) + (1)(-1) = 2$, which exceeds the threshold value, and thus the unit's output is 1.

The fact that a weight can be positive or negative means that the corresponding input can have either an inhibiting or exciting effect on the receiving unit. (If the weight is negative, then a 1 at that input position reduces the weighted sum and thus tends to hold the effective input below the threshold value. In contrast, a positive weight causes the associated input to have an increasing effect on the weighted sum and thus increase the chances of that sum exceeding the threshold value.)

Figure 10.15 Representation of a processing unit

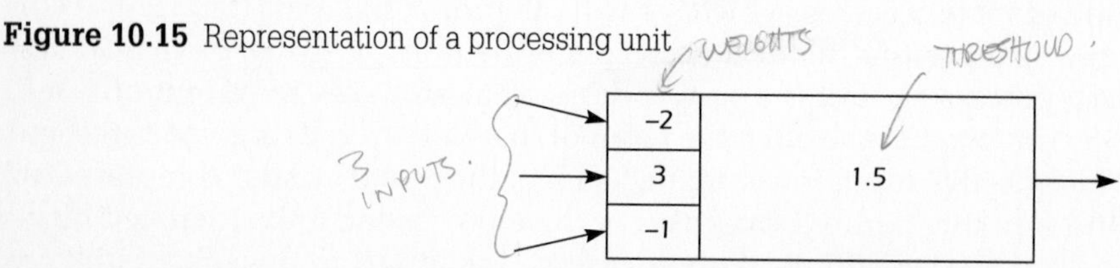

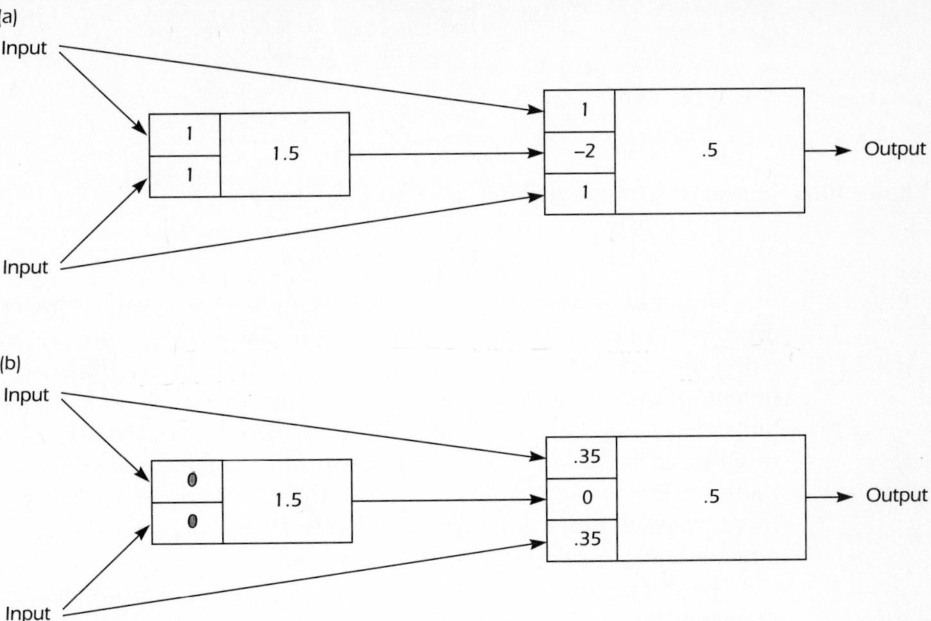

Figure 10.16 A neural network with two different programs

Moreover, the actual size of the weight controls the degree to which the corresponding input is allowed to inhibit or excite the receiving unit. Consequently, by adjusting the values of the weights throughout an artificial neural network, we can program the network to respond to different inputs in a predetermined manner.

As an example, the simple network presented in Fig. 10.16(a) is programmed to produce an output of 1 if its two inputs differ and an output of 0 otherwise. If, however, we change the weights to those shown in Fig. 10.16(b), we obtain a network that responds with a 1 if both of its inputs are 1s and with a 0 otherwise.

A Specific Application

To appreciate the power of artificial neural networks, let us return to the problem of character recognition. In particular, consider the problem of distinguishing between the uppercase letters C and T, as represented in Fig. 10.17. The problem is to identify either letter when it is placed in the field of vision, regardless of its orientation. All of the patterns in Fig. 10.18(a) should be identified as Cs, and all of those in part (b) should be recognized as Ts.

We have already alluded to the complexities involved when trying to solve such a problem in the traditional programming environment, in which template-matching techniques or feature extraction and evaluation are used. Indeed, the list of special cases we must foresee when designing such a system seems to go on forever. We are about to see, however, that the problem has a rather simple and elegant solution in terms of artificial neural networks.

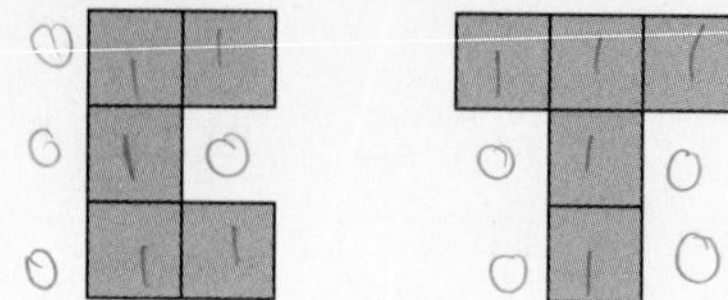

Figure 10.17 Uppercase C and uppercase T

We begin by assuming that each rectangle (each pixel) in the field of vision is attached to a detector that produces a 1 if that rectangle is covered by the letter being viewed and produces a 0 otherwise. We then use the outputs from these detectors as the inputs to our artificial neural network. This network itself contains two levels of processing units. The first level consists of a unit for each three-by-three block of rectangles in the field of view (see Fig. 10.19). Each of these units has nine inputs, to which the detectors associated with that unit's three-by-three block are attached. (Note that each detector provides input to nine of the processing units at the first level.)

The second level of our network consists of a single processing unit, with a separate input for each of the units in the first level. This processing unit has a threshold value of .5, and each of its inputs is associated with a weight of 1. Thus this top-level unit produces an output of 1 if and only if at least one of its inputs is 1.

Each lower-level processing unit has the threshold value of .5. Each input is given a weight of −1, except for the input associated with that unit's middle square, which is given a weight of 2. Each unit can therefore produce an output of 1 if and only if it receives a 1 from at most two of its detectors, one of which must be associated with the square in the center of the unit's three-by-three block.

Note that if a portion of the uppercase C covers the middle square of any three-by-three block, then the letter must also cover two or more additional

Figure 10.18 Various orientations of the letters C and T

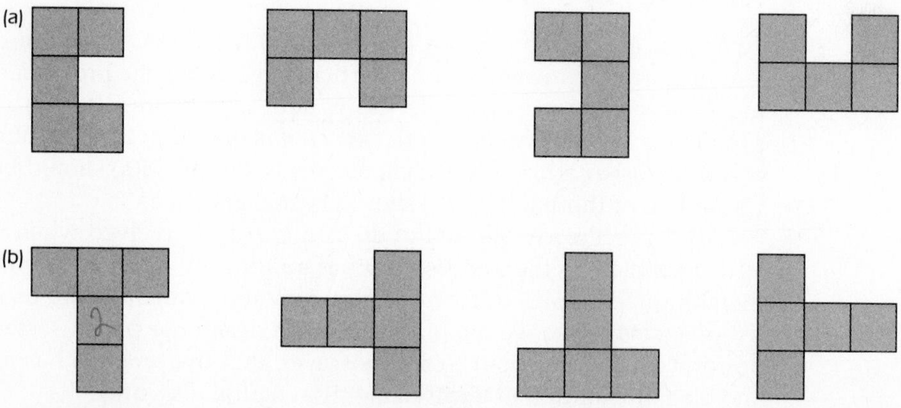

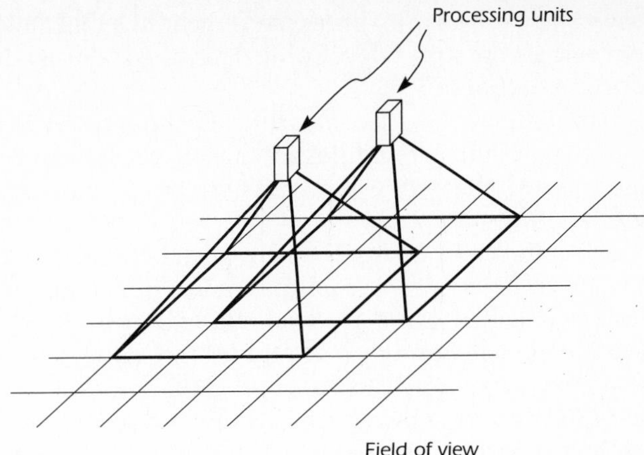
Processing units
Field of view

Figure 10.19 Two lower-level processing units and their three-by-three blocks in the field of view

squares in the block. Therefore, if the uppercase C is the letter in the field of view, all of the lower-level processing units produce an output of 0, and hence the upper-level unit also produces an output of 0.

In contrast, suppose the letter in the field of view is the uppercase T, and consider the three-by-three block whose center is the square covered by the bottom of the T's stem (Fig. 10.20). The processing unit assigned to this square receives an effective input of 1 (2 from the center pixel and −1 from the other pixel

Figure 10.20 The three-by-three block whose center square contains the bottom of the T's stem

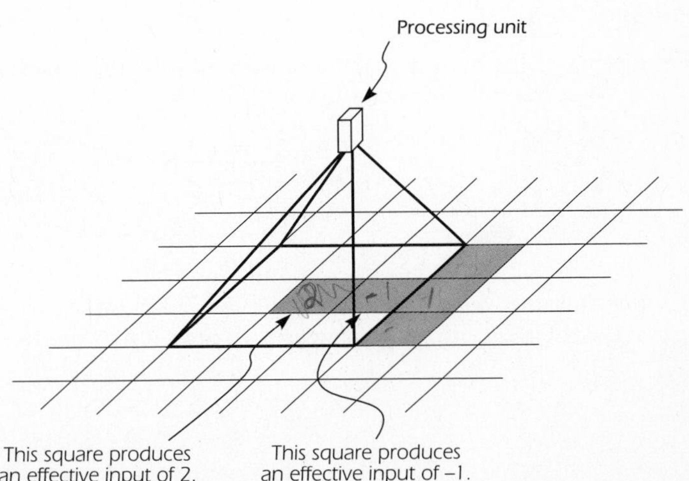
Processing unit
This square produces an effective input of 2.
This square produces an effective input of –1.

covered by the stem). This exceeds the unit's threshold, so the unit sends an output of 1 to the upper-level unit. This, then, causes the upper-level unit to produce an output of 1.

In summary, we have an artificial neural network that distinguishes between the letters C and T, regardless of the letter's orientation in the field of view: If the letter is a C, the network produces a 0 as its output; if the letter is a T, the network outputs a 1.

Of course, the ability to distinguish between just two letters is a far cry from the image-processing capabilities of the human mind. But the elegance of the solutions obtained using artificial neural networks, especially when compared to those obtained through more traditional approaches, indicates that further research in the area is justified.

Major effort is being applied toward solving the problems associated with designing and programming artificial neural networks. Typical goals relating to network design include determining how many processing units and how many levels of units are required to solve certain problems and what patterns of connections between these units are most productive. As for the subject of network programming, we have already mentioned that the task of programming an artificial neural network is that of assigning the proper weights to the various processing unit inputs throughout the system. The most popular way of doing this at the present is to perform a repetitive training process, in which sample inputs are applied to the network and then the weights are adjusted by small increments so that the actual output of the network approaches the desired output. As this process is repeated among the sample inputs, one hopes that the weights require less and less adjusting until the network begins to perform correctly over the entire range of sample data. Current research is aimed at determining how the weights can be adjusted during this training process so that each new adjustment leads toward the overall goal rather than destroying the progress made on the previous samples.

Questions/Exercises

1. What is the output of the following processing unit when both its inputs are 1s? What about the input patterns 0, 0; 0, 1; and 1, 0?

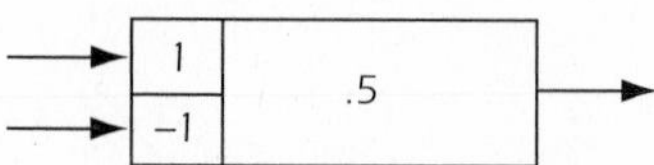

2. Adjust the weights and threshold value of the following processing unit so that its output is 1 if and only if at least two of its inputs are 1s.

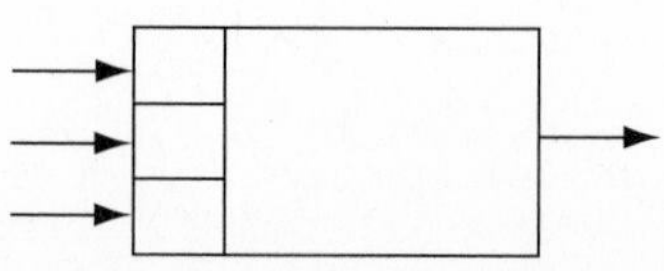

3. Design an artificial neural network that can detect which of the following two patterns is in its field of view.

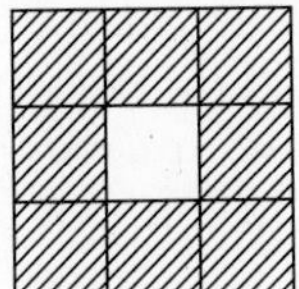
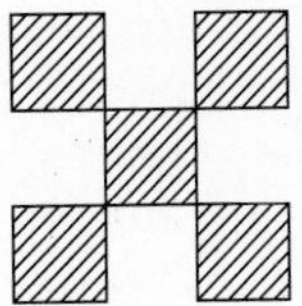

4. Design an artificial neural network that can detect which of the following two patterns is in its field of view.

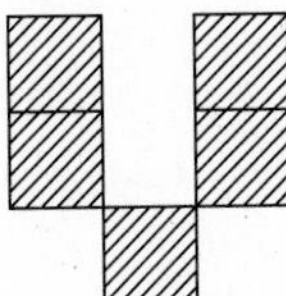
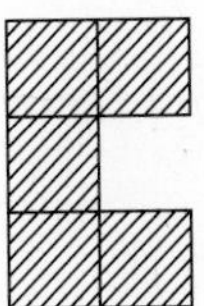

10.7 Applications of Artificial Intelligence

Having considered some of the techniques used in artificial intelligence, we turn now to the areas in which such techniques have found or are finding applications.

Language Processing

We begin with the task of translating statements from one language to another. Here, we find either traditional or artificial intelligence systems being used, depending on the languages involved. The distinction centers on whether the semantics of a statement must be considered to produce the translation. For instance, traditional programming languages are designed so that they can be translated through the rather straightforward process of essentially finding the original statement (or statement part) in a table in which it is stored along with its translated equivalent. The machine is therefore never called upon to understand the statements being translated; it must merely recognize their syntax. We therefore classify such applications as being in the range of traditional computer applications.

The problem of translating natural languages such as English, German, and Latin, however, usually requires an understanding of a sentence before a correct translation can be made. For example, the task of translating the sentences

> Norman Rockwell painted people.

and

> Cinderella had a ball.

cannot be accomplished by merely translating each word. Instead, to translate these sentences requires the ability to understand them.

Developing computers that can understand natural language has become a major research area in artificial intelligence. It is also an area that demonstrates how challenging research in artificial intelligence can become.

One problem in natural language processing is that people do not always conform to rules when they speak. In some cases they do not even say what they mean. For example,

Do you know what time it is?

often means "Please tell me what time it is," or if the speaker has been waiting for a long time, it may mean "You are very late."

To unravel the meaning of a statement in a natural language therefore requires several levels of analysis. The first of these is **syntactic analysis** whose major component is parsing. It is here that the subject of the sentence

Mary gave John a black eye.

is recognized as *Mary* while the subject of

John got a black eye from Mary.

is found to be *John.*

Another level of analysis is called **semantic analysis.** In contrast to the parsing process, which merely identifies the grammatical role of each word, semantic analysis is charged with the task of identifying the semantic role of each word in the statement. Semantic analysis seeks to identify such things as the action described, the agent of that action (which may or may not be the subject of the sentence), and the object of the action. It is through semantic analysis that the sentences "Mary gave John a black eye" and "John got a black eye from Mary" would be recognized as saying the same thing.

A third level of analysis is **contextual analysis.** It is at this level that the context of the sentence is brought into the understanding process. For example, it is easy to identify the grammatical role of each word in the sentence

The bat slipped from his hand.

We can even perform semantic analysis by identifying the action involved as *slipping,* the agent as *bat,* and so on. But it is not until we consider the context of the statement that its meaning becomes clear. Indeed, it has a different meaning in the context of a baseball player than it does in the context of exploring a cave. And it is at the contextual level that the true meaning of the question "Do you know what time it is?" would finally be revealed.

We should note that the various levels of analysis—syntactic, semantic, and contextual—are not necessarily independent. The subject of the sentence

Stampeding cattle can be dangerous.

is the noun *cattle* (modified by the adjective *stampeding*) if we envision the cattle stampeding on their own. But, the subject is the gerund *stampeding* (with object *cattle*) in the context of a troublemaker whose entertainment consists of starting stampedes.

Although we introduced the topic of natural language processing in the context of translation, the major directions of research in the subject today are found in the problems of **information retrieval** and **information extraction.** Information retrieval refers to the task of identifying documents that relate to the topic at hand. An example is the problem faced by attorneys when trying to find all the case histories that relate to current litigation. We will return to this example shortly in the context of database retrieval.

Information extraction refers to the task of extracting information from documents so that it takes a form that is useful in other applications. This may mean identifying the answer to a specific question or recording the information in a form from which questions can be answered at a later date. One such form is known as a template. It is essentially a questionnaire in which specifics are recorded. For example, consider a system for reading a newspaper. The system may make use of a variety of templates, one for each type of article that may appear in a newspaper. If the system identifies an article as reporting on a burglary, it would proceed by trying to fill in the slots in the burglary template. This template would probably request such items as the address of the burglary, the time and date of the burglary, the items taken, and so on. In contrast, if the system identifies an article as reporting on a natural disaster, it would fill in the natural disaster template, which would lead the system toward identifying the type of disaster, amount of damage, and so on.

Another form in which information extractors record information is known as a **semantic net.** This is essentially a large linked data structure in which pointers are used to indicate associations among the data items. Figure 10.21 shows part of a semantic net in which the information obtained from the sentence

Mary hit John.

has been circled.

Robotics

Another application of artificial intelligence is found in the area of robotics or, from a less flamboyant perspective, machinery control. Consider the use of computer-controlled systems in factory assembly lines. In this setting a machine is often asked to repeat a task over and over in an identical way (or at least such that any variations can be handled in a straightforward manner). The important point is that the machine performs its task in a controlled environment; if the task is to pick up assemblies and place them in boxes, the assemblies arrive on a conveyer belt at regular intervals, and full boxes are consistently replaced by empty ones in the same location. The machine does not really pick up an assembly but merely closes its gripper at a particular time at a particular location and moves its arm to another location where, rather than placing the assembly in a box, it merely opens its gripper. Most would agree, then, that intelligence is not embedded in such an application.

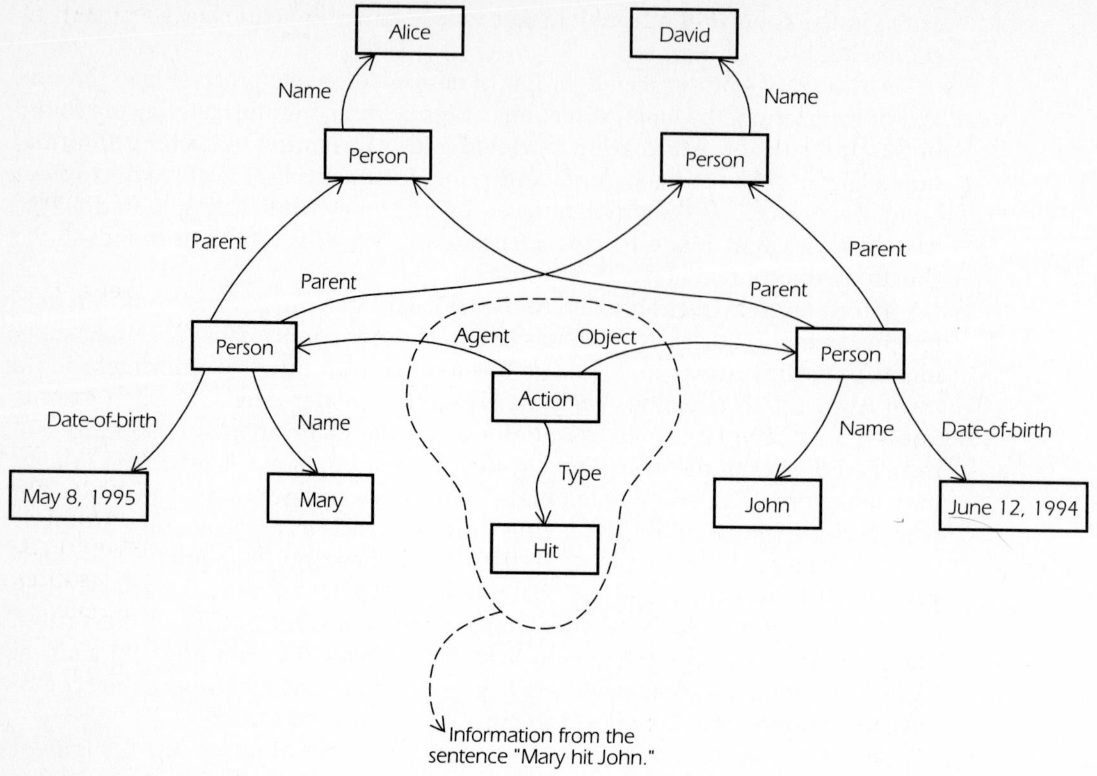

Figure 10.21 A semantic net

A major difference arises if the machine must perform its task in an uncontrolled environment. Prominent examples occur in uninhabitable and unknown environments, as found in such exotic pursuits as space exploration, or even in our factory assembly lines. Indeed, slight modifications of the task of picking up assemblies previously cited can result in the machine's being required to exhibit significant intelligent characteristics. For example, suppose the assemblies are delivered in a box containing an assortment of other parts rather than being isolated on a conveyer belt. The machine's task includes recognizing the correct assemblies, moving other parts out of the way, and picking up the correct objects. Assuming that the objects are placed in the box in an arbitrary manner, the retrieval of each assembly requires a unique sequence of steps that must be developed within the machine itself. Moreover, the machine must monitor and comprehend the situation constantly because parts in the box might shift, which would cause the required activities to change.

Such concerns fall within the scope of artificial intelligence and comprise much of the subject of robotics. Since successes in this area can readily result in financial gain, it is not surprising that this subject has attracted major attention from the industrial sector of our society and that corresponding progress has been made.

Database Systems

Next we consider data storage and retrieval systems. These systems represent a major application of natural language processing systems. The goal is to be able to request information from these systems by means of a natural language rather than requiring the human using the system to conform to a special and somewhat technical query language. However, artificial intelligence techniques are also used in the process of actually answering the question posed by the user.

Along these lines, traditional systems can merely retrieve facts that are explicitly requested and previously stored, whereas the goal of artificial intelligence systems is to provide for the retrieval of both information that is related although not directly requested and information not explicitly stored. A need for the former capabilities is found in legal searches. A lawyer might need to retrieve information about all previous cases relating to the present litigation; however, whether a case relates to the current one is a vague concept requiring judgment. A common approach to this problem taken by today's computer systems is to request the searcher to identify key words and phrases that should appear in any relevant case. The system then searches through all the case histories and retrieves those cases containing these words and phrases. Of course, such a system is really merely a sieve that reduces the number of cases that must be reviewed by the lawyer and may even overlook the most important case because it deals with "minors" rather than with "infants." A truly intelligent system, however, would produce a more reliable selection.

With regard to the ability to reply with information not explicitly stored, consider a database consisting of information about the presidents of the United States. When asked if there has ever been a president who was 10 feet tall, a traditional system would not be able to reply with the answer unless the height of each president was actually stored in the database. On the other hand, an intelligent system could reply correctly without knowing each president's height. The line of reasoning might go like this: If there had been a president who was 10 feet tall, that would have been significant and would be stored in the database. Therefore, since no president is recorded as being 10 feet tall, there have been no such presidents.

The conclusion that there have not been presidents who were 10 feet tall involves an important concept in database design—the distinction between closed-world databases and open-world databases. Loosely speaking, a closed-world database is one that is assumed to contain all true facts about the topic involved, whereas an open-world database does not encompass this assumption. The ability to reject the hypothesis of a 10-foot president in the previous example was based on the closed-world assumption that if the fact is not recorded then it must be false.

Although the closed-world assumption appears innocent enough on the surface, its application can lead to subtle complications. Consider a database consisting of the single statement

Item A is overstocked, or item B is overstocked.

From this statement alone we cannot conclude that item A is in fact overstocked. Thus the closed-world assumption forces us to conclude that

Item A is not overstocked.

In a similar manner, the closed-world assumption forces us to conclude that

Item B is not overstocked.

We see, then, that the closed-world assumption has led us to the contradictory conclusion that although item A or item B is overstocked, neither of them is overstocked. Understanding the limitations of such innocent-looking reasoning techniques is a goal of current research in artificial intelligence.

Still another goal of artificial intelligence research within the database environment deals with the problem of figuring out what the user of the system really wants to know or should be told instead of literally answering the question posed. Suppose we have a database consisting of the courses taught by the professors at a university along with the grades they awarded the students. Consider the following sequence of events: We ask the database for the number of A grades awarded by Professor Johnson last semester. The database replies, "none." We conclude that Professor Johnson was a rather demanding instructor and ask for the number of F grades awarded by Professor Johnson last semester. Again, the database replies, "none." We decide that Professor Johnson considers all students to be average except in extreme cases, so we ask for the number of C grades awarded by Professor Johnson last semester. The database again replies, "none." At this point we begin to get suspicious and ask whether Professor Johnson taught a course last semester. The database replies, "no." If only it had said so in the first place!

Expert Systems

An important extension of the intelligent database concept is the development of **expert systems**—software packages designed to assist humans in situations in which an expert in a specific area is required. These systems are designed to simulate the cause-and-effect reasoning that experts would accomplish if confronted with the same situations. Thus a medical expert system will propose the same procedure as a medical expert who knows that a biopsy should be performed if an abnormality is noticed and an X ray shows the presence of mass in that location.

It follows that a major task in constructing an expert system is to obtain the required knowledge from an expert. How this can be done has become an important area of research. The problem is actually twofold. One task is to procure and maintain the expert's cooperation—an undertaking that may not be easy because the questioning involved is likely to be long and frustrating, and the expert may not wish to relinquish knowledge to a system that might ultimately take the expert's place. The other complicating factor is that most experts have never considered what reasoning process they use in reaching their conclusions. When asked, "How did you know to do that?" they often reply, "I don't know."

Once these acquisition problems are overcome, the knowledge gained from the expert must be organized into a format compatible with a software system. This organization is often done by expressing the knowledge as a collection of rules in the form of if-then statements. For instance, the rule that an abnormality, confirmed by X-rays, leads to the performance of a biopsy can be expressed as

if abnormality noticed and
    X ray shows presence of mass
then perform biopsy

(Those who read the optional section on declarative programming in Chapter 5 will recognize the similarity between the structure of an expert system and that of a Prolog program. This similarity is a major reason for the popularity of Prolog in the field of artificial intelligence. Indeed, Prolog is an excellent language in which to develop an expert system.)

Notice the similarity between the rules of an expert system and the productions of a production system. The "if" portion of the rule essentially states the preconditions for performing or concluding the statement found in the "then" portion. Indeed, many expert systems are essentially production systems, with the rules obtained from the human expert being the productions and the underlying reasoning based on these rules being simulated by the control system. In this context the collection of productions is often called the system's knowledge base, and the control system is sometimes referred to as an inference engine.

Do not be misled, however, into thinking that an expert system is merely a large version of the puzzle-solving system discussed earlier. Some expert systems are organized as collections of production systems that combine their efforts to solve problems. Examples include expert systems that are based on the blackboard model in which several problem-solving systems, called knowledge sources, share a common storage area called the blackboard. This blackboard contains the current state of the problem being solved and, since it is shared by all the knowledge sources, provides a medium through which the knowledge sources can contribute to the problem's solution. To coordinate the activities of the knowledge sources, a control module is provided that is given the task of activating the appropriate knowledge source at the appropriate time. In the terminology of the blackboard model, this control module is said to determine the "focus of attention" of the system.

Another distinction between an expert system and a simple production system is that an expert system is not necessarily charged with reaching a predetermined goal but is more likely to be charged with deriving well-founded advice. This means that the heuristics used are not measurements of closeness to a goal, because no precise goal is actually present. Rather, heuristics used in expert systems tend to be the rules of thumb used by the human expert.

Our claim that no precise goal may exist in the setting of an expert system may bother you, so let us consider this claim a bit further. Suppose either an expert or an expert system is charged with the problem of diagnosing diseases. Ideally, one would like both systems to conclude with a definitive statement of the form "The disease is X," where in place of X the statement gives the name of the disease present. Unfortunately, such precision may not be possible. Instead, the best answer might be "The disease is most likely X" or perhaps "The disease is either X or Y. Please perform the following test to determine which is more likely." Because of this ambiguity, the control system within an expert system may choose to follow several paths through the system's state graph and report on the results of each. Indeed, if the production applied at some state is

```
if rheumatoid factor present and
     patient has pain in joints
then 80% chance of rheumatoid arthritis
```

then any further reasoning based on the fact that the disease is rheumatoid arthritis has the potential of being invalid.

As in other research areas, early applications of expert systems were limited to only a few areas. Today, however, the number of areas in which expert systems find applications is extensive. One catalyst for this expansion was the realization that an expert system can be separated into its reasoning component and its knowledge component. By removing the knowledge base from an existing expert system, one is left with a system of reasoning routines that is likely to be applicable in other settings as well. New expert systems in other areas can therefore be constructed merely by attaching a new knowledge base to this already existing reasoning system. This is essentially the observation that the control system we developed for solving the eight-puzzle can be applied to other problems merely by replacing the eight-puzzle productions with the productions representing those other problems.

Questions/Exercises

1. Identify the ambiguities involved when translating the sentence "They are racing horses."
2. Compare the results of parsing the following two sentences. Then, explain how the sentences differ semantically.

   The farmer built the fence in the field.
   The farmer built the fence in the winter.
3. Based on the semantic net in Fig. 10.21, what is the family relationship between Mary and John?
4. A database about magazine subscribers typically contains a list of subscribers to each magazine but does not contain a list of those who do not subscribe. How, then, does such a database determine that a person does not subscribe to a particular magazine?
5. What is the difference between a traditional database and a knowledge base for an expert system?

CHAPTER REVIEW PROBLEMS

1. Sometimes the ability to answer a question depends as much on knowing what facts are known as on the facts themselves. For example, suppose databases A and B both contain a complete list of employees who belong to the company's health insurance program, but only database A is aware that the list is complete. What could database A conclude about a member who was not on its list that database B could not?
2. In the text we briefly discussed the problems of understanding natural languages as opposed to formal programming languages. As an example of the complexities involved in the case of natural languages, identify situations in which the question "Do you know what time it is?" has different meanings.
3. As demonstrated by Problem 2, humans may use a question for a purpose other than asking. An example is "Do you know that your tire is flat?" which is used to inform rather than to ask. Give examples of questions used to reassure, to warn, and to criticize.
4. Compare the roles of the prepositional phrases in the following two sentences (that differ by only one word):

   The pigpen was built by the barn.
   The pigpen was built by the farmer.

5. If a researcher uses computer models for studying the memorization capabilities and processes of the human mind, do the programs developed for the machine necessarily memorize to the best of the machine's abilities? Explain.
6. Which of the following activities do you expect to be performance oriented and which are simulation oriented?
   a. The design of a flight simulator
   b. The design of an automatic pilot system
   c. The design of a database dealing with library materials
   d. The design of a model of a nation's economy for testing theories
   e. The design of a program for monitoring a patient's vital signs
7. Identify a small set of geometric properties that can be used to distinguish between the symbols O, G, C, and Q.
8. Describe the similarities between the technique of identifying characteristics by comparing them to templates and the error-correcting codes discussed in Chapter 1.
9. Describe two interpretations of the following line drawing based on whether the "corner" marked A is convex or concave:

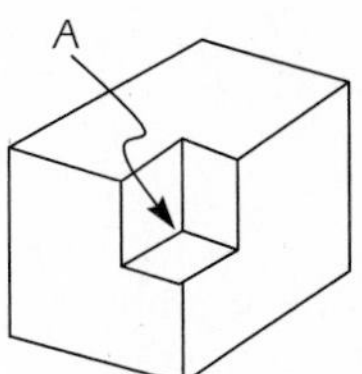

10. In the setting of a production system, what is the difference between a state graph and a search tree?
11. Characterize the task of solving the Rubik's cube as a production system. (What are the states, the productions, and so on?)
12. Characterize the task of developing a software system in terms of a production system.
13. In the text, we mentioned that a production system is often used as a technique for drawing conclusions from known facts. The states of the system are the facts known to be true at each stage of the reasoning process, and the productions are the rules of logic for manipulating the known facts. Identify some rules of logic that allow the conclusion "John is tall" to be obtained from the facts that "John is a basketball player," "Basketball players are not short," and "John is either short or tall."
14. The following tree represents possible moves in a competitive game, showing that player X currently has a choice between move A and move B. Following the move of player X, player Y is allowed to select a move, and then player X is allowed to select the last move of the game. The leaf nodes of the tree are labeled W, L, or T, depending on whether that ending

represents a win, loss, or tie for player X. Should player X select move A or move B? Why? How does selecting a "production" in a competitive atmosphere differ from a one-person game such as the eight-puzzle?

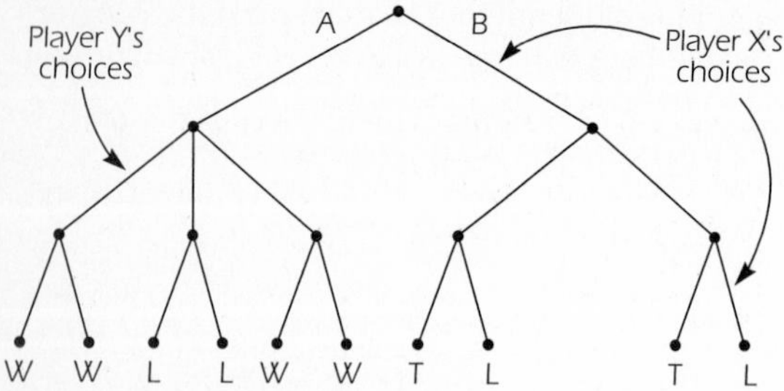

15. By considering the manipulation rules of algebra as productions, problems involving the simplification of algebraic expression can be solved in the setting of a production system. Identify a set of algebraic productions that allow the equation $3/(2x + 1) = 2/(2x - 2)$ to be reduced to the form $x = 4$. What are some rules of thumb (that is, heuristic rules) used when performing such algebraic simplifications?

16. Draw the search tree that is generated by a breadth-first search in an attempt to solve the eight-puzzle from the following start state without using the assistance of any heuristic information.

	1	3
4	2	5
7	8	6

17. Draw the search tree that is generated by the algorithm of Fig. 10.9 in an attempt to solve the eight-puzzle from the start state in Problem 16 if the number of tiles out of place is used as a heuristic.

18. Draw the search tree that is generated by the algorithm of Fig. 10.9 in an attempt to solve the eight-puzzle from the following start state, assuming the heuristic used is the same as that developed in Section 10.5.

1	2	3
5	7	6
4		8

19. What is the distinction between the technique of deciding which way to go when applying the binary search to a list stored as a tree (Chapter 8) and the use of a heuristic when searching for a goal state in the context of a production system?

20. Note that if a state in the state graph of a production system has an extremely low heuristic value in comparison to the other states and if there is a production from that state to itself, the algorithm in Fig. 10.9 can get caught in the loop of considering that state over and over again. Show that if the cost of executing any production in the system is at least one, then by computing the projected cost to be the sum of the heuristic value plus the cost of reaching the state along the path being traversed, this endless looping process will be avoided.

21. What heuristic do you use when searching for a route between two cities on a large road map?

22. List two properties that a heuristic should have if it is to be useful in a production system.

23. Suppose you have two buckets. One has a capacity of exactly 3 liters; the other has a capacity of 5 liters. You can pour water from one bucket to another, empty a bucket, or fill a bucket at any time. Your problem is to place exactly 4 liters of water in the 5-liter bucket. Formulate this problem as a production system.

24. Suppose your job is to supervise the loading of two trucks, each of which can carry at most 14 tons. The cargo is a variety of crates whose total weight is 28 tons but whose individual weights vary from crate to crate. The weight of each crate is marked on its side. What heuristic would you use for dividing the crates between the two trucks?

25. Design an artificial neural network that can tell which of the following two patterns is in its field of view.

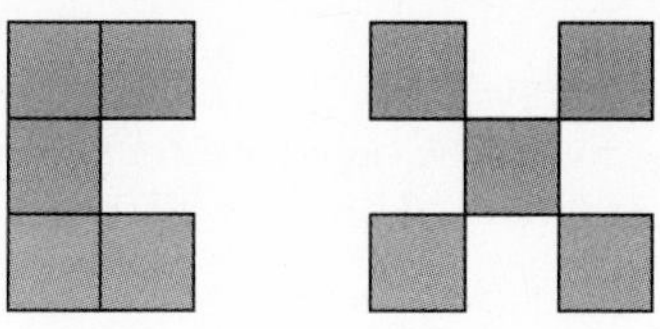

26. Design an artificial neural network that can tell which of the following two patterns is in its field of view.

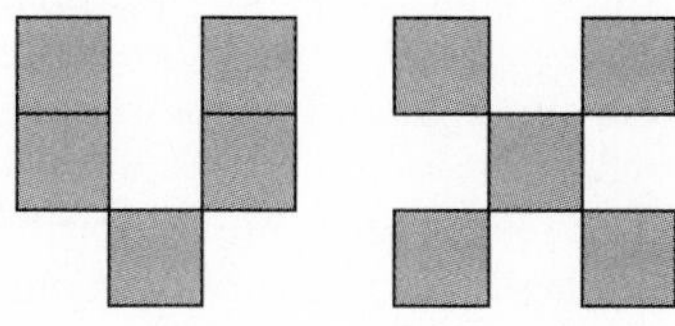

27. Design an artificial neural network that can tell which of the following four patterns is in its field of view.

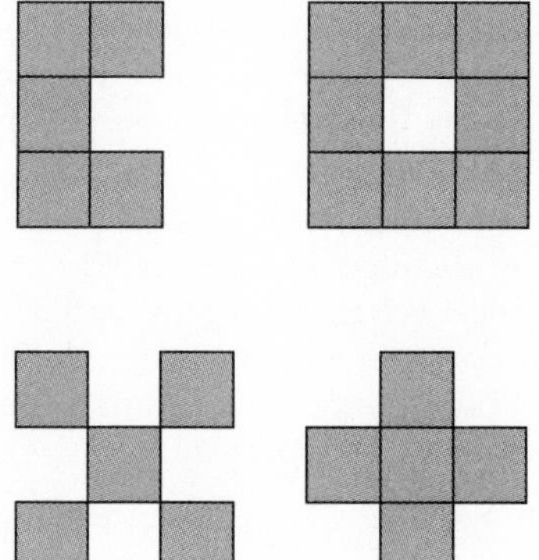

28. How do the results of parsing the following two sentences differ? How do the results of semantic analysis differ?

Theodore rode the zebra.
The zebra was ridden by Theodore.

29. How do the results of parsing the following two sentences differ? How do the results of semantic analysis differ?

If $X = 5$ then add 1 to X else subtract 1 from X.
If $X \neq 5$ then subtract 1 from X else add 1 to X.

30. Give an example in which the closed-world assumption leads to a contradiction.

31. Give two examples where the closed-world assumption is commonly used.

32. Adjust the weights and threshold values in the artificial neural network in Fig. 10.17 so that its output is 1 when both inputs are the same (both 0 or both 1) and 0 when the inputs are different (one being 0 while the other is 1).

33. Draw a diagram similar to Fig. 10.4 representing the process of simplifying the algebraic expression $7x + 3 = 3x - 5$ to the expression $x = -2$.

34. Expand your answer to the previous problem to show other paths that a control system might pursue when attempting to solve the problem.

35. Draw a diagram similar to Fig. 10.4 representing the reasoning process involved when concluding that "Polly can fly" from the initial facts "Polly is a parrot," "A parrot is a bird," and "All birds can fly."

36. In contrast to the statement in the preceding problem, some birds, such as an ostrich or a robin with a broken wing, cannot fly. Indeed, it would not seem reasonable to construct a deductive reasoning system in which all the exceptions to the statement "All birds can fly" are explicitly listed. How then do we as humans decide whether a particular bird can or cannot fly?

37. Explain how the semantics of the sentence "I met the fat lady's husband" depend on the context.

38. Formulate the problem of traveling from one city to another as a production system. What are the states? What are the productions?

39. Suppose you must perform three tasks, A, B, and C, that can be performed in any order (but not simultaneously). Formulate your problem as a production system and draw its state graph.

40. How does the state graph in the previous problem change if task C must be performed before task A?

41. Changes in the context of a sentence can change the significance of the sentence as well as its meaning. In the context of Fig. 10.21, how would the significance of the sentence "Mary hit John." change if the birthdates were in the 1960s rather than the 1990s? What if one were in the 1960s and the other in the 1990s?

42. Draw a semantic net representing the information in the following paragraph.

    Donna threw the ball to Jack, who hit it into center field. The center fielder tried to catch it, but it bounced off the wall instead.

QUESTIONS OF ETHICS

The following questions are provided to help you understand some of the ethical/social/legal issues associated with the field of computing as well as investigate your own beliefs and their foundations. The goal is not merely to answer these questions. You should also consider why you answered as you did and whether your justifications are consistent from one question to the next.

1. To what extent should researchers in nuclear power, genetic engineering, and artificial intelligence be held responsible for the way the results of their work are used?
2. How would you distinguish between intelligence and simulated intelligence? Do you believe there is a difference?
3. Suppose a computerized medical expert system gains a reputation within the medical community for giving sound advice. To what extent should a physician allow that system to alter his or her decisions regarding the treatment of patients? (If the physician gives a treatment contrary to that proposed by the expert system and the system turns out to be right, is the physician guilty of malpractice?) In general, if an expert system becomes well known within a field, to what degree could it hamper, rather than enhance, the ability of human experts when making their own judgments?
4. Many would argue that a computer's actions are merely consequences of how it was programmed, and thus a computer cannot possess free will. In turn, a computer should not be held responsible for its actions. Is a human's mind a computer? Are humans preprogrammed at birth? Are humans programmed by their environments? Are humans responsible for their actions?
5. Are there avenues that science should not pursue even though it may be capable of doing so? For instance, if it becomes possible to construct a machine with perception and reasoning skills comparable to those of humans, would the construction of such a machine be appropriate? What issues could the existence of such a machine raise? What are some of the issues being raised today by advancements in other scientific fields?
6. History abounds with instances in which the work of scientists and artists was affected by the political, religious, or other social influences of their times. In what ways are such issues affecting current scientific efforts? What about computer science in particular?

ADDITIONAL ACTIVITIES

1. Write a program that matches input symbols to predefined templates and reports on its findings. Input the symbols in the form of a matrix of 0s and 1s, where 0s represent white pixels of the input image and 1s represent black pixels. Design your program so that it does not require an exact match but allows for slight imperfections. Experiment with the problem of distinguishing between the symbols O, Q, and C.

2. Implement the puzzle-solving algorithm in Fig. 10.9. Design your system to accept the initial puzzle state in the form of a three-by-three matrix and to display the solution as a series of such matrices. You may want to experiment with different heuristics for determining the projected cost.
3. Write a program that changes simple statements of the form "I am . . ." into questions of the form "Why are you . . . ?" Does your program correctly handle the statement "I am your friend"? (It should change "your" to "my" to produce "Why are you my friend?")
4. Write two programs, one performance oriented and the other simulation oriented, to play tic-tac-toe.

ADDITIONAL READING

Allen, J. *Natural Language Understanding.* Redwood City, Calif.: Benjamin/Cummings, 1987.

Pearl, J. *Heuristics.* Reading, Mass.: Addison-Wesley, 1984.

Rich, E., and K. Knight, *Artificial Intelligence,* 2nd ed. New York: McGraw-Hill, 1991.

Rumelhart, D. E., and J. L. McClelland, *Parallel Distributed Processing.* Cambridge, Mass.: MIT Press, 1986.

Tanimoto, S. L. *The Elements of Artificial Intelligence Using Common Lisp,* 2nd ed. New York: Computer Science Press, 1995.

Weizenbaum, J. *Computer Power and Human Reason.* New York: W. H. Freeman and Co., 1979.

Zurada, J. M. *Introduction to Artificial Neural Systems.* St. Paul, Minn.: West, 1992.

CHAPTER ELEVEN

Theory of Computation

11.1 A Bare Bones Programming Language
- Data Description Statements
- Process Description Statements
- The Scope of Bare Bones

11.2 Turing Machines
- Turing Machine Fundamentals
- A Specific Example

11.3 Computable Functions
- Functions and Their Computation
- The Church–Turing Thesis
- The Universality of Bare Bones

11.4 A Noncomputable Function
- Some Preliminaries
- The Halting Problem

11.5 Complexity and Its Measure
- Complexity of the Insertion Sort
- Complexity of the Quick Sort
- Orders of Complexity

11.6 Problem Classification
- Polynomial Problems
- Nonpolynomial Problems
- NP Problems

In this chapter we discuss some theoretical ideas founded on the question of what algorithmic machines can and cannot do. We start by introducing a very simple programming language. Next, we see that any problem that can be solved on a modern computer has a solution that can be expressed in that language. (If a programming language is designed to encompass the features of this simple language, it is guaranteed to provide a means of expressing a solution to any problem that the machine is capable of solving.) Using this language, we then discover that there are problems that today's machines cannot solve and that apparently no future algorithmic machine will be able to solve. Finally, we find that even among the machine-solvable problems, there are problems whose solutions are so complex that they are apparently unsolvable from any practical point of view.

Many of the results in this chapter were originally obtained in the early twentieth century by mathematicians working in the area of mathematics known as logic and foundations. Thus many of the points about the problem-solving ability of modern machines summarized here were known well before today's technology evolved. Today, the subject is known as the theory of computation, and although born within mathematics, it is now classified by many as computer science.

Regardless of its classification, the subject presents a truly fascinating study of the power and limitations of mathematical reasoning. Paramount in the subject is the paper published by the German mathematician Kurt Gödel in 1931 that essentially shows that within any mathematical system encompassing the system of natural numbers (0, 1, 2, 3, . . .) and the arithmetic operations of addition and multiplication, statements exist that can be neither proven nor disproven. This startling result implies that a complete understanding of even our "simple" arithmetic system lies beyond the capabilities of algorithmic machines.

11.1 A Bare Bones Programming Language

Let us assume that we have been asked to design a new imperative programming language that can serve as a general-purpose programming language well into the future. Our task is complicated by the fact that we cannot foresee the particular applications that the future will bring. How, then, can we guarantee that our language will contain those features required to express solutions to any problems future programmers may encounter?

Our answer is to design our language to encompass the power of algorithmic processes themselves. That is, we want to ensure that if a problem can be solved algorithmicly, then an algorithm for solving that problem can be expressed in our language. Hence, if a future programmer finds that a problem cannot be solved using our language, then the reason will not be a fault of our language. Instead, it will be that there is not an algorithm for solving the problem. A programming language with this property is called a **universal programming language.**

Let us also assume that considerations of expense dictate that we not provide an abundance of features that merely enhance convenience. Our task is to design a powerful yet concise programming language.

In this section we describe an imperative programming language that fulfills these requirements. Because our language has few of the conveniences found in other languages, it is fitting that we refer to it as Bare Bones. Indeed, our language isolates the minimum requirements of a general-purpose programming language.

Our description of Bare Bones follows the format of the discussion of programming languages in Chapter 5. We first present the language features for data description, followed by the assignment statements, and then we discuss the control statements in the language.

Data Description Statements

As we have seen, the data description statements found in high-level programming languages allow programmers the luxury of thinking in terms of arrays of numeric values and strings of alphabetic characters, even though the machine itself does not associate interpretations to the bit patterns representing these objects. The machine merely manipulates the patterns as directed by the instructions being executed. Before being presented to a machine for execution, a high-level instruction directing that two characters in a string be interchanged must be translated into machine-level instructions to interchange two bit patterns.

In turn, the design of a programming language can be simplified by forcing the programmer to express all operations in terms of bit patterns in the first place. Such a language has a single data type and structure, so it does not need data description statements.

For simplicity sake, our Bare Bones language adopts this approach. All variables are considered to be of type "bit pattern of any length." Thus in a Bare Bones program we do not need a declarative part in which variable names and their associated properties are described; we can simply begin using the names as they are required in the procedural part of the program.

Of course, a translator for our Bare Bones language must be able to distinguish variable names from the other terms. This is done by designing the syntax of Bare Bones so that the role of any term can be identified by its context. For this purpose, we specify that variable names consist only of letters from the traditional alphabet. Thus the strings XYZ, Bill, and abcdefghi can be used as variable names, whereas 2G5, %o, or x.y cannot. Furthermore, we adopt the policy of terminating each statement with a semicolon so that a translator can easily separate statements.

Process Description Statements

Bare Bones contains only three assignment statements, each of which takes the form of modifying the contents of the variable identified in the statement. The first allows us to associate a string of zeros with a variable name. Its syntax is

clear *name;*

where *name* can be any legal variable name.

The other assignment statements are essentially opposites of each other:

incr *name;*

and

decr *name;*

Again, *name* represents any legal variable name. The first of these statements increments the value associated with the identified variable. Here the term *increment* refers to the interpretation of bit patterns as representing numeric values in base two notation and means to change the pattern to represent the next larger integer. To illustrate, if the pattern 101 is associated with the variable Y before the statement

```
incr Y;
```

is executed, the pattern 110 is associated with Y afterward. That is, 1 is added to the value assigned to Y.

In contrast, the statement decr *name;* is used to decrement the value associated with the identified variable or, in other words, to decrease the represented value by one. An exception is when the identified variable is already associated with zero, in which case this statement leaves the value unaltered. Therefore, if the value associated with Y is 101 before the statement

```
decr Y;
```

is executed, the pattern 100 is associated with Y afterward. However, if the value of Y had been zero before executing the statement, the value would remain zero after execution.

Bare Bones contains only one control structure represented by a while-end statement pair. The statement sequence

```
while name not 0 do;
         .
         .
         .
end;
```

(where *name* represents any legal variable name) causes any statement or statement sequence positioned between the while and end statements to be repeated as long as the value of the variable *name* is not zero. To be more precise, when a while-end structure is encountered during program execution, the value of the identified variable is first compared to zero. If it is zero, the structure is skipped and execution continues with the statement following the end statement. If, however, the variable's value is not zero, the statement sequence within the while-end structure is executed and control is returned to the while statement, whereupon the comparison is conducted again. Note that the burden of loop control is partially placed on the programmer, who must explicitly request that the variable's value be altered within the loop body to avoid an infinite loop. For instance, the sequence

```
incr X;
while X not 0 do;
    incr Z;
end;
```

results in an infinite process because the value associated with X can never be zero, whereas the sequence

```
clear Z;
while X not 0 do;
    incr Z;
    decr X;
end;
```

ultimately terminates with the effect of transferring the value initially associated with X to the variable Z.

Observe that while and end statements must appear in pairs with the while statement appearing first. However, a while-end statement pair may appear within the instructions being repeated by another while-end pair. In such a case

```
clear Z;
while X not 0 do;
  clear W;
  while Y not 0 do;
    incr Z;
    incr W;
    decr Y;
  end;
  while W not 0 do;
    incr Y;
    decr W;
  end;
  decr X;
end;
```

Figure 11.1 A Bare Bones program for computing $X \times Y$

the pairing of while and end statements is accomplished by scanning the program in its written form from beginning to end while associating each end statement with the nearest preceding while statement not yet paired. Although not syntactically necessary, we often use indentation to enhance the readability of such structures.

As a closing example, the instruction sequence in Fig. 11.1 results in the product of the values associated with X and Y being associated with Z, although it has the side effect of destroying any nonzero value that may have been associated with X. (The while-end structure controlled by the variable W has the effect of restoring the original value of Y.)

Finally, we note that a Bare Bones program terminates when the end of the list of instructions is reached.

The Scope of Bare Bones

Keep in mind that although we set the stage for this section with a proposal for a usable programming language, our goal is actually to investigate what is possible, not what is practical. Bare Bones would probably prove to be more awkward than most machine languages if used in an applied setting. On the other hand, in Sections 11.2 and 11.3 we argue that this simple language fulfills our goal of providing a no-frills universal programming language.

Although not practical in an application programming environment, languages such as Bare Bones find use within theoretical computer science. For example, in Appendix E we use Bare Bones as a tool to settle the question regarding the equivalence of iterative and recursive structures raised in Chapter 4. There we find that our suspicion of equivalence was, in fact, justified.

For now, we support our claims regarding the power of Bare Bones by demonstrating how its use allows the expression of some elementary operations. We first note that with a combination of the assignment statements, any value (any bit pattern) can be associated with a given variable. For example, the following sequence assigns the bit pattern 11 (the binary representation for 3) to the variable X by first clearing any previous association and then incrementing its value three times:

```
clear X;
incr X;
incr X;
incr X;
```

Another common activity in programs is to move data from one location to another. In terms of Bare Bones, this means that we need to be able to assign to one variable a bit pattern previously assigned to another. This can be accomplished by first clearing the destination and then incrementing it an appropriate number of times. In fact, we have already observed that the sequence

```
clear Z;
while X not 0 do;
      incr Z;
      decr X;
end;
```

transfers the value associated with X to Z. On the other hand, this sequence has the side effect of destroying the original value of X. To correct for this, we can introduce an auxiliary variable to which we first transfer the subject value from its initial location. We then use this auxiliary variable as the data source from which we restore the original variable while placing the subject value in the desired destination. In this manner, the movement of Tax to Extra can be accomplished by the sequence shown in Fig. 11.2.

We adopt the syntax

move *name1* to *name2*;

(where *name1* and *name2* represent variable names) as a shorthand notation for a statement structure of the form in Fig. 11.2. Thus, although Bare Bones itself does not have an explicit move instruction, we often write programs as though it did, with the understanding that to convert such informal programs into real Bare Bones programs, one must replace the move statements with their equivalent

Figure 11.2 A Bare Bones implementation of the instruction "move Tax to Extra"

```
clear Aux;
clear Extra;
while Tax not 0 do;
  incr Aux;
  decr Tax;
end;
while Aux not 0 do;
  incr Tax;
  incr Extra;
  decr Aux;
end;
```

while-end structures using an auxiliary variable whose name does not clash with a name already used elsewhere in the program.

Questions/Exercises

1. Show that the statement Invert X; (whose action is to convert the value of X to zero if its initial value is nonzero and to 1 if its initial value is zero) can be simulated by a Bare Bones program segment.
2. Show that even our simple Bare Bones language contains more statements than necessary by showing that the clear statement can be replaced with combinations of other statements in the language.
3. Show that the if-then-else structure can be simulated using Bare Bones. That is, write a program sequence in Bare Bones that simulates the action of the statement

   ```
   if X not 0 then S1 else S2;
   ```

   where S1 and S2 represent arbitrary statement sequences.
4. Show that each of the Bare Bones statements can be expressed in terms of the machine language of Appendix C. (Bare Bones can be used as a programming language for such a machine.)
5. How can negative numbers be dealt with in Bare Bones?

11.2 Turing Machines

In Section 11.1 we claimed that Bare Bones is a universal programming language, meaning that with Bare Bones we can express a solution for any problem that algorithmic machines are capable of solving. We discuss this claim in more detail in Section 11.3, but first we must develop a better understanding of the capabilities of algorithmic machines themselves.

Turing Machine Fundamentals

We now consider the class of computing machines known as **Turing machines.** These machines were introduced by Alan M. Turing in 1936 as a tool for studying the power of algorithmic processes and are still used for that purpose today. Keep in mind that Turing "invented" these machines before technology could produce them. Thus a Turing machine is a conceptual device rather than an actual machine. Although today we often think of a Turing machine as an electronic device, Turing originally envisioned these machines in terms of a human performing a calculation with pencil and paper.

A Turing machine consists of a control unit that can read and write symbols on a tape by means of a read/write head (Fig. 11.3). The tape extends indefinitely at both ends and is divided into cells, each of which can contain any one of a finite set of symbols. This set is called the machine's alphabet.

At any time during a Turing machine's computation, the machine must be in one of a finite number of conditions, called states. A Turing machine's computa-

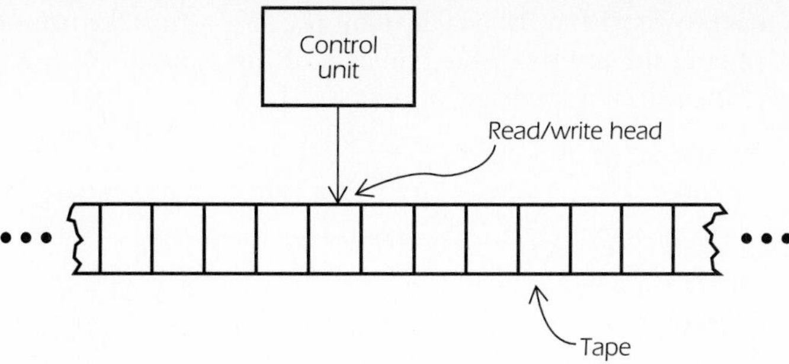

Figure 11.3 The components of a Turing machine

tion begins in a special state called the start state and ceases when the machine reaches another special state known as the halt state.

A Turing machine's computation consists of a sequence of steps that are executed by the machine's control unit. Each step consists of observing the symbol in the current tape cell (the one under the read-write head), writing a symbol in that cell, possibly moving the read-write head one cell to the left or right, and then shifting states. The exact action to be performed is determined by a program that tells the control unit what to do based on the machine's state and the contents of the current tape cell.

Being conceptual in nature, a Turing machine can be implemented in a variety of forms. In fact, today's computers are actually Turing machines (except that their memories are finite, whereas an abstract Turing machine has an unlimited supply of tape). The CPU is the control unit, whose states are the various bit patterns that can be assigned to the registers; the machine's memory takes the place of the traditional tape storage system; and the alphabet consists of the symbols 0 and 1.

This similarity between Turing machines and the machines of today is not completely coincidental. It was Turing's objective to design an abstract machine that captured the essence of computational processes. It is fitting, then, for the machines of today to incorporate the basic features identified by Turing.

The significance of Turing machines in theoretical computer science lies in the conjecture that (according to the Church–Turing thesis, which we will discuss later) the computational power of Turing machines is as great as any algorithmic system. That is, if a problem cannot be solved by a Turing machine, then it cannot be solved by any algorithmic system. Thus Turing machines are simple in design yet represent a theoretical bound on the capabilities of actual machines. In turn, Turing machines are useful as tools for investigating the limitations of algorithmic machines and of algorithmic processes themselves.

A Specific Example

We now consider an example of a specific Turing machine. For this purpose, we represent the machine's tape as a horizontal strip divided into cells in which we can record symbols from the machine's alphabet. We indicate the machine's current position on the tape by placing a pointer under the current cell. The alphabet for our example consists of the symbols 0, 1, and *. The tape of our machine might appear as follows:

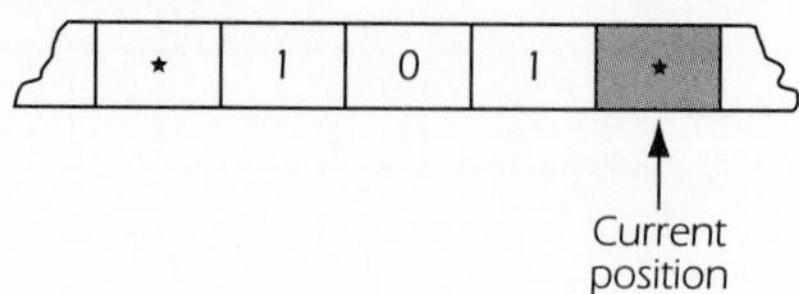

By interpreting a string of symbols on the tape as representing binary numbers separated by asterisks, we recognize that this particular tape contains the value 5. Our Turing machine is designed to increment such a value on the tape by 1. More precisely, it assumes that the starting position is at an asterisk marking the right end of a string of 0s and 1s, and it proceeds to alter the bit pattern to the left so that it represents the next larger integer.

The states for our machine are START, ADD, CARRY, NO CARRY, OVERFLOW, RETURN, and HALT. The actions corresponding to each of these states and the content of the current cell are described in the table in Fig. 11.4. We assume that the machine always begins in the START state.

Let us apply this machine to the tape pictured earlier that contains the value 5. Observe that when in the START state with the current cell containing * (as is our case), we are instructed by the table to rewrite the *, move our position one cell to the left, and enter the ADD state. Having done this, our situation can be described as follows:

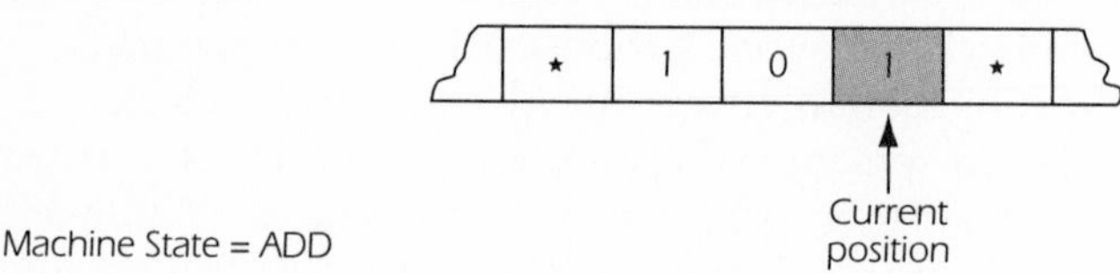

To proceed, we look at the table to see what to do when in the ADD state with the current cell containing 1. The table tells us to replace the 1 in the current cell with 0, move one cell to the left, and enter the CARRY state. Our situation can then be described by the following:

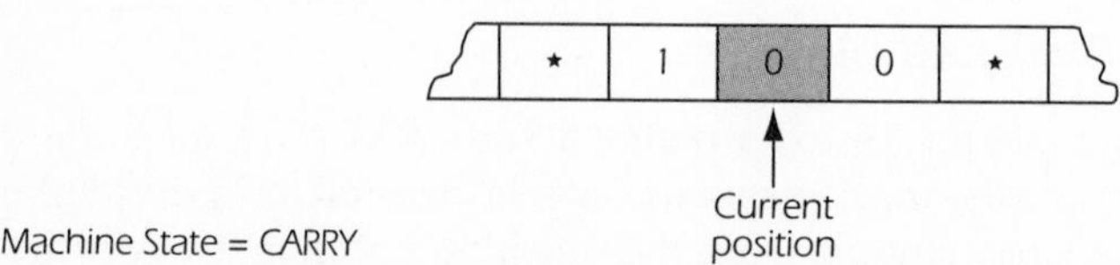

Current state	Current cell content	Value to write	Direction to move	New state to enter
START	*	*	Left	ADD
ADD	0	1	Left	NO CARRY
ADD	1	0	Left	CARRY
ADD	*	*	Right	HALT
CARRY	0	1	Left	NO CARRY
CARRY	1	0	Left	CARRY
CARRY	*	1	Left	OVERFLOW
NO CARRY	0	0	Left	NO CARRY
NO CARRY	1	1	Left	NO CARRY
NO CARRY	*	*	Right	RETURN
OVERFLOW	(ignored)	*	Right	RETURN
RETURN	0	0	Right	RETURN
RETURN	1	1	Right	RETURN
RETURN	*	*	No move	HALT

Figure 11.4 A Turing machine for incrementing a value

We again refer to the table to see what to do next and find that when in the CARRY state with the current cell containing 0, we should replace the 0 with 1, move one cell to the left, and enter the NO CARRY state. After doing this our situation is as follows:

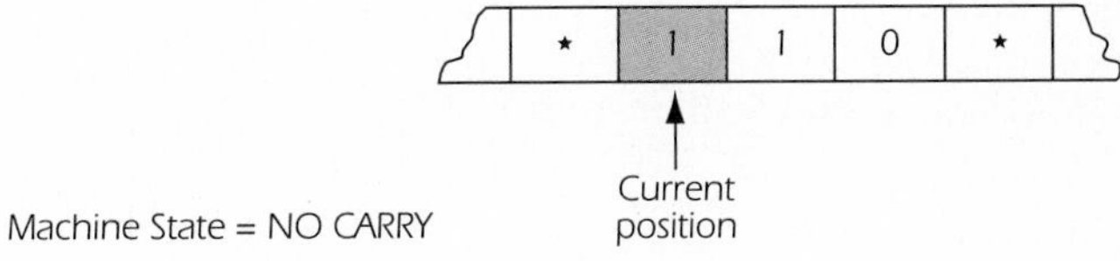

From this situation, the table instructs us to proceed by replacing the 1 in the current cell with another 1, move one cell to the left, and remain in the NO CARRY state. Consequently, we find our machine in the following condition:

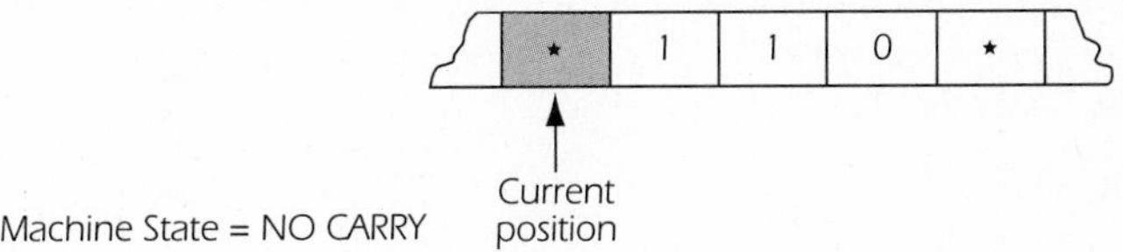

Now the table tells us to rewrite the asterisk in the current cell, move one position to the right, and enter the RETURN state. Continuing in this fashion, we remain in the RETURN state as we move back to the right cell by cell until we finally arrive at the condition as follows:

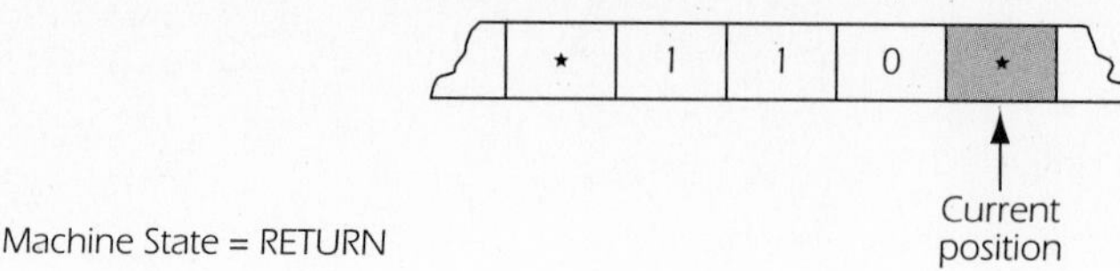

At this point, we see that the table instructs us to rewrite the asterisk in the current cell and HALT. The machine thus stops in the following configuration (the symbols on the tape now represent the value 6 as desired):

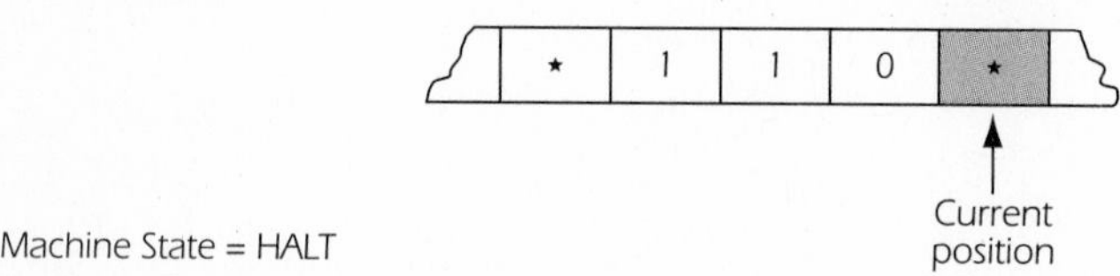

In closing, we note that this example has shown how a Turing machine might perform the action described by the statement

```
incr X;
```

in the Bare Bones language of Section 11.1.

Questions/Exercises

1. Apply the Turing machine described in this section, starting with the following initial status:

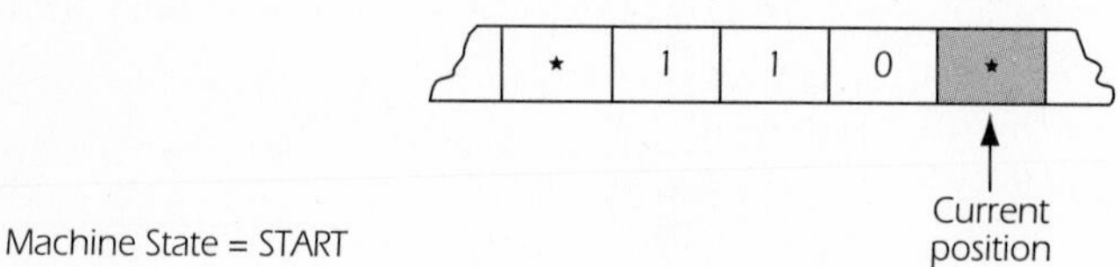

2. Describe a Turing machine that replaces a string of zeroes and ones with a single zero.
3. Describe a Turing machine that decrements the value on the tape if it is greater than zero or leaves the value unaltered if it is zero.
4. Identify an everyday situation in which calculating takes place. How is that situation analogous to a Turing machine?

11.3 Computable Functions

Our goal is to use Turing machines to investigate the power of our Bare Bones language. But first we need a method of measuring computing power.

Functions and Their Computation

The measure of computing power we need is available in the concept of computable functions. To explain, let us consider the actions of a computer at a very fundamental level. If we were to take snapshots of the machine's storage facilities before and after executing a program, we would find one collection of bit values before the execution and another collection afterward. All a program actually does, after all, is direct the conversion of some initial collection of bits, which we will call the input, into another collection, which we will call the output.

This association between inputs and outputs is called a **function.** Many functions are so common that they have been given names, such as addition, which with each input pair associates an output value equal to the sum of the inputs; multiplication, which again accepts an input pair but produces an output equal to the product of the inputs; and the successor function, which with each input value associates an output that is one greater than the input.

The process of determining an output of a function from its input is called *computing the function.* In turn, the action of any algorithmic machine can be considered that of computing a function. This insight provides a means of measuring the computational powers of machines or, in fact, any computational system. We need merely identify the functions it is capable of computing and use this set as the measure. If one machine or algorithmic system is capable of computing more functions than another, the former is considered the more powerful.

Consider, for example, a system in which function outputs are predetermined and recorded in a table along with their associated inputs. Each time the output of a function is required we merely look for the given input in the table and find the required output. Such systems are convenient but limited, because many functions cannot be represented in tabular form. An example is shown in Fig. 11.5 where we have attempted to display the successor function. Since there is no limit to the list of possible input/output pairs, the table is destined to be incomplete. The addition function suffers the same fate—no table can display all the possible inputs and outputs for addition.

Another approach for finding function outputs would be to describe how to compute the output rather than trying to display all possible input/output combinations. We could, for example, use algebraic formulas to describe the input/output associations of many functions. To describe the function whose output is the value of an original investment of P that has earned an annually compounded interest rate of r for n years, we would write

$$V = P(1 + r)^n$$

which describes how the computation is done rather than presenting the results in tabular form. Indeed, the algebraic formula itself is a description of an

Input	Output
0	1
1	10
10	11
11	100
100	101
101	110
110	111
111	1000
1000	1001
.	.
.	.
.	.

Figure 11.5 The successor function

algorithm for calculating the function's output, given any particular inputs. The successor function would be described by

$$Output = Input + 1$$

But, the expressive power of algebraic formulas has its limitations as well. There are functions whose input/output relationships are too complex to be described by algebraic manipulation of the function's input value. Examples include the trigonometric functions such as sine and cosine. If pressed to calculate the sine of 38 degrees, you might draw the appropriate triangle, measure its side, and calculate the desired ratio—a process that cannot be expressed in terms of algebraic manipulations of the value 38. Your pocket calculator also struggles with the task of computing the sine of 38 degrees. In reality, it is forced to apply rather sophisticated mathematical techniques to obtain a very good approximation to the sine of 38 degrees, which it reports to you as being the exact answer.

We see, then, that as we consider functions whose input/output relationships are more and more complex, we are forced to find more complex algorithms for computing the relationships and more powerful techniques for describing these algorithms.

A striking result from mathematics is that there are functions whose input/output relationships are so complex that there is no well-defined, step-by-step process for determining the function's output based on its input value. That is, there are functions whose input/output relationships cannot be determined by any algorithmic means. These functions are said to be noncomputable, whereas the functions whose output values can be determined algorithmically from their input values are said to be **computable.**

Since there is no algorithmic method of finding the output values of the noncomputable functions, these functions lie beyond the powers of today's, as well as tomorrow's, computers. Thus understanding the boundary between the computable and noncomputable functions is equivalent to understanding the limitations of computers in general. The Church–Turing thesis represents an important step toward identifying this boundary.

The Church–Turing Thesis

We have already seen that finite tables and algebraic formulas are insufficient for describing the input/output relationships of all computable functions. For example, we claimed that the trigonometric functions cannot be described by either. Alan Turing developed the concept of a Turing machine in an attempt to establish a single context in which all the computable functions could be described.

Consider again the Turing machine example of Section 11.2. This machine can be used to find the output values for the successor function by placing the input value in its binary form on the tape, running the machine until it halts, and reading the output value from the tape. In other words, the Turing machine previously described actually calculates the successor function outputs for us. A function that can be computed in this manner by a Turing machine is said to be **Turing computable.**

Turing's conjecture was that the Turing computable functions were the same as the computable functions. In other words, he conjectured that the computational power of Turing machines encompasses that of any algorithmic process or, equivalently, that (in contrast to such approaches as tables and algebraic formulas) the Turing machine concept provides a context in which all the computable functions could be described. Today, this conjecture is often referred to as the **Church–Turing thesis,** in reference to the contributions made by both Alan Turing and Alonzo Church. Since Turing's initial work, much evidence has been collected to support this thesis, and today the Church–Turing thesis is widely accepted. That is, the computable functions and the Turing-computable functions are considered one and the same.

The significance of this conjecture is that it gives insight to the capabilities and limitations of computing machinery by identifying the set of Turing-computable functions as a test set to which the computational powers of various computational systems can be compared. In particular, if a computational system is capable of computing all the Turing-computable functions, it is considered to be a universal system.

The Universality of Bare Bones

As an example of the significance of the Church–Turing thesis, let us apply it to confirm our claim that Bare Bones is a universal programming language. First, we observe that any program written in Bare Bones can be thought of as directing the computation of a function by considering the initial values of certain variables (including all those with nonzero initial values) as the function's input and the values of certain variables (which may or may not be the same as those used for input) as the function's output. We merely execute the program, starting with the input variables containing the proper values, and observe the output variables when the program terminates.

Under these conditions the program

```
incr X;
```

describes the same function (the successor function) that is described by the Turing machine example of Section 11.2. Indeed, it increases the value associated with X by one. Likewise, by considering the variables X and Y as inputs and the variable Z as the output, the program

```
move Y to Z;
while X not 0 do;
    incr Z;
    decr X;
end;
```

describes the addition function.

Thus, we see that the Bare Bones programming language can be used to describe the input/output relationships of functions. In fact, researchers have shown that the Bare Bones programming language can be used to describe exactly the same input/output relationships that can be described by Turing machines.

This equivalence is what we need to complete our solution to the problem posed in Section 11.1 of developing a simple yet powerful programming language. Since any Turing-computable function can be computed by a program written in Bare Bones, then (by the Church–Turing thesis) any computable function can be computed by a program written in Bare Bones. That is, Bare Bones is a universal programming language in the sense that if an algorithm exists for solving a problem, then that problem can be solved by some Bare Bones program. In turn, Bare Bones could theoretically serve as a general-purpose programming language.

We say *theoretically* because such a language is certainly not as convenient as the high-level languages introduced in Chapter 5. However, each of those languages essentially contains the features of Bare Bones as its core. It is, in fact, this core that ensures the universality of each of those languages; all the other features in the various languages are included for convenience.

Questions/Exercises

1. Identify other functions whose output can be described as an algebraic expression involving its input.
2. Identify a function that cannot be described in terms of an algebraic formula. Is your function nonetheless computable?
3. Describe the function computed by the following Bare Bones program, assuming the function's input is represented by X and its output by Z:

```
clear Z;
while X not 0 do;
      incr Z;
      incr Z;
      decr X;
end;
```

4. Describe a Turing machine that ultimately halts for some inputs but never halts for others.

11.4 A Noncomputable Function

We now identify a function that is not Turing computable and so, by the Church–Turing thesis, is widely believed to be noncomputable in the general sense.

Some Preliminaries

Our presentation of a noncomputable function requires the understanding of two additional concepts. The first is Gödel numbering, which refers to a technique initially used by Kurt Gödel for assigning a unique nonnegative integer to each object in a collection. The objects in Gödel's case were such things as formulas and proofs. In our case, they are programs written in Bare Bones, Gödel's system was built around the properties of prime numbers and consisted of a more complex process than we need here. For our purpose, the process summarized in Fig. 11.6 suffices. We first consider any program written in Bare Bones as one single long string of characters (in which the instructions are separated by semicolons). We then code each character of this string into a bit pattern using the ASCII code. After this, any program appears as a long string of 0s and 1s that can be interpreted as representing a (rather large) number in binary notation. In this manner we can associate any program written in Bare Bones with a unique positive integer.

It is not important in our case whether the positive integers associated with the programs in Bare Bones are obtained by the process just described or by Gödel's original technique. The important point is that such an association is possible. Having established this possibility, we continue by assuming such an association has been carried out. Moreover, we call the number associated with a given program that program's **Gödel number.**

The second concept is that of a self-terminating program. Observe that any program written in Bare Bones must contain at least one variable name, and since each such variable consists of a string of letters, the names in a given program can be placed in alphabetical order. In terms of this order, we can speak of

Figure 11.6 Computing the Gödel number of a Bare Bones program

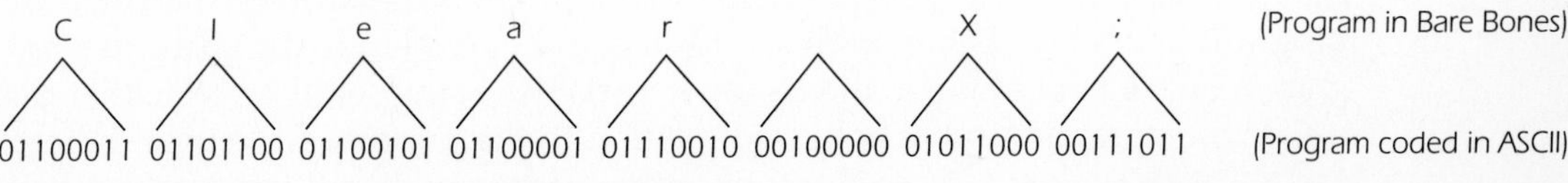

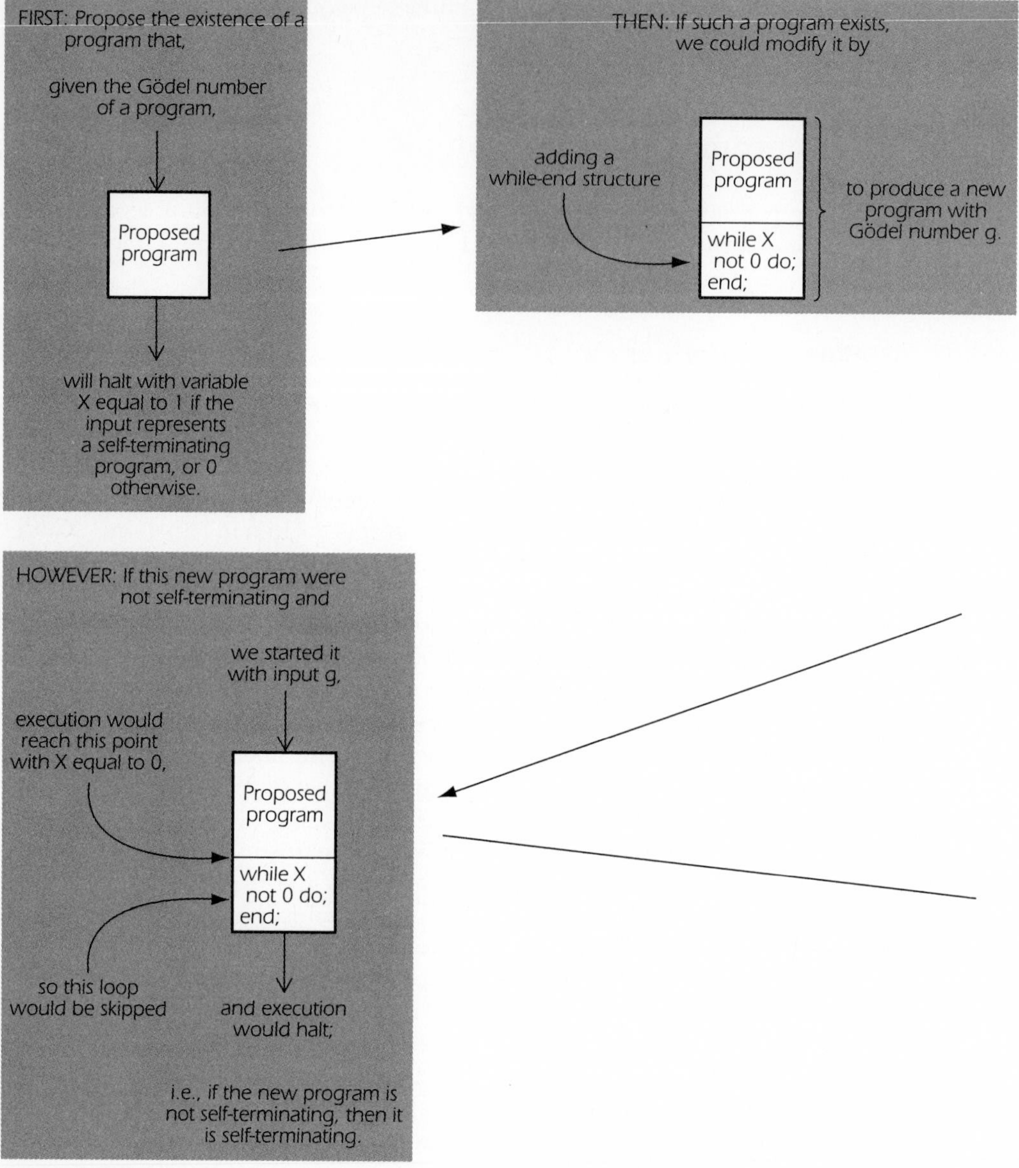

Figure 11.7 Proving the unsolvability of the halting program

the first variable of a program. We say that a program is **self-terminating** if the program halts after being started with its first variable initialized to the program's own Gödel number and its other variables being set to 0. (Note that this use of the program probably has no relation to the purpose for which the program was originally written.) Any program written in Bare Bones either is self-terminating or is not.

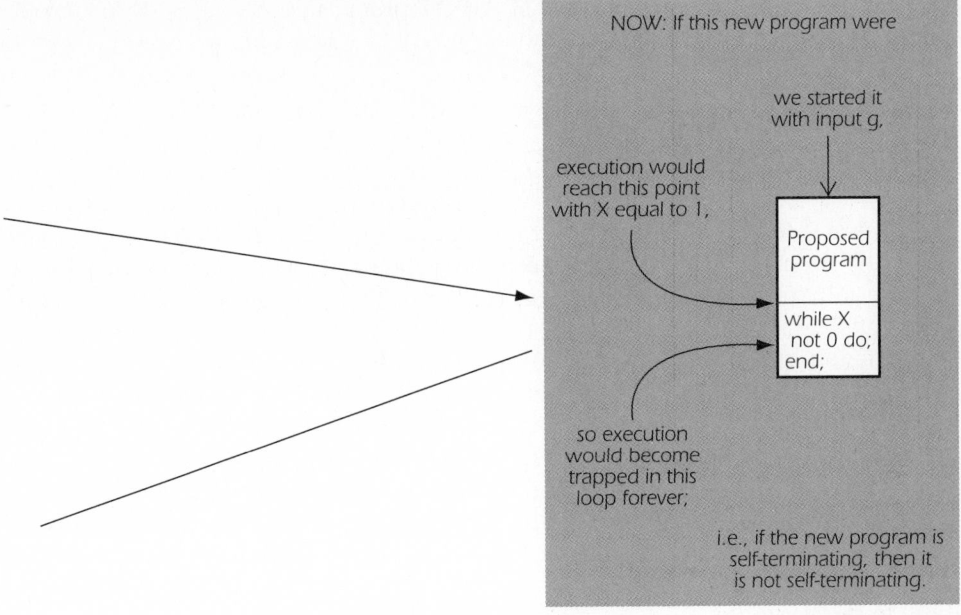

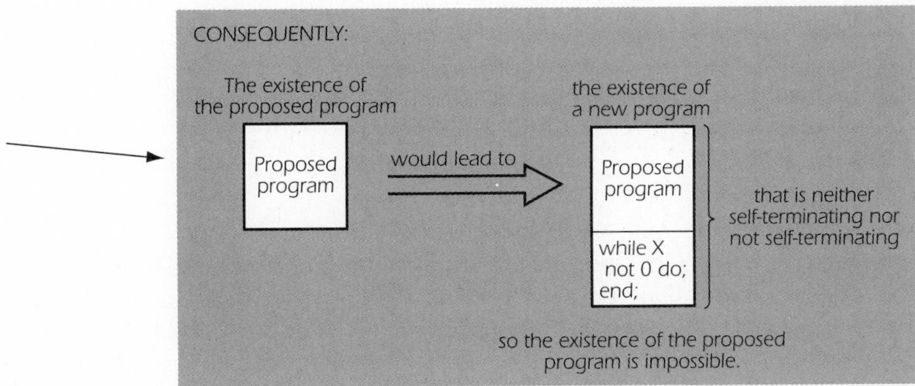

Figure 11.7 *(Continued)*

Essentially, a program is self-terminating if and only if it ultimately halts if started with itself as its input. Thus the concept of a self-terminating program involves self-reference—the idea of an object referring to itself. This ploy has repeatedly led to amazing results in mathematics from such informal curiosities as the statement "This statement is false" to the more serious paradox represented by the question "Does the set of all sets contain itself?" What we have done, then, in defining the concept of a self-terminating program, is to set the stage for a line of reasoning similar to "If it does, then it doesn't; but, if it doesn't, then it does," as we see shortly.

The Halting Problem

We are now in position to define a function that is not computable. It associates with each Gödel number of a program in Bare Bones (the function's input) a 1 or a 0 (the function's output) depending on whether the program in question is self-terminating. More precisely we will define the function so that Gödel numbers of self-terminating programs produce the output value 1 and Gödel numbers of non-self-terminating programs produce the output value 0.

The problem of computing this function is actually the problem of calculating whether programs ultimately halt after being started from a particular initial state; it is therefore commonly referred to as the **halting problem.**

Our task now is to show that the preceding function is not computable. To this end, we show that the assumption that it is computable leads to an impossible situation. Consequently, we are forced to conclude that the function is not computable.

Referring to Fig. 11.7, we proceed with the assumption that the function is computable. This means that there must be a program in Bare Bones that computes the function. In other words, there is a program that halts with its output either equal to 1 if its input variable was the Gödel number of a self-terminating program or equal to a 0 if not. We can assume that the variables in this program are named so that the input variable is the first in alphabetical order; otherwise we could simply rename them to have this property. Likewise, we may assume that the program's output variable is named X.

We could then modify the program by attaching the statements:

```
while X not 0 do;
end;
```

at its end, producing a new program. This new program must be either self-terminating or not. However, we are about to see that it can be neither! In particular, if this new program were self-terminating and we ran it with its input being equal to its own Gödel number, then when its execution reached the while statement that we added, the variable X would contain a 1. (To this point the new program is identical to the original program that produced a 1 if its input was the Gödel number of a self-terminating program.) At this point, the program's execution would be caught forever in the while-end structure because we made no provisions for X to be decremented within the loop. But this contradicts our assumption that the new program is self-terminating. Therefore we must conclude that the new program is not self-terminating.

If, however, this new program were not self-terminating and we executed it with its input being its own Gödel number, it would reach the added while statement with X being assigned the value 0. (This occurs because the statements preceding the while statement constitute the original program that produces an output of 0 when its input represents a program that is not self-terminating.) In this case, the loop in the while-end structure would be avoided and the program would halt. But this is the property of a self-terminating program, so we are forced to conclude that the new program is self-terminating, just as we were forced to conclude earlier that it is not self-terminating.

In summary, we see that we have the impossible situation of a program that on the one hand must be either self-terminating or not and on the other hand can be neither. Consequently, the assumption that led to this dilemma must be false. In other words, the function in question is not computable.

With this conclusion, we have found an example of a function that is not Turing computable and hence, by the Church–Turing thesis, accepted as being noncomputable in the general context. We can conclude that the halting problem is an example of an **unsolvable problem,** meaning that its solution requires finding the output of a noncomputable function and therefore lies beyond the capabilities of computing machinery.

In closing, we should relate what we have just discussed to the ideas in Chapter 10. There, a major underlying question was whether the powers of computing machines include those required for intelligence itself. We have now seen that there are limits to the abilities of machines that technology cannot overcome. They can solve only problems with algorithmic solutions. The question, then, is whether natural intelligence embodies more than the execution of algorithmic processes. Needless to say, this is a highly debatable and sometimes emotional issue.

Questions/Exercises

1. What value would our Gödel numbering technique associate with the following simple Bare Bones program?

```
decr X;
```

2. Is the program "incr X; decr Y;" self-terminating?
3. What is wrong with the following scenario?

   In a certain community, everyone owns his or her own house. The house painter of the community claims to paint all those and only those houses that are not painted by their owners.

   (*Hint:* Who paints the house painter's house?)

11.5 Complexity and Its Measure

In Section 11.4 we investigated problems in terms of their solvability. In this section and in Section 11.6 we are interested in the more down-to-earth issue of whether a solvable problem has a practical solution.

The tool used for our investigation is a measure of the **complexity** of a problem. Here again, we are using a term whose meaning should be clarified, because *complexity* means different things to different people. One interpretation deals with the amount of branching and decision making involved in a problem's solution. Intuition tells us that following a twisted and entwined list of directions is more complicated than following instructions in the sequential order in which they are listed. This is complexity from a software engineer's point of view. However, such an interpretation does not capture the concept of complexity from a machine's point of view. A machine does not really make any decisions when selecting the next instruction for execution but merely executes the instruction that is indicated by the program counter. Consequently, a machine can execute a set of tangled instructions as easily as it can execute a list of instructions in the order they are listed. Our intuitive interpretation therefore tends to measure the complexity of a solution's representation rather than the solution itself.

An interpretation that more accurately reflects the complexity of a solution is based on the number of steps that must be performed when executing the solution. Note that this is not the same as the number of instructions appearing in the written program. For example, a loop whose body consists of a single print statement but whose control requests the body's execution 100 times is equivalent to 100 print statements when executed. Such a routine is considered more complex than a list of 50 similar print statements, even though the latter appears longer in written form. The point to remember is that our meaning of *complexity* is ultimately concerned with the time it takes a machine to execute an algorithm and not with the size of the algorithm in its written form.

Keep in mind that what we are measuring with this concept is actually a property of a solution and not the problem directly. Different solutions to the same problem might well be associated with different degrees of complexity. To assign a level of complexity to a problem, we select the complexity of the simplest solution to the problem in question. Unfortunately, finding the simplest solution to a problem and knowing that it is the simplest is often a difficult problem in itself. In fact, mathematicians have shown that many problems do not have a simplest solution. That is, regardless of what algorithm we use to solve these problems, there is always a more efficient method waiting to be discovered. It is not surprising then that the exact complexity of many problems is still unknown.

In reality, when calculating the complexity of a solution, we do not try to count every step in the algorithm's execution. Rather, we concentrate on the significant or time-consuming steps. In defense of this looseness, we note that the major use of a complexity measure is in making comparisons in which only a relative measure is actually required. This might be in the form of comparing different solutions to the same problem (as we are about to do) or comparing different problems (as in Section 11.6).

Observe that we have already used these ideas to compare the sequential and binary search algorithms in Section 4.6. There we found that when faced with a sorted list of 30,000 entries, the sequential search would interrogate an average of 15,000 entries, whereas the binary search would consider at most 15.

Let us now consider the complexities of the insertion and quick sort algorithms. In each case it suffices to count the number of times two names are compared, because this activity dominates both algorithms. Of course, the number of such comparisons depends on the number of names in the list, so it is convenient to express the number of comparisons required in terms of the length of the list being sorted. For this purpose we use the letter n in the following discussion to represent the number of names in the list.

Complexity of the Insertion Sort

We begin with the insert sort (summarized in Fig. 4.12). Recall that the process involves selecting a list entry, called the pivot, comparing this entry to those preceding it until its proper place is found, and then inserting the pivot in this place. The first pivot chosen is the second list entry, the second chosen is the third entry, the third is the fourth entry, and so on. In the best possible case each pivot is already in its proper place and thus needs to be compared to only a single name before this is discovered. Thus, in the best case, applying the insertion sort to a list with n entries requires $n - 1$ comparisons. (The second entry is compared to one name, the third entry to one name, and so on.)

In contrast, the worst scenario is that each pivot is compared to all the preceding entries before its proper location can be found. This occurs if the original list is in reverse order. In this case the first pivot (the second list entry) is compared to one name, the second pivot (the third list entry) is compared to two names, and so on (Fig. 11.8). Thus the total number of comparisons when sorting a list of n entries is $1 + 2 + 3 + \cdots + n - 1$, which is equivalent to $n(n - 1)/2$ or $(1/2)(n^2 - n)$. In particular, if the list contained 10 entries, the sort process requires 45 comparisons.

Having analyzed the insertion sort in both the best and worst possible cases, we might also consider what we expect the average performance to be. In short, we expect each pivot to be compared to half of the entries preceding it. This results in half as many comparisons as were performed in the worst case, or a total of $n(n - 1)/4$ comparisons to sort a list of n names. If, for example, we use the insertion sort to sort a variety of lists of length 10, we expect the average number of comparisons per sort to be 22.5.

Figure 11.8 Applying the insertion sort in a worst-case situation

Initial list	Comparisons made for each pivot: 1	2	3	4	Sorted list
Elaine	Elaine	David	Carol	Barbara	Alfred
David	David	Elaine	David	Carol	Barbara
Carol	Carol	Carol	Elaine	David	Carol
Barbara	Barbara	Barbara	Barbara	Elaine	David
Alfred	Alfred	Alfred	Alfred	Alfred	Elaine

Complexity of the Quick Sort

Let us now analyze the quick sort algorithm (summarized in Fig. 4.18). We first consider the task of sorting a list that is already in the desired order. For example, consider the list Alice, Bob, Carol, David, and Elaine. In this case, the quick sort algorithm designates the first name as the pivot entry, compares it to each of the other names (performing $n - 1$ comparisons), and finally exchanges the pivot with itself. It then proceeds by sorting first the sublist in front of the pivot entry (a list of length 0) and then the sublist following the pivot entry (a list of length $n - 1$), as summarized in Fig. 11.9.

The list of length 0 requires no comparisons, but the list of length $n - 1$ requires $n - 2$ comparisons before further divisions take place. In particular, its first entry is designated as the pivot entry, then compared to each of the other entries (of which there are $n - 2$), and finally switched with itself. Note that this results in the creation of two new lists to be sorted (one of length $n - 2$ and the other of length 0) in a manner similar to the previous step that produced two lists (of length $n - 1$ and 0).

This process continues, with additional recursive activations of the algorithm being applied to shorter and shorter lists. Each such activation operates on a list whose length is 1 less than the previous activation and compares the first name of its list to the other names in its list before calling the next activation. Consequently, the first activation of the algorithm in the chain performs $n - 1$ comparisons, the next $n - 2$, the next $n - 3$, and so on. The total number of comparisons required is therefore

$$(n - 1) + (n - 2) + \cdots + 1 = (1/2)(n^2 - n)$$

Figure 11.9 The action of the quick sort algorithm when the pivot belongs at the first of the list

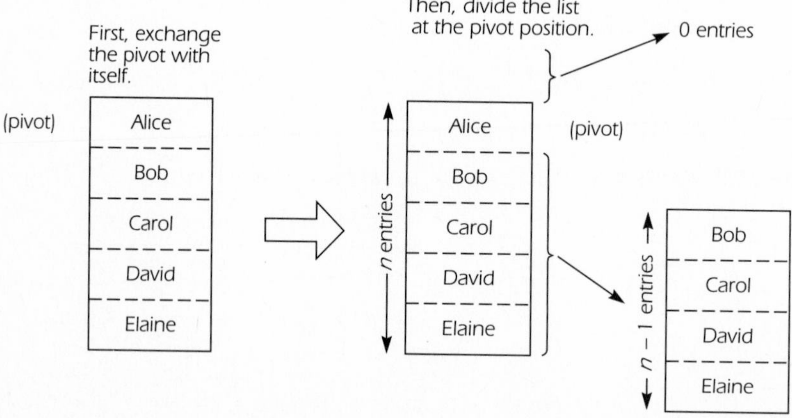

The quick sort algorithm approaches its task by dividing the original list into shorter lists, each of which should be easier to sort. Such a technique performs best when the lists produced from the division are both the same size and thus half the size of the original. However, it is at a disadvantage if the division results in "smaller" tasks almost as large as the original. This is exactly what happens in the previous example; therefore the preceding discussion constitutes a worst-case analysis of the quick sort algorithm.

We now turn to a best-case analysis. For this we assume that the original list is arranged so that each list division results in two lists as nearly equal in size as possible. In turn, the divide-and-conquer approach of the quick sort algorithm has its optimal effect.

Under these conditions the algorithm will first attack the list of n names in such a way that the initial sorting problem is reduced to two smaller problems of sorting lists, each of length approximately $n/2$. These two problems in turn are reduced to a total of four problems of sorting lists of length approximately $n/4$. This division process can be analyzed in terms of the tree structure in Fig. 11.10, where we use each node of the tree to represent a single problem in the recursive process and the branches below each node to represent the smaller problems resulting from the division. Hence, we can find the total number of comparisons that occur when sorting the initial list by adding together the number of comparisons that occur at each node.

Our first task is to determine the number of comparisons performed at each level of the tree. To avoid complications, however, we settle for a rough approximation. Observe that each node appearing across any level of the tree requests the sorting of a unique segment of the list. This sorting process is accomplished by dividing the node's segment into two shorter segments that are ultimately sorted by the nodes below. To perform this division requires no more comparisons than there are names in the segment. (The first name in the segment is compared to each of the other names.) Hence each level of the tree requires no more comparisons than the total number of names in its list segments, and since the

Figure 11.10 The hierarchy of problems generated by the quick sort algorithm

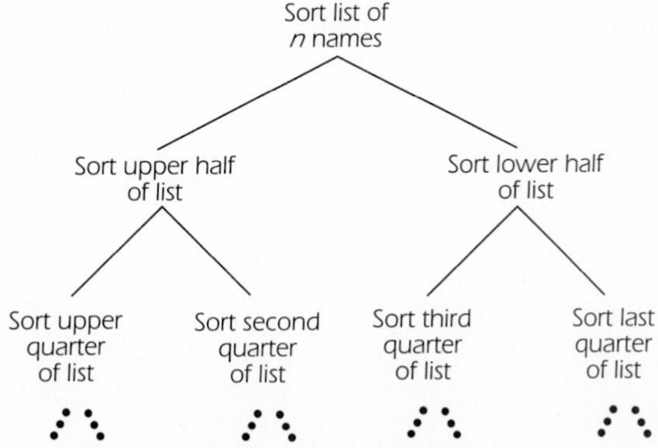

segments across a given level consist of disjoint portions of the original list, this total is no greater than the length of the original list. Consequently, each level of the tree requires no more than n comparisons. (Note that the bottom level is composed entirely of nodes representing the sorting of list segments of length 1 or 0 and thus requires no comparisons.)

Next we need to determine the number of levels (or the depth) of the tree. For this, observe that the division process continues until lists of length no greater than 1 are obtained. Thus the depth of the tree is equal to the number of times (starting with the number n) that we can repeatedly divide by 2 until the result is no larger than 1. This is nothing more than the logarithm of n (base two), which we write as $\lg n$.

Figure 11.11 is a table of base two logarithms of values from 10 to 1000. Note that the entries in the table do not have integer values, whereas the depth of a tree is an integer. To get the actual depth of the tree obtained from sorting a list of n names, we round the value of $\lg n$ up to the nearest integer. However, since the bottom level of the tree involves no comparisons, we can more accurately estimate the number of levels contributing to our comparison count by rounding the value of $\lg n$ down to the nearest integer. We denote this rounded value with the notation $\lfloor \lg n \rfloor$. Thus, we estimate that if the list in question contained 10 names, the tree would contain $\lfloor \lg 10 \rfloor = 3$ levels that involve comparisons.

Finally, by multiplying the number of contributing levels ($\lfloor \lg n \rfloor$) by the maximum number of comparisons in each level (n), we obtain $n\lfloor \lg n \rfloor$ as our best-case estimate of the number of comparisons required by the quick sort algorithm.

In summary, given an arbitrary list of n names, we expect quick sort to require between $n(\lfloor \lg n \rfloor)$ (best case) and $(1/2)(n^2 - n)$ (worst case) comparisons to sort it. In particular, when sorting a list of 10 names we would expect the quick sort to require between 30 and 45 comparisons.

(If you compare this projected performance to that of the insertion sort, you may wonder how the quick sort got its name. The answer is that the average performance of the quick sort algorithm tends to be closer to its best-case performance, which for large lists proves to be more efficient than the average

Figure 11.11 Logarithms (base two)

n	$\lg n$	n	$\lg n$
10	3.322	200	7.644
20	4.322	300	8.229
30	4.907	400	8.644
40	5.322	500	8.966
50	5.644	600	9.229
60	5.907	700	9.451
70	6.129	800	9.644
80	6.322	900	9.814
90	6.492	1000	9.966
100	6.644		

performance of the insertion sort. For example, given a collection of arbitrary lists containing 100 entries each, the average number of comparisons required by the insertion sort tends to be (100)(99)/4 = 2475, whereas the average performance of the quick sort is closer to 100 ($\lfloor \lg 100 \rfloor$) = 700.)

Orders of Complexity

Although we may have made some approximations when computing the complexities of the insertion sort and quick sort algorithms, we were actually more precise than many situations require as well as being more precise than other situations may justify. For instance, we measured the average complexity of the insertion sort to be $n(n - 1)/4 = (1/4)(n^2 - n)$, but for large values of n, the difference between $(1/4)(n^2 - n)$ and simply $(1/4)(n^2)$ becomes insignificant when compared to the size of the numbers involved. (When n is 100, the difference between the two expressions is 25, whereas the two expressions themselves are on the order of 2500.) Furthermore, for small values of n, the time required to execute the statements that we did not count (we counted only the number of times names were compared) could easily be significant in comparison to the computed complexity. In short, our claim that the average complexity of the insertion sort is $(1/4)(n^2 - n)$ is probably no more accurate than another's claim that the complexity is $(1/4)(n^2)$.

Moreover, if we use our complexity measure to estimate the actual time required to execute an algorithm, we find that differences between complexities such as $(1/4)n^2$ and simply n^2 have little significance. After all, distinctions determined by constant factors can be mitigated merely by executing the algorithm on different machines. On one machine, an algorithm may appear to have a complexity of $(1/4)n^2$, while on another, slower machine, the complexity might appear to be n^2. We see then that any constant coefficient involved in the computation of the complexity of an algorithm is more likely to be a property of the environment in which the algorithm is executed than of the algorithm itself.

Because of such uncertainties and variations, one rarely distinguishes between such expressions as $(1/4)(n^2 - n)$ and n^2 when determining the complexity of an algorithm. Instead, one tends to isolate the dominant term in the expression of the complexity while dropping any constant coefficients. In our case, although we computed the average complexity of the insertion sort to be $(1/4)(n^2 - n)$, we actually claim no more than that the insertion sort should be expected to require a time period proportional to n^2 or, using other terminology, that the complexity of the insertion sort is on the order of n^2.

Computer scientists use O-notation (read "big oh notation") to represent such approximate measures. For example, the complexity of the insertion sort is considered to be $O(n^2)$ (read "big oh of n squared" or "on the order of n squared"). After all is said and done, then, two algorithms whose complexities are computed to be $(1/2)(n^2 - 5n + 2)$ and $(2/3)(n^2 + 2n - 3)$ are considered to have essentially the same complexities, because both fall in the class of algorithms having complexity $O(n^2)$. In turn, both algorithms are considered more efficient than an algorithm in the class $O(n^3)$.

Questions/Exercises

1. Suppose we find that a machine programmed with our insertion sort algorithm requires an average of one second to sort a list of 100 names. How long do you estimate it takes to sort a list of 1000 names? How about 10,000?
2. If a machine required a minimum of one second to sort a list of 100 names using the quick sort algorithm, how long do you expect it to take to sort 1000 names?
3. How many comparisons does the quick sort algorithm require to sort a list of 10 names already in order?
4. Arrange the names Alice, Bill, Carol, David, Earl, Fred, and Gwen so as to require the least number of comparisons when sorted by the quick sort algorithm. How many comparisons would actually be required in this case?

11.6 Problem Classification

A **polynomial** (in x) is defined to be a mathematical expression of the form:

$$a_n x^n + a_{n-1} x^{n-1} + \cdots + a_1 x + a_0$$

where each subscripted a represents a constant numeric value, n represents a nonnegative integer, and x is called the polynomial's variable. Thus $3x^2 + 2x + 5$ is a polynomial (in x) and $w + 5$ is a polynomial (in w). Note that any polynomial describes a function by associating with each input an output value obtained by replacing the polynomial's variable with the input.

In contrast to polynomial expressions are the **exponential** expressions that have the form

$$b^{ax}$$

where a and b represent constant numeric values and x again represents a variable. The actual letter used to represent the variable is arbitrary; examples of exponential expressions include 4^{2x} and 2^w. As with polynomials, each exponential expression describes a function obtained by substituting the input in place of the expression's variable and performing the indicated operations.

The significance of exponential expressions for our purpose is that if the constant b is greater than one and a is positive, the value of the expression is larger than the value of any given polynomial if the input values are large enough. That is, if we pick any polynomial and proceed to compare its outputs to those of any exponential for similar inputs, as the inputs become larger we find that the outputs of the exponential eventually increase more rapidly than those of the polynomial and ultimately leave the polynomial outputs far behind.

Although an example of this phenomenon does not constitute a proof of its certainty, it is nonetheless instructive to take a look at the example given in the

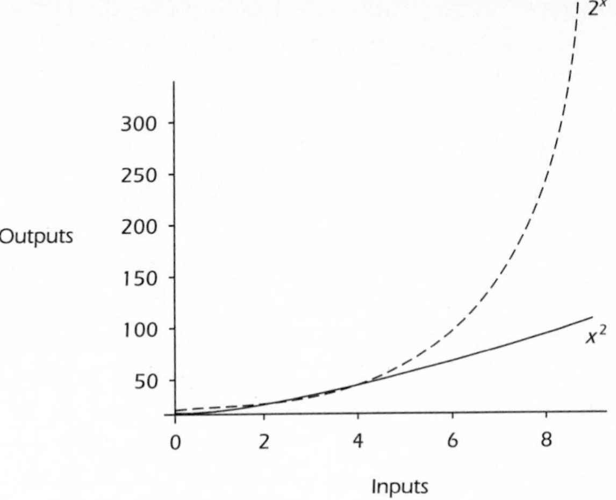

Figure 11.12 The exponential 2^x compared to the polynomial x^2

graph in Fig. 11.12. Here we compare the outputs of the polynomial x^2 to the exponential 2^x for input values in the range of 0 to 8. Note that although the exponential expression produces outputs smaller than those of the polynomial for some input values, its outputs overtake those of the polynomial as the inputs become larger.

Polynomial Problems

Observe that the complexities obtained in Section 11.5 either were polynomials themselves (such as $(1/4)n^2 - (1/4)n$) or were bounded by a polynomial (such as $n\lfloor \lg n \rfloor$). (An expression is bounded by a polynomial if the expression's value for each possible input is always less than or equal to the polynomial's value for the same input. Thus $n\lfloor \lg n \rfloor$ is bounded by the polynomial n^2.) As a result, the insertion and quick sort algorithms belong to the class known as **polynomial algorithms,** the class consisting of those algorithms whose complexity is bounded by a polynomial. Since our complexity is actually a measure of the time required to execute the algorithm, we often say that the algorithms in this class run in polynomial time.

This relationship between complexity and an algorithm's run time is the key to the importance of the class of polynomial algorithms. An algorithm that is not in this class is characterized by extremely long run times as the size of its input increases. For instance, the graph in Fig. 11.12 shows that an algorithm of complexity 2^n becomes unbearably time-consuming when applied to large inputs. Consequently, such algorithms are seldom practical for routine use.

As mentioned earlier, problems are assigned degrees of complexity based on the complexity of their solutions. Thus we find a class of problems, called **polynomial problems**, defined as being those problems with polynomial time solutions. Determining whether a theoretically solvable problem is in this class is of major importance because it is closely related to the question of whether the problem has a practical algorithmic solution.

Nonpolynomial Problems

Unfortunately, many solvable problems fall outside the class of polynomial problems. For example, consider the problem of listing all possible committees of size one or more that can be formed from a group of n people. Since there are $2^n - 1$ such committees (we allow a committee to consist of the entire group), any algorithm that solves this problem must have at least $2^n - 1$ steps and thus a complexity at least that large. In turn, this problem does not have a polynomial time solution, and hence any solution becomes enormously time consuming as the size of the group from which the committees are selected increases.

In contrast to our subcommittee problem, whose complexity is large merely because of the size of its output, problems exist whose complexities are large even though their ultimate output is merely a simple yes or no answer. An example involves the ability to answer questions about the truth of statements involving the addition of real numbers. For instance, we can easily recognize that the answer to the question "Is it true that there is a real number that when added to itself produces the value 6?" is yes, whereas the answer to "Is it true that there is a nonzero real number which when added to itself is 0?" is no. However, as such questions become more involved, our ability to answer them begins to fade. If we found ourselves faced with many such questions, we might be tempted to turn to a computer program for assistance. Unfortunately, the ability to answer these questions has been shown to require exponential time, so even a computer ultimately fails to produce timely answers as the questions become more involved.

NP Problems

Let us now consider the **Traveling Salesman problem.** It involves a traveling salesman who must visit each of his clients in different cities without exceeding his travel budget. His problem, then, is to find a path (starting from his home, connecting the cities involved, and returning to his home) whose total length does not exceed his allowed mileage.

The traditional solution to this problem is to consider each potential path in a systematic manner, comparing the length of each path to the mileage limit until either an acceptable path is found or all possibilities have been considered. This approach, however, does not produce a polynomial algorithm. As the number of cities increases, the number of paths that may require testing grows more rapidly than any polynomial. In turn, solving the Traveling Salesman problem in this manner is impractical for cases involving large numbers of cities.

We conclude that to solve this problem in a reasonable amount of time, we must find a faster algorithm. Our appetite is whetted by the observation that if a satisfactory path exists and we happen to select it first, our present algorithm terminates quite quickly. In particular, the following list of instructions can be executed quickly and has the potential of solving the problem:

```
Pick one of the possible paths, and compute its total distance.
If this distance is not greater than the allowable mileage,
  then declare a success
  else declare nothing.
```

However, this set of instructions is not an algorithm in the technical sense. Its first instruction is ambiguous, in that it does not specify which path is to be selected. The result of executing the instruction is therefore not predetermined at the moment prior to its execution. We say that such instructions are nondeterministic, and we call an "algorithm" containing such statements a **nondeterministic algorithm.**

Note that as the number of cities increases, the time required to execute the preceding nondeterministic algorithm grows relatively slowly. The process of selecting a path is merely that of producing a list of the cities, which can be done in a time proportional to the number of cities. Moreover, the time required to compute the total distance along the chosen path is also proportional to the number of cities to be visited, and the time required to compare this total to the mileage limit is independent of the number of cities. In turn, the time required to execute the nondeterministic algorithm is bounded by a polynomial. Thus it is possible to solve the Traveling Salesman problem by a nondeterministic algorithm in polynomial time.

Of course, our nondeterministic solution is not totally satisfactory. It relies on a lucky guess. But its existence is enough to suggest that perhaps there is a deterministic solution to the Traveling Salesman problem that runs in polynomial time. Whether or not this is true remains an open question. In fact, the Traveling Salesman problem is only one of many problems that are known to have nondeterministic solutions that execute in polynomial time but for which no deterministic polynomial time solution has yet been found. The tantalizing efficiency of the nondeterministic solutions to these problems causes some to hope that efficient deterministic solutions will be found someday, yet most believe that these problems are just complex enough to escape the capabilities of efficient deterministic algorithms.

A problem that can be solved in polynomial time by a nondeterministic algorithm is called a **nondeterministic polynomial problem,** or an **NP problem** for short. It is customary to denote the class of NP problems by **NP** and the class of polynomial problems by **P.** Note that all the problems in P all also in NP, since any (deterministic) algorithm can have a nondeterministic instruction added to it without affecting its performance.

Whether all of the NP problems are also in P, however, is an open question, as we have already observed in our discussion of the Traveling Salesman problem. In fact, this is perhaps the most widely known unsolved problem in computer science today. Its solution could have significant consequences. Security systems have been designed whose integrity relies on the enormous time required to solve the equivalent of a very large version of the Traveling Salesman problem. If it turns out that efficient solutions to such problems exist, these security systems will be compromised.

Efforts to resolve the question of whether the class NP is, in fact, the same as the class P have led to the discovery of a class of problems within the class NP

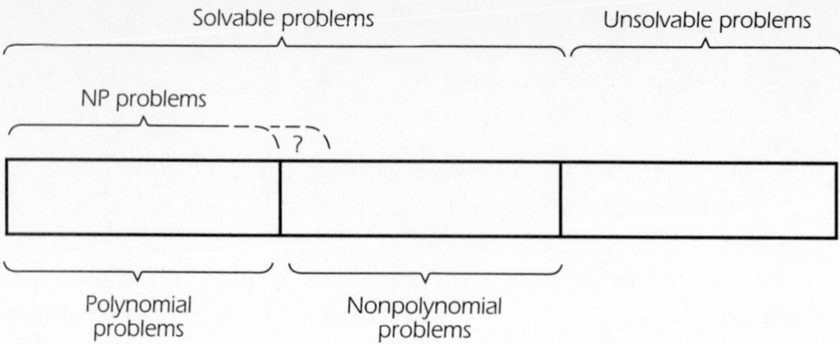

Figure 11.13 A graphic summation of problem classification

known as the **NP-complete problems.** These problems have the property that a polynomial time solution for any of them would provide a polynomial time solution for all the other problems in NP as well. That is, if a (deterministic) algorithm can be found that solves one of the NP-complete problems in polynomial time, then that algorithm can be extended to solve any other problem in NP in polynomial time. In turn, the class NP would be the same as the class P. The Traveling Salesman problem is an example of an NP-complete problem.

In summary, we have found that problems can be classified as either solvable (having an algorithmic solution) or unsolvable (not having an algorithmic solution), as depicted in Fig. 11.13. Moreover, within the class of solvable problems are two subclasses. One is the collection of polynomial problems considered to have practical solutions. The second is the collection of nonpolynomial problems whose solutions are considered to be practical for only relatively small or carefully selected inputs. Finally, there are the mysterious NP problems that thus far have evaded precise classification. They are contained in the class of solvable problems and contain the polynomial problems. Whether there are true polynomial solutions to all the NP problems remains an open question.

Questions/Exercises

1. For the same input value, does a polynomial expression always produce a value less than a given exponential?
2. List all of the subcommittees that can be formed from a committee consisting of the two members Alice and Bill. List all the subcommittees that can be formed from the committee consisting of Alice, Bill, and Carol. What about the subcommittees from Alice, Bill, Carol, and David?
3. Give an example of a problem in each of the following classes:

   polynomial problems
   nonpolynomial problems

   Give an example of an NP problem that as yet has not been shown to be a polynomial problem.

CHAPTER REVIEW PROBLEMS

1. Show how a structure of the form

```
while X equals 0 do;
   .
   .
   .
end;
```

   can be simulated with Bare Bones.

2. Write a Bare Bones program that places a 1 in the variable Z if the variable X is less than or equal to the variable Y and places a 0 in the variable Z if it is greater.
3. Write a Bare Bones program that places the Xth power of 2 in the variable Z.
4. In each of the following cases write a program sequence in Bare Bones that performs the indicated activity:
   a. Assign 0 to Z if the value of X is even; otherwise assign 1 to Z.
   b. Calculate the sum of the integers from 0 to X.
5. Write a Bare Bones routine that divides the value of X by the value of Y. Disregard any remainder; that is, 1 divided by 2 produces 0, and 5 divided by 3 produces 1.
6. The example of a Turing machine that never halts given in the text used the fact that the tape was infinitely long. Design a Turing machine that never halts but uses no more than a single cell on its tape.
7. Design a Turing machine that places 0s in all the cells to the left of the current cell until it reaches a cell containing an asterisk.
8. Suppose a pattern of 0s and 1s on the tape of a Turing machine is delimited by asterisks at either end. Design a Turing machine that rotates this pattern one cell to the left, assuming that the machine starts with the current cell being the asterisk at the right end of the pattern.
9. Design a Turing machine that reverses the pattern of 0s and 1s that it finds between the current cell (which contains an asterisk) and the first asterisk to the left.
10. Summarize the Church–Turing thesis.
11. What value does our Gödel numbering technique associate with the program "incr A;"?
12. What Bare Bones program is represented by the number

    28,258,975,461,955,643

    when using our Gödel numbering system described in this chapter?
13. Is the following Bare Bones program self-terminating?

```
while X not 0 do;
end;
```

14. Analyze the validity of the following two statements:

    The next statement is true.
    The above statement is false.

15. Analyze the validity of the statement "The cook on a ship cooks for all those and only those who do not cook for themselves."
16. Summarize the significance of the halting problem in the field of theoretical computer science.
17. Is the problem of searching through a list for a particular entry a polynomial problem? Justify your answer.
18. Compute the complexity of the traditional grade school algorithms for addition and multiplication. That is, if asked to add two numbers each having n digits, how many individual additions must be performed, and if requested to multiply two n-digit numbers, how many individual multiplications are required?
19. Is a polynomial solution to a problem always better than an exponential solution? Explain.
20. Does the fact that a problem has a polynomial solution mean that it can always be solved in a practical amount of time? Explain.
21. Given the problem of dividing a group (of an even number of people) into two disjoint subgroups of equal size so that the difference between the total ages of each subgroup is as large as possible, Charlie Programmer proposes the solution of forming all possible subgroup pairs, computing the difference between the age totals of each pair, and selecting the pair with the largest difference. Mary Programmer, on the other hand, proposes that the original group first be sorted by age and then divided into two subgroups by forming one

subgroup from the younger half of the sorted group and the other from the older half. What is the complexity of each of these solutions? Is the problem itself of polynomial, NP, or nonpolynomial complexity?

22. Sometimes a slight change in a problem can significantly alter the form of its solution. For example, find a simple solution to the following problem and determine its complexity class:

> Divide a group of people into two disjoint subgroups (of arbitrary size) such that the difference in the total ages of the members of the two subgroups is as large as possible.

Now change the problem so that the desired difference is as small as possible. What is the complexity of your solution?

23. From the following list, extract a collection of numbers whose sum is 3165:

> 26, 39, 104, 195, 403, 504, 793, 995, 1156, 1673

What is the complexity of your technique for solving this problem? Does this appear to be a polynomial problem or a nonpolynomial problem?

24. Is the following algorithm deterministic? Explain your answer.

```
procedure mystery (Number)
if (Number >5)
    then (answer "yes")
    else (pick a value less than 5 and
          give this number as the answer)
```

25. Is the following algorithm deterministic? Explain your answer.

> Drive straight ahead.
> At the third intersection, ask the person standing on the corner if you should turn right or left.
> Turn according to that person's directions.
> Drive two more blocks and stop there.

26. Identify the points of nondeterminism in the following algorithm:

```
Select three numbers between 1 and 100.
If (the sum of the selected numbers is greater
  than 150)
    then (answer "yes")
    else (select one of the chosen numbers and
          give that number as the answer)
```

27. Does the following algorithm have a polynomial or nonpolynomial time complexity? Explain your answer.

```
procedure mystery (ListOfNumbers)
Pick a collection of numbers from ListOfNumbers.
if (the numbers in that collection add to 125)
    then (answer "yes")
    else (do not give an answer)
```

28. Which of the following problems are in the class P?

a. A problem with complexity n^2
b. A problem with complexity 3^n
c. A problem with complexity $n^2 + 2^n$
d. A problem with complexity $n!$

29. Summarize the distinction between stating that a problem is a polynomial problem and stating that it is a nondeterministic polynomial problem.

30. Give an example of a problem that is in both the class P and the class NP.

31. Suppose you are given two algorithms for solving the same problem. One algorithm has time complexity n^4 and the other has time complexity 4^n. For what size inputs is the former more efficient than the latter?

32. Summarize the significance of Turing machines in the field of theoretical computer science.

33. Summarize the Church–Turing thesis.

34. How many comparisons between names are made if the quick sort algorithm (Fig. 4.18) is applied to the list Alice, Bob, Carol, and David? How many are required if the list was Alice, Bob, Carol, David, and Elaine?

35. Give an example of a problem in each of the categories represented in Fig. 11.13.

36. Arrange the names Brenda, Doris, Raymond, Steve, Timothy, and William in an order that requires the least number of comparisons when sorted by the quick sort algorithm (Fig. 4.18).

37. What is the largest number of entries that are interrogated if the binary search algorithm (Fig. 4.14) is applied to a list of 4000 names? How does this compare to the sequential search (Fig. 4.7)?

38. Design an algorithm for finding integer solutions for equations of the form $x^2 + y^2 = n$, where n is some given positive integer. Determine the time complexity of your algorithm.

39. Design an algorithm for determining whether a given positive integer (the input value) is prime. How does the time required by your algorithm depend on the input value?

40. The following algorithm for sorting a list is called the bubble sort. How many comparisons between list entries does the bubble sort require when applied to a list of n entries?

```
procedure BubbleSort (List)
Assign Counter the value 1;
while (Counter < number of entries in List) do
    [Assign n the number of entries in List;
     while (n > 1) do
          (if (the nth List entry is less than the
               entry preceding it)
             then (interchange the nth entry
                    with the preceding entry)
          Subtract 1 from n)]
```

QUESTIONS OF ETHICS

The following questions are provided to help you understand some of the ethical/social/legal issues associated with the field of computing as well as investigate your own beliefs and their foundations. The goal is not merely to answer these questions. You should also consider why you answered as you did and whether your justifications are consistent from one question to the next.

1. Suppose a department's computers are all connected by a network and the department manager has software that allows him or her to observe what is being done on each machine in the department at any time. What rights does the department manager have regarding the use of that software? What rights do the department's employees have regarding the use of that software?

2. Can releasing the results of a survey affect public opinion? Can the speed of today's technology be used to affect the survey itself? Would it be ethical to do so? What if the survey were in the form of an election?

3. If the human mind is an algorithmic device, what consequences does Turing's thesis have in regards to humanity?

4. Note that the Traveling Salesman problem could be solved quickly if one guesses correctly. Some computer security systems rely on the time required to solve problems such as the Traveling Salesman problem. Is it ethical to base the security of a nation's defense on the inability of an adversary to solve such a problem in a timely manner?

ADDITIONAL ACTIVITIES

1. Identify a small collection of instructions in a programming language you know that collectively provide all the features of Bare Bones. Show how each Bare Bones statement can be simulated with the instructions you picked.

2. Write a program to list all the numbers that can be obtained by rearranging the various groupings of digits appearing in a given number. For example, if the input is 13, your program should produce the values 1, 3, 13, and 31. Why would you not want to execute this program for large input values?

3. Rewrite the program of Activity 3 so that it prints only those rearrangements whose digits total a particular value. What techniques can you apply to increase the efficiency of your solution?

4. Write a program to simulate a Turing machine.

5. Write a program for computing the Gödel numbers of Bare Bones programs using the numbering system adopted in the text.

6. Write a translator that translates programs from Bare Bones into the machine language described in Appendix C.

ADDITIONAL READING

Brookshear, J. G. *Theory of Computation.* Redwood City, Calif.: Benjamin/Cummings, 1989.

Cohen, D. I. A. *Introduction to Computer Theory,* revised ed. New York: John Wiley and Sons, 1991.

Garey, M. R., and D. S. Johnson, *Computers and Intractability.* New York: W. H. Freeman and Co., 1979.

Hofstadter, D. R. *Gödel, Escher, Bach: An Eternal Golden Braid.* St. Paul, Minn.: Vintage Book Co., 1980.

Lewis, H. R., and C. H. Papadimitriou, *Elements of the Theory of Computation.* Englewood Cliffs, N.J.: Prentice-Hall, 1981.

Sipser, M. *Introduction to the Theory of Computation.* Boston: PWS, 1996.

APPENDICES

Appendix A ASCII

Appendix B Circuits to Manipulate Two's Complement Representations

Appendix C A Typical Machine Language

Appendix D Program Examples

Appendix E The Equivalence of Iterative and Recursive Structures

Appendix F Answers to Questions/Exercises

APPENDIX A

ASCII

The following is a partial listing of ASCII code, in which each bit pattern has been extended with a 0 on its left to produce the eight-bit pattern commonly used today.

Symbol	*ASCII*	*Symbol*	*ASCII*	*Symbol*	*ASCII*
(space)	00100000	?	00111111	^	01011110
!	00100001	@	01000000	–	01011111
″	00100010	A	01000001	a	01100001
#	00100011	B	01000010	b	01100010
$	00100100	C	01000011	c	01100011
%	00100101	D	01000100	d	01100100
&	00100110	E	01000101	e	01100101
'	00100111	F	01000110	f	01100110
(	00101000	G	01000111	g	01100111
)	00101001	H	01001000	h	01101000
*	00101010	I	01001001	i	01101001
+	00101011	J	01001010	j	01101010
,	00101100	K	01001011	k	01101011
-	00101101	L	01001100	l	01101100
.	00101110	M	01001101	m	01101101
/	00101111	N	01001110	n	01101110
0	00110000	O	01001111	o	01101111
1	00110001	P	01010000	p	01110000
2	00110010	Q	01010001	q	01110001
3	00110011	R	01010010	r	01110010
4	00110100	S	01010011	s	01110011
5	00110101	T	01010100	t	01110100
6	00110110	U	01010101	u	01110101
7	00110111	V	01010110	v	01110110
8	00111000	W	01010111	w	01110111
9	00111001	X	01011000	x	01111000
:	00111010	Y	01011001	y	01111001
;	00111011	Z	01011010	z	01111010
<	00111100	[	01011011	{	01111011
=	00111101	\	01011100	}	01111101
>	00111110	]	01011101		

APPENDIX B

Circuits to Manipulate Two's Complement Representations

In this appendix we present circuits for negating and adding values represented in two's complement notation. We begin with the circuit in Fig. B.1 that converts a four-bit two's complement representation to the representation for the negative of that value. For example, given the two's complement representation of 3, the circuit produces the representation for −3. It does this by following the same algorithm as presented in the text. That is, it copies the pattern from right to left until a 1 has been copied and then complements each remaining bit as it is moved from the input to the output. Since one input of the rightmost XOR gate is fixed at 0, this gate will merely pass its input to the output. However, this output is also passed to the left as one of the inputs to the next XOR gate. If this output is 1, the next XOR gate will complement its input bit as it passes to the

Figure B.1 A circuit that negates a two's complement pattern

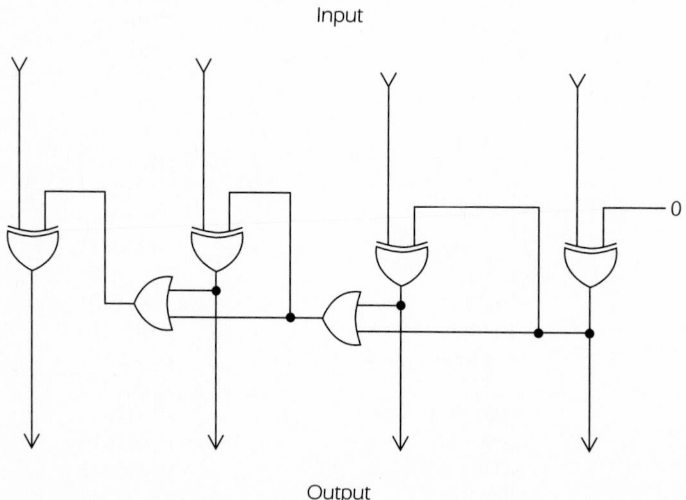

output. Moreover, this 1 will also be passed to the left through the OR gate to affect the next gate as well. In this manner, the first 1 that is copied to the output will also be passed to the left, where it will cause all the remaining bits to be complemented as they are moved to the output.

Next, let us consider the process of adding two values represented in two's complement notation. In particular, when solving the problem

$$\begin{array}{r} 0110 \\ \underline{+\ 1011} \end{array}$$

we proceed from right to left in a column-by-column manner, executing the same algorithm for each column. Thus once we obtain a circuit for adding one column of such a problem, we can construct a circuit for adding many columns merely by repeating the single-column circuit.

The algorithm for adding a single column in a multiple-column addition problem is to add the two values in the current column, add that sum to any carry from the previous column, write the least significant bit of this sum in the answer, and transfer any carry to the next column. The circuit in Fig. B.2 follows this same algorithm. The upper XOR gate determines the sum of the two input bits. The lower XOR gate adds this sum to the value carried from the previous column. The two AND gates together with the OR gate pass any carry to the left.

Figure B.2 A circuit to add a single column in a multiple-column addition problem.

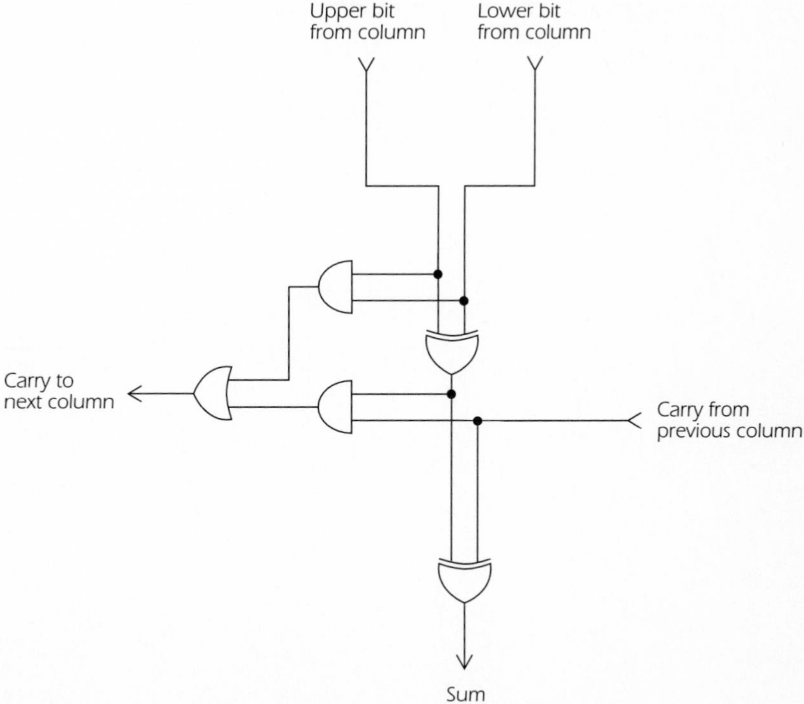

In particular, a carry of 1 will be produced if the original two input bits in this column were 1 or if the sum of these bits and the carry were both 1.

Figure B.3 shows how copies of this single-column circuit can be used to produce a circuit that computes the sum of two values represented in a four-bit two's complement system. Each rectangle represents a copy of the single-column addition circuit. Note that the carry value given to the rightmost rectangle is always 0 because there is no carry from a previous column. In a similar manner, the carry produced from the leftmost rectangle is ignored.

Figure B.3 A circuit for adding two values in two's complement notation using four copies of the circuit in Fig. B.2.

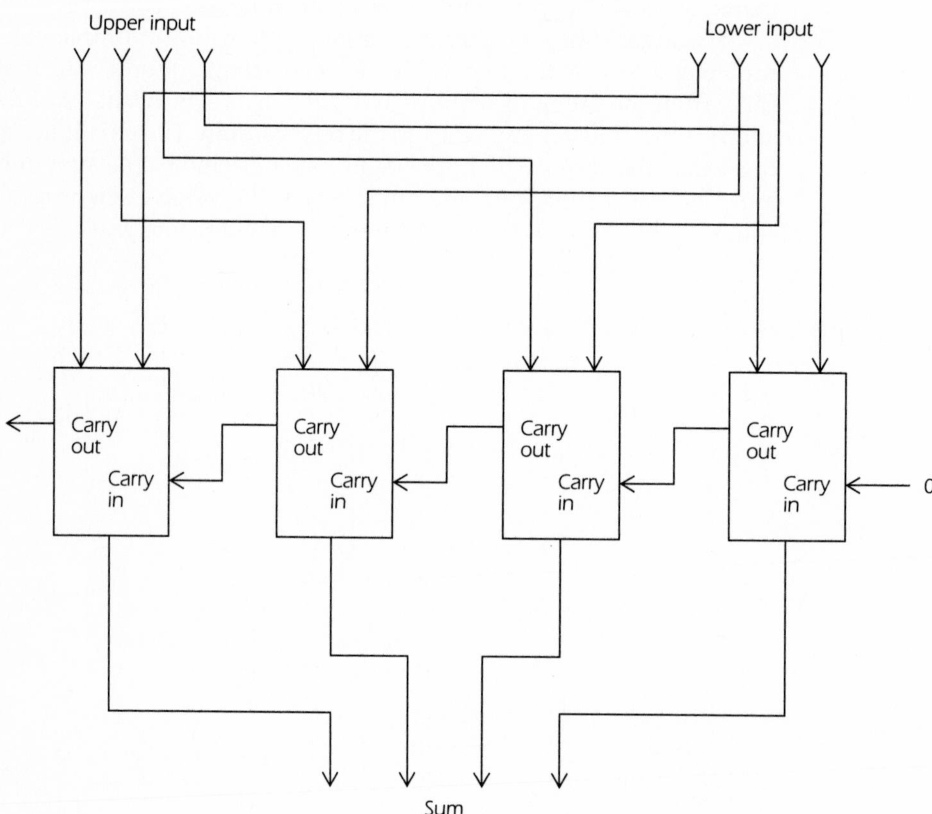

APPENDIX C

A Typical Machine Language

Machine Architecture

The machine has 16 general-purpose registers numbered 0 through F (in hexadecimal). Each register is one byte (eight bits) long. For identifying registers within instructions, each register is assigned the unique four-bit pattern that represents its register number. Thus register 0 is identified by 0000 (hexadecimal 0), and register 4 is identified by 0100 (hexadecimal 4).

Main memory consists of 256 cells. Each cell contains eight bits (or one byte) of data. Since there are 256 cells in memory, each cell is assigned a unique address consisting of an integer in the range of 0 to 255. An address can therefore be represented by a pattern of eight bits ranging from 00000000 to 11111111 (or a hexadecimal value in the range of 00 to FF).

Floating-point values are assumed to be stored in the format, which is shown as follows.

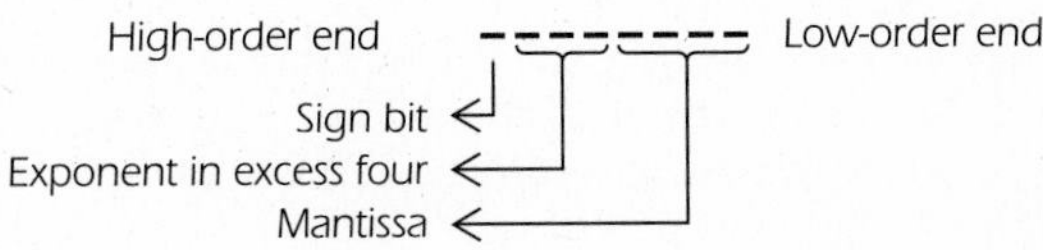

Machine Language

Each machine instruction is two bytes long. The first four bits consist of the op-code; the last 12 bits make up the operand field. The following table lists the instructions in hexadecimal notation together with a short description of each. The letters R, S, and T are used in place of hexadecimal digits in those fields representing a register identifier that varies depending on the particular application of the instruction. The letters X and Y are used in lieu of hexadecimal digits in variable fields not representing a register.

Op-code	*Operand*	*Description*
1	RXY	LOAD the register R with the bit pattern found in the memory cell whose address is XY. *Example:* 14A3 would cause the contents of the memory cell located at address A3 to be placed in register 4.
2	RXY	LOAD the register R with the bit pattern XY. *Example:* 20A3 would cause the value A3 to be placed in register 0.
3	RXY	STORE the bit pattern found in register R in the memory cell whose address is XY. *Example:* 35B1 would cause the contents of register 5 to be placed in the memory cell whose address is B1.
4	0RS	MOVE the bit pattern found in register R to register S. *Example:* 40A4 would cause the contents of register A to be copied into register 4.
5	RST	ADD the bit patterns in registers S and T as though they were two's complement representations and leave the result in register R. *Example:* 5726 would cause the binary values in registers 2 and 6 to be added and the sum placed in register 7.
6	RST	ADD the bit patterns in registers S and T as though they represented values in floating-point notation and leave the floating-point result in register R. *Example:* 634E would cause the values in registers 4 and E to be added as floating-point values and the result to be placed in register 3.
7	RST	OR the bit patterns in registers S and T and place the result in register R. *Example:* 7CB4 would cause the result of ORing the contents of registers B and 4 to be placed in register C.
8	RST	AND the bit patterns in register S and T and place the result in register R. *Example:* 8045 would cause the result of ANDing the contents of registers 4 and 5 to be placed in register 0.
9	RST	EXCLUSIVE OR the bit patterns in registers S and T and place the result in register R. *Example:* 95F3 would cause the result of EXCLUSIVE ORing the contents of registers F and 3 to be placed in register 5.
A	R0X	ROTATE the bit pattern in register R one bit to the right X times. Each time place the bit that started at the low-order end at the high-order end. *Example:* A403 would cause the contents of register 4 to be rotated 3 bits to the right in a circular fashion.
B	RXY	JUMP to the instruction located in the memory cell at address XY if the bit pattern in register R is equal to the bit pattern in register number 0. Otherwise, continue with the normal sequence of execution. *Example:* B43C would first compare the contents of register 4 with the contents of register 0. If the two were equal, the execution sequence would be altered so that the next instruction executed would be the one located at memory address 3C. Otherwise, program execution would continue in its normal sequence.
C	000	HALT execution. *Example:* C000 would cause program execution to stop.

APPENDIX D

Program Examples

This appendix presents sample programs in the languages Ada, C, C++, FORTRAN, Java, and Pascal. Each program receives a list of names typed at the keyboard, sorts the list using the insertion sort algorithm, and prints the sorted list on the monitor screen.

Ada

The language Ada, named after Augusta Ada Byron (1815–1851), who was an assistant of Charles Babbage and the daughter of poet Lord Byron, was developed at the initiative of the U.S. Department of Defense in an attempt to obtain a single, general-purpose language for all its software development needs. A major emphasis during Ada's design was to incorporate features for programming real-time computer systems used as a part of larger machines, such as missile guidance systems, environmental control systems within buildings, and control systems in automobiles and small home appliances. Ada thus contains features for expressing activities in parallel processing environments as well as convenient techniques for handling special cases (called exceptions) that might arise in the application environment. The newest version of Ada, known as Ada 95, embraces the object-oriented paradigm.

Figure D.1 presents a sample Ada program.

C

The language C was developed by Dennis Ritchie at Bell Laboratories in the early 1970s. Although originally designed as a language for developing operating systems and compilers, C has obtained popularity throughout the programming community and is enjoying the benefits of standardization through the efforts of the American National Standards Institute.

```
--Program to manipulate a list
with TEXT_IO;
use TEXT_IO;
procedure MAIN is
    subtype NAME_TYPE is STRING (1 .. 8);
    LIST_LENGTH: constant : = 10;
    NAMES: array (1 .. LIST_LENGTH) of NAME_TYPE;
    PIVOT: NAME_TYPE;
    HOLE: INTEGER;
begin
--First, get the names from the terminal.
    for K in 1 .. LIST_LENGTH loop
      GET(NAMES(K));
    end loop;
--Sort the list (HOLE contains the location of the
--                hole in the list from the time the
--                pivot is removed until it is
--                reinserted.)
    for N in 2 .. LIST_LENGTH loop
      PIVOT := NAMES(N);
      HOLE := N;
      for M in reverse 1 .. N - 1 loop
        if NAMES(M) > PIVOT
            then NAMES(M + 1) := NAMES(M);
            else exit;
        end if;
        HOLE := M;
      end loop;
      NAMES(HOLE) := PIVOT;
    end loop;
--Now, print the sorted list.
    for K in 1 .. LIST_LENGTH loop
      NEW_LINE;
      PUT(NAMES(K));
    end loop;
end MAIN;
```

Figure D.1 A sample Ada program

C was originally envisioned as merely a step up from machine language. Consequently, its syntax is terse compared to other high-level languages that use complete English words to express some primitives that are represented by special symbols in C. This terseness is one of the reasons for C's popularity, because it allows for efficient representations of complex algorithms. (Often a concise representation is more readable than a lengthy one.)

Figure D.2 presents a sample program in C.

C++

The language C++ was developed by Bjarne Stroustrup at Bell Laboratories as an enhanced version of the language C. The goal was to produce a language compatible with the object-oriented paradigm.

```
/* Program to manipulate a list */

#include <stdio.h>
#include <string.h>

main ()
{
  char names[10][9],pivot[9];
  int i,j;

/*get the names */
  for (i = 0;i < 10;++i)
    scanf("%s",names[i]);

/*sort the list */
  for (i = 1;i < 10;++i)
  {
    strcpy(pivot,names[i]);
    j = i - 1;
    while ((j >= 0)&&(strcmp(pivot,names[j]) < 0))
      {strcpy(names[j+1],names[j]);--j;};
    strcpy(names[j+1], pivot);
  }

/*print the sorted list */
  for (i = 0;i < 10; ++i)
    printf("%s\n",names[i]);
}
```

Figure D.2 A sample C program

Figure D.3 presents an implementation of the insertion sort algorithm in C++. The last four statements in this program request that an object named `namelist` be established having "type" `list` and that this new object perform the operations `getnames`, `sortnames`, and `printnames` on itself. The preceding portion of the program defines the properties that any object of "type" `list` is to possess. In particular, any such object is to contain of an internal array of characters called `names` and three operations called `getnames`, `sortlist`, and `printnames`. Note that the definitions of these operations are the same as portions of the C language program in Fig. D.2. The difference is that in the C++program these operations are considered to be a part of an object's properties, whereas in the C program they are considered as units within the procedural part of the program.

FORTRAN

FORTRAN is an acronym for FORmula TRANslator. This language was one of the first high-level languages developed (announced in 1957) and the first to gain wide acceptance within the computing community. Over the years its official description has undergone numerous extensions, so you may hear computer scientists mention FORTRAN IV or FORTRAN 77. The latest in the series is FORTRAN 90, which extended FORTRAN 77 to include such features as

```
// Program to manipulate a list

#include <iostream.h>
#include <string.h>
const int ListLength = 10;

// All list objects contain a list of names and three public
// methods called getnames, sortlist, and printnames.

class list
{private:
  char names[ListLength][9]:

public:

void getnames()
{int i;
 for (i = 0; i < ListLength; ++i)
   cin >> names[i]:
}

void sortlist()
{int i,j:
 char pivot[9];
 for (i = 1; i < ListLength; ++1)
  {strcpy(pivot, names[i]);
   j = i - 1;
   while ((j >= o) && (strcmp(pivot, names [j]) < 0))
     {strcpy(names[j+1], names[j]);
      --j;
     }
   strcpy(names[j+1], pivot);
  }
}

void printnames()
{int i;
 cout < endl;
 for (i = 0; i < ListLength; ++i)
   cout < names[i] < endl;
}
};

// Establish an object called namelist and ask it to
// collect some names, sort them, and print the list.

void main()
{list namelist;
 namelist.getnames();
 namelist.sortlist();
 namelist.pritnames();
}
```

Figure D.3 A sample C++ program

recursion and user-defined data types. Although criticized by many, FORTRAN continues to be a popular language within the scientific community. In particular, many numerical analysis and statistical packages are, and will probably continue to be, written in FORTRAN. Figure D.4 presents a sample program in FORTRAN.

Java

Java is an object-oriented language developed by Sun Microsystems in the early 1990s. Its designers borrowed heavily from C and C++. Being a new language, Java has not had the benefits of standardization. Indeed, the language is still in its early evolutionary stage.

The excitement over Java stems from its promise of becoming a standard by which programs, known as **Java applets,** can be transported over the Internet in an executable form and run on any host machine. With this capability, hypertext documents, which are static in nature, can be replaced by dynamic programs with which the user can interact. Note that this technology is a step beyond video "documents" that are dynamic but do not offer interactive capabilities.

Figure D.5 presents a sample program in Java. Note the resemblance between Java and C++.

Figure D.4 A sample FORTRAN program

```
!    Program to manipulate a list
       INTEGER J,K
       CHARACTER(LEN=8) Pivot
       CHARACTER(LEN=8) DIMENSION(10) Names
!    First, get the names.
       READ(UNIT=5, FMT=100) (Names(K), K=1,10)
100    FORMAT(A8)
!        Now, sort the list.
OuterLoop: DO J=2,10
            Pivot = Names(J)
 InnerLoop: DO K=J-1, 1,-1
             IF (Names(K) .GT. Pivot) THEN
                    Names(K+1) = Names(K)
                 ELSE
                   EXIT InnerLoop
             ENDIF
             END DO InnerLoop
            Names(K+1) = Pivot
            END DO OuterLoop
!    Now, print the sorted list.
       WRITE(UNIT=6,FMT=400) (Names(K),K=1,10)
400    FORMAT ('',A8)
       END
```

```
// Program to manipulate a list

import java.io.*;

// All list objects contain a list of names and three public
// methods called getnames, sortlist, and printnames.

class list
  final int ListLength = 10;
  private String[] names;
  public list() {
    names = new String[ListLength];
  }
  public void getnames() {
    int i;
    DataInput data = new DataInputStream(System.in);
    for (i=0; i < ListLength; i++)
      try {names[i] = data.readLine();
          }
      catch(IOException e) {};
  }
public void sortnames() {
  int i,j;
  String pivot;
  for (i=1; i < ListLength; i++) {
    pivot = names[i];
    j = i - 1;
    while ((j >= 0) && (pivot.compareTo(names[j]) < 0)) {
      names[j+1] = names[j];
      j--;
    }
    names[j+1] = pivot;
  }
}
public void printnames() {
  int i;
  for (i=0; i < ListLength; i++)
    System.out.println(names[i]);
}
}

// Establish an object called namelist and ask it to
// collect some names, sort them, and print the results.

class sort {
  public static void main(String args[]){
    list namelist = new list();
    namelist.getnames();
    namelist.sortnames();
    namelist.printnames();
  }
}
```

Figure D.5 A sample Java program

Pascal

Pascal is named after the French mathematician and inventor Blaise Pascal (1623–1662). Announced by Niklaus Wirth in 1971, it incorporates many of the later design features such as an emphasis on data type in addition to structure, a free-format syntax, and numerous control structures. Today, Pascal is used mainly in computer science education because its design reinforces an organized approach to program development. Figure D.6 presents a sample program in Pascal.

Figure D.6 A sample Pascal program

```
    {Program to manipulate a list}
program InsertSort(input, Output);
const
    Blanks = '                ';
    ListLength = 10;
type
    NameType = packed array [1 .. 8] of char;
var
    Names:array[1 .. ListLength] of NameType;
    Pivot: NameType;
    LocationFound: Boolean;
    J,M,N: Integer;
{GetName is a procedure for reading an entire name.}
procedure GetName(var Name: NameType);
var J: Integer;
begin J := 1;
    repeat read(Name[J]); J := j + 1;until (J > 8) or eoln;
    readin
end;
begin
{First, get the names from the terminal.}
    for J := 1 to ListLength do
        begin Names[J] := Blanks; GetName(Names[J]) end;
{Sort the list.}
    N := 2;
    repeat
        Pivot := Names[N];
        M := N - 1;
        LocationFound := false;
        while (not LocationFound) do
            if Names[M] > Pivot
                then begin Names[M+1] := Names[M];
                           M := M - 1;
                           if M = 0 then LocationFound := true
                             end
                else LocationFound := true;
            Names[M+1] := Pivot;
            N := N + 1
      until N > ListLength;
{Now print the sorted list.}
      for J := 1 to ListLength do writein (Names[J])
end.
```

APPENDIX E

The Equivalence of Iterative and Recursive Structures

In this appendix, we use our Bare Bones language of Chapter 11 as a tool to answer the question posed in Chapter 4 regarding the relative power of iterative and recursive structures. Recall that Bare Bones contains only three assignment statements (clear, incr, and decr) and one control structure (constructed from a while-end statement pair). Moreover, this simple language has the same computing power as a Turing machine; thus, if we accept the Church–Turing thesis, we may conclude that any problem with an algorithmic solution has a solution expressible in Bare Bones.

The first step in the comparison of iterative and recursive structures is to replace the iterative structure of Bare Bones with a recursive structure. We do this by removing the while and end statements from the language and in their place providing the ability to divide a Bare Bones program into units along with the ability to call one of these units from another location in the program. More precisely, we propose that each program in the modified language can consist of a number of syntactically disjoint program units. We suppose that each program must contain exactly one unit called MAIN having the syntactic structure of

```
MAIN: begin;
        .
        .
        .
      end;
```

(where the dots represent other Bare Bones statements) and perhaps other units (semantically subordinate to MAIN) that have the structure

```
unit: begin;
        .
        .
        .
      return;
```

(where unit represents the unit's name that has the same syntax as variable names). The semantics of this unit system is that the program always begins execution at the beginning of the unit MAIN and halts when that unit's end statement is reached. Other program units can be called as subprograms by means of the conditional statement

```
if name not 0 perform unit;
```

(where name represents any variable name and unit represents any of the program unit names other than MAIN). Moreover, we allow the units other than MAIN to call themselves recursively.

With these added features, we can simulate the old while-end structure. For example, a Bare Bones program of the form

```
while X not 0 do;
  S;
end;
```

(where S represents any sequence of Bare Bones statements) can be replaced by the unit structure

```
MAIN: begin;
       if X not 0 perform unitA;
       end;
unitA: begin;
       S;
       if X not 0 perform unitA;
       return;
```

Consequently, we may conclude that the modified language has all the capabilities of the original Bare Bones.

It can also be shown that any problem that can be solved using the modified language can be solved using Bare Bones. One method of doing this is to show how any algorithm expressed in the modified language could be written in the original Bare Bones. However, this involves an explicit description of how recursive structures can be simulated with the while-end structure of Bare Bones, which in turn requires that we describe how the environments of the various unit activations can be saved in a stack storage structure using Bare Bones.

For our purpose, it is simpler to rely on the Church–Turing thesis as presented in Chapter 11. In particular, the Church–Turing thesis, combined with the fact that Bare Bones has the same power as Turing machines, dictates that no language can be more powerful than our original Bare Bones. We can thus conclude immediately that any problem solvable in our modified language can also be solved using Bare Bones.

We can then see that the power of the modified language is the same as that of the original Bare Bones. The only distinction between the two languages is that one provides an iterative control structure and the other provides recursion. We must therefore conclude that the two control structures are, in fact, equivalent in terms of computing power.

APPENDIX F

Answers to Questions/Exercises

PART ONE

Chapter 1

Section 1.1

1. One and only one of the upper two inputs must be 1, and the lowest input must be 1.
2. The 1 on the lower input is negated to 0 by the NOT gate, causing the output of the AND gate to become 0. Thus both inputs to the OR gate are 0 (remember that the upper input to the flip-flop is held at 0) so the output of the OR gate becomes 0. This means that the output of the AND gate will remain 0 after the lower input to the flip-flop returns to 0.
3. The output of the upper OR gate will become 1, causing the upper NOT gate to produce an output of 0. This will cause the lower OR gate to produce a 0, causing the lower NOT gate to produce a 1. This 1 is seen as the output of the flip-flop as well as being fed back to the upper OR gate, where it holds the output of that gate at 1, even after the flip-flop's input has returned to 0.
4. a. 6AF2 b. E85517 c. 48
5. a. 0101111110110010111
   b. 0110000100001010
   c. 1010101111001101
   d. 0000000100000000

Section 1.2

1. In the first case, memory cell number 6 ends up containing the value 5. In the second case, it ends up with the value 8.
2. Step 1 erases the original value in cell number 3 when the new value is written there. Consequently, step 2 does not place the original value from cell number 3 in cell number 2. The result is that both cells end up with the value that was originally in cell number 2. A correct procedure is the following:
   Step 1. Move the contents of cell number 2 to cell number 1.
   Step 2. Move the contents of cell number 3 to cell number 2.
   Step 3. Move the contents of cell number 1 to cell number 3.
3. 32768 bits.

Section 1.3

1. Faster retrieval of data and higher transfer rates.
2. The point to remember here is that the slowness of mechanical motion compared with the speed of the internal functioning of the computer dictates that we minimize the number of times we must move the read/write heads. If we fill a complete surface before starting the next, we must move the read/write head each time we finish with a track. The number of moves therefore is approximately the same as the total number of tracks on the two surfaces. If, however, we alternate between surfaces by electronically switching between the read/write heads on the two surfaces, we must mechanically move the read/write heads only after each pair of tracks has been filled. This

technique requires half the number of mechanical motions as the previous technique and is therefore preferred.

3. In this application, a constant expansion and shrinking takes place within the data. If the information were stored on tape, this would result in an endless rewriting process to accommodate the upheaval taking place within the data. (One envisions the last block of the data yo-yoing back and forth as reservations earlier on the tape are made, dropped, or become outdated.) When using disk storage, however, each change affects only the portion of the data stored on the track involved. Consequently, much less rewriting of data is required when updates are made.
4. Spreading logical records across different sectors means that more than one sector must be retrieved from the disk to obtain a complete logical record. The time required to retrieve these additional sectors could easily outweigh the benefits of saving storage space.

Section 1.4

1. Computer science.
2. The two patterns are the same, except that the sixth bit from the low-order end is always 0 for uppercase and 1 for lowercase.
3. a. 01010111 01101000 01100101 01110010 01100101 00100000 01100001 01110010 01100101 00100000 01111001 01101111 01110101 00111111
   b. 00100010 01001000 01101111 01110111 00111111 00100010 00100000 01000011 01101000 01100101 01110010 01111001 01101100 00100000 01100001 01110011 01101011 01100101 01100100 00101110
   c. 00110010 00101011 00110011 00111101 00110101 00101110
4.

5. a. 5 b. 9 c. 11 d. 6 e. 16 f. 18
6. a. 110 b. 1101 c. 1011 d. 10010 e. 11011 f. 100
7. In 24 bits, we can store 3 symbols using ASCII. Thus we can store values as large as 999. However, if we use the bits as binary digits, we can store values up to 16,777,215.
8. a. 15.15 b. 51.0.128 c. 10.160

Section 1.5

1. a. 42 b. 33 c. 23 d. 6 e. 31
2. a. 100000 b. 1000000 c. 1100000 d. 1111 e. 11011
3. a. $3\frac{1}{4}$ b. $5\frac{7}{8}$ c. $2\frac{1}{2}$ d. $6\frac{3}{8}$ e. $\frac{5}{8}$
4. a. 100.1 b. 10.11 c. 1.001 d. 0.0101 e. 101.101
5. a. 100111 b. 1011.110 c. 100000 d. 1000.00

Section 1.6

1. a. 6 since $1110 \rightarrow 14 - 8$
   b. -1 since $0111 \rightarrow 7 - 8$
   c. 0 since $1000 \rightarrow 8 - 8$
   d. -6 since $0010 \rightarrow 2 - 8$
   e. -8 since $0000 \rightarrow 0 - 8$
   f. 1 since $1001 \rightarrow 9 - 8$
2. a. 1101 since $5 + 8 = 13 \rightarrow 1101$
   b. 0011 since $-5 + 8 = 3 \rightarrow 0011$
   c. 1011 since $3 + 8 = 11 \rightarrow 1011$
   d. 1000 since $0 + 8 = 8 \rightarrow 1000$
   e. 1111 since $7 + 8 = 15 \rightarrow 1111$
   f. 0000 since $-8 + 8 = 0 \rightarrow 0000$
3. No. The largest value that can be stored in excess eight notation is 7, represented by 1111. To represent a larger value, at least excess 16 (which uses patterns of 5 bits) must be used. Similarly, 6 cannot be represented in excess four notation. (The largest value that can be represented in excess four notation is 3.)
4. a. 3 b. 15 c. -4 d. -6 e. 0 f. -16
5. a. 00000110 b. 11111010 c. 11101111 d. 00001101 e. 11111111 f. 00000000
6. a. 11111111 b. 10101011 c. 00000100 d. 00000010 e. 00000000 f. 10000001
7. a. With 4 bits the largest value is 7 and the smallest is -8.

b. With 6 bits the largest value is 31 and the smallest is −32.
c. With 8 bits the largest value is 127 and the smallest is −128.

8. a.
$$\begin{array}{r} 0101 \\ \underline{+0010} \\ 0111 \end{array} \rightarrow \begin{array}{r} 5 \\ \underline{+2} \\ 7 \end{array}$$

b.
$$\begin{array}{r} 0011 \\ \underline{+0001} \\ 0100 \end{array} \rightarrow \begin{array}{r} 3 \\ \underline{+1} \\ 4 \end{array}$$

c.
$$\begin{array}{r} 0101 \\ \underline{+1010} \\ 1111 \end{array} \rightarrow \begin{array}{r} 5 \\ \underline{+(-6)} \\ -1 \end{array}$$

d.
$$\begin{array}{r} 1110 \\ \underline{+0011} \\ 0001 \end{array} \rightarrow \begin{array}{r} (-2) \\ \underline{+\ 3} \\ 1 \end{array}$$

e.
$$\begin{array}{r} 1010 \\ \underline{+1110} \\ 1000 \end{array} \rightarrow \begin{array}{r} (-6) \\ \underline{+(-2)} \\ (-8) \end{array}$$

9. a.
$$\begin{array}{r} 0100 \\ \underline{+0011 \rightarrow} \\ 0111 \rightarrow \end{array} \begin{array}{r} 4 \\ \underline{+3} \\ 7 \end{array}$$

b.
$$\begin{array}{r} 0101 \\ \underline{+0110 \rightarrow} \\ 1011 \rightarrow \end{array} \begin{array}{r} 5 \\ \underline{+6} \\ -5 \end{array}$$ (incorrect due to overflow)

c.
$$\begin{array}{r} 1010 \\ \underline{+1010 \rightarrow} \\ 0100 \rightarrow \end{array} \begin{array}{r} (-6) \\ \underline{+(-6)} \\ 4 \end{array}$$ (incorrect due to overflow)

d.
$$\begin{array}{r} 1010 \\ \underline{+0111 \rightarrow} \\ 0001 \rightarrow \end{array} \begin{array}{r} (-6) \\ \underline{+7} \\ 1 \end{array}$$

e.
$$\begin{array}{r} 0111 \\ \underline{+0001 \rightarrow} \\ 1000 \rightarrow \end{array} \begin{array}{r} 7 \\ \underline{+1} \\ -8 \end{array}$$ (incorrect due to overflow)

10. a.
$$\begin{array}{rrr} 6 & 0110 & \\ \underline{+1 \rightarrow} & \underline{+0001} & \\ & 0111 \rightarrow & 7 \end{array}$$

b.
$$\begin{array}{rrrr} 3 & 0011 & 0011 & \\ \underline{-2 \rightarrow} & \underline{+0010 \rightarrow} & \underline{+1110} & \\ & & 0001 \rightarrow & 1 \end{array}$$

c.
$$\begin{array}{rrrr} 4 & 0100 & 0100 & \\ \underline{-6 \rightarrow} & \underline{+0110 \rightarrow} & \underline{+1010} & \\ & & 1110 \rightarrow & -2 \end{array}$$

d.
$$\begin{array}{rrrr} 2 & 0010 & & \\ \underline{+4 \rightarrow} & \underline{+0100} & & \\ & 0110 \rightarrow & & 6 \end{array}$$

e.
$$\begin{array}{rrrr} 1 & 0001 & 0001 & \\ \underline{-5 \rightarrow} & \underline{+0101 \rightarrow} & \underline{+1011} & \\ & & 1110 \rightarrow & -4 \end{array}$$

11. No. Overflow occurs when an attempt is made to store a number that is too large for the system being used. When adding a positive value to a negative value, the result must be between the values being added. Thus, if the original values are small enough to be stored, the result is also.

Section 1.7

1. a. $\frac{5}{8}$ b. $3\frac{1}{4}$ c. $\frac{9}{32}$ d. $-1\frac{1}{2}$ e. $-\frac{11}{64}$

2. a. 01101011 b. 01111010 (round-off error)
c. 01001100 d. 11101110
e. 11111000 (round-off error)

3. 01001001 ($\frac{9}{16}$) is larger than 00111101 ($\frac{13}{32}$). The following is a simple way of determining which of two patterns represents the larger value:

Case 1. If the sign bits are different, the larger is the one with 0 sign bit.

Case 2. If the sign bits are both 0, scan the remaining portions of the patterns from left to right until a bit position is found where the two patterns differ. The pattern containing the 1 in this position represents the larger value.

Case 3. If the sign bits are both 1, scan the remaining portions of the patterns from left to right until a bit position is found where the two patterns differ. The pattern containing the 0 in this position represents the larger value.

The simplicity of this comparison process is one of the reasons for representing the exponent in floating-point systems with an excess notation rather than with two's complement.

4. The largest value would be $7\frac{1}{2}$, which is represented by the pattern 01111111. As for the smallest positive value, you could argue that there are two "correct" answers. First, if you stick to the coding process described in the text, which requires the most significant bit of the mantissa to be 1 (called normalized form), the answer is $\frac{1}{32}$, which is represented by the pattern 00001000. However, most machines do not impose this restriction for values close to 0. For such a machine, the correct answer is $\frac{1}{256}$ represented by 00000001.

Section 1.8

1. b, c, and e.

2. Yes. If an even number of errors occurs in one byte, the parity technique does not detect them.

3. In this case, errors occur in bytes a and d of question 1. The answer to question 2 remains the same.
4. a. 001010111 001101000 101100101
101110010 101100101 100100000
001100001 101110010 101100101
000100000 001111001 101101111
001110101 100111111

   b. 100100010 101001000 101101111
101110111 100111111 100100010
000100000 001000011 001101000
101100101 101110010 001111001
101101100 000100000 001100001
001110011 001101011 101100101
001100100 100101110

   c. 000110010 100101011 100110011
000111101 100110101 100101110
5. a. BED b. CAB c. HEAD
6. One solution is the following:
A 00000
B 11100
C 01111
D 10011

Chapter 2

Section 2.1

1. On small machines this is often a two-step process consisting of first reading the contents from the first cell into a register and then writing it into the destination cell. On most large machines, this activity appears as one event.
2. The value to be written, the address of the cell in which to write, and the command to write.
3. The term *move* often carries the connotation of removing from one location and placing in another, thus leaving a hole behind. In most cases within a machine, this removal does not take place. Rather, the object being moved is most often copied (or cloned) into the new location.
4. A common technique, called relative addressing, is to state how far rather than where to jump. For example, an instruction might be to jump forward three instructions or jump backward two instructions. You should note, however, that such statements must be altered if additional instructions are later inserted between the origin and the destination of the jump.
5. This could be argued either way. The instruction is stated in the form of a conditional jump. However, because the condition that 0 be equal to 0 is always satisfied, the jump will always be made as if there were no condition stated at all. You will often find machines with such instructions in their repertoires because it provides an efficient design. For example, if a machine is designed to execute an instruction with a structure such as "If . . . jump to . . ." this instruction form can be used to express both conditional and unconditional jumps.

Section 2.2

1. 156C = 0001010101101100
166D = 0001011001101101
5056 = 0101000001010110
306E = 0011000001101110
C000 = 1100000000000000
2. a. STORE the contents of register 6 in memory cell number 8A.
   b. JUMP to location DE if the contents of register A equals that of register 0.
   c. AND the contents of registers 3 and C, leaving the result in register 0.
   d. MOVE the contents of register F to register 4.
3. The instruction 15AB requires that the CPU query the memory circuitry for the contents of the memory cell at address AB. This value, when obtained from memory, is then placed in register 5. The instruction 25AB does not require such a request of memory. Rather, the value AB is placed in register 5.
4. a. 2356 b. A503 c. B7F3 d. 80A5

Section 2.3

1. Hexadecimal 34
2. a. 0F b. C3
3. a. 00 b. 01 c. four times
4. It halts. This is an example of what is often called self-modifying code. That is, the program modifies itself. Note that the first two instructions place hexadecimal C0 at memory location F8, and the next two instructions place 00 at location F9. Thus, by the time the machine reaches the instruction at F8, the halt instruction (C000) has been placed there.

Section 2.4

1. One set of registers is used for fetching, decoding, and executing microinstructions, while the other set is used for fetching, decoding, and executing the machine-language instructions as directed by the microprogram.
2. The pipe would contain the instructions B1B0 (being executed), 5002 (being decoded), and B0AA (being fetched). If the value in register 0 is equal to the value in register 1, the jump to location B0 is executed, and the effort expended on the last two of these instructions is wasted.
3. If no precautions are taken, the information at memory locations F8 and F9 is fetched as an instruction before the previous part of the program has had a chance to modify these cells.
4. a. The CPU that is trying to add 1 to the cell can first read the value in the cell. Following this the other CPU reads the cell's value. (Note that at this point both CPUs have retrieved the same value.) If the first CPU now finishes its addition and writes its result back in the cell before the second finishes its subtraction and writes its result, the final value in the cell reflects only the activity of the second CPU.
   b. The CPUs might read the data from the cell as before, but this time the second CPU might write its result before the first. Thus, only the activity of the first CPU is reflected in the cell's final value.

Section 2.5

1. a. 00001011 b. 10000000 c. 00101101
   d. 11101011 e. 11101111 f. 11111111
   g. 11100000 h. 01101111 i. 11010010
2. 0011100 with the AND operation
3. 0011100 with the XOR operation
4. a. The final result is 0 if the string contained an odd number of 1s. Otherwise it is 1.
   b. The result is the value of the parity bit for even parity.
5. The logical XOR operation mirrors addition except for the case where both operands are 1, in which case the XOR produces a 0, whereas the sum is 10. (Thus the XOR operation can be considered an addition operation with no carry.)
6. Use AND with the mask 01011111 to change lowercase to uppercase. Use OR with 00100000 to change uppercase to lowercase.
7. a. 01001101 b. 11100001 c. 11101111
8. a. 57 b. B8 c. 6F d. 6A
9. 5
10. 00110110 in two's complement. 01011110 in floating-point. The point here is that the procedure used to add the values is different depending on the interpretation given the bit patterns.
11. One solution is:
    12A7 (LOAD register 2 with the contents of memory cell A7.)
    2380 (LOAD register 3 with the value 80.)
    7023 (OR registers 2 and 3 leaving the result in register 0.)
    30A7 (STORE contents of register 0 in memory cell A7.)
    C000 (HALT.)
12. One solution is:
    15E0 (LOAD register 5 with the contents of memory cell E0.)
    A502 (ROTATE 2 bits to the right the contents of register 5.)
    260F (LOAD register 6 with the value 0F.)
    8056 (AND registers 5 and 6, leaving the result in register 0.)
    30E1 (STORE the contents of register 0 in memory cell E1.)
    C000 (HALT.)

Section 2.6

1. Since each state communicated represents 3 bits, the measure of bps is three times the baud rate.
2. a. 37B6
   b. One million times
   c. No. A typical page of text contains less than 4000 characters. Thus the ability to print five pages in a minute indicates a printing rate of no more than 20,000 characters per minute, which is much less than one million characters per second. (The point is that a computer can send characters to a printer much faster than the printer can

print them; thus the printer needs a way of telling the computer to wait.)

3. The 13 disks together have a capacity of 18.72MB, which might tempt you to answer yes. However, most software is shipped in a compressed form. The data compression techniques used for this purpose can have compression ratios of as much as 2.6 to 1, meaning that the 13 disks could contain more than 40MB of software. The answer is that you will probably have to buy a larger hard drive.
4. Relative encoding, using a Huffman code, and Lempel–Ziv encoding.

PART TWO
Chapter 3
Section 3.1

1. A traditional example is the line of people waiting to buy tickets to an event. In this case there always seems to be someone who tries to "break in line," which would violate the FIFO structure.
2. Options (b) and (c).
3. Real-time processing refers to coordinating the execution of a program with activities in the machine's environment. Interactive processing refers to a person's interaction with a program as it executes. Good real-time characteristics are needed for successful interactive processing.
4. Time-sharing is the technique by which multitasking is accomplished on a single-processor machine.

Section 3.2

1. *Command processor:* Communicates with the machine's environment.
   File manager: Coordinates the use of the machine's mass storage.
   Device drivers: Handles communication with the machine's peripheral devices.
   Memory manager: Coordinates the use of the machine's main memory.
   Scheduler: Coordinates the processes in the system.
   Dispatcher: Controls the assignment of processes to CPU time.
2. The line is vague, and the distinction is often in the eye of the beholder. Roughly speaking, utility software performs basic, universal tasks, whereas application software performs tasks unique to the machine's application.
3. Virtual memory is the imaginary memory space whose apparent presence is created by the process of swapping data and programs back and forth between main memory and mass storage.
4. When the machine is turned on, the CPU begins executing the bootstrap, which resides in ROM. This bootstrap directs the CPU through the process of transferring the operating system from mass storage into the volatile area of main memory. When this transfer is complete, the bootstrap directs the CPU to jump to the operating system.

Section 3.3

1. A program is a set of directions. A process is the action of following those directions.
2. The CPU completes its current fetch–decode–execute cycle, saves the state of the current process, and sets its program counter to a predetermined value (which is the location of the interrupt handler). Thus the next instruction executed will be the first instruction within the interrupt handler.
3. They could be given higher priorities so that they would be given preference by the dispatcher. Another option would be to give the higher-priority processes longer time slices.
4. The machine would provide 18 processes a complete quantum in one second.
5. A total of $^{10}/_{11}$ of the machine's time would be spent actually performing processes. When a process requests an I/O activity, its time slice is terminated while the controller performs the request. Thus, if each process made such a request after only 5 milliseconds of its quantum, the efficiency of the machine would drop to ½. That is, the machine would spend as much time making context switches as it would executing processes.
6. How about a mail order business and its clients, a stock broker and his or her clients, or a pharmacist and his or her customers?

Section 3.4

1. This system guarantees that the resource is not used by more than one process at a time; however, it dictates that the resource be allocated in a strictly alternating fashion. Once a process has used and relinquished the resource, it must wait for the other process to use the resource before the original process can access it again. This is true even if the first process needs the resource right away and the other process won't need it for some time.

2. If two cars enter opposite ends of the tunnel at the same time, they will not be aware of the other's presence. The process of entering and turning on the lights is another example of a critical region, or in this case we might call it a critical process. In this terminology, we could summarize the flaw by saying that cars at opposite ends of the tunnel could execute the critical process at the same time.

3. a. This guarantees that the nonshareable resource is not required and allocated on a partial basis; that is, a car is given the whole bridge or nothing at all.
   b. This means that the nonshareable resource can be forcibly retrieved.
   c. This makes the nonshareable resource shareable, which removes the competition.

4. A sequence of arrows that form a closed loop in the directed graph. It is on this observation that techniques have been developed, allowing some operating systems to recognize the existence of deadlock and consequently to take appropriate corrective action.

Section 3.5

1. An open network is one whose specifications and protocols are public, allowing different vendors to produce compatible products.

2. A router is a machine connecting two networks. More technically, a router is a machine connecting two networks that use the same protocols. The term *gateway* is used to refer to a machine connecting two networks that use different protocols.

3. The complete Internet address of a host consists of the network identifier and the host address.

4. A URL is essentially the address of a document in the World Wide Web. A browser is a program that assists a user in accessing hypertext.

5. Any break in the ring would disrupt communication. If messages could be transferred in either direction, one break in the ring would not disrupt communication.

Section 3.6

1. The link layer receives the message and hands it to the network layer. The network layer notes that the message is for another host, attaches another intermediate destination address to the message, and gives the message back to the link layer.

2. Unlike TCP, UDP is a connectionless protocol that does not confirm that the message was received at the destination.

3. Each message is assigned a hop count that determines the maximum number of times the message will be relayed.

4. Nothing really. A programmer at any host could modify the software at that host to keep such records. This is why sensitive data should be encrypted.

Chapter 4

Section 4.1

1. A process is the activity of executing an algorithm. A program is a representation of an algorithm.

2. In the introductory chapter we cited algorithms for playing music, operating washing machines, constructing models, performing magic tricks, and the Euclidean algorithm. Many of the "algorithms" you meet in everyday life fail to be algorithms according to our formal definition. The example of the long-division algorithm was cited in the text. Another is the algorithm executed by a clock that continues to advance its hands and ring its chimes day after day.

3. The informal definition fails to require that the steps be ordered and unambiguous. It merely hints at the requirements that the steps be executable and lead to an end.

4. There are two points here. The first is that the instructions define a nonterminating process. In reality, however, the process will ultimately reach the state in which there are no coins in your pocket. In fact, this may be the starting state. At this point the problem is that of ambiguity. The algorithm, as represented, does not tell us what to do in this situation.

Section 4.2

1. One example is found in the composition of matter. At one level, the primitives are considered molecules, yet these particles are actually composites made up of atoms, which in turn are composed of electrons, protons, and neutrons. Today, we know that even these "primitives" are composites.
2. Once a procedure is correctly constructed, it can be used as a building block for larger program structures without reconsidering the procedure's internal composition.
3.
```
assign X the value of the larger input;
assign Y the value of the smaller input;
while (Y not zero) do
      (assign Remainder the value of the
           remainder after dividing X by Y;
       assign Y the value of Y;
       assign Y the value of Remainder)
assign GCD the value of X
```
4. All other colors of light can be produced by combining red, blue, and green. Thus a television picture tube is designed to produce these three basic colors.

Section 4.3

1. a.
```
if (n = 1 or n = 2)
   then (the answer is the list containing the
         single value n)
   else (Divide n by 3, obtaining a quotient q
         and a remainder r.
      if r = 0
         then the answer is the list containing
           q 3s;
      if r = 1
         then the answer is the list containing
           q − 1 3s and two 2s;
      if r = 2
         then the answer is the list containing
           q 3s and one 2)
```
   b. The result would be the list containing 667 threes.
   c. You probably experimented with small input values until you began to see a pattern.
2. a. Yes. *Hint:* Place the first tile in the center so that it avoids the quadrant containing the hole while covering one square from each of the other quadrants. Each quadrant then represents a smaller version of the original problem.
   b. The board with a single hole contains $2^{2n} - 1$ squares, and each tile covers exactly three squares.
   c. Parts (a) and (b) of this question provide an excellent example of how knowing a solution to one problem helps solve another. See Polya's fourth phase.
3. It says, "This is the correct answer."

Section 4.4

1. Change the test in the while statement to read "target value not equal to current entry and there remain entries to be considered."
2.
```
assign Z the value 0;
assign X the value 1;
repeat (assign Z the value Z + X;
        assign X the value X + 1)
until (X = 6)
```
3.

Cheryl	Alice	Alice
George	Cheryl	Bob
Alice	George	Cheryl
Bob	Bob	George

4. It is a waste of time to insist on placing the pivot above an identical entry in the list. For instance, make the proposed change and then try the new program on a list in which all entries are the same.

Section 4.5

1. The first sublist consists of the names following Henry—that is, Irene, Joe, Karl, Larry, Mary, Nancy, and Oliver. Next are the names from this list preceding Larry—that is, Irene, Joe, and Karl. At this point, the search process would find the target Joe at the center of the sublist in question.
2. 8, 17
3.

Bob	Alice
Alice	Bob
Carol	Carol
Larry	Larry
John	John

4. This is an example of how unintelligent an algorithm can be. Rather than recognize that no work is needed, the algorithm ultimately picks each name as the pivot entry and ends up replacing it with itself.

   If the input list is in reverse order, the effect of the algorithm is to exchange the first name with the last, then exchange the new first name with itself, and then turn its attention to the portion of the list between the first and last entries.

5. The effect is that the first occurrence of the name is interchanged with the last, then the first with the next-to-the-last, and so on, until the first occurrence is exchanged with the second.

Section 4.6

1. No. The answer is not correct, although it may sound right. The truth is that two of the three cards are the same on both sides. Thus the probability of picking such a card is two-thirds.
2. No. If the dividend is less than the divisor, such as in $3/7$, the answer given is 1, although it should be 0.
3. No. If the value of X is zero and the value of Y is nonzero, the answer given will not be correct.
4. Each time the test for termination is conducted, the statement "Sum = $1 + 2 + \cdots + I$ and I less than or equal to N" is true. Combining this with the termination condition "I greater than or equal to N" produces the desired conclusion "Sum = $1 + 2 + \cdots + N$." Since I is initialized at zero and incremented by one each time through the loop, its value must ultimately reach that of N.

Chapter 5

Section 5.1

1. A program in a third-generation language is machine independent in the sense that its steps are not stated in terms of the machine's attributes such as registers and memory cell addresses. On the other hand, it is machine dependent in the sense that arithmetic overflow and round-off errors will still occur.
2. The major distinction is that an assembler translates each instruction in the source program into a single machine instruction, whereas a compiler often produces many machine-language instructions to obtain the equivalent of a single source program instruction.
3. The declarative paradigm is based on developing a description of the problem to be solved. The functional paradigm forces the programmer to describe the problems solution in terms of solutions to smaller problems. The object-oriented paradigm places emphasis on describing the components in the problem's environment.
4. The later-generation languages allow the program to be expressed more in terms of the problem's environment and less in terms of computer gibberish than do the earlier-generation languages.

Section 5.2

1. Using a descriptive constant can improve the accessibility of the program.
2. A declarative statement describes terminology; an imperative statement describes steps in an algorithm.
3. Integer, real, character, and Boolean
4. The if-then-else and while loop structures are very common.
5. All components of a homogeneous array have the same type.

Section 5.3

1. A local variable is accessible only within a program unit such as a procedure; a global variable is accessible programwide.
2. A function is a procedure that returns a value associated with the function's name.
3. Because that is what they are. I/O operations are actually calls to routines within the machine's operating system.
4. A formal parameter is an identifier within a procedure. It serves as a placeholder for the value, the actual parameter, that is passed to the procedure when the procedure is called.

Section 5.4

1. *Lexical analysis:* the process of identifying tokens.

   Parsing: the process of recognizing the grammatical structure of the program.

   Code generation: the process of producing the instructions in the object program.
2. A symbol table is the record of information the parser has obtained from the program's declarative statements.
3. 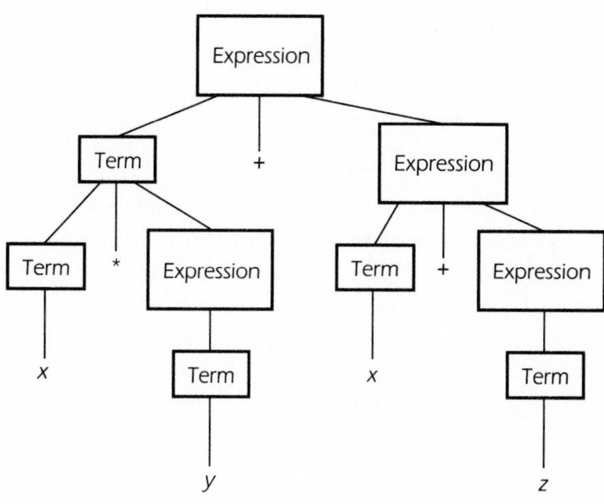

4. They are one or more instances of the substrings

   forward backward cha cha cha
   backward forward cha cha cha
   swing right cha cha cha
   swing left cha cha cha

Section 5.5

1. Only part (c).
2. Start the critical region with an in statement to retrieve a tuple of a particular type from the tuple space and close the critical region with an out statement to replace the tuple. Then, place a single tuple of that type in the tuple space. Any process trying to enter the critical region must first retrieve the tuple, and because there is only one such tuple, only one process is allowed in the critical region at a time.
3. a. The process executing this statement is blocked because there is no tuple of the form (4, 2) in the tuple space to be retrieved.
   b. A tuple of the form (8, 3.4) is placed in the tuple space.
   c. The variable Value is assigned the value 5. The tuple (5, 7) remains in the tuple space.
   d. The tuple (5, 7) is retrieved from the tuple space, and Value is given the value 5.

Section 5.6

1. R, T, and V. For instance, we can show that R is a consequence by adding its negation to the collection and showing that resolution can lead to the empty statement, as shown here:

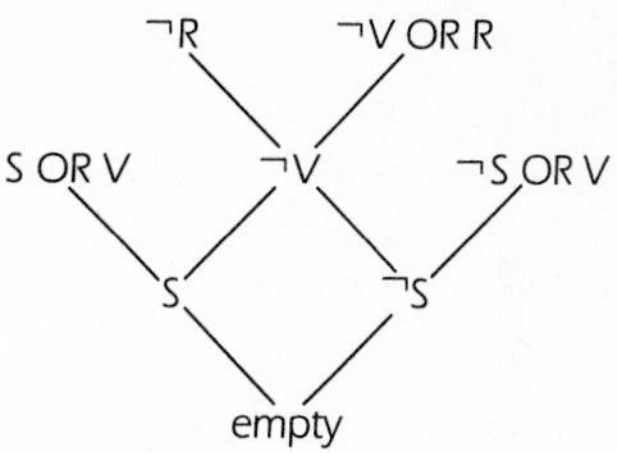

2. No. The collection is inconsistent, since resolution can lead to the empty statement, as shown here:

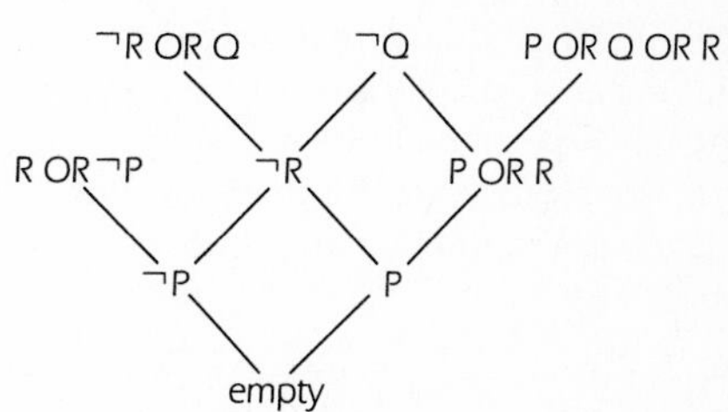

3. a. thriftier(sue, carol)
   thriftier(sue, john)
   b. thriftier(sue, carol)
   thriftier(bill, carol)
   c. thriftier(carol, john)
   thriftier(bill, sue)
   thriftier(sue, carol)
   thriftier(bill, sue)
   thriftier(sue, john)

Chapter 6

Section 6.1

1. A long sequence of assignment statements is not as complex in the context of program design as a few nested if statements.
2. One approach is to intentionally place some errors in the software when it is designed. Then, after the software has supposedly been debugged, check to see how many of the original errors are still present. If 5 of the 7 original errors have been removed, then conclude that only $\frac{5}{7}$ of the total errors in the software have been removed.
3. How about the number of errors found after a fixed period of use? One problem here is that this value cannot be measured in advance.

Section 6.2

1. System requirements are stated in terms of the application environment, whereas the specifications are stated in technical terms and identify how the requirements will be met.
2. The analysis phase concentrates on what the proposed system must accomplish. The design phase concentrates on how the system accomplishes its goals. The implementation phase concentrates on the actual construction of the system. The testing phase concentrates on making sure that the system does what it is intended to do.
3. The traditional waterfall approach dictates that the analysis, design, implementation, and testing phases be performed in a linear manner. The prototyping model allows for a more relaxed trial-and-error approach.

Section 6.3

1. The chapters of a novel build on one another, whereas the sections in an encyclopedia are largely independent. Hence a novel has more coupling between its chapters than an encyclopedia has between its sections. However, the sections within an encyclopedia probably have a higher level of cohesion than the chapters in a novel.
2. Explicit coupling includes the identification of the trump suit, which hand is dummy, who will lead, and so on. Insights gained from the bidding process, such as who holds which cards, can be considered implicit coupling.
3. This is a tough one. From one point of view, we could start by placing everything in a single module. This would result in little cohesion and no coupling at all. If we then begin to divide this single module into smaller ones, the result would be an increase in coupling. We might therefore conclude that increasing cohesion tends to increase coupling.

   On the other hand, suppose the problem at hand naturally divides into three very cohesive modules, which we will call A, B, and C. If our original design did not observe this natural division (for example, half of task A might be placed with half of task B, and so on), we would expect the cohesion to be low and the coupling high. In this case, redesigning the system by isolating tasks A, B, and C into separate modules would most likely decrease intermodule coupling as intramodule cohesion increases.
4. a. The common goal or interest of the club members. As various club activities are undertaken, committees and subcommittees are often formed to organize them. This can be viewed as a natural tendency to maximize cohesion. The cohesion of the club as a whole is weak compared with the specific tasks of the committees. Also, the duties of the officers of a club are modularized according to function. For example, the president presides over meetings, the secretary maintains records, and the treasurer manages the finances.

   b. The registration of students. This activity is normally broken into its functional components to obtain a greater degree of cohesion. For example, one component might deal with confirming admission, another with selecting courses, still another with paying fees.

   c. The marketing of merchandise. Here again we find a natural tendency to seek greater cohesion within the organization. In this case, it results in the formation of departments based on the type of merchandise being sold. In addition, we find the management divided according to function in a similar manner to the officers in a club.

d. The conveying of information. Again observe the natural desire to increase cohesion by subdivision. Newspapers are divided into sections according to subject matter.

Section 6.4

1.

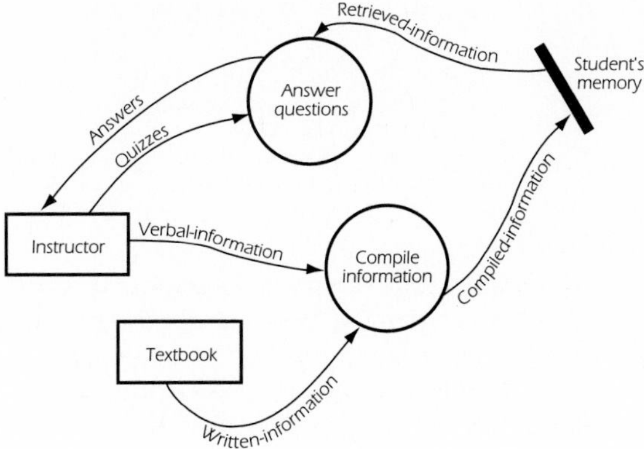

2.

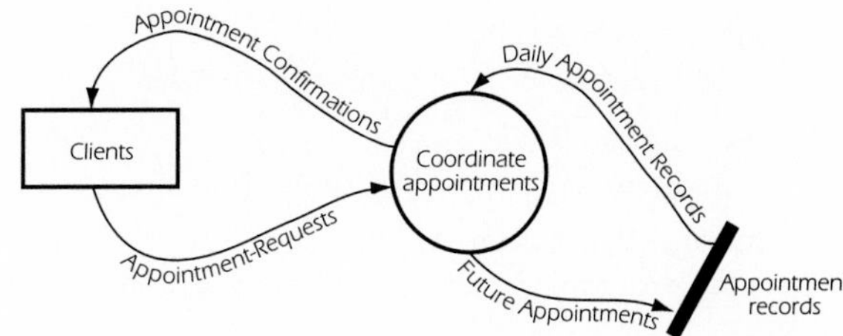

3. A dataflow diagram is a representation of the paths through which information flows through a system. An entity-relationship diagram is a pictorial representation of the various items of information in a system and how each item relates to the others. A data dictionary is a depository of information relating to the various data items in a software system.
4. The relationship between a company and its flights is one-to-many. The relationship between flights and passengers, as well as between companies and passengers, is many-to-many.

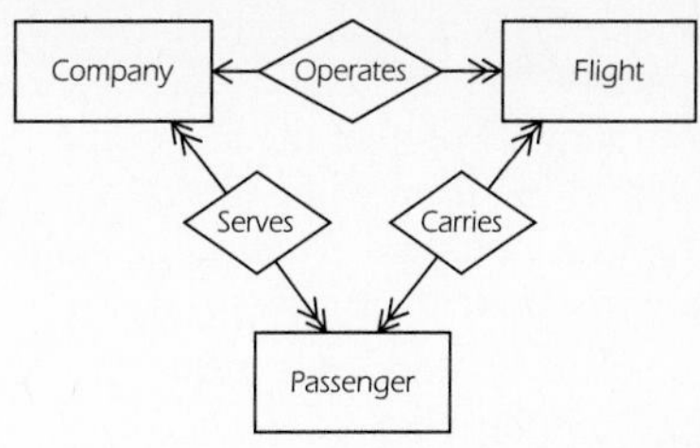

Section 6.5

1. In accompanying manuals, within the source program in the form of comments and well-written code, through interactive messages that the program itself writes at a terminal, through data dictionaries, and in the form of design documents such as structure charts, dataflow diagrams, and entity-relationship diagrams.
2. In both the development and modification phases. The point is that modifications must be documented as thoroughly as the original program. (It's also true that software is documented while in its use phase. For example, a user of the system might discover problems, which are then reported in the system user's manual. Moreover, books written on the use and design of popular software systems are common. These are often written by people other than the original designers and after the software has been in use for some time and has gained popularity.)
3. Different people will have different opinions on this one. Some will argue that the program is the point of the whole project and thus is naturally the more important. Others will argue that a program is worth nothing if it is not documented, because if you can't understand a program, you can't use it or modify it. Moreover, with good documentation, the task of creating the program can be "easily" re-created.

Section 6.6

1. This is a problem the courts must resolve. It would certainly involve more than just the format of the program and choice of variable names.
2. Copyright and patent laws benefit society because they encourage creators of new products

to make them available to the public. Trade secret laws benefit society because they allow a company to protect the steps in a product's development from competitors. Without such protection, companies would hesitate to make major investments in new products.

3. A disclaimer does not protect a company against negligence.

PART THREE

Chapter 7

Section 7.1

1. 5 3 7 4 2 8 1 9 6
2. If R is the number of rows in the matrix, the formula is $R(J - 1) + (I - 1)$.
3. From the beginning address of 25, we must skip over $11(3 - 1) + (6 - 1) = 27$ entries in the matrix, each of which occupies two memory cells. Thus we must skip over 54 memory cells. The final address can therefore be found by adding 54 to the address of the first entry, resulting in the address of 79.
4. $(C \times I) + J$

Section 7.2

1. As an example, to find the fifth entry in a dense list, multiply the number of cells in each entry by 4 and add the result to the address of the first entry. The situation is quite different in the case of the linked list because the address of the fifth entry is in no way related to the address of the first. Thus, to find the fifth entry, one must actually traverse each preceding entry.
2. The head pointer contains the NIL value.
3. **assign** Last **the value** of the last name to be printed
   assign Finished **the value** false
   assign Current Pointer **the value** in the head pointer;
   while (Current Pointer not NIL and Finished = false) **do**
   (print the entry pointed to by Current Pointer,
   if (the name just printed = Last) **then**
   (**assign** Finished **the value** true)
   assign Current Pointer **the value** in the pointer cell in the entry pointed to by Current Pointer)
4. **assign** Current **the value** in the head pointer
   assign Previous **the value** NIL
   assign Found **the value** false
   while (Current not NIL and Found is false) **do**
   (**if** (the entry pointed to by Current is the target entry)
   then (**assign** Found **the value** true)
   else (**assign** Previous **the value** of Current;
   assign Current **the value** in the pointer cell of the entry pointed to by Current))
   if (Found is true) **then**
   (**if** (Previous = NIL)
   then (**assign** head pointer **the value** in the pointer cell of the entry pointed to by Current)
   else (**assign** the pointer cell in the entry pointed to by Previous **the value** in the pointer cell in the entry pointed to by Current))

Section 7.3

1. One traditional example is the stack of trays in a cafeteria. Many of these set-ups are spring-loaded to keep the top tray at a convenient level. In this case, the term *push* is truly representative of the process of adding more entries to the stack.
2.

Activity	*Stack immediately following activity*
Main program calls subprogram A.	Position in main
Subprogram A calls subprogram B.	Position in A Position in main
Subprogram B completes.	Position in main
Subprogram A calls subprogram C.	Position in A Position in main
Subprogram C completes.	Position in main
Subprogram A completes.	Stack empty.

3. The stack pointer points to the cell immediately below the base of the stack.
4. **If** (the stack pointer points below the stack base) **then** (exit with error message)
   Extract the stack entry pointed to by the stack pointer;
   Adjust the stack pointer to point to the next lower stack entry
5. Represent the stack as a one-dimensional array and the stack pointer as a variable of integer type. Then use this stack pointer to

maintain a record of the position of the stack's top within the array rather than of the exact memory address.

Section 7.4

1.

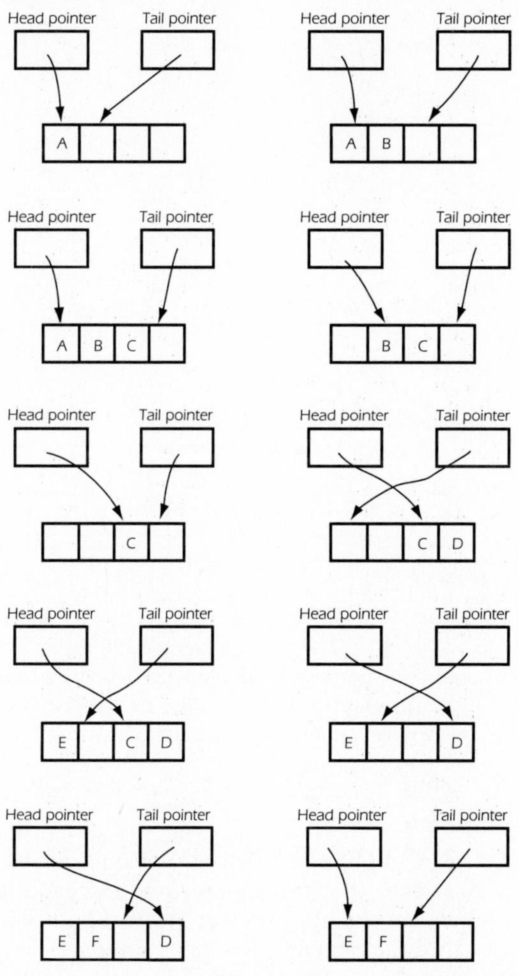

2. Both empty and full conditions are indicated by the equal head and tail pointers. Thus additional information is required to distinguish between the two conditions.

3. **if** (Full is true) **then** (exit with error message)
Store the new entry in the location pointed to by the tail pointer;
Advance the tail pointer;
If (the tail pointer points beyond the reserved block)
then (alter the tail pointer to point to the first cell of the reserved block)
if (head pointer = tail pointer)
then (assign Full the value true)

Section 7.5

1. The root is 11, the leaf nodes are 1, 2, 6, 3, and 4. There are four Qy subtrees below the node 9, with roots 5, 1, 2, and 6. The nodes 9 and 10 are siblings, as are 5 and 6, 1 and 2, and 7 and 8.
2. The root pointer is NIL.
3.

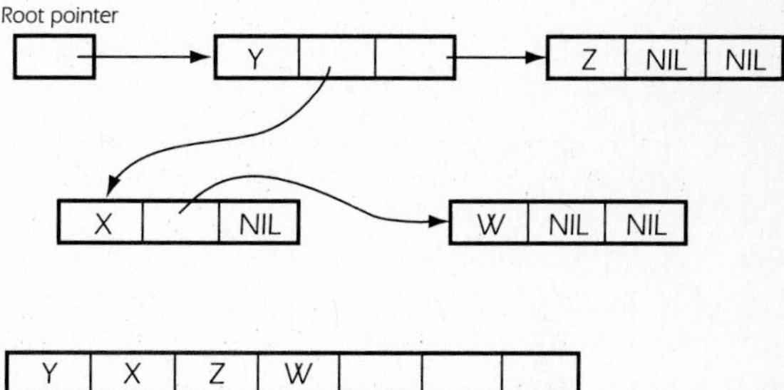

4.

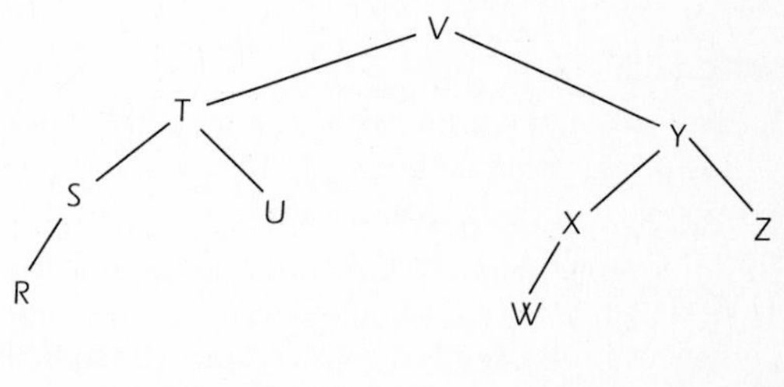

5. When searching for J:

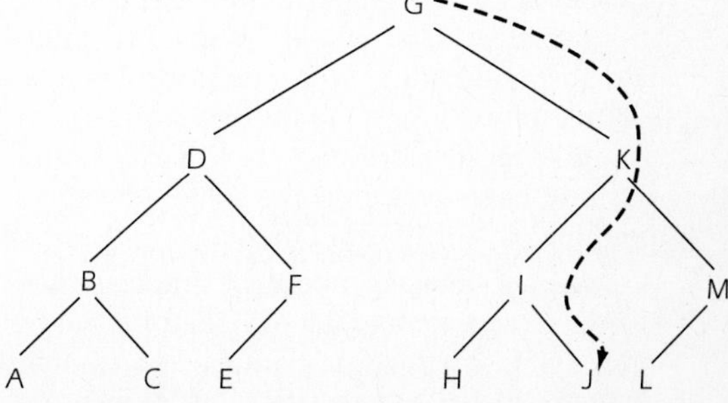

When searching for P:

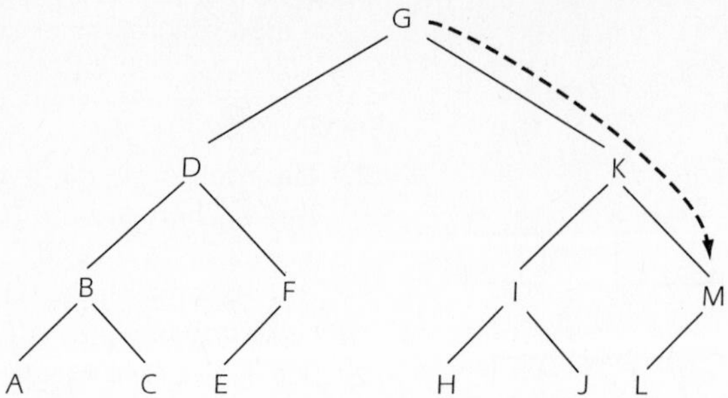

6.

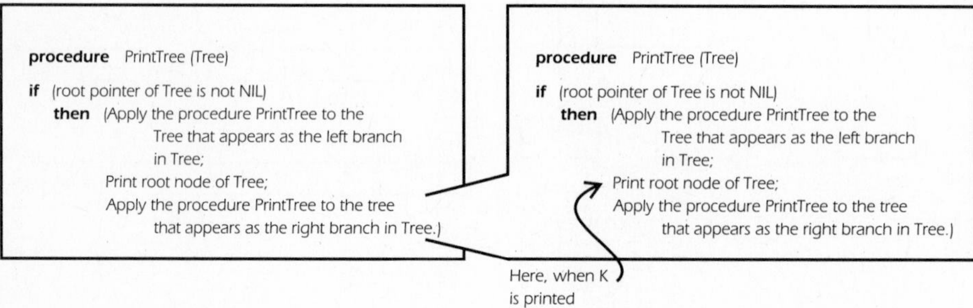

Section 7.6

1. Deposits and withdrawals to and from a checking account can be executed only through specific procedures that are supported by laws.
2. An abstract data type is a concept; an instance of that data type is an actual object of that type. For example, dog is a type of animal, whereas Lassie and Rex are instances of that type.
3. A traditional program module is normally designed to carry out a specific procedure and thus consists of a single routine. An instance of an abstract data type is designed to simulate the underlying type and thus may be capable of executing several procedures. For example, an instance of a stack is capable of pushing new entries on the stack as well as popping old entries from the stack.
4. A queue of integers might be implemented using either a contiguous or linked list as the underlying structure; or, perhaps as a circular queue restricted to a specific block of memory cells or a roaming block of cells, although this latter implementation would prove dangerous to the other data structures residing in memory.

Section 7.7

1. One might be an escalator that should be able to receive shoppers at one level and deposit them at another. Another might be an entrance that should be able to introduce new shoppers into the system while removing others from the system.
2. Each object package contains those routines used to simulate the abstract object being represented.
3. A single object often consists of separate routines for performing the various operations on the object. For example, a stack object would have routines for pushing and popping entries. Each of these routines could be implemented as a submodule of the object.

Chapter 8

Section 8.1

1. You should be led through these beginning stages:

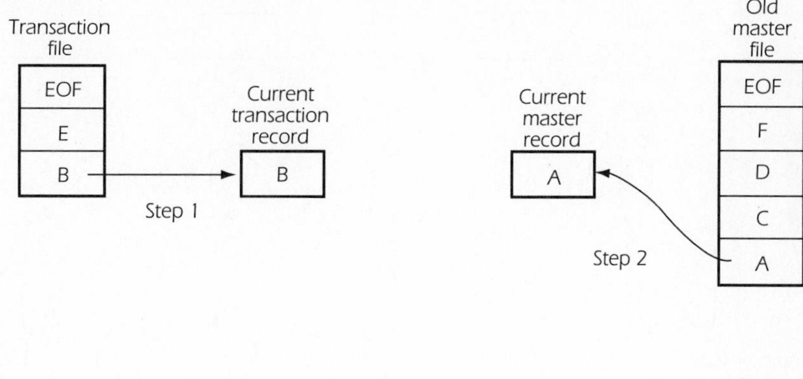

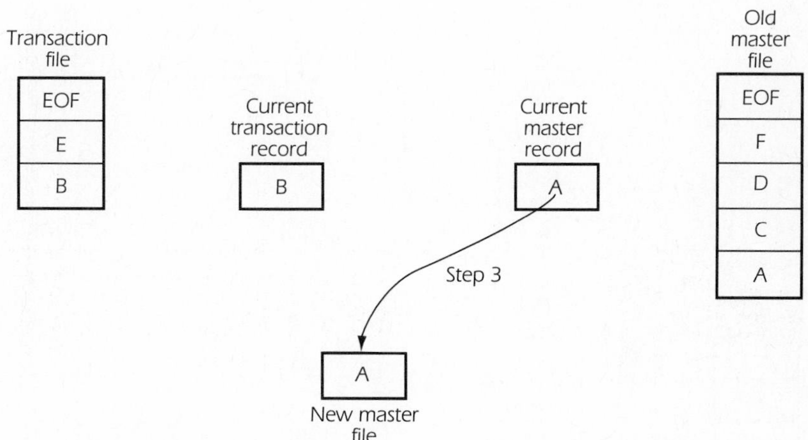

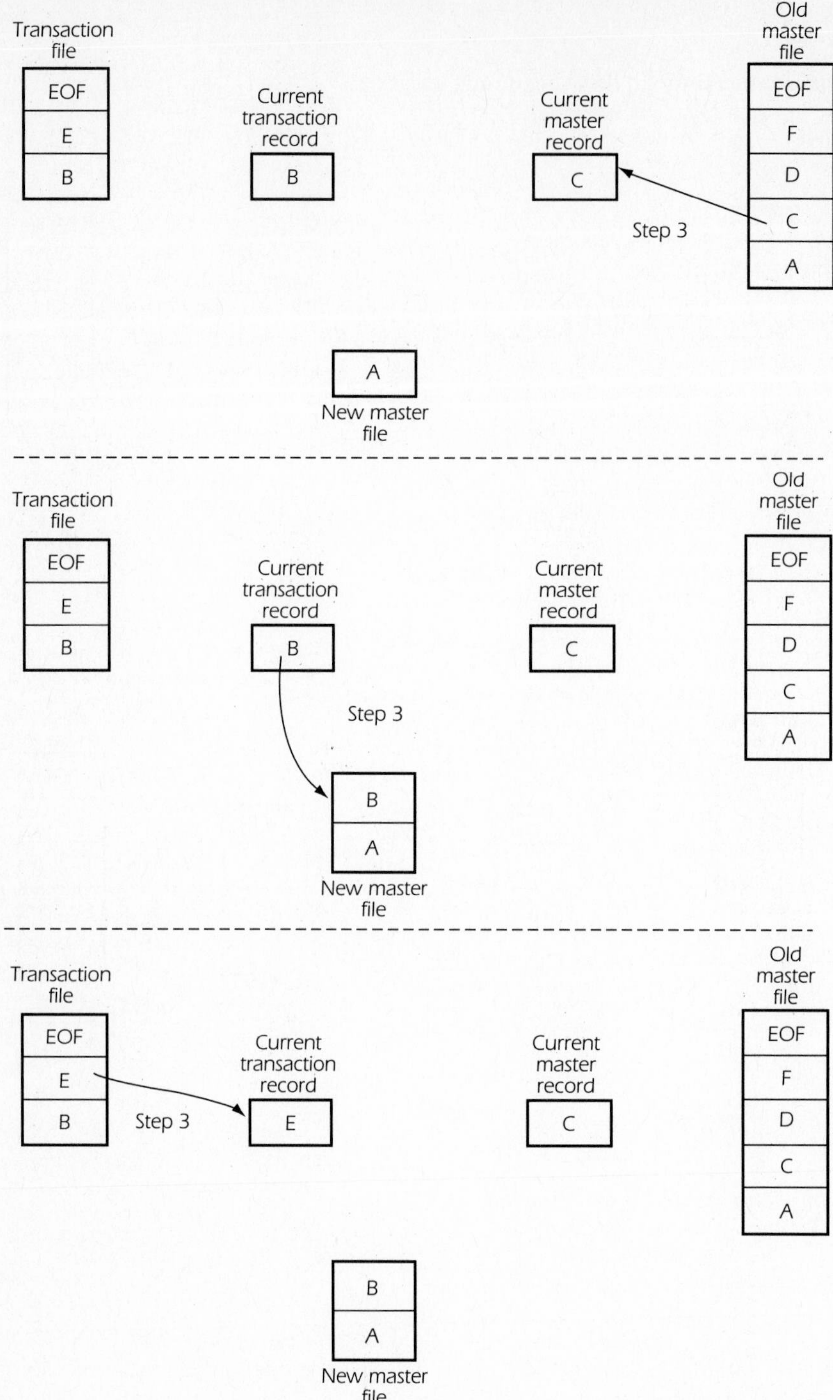
Transaction file
EOF
E
B
Current transaction record
B
Current master record
C
Old master file
EOF
F
D
C
A
Step 3
A
New master file
Transaction file
EOF
E
B
Current transaction record
B
Current master record
C
Old master file
EOF
F
D
C
A
Step 3
B
A
New master file
Transaction file
EOF
E
B
Step 3
Current transaction record
E
Current master record
C
Old master file
EOF
F
D
C
A
B
A
New master file

2. The idea is to first divide the file to be stored into many separate files containing one record each. Next, group the one-record files into pairs, and within each pair designate one file as the transaction file and the other as the old master. Since each file is sorted (it has only one record), we can now apply the merge algorithm to each pair. This results in half as many files, each with two records. Furthermore, each of these two-record files is sorted. We can group them into pairs, call one member of each pair the transaction file and the other the old master file, and again apply the merge algorithm to the pairs. Again we find ourselves with fewer but larger files, each of which is sorted. Continuing in this fashion, we are ultimately left with only one file that consists of all the original records but in sorted order. (If an odd number of files occur at any stage of this process, we need merely to set the odd one aside and pair it with one of the larger files in the next stage.)

3.
```
Read a record (called the current transaction record)
   from the transaction file.
Read a record (called the current master record)
   from the old master file.
while (neither record is a sentinel) do
   [if (the key field of the current transaction record
        is less than that of the current master record)
     then (write the current transaction record on the
            new master file and read the next record
            from the transaction file)
     else (write the current master record on the new
            master file and read the next record from
            the old master file)]
while (the current master record is not the sentinel) do
    (write the current master record on the new
     master file and read the next record from the old
        master file)
while (the current transaction record is not the
          sentinel) do
   (write the current transaction record on the new
   master file and read the next record from the
   transaction file)
Write a sentinel record on the new master file.
```

Section 8.2

1. A text file is essentially a sequential file in which each record is a single symbol.
2. Documents processed by word processors (letters, manuscripts, memoranda, brochures) are normally stored as text files. Mail transferred via e-mail is also normally handled as text files.
3. Normally a large part of the document is held in main memory, allowing random access to that portion of the document. However, as the latter portion of the document is processed, the earlier portion may be placed in mass storage. If one then wanted to back up this earlier portion, and that portion had been stored as a text file, then the processor would have to read from the beginning of the document to find the part to be updated.

Section 8.3

1. Suppose the entries in the index are the smallest key field values from each segment and we are looking for the record with key field value 7. If the first entry in the index is 5, we do not know whether or not the target record is in the segment represented by this entry. Thus we must go on to the next entry. If this next entry is 11, we can conclude that the previous entry is the one we need, because our target key field, 7, is less than 11. Consequently, we must backtrack to the previous index entry to continue the search.

   In contrast, suppose the entries in the index are the largest key field value from each segment. When looking for the entry 7, we might first find the entry 10. Since 10 is larger than the target key field value, we can conclude immediately that this is the segment of interest, without going further in the index.
2. The purpose is to provide both direct and sequential access to the file. As pointed out in the section, sequential access is possible in an indexed file if the index is constructed so that it can be traversed sequentially, as we did in the tree structure in Chapter 7. On the other hand, if the file is designed as an indexed sequential file, sequential processing might well be carried out more efficiently.
3. A list, in some cases, is easier to update. On the other hand, searching for an entry can take significantly more time than in the case of a tree.
4. It depends on how generally you interpret "the technique presented in this section." The

point is that the partial-index system we presented relies on each physical segment being a contiguous part of the overall sorted file. Since the file cannot be physically divided according to two different orders, the technique could not literally be applied to different key fields in the same file. On the other hand, approximations to the technique can be implemented using a pointer system to represent the second order. Since an index based on this additional system is less efficient than the one based on the physical storage order, we normally use it for the key field that is used less frequently.

Section 8.4

1. This is a good example of the kinds of things that must be considered when selecting a hash algorithm. In this case using the first three digits of the Social Security numbers is a poor choice because these digits represent the area of the country in which the number was assigned. Consequently, citizens in one area of the country tend to have the same starting digits in their Social Security numbers, and this would result in more clustering than normal in the hashed file.
2. A poorly chosen hash algorithm results in more clustering than normal and thus in more overflow. Since the overflow from each section of mass storage is organized as a linked list, searching through the overflow records is essentially searching a sequential file.
3. The section assignments are as follows:
   a. 0 b. 0 c. 3 d. 0 e. 3
   f. 3 g. 3 h. 3 i. 3 j. 0
   Thus all the records hash into buckets 0 and 3, leaving buckets 1, 2, 4, and 5 empty. The problem here is that the number of buckets being used (6) and the key field values have the common factor of 3. (You might try rehashing these key field values using 7 buckets and see what improvement you find.)
4. The point here is that we are essentially applying a hash algorithm to place the people in the group into one of 365 categories. The hash algorithm, of course, is the calculation of one's birthday. The amazing thing is that only 23 people are required before the probability is in favor of at least two of the birthdays being the same. In terms of a hashed file this indicates that when hashing records into 365 available buckets of mass storage, clustering is likely to be present after only 23 records have been entered.

Section 8.5

1. The operating system first searches the index to find which segment should be interrogated. Having established the desired segment number, the operating system might then check to see whether that segment is already in main memory (it may be the same segment that was previously accessed). If it is already in main memory, the operating system searches it and relays the correct record to the program. Otherwise, the segment must be retrieved from mass storage and then searched.
2. The operating system in a time-sharing environment does its best to use all time efficiently. If the required storage segment is not already in main memory, the operating system asks the controller of the disk drive to retrieve the correct segment; but rather than wait for the data to arrive, the operating system terminates the original process's time slice and starts another process. After the controller has placed the requested segment in main memory, the operating system returns to the original process, gives it the record it needed, and allows it to continue execution in the normal sequence of time slices.
3. No. For some reason this is a common mistake made by beginning programmers. Keep in mind that an index for a file must be maintained as the file is initially constructed and later modified. The operating system cannot perform the magic of creating an index for a previously nonindexed file.

Chapter 9

Section 9.1

1. The purchasing department would be interested in inventory records to place orders for more raw goods, whereas the accounting department would need the information to balance the books.
2. Employee, student, alumni, finance, registration, equipment/supplies, and so on.

3. The subschema for the purchasing department would probably include the addresses of the various manufacturers who supply the parts in inventory and perhaps the name of the sales representative for each of these companies. The subschema for the accounting department would probably not include this information.

Section 9.2

1. No. The use of file systems invariably dictates that the application program be expressed in terms of the actual organization of records in the file. Thus a change in the record structure would require changes in all programs accessing that file.
2.

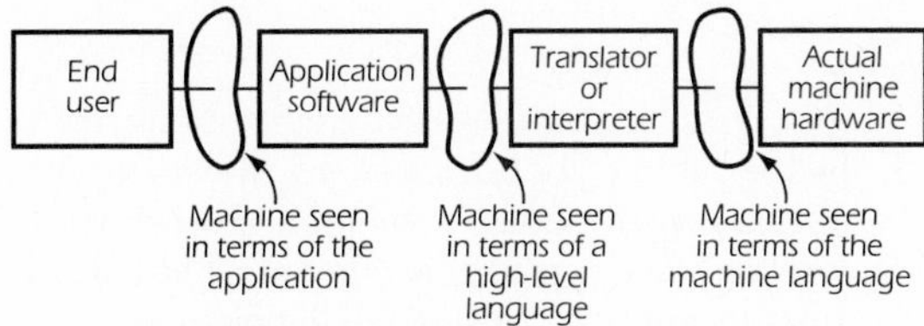

3. The application software translates the user's requests from the terminology of the application into terminology compatible with the database management system. The database management system in turn converts the requests into a form understood by the routines that actually manipulate the data in mass storage. These last routines perform the retrieval of data.

Section 9.3

1. a. G. Jerry Smith
   b. Cheryl H. Clark
   c. S26Z
2. One solution is

```
TEMP ← SELECT from JOB
          where Dept = "PERSONNEL"
LIST ← PROJECT JobTitle from TEMP
```

   In some systems this results in a list with a job title repeated, depending on how many times it occurred in the personnel department. That is, our list may contain numerous occurrences of the title secretary. It is more common, however, to design the PROJECT operation so that it removes duplicate tuples from the resulting relation.
3. One solution is

```
TEMP1 ←JOIN JOB and ASSIGNMENT
          where JOB.JobId =
          ASSIGNMENT.JobId
TEMP2 ←SELECT from TEMP1
          where TermDate = "*"
TEMP3 ←JOIN EMPLOYEE and TEMP2
          where EMPLOYEE.EmplId =
          TEMP2.EmplId
RESULT ←PROJECT Name, Dept from TEMP3
```

4.

```
select JobTitle
from JOB
where Dept = "PERSONEL"

select EMPLOYEE.Name, JOB.Dept
from JOB, ASSIGNMENT, and EMPLOYEE
where (Job.Job = ASSIGNMENT.JobId) and
      (ASSIGNMENT.EmplId = EMPLOYEE.EmplID)
      and
      (ASSIGNMENT.TermDate = "*")
```

5. The model itself does not provide data independence. This is a property of the data management system. Data independence is achieved by providing the data management system the ability to present a consistent relational organization to the application software even though the actual organization may change.
6. Through common attributes. For instance, the EMPLOYEE relation in this section is tied to the ASSIGNMENT relation via the attribute EmplId, and the ASSIGNMENT relation is tied to the JOB relation by the attribute JobId. Attributes used to connect relations like this are sometimes called connection attributes.

Section 9.4

1. There may be methods for assigning and retrieving the StartDate as well as the TermDate. Another method may be provided for reporting the total time in service.
2. One approach is to establish an object for each type of product in inventory. Each of these objects could maintain the total inventory of its product, the cost of the product, and links to the outstanding orders for the product.
3. As indicated at the beginning of this section, object-oriented databases appear to handle

composite data types more easily than relational databases. Moreover, the fact that objects can contain methods that take an active role in answering questions promises to give object-oriented databases an advantage over relational databases whose relations merely hold the data.

Section 9.5

1. Once a transaction has reached its commit point, the database management system accepts the responsibility of seeing that the complete transaction is performed on the database. A transaction that has not reached its commit point does not have such assurance. If problems arise, it may have to be resubmitted.

2. One approach would be to stop interweaving transactions for an instant so that all current transactions can be completed in full. This would establish a point at which a future cascading rollback would terminate.

3. A balance of $100 would result if the transactions were executed one a time. A balance of $200 would result if the first transaction executed after the second transaction retrieved the original balance and before that second transaction stored its new balance. A balance of $300 would result if the second transaction after the first retrieved the original balance and before the first transaction stored its new balance.

4. a. If no other transaction has exclusive access, the shared access will be granted.
   b. If another transaction already has some form of access, the database management system will normally make the new transaction wait, or it could rollback the other transactions and give access to the new transaction.

5. Deadlock would occur if each of two transactions acquired exclusive access to different items and then required access to the other.

6. The deadlock above could be removed by rolling back one of the transactions (using the log) and giving the other transaction access to the data item previously held by the first.

PART FOUR

Chapter 10

Section 10.1

1. Our purpose here is not to give a decisive answer to this issue but to use it to show how delicate the argument over the existence of intelligence really is.
2. Although most of us would probably say no, we would probably claim that if a human dispensed the same products in a similar atmosphere, awareness would be present even though we might not be able to explain the distinction.

Section 10.2

1. In the remote control case, the system needs only to relay the picture, whereas to use the picture for maneuvering, the robot must be able to "understand" the meaning of the picture.
2. The possible interpretations for one section of the drawing do not match any of those of another section. To embed this insight into a program, one might isolate the interpretations allowable for various line junctions and then write a program that tries to find a set of compatible interpretations (one for each junction). In fact, if you stop and think about it, this is probably what your own senses did in trying to evaluate the drawing. Did you detect your eyes scanning back and forth between the two ends of the drawing as your senses tried to piece possible interpretations together? (If this subject interests you, you'll want to read about the work of people such as D. A. Huffman, M. B. Clowes, and D. Waltz.)

Section 10.3

1. Production systems provide a uniform approach to a variety of problems. That is, although apparently different in their original form, all problems reformulated into terms of

production systems become the problem of finding a path through a state graph.

2.

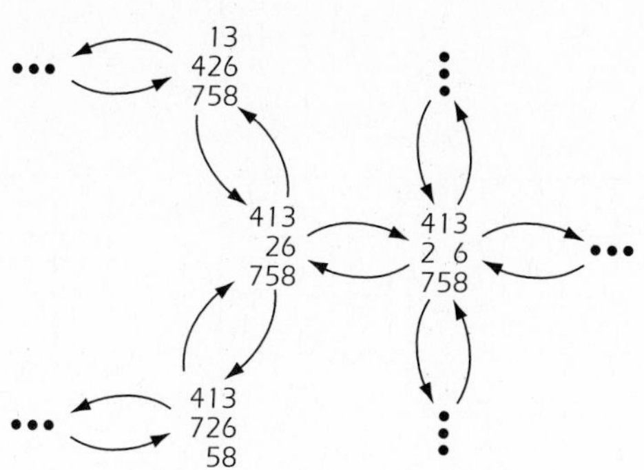

3. The states might include that of starting the maze, finishing the maze, deciding which way to go from the current position, or being stuck at a dead end. These individual states are so closely associated with particular positions in the maze that we can identify them by the positions labeled as follows. Thus we can speak of being in state S (the starting state), state B (deciding which way to go from that position), or state G (having reached the goal).

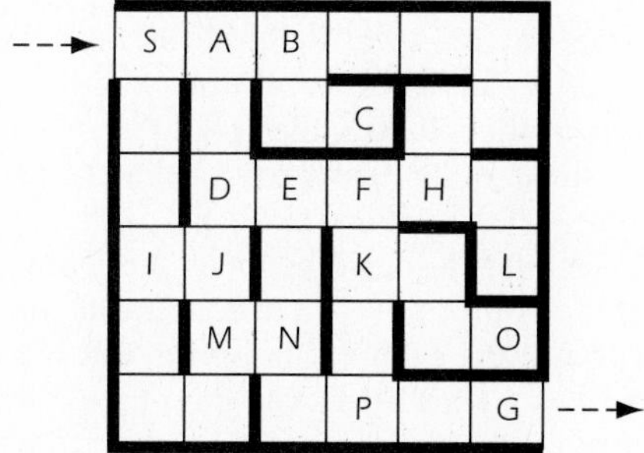

The productions consist of the movements from one location to another. Thus the state graph has the following form:

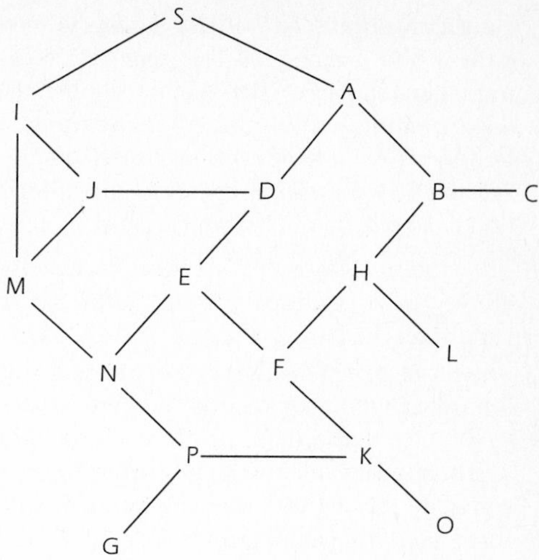

Section 10.4

1. The tree is four moves deep. The upper portion appears as follows:

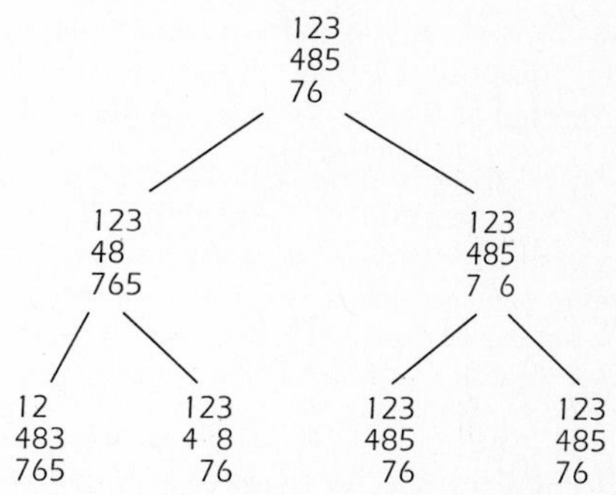

2. Less of the tree needs to be constructed, thus saving both time and storage space.
3. The task requires too much paper as well as too much time.

Section 10.5

1. Our heuristic system for solving the eight-puzzle is based on an analysis of the immediate situation, just as that of the mountain climber. This short-sightedness is what allowed our

algorithm to proceed initially along the wrong path in the example of this section just as a mountain climber can be led into trouble by always plotting a course based only on the local terrain. (This analogy often causes heuristic systems based on local or immediate information to be called hill-climbing systems.)

2. The system rotates the 5, 6, and 8 tiles either clockwise or counterclockwise until the goal state is reached.
3. The problem here is that our heuristic scheme ignores the value of keeping the hole adjacent to the tiles that are out of place. If the hole is surrounded by tiles in their correct position, some of these tiles must be moved before those tiles still seeking their correct place can be moved. Thus it is incorrect to consider all those tiles surrounding the hole as actually being correct. To fix this flaw, we might first observe that a tile in its correct position but blocking the hole from incorrectly positioned tiles must be moved away from its correct position and later moved back. Thus each correctly positioned tile on a path between the hole and the nearest incorrectly positioned tile accounts for at least two moves in the remaining solution. We can therefore modify our projected cost calculation as follows:

   First, calculate the projected cost as before. However, if the hole is totally isolated from the incorrectly positioned tiles, find a shortest path between the hole and an incorrectly positioned tile, multiply the number of tiles on this path by two, and add the resulting value to the previous projected cost.

   With this system, the leaf nodes in Fig. 10.10 have projected costs of 6, 6, and 4 (from left to right), and thus the correct branch is pursued initially.

   Our new system is not foolproof. For example, consider the following configuration. The solution is to slide the 5 tile down, rotate the top two rows clockwise until those tiles are correct, move the 5 tile back up, and finally move the 8 tile to its correct position. However, our new heuristic system wants us to start by moving the 8 tile, because the state obtained by this initial move has a projected cost of only 6 compared with the other options that have costs of 8.

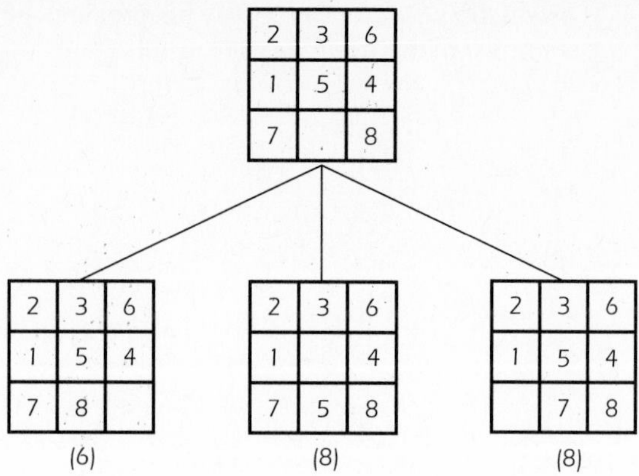

4. The search tree is little more than a linked list representing the result of depth-first search without a depth limit, because the "leftmost leaf node with the smallest projected cost" is always the leftmost leaf node. Thus the search tree consists of only the leftmost possible path.

Section 10.6

1. All patterns produce an output of 0 except for the pattern 1, 0, which produces an output of 1.
2. Assign a weight of 1 to each input, and assign the unit a threshold value of 1.5.
3. Design a two-level network as described in the text. The lower-level units should assign each of their inputs the weight 1 and have a threshold of 7½. Thus one of these units outputs a 1 if the pattern in the field of view is the circle; otherwise, all the lower-level units produce an output of 0. In turn, if the upper-level unit assigns each of its inputs the weight 1 and has a threshold of ½, then the entire network produces a 1 when the pattern is a circle and a 0 when the pattern is an X.
4. Design a two-level network as described in the text. Each lower-level unit should have a threshold of 2½, assign the weight of 0 to the corner squares in its field of view, and assign the weight of 1 to the other squares. The only way one of these units can produce a 1 as its output is to have the C pattern in its field of view. In fact, if this is the pattern, two lower-

level units produce an output of 1. Thus, if the upper-level unit assigns each of its inputs the weight 1 and has a threshold of 1, then it produces an output of 1 when the pattern in the field of view is the C and an output of 0 when the pattern is the V.

Section 10.7

1. Is the sentence describing what kind of horses they are, or is it telling what some people are doing?
2. The parsing process produces identical structures, but the semantic analysis recognizes that the prepositional phrase in the first sentence tells where the fence was built, whereas the phrase in the second sentence tells when the fence was built.
3. They are brother and sister.
4. It uses the closed-world assumption.
5. In many ways, the two are the same. However, traditional databases tend to contain only facts such as an employee's name, address, and so on, whereas knowledge bases tend to include rules such as "if raining, check rain gauge" that can be used to direct the reasoning process.

Chapter 11

Section 11.1

1.
```
clear AUX;
incr AUX;
while X not 0 do;
  clear X;
  clear AUX;
end;
while AUX not 0 do;
  incr X;
  clear AUX;
end;
```

2.
```
while X not 0 do;
  decr X;
end;
```

3.
```
move X to AUX;
while AUX not 0 do;
  S1
  clear AUX;
end;
move X to AUX;
invert AUX;
while AUX not 0 do;
  S2
  clear AUX;
end;
while X not 0 do;
  clear AUX;
  clear X;
```

4. If we assume that X refers to the memory cell at address 40 and that each program segment starts at location 00, we have the following conversion table:

	Address	*Contents*
clear X;	00	20
	01	00
	02	30
	03	40

	Address	*Contents*
incr X;	00	11
	01	40
	02	20
	03	01
	04	50
	05	01
	06	30
	07	40

	Address	*Contents*
decr X;	00	20
	01	00
	02	23
	03	00
	04	11
	05	40
	06	22
	07	01
	08	B1
	09	10
	0A	40
	0B	03
	0C	50
	0D	02
	0E	B1
	0F	06
	10	33
	11	40

	Address	Contents
while X not	00	20
0 do;	01	00
.	02	11
.	03	40
.	04	B1
end;	05	WZ
	.	.
	.	.
	.	.
	WX	B0
	WY	00

5. Just as in a real machine, negative numbers could be dealt with via a coding system. For example, the rightmost bit in each string can be used as a sign but with the remaining bits used to represent the magnitude of the value.

Section 11.2

1. The result is the following diagram:

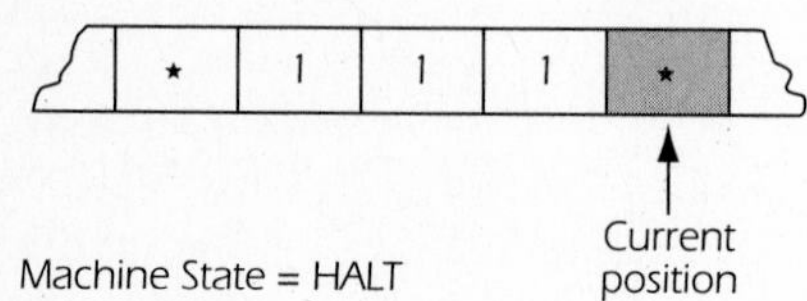

2.

Current state	Cell content	Value to write	Direction to move	New state to enter
START	*	*	left	STATE 1
STATE 1	0	0	left	STATE 2
STATE 1	1	0	left	STATE 2
STATE 1	*	0	left	STATE 2
STATE 2	0	*	right	STATE 3
STATE 2	1	*	right	STATE 3
STATE 2	*	*	right	STATE 3
STATE 3	0	0	right	HALT
STATE 3	1	0	right	HALT

3.

Current state	Current cell content	Value to write	Direction to move	New state to enter
START	*	*	left	SUBTRACT
SUBTRACT	0	1	left	BORROW
SUBTRACT	1	0	left	NO BORROW
BORROW	0	1	left	BORROW
BORROW	1	0	left	NO BORROW
BORROW	*	*	right	ZERO
NO BORROW	0	0	left	NO BORROW
NO BORROW	1	1	left	NO BORROW
NO BORROW	*	*	right	RETURN
ZERO	0	0	right	ZERO
ZERO	1	0	right	ZERO
ZERO	*	*	no move	HALT
RETURN	0	0	right	RETURN
RETURN	1	1	right	RETURN
RETURN	*	*	no move	HALT

4. The point here is that the concept of a Turing machine is supposed to capture the meaning of "to compute." That is, any time a situation occurs in which computing is taking place, the components and activities of a Turing machine should be present. For example, a person figuring income tax is doing a certain degree of computing. The computing machine is the person and the tape is represented by the paper on which values are recorded.

Section 11.3

1. The computation of a loan payment, the area of a circle, or a car's mileage.
2. Mathematicians call such functions transcendental functions. Examples include the logarithmic and trigonometric functions. These particular examples can still be computed but not by algebraic means. For example, the trigonometric functions can be calculated by actually drawing the triangle involved, measuring its sides, and only then turning to the algebraic operation of dividing.
3. The function is multiplication by 2.
4. The machine described by the following table halts if started with an even input but never halts if started with an odd input:

Current state	Cell content	Value to write	Direction to move	New state to enter
START	*	*	left	STATE 1
STATE 1	0	0	right	HALT
STATE 1	1	1	no move	STATE 1
STATE 1	*	*	no move	STATE 1

Section 11.4

1.

decr X;	(program)
↓	
0110010001100101011000110111001000100000010110000111011	(ASCII code)
↓	
28,258,975,461,955,643	(Gödel number in base ten)

2. Yes. In fact, this program halts for any input value. Thus it must halt if its input is its own Gödel number.
3. The point here is that the logic is the same as in our argument that the halting problem does not have an algorithmic solution. If the house painter paints his or her own house, he or she doesn't and vice versa.

Section 11.5

1. If the machine can sort 100 names in one second, it can perform (¼) (10,000 −100) comparisons in one second. This means that each comparison takes approximately 0.0004 second. Consequently, sorting 1000 names [which requires an average of (¼) (1,000,000 − 1000) comparison]requires roughly 100 seconds or 1⅔ minutes.
2. To sort a list of 100 names using the quick sort algorithm requires at least 100 [lg 100] = 600 comparisons. Since it takes the machine one second to do this, it requires about 0.0016 second for each comparison. Because to sort a list of 1000 names requires at least 100 [lg 1000] = 9000 comparisons, at least 15 seconds is required.
3. Surprising as it may seem, this is a worst-case example for the quick sort algorithm. Thus, to sort 10 names requires ½ (100 − 10) or 45 comparisons.
4. The list David, Carol, Alice, Bill, Gwen, Earl, Fred requires only 10 comparisons.

Section 11.6

1. No. Depending on which polynomial and exponential are compared, either may be small in comparison to the other for small inputs. In fact, it is true that exponential algorithms are sometimes preferred as opposed to polynomial ones when the application involves only small inputs.
2. From Alice and Bill we could form these three subcommittees:
   1. Alice
   2. Bill
   3. Alice, Bill

   From Alice, Bill, and Carol we could form these subcommittees:
   1. Alice
   2. Bill
   3. Carol
   4. Alice, Bill
   5. Alice, Carol
   6. Bill, Carol
   7. Alice, Bill, Carol

   From Alice, Bill, Carol, and David we could obtain 15 different subcommittees. The point here is that the number of subcommittees is growing exponentially, and from this point on, the job of listing all the possibilities becomes a laborious task.
3. Within the class of polynomial problems is the sorting problem, which can be solved by polynomial algorithms such as the insertion sort or the quick sort.

   Within the class of nonpolynomial problems is the task of listing all the subcommittees that could be formed from a given parent committee.

   Any polynomial problem is an NP problem. The Traveling Salesman problem is an example of an NP problem that has not been shown to be a polynomial problem.

Index

Abacus 6
Abstract data type 289
Abstraction 10
Abstract tools 10
Access time 26
Actual parameter 206
Ada 193, 194, 195, 197, 201, 202, 205, 219, 291
Address 23
Address polynomial 264
Adobe Systems 34
Aiken, Howard 8
Algebraic coding theory 51
Algorithm 2, 131–133
  discovery of 140–146
  complexity/efficiency of 171–172, 415–421
Algorithmic machine 6
American National Standards Institute (ANSI) 30, 186, 343, 439
American Standard Code for Information Interchange (ASCII) 30, 48, 83
AND 16, 75
Apple Computer, Inc. 34
Application layer (Internet) 121
Application software 96, 122
Arc 280, 364
Argument (of a predicate) 225
Arithmetic/logic unit 59
Arithmetic shift 77
Array 262
  heterogeneous 196
  homogeneous 196
Artificial intelligence 357
  performance-oriented approach 359
  simulation-oriented approach 359
Artificial neural network 74, 377
ASCII. *See* American Standard Code for Information Interchange
Assembler 185
Assembly language 185
Assertions 174
  in algorithm development 162–165
  in proof of correctness 174–176
Assignment statements 197
Association for Computing Machinery (ACM) 234
Atanasoff, John 8
Attribute 334
Axiom 174, 366

Babbage, Charles 6, 439
Backtracking 272
Balanced tree 282
Bare Bones language 397
Base case 161
Base Two. *See* Binary system
Batch processing 92
Baud rate 82
Bell Laboratories 8, 439, 440
Berry, Clifford 8
Binary notation 31. (*See also* Binary system)
Binary search 155
  complexity of 172

Binary system 35
Binary tree 281
Bit 16
Bit map 34, 75
Bits per second (bps) 82
Blackboard model 389
Body (of a loop) 148
Boole, George 16
Boolean data type 195
Boolean operations 16
Booting 100
Bootstrap 101
Borland International 192, 321
Borne shell 97
Bottom-up design 245
Bottom-up methodology 144
Bps. *See* Bits per second
Breadth-first search 370
Browser 115
Buffer 80, 309
Buffering 80
Bus 59, 80
Byron, Augusta Ada 439
Byte 22

C 193, 194, 195, 196, 197, 201, 202, 205, 209, 210, 219, 262, 305, 310, 315, 320, 322, 439
C++ 193, 194, 195, 197, 201, 202, 205, 209, 262, 292, 295, 305, 306, 310, 322, 440
Cache memory 59
Carrier Sense, Multiple Access with Collision Detection (CSMA/CD) 118, 123
Cascading rollback 348
CASE. *See* Computer-aided software engineering
Case control structure 200
CD. *See* Compact disk
CD-ROM 27
Cell (memory) 22
Central processing unit (CPU) 59
Character data type 195
Children (in a tree) 280
Chip 20
Church, Alonzo 409
Church–Turing thesis 403, 409, 410, 411, 446, 447
Circular queue 277
CISC. *See* Complex instruction set computer
Class 294
Clause form 223
Client 104
Client/Server model 104
Closed-world assumption 387
Close statement 322
Code generation 215
Code generator 211
Code optimization 216
Coercion 215
Cohesion (intramodule) 243
COLOSSUS 8
Column major order 263
Comments 200
Commit point 347
Commit/Rollback protocol 347
Compact disk 27
Compiler 186
Complement 41
Complex instruction set computer (CISC) 71
Complexity 416
  of binary search 172
  of insertion sort 417
  of quick sort 418
  of sequential search 171, 416
  orders of 421
Computable function 407
Computer-aided design (CAD) 34
Computer-aided software engineering (CASE) 238
Concatenation 199
Conditional jump 61
Connectionless protocol 125
Constant 194
Constructor 296
Contextual analysis 384
Contiguous list. *See* List
Control coupling 241
Controller 79
Control of repetitive structures
  iteration (looping) 148–151
  recursion 161–162
Control statements 200
Control unit 59
Copyright law 252

Core 20
Core wars 85
Coupling (intermodule) 241
CPU. *See* Central processing unit
Critical region 107, 221
C shell 97
CSMA / CD. *See* Carrier Sense, Multiple Access with Collision Detection

Database 328, 387
Database administrator (DBA) 329
Database management system (DBMS) 332
Database model 333
Data compression 82
Data coupling 241
Data dictionary 249
Dataflow diagram 247
Data independence 332
Data Processing Management Association (DPMA) 234
Data structure 196
Data type 195, 288
  Boolean 195
  character 195
  integer 195
  real 195
Deadlock 107
Debugging 184
Declaration part (of a program unit) 193
Declarative programming. *See* Programming paradigms
Declarative statements 193
Defense Advanced Research Projects Agency (DARPA) 111
Deferred update protocol 347
Degenerative case 161
Delphi 192
Depth (of a tree) 280
Depth-first search 370
Device driver 99
Direct access file 315
Direct memory access (DMA) 79
Directory 99, 312
Disclaimers 253
Diskette 26
Disk storage 25
Dispatcher 100
Distributed database 332
DMA. *See* Direct memory access
DOCTOR (ELIZA) program 359
Documentation 200–203, 250
Domain 111
Domain name 113
Dotted decimal notation 35
Double precision 43
DXF 34

Eckert, J. Presper 8, 62
Editor 217
Effective 132
Effective input (of a processing unit) 377
Eight-puzzle 361
E-mail 114
Encapsulation 291
End-of-file (EOF) mark 303
ENIAC 8
Entity-relationship diagram 247
ELIZA 359
EOF. *See* End-of-file mark
Error-correcting code 49
Ethics, role of 11
Euclid 3
Euclidean algorithm 3, 140
Euclidean geometry 174
Even parity 49
Evolutionay prototyping 238
Excess notation 38
Exclusive lock 349
Exclusive or (XOR) 16, 75
Expert systems 388
Exponent field 44
Exponential expression 422

Factorial 179
Feature evaluation 362
Feature extraction 362
Fibonacci sequence 178
Field 303
FIFO. *See* First in, first out
Fifth-generation language 187
File 25
  management of 98, 321–323
  organization of 302–320
File control block 321
File descriptor 99, 321

File manager 98
Flip-flop 17, 20
First-generation language 185
First in, first out (FIFO) 93
First-order predicate logic 223
Fixed-format language 211
Floating-point notation 33, 44
 normalized form 450
Floppy disk 26
Flowchart 150
Folder 99
Formal parameter 206
Formatted I/O 209, 305
Formatting (a disk) 26
For statement 201
FORTRAN 193, 194, 195, 199, 202, 205, 219, 321, 322, 441
Fourth-generation language 187
Free-format language 211
Frequency-dependent code 83
Full tree 282
Function
 abstract 190, 407
 computation of 407
 program unit 139, 207
Functional cohesion 243
Functional programming. *See* Programming paradigms

Garbage collection 269
Gate 17
Gateway 111
GB. *See* Gigabyte
General-purpose register 59
GIF 34
Gigabyte 23
Global variable 205
Gödel, Kurt 5, 397, 411
Gödel number 411, 414
Gödel's incompleteness theorem 5, 9
Goto statement 199
Graph 364
Graphical user interface (GUI) 97
GUI. *See* Graphical user interface

Halting problem 414
Hamming, R. W. 50
Hamming distance 50
Handshaking 81
Hard disk 26
Hardware 3
Harvard University 8
Hash algorithm 316
Hashed file 316
Head (of a queue) 275
Head pointer 267, 276
Help packages 250
Heuristic 372
Hexadecimal notation 21
High-order end 24
Hollerith, Herman 8
Host 111
Host address 113
Host language 333
HTML. *See* Hypertext Markup Language
Huffman code 83
Hypermedia 115
Hypertext 114
Hypertext Markup Language (HTML) 116

IBM 8, 98, 343
Identifiers 184
If statement 137, 200
Image analysis 361
Imperative statements 193
Inconsistent 223
Incorrect summary problem 348
Incubation period 143
Indexed file 311
Indexed sequential file 315
Inference engine 389
Information extraction 385
Information retrieval 385
Inheritance 294
Input/output (I/O) 61
Input/output instructions (machine level) 61, 81
Input/output program statements 208–209
Insertion sort 154
 complexity of 417
Instance (of a data type) 289
Institute of Electrical and Electronics Engineering (IEEE) 234
Instruction pointer 265

Instruction register 66
Integer data type 195
Integrated software 187
Interactive processing 93
Internal documentation 200
International Standards Organization (ISO) 30, 124, 187
Internet 95, 110, 111
Internet addressing 111
Internet Network Information Center (InterNIC) 111
Internet Protocol (IP) 124, 125
InterNIC. *See* Internet Network Information Center
Interprocess communication 102
Interrupt 80, 103
Interrupt handler 103
Inverted file 311
I/O. *See* Input/output
Iowa State College (University) 8
IP. *See* Internet Protocol
ISO. *See* International Standards Organization
Iterative structure 146, 148–151, 200–201, 400

Jacquard, Joseph 7
Jacquard loom 7
Java 193, 194, 195, 199, 201, 202, 205, 262, 295, 433
Java applets 443
JCL (job control language) 93
Job queue 92
JOIN (database operation) 339
JPEG 34

KB. *See* Kilobyte
Kernel 98
Key field 304
Key words 212
Kill (a process) 108
Kilobyte 23
Knowledge base 389
Korn shell 93

LAN. *See* Local area network
Language processing 383
Last in, first out (LIFO) 271
Latency time 26
Leaf node 280
Least significant bit 24
Left child pointer 281
Lempel–Ziv encoding 83
Lexical analysis 211
Lexical analyzer 211
Liebniz, Gottfried Wilhelm 6
LIFO. *See* Last in, first out
Linda 219
Linker 216
Link layer (Internet) 122, 125
LISP 191, 219
List
  contiguous 267, 283
  linked 267
Literal 194
Load balancing 74, 95
Loader 216
Load module 216
Local area network (LAN) 110
Local variables 204
Locking protocol 349
Logical cohesion 243
Logical deduction 222
Logical record 29
Logical shift 77
Logic programming 187
Loop invariant 175
Loop structures 148. (*See also* Iterative structure)
Lost update problem 384
Low-order end 24
Lynx 115

Machine cycle 66
Machine independence 185, 186
Machine instructions 60
  AND 75, 76
  BRANCH 61
  I/O 61
  JUMP 61, 65
  LOAD 61, 80
  OR 75, 76
  ROTATE 61, 76
  SHIFT 61, 76, 77
  STORE 61, 80
  Test-and-set 107
  XOR (exclusive or) 75, 76
Machine language 63, 184

Main memory 22
Mantissa field 44
Many-to-many relationship 247
Mariner 18 space probe 234
Mark I 8
Mask 75
Masking 75
Mass storage 25
Master file 308
Mauchly, John 8
MB. *See* Megabyte
Megabyte 23
Member function 282
Memory leak 269
Memory manager 99
Memory mapped I/O 80
Merge sort 308
Method 292
Metric 233
Micromemory 71
Microprogram 71
Microsecond 53
Microsoft Corporation 192
Millisecond 26, 171
MIMD 73
MIPS 69
Mnemonic 184
Modem 82
Modular design 236–237, 239–244
Modularity 239
Module 139
Moore School of Engineering 8, 62
Mosaic 115
Most significant bit 24
Mouse 97
MPEG 34
MS-DOS 97
Multitasking 94

Name server 114
Nanosecond 26, 72
Netscape Navigator 115
Network 94
Network identifier 111
Network layer (Internet) 122
Network security 116
Network topologies 111
Neuron 74
NIL pointer 268
Node 280, 364
Nondeterministic algorithm 425
Nondeterministic polynomial (NP) problems 425
Nondisclosure agreement 253
Nonloss decomposition 337
Nonpolynomial problems 424
Nonterminal 212
Normal forms 337
Normalized form 450
NOT 16
NP problems 425. (*See also* Nondeterministic polynomial problems)
Numerical analysis 47

Object 292
Object-oriented database 345
Object-oriented design 240
Object-oriented programming 191, 292–296. (*See also* Programming paradigms)
Object program 211
Odd parity 49
Off-line 25
One-to-many relationship 247
On-line 25
O-notation 421
OOP. *See* Object-oriented programming
Op-code 63
Open network 110
Open statement 321
Open System Interconnect (OSI) 124
Operand 63
Operating system 91, 216
Operator precedence 198
OR 16, 75
OSI. *See* Open System Interconnect
OSI reference model 124
Overflow error 43
Overloading 199

P 425. (*See also* Polynomial problems)
Packet 121
Page (memory) 100
Parallel algorithm 131
Parallel communication 81

Parallel computing 219
Parallel processing 73
Parameter 205
  passed by reference 206
  passed by value 206
Parent node 280
Parity bit 48
Parse tree 212
Parser 211
Parsing 211
Partial index 313
Pascal 193, 194, 195, 196, 197, 201, 202, 205, 209, 210, 219, 267, 305, 309, 321, 322, 445
Pascal, Blaise 8, 445
Patent law 252
Path 99
PC. *See* Personal computer
Personal computer 9
Physical record 28
Pipelining 72
Pixel 34
Poincare, H. 143
Pointer 265
Polya, G. 141, 237
Polymorphism 296
Polynomial algorithm 423
Polynomial expression 422
Polynomial problems 423, 425
Pop (stack operation) 271
Port 81
PostScript 34
Precedence (of operators) 198
Preconditions 174
Predicate 225
Primary key 311
Primitive 134
Problem solving 140–146
Procedural part (of a program unit) 193
Procedural programming. *See* Programming paradigms
Procedure 139, 204
Procedure's header 204
Process 102, 131
Processing unit 377
Process state 102
Process switch 103
Process table 103
Production system 363
  control system 364
  goal state 364
  production 364
  start state 363
Program 3, 131
Program counter 66, 265
Programming language 135
Programming paradigms 188
  declarative 187, 189, 222–227
  functional 190, 203
  imperative 189
  object-oriented 191, 203
  procedural 189
PROJECT (database operation) 338
Projected cost 373
Prolog 219, 225
Proof of correctness 174
Protocol 117
Prototyping 238
Pseudocode 136
Push (stack operation) 271

Quantum 103
Queue 275
Quick sort 166
  complexity of 418

Radix point 37
RAM. *See* Random access memory
Random access file 315
Random access memory (RAM) 24
Ravel, Maurice 114
Read-only memory (ROM) 100
Ready (process) 103
Real data type 195
Real-time processing 93
Recursion 161
Recursive structures 155–170, 400
Reduced instruction set computer (RISC) 71
Register 59
Relation 333
Relational database model 333
Relative addressing 451
Relocatable module 217
Repeat control structure 151
Requirements (of software) 236
Reserved words 212
Resolution 222

Resolvent 223
Right-child pointer 281
Ring network 118
RISC. *See* Reduced instruction set computer
Ritchie, Dennis 439
Robotics 385
Rogerian thesis 360
Roll back 348
ROM. *See* Read-only memory
Root node 280
Root pointer 281
Rotation delay 26
Round-off error 46
Router 111
Row major order 263

Scalable fonts 34
Scaling 95
Scheduler 100
Schema 330
Search tree 368
Secondary key 311
Secondary memory 25
Second-generation language 185
Sectors 25
Seek time 26
SELECT (database operation) 338
Self-reference 412
Self-terminating program 411
Semantic analysis 384
Semantic net 385
Semantics 135
Semaphore 107
Sentinel 303
Sequential access file 315
Sequential file 303
Sequential search 148
  complexity of 171, 311, 416
Serial communication 82
Server 105
Set theory 174
Shared lock 349
Shell 97
Siblings (in a tree) 280
Side effect 242
Sign bit 38, 44
SIMD 73
SISD 73
Software 3
Software engineering 232
Software life cycle 234
Software verification 172–176
Source program 211
Special-purpose register 59
Specifications (of software) 175, 201, 236
Spooling 109
SQL. *See* Structured Query Language
Stack 271
Stack pointer 273
Starvation 128
State
  of process 102
  of production system 363
  of Turing machine 402
State graph 364
Stepwise refinement 144
Stibitz, George 8
Stored program concept 62
Streaming tape unit 27
Strongly typed 215
Stroustrup, Bjarne 440
Structure chart 239
Structured programming 200
Structured Query Language 343
Stub 237
Subprogram 139
Subroutine 139
Subschema 330
Subtree 280
Successor function 407, 408, 410
Sun Microsystems 443
Symbol table 215
Synapse 74
Syntactic analysis 384
Syntax 135
Syntax diagram 212
System documentation 250
System requirements 236
System software 96
System specifications 236
System/360 (IBM) 98

Tail (of a queue) 275
Tail pointer 276

Tape storage 27
TCP. *See* Transmission Control Protocol
TCP/IP 111, 124
Terminal (in a syntax diagram) 212
Terminal node 280
Test-and-set instruction 107
Text file 308
Third-generation language 186
Throughput 72
Throwaway prototyping 238
TIFF 34
Time-sharing 94
Time slice 94, 103
Token (in a network) 118, 122
Token (in a translator) 211
Top-down design 244
Top-down methodology 144
Top of stack 271
Towers of Hanoi 179, 180
Track 25
Trade secret law 253
Transaction file 308
Transcendental functions 472
Transfer rate 26
Translation 211
Translator 186
Transmission Control Protocol (TCP) 124, 125
Transport layer (Internet) 122, 125
Trapdoor 116
Traveling salesman problem 424, 426
Tree 212, 280, 313, 419
TrueType 34
Tuple (in Linda) 219
Tuple (in a relation) 334
Tuple space 220
Turbo Pascal 321
Turing, Alan M. 359, 402, 409
Turing computable 409
Turing machine 402
Turing test 359
Twins (in a tree) 280
Two's complement notation 33, 40
Type. *See* Data type

UDP. *See* User Datagram Protocol
Unconditional jump 61
Unicode 30
Unification 225
Uniform resource locator (URL) 265
Universal programming language 397, 410
University of Pennsylvania 8
UNIX 97
Unsolvable problem 415
URL. *See* Uniform resource locator
User Datagram Protocol (UDP) 124, 125
User-defined type 288
User documentation 250
Utility software 96, 122

Variable 194
Virtual memory 100
Virus 116
Visual Basic 192
von Helmholtz, H. 143
von Neumann bottleneck 80
von Neumann, John 62

WAN, *See* Wide area network
Waiting (process) 103
Waterfall model 237
Weight (in a processing unit) 378
Weighted sum 377
Weizenbaum, Joseph 359
While control structure 138, 150, 200
Wide area network (WAN) 110
Windows 97
Wirth, Niklaus 445
World Wide Web 115
Worm 117
Wound-wait protocol 349

XOR. *See* Exclusive or